# The Cry of the Tomahawk

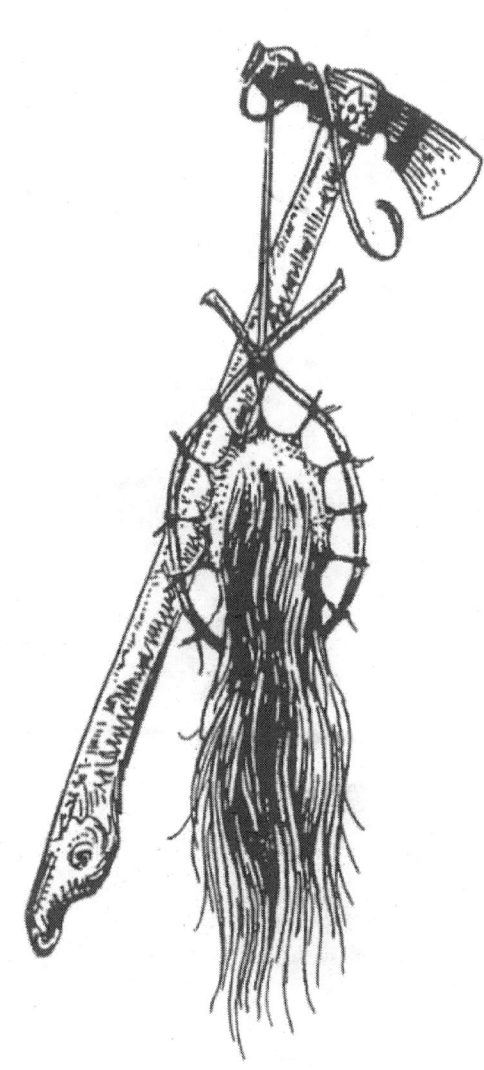

One of the mighty warriors of the "Six Nations."

## Prologue

Trees blanketed the ancient mountains. Under the trees and upon the ancient earth beneath them many feet trod through the eons, all leaving a little of their essence with their passing. They were known as Mohican, Conoy, Onondaga, Mohawk, Cayuga, Seneca, Oneida, Tuscarora, Saponie, Nanticoke, Shawnee, and Lenni Lanape to name a few whom have not been lost to the ages. Here, along the banks of the Susquehanna River and in the Endless Mountains surrounding them, they raised their families, hunted, fished, gathered, farmed, and simply lived.

Young warriors strode along the riverbanks hand in hand with young maidens planning their futures together. Mothers bore children. Fathers beamed with pride. Their story, along with countless similar stories, lay under the trees and hidden in their deep shadows, their spirits etching themselves in the very heart of the earth itself, whispering on the ancient winds of time not to be forgotten.

They walked, lived, and passed in the great shadows for thousands of years before the arrival of new faces, white faces, bearing new and strange ways. Ways which collided with the ancient people's ways. Their eyes burned with a different light, born of a different flame.

The flame started as all flames, but a mere spark; a few emissaries, explorers, and traders, but steadily grew, eventually engulfing all with its burning passion and conquering all in its path. Through their eyes-*white eyes*-reflected an entirely different vision and concept of the future. Right or wrong, they, along with their guns, germs, and steel, swept over the ancient peoples, changing all forever.

The white eyes ventured forth from their footholds on the coasts and trudged inland, carrying their visions with them. But their eyes gazed upon the land differently. Their hearts seemed to beat with an indifference to all not of their kind. They came as a mere drizzle which grew into a torrential rain, flooding all before them. In the end, only their vision remained, only their feet trod across the ancient land.

This is the story of one of the many struggles born of this clash of cultures, and how the white eyes, though victorious in the end, were, and will be forever haunted by *the cry of the tomahawk*.

We must never forget the whispers across the ages, and hear in their faint echoes the lessons they bear, even though they may be hushed by the roar of modern life. Let us never forget those whom came before, lest we forget a part of ourselves. Hear their whispers across the ages in their story echoing across time to us, their posterity. Lest we forget.

James B. Miller
May 4, 2010

*This book is dedicated to my grandson Cayleb Wayne Scott Sobczyk*

## Chapters

| Chapter | Title | Page |
|---|---|---|
| Chapter One | Noah's Web: The Massacre of 1763 | 9 |
| Chapter Two | The Cross of 1763 | 18 |
| Chapter Three | Rampart Rocks: Pennamite-Yankee battle of 1775 | 28 |
| Chapter Four | Wyoming Stands | 35 |
| Chapter Five | Town Meeting | 39 |
| Chapter Six | Treaty with the Six Nations | 44 |
| Chapter Seven | Dear Bethiah | 54 |
| Chapter Eight | Queen Esther's Town | 61 |
| Chapter Nine | Tories and Traitors | 71 |
| Chapter Ten | Fort Jenkins | 75 |
| Chapter Eleven | York's Place at Wyalusing | 80 |
| Chapter Twelve | Dealing with Tories | 83 |
| Chapter Thirteen | The Tories' Revenge | 89 |
| Chapter Fourteen | The capture of John Jenkins | 94 |
| Chapter Fifteen | A cruel trek | 99 |
| Chapter Sixteen | Chemung Village | 102 |
| Chapter Seventeen | Red Jacket | 107 |
| Chapter Eighteen | Off to Fort Niagara | 112 |
| Chapter Nineteen | Painted Post | 117 |
| Chapter Twenty | Old Man Fitz | 122 |
| Chapter Twenty One | The flax break | 127 |
| Chapter Twenty Two | The Foxes of the Susquehanna | 131 |
| Chapter Twenty Three | Collecting Tories | 135 |
| Chapter Twenty Four | A Neighbor's Betrayal | 144 |
| Chapter Twenty Five | Secord's Word | 153 |
| Chapter Twenty Six | Up River Rescue | 162 |
| Chapter Twenty Seven | Prisoners of Fort Niagara | 168 |
| Chapter Twenty Eight | Poor Pickering | 171 |
| Chapter Twenty Nine | The Hole at Niagara | 176 |
| Chapter Thirty | The Ghoul | 179 |
| Chapter Thirty One | A friend, a enemy | 187 |
| Chapter Thirty Two | The Stropes are taken | 193 |
| Chapter Thirty Three | The babe Rudolf | 201 |
| Chapter Thirty Four | Tioga Point | 208 |
| Chapter Thirty Five | Jenkins Returns | 212 |
| Chapter Thirty Six | Tunkhannock | 216 |
| Chapter Thirty Seven | Fate's Warning | 219 |
| Chapter Thirty Eight | Queen Esther's War | 223 |
| Chapter Thirty Nine | White Dog Sacrifice | 230 |
| Chapter Forty | Brant & Butler | 234 |
| Chapter Forty One | The Scouts | 238 |
| Chapter Forty Two | Escape! | 242 |
| Chapter Forty Three | Jenkins' Wedding | 245 |
| Chapter Forty Four | Gucingerachton | 250 |
| Chapter Forty Five | A Tory's Promise | 253 |
| Chapter Forty Six | The Harding Massacre | 256 |
| Chapter Forty Seven | Bailey's Farm | 261 |
| Chapter Forty Eight | Young John Hadsall survives | 270 |
| Chapter Forty Nine | Gencho's Ambush | 273 |

| | | |
|---|---|---|
| Chapter Fifty | Esther Mourns | Page 279 |
| Chapter Fifty One | Fort Wintermoot | Page 283 |
| Chapter Fifty Two | Fort Jenkins capitulates | Page 287 |
| Chapter Fifty Three | Parley | Page 292 |
| Chapter Fifty Four | Muster for Battle! | Page 299 |
| Chapter Fifty Five | Drummer Strike Up! | Page 306 |
| Chapter Fifty Six | A Spirited March | Page 313 |
| Chapter Fifty Seven | Every Man to his Duty! | Page 317 |
| Chapter Fifty Eight | Perfect! All so Perfect! | Page 322 |
| Chapter Fifty Nine | The Battle | Page 325 |
| Chapter Sixty | Targeting | Page 342 |
| Chapter Sixty One | Go where the Rabbit won't go! | Page 346 |
| Chapter Sixty Two | Forty Fort | Page 350 |
| Chapter Sixty Three | The Horrors of War | Page 355 |
| Chapter Sixty Four | The Hanover Boys | Page 360 |
| Chapter Sixty Five | Save a Guinea | Page 363 |
| Chapter Sixty Six | Fratricide | Page 366 |
| Chapter Sixty Seven | The Horse's Tail | Page 374 |
| Chapter Sixty Eight | The Horrible Aftermath | Page 377 |
| Chapter Sixty Nine | Zebulon Butler Departs | Page 383 |
| Chapter Seventy | Queen Esther's Rock | Page 389 |
| Chapter Seventy One | Carey's Adoption | Page 398 |
| Chapter Seventy Two | Back from the Dead | Page 401 |
| Chapter Seventy Three | The eerie shadows | Page 405 |
| Chapter Seventy Four | Pittston Fort | Page 408 |
| Chapter Seventy Five | Godspeed John Jenkins | Page 415 |
| Chapter Seventy Six | The Upper Road | Page 422 |
| Chapter Seventy Seven | Death Along the Lackawanna | Page 427 |
| Chapter Seventy Eight | Liberty Rises from the Ashes | Page 431 |
| Chapter Seventy Nine | Curbing the Indians | Page 439 |
| Chapter Eighty | Butler claims Forty Fort | Page 443 |
| Chapter Eighty One | Jenkins' Ride | Page 449 |
| Chapter Eighty Two | Life born anew | Page 452 |
| Chapter Eighty Three | The Stroke of a Quill Pen | Page 457 |
| Chapter Eighty Four | We must! | Page 462 |
| Chapter Eighty Five | The Ludicrous and Sad | Page 466 |
| Chapter Eighty Six | Bullock's farm | Page 475 |
| Chapter Eighty Seven | Promises made, promises broken | Page 479 |
| Chapter Eighty Eight | Hollenback's relief | Page 486 |
| Chapter Eighty Nine | Odd old Friends | Page 490 |
| Chapter Ninety | The Great Runaway | Page 496 |
| Chapter Ninety One | The Best Laid Plans | Page 499 |
| Chapter Ninety Two | A woman's sufferings | Page 502 |
| Chapter Ninety Three | Indian Butler Departs | Page 508 |
| Chapter Ninety Four | Fort Penn's Refuge | Page 511 |
| Letters of witnesses | | Page 516 |

## Chapter One
### Noah's Web: The Massacre of 1763

A mist rose from the valley in the pale autumn morning. Lush fields of ripening grain waved in the gentle breeze. Now and then tri-cornered hats bobbed through the trails intersecting the fertile fields. Diligent settlers went about the work of the day; leading oxcarts along the trails criss-crossing the valley, gathering wood from the thick forests bracing the valley, and tending to the other necessary tasks of life on the frontier.

One of the settlers, Noah Hopkins, stopped along the trail climbing one of the mountains bracing the valley. Gazing down, he drank in the beauty before him, letting out a long sigh. 1763; it proved to be a good year for the Connecticut settlers of *Wyoming**. 1764 held even greater promise. More settlers would certainly pour in from Connecticut come spring, spurred on by his and his fellow pioneers' success.

A tremendous sense of pride swelled his chest in recognition of the great efforts each golden field below represented. His, and many of his fellows' toil, blood, and sweat cleared those fields. In that, a piece of their hearts bond them to this virgin land. Remembering the rough, rocky, and hard soil of Connecticut, he felt well of his decision to purchase a share in the Susquehanna Land Company.

The Wyoming Valley stretched out before him. Glints of crimson, yellow, and gold speckled the trees and teased the mist slowly rising from the valley. The beautiful Susquehanna River wound its way through it all on its relentless quest for the sea. A more serine place did not exist in all of God's creation, at least not for Noah and his fellows. He silently bowed his head and mouthed a quick prayer for Providence's continued protection of their isolated haven amidst the wilderness. Bless this land Lord. Bless these people.

Others of his race knew of this handsome valley but did not settle in it. Their loss, Noah reasoned. He wondered of their rants, especially of the most recent, delivered by one of the *Moravian* missionaries passing through to preach to the Indians at Wyalusing, warning them to vacate the valley before they met reprisals from the Iroquois to the north or from the Pennsylvanians to the south.

Let them come, Noah reasoned, for he felt their claim on the land to be most solid. The King's Connecticut Charter of 1662 and the Albany Treaty of 1754 assured their right of soil. The others' claims all fell flat in the face of the two documents. If honor and fair play dwelt at all in their detractors' hearts, their claim would prevail. If not, they would find dire

*\*Wyoming at the time of the American Revolution was considered to be the area along the Susquehanna River from Tioga Point(present Athens Pa.) to present Nescopeck Pa.*

and severe consequences in contesting Wyoming's rightful claim. Any attempt to usurp this soil would be met by whatever force necessary.

Turning, Noah trudged slowly up the trail, whistling to relieve his mind of such anxious thoughts. He had noticed the bright yellow leaves of Ginseng along the trail yesterday. Its root, highly prized in the Far East, brought a good price when taken to Philadelphia to be sold and shipped. Thus, he brought along a long walking stick to tap the head of any rattlesnake he encountered to dispatch it, a sack to hold his prize, and a small metal implement to help pry the root from the earth.

Spying a hint of the prized plant down the trail to his left he started for it, stopping suddenly from the distinct report of gunshots. Standing perfectly still he listened intently for a moment. The crisp and still morning air remained silent. His heart pounded in his ears. Just somebody shooting at one of the ever-present wolves plaguing the valley or a catamount, he reasoned, staying deathly still. His eyes fell to the Ginseng plant below him.

He bent down, ready to claim his prize.

A series of loud gunshots jolted him up from the ground, his eyes alive with fear. Haunting yells and screams echoed from the valley below. More gunshots joined the yells. Cry tinged with fear filled the air.

Immediately turning, he rambled down the path toward, rather than away from, the cries of horror. Something is happening, he told himself. Something terrible.

The screams and yells increased, along with the report of many more firelocks, hastening his steps all the more. Skidding to a stop upon the spot from which he had beheld the valley's beauty but a few minutes before he gasped at the sight below him.

Smoke already started rising from cabins along the river, set alight by scurrying painted men clenching firebrands in their hands and darting about them. People rushed from the barns and cabins, to and fro, mercilessly pursued by gruesomely painted men. Firelocks spew angry puffs of smoke from the end of them, felling many unfortunate souls. Tomahawks waved in the air, coming down hard on many fugitives running from the flaming cabins. Spears flew and struck several others. Triumphant war whoops mingled with the cries of terror.

Noah paled at the horrible sight below him, cursing himself for not bringing along his rifle. His feet suddenly felt like a ton of bricks. Solid fear gripped him. His mind seemed to pour out of his ears.

A rustle to his rear stood the hair on the nape of his neck on end. He turned ever so slowly. Several of the painted devils crept cautiously along the trailside behind him. They stopped all at once, each slowly turning toward him.

Dark and piercing eyes, awash with a stern look of death, stared back at him. None of the painted men even blinked or looked down to the firelocks they gripped tightly in their hands. Their thumbs all clicked back the hammers of the firelocks at the same time.

The clicks sounded loudly in his mind, alerting all of his senses in an instant. His feet instantly lightened. In another instant he ran madly down the trail. His fingers instinctively relaxed, dropping the stick, bag, and metal implement in his wake. Survival meant getting away quickly.

War whoops assaulted the air to his rear. Several distinct buzzing sounds passed close to his person. Scrunching his shoulders, he plowed headlong down the side of the trail and into the forest. Saplings and low branches snapped from his flailing hands in his mad plunge for freedom and life. Slick leaves under his feet made them fly from under him, sending him slipping and sliding down the mountainside.

Rolling over and over, welcoming the increasing momentum, and praying the hand of God held him in his grasp. A great fallen tree suddenly stopped him with a thud. Frantically, he tumbled over it to shield himself from his pursuers. His breath raced in his heaving chest. He cursed it for its noise, his eyes darting all around, seeking any avenue of further escape. His heart pounded in fear of his antagonists pouring over the log and quickly dispatching him, or worse. The thought of being the object of their cruel ritualized torture festivals made him cringe.

Seeing nothing but the steep leaf-covered mountainside below, he tried to stand, falling under the slippery leaves again. His fingers clawed into the rough bark of the fallen tree, tearing it in a desperate effort to use it for leverage. His feet slipped again despite his hold on the tree and he cursed the noise of his rash acts under his heaving breaths.

His eyes shot all around again. His deep and rapid breaths, along with his flailing feet, roared over the sound of his thudding heart in his ears. He must do something! They must be near! In sheer desperation his eyes locked on the dark end of the hollow log facing him. Without a moment's hesitation he scampered into the dark hole, hoping it not to be too late. Hoping to live another day.

Clawing his way deep inside the huge log he scrunched himself in the smallest ball possible. He froze, silently scolding himself not to draw such deep breaths, despite of his urgent need for air. Finally bringing his breath under control, he listened.

No noise sounded around him, save the distant horrible whoops and screams from the valley below. Suddenly his eyes shot straight toward the opening of the log, catching a slight movement. A huge spider slid down on a long silken string and started weaving a web, apparently oblivious of the bulging eyes full of terror shinning at it from the deep recesses of the log.

Noah felt a strange fascination watching the spider weave its intricate web. The sun glistened off the slender silken threads. Odd, somewhat eerie, but somehow beautiful, he thought, as all God's creations. Here, huddled in this log, hiding from certain death amid the screams of those less fortunate below, he witnessed Providence and praised it, silently, but full-heartedly. He recognized Providence's hand and blessed it. The web provided the perfect shield from the prying eyes of the demons pursuing him. Halleluiah!

He did not wait on the demons long. A slight thud sounded on top of the log, followed by another, then another. His breath went away again.

The slight rustle of a few leaves about the mouth of the log made him shrink back into its shadows even further. A shadow, then a head, appeared in the light of the opening. The head moved from side to side, peering into the web. Its dark and unforgiving eyes shone from a face painted red. No sign of mercy or humanity shone through them, only the cruel intensity of a hunter's eye embodied them. They widened, not in recognition, but with a start from a hand placed on his shoulder. The eyes turned and looked with contempt toward the intrusive hand. A gruff and disgusted grunt followed.

The eyes, burning with disgust, rose from the entrance of the log. Two pairs of legs covered with leather leggings appeared in their place.

Noah did not move a muscle, even to breathe. Had the devils seen him? Was this just one of their cruel games? These, and other anxious thoughts, raced through his mind. God's shield, even if only the silken threads of a spider's web, would shield him. He felt certain of it and drew great strength from it. Thy will be done.

The legs took a few steps from the log. Both of the braves squatted but a few feet from the web. Their eyes now darted to and fro, seemingly befuddled by the sudden disappearance of their prey. After a long moment of contemplation both braves looked to the sky, apparently mystified by the sudden disembodiment of their prey.

A spine-tingling wail broke both of them from their confused gazes. They both yelled and immediately stood in response. One of them promptly broke into a wild run down the mountainside. The other started to move, but then suddenly stopped. Turning back to the web, he bent down before it. His hand fell to the bullet bag on his belt and jingled it for an awful second. The fingers of the other hand rose to the fragile web, gently touching it. It jiggled and danced from the force of the touch. The spider scurried for cover up one of its sides. The eyes of the brave followed it, lifting from their stare into the log.

A loud yell erupted from the brave, sending his head reeling back from its force. The warrior stood, raised his rifle in the air and darted after his comrade, leaving Noah with his heart thudding uncontrollably in his ears.

He listened, daring not to breathe, waiting for the warrior's yelps to fade in the distance. After a long moment he finally gasped for breath. Breathing the blessed air never felt so good. But he soon lost his sense of relief to the sounds of horror filtering through the air from below. Once again he cursed himself for not bringing his rifle.

The horror he had just escaped played at his thoughts. Contempt filled his soul. Contempt for the painted devils of the forest. His contempt grew into a burning rage for the savage devils, and for himself for not heeding the many warnings. If only he had not forgotten his rifle!

The cries and shouts of anguish from the valley below intensified his rage and feeling of helplessness. But what could he do? If he crept forth from his haven death hovered all around; he had seen it. He had barely escaped it.

Trying to find anyway to clear his mind, he squeezed back into the log and clenched his teeth, staring blankly at the spider web. It jiggled, giving his heart a start, but to his relief the spider scampered back down the web and took its place in the center of it. Mesmerized by it he now sit perfectly still, waiting for its unwary prey to be caught in its awaiting web. Much as he, Noah thought to himself. A web awaited him outside the sanctuary of the log. A web of certain death.

Patience, he whispered ever so slightly to himself, patience. Leaning back he rested his head against the log, praying for the sounds of anguish to fade. Somehow he drifted into an uneasy sleep, wishing to escape the nightmares of the day. He only hoped they did not pursue him in his dreams.

But the anguish followed. He soon awoke, twisting and screaming inside the log. Coming to his senses almost immediately, he sat painfully still, listening intently for any telltale sounds of discovery from his merciless foes. Darkness and silence filled the air.

After a few tense moments he crawled to the end of the log and stared into the pitch-black night. Suddenly he felt a silky substance at his cheek. It jiggled. He waited for his friend, the spider, to scamper away from the unintentional danger he bore. Ever so gently, he pushed just enough of the web aside to make way for him. Ironically, he almost mouthed a thank you to the life-saving spider before regaining his composure.

An eerie silence greeted him outside the log. Standing erect, he slowly surveyed the area with a cautious eye. Nothing stirred on the slope around him. No wails crept from the valley. Only the heavy and desperate sense of dread clinging to the wake of every disaster filled the silent air. In wake of a massacre nothing stirred.

Taking a deep breath he stared down into the valley below. Lurid flames speckled the valley with no movement but glowing embers rising into the still air. He could act now, he told himself. He stepped forwards, mentally bracing himself for the horrors he knew awaited him in the valley below.

Reaching the bottom of the mountain he watched the morning glow of dawn slowly creep over the mountains. He hurriedly trotted down the trail, hoping to meet anyone besides an Indian. He did not go far before he met his wish with a great sense of dread.

Someone, or what had once been someone, lie at his feet along the trail. The clump of mangled flesh did not move. It lie face down, the clothing on its back ripped into shreds. Pools of blood laid all around it. Ever so slowly he rolled the body over onto its back. Bulging eyes, still alive with the terror of the last sight they witnessed, stared up to him. Deep slashes covered its face and upper torso, making it impossible to recognize it as anyone whom he had once known. A quick prayer rolled off his tongue before he rose and continued on his macabre quest.

But a few rods up the trail another body greeted him. To his relief no telltale signs of torture desecrated it. It lie face up, its eyes closed, looking for all the world to be merely sleeping, except for the gaping hole in the middle of its chest. Stepping toward the slain soul he suddenly halted. This face he knew. Nathaniel Terry. A good man. A good friend. He and his brother Parshall had been among the first to enter the valley. They both shared such high hopes for Wyoming, now one of them lay dead on the fields which had once held such promise. He looked down and silently prayed that the mangled mass of flesh he first encountered had not been Parshall. Muttering another quick prayer he trudged further down the trail.

Smoldering cabins soon spread before him. He stumbled toward a mill and blockhouse on Mill Creek, knowing any survivors would gather there.

Reaching the mill he fell to his knees, overcome by the sight before him. No survivors gathered here, only the dead awaited him. Men lie strewn in a crowded circle around a cross of logs hastily set in the ground. Awls stood erect in each and every eye socket. Pitchforks, spears, and arrows pierced many of the slain, rising in the air as markers of the gruesome task. Disgust mixed with pity overwhelmed his soul.

Stumbling incoherently through the bodies he stopped, gasping in recognition of the faces he encountered. Just a few hours before these very faces smiled at him, alive and full of hope. "My God, my God," he mumbled through his grief. "What hell hath come to Wyoming?" His eyes swirled around in his head. He fell, overcome with the scene of death. He closed his eyes to block it out. "Oh my, oh my," he muttered, collapsing in grief to the ground with a thud. He felt something warm at his feet, smoldering embers from a fire once circling the bottom of the post, he realized. The air, poisoned by rotting human flesh, hung dead.

He reached out, feeling the wooden post before him. Feeling a wet and slimy sensation he flung his hands away and quickly rose, forcing his eyes open. He looked to his hands. Turning his red palms up, he stared in horror at the blood and slime covering them. His eyes slowly gazed to the cross covered with blood. Tears flooded his eyes. Falling to his knees he bowed his head in pure anguish.

Catching his panting breath through great sobs he forced his eyes back to the cross. Creeping up the length of it his eyes beheld the pitiful creature stretched upon it. Many cuts and abrasions covered the half-roasted remains. Torn and cut breasts, along with long flowing blood-matted strands of red hair from the fringes of the head, identified the tortured soul as a woman. Her head bowed down to her chest, revealing a bright red spot atop her skull. Tattered and burned rags danced in bloody strips about her body. Outstretched arms held her in place on the cross from which her mutilated body hung. Nails hammered into her wrists still trickled blood. Leather thongs covered her balled fists. A few of them burned away revealing hinges, apparently placed in her hands red-hot. No feet dangled from her legs, but lie detached and thrown into the smoldering ashes at the foot of the cross.

A solid fear, one greater than any he felt before, even yesterday, gripped him. The savages may still be lurking about! He must get to the settlements along the Delaware River for help! These souls, he thought, gazing up at the poor woman hanging from the cross, must be avenged!

A deep and burning rage in his empty stomach came alive. He must get food before he struggled through the wilderness. Turning away from the cross and death circle, he gazed about the ruined valley. Nothing but devastation fell under his sorrowful eyes.

He ran pell-mell toward the river, hoping the cabins on the far shore faired better than the ones around him. Creeping out into the swirling waters he dove into them, madly swimming for the far shore. Rambling up the riverbank his heart sank. Smoke wisped in the air from charred ruins. He stumbled to a few bodies lying among the ruins, feeling relief from his decision to keep his family in Connecticut. Remembering the sight of his burned-out cabin on the other shore he shunned the thought of his family in it. Refusing to let them come with him had saved their lives. But still the thought brought little relief to his soul watching the poor unfortunates lying about. What hell hath come to Wyoming? A savage hell. A vengeful, merciless, and cruel hell.

Silently he added the numbers of unfortunates he saw so far in his mind. With great relief he realized the numbers did not represent the total population. Many must have escaped, or, he thought with dread, have been taken prisoner. Either way, one thing remained constant, he was alone, except for the dead.

He looked sullenly down the great Susquehanna River, dreading the thought of the Pennamites. Whether they had something to do with this or not, they would hold little sympathy for he and the others. He knew the only hope of sympathy lie on the Delaware River, directly east.

A rage burned within him at the thought of his fellow white men instigating this massacre. Biting his lip he fell to his knees, cursing and mumbling vows of revenge. No! He finally rebuked himself. Now is not the time! The Pennamite matter would be dealt with latter by he and his fellow New Englanders. First he had to survive, for his family and for the unfortunate souls lying around him. Blood covered this land. Only blood shed in the name of justice would cleanse it in return.

He swam the river again and again but still found nothing of value on either side of the river. What few buildings remaining bore nothing to help him. No survivors. No food. No weapons.

He stumbled crestfallen down the west bank of the river in his dripping clothes, dreading another swim back across the river. But he must find something! Sixty miles of untamed wilderness lie before him and safety, crawling with rattlesnakes, panthers, wolves, and savages.

His knees fell to his knees, weak with grief. A grief coupled with a deep sense of loneliness. He let out a furious and frustrated groan, letting it push his head back. As his head lowered his eyes caught sight of feathers lying just over the crest of the trail. A dead Indian? He suddenly realized not one of the enemy lay among the slain.

A rage swept through his veins. His fists tightened. Rising to his feet he marched steadfastly toward the feathers, ready to vent his anger upon the living or the dead. Coming within sight of the clump of feathers he stopped, looking dumfound at the dead turkey lying across the trail.

Someone must have shot it and dropped it when the massacre started! Now it left him a feast! A feast for strength so he could make his escape!

Muttering a quick prayer he scooped up the turkey, holding it tightly to his chest. He looked all around, cradling his prize.

He started feverously plucking the bird, cursing the stubborn and smelly feathers. Fire! He needed fire! His mind thought back to a iron pot lying among the ashes of a cabin he just passed. Sprinting back to the burned-out cabin, still clutching the bird to his chest he kicked aside some debris, gathering up the pot. Gathering a few half-charred timbers he knelt down to some glowing embers. Angrily blowing them back to life, he fueled the fire. It quickly blazed to life. "Life-giving fire, thank you dear God," he muttered. "Now I must get water!"

Grabbing the pot he quickly filled it with river water. In what seemed an eternity the water boiled, loosening the tough feathers. Quickly fashioning a spit across the flames he hastily roasted his prize, ever mindful of the sun high in the sky.

Pennamites to the south. Indians to the north and west. It left only one way. One way to live. One way to carry the horrors he had witnessed back to the world.

Gnawing at the half-cooked bird he quelled the rage burning in his empty stomach. Stuffing his shirt with great chunks of the bird's half-cooked flesh he turned to the east, plunging into the river one last time.

Climbing to the east shore he ran without looking back, gauging his advance by the long shadows cast by the sun behind him. The shadows grew deeper and deeper into the dense forest, creating a foreboding column of darkness under the tall trees. But onward he trod, knowing the threats lying in the shadows to his front weighed lightly against what lie in the shadows behind him.

A deep sense of terrible resolve filled him. This massacre must be avenged! It had to be! He must get word to the Delaware River settlements!

The memory of the abode of happiness and hope just a morning ago played at his soul, feeding his steps, and his resolve.

Wyoming, in very truth, lay deserted and forsaken with his passing. It must be avenged!

## Chapter Two
*The Cross of 1763*

Major Asher Clayton sat stoically in his saddle watching the troops of his command file past him on the trail below. He clasp his hands tightly on the pommel of his saddle deep in thought, so deep in thought he did not notice the captain of one of his companies riding up to him.

The captain reined his horse to stop, waiting anxiously to be recognized. His eyes followed the major's eyes down to the column of mounted men filing along the trail below them. He knew the major to be a deep-thinking man, but also strictly military; just what he expected from one whom held a King's commission of rank. He waited for the longest moment before clearing his throat, not wishing to gain his commander's scorn by speaking out of turn.

"Yes, Captain Stewart?" Clayton muttered without breaking his gaze upon the men.

"They're a great lot, that bunch, just the kind we need to do a proper job of clearing these parts of the red menace," Lazarus Stewart flatly stated with a sake of his head and a self-satisfied grin.

Major Clayton sighed. The captains of the Paxton Rangers hinted of their desire to exterminate all Indians, despite their agreement of orders to the contrary. They figured it to be a necessity to march upon Wyalusing and hinted about it all along the trail from Fort Augusta. Now, but a few miles from their destination, the Wyoming Valley, the major expected the hints to grow into a demand. A loud demand. No matter, he already considered their proposal and rehearsed a comment in his mind long ago. Miles ago.

"Our orders are clear, fine sir," he said, drawing a snuff box from his waistcoat pocket to sniff a pinch of finely pulverized tobacco. "We are to proceed to Wyoming and destroy the grains or whatever else is left behind by the New Englanders whom have been ordered out of the valley, and," he added after a long pause, "intercept any war parties of hostiles returning from raids on Northampton."

Wheeling his horse about he rode toward the front of the column, leaving the captain before he could reply.

After a long moment he called "See to your company, Captain!" back over his shoulder.

"Just what I expected," Lazarus scoffed under his breath, "from one whom holds a King's commission."

Spurring his horse down to the column he rode up next to another officer riding in the long single file of men and horses.

"Good day Lieutenant Hunter," he said. Hunter had only joined the expedition the day before, which had not given Lazarus enough time to sum up the new officer's feelings about the Indian question. After all, though new, Hunter already had the ear of the commander of Fort Augusta, Colonel Burd. Perhaps he shared the feelings of the Paxton Rangers. Any ally, or any port, proved good in a storm.

"I think it to be most foolish to proceed any further without detaching a strong scout," Lazarus said to the silent man. "It's most unwise to approach any hostile land without a look ahead. Most unwise."

Hunter rolled an eye toward the brash frontier captain.

"Hostile Indians or Yankees, makes no difference, both are headstrong vagabonds," Lazarus continued, undaunted by Hunter's silence.

"Major Clayton is in command," Hunter finally snapped. "He has my, as well as Colonel Burd's, complete confidence." With glaring eyes he turned, looking back down the column. "Is not your place with your company, sir?"

Lazarus smiled. Now he knew. "Just trying to save scalps," he muttered. Reining his horse about he trotted back along the tight column.

A rushing courier quickly overtook the retreating captain. "We are approaching Wyoming!" he announced loudly. "All officers to the front at once!"

Stewart and three other horsemen immediately answered the call, galloping hard for the front of the column. They found Major Clayton standing atop a large boulder overlooking the valley below him. He held a spyglass to his eye and continued staring through it. The officers all raised themselves high in their saddles, craning their necks to gaze into the valley below.

"Well, gentlemen," Clayton finally said, still staring intently through the spyglass. "We have a situation on our hands." Lowering the spyglass from his eye he slowly turned toward the anxious officers.

After drawing a long breath of consideration he said, "Captain Stewart, you and your rangers get down into the valley and secure it."

Stewart instantly whooped and waved his hat back to his rangers in triumph.

The company of rangers spurt forth, galloping madly toward their awaiting captain.

"What of hostiles, Major?" Stewart asked, twirling about on his anxious mount.

Clayton looked down deep in thought and raised his head again. "If you encounter any hostile Indians do as you may," he answered.

"Just what I wanted to hear, fine sir, yes, indeed!" Stewart said with a whoop. Raising his rifle high in the air he led the mounted rangers headlong down the trail into the valley. They thundered down the trail post haste, each raising their rifles to the ready. Their burning rage, thirst for revenge, and thrill for the hunt echoed from their yelling throats, spreading like a contagion among the remaining companies. Soon horses nervously milled about, sensing the angst of the men on their backs. A lone whoop from somewhere along their line grew into a chorus. Long rifles and muskets rose in their anxious hands. They lived on the frontier, too. They had cabins gracing the fringes of the frontier full of their loved ones and their prosperity. Hostiles threatened them also.

"Sometimes there is a need for such men as the Paxton Rangers," Clayton said to the remaining captains. "Unfortunately."

The officers nodded, struggling to hold back the reins of their jittery horses.

"Advance!" Clayton suddenly ordered, raising his hand and turning his mount toward the trail. He trotted at a carefully controlled gait, seeming oblivious to the anxious men following him. The men following soon followed suit, impressed by the disciplined example of their graceful leader. Refinement and culture soothed the beast.

Also, the further they followed in the wake of the *'mad'* rangers the more their anger melted into a hollow and foreboding sense of the unknown. The chilly winds of Autumn howled a melancholy wail through the mountain pines. Through the breaks in the foliage from the falling leaves wisps of smoke rose from the valley below. The ranger's whoops faded in the valley. The further they descended the trail the less birds chirped. The less squirrels scampered through the trees. An eerie silence hung in the air. A solemn mood swept through the ranks. Rifles shifted in increasingly anxious hands. Eyes peered into the gloomy forest surrounding them. A growing stench fouled nostrils.

After what seemed a march of a hundred miles, they finally filed off the trail into the river flat. Morbid looks shone from the faces of the silent rangers milling about. All remnants of their former boisterous attitudes somehow melted from their faces. Following the rangers' lead, they filed to a stop near a burned-out blockhouse.

Captain Stewart and a few other rangers stood nearby, circling the foot of a charred and rough wooden cross. Pitchfork handles and spear handles stood erect in the many bodies circled about the foot of a cross. None of the rangers spoke more than an angry mumble, especially Stewart, whom stood staring at the tortured soul hanging from the cross. His grim eyes betrayed nothing but frustration. He clenched his rifle tightly in his white-fisted knuckles. He gasped against the stench.

Major Clayton dismounted, slowly sliding his sword back into its sheath. He carefully walked through the circle of bodies. The stench made him wince, but he quickly regained his composure and continued to the morbid cross. Pulling a small handkerchief from his pocket he covered his mouth against the growing stench. He had too.

"Their tracks lead to Wyalusing," Stewart reported through gritted teeth, still staring grimly at the woman stretched on the cross.

Clayton said nothing, but just let out a huff through the handkerchief.

"Seeing how fresh the signs are, we could probably still catch the devils," Stewart said, his eyes widening.

Clayton ignored Stewart's remarks and strolled around the cross, staring at the woman. "Ghastly," he said under his breath, more to himself than to anyone else. He coughed against the stench.

"What are your orders, sir?" Lieutenant Hunter called from his horse.

Clayton sighed, lowering the handkerchief from his mouth. He cast a pitiful eye to the woman on the cross before stuffing the handkerchief back into his fine waistcoat's pocket. Slowly turning, he walked back toward the column of men. "Form a burial party at once for these unfortunate souls," he said to Hunter.

Hunter nodded and immediately waved a hand back to his awaiting men. They all promptly dismounted.

"You should find shovels, pickaxes and such around," Clayton said, motioning to the surrounding half-burned buildings and smoldering cabins.

"These are Christian people!" Stewart's voice echoed from the circle of dead men around the cross. "Good Christian people!"

"Yes they are," Clayton said, turning toward the angry voice. "They shall receive a proper Christian burial at that."

Stewart raised his rifle and marched directly toward the haughty officer. "Can't you see what the murdering red bastards did!?!" he exclaimed. "Their tracks, still fresh, may I need remind you, lead upriver to Wyalusing!" He gruffly turned, fit to be tied, and stomped back to his horse. His men did the same.

"Sir!" Hunter admonished him. "Remember your place! Attend to your work!"

"My work, fine sir, is to defend the innocents along the frontier from the savage and murdering devils! And I intend to attend to that work!" Raising his rifle high over his head he lifted a tomahawk from his belt. "This is all the savage understands!" he said, shoving the tomahawk back into his belt. Mounting, he reined his horse back on its haunches and trotted up to the major. "It is all he shall ever understand!"

"Sir," Clayton said before he reached him. "Post pickets all around the perimeter, we shall camp in the next field, upwind."

"Pickets my arse!" Stewart yelled. "I am off to Wyalusing and then to Tioga Point!" Galloping around in a circle he screamed "Who is with me?"

"Compose yourself Captain!" Clayton barked at him.

"If we ride now we'll perhaps overtake them by first light!" Stewart railed over Clayton's protests.

Clayton waved a hand to a nearby captain to come forth. John Brady galloped forwards, closely followed by his friend and fellow captain, Hawkins Boone.

"Control your mate here, or I shall have him put in irons!" Clayton flatly stated to the two captains.

Gaining a whiff from a breeze flowing from the circle of bodies both men winced before nodding to the upset major. With sour looks of contempt they turned toward their unruly comrade.

"Come now, Lazarus," Brady pleaded, "we mustn't quarrel amongst ourselves, especially out here in the sugarbush."

"John Brady, fine sir," Stewart scoffed. "I never thought there'd come a day I hear a coward's breath from the likes of you."

Brady clutched his rifle and raised it to his chest.

"There's no call for such talk!" Hawkins Boone immediately shouted. He carefully reached out and laid a hand on Brady's rifle, slowly easing it back down.

"Nor from the likes of you, Captain Boone," Stewart continued, abruptly wheeling his horse around to face the cross. The stench made his gasp. "Look at her!" he said, raising his rifle barrel toward the limp woman's body. "That could easily be any of our wives or daughters up there! God forbid! Your's or mine! Are we to cower so low just to please the Quakers sitting warm by their hearths in far off Philadelphia? I tell you, from this woman's lips, which can speak no more, or plead no more, they do not give a damn about any on the frontier, but only the savage! Look! All of you look! Are we to share a poltroon's blindness to truth? No! We must not! This poor woman, Christian woman, beckons to us all from beyond to avenge her tortured soul! Look! Look at her and bear witness of what the savage is capable of! As men we must act! We must pursue the wolves to their lair!" He turned toward Clayton. "Your orders are to intercept the hostiles if you can! Well, here you can! Don't let the chance slip away! Follow your orders! Ride to Wyalusing! The day grows long! If you lack the stomach for such work make way for those whom do not! Avenge these murdered souls! In the name of the most holy I beg you, sir, on his behalf! For justice it is I speak! Fine sir! Simple justice!"

Brady and Boone did not move, but stood ever so still, contemplating their fellow captain's words. The ranks milled about uneasily. The words touched them, also. Ceasing their work, they too stood still, looking up to the poor woman stretched across the cross and down to the tortured bodies strewn about the ground.

Clayton, noticing the effect the bombastic captain had on everyone had had enough of him. Drawing his sword he pointed it straight at Stewart. "For the very last time, my dear Captain," he said through gritted teeth, "calm down!"

Stewart glared at him, but said nothing. No one spoke for the longest moment.

"Well now," Stewart finally said through his own clenched teeth. "If that were a Clayton hanging up there I mite reckon your attitude to be quite different, fine sir!"

Clayton bit his lip, jabbing his sword in the air between the them, but carefully checking his thrust. This ranger captain did have a way with words, and of getting under one's skin.

The chilly wind grew, somehow intensifying rather than lessening the stench. Wisps of smoke danced in the foul air from the cabins and fields. An eerie howl rode on it from the depths of the forest. The beasts of the forest howled in protest of the interlopers whom spoiled their feast. They wished to claim the rotting spoils of war. They wished to claim the rights of the wilderness.

Each man felt the same chill run down his spine. Many pulled their hunting frocks tight against the breeze, but it did little to quell the growing chill spreading through their hearts. The sudden realization of just how many miles lay between them and civilization shone clear in each of their eyes, and hearts. The stark reality of their isolation drifted on each of the eerie howls.

"We shall bury these dead properly!" the voice of their commander sounded above the eerie howls. "We shall see to the other matters on the morrow."

Stewart, nor any other voice, offered any protest. The forbidding and deep veil of darkness descending over the forsaken valley amplified the need of interdependency. They needed to band together this night to ensure they lived to see the light of the next day. Too many devils lie cloaked in the darkness, ready to strike at any weak point. Together they offered no weak point. Together their chances of survival greatly increased.

Each man went about setting up their camp, hoping to find some semblance of order in performing their tasks. The burial party dutifully worked in torchlight. Pickets posted themselves at every approach to the morose camp without direction from their captains. Each man knew his duty. Each man had to protect the whole of the lot, and in that himself.

Nonetheless, morning broke none too soon for the anxious pickets. With light came clear sight, vanquishing the devils lurking in the shadows deep within the forest. Now the howls and calls of beasts seemed much less threatening, though they still cringed at the call of a turkey or caw of a crow. The devils of the Six Nations imitated the animals' calls and used them to communicate in the shadows, striking from them to perhaps finish their work of the previous day.

"Captain's call!" a commanding voice announced, breaking the eerie silence. The officers quickly responded from around huddled campfires. They found their commander milling about the newly dug graves of the poor unfortunates.

He did not say a word upon their approach, or turn to face them. His eyes looked up the winding river to the north, deep in thought.

The officers minded their tongues and waited, even bold Lazarus Stewart.

"You know gentlemen," Clayton finally said without turning toward them. The river seemed more interesting to him. More foreboding. "Governor Hamilton explicitly forbade this expedition to advance upon Chief Papoonhank and other so-called religious Indians residing at Wyalusing until as such time we learn they harbor or receive any hostiles. If that should turn out to be the case, they richly deserve whatever retribution their mischief warrants."

"The trail is clear and runs directly to Wyalusing," Stewart said, suddenly feeling his tongue free to move. Perhaps some commonsense etched itself into the pompous officer last night through the howls of the uneasy wilderness. The wilderness played by its own harsh rules, civility be damned. "The signs of plunder they are burdened with shows all along it," he added, turning toward the graves. "Plunder from these innocents. They aren't even attempting to mask their trail."

"Yes, it seems so," Clayton said, looking down soulfully to the ground. He kicked up some of it with an angry scuff of his boot. "That is why I called this council. What say you all, gentlemen?"

Shaking his head and letting out a disgusted grunt, John Brady spoke first. "This is enough to try the patience of a saint, it is!" he said.

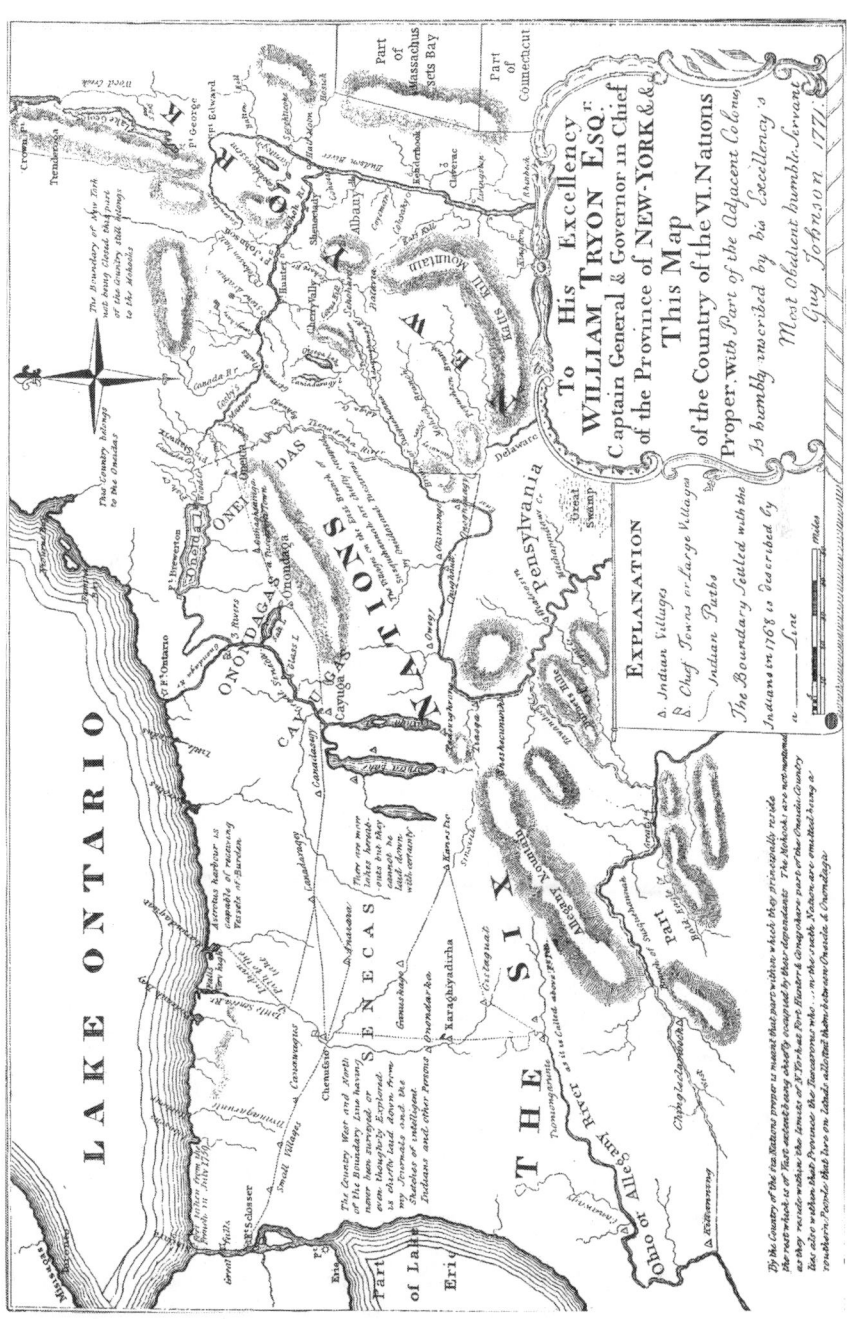

"How many more poor souls lay dead in Northampton by the free hand of these ruthless devils?" Hawkins Boone added. "God forbid, but I'm with Lazarus. We must stop them, or at least bloody their damn noses a bit so they'll think twice before doing any more devilish acts such as this! My God, simple humanity and justice demand we act!"

"Indeed," Lieutenant Hunter agreed.

Clayton slowly clasped his hands behind his back and turned to face the apprehensive officers. The same cold stare shot back at him from every eye. But one must not behave rashly, with all abandon, fueled by furious emotions. Calm, rational, heads must prevail for justice to be properly administered. That is why he held a King's Commission from the Provincial Governor and the others did not. Rash men do rash acts. But still, the poor tortured souls lying about cried loudly from the grave for vengeance. He stood here, at the foot of their graves, not in some high post far away from it all. A lot could be gained from an successful expedition into the Indian's own country. Successful, that remained the key to silence any criticizing tongue from those in high places far from the horrors. Distance bred tolerance and indifference. Proximity bred humanity, and a thirst for vengeance. Raising his head high, he turned and looked directly into Lazarus Stewart's eyes.

"Sir!" a voice interrupted him before a syllable rolled from his tongue, "a rider approaches!"

They all rushed toward the noise of the thudding hooves. The rider rode hard, indifferent to stealth, a necessity in this wilderness. The rider's message must be most urgent for him to act so rashly. The horse soon appeared from the speckled leaves of the forest. It's master reined the lathered steed to a stop in front of the gathering of officers and swung one leg over the saddle, plopping down squarely in front of Major Clayton. "Dispatch from Colonel Burd, sir!" he reported through rushed breaths.

Clayton grabbed the dispatch and took a few steps away from the others before reading it. He promptly folded it and stuck it into his fine waistcoat's pocket. Colonel Burd, he thought, a man of impeccable timing. He turned toward the officers wearing a slight frown. "Captains!" he said, "lay waste to the remaining grains and buildings at once! Leave nothing! Nothing!" Puzzled and disappointed eyes searched his eyes for reason. "Get to it! At once!" he said. "For Colonel Burd has recalled us to Fort Augusta, posthaste!"

Lazarus Stewart stood firm.

Clayton hastily took off his gloves and slapped them in his hand. He stared directly into the ranger captain's cold eyes. "When your

Colonel Elder volunteered the Paxtang Rangers for this expedition he did so with the explicit understanding they would follow Colonel Burd's orders!" he said. "Do you intend to honor his word?"

A burning stare shot back at Clayton. Stewart rubbed his chin. "Rangers! " he finally barked in frustration, "you heard the orders! Carry them out! Posthaste!"

He gruffly mounted his horse and rode next to Captain Brady sitting quietly atop his own mount and watching the troops raze the valley. "These people may be misguided, these Yankees, but they are brave," he said, raising his chin and casting an eye to Brady.

Brady shook his head. "It is truly horrible what happened here to these people, but they were interlopers, given fair warning, Lazarus," he said. "They had been ordered to remove themselves and they chose to ignore it. The command given by a King's official, no less."

"Yes," Lazarus snarled, "the Kings officials, I know of their caring by counting the scalps taken all along this frontier, both upriver and down!"

Brady stared at him without saying a word.

"This is not over," Lazarus answered his cold stare. "Interlopers, intruders, or whatever, these people have a zeal lacking within the complacent hearts of the King's officials and other people trying to settle this land. I, for one," he added, "will not forget what I have seen this day in this valley." Dropping the reins in his hand he raised an angry fist to the sky.

"Nor shall any of us," Brady said under his breath.

The two men sat and watched the men bustle about them, lighting torches, trampling grain under their horses' hooves, demolishing and setting alight the few remaining structures. Structures built by men of strong heart and zeal. But now they finished what the savage started. Lazarus closed his eyes against the frustrating thought, recognizing the irony of it all. The lust for land made fools of them all.

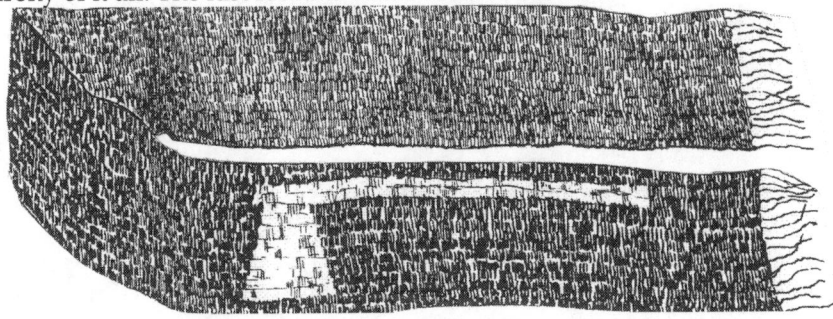

## Chapter Three
*Rampart Rocks: Pennamite-Yankee battle 1775*

"I remember the massacre of 1763, I do, the savages were never as fierce, still sends shivers down my spine when I think on it," Squire Jenkins said to his son. "Then we returned in '69, and had troubles and struggles with the Pennamites all the way up to '71. Thought we had driven the rascals away for good, we did, but alas now we're here in '75, near Christmas and all, and it goes on. And what with the troubles with the Crown and all? What times we live in son, what times. Troubled times indeed."

The old man's lonely words and equally lonely gaze played hard at his son's soul. Those eyes, his son mused, the sights they have endured. He wondered of the past struggles shining so clear in those tired old eyes, eyes soon to endure more struggles, unfortunately. But he held his tongue in respect. He knew his father talked to ease his mind. He did not blame him.

He turned his eyes to the long plain stretching out before them, soon to be filled by hundreds of rascals, the Pennamites, marching upon them flush with victory from destroying their settlements of Charleston and Judea on the West Branch of the mighty Susquehanna River. Now they marched, hundreds strong, to finish their task. Here they marched to drive them out, even though they held a Charter from the King predating any Pennamite Charter. Even though they purchased the land from the Six Nations way back in 1754. Higher and more influential powers declared them all null and void. Money held sway over justice. The Penns and their land-hungry speculator friends held sway over the law. Their position and inherited power precluded everything but the true hearts standing here to defend their rightful homes. Power be damned. Money be damned. Social position be damned.

Gazing up, his eyes ran along the natural formation of rocks around them. They formed a natural barrier from the approaches along the river to the south, and proved formable indeed. The few breaks in them being buttressed up with great fallen logs and rocks made him feel quite certain of their strength, no matter what number assaulted them.

Captain Butler you have outdone yourself, he thought. He chose the perfect defense. The rocks and ledges of *Rampart Rocks* proved an impassable obstacle to any force invading from the south. He only wished such a natural barrier shielded them to the north against an equal, and perhaps more formable foe, the Six Nations. The talk of erecting a fort at Wyalusing always fell short of fruition. Frustrating indeed, but one foe at a time, he reassured himself. One foe at a time.

He turned back to the sight in front of him. Only one small gap lay between the rocks, forcing any invading force to funnel through it. A smaller force could hold out indefinitely against a larger one. "Brilliant defense," he muttered aloud. "Brilliant defense."

"Yes," his father instantly answered. "With men such as we have now the massacre of '63 will never happen again!" He beamed with pride at the long line of two hundred or so men huddled around fires and manning the defensive works around them. Waving his arms around he hugged his stout torso against the chill. Both he and his son looked to the inviting warmth of the numerous campfires behind the line.

"What say you, Ensign Jenkins?" the elder Jenkins asked his son. "Shall we warm ourselves against the morning chill? I say sleeping out here in the frigid cold all night may be fine for those of the younger sort, but I dare say it its hard on old bones, they chill more, I am afraid."

The ensign smiled and took his father by the arm, handing the elder his cane with his other hand.

Another officer, Captain Butler, strolled by them on an inspection of the line. He seemed to anticipate their intentions. "You may warm yourselves," he said, "but be sure to keep your firelocks at the ready. I have a feeling Ensign Alden shall be greeting Mr. Plunkett and his lot soon. Then we shall have some sport!"

"Splendid job, old man!" Squire Jenkins had to say. "You have positioned our troops brilliantly. I dare say these rocks could hold back Caesar's Legions! And the rapids, by God, they shall force them to leave their bateaux and advance by land, the only passage being covered by our guard. Brilliant!"

"Thank you Squire," Butler answered. "I appreciate your confidence." He carefully brought a spyglass to his eye and scanned the far bank of the Susquehanna.

"No need to worry about the east bank,," Ensign Jenkins said. "Lazarus Stewart and the Paxtang Boys will make quick work of any advancing on their front."

"The conflict shall be a sharp one," Butler said, slowing lowering the spyglass. He looked soulfully down to the ground and then up to Squire Jenkins. "But I, for one, and ready to forfeit my life, if need be, for my country."

Neither of the Jenkins men said a word in response. Butler placed the spyglass in his haversack and looked up the line. "I know every man shall due his duty this day, if need be," he said. "Now warm yourselves gentlemen, while you still can."

Both men stumbled to a nearby fire, giving leave to their

commander.

Two other men, each with an armload of wood, soon walked up to the fire. The elder of the two dropped a log on the fire and quickly instructed his son to stir the coals to get the fire blazing again. Rubbing his hands against the chill he looked up to the Jenkins men with a smile. "It's been a mild season so far," he said, crouching close to the fire, "but the chill of this day cuts to the bone."

"That it does, my dear Thomas," Squire Jenkins answered. "It's much too cold for a pair of old souls such as you and I, I dare say. This work is for the young of heart and body, it is."

Pounding hooves tore their attention to the trail from Forty Fort.

"Aye, 'tis Martha, is it not Solomon?" Thomas asked the teenager kneeling beside him.

Solomon quickly rose. "Yes, I believe it is, Father," he said, watching the horses gallop into view.

"You have a fine daughter there, Thomas," the elder Jenkins said, rubbing his hands against the chilly air. "Without her running supplies to this place it would indeed be much more miserable. A full belly staves off the cold."

The young woman thundered into camp to welcoming cheers. Reining up her horses she jumped down from her mount, hastily passing the lead of the packhorses to a sea of eager hands. They immediately relieved the animals of their packs.

"Papa!" Martha said, tying the reins of her mount to a nearby tree branch. She eagerly trotted to her father's fire. "Have you any word?" she asked.

"No, not yet, my darling," Thomas answered, looking down to the breastworks. "But soon, I am told."

Thomas reached out and gave his daughter a great hug. Pride beamed from his face. "I thank God for blessing me with such fine children," he said to both of his children.

Martha smiled and pulled her haversack over her head and shoulder. Kneeling, she pulled a small bundle from it, carefully laying it on a flat stone by the fireside. She gingerly unfolded the cloth wrapping on the bundle. "Here Papa," she said, raising her hand to him. "Mother made these fresh biscuits for you." She handed some to Solomon also. "Squire? Ensign?" she asked with an outstretched hand to the other two men. Nodding, they gratefully accepted her generosity.

"Everyone back at Forty Fort is on edge," she said, holding her palms toward the warming flames. "No one knows what shall happen." She looked to the line of breastworks beyond the fire. "It has been said that Colonel Plunkett has an army of well over seven hundred men. No one has heard from poor Benjamin Shoemaker or Daniel Harvey since they headed for Middletown weeks ago. Some fear foul play."

"We've struggled afore, and we shall overcome, just as we always have," Squire Jenkins said. "For God is with the righteous and pure of heart. He shall not allow Plunkett and his like to triumph no more than the rascals did in seventy-one. Drove them out then, and we shall now!"

Martha raised an eyebrow and slowly looked around. Her eyes stopped on the next fire. The men huddling around it held odd weapons. Several held scythe blades fastened to long poles, projecting the curved blades as straight as possible; formidable weapons in close quarters, but otherwise useless. A few other brazen souls held mere sickles or poles sharpened to a point. She adverted her gaze.

"Father Times," Solomon said, noticing her gaze. "That's what we call them. But they'll do the job, they will, if need be, Sis, so don't you fret none."

Martha blushed. She had no desire to cast doubt, but only encouragement to these brave defenders of the valley. "Some say Colonel Stroud has even had a change of heart," she said in an effort to change the subject.

"Now, child, let us be of stout heart," Squire Jenkins said. "I know the good colonel personally and will vouch for his character. He is a fine man, not all Pennamites are of the same heart."

"Yes Squire, I am only telling what I've heard."

The old man smiled.

"Come now," Thomas said, devouring the rest of his biscuit. "Let's see what else your fine mother has sent. What's in the rest of your poke?"

Martha grinned and reached into the haversack. "We have some chocolate, coffee, more biscuits, and a fine hunk of boiled pork."

"That's great, you and your mother are indeed fine woman!"

Solomon helped her empty the haversack and pass its contents to eager hands. He emptied a gourd full of water into a pot on a hot stone by the fire. Wrapping some coffee grounds in a cloth he gently pounded them on a rock with the blunt end of his tomahawk. "Won't be long, Squire," he said, pouring the smashed beans into the pot. "We'll soon have a brisk pot of coffee."

"To your posts! To your posts!" a call suddenly rang down the line of fires. Men instantly dropped everything but their weapons and poured behind the awaiting breastworks.

Martha trotted to her horse and drew the old firelock hanging on the side of her saddle.

Her father's quick eye caught her actions. "Now, Miss Martha, you attend to your work and let we men attend to ours," he called to her. "You ride back and keep fetching us supplies!"

She attempted to protest but her father's stern eye made her reconsider. Pointing a finger at her he turned and took his place at the breastworks.

Martha turned her eyes to the old and young men standing in reserve with their hand-made weapons and then down to the old Queen Anne musket in her hands. She walked up to the nearest man. "Get one for me," she said, handing the firelock to a grateful old man. She turned and grabbed the powder horn and shot bag from the pummel of her saddle. "Make good use of it," she said, locking eyes with the old man as she passed him the horn and bag. "Our homes and very lives depend upon your zeal today." She cast a long eye to all the faces around her. "The fate of Wyoming rests in all your hands today! Be strong ye men of Wyoming!" With that she mounted and gathered the reins of the packhorses. "I expect ole Trusty back after all this ruckus, nonetheless for the wear!" she called back over her shoulder before galloping hard up the trail back to Forty Fort. She had to get away before the first shot rang out. If not, she knew she would find it impossible to leave. She would not bear the label of disobedient child. Her dear father and brother had enough to deal with at the moment.

Every eye along the line of breastworks watched some movement at the far end of Nanticoke Flats. Muskets and rifles rose all along the line.

"It's Alden and his men!" Butler's voice boomed along the anxious line. "Hold your fire!"

Some twenty men filed from the woods and onto the flats in good order. Martial airs sounded far to their rear. The twenty men soon scampered over the ramparts of logs and rocks, helped here and there by eager hands.

"They're advancing," Ensign Alden promptly reported to Captain Butler.

"Yes," Butler said. "I hear." Looking up and down the breastworks for a long moment he bowed his head, listening to the music grow closer. "Fire the first volley over their heads!" His order echoed down the silent breastworks.

The shrill of fifes and thudding of drums grew louder, echoing through each of the brave Wyoming men's souls. Hands grew tight around firelocks just the same. Their bold enemies drew close, confident and sure of their triumph, which meant the Wyoming Yankees' demise. No. Not here. Not now.

All eyes burned with a new radiance upon sight of the sharply marching column rising on the far side of the flats. Two proud men sat tall in saddle in the lead. One dressed in an immaculate uniform with a large ostrich feather dancing in the breeze atop his finely embroidered hat. The other dressed no finer than any other in the masses of men marching behind them. A large dog ran to and fro about the two horsemen. Spirited airs from fifes and drums hastened their march.

They marched to the beat toward the breastworks when suddenly an order to halt rang out. The music immediately ceased. The finely dressed man reined his horse sideways and stared wide-eyed at the massive breastworks. "My God what breastworks!" he exclaimed.

Some two hundred firelocks barked in response. Hundreds of whizzing balls peppered the air above the Pennamites heads, cracking branches in the trees to their rear.

The dog yelped and ran away with its tail tucked between its legs, followed closely by the horsemen, musicians, and soldiers. Drums rolled out of hands and fifes crumbled under the feet of hordes of panic-stricken men.

As the smoke cleared a rousing cheer erupted from the breastworks. "There you be!" a voice announced after the cheer. "There's the resolve of the Pennamites!"

"It's not over yet!" Butler's voice warned loudly. "Hold fast and stand ready!" He raised his spyglass to his eye and scanned the plain below. The backs of the last Pennamite soldiers disappeared among the trees at the southern end of the plain. Silence once again prevailed all along the breastworks as searching eyes scanned the plain below for movement. After a few anxious moments a cry sounded down the line. "Look to the river!" the voice warned. "There are bateaux on the river!"

Intense and anxious eyes watched two large flat-bottomed boats pole up the river against the strong current. Rifle and musket barrels turned obliquely toward them.

"They are too far down river!" Butler said. "The trees and riverbank shield them! Stand easy and wait, lads!"

The fully loaded boats suddenly turned toward the east bank of the Susquehanna. The anxious eyes of the crowded soldiers in them stared up at the far breastworks, relieved to be heading to the opposite shore. The small cannon on the bow of the first boat turned toward it. A tall and properly attired gentlemen glared at the breastworks from the bow of the second boat. Lifting one foot up on the bow, he scoffed at the out-of-range firelocks bristling along the breastworks. A dog lifted its head up from below the gunwales and perched itself along side the man, its ears erect and sniffing the air. The gentlemen and his crew ignored the taunts and insults echoing down the river from the breastworks.

Oars replaced the poles and plowed all the more madly against the current as the taunts grew louder. The oarsmen heaved against the strong current. Slowly, they inched toward the shore.

A crunch sounded in the air, much to the dismay of the oarsmen. Their loud curses soon filled the air. A thin sheet of invisible ice jutting out from the shoreline checked the progress of the lead vessel. Angry men slammed at the ice with poles and oars, lowering their weapons, and their guard, for a fateful moment.

Fire immediately burst through the trees dotting the shoreline. A man instantly fell from the first boat, his oar falling and hitting the ice with a sharp ping. The dog fell with a thud. The gentlemen collapsed hard below the gunwales. The first to fall never to breathe again, while the other screamed "Retreat! Retreat!" atop his harried breaths.

"Don't fire! Don't fire!" another man pleaded at the top of his lungs. "It's Shoemaker and Harvey! They have us as hostages!"

The fire from the shoreline immediately ceased in response to the plea, but fire from anxious Pennamites farther down the opposite bank peppered the woods. The boats swirled away in the current, drifting down the river, much to the relief of their occupants.

The Yankees behind the breastworks could hold their fire no longer. A rain of shots poured down on the drifting boats. Spurts of water gushed all around them from near-misses. Thuds sounded in the gunwales. No one, be he friend or foe, dared raise his head over the sides of the boats. The shots faded as the boats finally gained the swift current of the rapids and sped through the whitecaps like an arrow.

Once again a loud cheer erupted from the line of breastworks. Captain Butler stood uneasily despite the sea of confidence flowing over his troops. Gazing over his shoulder at the sun already low on the horizon he wondering what the morrow might bring.

## Chapter Four
*Wyoming stands*

As dawn broke through the dull-gray clouds the breastworks bustled with activity. A group of men rambled off further to the right of the line, melding into the trees and rocks until they disappeared completely out of sight.

Meanwhile, Captain Butler and his officers hurried up and down the line, checking firelocks and ammunition. Proud smiles met them. Butler met the all the praising voices with stern warnings that it might not be over yet. He cautioned all, especially his officers, to remain on guard.

His warning quickly came to fruition. Anxious calls rolled up the line from the river. A lone canoe made its way through the swirling currents from the opposite side of the Susquehanna. Two men hurriedly beached the canoe and trotted up the bank to the breastworks.

Butler met them halfway. His second, Nathan Denison, followed. The two buckskin-clad rangers proudly approached the officers. Self-satisfied grins stretched from ear to ear across their faces. The first man nodded at Butler and eagerly shook Denison's hand. "We got 'em Nathan!" he said. "And we got 'em good!"

"Yes, Lazarus," Denison said. "Splendid show!" He rolled an eye to Captain Butler. Lazarus' smile disappeared. He turned toward Captain Butler. "Lost one man, Bowen, was a good soul, he'll be missed, but we set them on their heels, by God we did!" he reported.

Butler nodded and looked to the far shore.

"Left Mckarrachan in charge," Lazarus said. "We came to report."

"Very well," Butler said. "You and your man take position along the line."

"We're just here to report," Lazarus said, looking over his shoulder to the opposite shore. "We've got to get back!"

"If it's blood you seek, you'll find it here," Butler said. "They'll be attacking on our front this day."

Lazarus raised and eyebrow. His friend bore the same surprised look. Everyone assumed they had taught the pesky Pennamites a proper lesson by their show of force yesterday.

"Plunkett will try again," Butler answered the curious looks. "He won't want to lose face with his masters in Philadelphia."

"Well, we'll just give them the boot again!" Lazarus said. "The thick-headed fools." He and his friend immediately strutted to the line.

Butler and Denison followed, taking their place in the center of the breastworks. Nothing stirred to their front but a few crows scavenging through the abandoned haversacks and bundles left by the hastily retreating Pennamites the day before. One curiously sat atop an abandoned drum as if on guard. Many eyes watched the odd bird. Turning suddenly, it rose into the sky, cawing a warning all the way.

Pennamite soldiers immediately filed into the field from the trees behind it. At the harsh commands of their officers they scattered about the plain, seeking cover behind trees, bushes, and rocks. A deathly silence hung in the air as partisans on both sides waited with pounding hearts. Soon the aggressors crept forward, becoming bolder with each step taken without confrontation.

Butler and Denison watched with dry throats. Every Yankee sat anxiously awaiting the command to fire. The Pennamites grew closer and closer, apparently saving their shots until they couldn't miss.

Clearing his dry throat Denison looked to Butler, but the man's eyes showed blank. He stared straight ahead, ignoring his increasingly nervous second. Finally, Butler cleared his own throat and shouted "Fire!"

Firelocks blazed to life from each side. Smoke instantly clouded the field. A man spun through it from the breastworks, clutching at his throat to check the flow of his life's blood spurting from it. He quickly fell dead, his eyes bulging with fear.

Balls whizzed all about the breastworks, thudding into logs and pinging off rocks. A spirited exchange resulted.

Butler drew his pistols from his belt and fired both at the advancing Pennamites. Quickly reloading them he cocked an eye to the right and up the sloping rocks. "Send a messenger to Ransom!" he called to Denison. "They're trying to flank us on the right! Tell him to check them! We'll keep an eye on him and send help if need be!"

Denison immediately waved to one of the lads in the reserve. He barked the orders to him and watched him disappear into the woods to the right. A ball smashed into the log to his front, sending splinters flying in the air. Lifting his rifle, he took careful aim. A surprised Pennamite fell from the angry report of his rifle. "Pour it into them lads!" he said, quickly reloading his weapon.

Farther down the line Ensign Jenkins fired as fast as he could load. All the while he stole glances to his aged father on his right, ever mindful of the balls whizzing about their ears. A man twirled from the line to his father's side, angrily cursing and clutching his bleeding arm. Another whom took his place in line fell limp, no doubt the victim of the same Pennamite rifleman.

The men from the reserve tended to both men while others grabbed their weapons and took their place along the breastworks. One of them fell before he even brought his firelock to his shoulder.

Young Jenkins peered through the smoke, fearing when the marksman would turn his eye to his father. A ball skimmed along his father's weapon, forcing it from his hands. "My God, that was close!" he said, bending down to retrieve his weapon. "But it'll still shoot!"

Young Jenkins wasted no time. He bent down low and peered under the smoke, noticing a man ducking behind a large rock a few rods to their front. No doubt the marksman.

The man spun around the tree and fired again, disappearing like a specter before Jenkins could draw a bead on him. His father scrunched his shoulders as if an angry bee buzzed about his head.

Young Jenkins drew a long breath and waited, ignoring the temptation to fire at a more convenient target. The next shot from the specter would be sure to hit his father and no coaxing or argument from him could convince his father to retreat from the line. He knew it. His father seemed oblivious to the danger. Brave, but perhaps foolish. Both played closely to one another in a man's heart.

A ball whizzed past his own ear but he ignored it, waiting out the specter. A dark hat rose above the smoke over the large rock. He fired. The hat spun wildly in the air. He quickly reloaded his rifle without looking down to it, his eyes locked on the rock.

After a few anxious seconds he smiled at his father, certain he had eliminated the threat. Turning his sights to another brazen invader, he fell another Pennamite, cheering in triumph.

Further to the left Lazarus Stewart stood tall atop the breastworks, laughing at those ducking behind them to load after firing. The hail of lead seemed to only invigorate him. The brashness of the ranger caught the attention of his friend, Nathan Denison. "Lazarus!" he yelled to him. "Get down, you damn fool, before you lose your head!"

"Not a chance!" Lazarus screamed back at him. "I've been waiting to settle with these Quaker bastards and their pawns too long to be timid now!" He turned to his friend just long enough to smile. "It's glorious!" he yelled through his grin. "Justice served full!"

A thunderous commotion to the right rose above the sounds. Screaming and howling men scampered up to the ridge, determined and fueled by a shared rage. A rain of lead answered their fury, checking them just before the breastworks, sending them tumbling pell-mell back down the ridge with an equal emotion for self-preservation.

Butler yelled in approval of the sight. Cheers flowed all down the breastworks watching the retreat from the left of the Pennamite line, spreading like a contagion through the rest of their line. Yankee after Yankee danced atop the breastworks, ecstatic with their victory over the larger and better armed force of Pennamites. Their solid resolve and audacity held the day. A sense of invincibility swelled each of their chests.

Wyoming stood tall this day! Wyoming triumphed this day!

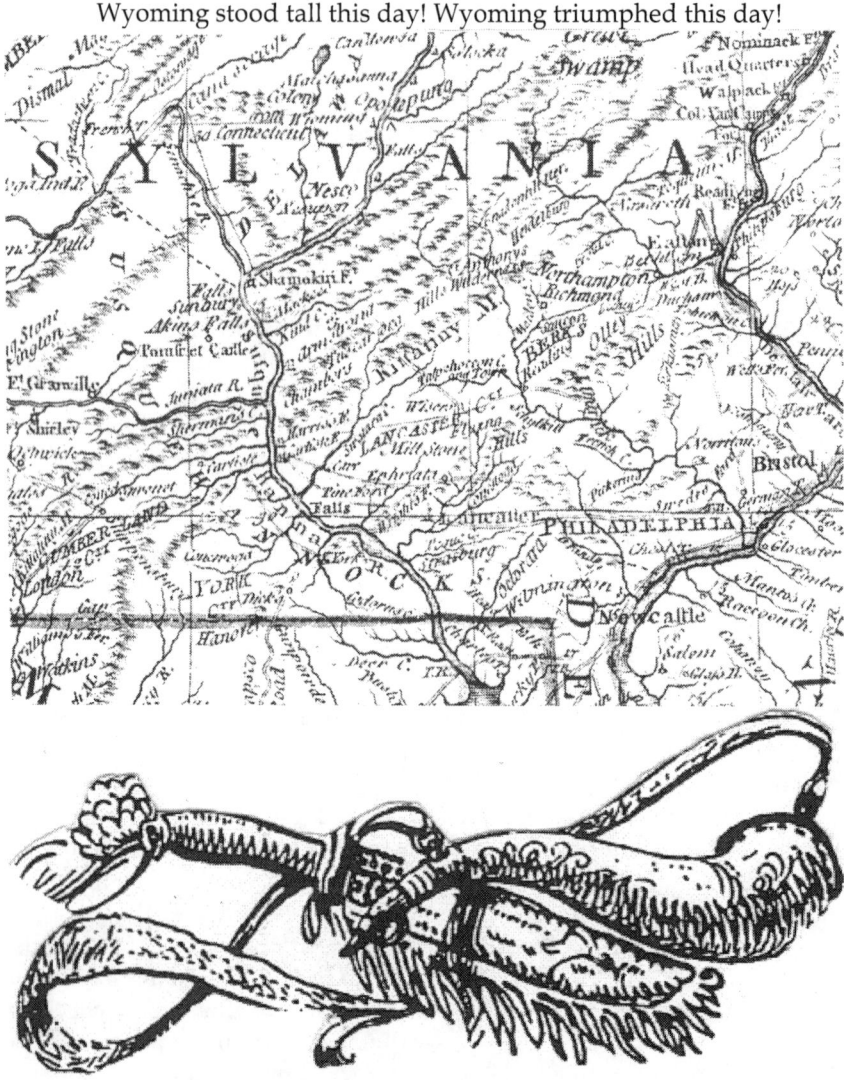

## Chapter Five
*Town Meeting*

Chilled breaths rose in the crisp air from the heavily cloaked masses filling the green at Wilkes-Barre. No one seemed to pay the chill much mind, though; for all of Wyoming rang with cheers over their recent triumphant battle with the Pennamites. People watched the proceedings of the town meeting, listening intently to the selectmen weighing and debating one issue after another, while some, mostly the younger ones, thought of the upcoming festivities after the meeting. The rigid Puritanism of the times allowed few amusements and the town meetings became a place of business as well as amusement. Every heart looked forward to the wrestling matches, foot races, and other activities. Barrels of rum also livened the festivities.

Pride swelled John Jenkins' chest at the sight of it all. He yelled a great huzza at every call for one. People shuffled and moved all about him and his party. He smiled at every rude shove or foot on his shoe. Nothing mattered but the meeting and what it represented, victory! His eyes little noticed a pair of eyes staring at him from the edge of the green.

Bethiah Harris stood at the edge of the green, the hood of her cloak all but covering her head. She broke her stare at her beau once and awhile, fearing someone might notice her provocative gaze. How would she explain such a forward attitude? Proper young women of fine stock and bearing shunned such behavior. She had to play her cards right.

Gazing about the sea of faces she smiled to one or two, but always broke her glance at them before becoming to familiar, especially when she locked eyes with a certain young gentleman.

Normally she would welcome all the attention. Her welcoming smile and graceful mannerisms made her the favorite of all of Wyoming. But now, as she stepped out and strolled through the crowded green, she wished to be noticed by just one, John Jenkins, the handsome young man standing by his father, Squire Jenkins, one of the most respected and distinguished men of the valley. Bowing her head she walked steadfastly toward Squire. She finally shuffled triumphantly up to him and pulled back her hood, exposing her graceful beauty. "Good day Squire Jenkins," she said with a beaming smile.

"Why Bethiah, you are as radiant as the noonday sun," Squire Jenkins greeted her. "Your efforts in producing gunpowder in our recent troubles is greatly appreciated by all, I do most assure you, fine lady!"

"Oh, Squire, it was no problem, I assure you, fine sir," she said with a curtsy. "There are many others involved, sir, why if Mathias Hollenback had not secured a pounder all of our efforts would had been for not."

"Oh, yes, yes, my dear," he answered. "Hearty thanks to all! What with all the tearing up of cabin floors for saltpeter and all, such work!" He grinned and looked to his wife by his side. "Yes," he added, "thank God for all the good ladies of Wyoming."

She smiled and clutched her husband's elbow to her.

"You know, of course, my fine wife, and sons John and Stephen," Squire said, spreading his hand toward them.

"Yes," Bethiah said. "They are fine indeed."

Stephen smiled at her and she smiled back, but her eyes beamed when they met John's. The rough young lad suddenly felt his knees go weak. He managed to crack a nervous smile at the stunningly beautiful young woman. A loud call from the assembly saved him from the awkward moment. Touching his hat he feigned interest in it, stealing a glance at the beautiful young delight before him every now and then.

"Voted!" a loud voice announced. "Christopher Avery chosen Agent for this town of *Westmoreland*, to proceed forthwith to his Honorable Governor of this colony, and lay our distressed case before him. And so say we assembled here that Obadiah Gore Jr., be appointed to proceed to Philadelphia and lay before the Honorable Continental Congress, the late invasion made by the Tory party of the Pennsylvania people."

The speaker stopped, quickly exchanging some papers with a man standing below him. "Voted," he continued after adjusting his spectacles, "that Titus Hinman and Perrin Ross be appointed to collect charity of the people for the support of the recent widows of the late action against the invasion." With that the town meeting drew to a close.

Everyone turned, shook hands, and otherwise congratulated one another. Gradually the crowds broke apart and headed to the festivities. Men and boys gathered around two men standing a few rods apart glaring at one another. With a great shout they suddenly charged one another. After colliding, they tumbled to the ground wrestling. Others gathered around numerous foot races, always popular at such events.

John Jenkins stood awkwardly at Bethiah's side. She coyly smiled and greeted the sea of eager men quickly surrounding her, all the while watching John out of the corner of her eye. She wished for but one moment to wave away the constraints of proper society, but quickly subdued the thought, hoping her eyes did not betray her thoughts. She masked her thoughts again with her polite smile but secretly wished to just take John by the hand and disappear somewhere alone with the handsome lad. With each glance at him she fought to ease her frustration and therefore erase the telltale emotions from her face. Suddenly a loud and bombastic man burst through the crowd, drawing attention from her. She sighed in relief.

The bombastic man strutted proudly with two lads holding poles behind him. His loud voice boomed, announcing his intentions to amaze one and all. The crowd, as well as John and Bethiah, followed his call.

Noticing a rock in front of she and John, who began to outdistance her, she feigned a stumble. John instantly grabbed her arm, steadying her. "Why thank you John," she said with a smile from ear to ear.

"Well," John said, his smile just as wide, "it is my pleasure."

They both watched the crowd draw away.

"We had best be on our way," John said after the longest moment. A nervous glimpse passed between them. After another long moment they continued walking; but this time truly together.

The loud man, Hibberd, noticed their approach. Grinning, he pushed his sleeves back, waving to the lads holding the poles. A length of hemp rope stretched between the poles. Hibberd waved to the lads to stretch the poles taunt and walked between the poles with his arms outstretched, gesturing to the lads until the rope stretched taunt just high enough to touch the hair atop of his head. Bearing a self-satisfied grin he finally stepped back, giving the crowd a courteous bow.

Welcoming the cheers, he stepped back a rod or two. Glancing around he raised his arms in the air to heighten the cheers, then, without warning, ran like a deer, his feet barely touching the earth, and jumped, clearing the rope with ease. The crowd exploded with cheers. John and Bethiah both found themselves joining in the revelry. Their clapping and cheers broke the great smile across each of their faces as they noticed each other's gaze. A gruff hand from nowhere suddenly landed on John's shoulder, breaking the mood.

"John Jenkins!" a voice boomed. "Hibberd may leap like a deer, but none," the man said, shaking his finger, "can beat Obadiah Gore in a foot race!" The man stepped back, his chest swelling with pride.

"Well, Obadiah," John said. "I do not know about that!"

"What is this, fair lady?" Obadiah asked, raising an eyebrow at Bethiah. "A challenge?"

John nodded and waved his arm forward. "See the tree over yonder across the green?" he asked, etching a line in the dirt with his heel in front of them. "It'll be from this line to yonder tree!"

Obadiah lifted the hat from his head, gracefully handing it to Bethiah. Tugging at his breeches he crouched down into a starting position. John did the same to the cheers of the crowd gathering around them. The crowd parted and backed away until a corridor of people stretched from the line to the tree. A wobbly soul strutted up to the two crouching men holding a mug of rum in his hand. Drawing a handkerchief from his waistcoat pocket he waved it over his head. Taking a great gulp from the mug he announced, "at the fall of this flag the contest shall begin!" After letting out a long belch he staggered a step or two away, dropping the handkerchief after another loud belch.

The two men instantly darted down the gauntlet of waving arms and staggering people. Both ignored them, running steadfastly to the tree. Neither heard any sounds but the thudding of their hearts. Both men felt nothing but their thudding footsteps on the frozen earth. The tree seemed a distant trophy to both men. For one it meant proof of his agility, for the other it meant proof of his worthiness as a suitor. John Jenkins finally thundered past the tree but a hairsbreadth before Obadiah plummeted past it.

"That was a close one!" a man standing by the tree proclaimed. "But," he continued, grabbing John by the hand and raising it in the air, "we have a clear winner!"

The crowd swarmed around the tree, many a hand holding a full mug of rum. They cheered and clamored about, congratulating both men and offering them a drink from their mugs.

"You're still as agile as a deer, John," Obadiah said through gulps of rum. "But you have to admit it was close!"

"That it was, Obadiah!" John said, raising a mug of cheer to his lips. "That it was!" A smile stretched across his face upon sight of Bethiah emerging from the crowd, forcing an involuntary gasp from his suddenly dry throat. Her beauty took his breath away every time he saw her.

"You two would give a rabbit a good run!" she said, handing both men their hats.

"Today you stretched your neck just long enough," Obadiah said. "But the morrow is another matter! Then we shall see!"

"This hare intends to remain agile through all his days," John answered. They both smiled and drank heartily from their mugs.

"Here! Here!" Obadiah called to a man struggling through the crowd with a great bucket. The man nodded, placing the bucket before Obadiah. Producing his own mug from under his cloak he dipped it into the bucket along with the two men. "Here's to Mr. Plunkett and his great, but failed, mind you, expedition!" he said, raising his mug high. "Here! Here!" came an instant reply from the other two men. All of the mugs came together in salute. The warm rum tamed the chill. The camaraderie warmed their hearts. The years of struggle seemed behind them with their recent victory. It proved their mettle to any future adversaries, white or red-skinned. As the bucket of rum emptied the crowd melted away to the many other displays of prowess. The trio thanked the man with the bucket of cheer and walked away from the tree.

An iron bar sailing through the air over the heads of another crowd caught their attention. They followed it, noticing another sailing just behind the first. It far outdistanced the first.

"There!" Obadiah said, pointing to it. "That would be Franklin fer sure!"

John nodded, taking Bethiah's hand soft hand into his own.

Obadiah led them through the crowd, parting it as they went. Soon they emerged through the throngs of people and Obadiah raised his hand toward a tall man receiving many congratulatory pats on his back. "See," he said, "I told you. No one can throw the bar as far as John Franklin! He's a mountain of a man, he is. A damn big mountain!"

"That's for certain," John said.

Franklin noticed them and promptly excused himself from the crowd, walking toward the trio. He removed his slouch hat just as he neared them and bowed.

"That is how one throws the bar," he said with a wink of his eye.

"John Franklin, if it comes to blows with either Tory or Indian, I hope I am with you!" John said.

"And I'd be proud to have you," Franklin said. "And you too, Obadiah!

"We are all proud of the men of this valley," Bethiah said. "There is no finer lot to be found in any other country."

"We appreciate your confidence, fine lady," Franklin said.

"It is well deserved, fine sir," Bethiah answered.

They all stood watching the grand spectacle unfolding all around the green. The spirit of the people seemed contagious. Cheers echoed through the air and people embraced all around. The surrounding mountains resounded with their roars. The wrestling matches, trip and twitch matches, throwing of the bar, and numerous foot races attested to the masculinity of Wyoming. The many happy woman and frolicking children proved the virility and vitality of the men as well. Wyoming lived and bloomed with an exuberant confidence which fostered a terrible resolve against anybody fool enough to threaten the beautiful refuge carved out of the unforgiving wilderness.

## Chapter Six
### Treaty with the Six Nations

John Jenkins watched the sparks from the huge fire dance in the night sky. Watching the flitting fire flecks disappear in the dark sky he prayed the hopes of the men sitting around the fire did not rise with them and fade into the heavens the higher they rose. The hopes of both white and red men. War among these people would be devastating for both sides.

Word of a meeting at Oswego between *Sir Guy Johnson* and the leading chiefs of the Six Nations caused such a concern in these uneasy times that the citizens of Wyoming demanded a meeting. So Zebulon Butler, now Lt. Colonel Butler, called this council at Wilkes-Barre to ease the worries of both sides. Now they gathered, each with a suspicious eye on the another, but both seeming to want peace.

John stood just beyond the fire with his back toward the unfinished palisades of Fort Wilkes-Barre. Many others milled around him, anxiously listening and waiting. None carried weapons but a few cautious souls behind the unfinished walls of the fort. Colonel Butler ordered that no firelocks be present; not within the sight of the Indians, at least.

The Indians mingled just beyond their side of the fire. A few stern-faced warriors stood an equal distance away as John and his fellow settlers did on their side of the fire. If everything remained equal, so would the chance for peace. Behind the warriors many other natives busied themselves attending to their camp. They seemed indifferent to the talk around the great fire. Women tended to fires and cooked. Cradles hung in low branches of trees surrounding the camp. A few dogs mingled about the camp. Buckskin and elk hide pallets lay strewn all about the green. Strong fragrances from the Indians' fires filled the air with the smell of sweet grass, wild herbs and spices; none the least as the strong smell of tobacco from the handfuls of it the lead chief constantly threw into the flames of the council fire.

A lone woman, somehow appearing different from the others in bearing as well as dress, stood a few yards behind the chiefs sitting around the fire. She stood with her arms crossed and her head bent to one side, intently listening to every word. She seemed somehow regal in her bearing. Silver glistened in the firelight from the many ornaments bedecking her clothing. Wisps of her raven hair danced in an occasional breeze. Her piercing dark eyes somehow demanded attention.

John recognized her immediately as the one they called Queen Esther; a woman of some high standing whom held sway over a village upriver some sixty miles by Tioga Point. He, as well as many other settlers, had dealings with her before. She always warmly welcomed him with an open hand and with her broken English heartily conveyed her deep wish that the two peoples live in an everlasting peace. Her presence and intense interest in the proceedings eased John's worries. Looking back over his shoulder to the people huddled at the fort's gate he caught a glimpse of Bethiah and other Yankee women standing just inside it. Yes, peace must prevail.

The rambling tongue of the buckskin-clad warrior standing by the fire also brought some relief to his worries as every other word he said began with *'brother'*. The chief talked on and on without any sign of ending. The sparkle in his dark eyes when he spoke of war every now and then broke the tedium. Every eye looked up to him upon mention of the word. A word they all detested. A word which never had come to fruition between Six Nations and the Wyoming Yankees, thankfully. Finally, with a slight bow of his head, the chief sat down.

"Captain John Mohawk," Colonel Butler said, rising from his place around the fire. "Your words, brother, are rich and full of hope! A hope of peace between our two peoples! We must not let the troubles between ourselves and the King cloud our eyes to our lives here, far from the King. We must not hear *the cry of the tomahawk* on the Susquehanna!"

Reverend Johnson stood interpreting Butler's words. Butler watched each of the chiefs as Johnson fed him his words. A few guttural responses made him wince. Raising his hands high, he stepped forward.

"The quarrel between us people, we Americans, and the King, must not make us enemies!" he proclaimed. Johnson found no need to interpret these words. Butler's forceful mannerisms spoke louder than his words.

A grunt from behind the sitting chiefs made them all turn around. Esther stared deathly at Captain John. The chief turned and stared at the fire in silence for an awful moment before slowly lifting his head. He carefully scanned all the eyes on the opposite side of the fire.

"Brothers," he said, "we need peace, all of us." He raised his eyes to the fort rising behind the white men. "Brothers, you must not build a fort at Wyalusing as you want for it will come between us as we have built a fine new road at Wyalusing. Listen to my words."

Butler did not say a word but merely sat back down.

The chief rose in his place holding a belt of wampum. "Brothers," he said, "we desire that Wyoming may be a place appointed where the great men may meet, and have a fire, which shall forever be called *Wyomick*, where we shall judge best how to prevent any jealousies or uneasy thoughts that may arise, and thereby preserve our friendship." He shook the belt of wampum at the white men. "Brothers! What we say is not from our lips but from our hearts! If any Indians of little note should speak otherwise, you must pay no regard to them, but observe what has been said and written by the chiefs, which may be depended on."

His eyes glared. They rose to the moon in the great night sky. "Brothers we all live under the same great sky!" He slowly walked around the fire, staring with his dark eyes through the dancing flames to the white men on the other side of it. When he felt certain he had all their attention he turned to the Indian families to his rear. "Brothers," he continued after a long moment, "my people would greatly appreciate a gift of flour. Our rifles are in need of repair as are our knives. They need to be in good order for our hunts. A flag you fly would be a great gift to show our people are one and at peace! Brothers! This is all we ask. We are all of one mind, and we are all for peace." With that he nodded to the white men and to his fellow chiefs before gracefully sitting back down.

Butler, as well as the other white men, remained silent. Nathan Denison, now Colonel of the newly formed *Twenty-fourth Regiment of Connecticut Militia*, finally leaned toward Butler, whispering in his ear. Several of the other white men did the same. Their counterparts across the fire said nothing, but just stared stoically at them through the flames.

"See!" a voice startled John from behind. "They play with us with their words."

John looked to the man without agreeing with him.

"I tell you none of them are to be trusted," the man continued, slowly stepping to John's side. Raising an eyebrow he rolled his eyes down to his hand inside his hunting frock. He rubbed the butt of a pistol stuck in the waist of his breeches.

"There is no call for that, Sam," John whispered.

"You are far too trusting, John," Sam said, staring at the fire. It reflected in his eyes as he slowly stroked the butt of the pistol. His eyes bore a deep thought, a thought from the deepest part of his soul. Parts of the soul which harbored love and its counterpart, hatred. He shook his head, spilling the emotion from his eyes through his tongue. "I tell you more enemies lie just within our sight than in the of whole Six Nations," he said. "It is just the way of it. You know it as well as I. There is no dodging the truth. Land, when it all comes down to it, it is simply land. Land and property, property breeds wealth and wealth breeds corruption. It is all power in the end, it turns men's spirits topsy-turvy. In the end who knows who is friend or foe? Dark it is. Dark, but simple, in the end." Lifting his hand from the pistol, he waved it toward the fire. "Look at Secord down there," he continued, raising his voice. "It is well he sits so close to good Captain Durkee so as he can keep an eye on him."

He waited for a moment for a response but only a strange silence answered him. A few indifferent eyes glanced to him. "I and Simon Spalding had a good talk about the man Secord when I surveyed Long Township," he said just as loudly. "The man is not to be trusted! How he got on the Committee of Safety is well beyond me! Everyone knows he is lukewarm at best toward our cause! Borderline Tory!"

The man Secord turned, looking back at the two men with a scowl. Durkee watched the man's reaction out of the corner of his eye and waved a hand nonchalantly behind him for them to desist.

"Lower your voice, Sam," John said. "That is an order from one also on the Committee of Safety! We don't need any of that just now."

"What?" Sam scoffed. "The truth?" He flung his hands in the air and retreated back into the fort. "I, for one, prefer to see things as they are, not as I wish them to be!" he called out loudly in his wake.

John watched the man with a stern eye until he disappeared behind the fort's gate. He knew he shared a wave of relief with everyone. They really didn't need such talk at this time.

Butler rose, hoping to draw attention from the disturbance. "We have heard from the Great Head at Onondaga through John Mohawk," he said. "We beseech all of the Six Nations to remain at peace with the people of Wyoming. Our blacksmiths are at their disposal. We shall share our flour, but as for our flag, I have not the authority to issue such a gift. I must consult Congress on such a matter."

Captain John rose as Butler sat down. A smug smile stretched across his face. He raised his arms once again to the heavens. "You, brother, Butler, for your wisdom, shall be known at the great fire as *Koorenghloognana*."

Reverend Johnson quickly rose to his feet and bowed to the chief. The chief waved an approving hand to him. "Great Tree," he said. "It means Great Tree." He wasted no time sitting back down.

Butler smiled and looked up to the grinning chief. Captain John raised his hands slowly to the heavens and then back down to the fire before sitting back down, throwing a last handful of tobacco into the flames.

Butler turned his eyes to Johnson. The interpreter nodded. Butler rose to his feet. "These proceedings are closed," he flatly stated.

Men from both sides of the fire rose and melded into little groups for conversation. A few Indians ignored their counterparts and rejoined their camp.

John's eye fell to the group which held his father and the Indian Queen Esther. He slowly approached, not wishing to seem an intruder.

"Ah," a voice whined from the group upon his approach. "Young Chickens! It good to see you!"

John smiled at the Indian Queen, despite her misinterpretation of his name. She broke from the group and took a few steps toward him with outstretched arms. She took him by the arm immediately.

"My dear Esther it is grand to see you again," he said to the forward Queen. She smiled, nodding profusely. She tightened her grip on his arm and led him into the folds of the little group.

"Old Chickens," she said with a warm smile to Squire, "your son, he grow strong since I last see him!"

"Yes," Squire Jenkins said. "He is becoming quite a man." They both nodded in approval of John.

"I did not mean to intrude," John said.

"Nonsense," another man said with a welcoming smile, "you, as a member of the Committee of safety, as I, should have taken your place around the fire." Raising his hand he shook John's.

"Yes, Mr. Secord," John answered, "but the Committee was already well represented."

"Call me John, lad, no need to be so formal," Secord said with a disarming smile to the Queen holding tightly to John's arm. "We are all friends here. Do not let blood boil from the foul fires of suspicion."

"I apologize for Sam Gordon," John immediately said. "He just has a bad case of nerves."

"Nerves, or nerve, indeed," John Secord said.

"Yes," Squire Jenkins interjected, "but we must not let a few jitters from the outside world disrupt our situation here, fine sirs." He bowed his head toward the Indian Queen. "And fine ladies. You, my dear Esther, and all your people, are welcome to trade at Wyoming anytime."

"Yes," Colonel Denison said, joining the group after listening just to the side of it. "Esther, you must promise to bring more Indians to trade with us here at Wyoming!"

The Queen turned a suspicious eye to the colonel but said nothing.

"I shall be surveying upriver soon," John Jenkins said.

"You, Young Chickens," the Queen said, gently releasing his arm, "always welcome at my village." Stepping back, she slowly made her way to the Indian camp. Her twinkling silver trinkets adorning her dress shone in the moonlight. The moonlight reflected off her raven hair in deep shades of dark blue and black.

"A rather spooky woman." Denison could not help but mutter under his breath.

"Yes," Squire said as they all gazed at the massive Indian camp, "aren't they all?"

"The Moravians did little to enlighten them," Denison added.

"They have their ways, and we have ours," Secord said. "That is all there is to it," he added, shrugging his shoulders at the strange looks his comment provoked from the others. He traded with the Indians and had laid many a trap with them before coming to settle about Tunkhannock. He learned to respect their ways and now looked upon them as he would any people of equal standing. Their society possessed advantages and disadvantages and he had come to prefer their company to many of the impudent white people he met now. Bad men stained both races. As for Tory or Patriot each had an equal yoke of burden. He preferred neither. He would just the same be left out of it all anyways.

Denison huffed, raising an eyebrow toward the man. "They are still heathen," he said.

"Yes, in some eyes," Secord said, "but perhaps not in others."

Colonel Butler strode into the middle of the group, much to John Jenkins' relief. He could not help but notice the growing divide between the upriver settlers and those of the lower settlements. The differences of opinion about the natives only heightened his growing realization of the widening riff between them. The few upriver settlers whom did attend the council remained separate from the others and made their own camp down by the river. Few others, including Secord, actually stayed to mingle after the council had adjourned. Now to have Denison and Secord at each other's throats seemed very detrimental to the settlers' increasingly fragile union. The pangs of discord reached far into the wilderness and touched Wyoming, even in its isolation. Butler could not have arrived at a more appropriate moment to defuse the situation.

"I have conferred with the others," Butler announced, turning his eyes to the various other groups of huddling white men. "It is theirs, as well as my contention, that a dispatch be sent posthaste to the Honorable Roger Sherman in Congress as to these proceedings. What say ye, gentlemen?"

"Why certainly," Denison said. "Why should they want a flag?"

"To use in deception for some future mischievous event to their advantage, no doubt," Squire Jenkins said.

"Let us pray not," Captain Durkee said. "An Indian war would be most devastating."

Each man looked with a concerned eye to the newly elected captain of one of the independent companies ordered to be formed by Congress to protect Wyoming from just such an occurrence. Dread dripped from each man's face.

"If calmer heads prevail we have nothing to fear," Secord said. "We must learn to be less forceful in our approach to one another. Others have opinions also. We must respect one another. It is the only way to keep the peace."

"Yes," Denison said, "opinions are fine as long as they are not acted upon."

"Enough!" Butler scolded both men, keeping a wary eye on a few Indians listening intently from a safe distance. They seemed to have lost their stoic looks and indifferent attitudes. Butler could not help but wonder if their sudden keen interest did not have something to do with Secord's presence. "There are more pressing matters at hand!" he added.

Before either man could respond thundering hooves echoed in the air. Every eye turned to the intruders galloping hard for the fort. Several Indians scrambled for their weapons. The stern look of the rushing riders in their direction fed their fear.

Lazarus Stewart, his eyes alive with a burning hatred, let out a loud war whoop, reining his mount to a hard stop. The half-dozen or so riders circling him let out their own war whoops right after his. They threateningly stared at and taunted the Indians, raising their weapons at them with each new whoop escaping their lungs.

Butler, visibly shaken, grabbed at the fine beaver hat on his head and clenched it tightly in his fists. Vexed on what to do next, he strode forward, waving his ruined hat at the intruders. "I explicitly ordered no firelocks be present at this council!" he screamed at the brash young men.

It did little to quell the fire in their eyes. It only fueled it.

"Begging your pardon, fine sir!" Stewart snarled. "You best take a look yonder to the red devils! I dare say the only good one of their lot is a dead one!"

Tomahawks and firelocks bristled in the firelight from the many fires dotting the Indian camp. More and more Indians emerged from under blankets and animal skins. Dark eyes stared back at the white men, stern and ready for a fight.

"Come now!" Denison said, joining Colonel Butler in the middle of the circling rangers. "This is a peaceful meeting! Lazarus! Desist and disperse your men at once!"

Stewart stared over the heads of the leaders and through the dancing flames to the dark eyes intently watching them from the Indian camp. He did not care much for the haughty Colonel Butler, but he and Denison had become fast friends. Denison admired Lazarus' bravery and Lazarus admired Denison's determination to keep Wyoming alive at all costs. Such men of grit had to admire one another.

"Fine!" Lazarus finally conceded, throwing one leg over the saddle. He sat staring defiantly at the two Wyoming officers before finally plopping down from the saddle. "Fine, gentlemen!" he snapped. "But be sure to take any words from their mouths with a grain of salt!"

"Deal with them!" Butler said through clenched teeth to Denison, barely containing his absolute rage. He rambled off toward his home but a few rods from the green, still clenching his ruined hat.

Denison nodded, giving him leave. Marching to his rash friend he put a stern hand on his shoulder. His other fell to the rifle clenched tightly in his friend's hands. "There is no need for this," he said, slowly slipping the weapon from Lazarus' hands and placing it back into the sheath on his saddle. "Not now, anyway," he added under his breath.

Lazarus raised his upper lip, shaking his head in disgust. "I'll be keeping this handy just the same," he said with a glint in his eye. His hand rubbed the butt of a pistol stuck in his belt.

"Fine," Denison said with a concerned half-smile. Lazarus' men grumbled, but soon led their horses through the gate of the unfinished fort. Denison handed the reins of Lazarus' horse to one of them and slowly led Stewart away. The further he could distance Stewart from his men, the better. He slowly glanced over his shoulder at the Indian camp while leading his disgruntled friend from the green. To his relief, many of the swarthy Indians went back to their tasks as if nothing had happened. Only a few dark eyes from a scattering of warriors watched them until they disappeared behind a cabin door. They too then went about their business, but this time with their rifles in plain view.

Out of sight, out of mind, Denison hoped while latching the door behind them.

Just then a gentle hand touched John Jenkins' shoulder, breaking his gaze at the whole spectacle. He turned to see the welcoming eyes of Bethiah. Somehow it eased his thoughts about the tense situation.

"Oh John," Bethiah said, "I don't like the look of things!" What will happen if the Indians are provoked any further?" She paused for a moment. "It is too horrible to imagine! Oh, dear God, spare us!"

"Come now," John reassured her. "Everything is fine. Don't mind Lazarus and Sam, they're a bit anxious is all."

Her eyes still mirrored concern. She wanted to believe him, but the angst in the air forbade it. She fell to his chest, despite polite society.

He instantly wrapped his strong arms around her. She felt good, somehow foreign to all he had ever known, but good. Her soft brown hair fell softly against his chin. He inhaled her sweat aroma. Oh, Beth, he thought, I wish this drama would all fade. Then he could make something of himself and build a new, strong, life in this wilderness. Virgin lands lay all around. All this land would need the surveyor's eye. Something he possessed. If peace could just prevail, a small fortune could be made in surveying alone. Then he could ask for her hand as a man of means and stature. If only the upriver settlers would embrace the cause. Without their resistance the Indians could then be persuaded to remain peaceful. Peace remained the key, but he would go on no matter what; be it in the comforting and warming air of peace, or the in the harsh winds of war.

Suddenly Beth let out a muffled cry in his strong chest, tightening her embrace. An instant latter he felt a bony hand grip his shoulder. Beth's embrace grew tighter. Wincing, he strained his head to look behind him and upon the rude intruder. Footsteps retreated behind him. The terror reflected in Beth's eyes instinctively caused him to push her to his far side to protect her. Gripping her ever so tightly he wheeled about toward the intruder. From the gloomy shadows behind them showed a specter, wild and dark hair outlined the head, with silver glistening in the bright moonlight from its colorfully clad form.

"Young Chickens?" a voice drifted on a whisper from the shadows. In another instant a form also advanced from the shadows. "It only me, no fear." Queen Esther slowly stepped into the light cast from the great council fire. Raising her hands she scrunched her shoulders.

Her face bore a confused look.

"Esther?" John asked in relief. Beth kept to his side, straight as a ramrod. She did not utter a word, but just stared at the Indian Queen.

John looked down to her, suddenly feeling a bit embarrassed by her fear. He tried to imagine how she felt, but he knew Esther to be completely harmless, always greeting whites with an open hand and professing her heartfelt desire for peace. No one could fake such a pure emotion, not that he knew of, anyways. But to Beth she remained a savage of the forest, ready to pounce and wreak havoc upon Wyoming at the first opportunity.

"Chickens," Esther said, taking a careful step forward. A smile grew across her face. Cocking her head she gazed sympathetically into Beth's eyes. Terror beamed back at her.

"It fine," Esther said. "You fine woman," she added, pointing a long bony finger at Beth. "She will bring fine strong childs!"

"Yes," John agreed. "She is most fine indeed."

Esther laughed and shook her head. "You no need fear, young one," she said, turning a hand toward the Indian camp. "Indians here in peace. Want peace, are not so, Young Chickens?"

"I most certainly hope so," he answered with a nervous smile.

"Ah," Esther said, despite of Beth's continuing fear. "Sweet love." She stood for a moment as if pondering the past. "I have once," she said with a downcast eye. "He *Eghobund*, he fine man! Great chief of *Schechscheequanink*. You remember, Young Chickens?"

"Yes, of course, he was a fine man and a great chief. If only he lived now. He too loved peace."

"He do live," Esther said, thumping her chest, "in here."

"Then I hope you shall follow his words in your heart."

"Oh I shall, Young Chickens, me promise."

Esther's eyes looked up and down the young couple again, seeming invigorated by their love. With a smile she turned and slowly walked back to the Indian camp.

Beth did not loosen her grip until the Queen disappeared well into the shadows of the camp. "Oh, John," she said on a careful whisper, "I fear for us all!" Her soulful eyes looked up to him. "Be careful around those people, please, be most careful."

"Yes, I shall my dear," he quietly answered. "You needn't worry on that, I promise, I most certainly shall be most careful."

## Chapter Seven
*Dear Bethiah*

John Jenkins shuffled along through the newly fallen snow with a wary eye. Glancing down at his Indian-made snowshoes for just a moment he felt teased by the thought of the wrinkly faced old Indian from whom he had purchased them. "Good shoes, Chickens, walk many, many moons," he said through his toothless grin over and over again. The scarcity of Indians around Wyoming now caused a heavy feeling in his chest. It is always better to have the fox near the henhouse to keep a close eye on it, he reasoned. Now the wily fox ran wild in the sugarbush.

After pausing for another look around he held his rifle, now his constant companion, tightly to his chest. The snow-capped mountains glistened under the brisk February sky. He listened intently to the sounds of the forest, birds chirping, chattering squirrels, the caw of a crow, all capable of giving him early warning of any mischief.

The stories flying around Wyoming and the reports from those inhabiting the upriver cabins echoed in his mind, sending a new chill down his spine. Increasing reports of Tory activity, especially of their growing influence among the Indians, made him uneasy at the least. Still, in the back of his mind, he held faith in Esther and her promise of peace.

His mind slipped to easier thoughts. Visions of Beth warmed his soul as well as his heart, melding slowly with the thoughts of the future of this great virgin land, just waiting to be settled, waiting to be tamed. In his mind's eye he envisioned Wyoming in the future, alive, thriving, and at peace. A settlement rivaling any in Connecticut or in any other colony.

The close caw of a crow snapped his mind back into the realities of the day. Lifting his rifle he stopped and awkwardly turned around, despite the clumsy snowshoes on his feet. No movement, save the flight of a lone crow and the dark clouds forming to his east, caught his careful eye. He let out a long sigh, cursing the telltale trail of his frosty breath in the air. He stood and waited, stealing a glance every now and then to his flanks out of the corner of his eye. His mind raced with thoughts of Tories, Indians, and wild beasts.

A sudden wind gust brought a change of direction to the breeze and a slight bustle in the trees to his rear. Shrugging his shoulders against the chill the gust bore he sniffed the air with its new smell of burning wood. The smell eased his apprehension. The smell must be from the Murphy's new cabin, he thought.

He drew a few more frosted breaths before turning and trudging toward the welcoming smell. The thought of the warm fire quickened his steps. Stopping on a slight knoll just before the Murphy's cabin he caught his frosted breaths and stared down at the welcoming cabin.

The smoke from the chimney hung low over the cabin as if it also found the bitter chill too much to bear. Winter with its silence coated the man-made haven among the trees with a pure white blanket. Beautiful, but deadly, he realized, trudging once again toward the cabin.

Why his friend John Murphy had built his cabin so far away from the settlement proper still puzzled him, even though his friend explained the assets of the land here about to him until he showed blue in the face. He glanced up to the huge and sprawling trees surrounding the cabin, a good sign, his friend had assured him, of the fertility of the soil. Still, to bring his new wife so far out on the fringes of Exeter seemed rash to him, no matter how fertile the soil.

Stumbling to the corner of the cabin he shouted, "Halloo!" before bending down to remove his snowshoes. Glancing at the door he noticed the rope attached to the latch through a hole in it had been pulled in, a good sign all in the cabin were safe and sound.

A shadow showed over the greased paper stretched taunt over a small square in the cabin's front wall near the door. The door slowly opened a crack. A rifle barrel, then a head, slowly peaked out of it.

"Why John Jenkins!" a voice cheerfully announced. "What took you so long my man? I was beginning to think, well, never mind that, you old bear!"

John Murphy immediately lowered his rifle and sat it down inside the door. Patting his friend on the back, he welcomed him into the cozy cabin. Elizabeth, his wife, quickly sat the wool in her hands down into a basket by her side and smiled. Another woman, looking shyly to the floor, raised her beaming face to the visitor. The wool card she held in her hand dropped to the floor with a sharp ping.

"Why Bethiah," Jenkins gasped, removing his hat. "What a pleasant surprise!" A display of wonderment covered his whole face.

An equal look blanketed Bethiah's face.

Murphy wondered how two people so blatantly attracted to one another remained apart. A fault of their own social conscience, he figured. Sometimes order betrayed the purity of love.

"She is here to help with the carding, is all," Murphy explained. "Purely a social call, just as yourself."

Jenkins smiled at the explanation since he received the invitation but yesterday. He had no doubt Bethiah received her invitation just as hastily. He raised a suspicious eyebrow to his friend.

Bethiah's face turned crimson. Graciously picking the card and wool up from the floor she sat back down on her stool by the hearth. She and Elizabeth shared a sly smile.

"Come John," Murphy said with an outstretched hand gesturing toward the hearth, "warm yourself by the fire."

Jenkins sat his rifle down by his friend's and followed him to the fire, but hints of concern still covered his face.

"What it is, John?" Murphy asked. He looked coyly about, catching Bethiah's school-girl gaze at his friend. "Oh, fear not," he said. "The lass's cousin Peter escorted her here and I am to take her back on the morrow."

Jenkins nodded, embarrassed of his telltale expression. "That is well and fine," he said, eagerly removing his thick blanket coat and opening his palms toward the warm fire. Trying to crack a disconcerting smile he feared it fell well short. What was he to do about Bethiah?

"Come, John," Murphy said, reaching for a small keg on a nearby shelf. "These are trying times fer sure, but we've been through worse! We'll be fine by the good graces of God, we will fer sure, my friend!"

"Yes," Elizabeth added, easing between the two men to stir a pot hanging by a lug pole over the fire with a long wooden spoon. "In the basin's plenty of stew meat!" With her other hand she lifted a string attached to a cloth sack sitting in another pot full of boiling water. "Plus pudding!"

Jenkins nodded to her.

Raising her spoon toward Bethiah she gestured to a rough hewn cupboard along the far wall. "Dear Beth," she said, "I think we are ready to serve."

Beth cheerfully rose and headed for the cupboard.

"Be a good lass and pass the jack on yer way," Murphy asked her. Opening the cupboard she quickly returned with a large leather mug. Murphy took it with a great smile of anticipation, quickly placing it under the spigot of the small keg.

"This is what I'm talking about!" he said, raising the full leather jack in the air. "Essence of lockjaw, 'tis good for what ails you!" After taking a long drink he handed the jack to his friend. Jenkins in turn took an equally long drink.

"No truer words have even been spoken!" Jenkins exclaimed. Wiping his chin on his sleeve he passed the jack back to his friend.

"Bring forth the charger!" Elizabeth said to Beth.

Beth lifted a huge pewter platter from the cupboard and laid it on the hearth.

"Hold it firm," Elizabeth warned, pouring the contents of the larger pot onto the platter. The two woman, each gripping opposite sides of the charger, placed it in the middle of the table.

"We've only two trenchers," Elizabeth explained, waving the men to the table. "I'm sure you two have no objection to sharing one."

"No, none at all," Beth said, smiling at the trencher she placed next to Jenkins.

"How do you like the forms and table board, John?" Murphy asked, running his hand over the smooth table top. "Weren't here when you last called, just finished it, in fact." Leaning his head back toward the cupboard he added "Made that, too," with pride.

Jenkins rubbed the table top and cast a long eye toward the cupboard. Its middle shelf curved in at the sides, rather than straight as the other two shelves. At the apex of the curve several pewter spoons sat nestled in the slots of a large holder. On the top shelf sat a silver teapot in its coveted place for show. The bright flowery leaves painted on its front made it stand out against the other crude implements. Porringers sat on pegs to its rear. A few large wooden bowls sat on the last shelf, meager, put practical, all that was needed on the frontier. Its fine walnut wood gave it a dignified look in the otherwise sparse cabin.

"Fine work, Johnny," Jenkins finally said to his beaming friend.

"Took the best part of a week, but was well worth it," Murphy said, suddenly grabbing Elizabeth and twirling her around to sit her on his lap. Heartily embracing her he quickly kissed her cheek. "Fine ladies need fine things!"

"Johnny," Elizabeth immediately admonished him. "Not now! We've company! Be the proper sort!"

"What?" Murphy asked. "Have I offended a raccoon, or possibly a bear? No fear! They've all holed up for the winter!"

She laughed and took the leather jack from his hand, taking a long drink before passing it to Beth.

Beth took a slight sip and passed it to Jenkins.

"Now we can sup!" Elizabeth said, rising from Johnny's lap. She carefully folded her dress behind her legs before sitting down.

"Now, being proper and all," Johnny said, "let us bow our heads and thank God for his good graces and for his protecting hand now and in the troubled times I fear are ahead." He paused for a moment. "We all here thank you dear Lord, for all your blessings, continuing life, and for your blessing on our little spot in the woods."

"Amen," the others said.

Elizabeth stood and carefully removed the cloth from the pudding.

"There you be," her husband said with a nod. "There be no finer cook in all of Wyoming!" He smiled to Beth. "Present company excluded, of course," he added. Taking a spoon he gruffly scooped a great gob of pudding onto the trencher sitting in front of him and his wife. "Dig in!" he urged his guests. Taking a bite he looked down at his spoon. "We haven't any forks as our fine Colonel Butler graces his table board with. We are not macaronis. The spoon and knife 'tis fine for our like!"

The mention of the colonel's name brought a somber mood to the table. Each became silent for a moment.

"Yes," Murphy broke the silence. "It's been a month and a fortnight since he went off to the Connecticut Line. May God bless and protect him from the Tories and Lobsters, the bloody-backed devils!"

"He, Major Judd, Captain Strong, Jamison and their company, Obadiah Gore and his company off with Colonel Wisner, and the two Westmoreland Companies," Jenkins added. "A lot of Wyoming's manhood is off serving the greater cause of liberty."

"It is most sad, the news of young Justice Porter," Elizabeth said. "He was well liked by all." They all bowed their heads in thought of the British cannonball that had cut the poor soul asunder in a late battle in New Jersey. "He was such a fine and jovial soul. Let our prayers and thoughts be with his poor suffering father and all those still serving in this struggle."

"I think I miss Obadiah the most," Beth said.

"Yes," Elizabeth agreed. "I miss my dear brother the most also. He is of stout heart." The faraway look in her eyes mirrored her concern.

"They are to be transferred from Wisner's New York regiment to the Connecticut Line, I've heard," Murphy said.

Elizabeth let a smile wipe her face clear of anguish.

"How is dear Anna holding up?" Beth asked.

"Oh, she is fine," Elizabeth answered. "She is as stout of heart as Obadiah is. Her heart is equal to her husband's."

"Trenton was quite a feather in our cap!" Murphy said. "Put the Hessians in their place, we did, after what the rascals did at New York! And Millstone! There's a victory for our Durkee's and Ransom's lots! Each got several dollars in prize money! Captain Ransom kept one of the forty wagons captured along with two fine English draft horses! They are all of stout heart indeed! The stoutest!"

"Here! Here!" Jenkins said "We all need to be stout of heart to see our liberties are no longer trampled by the King or the savages!"

"Well," Murphy said. "Not all of the stout hearted have left the valley. I and the good Ensign Jenkins are of the stoutest of hearts and shall remain here to protect our liberties from the foul hand of tyranny! We shall endure against all the rascals!"

"Father and I thought it best at the moment to stay," Jenkins said. "At least until we settle the problems upriver. I fear many a Tory lay up there, no matter what they profess."

"Aye," Murphy said, "I'd be keeping a close eye on the Wintermoots and Van Alstynes, especially since they've built that fort. Perhaps a fort about your father's place would not be such a bad idea come spring. From there we could counter any mischief from them."

"Father and I have similar feelings, as do many in the valley."

"That man Secord, John Secord, there beats a Tory heart, what of him?" Elizabeth asked. " My brother Obadiah is leery of him."

"Zebulon Marcy is keeping an eye on him," Jenkins said. "I'm to pay him a visit soon to see how he's getting along."

"That spirited soul Marcy says Secord aided the bloody-backed officers who escaped from New London. Says he helped them find their way upriver and from there on to Niagara. I can see the Tories using that area to help British officers escape to Niagara, the river provides a much easier way than overland. What mischief is upriver at Tioga I dare not wonder!"

"Oh, none of us dare think of it," Beth said. "John, be most careful of them. For the hundredth time I beg thee!"

Murphy smiled upon her professing her concern for Jenkins. "I think a letter of introduction should be forthcoming to Mr. Harris, Beth's good father." he said. "An introduction for courting."

Jenkins blushed.

Beth beamed upon hearing the suggestion that she and John court, for in her heart, and she hoped in his, they had already started.

Jenkins swallowed hard after being put on the spot by his friend. But apparently the time had come. "Well, Miss Harris," he said, standing tall from the table. "What say you to Johnny's suggestion?"

"Oh yes, dear John, oh yes!" Beth quickly answered.

"There you be!" Murphy said. "That being settled, let us partake in these fine victuals afore us!"

All immediately began to sup. John and Beth's appetite seemed ravenous after finally settling their longing for one another, or potential longing. Between their smiles they managed to empty their shared trencher well before Johnny and Elizabeth.

"Now, my good woman," Murphy said, pushing his full stomach back from the table, patting his hands on either side of it. "Time, my dear Elizabeth, to fetch the voider and clear the table, for I and John shall play a game of all-fours."

Rising from the table Elizabeth grabbed a deep basket at one end of the it. She pushed all the trenchers, spoons, napkins, and the large charger, into it from the table top. "Go sit by the fire 'til we've finished clearing the table proper," she said to the men. They dutifully stood and slowly walked to the fireplace. Murphy rested one arm around his friend's shoulder while he reached for his long clay pipe. A few whispers passed between them as they did between the women clearing the table.

"Hand me a spill from the spill box," Murphy asked John just before they sat down.

John Jenkins reached into a small wooden box placed by the mantle of the fireplace and handed a small curled shaving of wood to his friend.

Murphy smiled and bent down to the fire, igniting the larger end of the turn of wood. Lifting the lit piece of wood to his pipe he strongly inhaled, igniting the tobacco in his pipe. The strong fragrance of tobacco soon filled the air.

"Hand me the jack, my fair maiden, if you please," Murphy called back to the table.

Beth willfully answered the call, her wistful eyes beaming all the while at Jenkins as she passed the jack to Murphy's eager hands.

"That letter should be sent posthaste." Murphy urged his friend, noticing Beth's beauty in the firelight. She even cast a radiance in this dull light, he thought, breaking his gaze to his own wife. No matter what beauty past his eye, his wife always seemed the most radiant to him. He smiled from ear to ear at her until she coyly recognized his stare and smiled back at him. He looked down to his friend again. "A lass such as Bethiah should not be kept waiting," he said, "for many a suitor would like to court her, they would for sure. You are a lucky man, John."

John answered with a nod, knowing the truth of his friend's words. He stole another glance at Beth, drinking in her beauty. "No she should not," he said.

"It's not a time for timid souls in love or war," Murphy said with a wink.

## Chapter Eight
*Queen Esther's Town*

The fog gently lifted from the face of the swirling Susquehanna in the early morning light. The welcoming rays of the early spring sun shone brightly after the retreating fog. The glowing rays seemed to spark life anew in a village of some eighty well built cabins, bark huts, and wigwams along the bank of the winding river. It soon bustled with life. Women stood vigil over huge iron caldrons full of maple sap. The rhythmic thud of others pounding corn in wooden mortars echoed along the mountains surrounding the Indian hamlet. Across the river, at Tioga, at the confluence of the Susquehanna and Chemung Rivers, several canoes drifted on the waters in search of fish. The splash of nets hitting the water joined the sounds of life. Indian dogs trailed groups of carousing Indian children, now and then letting out a howl. Several striking white dogs stood out in their number, bred pure for religious sacrifices. For now, they roamed freely, ignorant of their true purpose.

All dwelled now as they had done for centuries before the dreaded white eyes had arrived. Nothing but painful change seemed to accompany the headstrong white eyes. To the white eyes no religion proved true but their own. No life seemed precious but on their terms, under their laws, and under their lies. How could such a people spread over the land like a pestilence? Did not the Great Spirit see their treachery? Perhaps the world did belong to such treacherous men, or would soon. Woe be to the Indian then. Woe be to the world then.

But the white eyes dwelled far away and stayed that way in the thoughts of the peaceful people performing their daily tasks of life. The white eyes called their land a wilderness. The Indians called it a heaven. What a contrast in ideas. What a contrast in peoples. Perhaps peace would prevail despite it all, most of the Indians prayed. Perhaps the white eyes would keep their distance. But knowing their lust and greed for land, none really believed it. But they must have something to cling to, some hope, even if potentially flawed.

Most clutched the fragile peace, hoping the white eyes would just let them live as they always had; with their own customs and with their own culture. Though the two cultures seemed as water and fire when they collided, the necessity of trade made it now necessary to deal with them. They must at least tolerate them, for the Indians had become dependent on the implements of white eyes, much to their consternation. Trade they must, so most begrudgingly accepted the white eyes' intrusions to some extent. But for most, they wished their contact to be at arm's length. So now most watched the two white men emerging from the trail from the south with mixed emotions. A few aged eyes stared gauntly at them, wondering of the past, and perhaps relieved they would not witness the future. A few eyes turned away completely, content to let others deal with the devils. Most warily watched each footstep of the pair of white men into the heart of their village, their haven, their home.

The white eyes marched boldly, as they always did, but for some reason their presence cut into the villagers' sense of solidarity this day. The white eyes no doubt carried news of their war with the King. A war which tore them, and somehow the Indians, apart in more ways than one. The white man's wars tore the fabric of peace in all of the world.

The white eyes trudged along with their confidence at first, but soon slowed after noticing the indifferent looks of the Indians turn into icy stares. One of them noticeably fidgeted with his rifle tucked underneath his arm until his comrade's touch steadied his movements. His fellow raised his nervous arm, pointing straight ahead without uttering a word. The former took the hint, locking his eyes on the building to which his friend pointed. Every part of his body tingled with fear. What had he got himself into? Peace with these savages? You may as well wish for water to turn into wine! Peace would take such a miracle. Dear God this long walk may be my last!

Children raced behind them with their hands to their faces ready to shield their eyes should the white devils look their way. The accompanying dogs howled at them. Women all around the village suddenly stopped staring and congregated around them. Their whispers filled the hushed air. Warriors, each bearing an indignant stare, watched their every move. One of the warriors raised his trade rifle, yelling at the top of his lungs. Others immediately joined him. He boldly led them on an intersecting track with the white eyes.

One of the white men's hands fell carefully to his pouch. His hand emerged a second later, bearing a long belt of woven beads. He held it high in the air, never slowing his footsteps.

The warriors winced upon sight of the belt and reluctantly adjusted their course, letting the white men proceed unmolested. An old white haired woman blanched at the warriors. Cursing them, she marched steadfastly toward the white men. Coming up behind them she yelled "Waasar hopeekomeetaa!" over and over to them. Her unearthly wail made both white men shudder, but they continued their trek nonetheless.

The woman slid to their side, continuing to wail.

Both white men looked down at the hunched-over ancient woman. Her filthy buckskin dress reeked. Her yellow and black sparse teeth showed with each wail. She raised her long and bony fingers, her nails caked by weeks of dirt, waving them one after another at the devils. She quickly scooped up a small drum along the way and began to pound on it, her long finger nails scratching across the head on it with each new thud. She spat and clutched the drum ever so tightly under her frail arm. "Waasar hopeekomeetaa!" she wailed between scratchy beats.

A tall warrior, seeming to be emboldened by the old woman's chants, walked up to the men, standing full and bold in their path. Spitting at their feet he raised a spear to stab at the air near the belt.

The white men stopped, but did not flinch, especially the one holding the wampum belt. His grim face bore a look of pure defiance.

More warriors encircled them, raising their weapons in a threatening manner. Their war whoops grew to a frightening crescendo. The warrior with the spear opened the blanket wrapped around him, exposing his chest. His free hand fell to his belt, drawing his tomahawk. Stabbing the spear in the ground he thumped his barrel chest, producing a fierce thud. His unblinking eyes locked on the two white devils.

The white men stood firm. A slight blow from one of the warriors to the rear caused one of them to slightly flinch, but he quickly regained his composure. They both remained steadfast in nature, fearing any sign of weakness now meant instant death; or an extremely painful and slow death. They preferred neither.

The other women, as well as the children, all joined the old woman with her nerve-racking chant. The thud of large water drums suddenly echoed in the increasingly tense air. Each thud reverberated in the white men's heads, eerily tingling down their spines on its way to their toes. Soon each of the white men scanned beyond the circling and threatening bevy of warriors as if seeking out a savior.

Their eyes fell to a few warriors standing on the fringes of the circle, one wearing a bright red British officer's jacket. Their indifferent eyes adverted the white men's pleading stares. Some even turned and retreated into cabins and huts to escape the loud ruckus.

Spears danced closer to the white men's heads with each passing moment. One or two of the jabs from the sharp weapons tore into the fringes of their hunting frocks. A particularly enterprising brave yanked the feather from one of the white men's hats and the buck tail from the other. Children dashed about their feet, clubbing them with small sticks. A few muskets fired into the air.

The two white men stood as rigid as statues in the middle of the melee. Neither dared flinch or even gasp. Blow after blow struck their backs. They ignored them.

The hoary old woman passed her drum along and pulled a knife from her belt. The crowd parted around her. She slowly advanced toward the white devils bearing a mischievous smile. Warriors crowded around her and behind the white devils, holding their spears and rifles ready to counter any sudden moves from the doomed men.

The old woman sneered, swirling the knife in the air in front of the white men's faces. It drew closer and closer to the men's throats, with the old hag smiling at the fear she caused in the men's eyes. Just then a gruff voice sounded loudly in an Indian tongue to the rear of the crowd. The crowd grew silent. All eyes immediately turned toward the voice.

The crowd parted to make way for a stately figure, her showy dress covered with silver broaches and trinkets. The woman marched through the crowd with the air of a true sovereign. All backed away at the mere wave of her hand. Stopping just short of the nervous white men she glared at them for the longest moment.

"Young Chickens!" she finally said with a smile from ear to ear. "What you do here? Why you come?"

"Oh, my dear Esther," John Jenkins immediately said. "We are here to see you, my dear Queen. What else?"

Queen Esther laughed and shook her head. She quickly waved for the crowd to disperse. "Jogo!" she commanded. "Jogo!"

The crowd reluctantly melted away, some casting a sour eye at the Queen for ruining their sport. Soon all but the Queen and hoary old woman stood by the white men.

Queen Esther cast a cold eye to the stubborn old hag, shouting "Jogo!" at her. The woman looked down to the ground with a lost look in her eyes. She slowly departed, shuffling her feet along the ground.

The Queen watched her go and looked to the white men again. She reached out, taking Jenkins by the hand. "You fool to come here," she said, leading him toward a large hewed-logged cabin in the middle of the village.

"This, my dear Esther," Jenkins said, gesturing to the man following them, "is John Sutton of Wyoming. He is accompanying me on this mission, which I might add, is truly peaceful in nature."

"Yes, Chickens" Esther said. "We talk in cabin, now no talk!"

A tall Indian, older and also somehow stately, stood just in front of the door to Esther's great cabin, or castle. He remained rigidly still, his hands hidden in the folds of the blanket covering him.

Jenkins recognized him immediately and nodded his head to his indifferent stare.

The Indian remained stoic.

His indifference concerned Jenkins. Being a surveyor, he knew many of the Indians, having frequent contact with the prominent ones. Job Chillaway knew him, as well as his father, very well, and had many dealings with them. He dwelled with the *Moravians* at Wyalusing before their exodus to lands farther west, away from the upcoming war and troubles about Wyoming. "Job," he finally said. "It is good to see you."

"It no good to see you, Young Jenkins," Chillaway said with a glaring eye. "You stay in Wyoming from now on! It no good if you lose scalp up here. What I tell you father if that happen?"

"Oh, do not worry about that, my friend," Jenkins said. "I intend to keep this hair to the grave."

"The grave come sooner than you think!" Chillaway said, rolling his eyes. "Indian Butler and Joseph Brant come all around here! Stir pot they do! Pot of war!" With that the tall Indian turned, walking away without so much as a passing glance back over his shoulder. "Tell all to stay downriver until storm of war passes!" he said loudly before disappearing around the corner of the cabin.

"He right," Esther said with a wave toward the cabin door. "Come, sit, my castle."

"Keep peeaatarwee waaasar hopeekomeetaa!" the old woman called from around the far corner of Esther's castle.

"Old Shawnee woman," Esther said, shaking her head. "She touched in head!"

"What is she carrying on about anyway?" Sutton asked.

"She say you make good broth," Esther said. "Pay no mind to her. Those ways long gone."

"Ways?" Sutton asked.

"Ways to boil you, my friend," Jenkins said, "and me, too."

Sutton's eyes bulged at Jenkins, who only smiled back at him, though both hurried into the cabin.

Sutton walked slowly around the long edifice, glancing in every dark corner with a suspicious eye. Fireplaces sat on both ends of the cabin, both with large flat stones in front of them. Hewn logs, set in the ground at intervals of ten feet, had grooves into which sat neatly fitted horizontal planks, making the walls. Various deer and bear skin pallets sat about the floor. A strange idol, resembling nothing he had ever seen of any religion, sat in a coveted spot in the center of the floor. Pots and wooden bowls sat on a long shelf along one of the walls. No chair greeted his weary backside. He finally plopped down onto one of the bear skins by one of the fireplaces.

Jenkins and Esther shuffled over to him. Esther's features

surprised him, now that he had a moment to look at her with an easy eye. He had heard of her, but being a mill owner, he never had any dealings with her. She stood tall over him, not very fleshy, and not as dark as the usual Indian. Her raven hair shone softly in the firelight. No high cheek bones sat on her oval face. Her long imported blue shirt reached just over her knees. Brightly colored stockings showed below the shirt and met beaded moccasins adorning her feet. She now donned a blanket Indian fashion over her upper torso, but her glittering ornaments still shone through its folds. One ornament in particular caught his eye, bringing great comfort to him. A silver cross dangled from her neck on a long white beaded necklace.

Esther smiled, noticing his wide-eyes staring at the cross. "Great Jehovah," she said, lifting the cross to her lips. She gently kissed it.

Sutton smiled back at her. "God is indeed in the wilderness," he whispered. He, being of the Society of Friends, found comfort in her apparent affection for God. At the same time his eyes fell to the idol, giving him an odd feeling. These people, these Indians, seemed caught between two worlds.

"Now, my dear Esther," Jenkins said. "I shall come down to business. We have come to secure the release of Dan Ingersoll."

Esther shook her head and looked down to the fire. "He go Niagara, you too late," she said.

Both of the men let out a groan of disappointment.

"It bad times, Chickens," Esther said. "Fox, he taken too, no long ago, just before you come. They take Fox to Quebec."

Jenkins' eyes lit up with concern. "Rudolf Fox?" he asked.

Esther nodded, slowly descended to one of the skins.

"What of Mother Fox and the children?" he asked. The thought of any harm coming to the good natured German and his humble little family living on the *Towanda Creek* made his blood run cold.

"No, no, just old Fox," Esther answered.

Jenkins took a deep breath before sitting down. He knew he could never convince Mother Fox to leave her vulnerable upriver cabin until she had word from Rudolf or he returned. The latter seemed improbable at the least. He scolded himself for not stopping at Fox's cabin on their trek upriver. Perhaps then they could have prevented Rudolf's abduction.

"There no thing you could do," Esther said. "Fox, he Rebel!"

"Oh my good Lord!" Sutton said.

"The Lord giveth and the Lord taketh away," Esther said.

Sutton straightened his back and stared at the Indian Queen, amazed by her quotation of the scriptures. "What do you think of all this debauchery?" he asked.

"No good for Indian or white!" Esther said. "Butler and Brant they come, turn peace away!"

"Yes, they do," Sutton answered. "But as good Christians we must keep the faith."

"Yes, yes," Esther agreed, fondling the cross dangling at the end of her necklace.

"Blessed are the peacemakers for they shall see the face of God," Sutton said.

"Those whom live by the sword shall surely die by it," Esther added.

Both white men beamed at her command of the scriptures. Her broken English found no way into them. She spoke clearly, as if in another voice.

The door suddenly opened and a large buckskin-clad robust woman bounded in the room. A mischievous smile stretched across her face. She sat a large pot in her hands before the fire. A pair of dogs slipped through the door she left open and immediately started howling at the white men. The woman yelled "Jogo!" and waved her hands toward the door. The dogs ignored her. She rose to her feet, cursing and kicking at them. After a quick chase the dogs scampered out the door. She slammed it behind them, muttering a few oaths in her native tongue.

Sutton's wide-eyes told all. His hands held his rifle with an iron grip.

"It fine," Esther said.

"Why do they howl like demons and not bark?" Sutton asked.

Jenkins laughed, amused by his jittery friend's ignorance of the Indians. "They are more akin to the wolf than our dogs," he explained.

"Yes," Esther said, pointing to the larger woman. She and the woman both grabbed some wooden bowls and spoons from the shelf. Sitting the bowls before their guests the large woman scooped the contents of the pot into the bowls.

"You sup," Esther said. "This my sister, Mary."

The larger woman showed the same hints of the white race about her round face. Her buckskin dress held fewer silver broaches and much less other colored ornaments than her sister's. A great smile suddenly erupted across her face. "You true, sister," she said, eying Jenkins, "he fetching white man!" Giggling, she hid her face in her hands.

Esther blushed and diverted attention to the bowls. "Ump Squaqch," she said. "It good! You eat!"

Sutton looked down to the festering stew and then to Jenkins.

"Pork," Jenkins explained. "They take a dead boar, throw it into a fire to burn off all its hair, then throw it into a iron pot with water and what herbs and such they can find in the forest and in their gardens."

"Entrails and all, I gather," Sutton asked, lifting his spoon from the substance.

"Yes," Jenkins said, taking a bite. "They waste but little."

"Ah," Esther said, puzzled by the white man's hesitation. "Grace!" She bowed her head. "God bless all, keep peace, amen."

Sutton nodded his head and let a polite smile creep across his face. Lifting the spoon reluctantly to his mouth, he jumped from a series of loud taunts sounding from beyond the cabin door. Dropping the spoon, he clutched his rifle.

Esther and Mary looked at each other. Jenkins sat deathly still. The whoops and yells continued unabated.

"You sit," Esther said, rolling her eyes toward the disturbance. "I go see what goes." She stood and ran a hand over her dress. Clutching the cross on her necklace she muttered what sounded like a prayer. Her dark eyes closed and then opened, bearing a stern look of resolve. Drawing a long breath, she opened the door with her sister at her heels.

Loud whoops and chants welcomed her. A dozen warriors sat atop a log near the front of the cabin. The old Shawnee woman stood to their side, lost in a series of chants. Some of the warriors stood and let out loud whoops. A few thumped their chests. Several discharged their weapons into the tense air.

Mary peeled away from Esther, seeking escape around the corner of the cabin. Esther watched her out of the corner of her eye. She shook her head at her deserting sister and threw back her shoulders. Her eyes narrowed on the obstinate warriors and chanting old woman.

The warriors shot stern looks back to her, increasing their whooping. A few furiously waved their hands in the direction of the cabin. Some spat upon the ground, showing their disgust.

The Queen suffered the abuse with regal bearing. Waiting patiently for the fury of the warriors to subside, she approached the log. Her calming tones seemed to subdue the anger in the warriors' voices. Kneeling down to the ground, she positioned herself between them and the door, promptly engaging in an earnest conversation with them.

Jenkins and Sutton slowly edged to the door, careful to remain in the shadows. Each listened intently to the tone of the conversation.

"What shall we do?" Sutton asked.

"What we have to do," Jenkins bluntly answered. "For it seems we have stumbled into a hornet's nest."

"What if those beasts Butler and Brant show up?" Sutton continued. "It shall surely mean our demise, or capture."

"They, my dear friend," Jenkins said, "may be at least of our worries, dreadful scoundrels as they are." Slowly lowering his rifle he checked the brace of pistols in his belt. "It is best we just wait," he added, "for now at least. Check your rifle just the same and if I light out of here be quick at my heels. Run like the very devil is after you, for I think he may well be at that."

"What of Esther?"

"We shall see. Pray for her, my dear friend, as well as for us."

"Can you make anything of their gibberish?"

"No, I only sense the anger in their tones."

Jenkins waved his friend back from the door and followed him. Stopping at the corner of the hearth he pointed at his weapon and then to the door. Sutton needed no words to understand his meaning. Raising his rifle he leveled it at the door. His mind raced with scenarios, but deep down he knew their lives now hung on the influence of the Indian Queen over her subjects. He muttered the Lord's Prayer on a whisper.

The seconds turned into minutes and the minutes dragged into hours until the white men surmised the day neared its end. They only moved to reconfigure their weapons in their tired hands or to take a drink, otherwise their weapons remained steadily fixed on the door. To their relief, as the shadows of the day grew longer, the chatter outside the door lessened to a minor rumble with an occasional angry outburst. The Queen's calming voice always followed.

Finally, the voices fell silent. The door crept open. Both men eased their hammers back upon sight of the smiling Queen. She stopped and turned to latch the door, waving both men to her.

"I no can do nothing with them," she admitted with a serious look. "Your guns no good, they too many. You be still until I call you!" Turning, she walked slowly through the door. Silence followed her.

Jenkins latched the door behind him, jumping back as a new series of war whoops sounded in the distance. Slowly, he backed away from the door. Training his rifle on it, he stood listening intently to the noises.

Huge fires crackled along with the whoops.

The hours grew longer and the crackling fires slowly died. The war whoops and chants flitted into nothingness. Soon only the occasional howls of the Indian dogs sounded in the still of the night air.

A slight knock thumped the door. Jenkins quickly put an ear to it. "Esther?" he whispered through the cracks in the door.

"Yes, Chickens, it me," a voice whispered back. "Open."

Lifting the latch, he opened the door just wide enough for the Queen to squeeze through it.

"You listen," she said on a whisper to the white men huddling around her. "You go river. Find canoe." Grabbing one of the spoons, she held it edgewise. "Hold paddle this way! Make no noise!"

The white men nodded.

Esther crept to the door, slowly cracking it open. Peeking out of it, she gestured for the men to follow her. The trio slipped through the sleeping village in the dark veil of the night. In no time they reached the riverbank and crept down it to a canoe landing.

"Now slip away," Esther said, slowly easing a canoe into the water. The white men carefully climbed into it, easing their rifles down into it before grabbing the paddles Esther handed to them.

"Godspeed," Esther said.

Both men nodded, but none the more than Sutton, relieved to say the least. He suddenly saw Jenkins in a new light. He possessed a certain courage to go among these dangerous savages. His insistence they travel by foot instead of horses showed great wisdom also, for they would have surely lost them here. His odd relationship with the Indian Queen had undoubtedly saved their skins, for now. "Godspeed to you also, Mr. Jenkins," he said in appreciation.

"Godspeed to us all," Jenkins whispered.

Esther watched the canoe slowly wind down the Susquehanna in the pale moonlight. She stood until it slipped well out of sight. A slight prayer crossed her lips before she sullenly turned back to the village, softly kissing the cross on the beaded necklace around her neck.

## Chapter Nine
### Tories and Traitors

Little clusters of settlers stood about the room. Slouch hats mixed with fine cocked hats sat tucked under their arms. Rough hunting frocks stood side by side fine waistcoats of gentlemen. A few grizzly beards shown among the sea of clean shaven faces. A small desk sat in the corner of the room, covered with papers and goose quills, as if the scene of some intense composition just a few moments ago. Elderly gentlemen filled the few chairs, their hands resting on the boots of their canes, listening and conversing with the younger men milling about them. Each of their hushed conversations dripped with concern. A hint of tobacco haunted the room from clay pipes set in the jaws of a few nervous souls. Worried looks blanketed the faces of most, young and old, rough or refined. The intensity of their conversations soon raised the pitch of their voices.

Colonel Denison responded by grabbing a paper from the desk and standing in the middle of the room. His raised hand held the paper high. "Gentlemen!" he said, "please! May I have your attention?"

The room slowly quieted.

"Mr. Sutton's and Lieutenant Jenkins' reports, as well as others, pertaining to the conditions upriver must be addressed!" Denison said, clearing his throat. "The Tory question must be addressed!"

"Here! Here!" came a unified cry from the assembled men.

Dennison waved his arms to subdue the resulting tumult. "Quite!" he said, pausing until silence once again prevailed. "As I said, in consequence of sundry reports from upriver a dangerous plot has been discovered! Yes! A plot is afoot by some rascals to bring about an Indian war!" The crowd erupted into shouting He patiently waited for the noise to dissipate. "In particular," he continued loudly, "we have intercepted a letter written by Nicholas Pickard to John Pickard, at the house of Casper Reed in Penn Township, a copy of which has been brought to us by Nathaniel Landon of Wyoming." He waved the paper in the air. After some grumbling he lowered it to read:" 'Worthy friend, as soon as the river is clear of ice we will march from every part. Therefore I would advise you as a friend to get out of the way, for we intend to cut all off. Perhaps by Easter I shall be with you; then I shall tell you further. Signed Nicholas Pickard.' That is all gentlemen."

"Pickard!" a voice yelled. "He is of that nest of Tories about the Tunkhannock Creek!"

"Many of those who had moved to Niagara have returned and took the freeman's oath," Denison said, gesturing toward Zebulon Marcy.

"It's only a ruse!" Marcy said. "I warned you all afore! It would be wise to heed my warning. Their hearts lay with the King!"

"What he speaks is true!" Sam Gordon said, stepping next to Denison. "Secord has moved to Tioga Point, but others remain. I propose that I be sent upriver on a scout to ascertain just whom among them be Tory or Patriot!"

"I have already ordered James Murray and James Espy in search of Nicholas and John Pickard," Denison reported. "I have also just written a letter to Roger Sherman in Congress informing him of all this." Looking about the room he raised an eyebrow to Sam Gordon. "Gordon's scout shall prove most productive, I believe," he added.

"I shall depart alone," Gordon said, "as to not arouse suspicion. I shall send word when I have completed my task and rendezvous with a force sufficient to apprehend the Tories about Wyalusing." He looked about the many faces. "I propose John Jenkins lead such a force."

"If it be fine with Lieutenant Jenkins, so be it," Denison said.

"It is fine with me," Jenkins said. "If God should suffer those slavish, serpentine wretches to influence the savages into acts of hostilities, it might be the cause of some blood shed, but make no doubt they would soon sicken of the bargain!"

A cheer rose from everyone.

"I say be wary of the Indians despite the damn Tories!" Lazarus Stewart's voice boomed above the cheers just enough to silence them.

"I am not so sure," James Sutton immediately said. "If it were not for the Indian Queen I and John should have truly suffered. We cannot condemn all the natives, for Queen Esther seems to have the correct views on religious and moral responsibilities and obligations."

Stewart grinned, slowly walking over to Sutton. "Must be the white in her," he scoffed.

"Here now!" Sutton said. "'There's no need for such talk!"

"When is the need then, my fine Quaker?" Stewart said. "I make fair wager that that rifle you took for protection from wolves, bears, and such, was held at the ready when you and fine Jenkins lay huddled in that Indian castle." He stared coldly in Sutton's eyes. "I had my fill of your like at Paxtang, telling us on the frontier under the threat of the scalping knife to be patient while your like sat safe and warm around hearths in Philadelphia. You fools even traded and armed them with tomahawks amidst all the turmoil! " He ran his fingers through his fine crop of hair. "I intend to keep these locks! Do not listen to their like, be they from Philadelphia or New England, and you shall keep yours!"

"Yes, Lazarus," Denison said. "You have said your piece, now my friend, allow others to speak."

"I say," Squire Jenkins said, "that work be doubled on all forts until they are completed! Our very lives may depend upon it!"

Cheers filled the room again. They filtered out through the precious few panes of Denison's two fine windows and into the ears of the masses bunched around them. But no approving cheers crept from their throats. Only deep looks of concern passed from eye to eye among the women and few men. They all moved in unison away from the windows, milling about the yard. A few nervous whispers flitted amongst them.

A pair of women in particular hustled over to a large maple tree in the far corner of the yard. "Oh, that boisterous Sam Gordon!" Bethiah Harris said to her companion. "What mischief has he weaved John into now, my dear Elizabeth?"

"Now just calm yourself," Elizabeth Murphy answered. She looked over to the corner of the house to her husband John standing with his hands clenching the barrel of his upended rifle. The intensity of his stare at a particular group of men standing uneasily about remained firm, despite of her waving at him to desist.

"Oh look to my John," Elizabeth said. "The way he is looking at the Wintermoots and Van Gorders is enough to provoke even the most mild mannered. We don't need this, not now at least!"

The door of the house suddenly opened and men plowed through it, congratulating and shaking each other's hands. After most exited, Denison stood in the doorway with upraised hands. "Hear ye! Hear ye!" he said. "All work is to be doubled on the forts forthwith! " Casting a sour gaze to the Wintermoots he added, "Especially Fort Jenkins in Exeter!"

The Wintermoots, father and sons, along with their companions, stood undeterred by the sudden attention. The way John Murphy had stared at them since they arrived left them callous to it to say the least. Mumbling something to one another, they slowly walked toward their horses tethered to a nearby fence. Slowly mounting, they nonchalantly rode away, paying no heed to the cold stares following them.

"No worries John," Murphy said to his friend now standing at his side. "I kept a sharp eye on them flatlanders all the time. They tried to act as if they did not care, but I could tell they marked every word."

"I dare say nothing can be done with them," Jenkins said. "They are as set in their ways as much as we are in ours."

"Still, we shall watch them," Murphy said. "If they would only move as Secord did. Why they stay puzzles me. There is an air of mischief about them. They must know they are under suspicion."

"Aye," Jenkins said, casting an eye in the direction from which they departed. "It worries me as well, my friend."

"Ah, my son!" Squire Jenkins said, turning from a group of men to his son and Murphy. "I see they cause you ire also!"

"Yes, Father, we must keep a wary eye on them, especially with their dealings with the Indians. Stewart may not be as light of mind as some think," John Jenkins said.

"Yes, I fear so," Squire Jenkins said. "I fear so."

"As do we all," Murphy added. "As do we all."

Squire Jenkins looked down to a bulge in his waistcoat and slowly produced a fine pistol from it. "Their indifference may only be answered by these," he said, nodding to the exposed butt of the pistol.

Both his son and Murphy nodded, swallowing hard against the growing lumps in their throats. They all would fight if they must, but all feared the repercussions of brash acts, and turned a wary eye from the pistol to the booming voice still demanding such a remedy to the situation from inside the house.

Lazarus Stewart's voice did carry so, and his deep voice had a way of sending foreboding chills down a man's spine.

Squire Jenkins slowly slid the pistol back into his waistcoat.

## Chapter Ten
*Fort Jenkins*

The crack of axes rang along the banks of the Susquehanna. Trees crashed in cadence to the sharp cracks, breaking the continuity of the lush forest. Still, the crows cawed, the birds chirped, and the squirrels chattered, mixing with the thuds of the axes and the groans of the oxen struggling to pull the great fallen logs. All of the sounds converged to one point along the riverbank at Exeter, just opposite Pittston in Wyoming.

Palisades slowly rose around the fine cabin of Squire Jenkins. Men and boys bustled around them, each engaged in their own tasks to raise Fort Jenkins. When the wind died similar sounds crept up the river from the opposite bank and just south of them. The settlers of Pittston worked just as diligently raising their stronger fort. Vertically planted pointed logs crept from two completed blockhouses and stretched toward a third. Its sheer size precluded it from being finished any time as soon as the simple stockade being raised around the Jenkins' cabin.

William Jenkins, the youngest of Squire Jenkins' four sons, struggled with a wooden bucket of small beer to the men raising one of the pointed logs into place. A thunder clap off in the distance gave him a start, causing him to slightly upset the bucket, spilling some of the beer. Turning, he looked over his shoulder to the threatening clouds billowing high into the sky behind him, paying no mind to the bucket and the beer spilling onto his bare feet. A gruff hand promptly relieved him of the bucket.

"Why, thanking you I am, son, but mind your bucket," Ben Harding said with a grin.

William glanced up to him and then back to the great black clouds. "It's a gonna storm ! It is fer sure!" he said.

Ben grabbed the noggin attached to the bucket by a long length of hemp cord and took a long drink. Smacking his lips, he passed the noggin to the awaiting hands of John Jenkins.

"He's a fine looking lad, John," Ben said with a nod toward the boy. "Growing fast and strong, just the sort we need to tame this wilderness."

John Jenkins raised an admiring eye to his young brother. "He is a fine lad indeed," he said, ruffling the lad's hair with his hand.

"Tom and I got Sally all saddled and ready!" William said, suddenly forgetting all about the storm clouds. "We did just as Ma told us! She says you're a gonna lead a scout up to Wyalusing to meet Sam Gordon and round up some of them Tories!" The boy's face beamed.

"That I am, dear Will," John said. "That I am!"

"You really think things are that bad up there?" Ben asked.

"I tell you, Ben," John said. "I fear nothing can be done with them to change their minds. It is just the way of it."

Ben looked up the rising palisades. "Only five more to be set," he said. "Stukeley's got the last few feet of the post trench almost dug. Are you sure you can't stay, John? We can get it done today, leastways get all the pales set." Gazing up to the darkening sky he added, "Bad storm's a brewing anyways."

Jenkins looked up the almost finished wall and then to the dark clouds beyond. He could not help but notice Stukeley digging all the more faster upon hearing his father's words.

"Wintermoot's got their fort all done," Ben added, wiping the sweat from his brow.

"It's the first of June," John said, "the date I agreed to meet Sam at Wyalusing."

"I know," Ben said. "But don't you think it can wait but one more day? I've got fields that need tending to upriver and with you taking most of the men with you those of us who stay will have to work all the longer and harder to get the last of the posts raised. Can't neglect the crops, remember what happen in seventy-three? You ask any of them that trudged through that snow to fetch sacks of grain to tote them on their backs in the dead of winter from the Delaware to here, and they'll tell ya, by thunder they will." He waved his hands in the air. "Besides, you may be all outfitted, but Phelps, Martin, and Murphy ain't, I'll grant you that fer sure! They' ain't had time, what with cutting logs all morning!" he added for good measure.

Ben no sooner finished his words before the moans of oxen sounded in the air. Tired voices accompanied the laborious groans of the strained team of oxen. The snap of a whip only hastened their grunts of defiance. "Get going!" a voice commanded. "Storm's a brewing!"

Jenkins and Harding both walked around the unfinished palisades to the noises. Two sweat-soaked men staggered to the side of the fort and laid their axes against the walls. Groaning, they collapsed to the grass. The man snapping the whip motioned with his free hand at the young boy holding the reins. The boy guided the oxen to a stop by the unfinished section of the wall. The oxen bellowed a last groan before also collapsing to the cool grass. Two other shirtless men unhitched the harness and ropes holding the logs, rolling the logs toward the wall.

"That, my friends," John Murphy announced from the grass, "is the last five posts." Yanking off his hat, he wiped his brow before falling and rolling face first in the grass. He groaned in exhaustion. Lifting his head he added, "We got plenty of smaller logs to finish the banquette, too." His head collapsed back down into the soft grass.

Young William hurried to the exhausted men with the bucket and noggin. Murphy rolled over just long enough to take a long drink before passing the noggin to his fellows sprawled about the grass around him. They all took their own long drinks.

A sudden and near loud clap of thunder made every eye turn to the threatening sky. Dark, rolling clouds filled the air. A strong breeze swept over the grass. Bright yellow flashes showed deep within the angry clouds. Nature bellowed her warning before exploding full.

"We had better take cover," Ben said. "Looks like it's gonna be quite a boomer!"

"Quocko!" one of the men called. "See to them oxen! Quick!"

A dark skinned man immediately rose from the grass. "Yes, marse," he said, stumbling toward the tired beasts. Hard raindrops started falling violently from the clouds. Quickly removing the harness and yoke from the oxen, he shooed them toward the Jenkins' barn. The barn door flailed in gusts of wind against them before a pair of dark hands grabbed the doors from the inside and slammed them closed.

The others gathered under the half-finished banquette along the inside of the palisades. At a sprint William ran off toward the cabin in the center of the stockade. The men working on the other parts of the fort raced to the barn or to the banquette on the other side of the fort. Just as all reached cover a mad hail exploded from the angry heavens.

Grape sized clumps of hail assaulted the trees surrounding the fort, pinging off the cedar shingles of the cabin's roof. The poles making up the wooden platform over the men's heads rang loud with it. All of the men hunkered down and looked up at the poles over their heads, moving every now and then to avoid the cold stream of water leaking through the gaps between the poles.

"Quite a boomer!" Ben said, raising his voice above the pinging hailstones. "It'll play hell on the crops! Hope it's just a cloud burst around here so as to spare the fields upriver!"

"Amen to that," Stukeley said with bulging eyes. Thunderstorms always gave him the willies. He looked anxiously to the silent men surrounding him. Their wide eyes offered him no solace. Scrunching his knees tight to his chest, he listened for the hail to ease up. Closing his eyes tight, he mouthed a prayer. To his astonishment the pinging stopped, replaced by the gentle patter of rain.

John Jenkins rose and stood to the edge of the banquette to watch the rain. It poured down with no sign of letting up. Casting an eye to Stukeley, he stared gauntly at him. The hail stopped, that was enough. One should not push his prayers.

"Looks as if we will be delayed in our departure," he said over his shoulder.

"Just as well," Murphy said. "Ain't had no time to make ready anyhow."

Jenkins turned and looked at Ben. He shrugged his shoulders.

"Well, can't fight the hand of God," Jenkins said. "We'll start at first light then."

"But what of storm damage?" William Martin asked. "I have a feeling the devil is to pay for this storm. I and my man Quocko may have to tend to things."

"Then stay," Jenkins said. "I have a bad feeling about Sam. I should have left this morning like I had planned."

"And we would have all got caught up in this fine weather," Murphy said, rolling his eyes toward the heavy rain. "I may be delayed because of this mess just the same, John."

Jenkins looked to Phelps.

He shook his head. "My crops and place may need attention too," he said.

"Then I shall go alone!" Jenkins said. "I shall stop and bring along Zebulon Marcy, he's always game!"

"Now look John," Ben Harding said. "Ingersoll is back. Dan Walters is back, too." He oddly laughed and slapped his knee. "That Dan Walters, there's one for you! Hear he had a chance to marry a fine Indian princess when they had him. They dressed him up all fancy and in the finery of a chief as to make him presentable and all, and what does the fool do? Backs out! So they stripped him and made him run the gauntlet! Whipped the fool something fierce, seen the scars myself, I has!" Laughing again, he shook his head. "Now look at him! He's married to a woman not unlike the common squaw when he could have had a princess graced with the fair beauty of all the Indian race!" He looked up to Jenkins with a sly eye. "Bet you've come across some fine Indian flesh, what with being a surveyor among their land and all."

Jenkins looked coldly at him.

"No offense, dear John," Ben said. "Why, Bethiah Harris is a fine woman, and is surely worth the wait."

"The Indians claim neutrality," Martin said, changing the sore subject before blows ensued. "I don't think they'll break their treaty with us, or the one they made at Easton."

"Sam's scout does not concern Indians, but Tories, remember!" Jenkins said through gritted teeth. He stared deathly at each man. "I'll set out on the morrow, first light! Alone if I have too!"

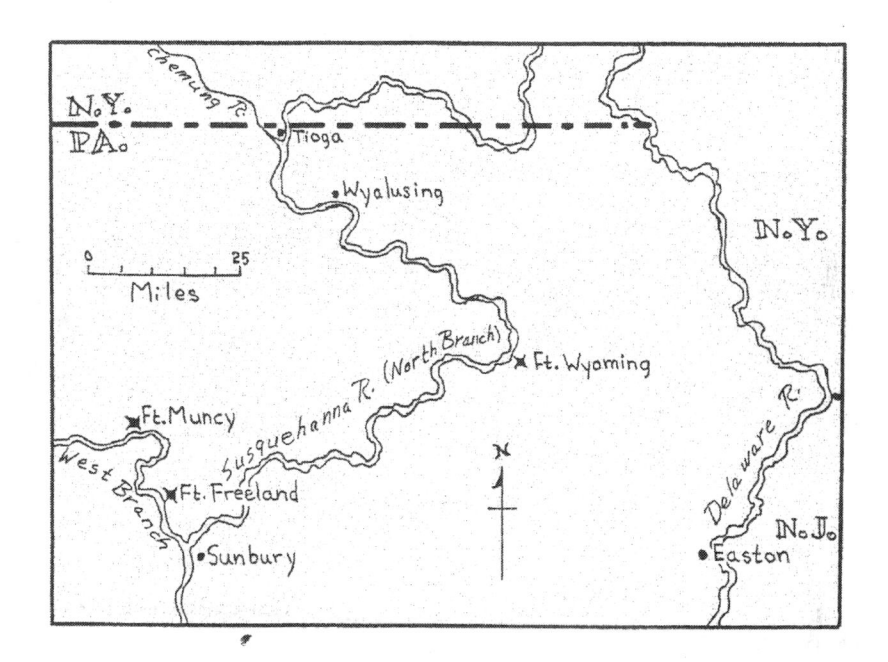

## Chapter Eleven
*York's place at Wyalusing*

The men emerging from the *Great Warrior Trail* at Wyalusing filed from it and onto Amos York's large farm. Reining their horses to a stop in the dooryard of the cabin, they waited. They nervously fingered their weapons laid across the pommels of their saddles. Some anxious thumbs played at the hammers of their rifles, ready to cock and fire in an instant. But aside from the few chickens milling about their mounts' hooves, nothing stirred in the farmyard.

Their leader rose high in his saddle, looking carefully around. The eyes of the men scanned the outbuildings and barn. No one uttered a word lest it betray a warning sound of some unseen and skulking foe. They lay everywhere, whether Tory or Indian, or so it seemed in this upriver country.

Their leader's hand slowly motioned for them to spread out further. Lifting one leg over his saddle, he slid down from it, holding his rifle at the ready. He stepped cautiously toward the eerily silent cabin door when it suddenly burst open full in his face. A man strode toward him, holding out his hand; his empty hand, lucky for him.

The man's smile stretched from ear to ear across his round little face. He eagerly sought out the leader's hand and shook it. "My God it's good to see you!" the man said, beaming at the wide-eyed men staring at him. "It's good to see you all, it is fer sure!" the man added.

A woman, followed by a brood of children, spilled from the door behind the smiling man. The woman fussed at her hair, suddenly conscious of how she appeared. Despite her worried look she managed to crack a half smile. "It is good to see you all!" she said.

"So I've heard," the leader said, gently taking his hand back. He nodded to the woman and looked back to the man. "What has you all spooked so, Amos?" he asked. "And what of Sam Gordon?"

"Oh John," Amos said, "the Tories are thick and all about, but have been behaving, until last night, that is."

"Sam?" John Jenkins asked again.

"Yes, poor Sam," Amos said, nervously looking about. "They took him! He waited, and with time his tongue got all the looser. He said you was a coming and started spouting on about the Tories and how they would soon be off to the Simsbury Mines Prison! One has to watch what one says around these parts, what with the Pauling boys and all."

"Was it they whom took him?"

"Don't know fer sure, two nights ago he said he needed to stretch his legs to relieve his mind of its angst, kept watching the trail to the south a wondering where you was. Well, that was the last we saw of him. His horse and trappings are in the barn still. They just took him."

"Do you think he's met with foul play?"

"No," Amos' wife said. "A Tioga Indian passed through this morning and said he passed a group of Tories heading upriver with one very glum prisoner. He described Sam to a down to his buttons, he did."

"Two nights ago!" Jenkins exclaimed, turning to the four horsemen behind him. "If I would have left when I wanted I could have prevented all this mischief!"

"Come now, John!" John Murphy said. "That is neither here nor there! You must not blame yourself! How were you to know?"

"I felt it, I did," Jenkins said through gritted teeth. "I grant you it will never happen again!"

Phelps, Martin, and Murphy sat silent on their mounts. The slave Quocko stared indifferently at him.

"The Pauling boys," Jenkins said, turning back to Amos. "Are you sure they had a hand in this mischief?"

Shaking his head he said, "No, not that I could swear in court to, at least. I just have my suspicions, is all. Nothing is for certain in these trying times."

Jenkins took the reins of his tired mount. It neighed, taking a few tired steps back.

"The horses are all played out, John," Murphy said. "They've two days head start on us. They are well into Indian country by now. Iroquois are not to be trifled with on their own land, least of all not by our sparse numbers!"

"What of the others upriver?" Jenkins asked Amos.

"Oh," Amos said, "you need not worry. The Indian said all is the same upriver. The Stropes and Foxes are unmolested."

"As of yet," Jenkins grumbled.

"Come," Amos said. "The sun has nearly set on this day. Your horses are spent. I've plenty of feed for them, as well as for you all." He looked to his wife. "Lucretia shall make you a fine meal."

Lucretia nodded and smiled.

"At least rest this night and consider all that has happened over a good meal among friends," Amos said.

"Sounds good to me," Martin said, quickly dismounting. He passed the reins of his mount to Quocko. "We've done all we can this day. Who knows what lays upriver? It is best we rest and return at first light to the Fort of the Forty to report this mischief."

Jenkins rubbed his chin with his free hand. He wanted to argue the question with Martin but his own saddle sore backside argued with him; through a burning pain. Besides, if they ventured after Gordon at night in Indian country all their scalps might just end up on some buck's lodge pole. He finally lifted his hand to Amos' shoulder. "We thank you for your hospitality," he said.

Relieved, the other men dismounted, handing the reins of their mounts to the eager hands of the York children milling about them.

"Now children," Amos said, "see their mounts to the barn, and stay out from underfoot!"

A young girl gently took the reins from Jenkins' hand. Politely smiling, he stepped back, watching Amos' family warmly greet his men and lead them into the cabin.

Taking a deep breath, he slipped away from the others, wishing to find some sense of solace from his anguish. Sam's fate played hard on him. If he would have just left when he wanted, things would be different, he mused over and over in his mind. Resting his hand on a fence post, he leaned his chin against it. The farm stretched out before him. Sheep lazily grazed in the field to his front. Behind a stone fence to the left of a barn pigs snorted. A huge corn crib sat just to the opposite side of the large barn. A winding snake rail fence wound through the larger fields beyond, partitioning them into different sections. Several horses grazed in one section. A dozen head of fine cattle milled about another. Fine plots of corn, rye, wheat, and flax danced in the gentle breezes rolling from the green hills beyond. Apple and peach trees dotted ample orchards by the farmhouse. Beyond the cabin the Susquehanna glistened in the late day sun.

A hand gently fell on his shoulder from behind, turning him to Amos' welcoming eyes. The farmer raised his own eyes to the beauty stretching out before them. "I never tire of this view," he said.

"You've done quite well here," Jenkins said. "It's beautiful."

"The thing is to keep it," Amos said. "That's the thing, indeed."

## Chapter Twelve
### *Dealing with Tories*

Zebulon Marcy, his eyes darting to and fro, hurriedly led three men down the tight trail along a bank of the Susquehanna River. Branches snapped in his wake, churning up muttered curses from those following him. His furious footsteps and the threat of snapping branches soon carried him well ahead of his comrades. After hearing a few more curses he slowed, allowing his fellows to catch up with him.

"Are you sure about this?" one of the panting men asked.

"As sure as the air I breathe!" Marcy answered. "Wortman's about, he's been sending messages up to Brant at Onoquaga. He's a damn Tory and proud of it! I'm glad Denison's finally doing something about the rascal!" he added, pointing his rifle barrel up the trail. "His cabin's near the tannery, but a few rods more is all!"

"Now just be easy with that rifle!" Captain Carr warned, glancing back to John Jenkins and Joel Phelps. Phelps still panted. "That goes for you all! We're just here to take him in, not execute him!"

Marcy lifted his thumb to lick it. With a right smart grin, he touched his front sight with his wet thumb. "You heard of Oriskany and Fort Stanwix, Captain?" he asked. "Seems we got some reckoning to do!"

Carr just rolled his eyes.

"Things are coming to a head with the Tories!" Marcy continued. "Them that strikes first will be the ones alive at the end of the day!" He took a long look around the mountains, green and majestic, and to the beautiful Susquehanna River winding through the valley below them. "It's our homes! Our land! No Pennamite or Tory is to have our homes while I still breathe God's sweet air!" Nodding his head, he raised his lower lip. Grim determination shone through his eyes.

"Take your place in the rear, Zebulon!" Carr ordered. He looked down to his own rifle, then back up the trail. Jenkins and Phelps took their places immediately behind him, making way for a disgruntled Zebulon Marcy.

"Take him as peaceful as possible, but be ready for anything," Captain Carr said before starting up the trail.

The group filed along the trail silently at first, wary of the overhanging branches. The peaceful sounds of the forest faded in the wake of their increasingly hurried footsteps. A deer darted out of their way, but they ignored the tempting target, lest it sound a warning to their true prey. Soon a clearing showed through the green leaves. The trail split just to the edge of the clearing.

Carr turned to Marcy, gesturing him to the left fork of the trail with his rifle barrel. Marcy instantly split off from them.

Carr led the others forward.

They all trotted up to the cabin nestled in the clearing, looking all around for sign of anyone. Stopping just at the corner of the cabin, they noticed a man standing near the far corner of it fumbling and cursing at an animal skin, trying in vain to attach it to a stretcher. The stoutly framed man stood with his buckskin-clad back turned toward them. Wisps of smoke drifted down around him from an odd breeze about the cabin's chimney, also obscuring the man's view. A gentle humming sounded from the open cabin door.

Carr stopped the men with a wave of his hand, eying the man's rifle leaning against the cabin just to his side. "Adam Wortman?" Carr called. "We are here to escort you to Forty Fort posthaste!"

Wortman raised his head but did not turn to confront the voice. He dropped the stretcher and hide to the ground.

The humming ceased. An equally stout framed woman popped her head out of the door, squinting in the early morning sun in the direction of Carr and his men. She dropped the bowl in her hand. "Oh Adam! " she gasped.

Wortman stood perfectly still.

Carr looked anxiously to his men and nodded his head to either side of him. The men spread out, raising their rifles at Wortman.

"Das Rebels Adam! Das no goot Rebels!" the woman shrieked from the door. "Shoot Adam! Shoot das Rebels!"

Wortman turned with one smooth motion and scooped up his rifle. Blindly aiming at one of the threatening men, he fired, knocking one of the rebels head over heals. The rebel's limp body slid down the crest of the trail, tumbling among fallen leaves and scrub brush.

Three rifles instantly barked in response.

Wortman flew backwards, thudding into the ground.

Carr and his men rushed forward with a spine-tingling wail. Phelps burst through the open door of the cabin. Jenkins skirted the cabin, scanning all around it with a quick eye. Carr drew his pistol, leveling it on Wortman's limp body.

"It's all clear!" Jenkins reported, scrambling back to Carr.

"He's dead," Carr said on a whisper to him. Lifting his pistol, he carefully approached the cabin door.

Jenkins stood over the body, madly reloading his rifle and looking around the clearing.

Phelps greeted Carr at the door, holding a terror-stricken woman by the arm. She gasped, madly clutching a kerchief to her mouth. "She's all," Phelps reported. "No sign of no one else at all."

Carr let his pistol fall to his side. Wiping the sweat from his brow, he gazed back to the lifeless body.

Mrs. Wortman's eyes followed his. She let out a long mournful wail and collapsed to her knees, crying profusely.

Carr shook his head. "Search the cabin," he said.

Phelps looked down to the crying Tory woman.

"Let her be," Carr said. "They've their dead, and we've ours."

John Jenkins looked down at Wortman with eyes of rage. He wanted to kick his lifeless body, but the crying woman made him reconsider. Just how were they to explain Zebulon Marcy's death to his widow? A brave man had fallen, brash perhaps, but nonetheless brave. His fists clenched his rifle. His knuckles showed white from the thought of having to go and collect his friend's body.

Carr turned to Jenkins, sensing his angst. He slowly walked up the trail to where he had seen his friend fall, shot full in the chest. Closing near the site, he bowed his head in grief. A slight bustle to his front instinctively raised his head. His wide eyes stared unbelievably at the specter stumbling up the bank brushing dirt from his breeches.

He stopped dead in his tracks, causing Jenkins to almost stumble into him. Jenkins stepped back, raising his rifle. Looking to the man stumbling up the bank, he blinked once, then twice, before gasping, "By God, I don't believe it!"

Zebulon Marcy grinned and stepped toward the dumfound men. He had never seen such a look in all his life as their faces' bore.

"Zebulon!" Phelps cried from the cabin door. Stumbling out the door, he gawked in amazement at the man returned from the dead. The woman stopped crying. Stunned, she looked wide-eyed at the ghost rebel.

Grinning from ear to ear, Marcy took a few steps forwards and stopped, putting a hand to his chest. He fingered a hole in the upper left part of his waistcoat, just over his heart.

Everyone still stared in awe.

Grimacing, he reached into the upper inside pocket of his waistcoat, one which he had had his misses sew into it for a special purpose. A special purpose which now had saved his life. He pulled out his metal tobacco tin, fingering a dent in it. The smile returned to his face. "Tobacco tin," he said to his wide-eyed fellows. "Proves tobacco can be good fer ya after all!"

His comrades immediately burst into cheers, each taking a turn shaking his hand and feeling the hole in his waistcoat. Marcy beamed at his incredible luck. "God is with us this day," he said. "And our cause!"

Adam Wortman's wife shook her head and glared at her husband's body. Marcy's words about God cut deep into her grief. She rose to her feet and stumbled toward her slain husband's body, collapsing in total grief before it. "Herr Marcy!" she managed to cry between great sobs of grief, "Der neck for dis!"

Marcy lifted an eyebrow toward the woman and showed the dented tin in triumph. "Better his blood than a Patriot's!" he said. He turned to his still wide-eyed friends. "Joel," he said, "be a good lad and fetch me rifle. I have a feeling I'll be needing it all the more sooner. I have a feeling Wyoming will be a needin' all the rifles it can get soon!"

"That is just what we're trying to prevent," Jenkins said, casting an eye to the sobbing woman. She quelled her crying just long enough to allow her the energy to crawl to her fallen husband's body. She laid a hand across his back and immediately commenced crying again.

Jenkins felt his rage wither away upon sight of the painfully grieving woman. Her face showed the full horrors of war. Hints of grief, hatred, horror, and disgust somehow melded with her features. Such a look disgusted Jenkins. In it somehow he no longer saw the face of an enemy, but of a human being.

He wondered how the king she so obediently followed would feel if he had witnessed the end result of his headstrong actions. Here, in a wilderness an ocean away, a woman lay grieving over the dead body of her husband, slain by people he had just recently called neighbors, and friends. The stupidity of war stared him stark in the face through the tear-strewn eyes of the grieving woman. Such a great step backwards is war for all of humanity, he thought. Such a waste!

His mind flitted back to Captain, now colonel, Butler in 1770, in the heart of the second Pennamite War, when they had constructed their fort but a thousands yards away from the Pennamite's structure. They had done this because no one really wanted to fight colony against colony, white man against white man, but neither would back down from their claim to soil, be it fraudulent or not. So there they sat, in kind of a cold war, staring down and trying to intimidate the other into retreating, thus adverting a horrible war. It was in the midst of the stand-off that Captain Butler walked with a flag of truce to parley with the Pennamites, proposing that the Pennamite leader come out with thirty men to meet him at a predetermined spot with his own thirty men. There they would settle the question once and for all. Leader against leader. Winner take all. What a wonderful idea. But, the days of honor having passed into the far reaches of time, the Pennamites scoffed at his idea.

Bloodshed had been the result, with the Pennamites losing anyway. The thought of King George sparring with George Washington brought a sense of pride to him. For he knew General Washington would undoubtedly emerge the victor of such a contest. Perhaps this is why the leaders thought the proposition ridiculous. A coward may hide behind massive armies of minions doing his dirty work. Such was the way of the world, with the exception of the brave General Washington. He forced his thoughts to the only comfort he knew, Bethiah. He prayed her eyes would never be strained by such torture. He could not help but stare at the grieving widow with great pity.

Carr watched the woman just as intensely as Jenkins, but turned away as the sobbing grew. "John, you stand watch here," he said, walking to the cabin door. "I shall search the cabin for papers."

Marcy walked to a large tree trunk nearby and sat on it. He rubbed his hand over his chest, casting an irritated eye to the sobbing woman. Joel Phelps walked over to him, standing his rifle on end to load it. "You'd be wise to load your rifle as well, Zeb," he said.

Marcy spat on the ground and said, "I'll tend to it directly, after I catch me breath. Never been shot afore. It does sting a mite."

Mrs. Wortman suddenly stopped crying and stood erect. Her eyes darted about. Rubbing her hand slowly along her husband's back, she quickly rolled him over onto it.

A mournful wail accompanied her action, alive with a sickly spattering sound. Flecks of blood spattered in the air from the man's mouth and onto his stunned wife's dress, but she didn't mind the sign of life. Immediately perking to life, she nestled his head to her quivering bosom. At the same time her hand searched along his chest, finding a gaping hole which whistled with each painful draw of his breath. Tearing a piece of her apron off, she placed it over the grisly wound. She looked up at the rebels with soulful eyes. "Herr Doctor," she pleaded. "You must fetch das doctor!"

Jenkins felt his jaw slacken. To hell with King George! He stood here and now, not him! He witnessed the result of war! He cringed in its face! Let all others, be they Rebel or Tory, be damned now! Kneeling down next to the exasperated woman and her quivering husband, he only saw the face of despair now. A human face.

"Das doctor, Herr Jenkins," bubbled through the frothy blood pouring from Adam Wortman's mouth. "Please, Herr Jenkins, please."

His wife could only look at him with pleading eyes.

"Joel!" he called over his shoulder. "Go back to the horses at Marcy's and ride at once to fetch Doctor William Hooker Smith!"

"A doctor?" Marcy asked, fingering a bullet out of his shot bag. Rolling it between his fingers, he followed it with his eyes. "This is the only doctoring he'll be requiring! It's the only doctor any of us would be sure to get if the shoe were on the other foot! A lead doctor!"

Jenkins ignored Marcy and stood tall. "Now Joel!" he said.

Phelps scratched his head, noticing Marcy's cold stare out of the corner of his eye. Another set of eyes, somehow more pleading, quickly caught his own eyes. The woman's pleading eyes spoke volumes to him, canceling the hatred embodying Marcy's eyes. He immediately turned, darting down the trail in a mad rush.

"Where is he off to?" Carr asked from inside the cabin.

"Off to do the right thing is all!" Jenkins answered.

Carr peaked out of the cabin door. "What?" he asked. "Is Wortman alive?"

"For the moment Captain," Jenkins answered, staring down Marcy to keep him at bay. "Have you any objections, Captain?"

"None at all," Carr said with a frown. "Is he off to the doctor?"

"Yes sir, he is, in fact," Jenkins said.

"Don't worry of me!" Marcy interrupted. "I'm fine and well, no thanks to that rat!" he added, casting a sour eye to the badly wounded Tory.

Both Jenkins and Carr stared at him with hollow eyes.

"My chest is a bit sore," Marcy continued, undeterred by the stares. "Leastways I won't be having to travel all the way down to Forty Fort to see the good doctor, now that he's coming up here for whatever misguided purpose. Some good will come of it, anyways!"

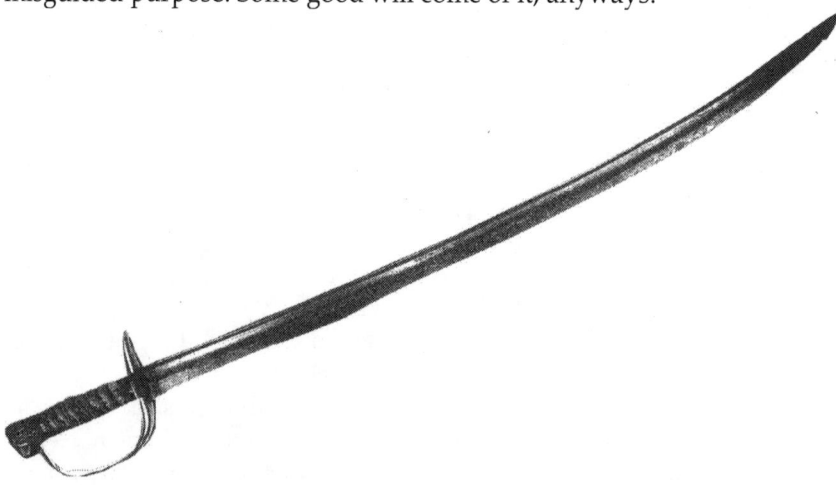

## Chapter Thirteen
### *The Tories' Revenge*

Crickets chirped in the late summer evening. Their song, along with the warm crackle of the fire, soothed all in the cabin into a deep sleep, save one, the master of the house. Zebulon Marcy sat in his hand-made favorite rocking chair by the crackling fire. He slowly rocked back and forth, smoking his pipe and watching the dancing flames, content with himself and his life. His other hand rubbed his favorite charm between its fingers; the dented tobacco tin which had save him from a Tory's ball.

But all had been set right, much by his efforts, he mused. Putnam Township had been cleared of all Tories. Captain Carr had collected two more before departing back to Forty Fort. Wortman, the Tory whom shot him, probably lay dying under a strong guard back at Forty Fort, what with the words Joel Phelps had said Doctor Smith said when he had summoned him to come treat the wounded Tory Wortman, 'I shall go, but if he is not dead now he will be when I get there!' The words of a true patriot like himself, Marcy mused.

Now, none but true men of the cause remained about Tunkhannock Creek, the Billings, Slocum, and Tripp families. All had cabins not far from his and swore an oath to come to one another's aid if trouble came calling; be it Tory or Indian trouble. York, Fitch, Kingsley, Eaton, and old man Fitzgerald provided a buffer between them and the Tory settlements about Tioga Point. As for the Fox, Van Valkenburg, and Strope families on the *Wysox* and *Towanda* Creeks, well, they would have to hope by continuing to treat the Indians kindly they would be spared their wrath. Zebulon himself scoffed at the idea. Even he, of little schooling, knew enough of history to know appeasement never worked. But they seemed confident in their presumptions even though Rudolf Fox still remained a prisoner of the very same Indians, taken because as the Indians said, 'He no good. He no King's man.' John Jenkins had gone to try and convince Mother Fox to come down to the safety of the lower settlements, but she adamantly refused to budge until Rudolf sent word or returned.

The fire crackled, breaking his train of thought. The chirps of the crickets played heavy on his eyelids. He soon nodded off into a deep sleep with the pipe dangling loosely from his mouth.

He slept so at ease he didn't hear the hushed footsteps outside the cabin door. A few twigs snapped and leaves rustled, despite the careful movements of the invaders. Eyes darted among the miscreants with each telltale noise. Their leader raised a hand to the door. To his relief found the latch string. He looked wide-eyed back to his minions.

They took the hint, standing deathly still after raising their weapons to the ready.

The leader looked down to the latch and carefully pulled on the string. The latch silently lifted. Easing the door open a crack, a sly smile slid across his face upon sight of the slumbering rebel in a rickety rocking chair by the glowing fire. He nodded to the others.

Holding his hand high in the air, he raised three fingers in the pale moonlight. The others crept behind him, positioning themselves to be ready to pounce upon the unsuspecting rebel upstart. One finger on their leader's hand fell. Then two fingers fell. Before the third finger fell to his palm the impetus of the others sent the leader through the door. They burst upon their slumbering prey all at once.

Marcy burst to life in an instant. His wild fists met jaws, sending some of the intruders flailing backwards before their sheer number forced him to the floor. Wrestling him, they finally pinned the rebel's hands behind his back, struggling to bind his writhing hands. Those struggling at his feet suffered several kicks to their faces before finally taming and binding his feet.

Another intruder darted madly about the cabin, pushing blankets aside from a bed with his long rifle's barrel. Screams met his assault. Shaking his head and clenching his teeth, he gestured threateningly with his rifle at a terrified woman on the bed. "Stay where you be!" he commanded a stunned Jerusha Marcy. Ignoring the command, she stumbled to her struggling husband, dragging blankets under her feet.

'"Stop the Rebel wench!" an order demanded of the rifleman. He instantly grabbed her by the scruff of her neck, flinging her into a corner. She immediately bounced back, but the butt of a rifle met her stomach with a ruthless thud. She gasped, collapsing to the floor.

She gazed up at her painted assailant through her gasping breaths, noticing blue eyes glinting in the firelight. They all dressed partly in Indian fashion, but their manners and accents betrayed their disguises. Blue eyed Indians, she thought. The worst of the lot! Tories!

"Stay where you be wench!" the painted rifleman warned.

"Tory bastards!" Jerusha promptly screamed.

"And mind yer tongue!" the rifleman exclaimed, pulling a knife from his belt with his free hand. "A woman's scalp brings the same price at Niagara!"

A hand to his shoulder instantly wheeled the rifleman about. The black painted face of his leader stared the rifleman dead in his eyes. White circles painted about his stern eyes somehow amplified his stare.

"No!" he said. "There will be none of that! We've come to administer justice, not barbarity!" He bowed his head with an apologetic eye to the woman and followed the others out the cabin door with their writhing and wriggling charge. He pushed the reluctant rifleman before him.

Jerusha struggled to her feet, gasping for breath. Pulling the blankets from about her feet, she looked up to the anxious eyes staring down at her from the darkness of the loft. "You children stay put!" she gasped. "Stay put!"

The children, too terrified to speak, sat mortified with solid fear.

Finally catching her breath, Jerusha stumbled toward the door. The blue-eyed Indians struggled with their charge but a few feet from the door. Squeezing past them in their confusion, she bolted down the trail, quickly disappearing into the night.

"There she be!" a voice called behind her. "Hurry about your business, for she's off to spread the alarm!"

The rifleman darted in the direction the woman disappeared, struggling with his urge to discharge his weapon. After a quick moment, he turned about in disgust, bringing the butt of his rifle down hard on Marcy's skull. The rebel finally fell limp.

"Now be quick about it!" the painted leader ordered. Backing away from the man, he motioned to the woods. Pulling a rope from over his shoulder he fashioned a loose in it while he trotted.

The others dragged Marcy's limp form toward the woods behind him. He led them off the trail and down into a nearby gully, sizing up the trees for the perfect branch. His eyes shined at a giant oak towering majestically in the moonlight. Scampering to it, he flung the rope over one of its great branches. In another instant he slid the rope over Marcy's neck. With a great pull he lifted him into the air.

Marcy groaned, suddenly coming back to life. Gasping, he dangled, twirling about in the still and misty air. His bulging eyes locked on the painted devils gloating below him. His legs kicked at them to no avail, only bringing muffled laughs in response. A few of them dodged his legs and pushed them, bringing more momentum to his spin. In another few seconds his gasps ceased.

Marcy swung still and lifeless from the end of the rope.

"How's that fer yer cause? "one of the Tory's scoffed.

They all stood and silently watched the body with satisfaction. The rifleman poked at it with his barrel and said, "There you have it, a just end for a traitor, and his cause."

Cries and yells from the cabin quickly broke their morbid stares. They rushed off into the prevailing darkness, satisfied justice had been served without so much as a passing glance behind them.

Jerusha darted about the trees, leading a party of hastily dressed men behind her. Waving a lighted pine knot in her hand all about her front, she madly searched the still forest. Pushing the pine knot low to the ground, she followed a trail of disturbed leaves and twigs left by the painted devils. Hastily wiping the tears from her eyes, she ignored the pleas from the men behind for her to slow down. She plowed forward despite them. She had to.

The men yelled even louder behind the scampering woman, thinking their loud announcements to fill every Tory found before them with lead would hasten the Tories' withdrawal. Several even discharged their weapons into the air. A blood churning scream hastened their feet to Jerusha.

They rushed to the glowing pine knot to their front, now sitting on the ground beside the trunk of a great oak tree. Jerusha clung tenaciously to the legs of a limp form hanging by a rope from one of its branches. She lifted with all her strength to ease the weight against the rope around her husband's neck.

A quick slash from a cutlass cut the rope, causing Jerusha and the body to fall to the ground. She instantly released her hold on the legs, clasping her husband's head in her hands. She stared in horror at his closed eyes. The head rolled limp on its neck. Someone picked up the pine knot, shining it on the face. Dark blue lips showed on a pale blue face. Jerusha wept uncontrollably. Her whole body trembled.

One of the hovering men, Billings, put a hand to her shoulder. Looking down to the lifeless body of his friend, he felt a great pity for Jerusha. He wanted to say something, but his throat went suddenly dry. Dropping the rifle in his other hand to the ground, he collapsed next to the grieving woman, taking her hand as she rocked back and forth.

The other men stomped about in frustration. Several muttered angry oaths against the Tories.

Jerusha stared through tear-strewn eyes at the blue face of her husband she rocked in her arms. Finally easing his head down to the ground, she let the back of her hand fall gently to his lips and suddenly stopped sobbing. She bent her head down to the lips, turning her ear to them. A wisp of air teased them. "He breathes!" she gasped.

Billings immediately leaned toward the lips. Hearing barely audible gasps, he slipped the loose rope over Marcy's head and shot it away from them. "He does breathe!" he announced to his stunned comrades. "By the grace of God he lives!" Everyone quickly helped him recover the man, twice back from the dead. A miracle indeed.

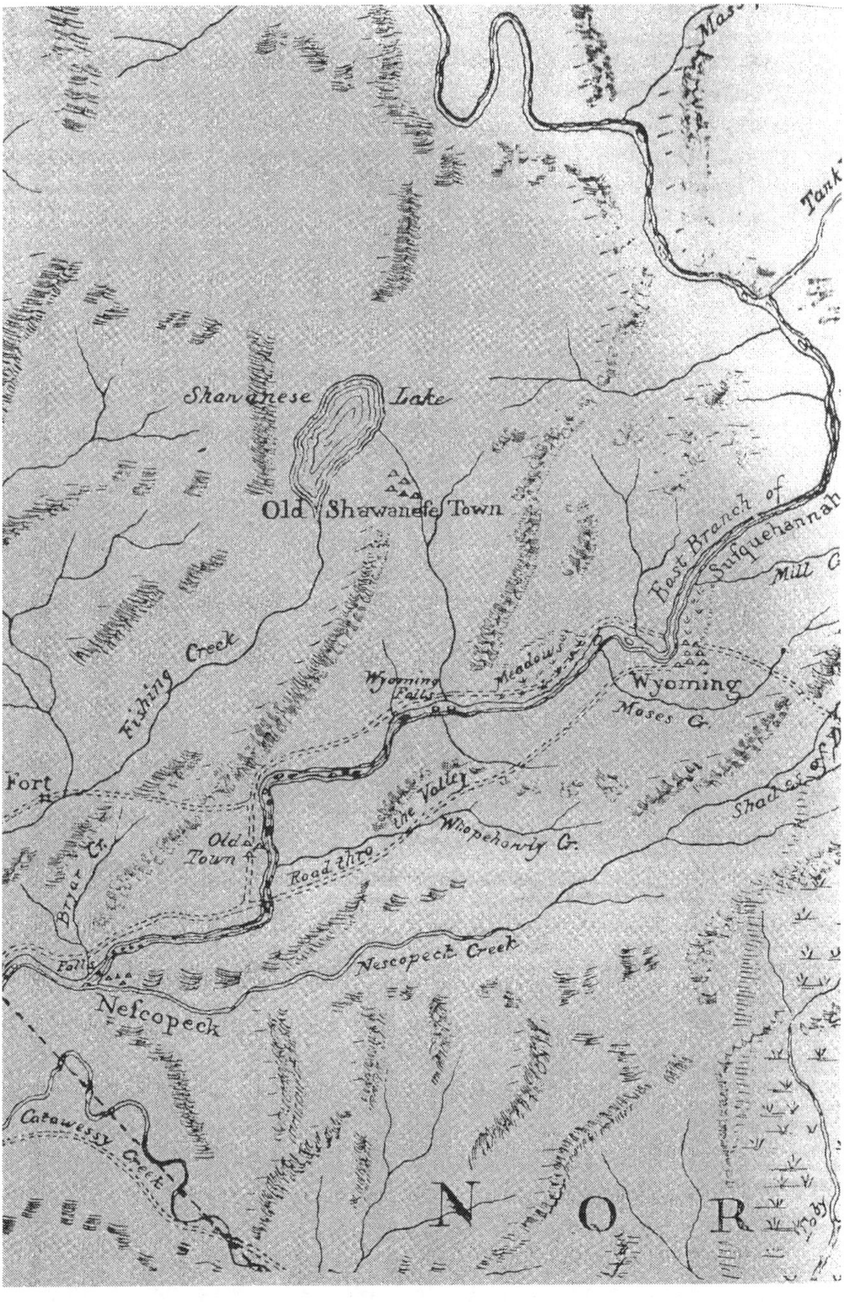
Shawanese Lake
Old Shawanese Town
East Branch of Susquehannah
Mill C
Fishing Creek
Wyoming Falls
Meadows
Wyoming
Moses C.
Fort
Old Town
the Valley
Road thro
Whopehonry C.
Shades of
Bryar C.
Falls
Nescopeck Creek
Nescopeck
Catawessy Creek
N O R

## Chapter Fourteen
### *The Capture of Lieutenant Jenkins*

John Jenkins stood on the narrow trail saddling the riverbank and stared down at the waters, wondering of his friend Sam Gordon taken but a few months ago. He still felt bad about missing the rendezvous with the man. He kicked at the hard face of the trail, well trodden by countless generations of Indians. Now his feet-the feet of the white man-tromped the trails, slowly changing the very nature of them and the land surrounding them forever. He imagined roads serving farms and many other trappings of civilization crisscrossing the land. He thought of just how many times he had broke chain to survey the hills and banks along the winding river. Land, rich beautiful land, though not yet tamed, stretched before him in the early morning sunlight of this crisp November morn. Pride swelled his chest, replacing his grief.

Along with the pride he suddenly felt a singular and unexpected affection for the men traveling with him; his band of brothers. Glancing over his shoulder, he watched them rise from their slumber. They toiled about the fire, stretching their muscles, boiling coffee, and preparing their frugal breakfasts. Frosty mists rose from their mouths in the chill of the morning. Horses neighed upon hearing the bustling men, eager for their own helping of oats.

"Come, John," Murphy called to him. "Warm your bones by the fire. Relax! Sometimes you think too much, my friend."

"We must make ready," he said, walking to the fire. Kneeling down, he rubbed his hands in the warmth of the fire. "Wyalusing's but five miles up the trail." He looked to the trail. "We can get there in the morning and perhaps make it all the way up to Fox's cabin this day."

None of the other three men said a word. A wary eye passed among them. Asa Stevens had led a scout of nine men up the river but a month before and dared not journey beyond Wyalusing. Stevens collected five suspected Tories. The Indians they encountered felt it suicide for them to venture any further upriver with less than a full company of men. Too many Tories hung about Tioga Point and Esther's Town, spreading their hatred and ill-will against the Yankees.

But Stevens differed in many ways to the bold lieutenant leading this scout of four men. The stern look in his eyes forbade any inkling of protest, no matter how sound the reasoning behind it.

"Ours is to protect," Jenkins said, noticing their questioning stares. "The frontier is ready to burst at the seams at any moment."

John Murphy nodded his head as did William Martin. Quocko grinned indifferently at all the men, passing Jenkins a tin cup of coffee.

Jenkins smiled and sipped the coffee. At least one of his men followed his orders without question. After a few bites of a hard biscuit and a bit of fried salt pork, he rose, stretching his arms wide. "Come on!" he said. "Let's get to it! Daylight's burning!"

The others rose in silence. Before long they trotted up the trail, Jenkins in the lead, followed by Martin and his man Quocko, with Murphy bringing up the rear. All rode silently, listening for any abnormal noises along the trailside. Every rifle lay across the pommel of their saddles, primed and ready for action. The fear of ambush-the favorite tactic of their adversaries-haunted every step.

The closer they trod toward Wyalusing, the tenser they became. A few cawing crows made their eyes dart among the shadows of the great towering trees along the trail, but to their relief nothing came of nature's warning. Their eyes soon lifted along the sheer cliff of rocks rising high to their right. A low plain stretched below it all the way to the riverbank to their left. Low scrub brush and other tangled vegetation infested the plain. In this tight few hundred yards of trail more apprehension plagued them than on any other part of it. It offered no escape to the right and great hiding places to the left. The perfect spot for an ambush.

Their eyes locked on the scrub brush, searching for any movement, ignoring the path to their front, and the lone rider sitting in the middle of it.

Jenkins' horse neighed, turning its master's eyes to the front again. Reining his horse sideways in the trail, he stopped the others. "What in heaven's name?" Martin asked, barely adverting a collision with him.

Jenkins did not say a word, but just motioned with his rifle to the horseman.

The obtrusive rider rode toward them, stopping but fifty feet away. He sat high in the saddle. His piercing blue eyes stared at them from under the wide brim of his slouch hat. Wisps of smoke rose from the pipe clenched in his teeth. He slowly clasped his hands on his saddle horn, giving no sign of giving way for the scouts.

Martin peered down the trail. "That's Parshall Terry!" he gasped. "He has turned Tory fer sure!"

Murphy reined his mount around, intently scanning the plain and the face of the cliff. Nothing moved, much to his relief.

"What in the blazes is he about?" Martin asked.

"I don't know," Jenkins said, reining his mount to face forward again. "Be on your guard 'til I find out!"

Terry sat oblivious to the apparent concern and apprehension he caused the rebel party. Slowly raising his hand to his pipe, he tapped its bowl on his saddle horn.

"Here!" Jenkins called to him. "Make way so we may pass!"

"I think not," Terry flatly stated.

Trouble, they all knew it.

Terry raised his pipe, pointing its stem to the plain below them. "It's a right smart nightmare in that sugarbush below!" he said. "Who knows what devils may be lurking in its folds?" Pulling back his coat, he revealed the butts of a brace of pistols tucked in his belt. Putting forked fingers to his lips, he whistled. Four mounted and heavily armed men immediately trotted up the trail to the rebel's rear. Two other men sprang from the tangled bushes on the plain below, raising their rifles. The click of their locks sounded in the still air. The horsemen carefully approached with their pistols leveled on the stunned rebels, riding to the side of each rebel.

"The rats have the drop on us," Murphy said.

"Now, my fine rebel, Mr. Jenkins," Terry said, riding forward. Two other mounted men rode up behind him, also leveling their pistols on the rebels.

Terry reined his horse to a stop just to the front of Jenkins, pointing the barrel of one of his pistols down to the ground. "Dismount, you traitorous rat!" he growled.

Quocko quickly raised his rifle, only to be walloped by the Tory at his side. His rifle flew into the air from the force of the blow. He tumbled head over heels to the ground below with a heavy thud.

One of the Tory riflemen advanced, leveling his rifle at Quocko. Other pistols and rifles quickly threatened the others.

"Now Lieutenant!" Terry screamed. He fully cocked his pistol and leveled it at Jenkins' head. "You sir, are my prisoner!"

"You will not get away with this!" Martin said. A rifle butt instantly slammed in his side, knocking him senseless to the ground. Another knocked Murphy to the ground before he too could react.

"We've only come for you, Mr. Jenkins," Terry said. "The sooner you do as you are told the sooner we'll be on our way! If their blood is to be shed, it shall be on your hands, fine sir, not mine!"

Jenkins stared at the man with a burning rage.

"Collect their weapons!" Terry ordered. One of the Tory riflemen gruffly gathered all their arms while a horseman collected their horses' reins, leading them away. Jenkins surrendered his rifle with a scowl.

Terry leaned forward on his horse. His fiendish eyes stared

down the pistol barrel he leveled at Jenkins' head. "You'll come or we'll end it here, prisoner or dead, makes no difference to me," he said.

"How can you be about this business?" Murphy suddenly raised his voice. "Your brothers, father, why all of your family, are patriots. Your betrayal is not only to your country, but to your very blood!"

"You feel the flat of Ransom's sword on your back for just stopping to buckle your shoe and then we'll see how you feel about it!" Terry answered. "We marched for days without so much as a morsel to quell our hunger! No shelter or nothing! Nothing but empty promises from the damned Congress! It took the flat of a sword to open my eyes to the foolishness. Be a Rebel for what? One master's as corrupt as the next! I prefer our proper King to those empty headed bastards of Congress!"

"How could a man's soul be so dark as to betray his own blood?" Murphy asked, unmoved by the Tory's explanation.

Terry flung himself from his horse. Stomping up to Murphy, he stared him straight in the eye, spitting at his feet. Through clenched teeth he muttered, "You mind your tongue or you'll be accompanying this rebel bastard Mr. Jenkins to who knows what hell or misfortune!"

Murphy stared indignantly back at him.

He brushed the brazen rebel's cheek with the barrel of his pistol. "Rebel scalps fetch a fine price at Fort Niagara, be sure to tell my dear brother Jonathan of that when you see him." Grabbing Murphy's rifle pouch, he tore it from him with a vicious yank.

Murphy bobbed, snarling in contempt of Terry and his men.

"Strip them of all but their shirts and britches," Terry commanded, turning back to his true object of contempt. Grabbing several lengths of rope looped over his saddle horn, he harshly bond Jenkins' hands. With another length of rope he fashioned a loop, placing it around his neck. A sharp tug pulled it taunt.

"Now," Terry said, leading Jenkins toward his horse, "you other men, your place is back downriver! Stay there and you will not be molested, but if ye be bold and brazen like this bastard and return, you will regret the day ye were born!" He spat upon the ground as if the words burned his tongue. "Now get!" he ordered. "And don't ya think of following or you'll find nothing but a corpse, minus its hair! This rebel officer's hair will bring as fine a price as his person. Keep that in mind."

The rebels reluctantly turned, disgraced and humiliated. They fumbled along at first, but gained momentum the further they stumbled from the place. One by one they turned, hoping to steal a glance at their forlorn leader. Each time they did a burning rage fueled their footsteps. In no time they trotted along, indifferent to the cold trail under their bare feet. The comfort and companionship of Forty Fort awaited them. They each shuddered to imagine what awaited John Jenkins.

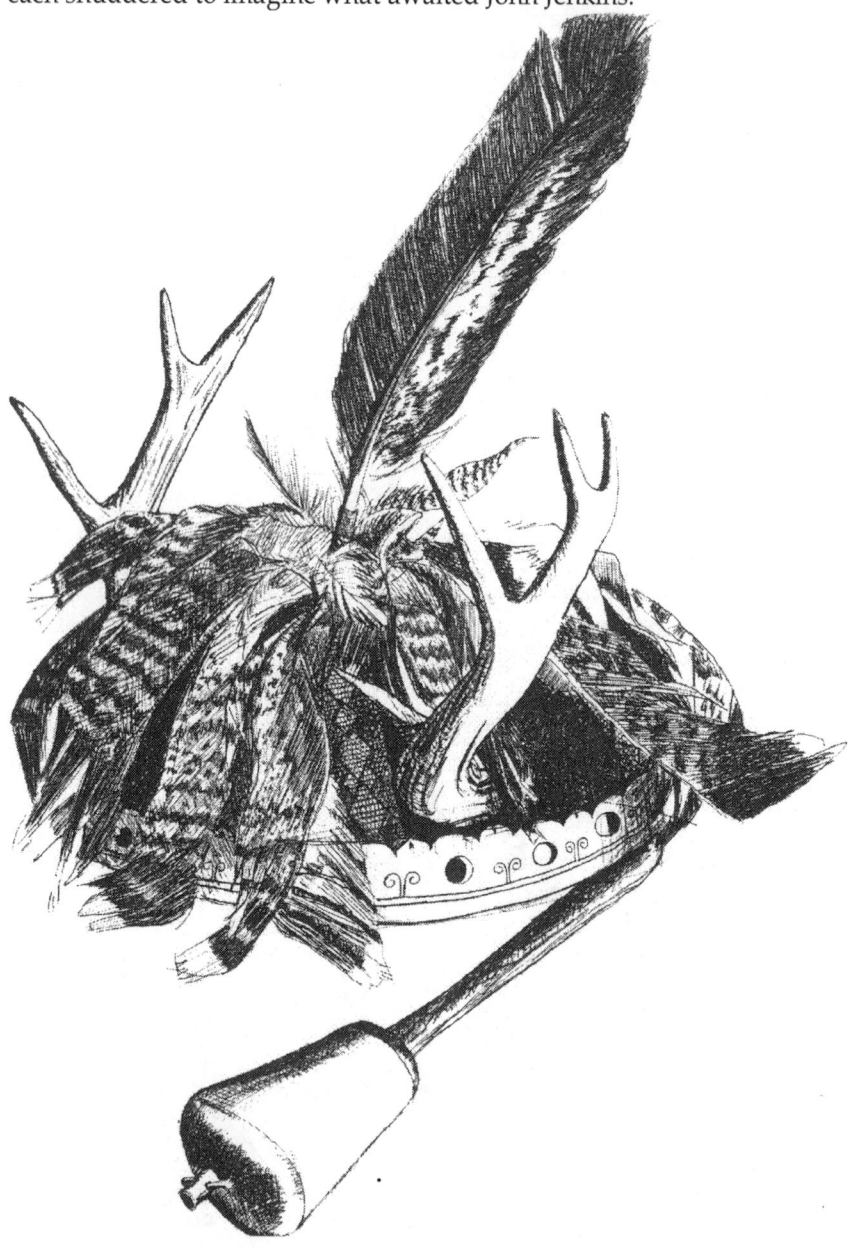

## Chapter Fifteen
### *A Cruel Trek*

The rope chafed John Jenkins' neck constantly, especially up the steep grades, causing him to lag behind his mounted captors. A sharp tug now and then reminded him to keep pace. He snarled once, but then held his tongue, not willing to give his captors the satisfaction of knowing the discomfort they caused him. They already had his most precious possession, his freedom. That was enough.

The further they trudged along, the more he noticed most of the Tories paid him no more mind than a they would a packhorse. They laughed and joked about the Continental Congress, George Washington, or some poor unfortunate they had burned out or captured on the frontier, or, curiously, of their Indian allies about Fort Niagara. He knew not to comment, even when some cruel remark rolled off their tongues about Wyoming. A bitter sense of betrayal burned deeply within him to hear such cutting remarks from those whom had once been such staunch friends and neighbors. War destroyed more than homes and lives. It poisoned the very nature of men toward one another.

Jenkins looked about the familiar land, wondering if he would ever again walk it a free man. Though the thought pained him deeply, he swallowed hard against it, so his sorrow wouldn't show upon his face. Instead, he found comfort in knowing that if he met some foul fate in the hands of these miscreants, a British officer in the hands of the American Army would meet the same fate in retaliation. An eye for an eye. An officer's blood for an officer's blood. Loose or not, these so-called rangers had orders. Someone pulled their strings from Fort Niagara, whom in turn had his strings pulled from someone across the sea. If he minded his tongue, and ways, he just might get through this thing, and return to Wyoming, and thus return to Bethiah.

Letting his mind drift back to comforting memories of he and Beth allowed him to escape the uncertainty of the moment. Picnics on the green at Wilkes-Barre, or high in the surrounding mountains, eased his mind now just as much as they did at the time they occurred. He remembered a gentle breeze teasing Beth's long brown hair and the sparkle of her pleasing eyes. The memory of her soft touch soothed his aching body and soul. The memories strengthened him with the resolve of true love. These Tories' hands played hard upon his body, not his soul.

He marked the landmarks, reasoning some twenty miles separated them from the place of his capture. In all that time they didn't stop but once, and then only long enough to relieve themselves. Haste marked their trek. Terry seemed eager, despite his bragging, to gain every inch of ground possible between his party and the lower settlements.

As the sun faded behind the mountains, Terry slowed his pace. He led them along another mile before stopping atop a hill in the waning sunlight. Sheshequin spread out below them; its small and warm cabins a welcome sight to the captors, as well as the captured. They needed no further urging to move down the tired trail.

An Indian stood before a particularly well built roughly hewn logged cabin with a lighted pine knot in his hand. He met and heartily welcomed Terry. "It go well, I see!" he said with a grin to Jenkins.

"Yes, Hopkins, it did indeed," Terry said, sliding from the saddle, rubbing his aching legs. "Been a long ride, didn't stop nary a minute along the trail. You never know what those crazy rebels will do."

The Indian Hopkins smiled and put a hand to Terry's shoulder. "Come all!" he said, waving toward the cabin door. "Plenty to eat! Plenty spirits! All well!" Laughing loudly, he looked back over his shoulder to the others. They all smiled at the invitation.

"Place him in the barn," Terry called over his shoulder almost as an afterthought. "Place a guard about him, I don't care who, work it out between yourselves, but make sure the guard's spelled proper throughout the night." With that he turned and disappeared into the warm cabin.

A Tory quickly took the rope and led Jenkins to the barn. Finding a post at the entrance to a stall, he tied the loose end of the rope to it. Gruffly slipping the loose from Jenkins' neck, he tied it over the other rope binding his hands. The numerous knots and winds of rope grew preposterous, giving Jenkins a sour feeling. They did not intend to give him a break in the least.

The Tory clumped up some straw in the empty stable and sat upon it, laying his rifle across his lap. He cocked it. Its snap brought a grin to his face. "Name's Gilbert Newberry," he announced. "Sergeant Newberry to you, Rebel! Now this can be as pleasant a night as circumstances will allow, or as unpleasant, it's up to you."

Jenkins did not say a word, but only stared down to the ground.

"Cat got your tongue?" Newberry asked. "If you behave you might get a morsel of food or a spot of rum to quench your thirst. But if you try anything, by Betsy, I'll blow a hole clean through your rebel carcass and my purse will swell by twelve pounds for your damn scalp! And no British officer will suffer any reprisal from a prisoner shot whilst escaping! Have we an understanding?"

A grumble answered him.

"I thought so," Newberry said, looking to his men putting the horses into the stables next to them. "Now don't you boys forget about your Sergeant out here in the night and fetch me some victuals! It's my good nature that I take the first watch anyways, don't none of you forget it, either! And one of you spell me in a couple hours, you here?"

Grumbles sounded from the other stalls. The men soon finished carrying for their tired mounts and disappeared into the cabins.

The night fell, and with it the warmth of the sun. Jenkins shivered and huddled in a stark corner, pondering his plight. It played heavily on his mind before he let his thoughts drift to the only comfort he had left, Beth's memory. He remembered her deep concern before he left on this very scout. With heartfelt tears, she begged him not to go, at least not until he had more men. Women possessed a strange sense of intuition. Beth's certainly proved true. He would not ignore her intuition again in the future, that is if fate allowed him to return to her.

He replayed her last motions in his mind, especially of how she had held his hand to her tear-strewn cheek. She held it there for the longest moment. He remembered the softness of her skin and the feel of her warm tears.

He gazed down at his hand through the eyes of memory now, in the dark corner of this filthy and cold stable. He struggled against the huge knots and coils of rope binding his hands to move but one finger of his left hand to touch the top of his right hand in a vain effort to feel something of her essence, if but a memory. Managed to slightly free one finger through the coils, he strained against the ropes. Triumphantly, he felt the spot on his right hand. The place of Beth's memory. The last place on his body she had touched, in what seemed a lifetime ago, and with her tears at that. A place of warmth and comfort. He rubbed it slowly with his finger, triggering a welcoming flood of memories. He slowly closed his eyes against the horror of this day and the uncertainty of this night.

Beth's touch would carry him through this living nightmare. When he finally made it back to Wyoming, he would marry her immediately, despite what life threw in their way. This he swore with a solemn oath to himself before drifting off into an uneasy sleep.

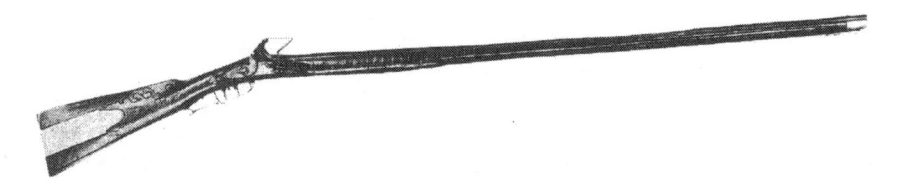

## Chapter Sixteen
*Chemung Village*

The party skirted around Queen Esther's Village, much to the angst of John Jenkins. The ray of hope that grew in his heart as they approached the village faded into despair. If only the Queen knew of his plight. She would use all of her vast influence to secure his release. But no eyes from the village even cast a curious gaze at the anxious party of white men hurrying through the woods around it.

Terry's gloating face stared down at him. "No," he said with a laugh. "We haven't time to visit this journey. The Queen shall miss your company fer sure. But such is war."

Muffled laughs accompanied his words.

Jenkins ignored them. He stumbled along, finding the weight of his heavy heart enough to keep his head bowed, and therefore his eyes, from sight of his cruel captors.

Soon the party trotted far beyond Tioga Point, and with it all familiarity of life and hope of being rescued flitted from Jenkins' mind. Tioga Point, the southern door of the Iroquois Confederacy, from which no white men, be he trader, surveyor, or whoever, passed without explicit permission, and lived. The Mohawk tribe guarded the eastern door. The Seneca tribe the west. The Cayuga tribe the south. From Tioga Point the *Forbidden Path*, amply named, for anyone passing without permission met immediate reprisals, branched off into the far reaches of the mighty Iroquois Confederacy. The land below Tioga Point and the West Branch of the Susquehanna had been filled with refugee and conquered tribes placed there as a buffer between the Confederacy and the white men to the south. All belonged to the Iroquois.

Terry and his Tories from Niagara had such explicit permission, as all about Wyoming feared. For from Iroquois country they could strike south at their settlements and then hastily retreat back into the protection of the Indian lands. A great arrangement for the Tories; a deadly one for Wyoming. Only a great invasion could ever penetrate Iroquois land and subdue their threat to the frontier. All else would simply be folly.

Thus Jenkins knew if he escaped now he would have to be extremely careful in exiting this country. If recaptured the gauntlet, torture, and a death unimaginable in its horrors would await him.

With these thoughts he trudged along, pulled ruthlessly by the rope around his neck by one of the mounted Loyalist Rangers. He wondered of his strength to survive the horrors awaiting him, but at the same time knew he had to stay alive for Beth, and all he believed. God would deliver him from this savage land, he knew it, somehow he just knew it. He need only bide his time. They could insult, degrade, and torture his body all they wanted, but his life could not be taken without the consent of God himself. For his soul belonged to God alone. Whatever cruelty inflicted upon him would be answered by his abusers before God. Let them forsake their own souls by their cruel actions.

The Chemung River, rather than the Susquehanna, flowed by the trailside now. The trail forked a little above Esther's Town and Jenkins looked with anticipation to which fork Terry led them. His fate lie entwined in the decision. If they followed to the left Niagara awaited him, with its Indians and frontier garrison. To the right Onoquaga awaited, Mohawk Joseph Brant's stronghold along the Susquehanna, and from there, possibly Albany. At Albany an prisoner exchange might await. At Niagara only cruel imprisonment awaited. He preferred Albany.

Without stopping to even consider the fork in the trail, Terry abruptly turned to the left. Jenkins' heart sank. He rubbed the spot on his hand until it turned red in response. "Oh Beth, Beth," he muttered under his breath. He needed her now more then ever, if only her memory.

The trail wound along the winding Susquehanna through virgin land. Only an occasional round patch of cleared ground used as a field for crops broke the trees of the vast forest. A few sparse huts and cabins sat along the trailside, also, usually by the round fields.

Jenkins watched the smoke spiral in the air from the cabins' chimneys, envious of the warmth it brought the cabins' inhabitants. The Tories seemed indifferent of the cabins, at most. Their eyes remained fixed on the trail ahead. The warming thoughts of the fires did not bother them,-as well they shouldn't-he mused, what with their long blanket coats and all. He wore only the small sailor's jacket he had been wearing when he had been captured. He recognized his own blanket coat on Sergeant Newberry's back. Forcing his mind from his anxious thoughts, he instead focused on the lay of the land, information he knew could prove advantageous for Wyoming later.

Suddenly Terry stopped, pointing down the riverbank. "Here we shall cross to Chemung," he said, glaring down to Jenkins. "Perhaps this shall wash some stink from your hide, Rebel!"

Jenkins held his tongue, despite the strong odors coming from all the rangers. Chemung, a war village, perhaps an exchange awaited him.

"No!" Terry called back to him as if reading his mind. "Niagara and the hole is to be your fate!" A sinister laugh followed.

With a cold splash, Terry's mount entered the river. The horse neighed in protest, only to be answered by its master's indifferent laugh.

Terry yanked on the reins, forcing the beast forward into the frigid waters. The others obediently plowed into the river after him. A sharp tug on the rope about Jenkins' neck forced him along, also.

Jenkins stumbled along the rocky bottom of the river. The cold water forced a sharp gasp from his heaving lungs. He needed no tug to coax him up the opposite riverbank.

A steep mountain rose to their right, no doubt the reason why Terry had led them along the leveler ground along the opposite bank. Still, by the chattering teeth of the others, they no doubt wished they had taken the steep trail, nonetheless.

"If it didn't take the stink off you, it took the warmth," Terry said, gesturing to the east. "Chemung is just a few rods away." Spirals of smoke rose above the trees in the direction to which he pointed with his filthy finger. The promise of warmth spirited them on with a steady gait.

Chemung, slightly larger than Esther's Town, spread out on a slight plateau on the east side of the river. Assorted bark huts and cabins circled two larger buildings in the center of the village. Windows, some no more than black holes, showed on many of the cabins. The common greased paper covered other windows, as was the fashion on the frontier, painted with figures of birds, animals, and fish. Some even held the coveted prize of the frontier, glass. Animal skins lashed to frames and stretchers leaned against walls or stood on their own supports. Some women laboriously scraped at some of the stretched hides. A somewhat rank, but almost pleasant odor of herbs mixed with grease, sweet grass, and wood smoke, permeated the air.

The ground felt harder underfoot the further they advanced into the village proper. Due to the chill, few, but the women scraping hides, ventured outside the cabins and huts. The few other Indians milling about stared blankly at the party of white men. Pulling their blankets tight around them, they whispered among themselves as the shivering white men passed.

The creak of a door on one of the large cabins broke the silence. A stout, but tall, white man in a green uniform strutted through it, marching steadfastly toward the party. Stopping a few yards from it, he raised his lower lip and asked "Terry, what have you brought along this time?"

The man walked over to Jenkins and looked him up and down. He tried to lock eyes with Jenkins, but the rebel's head remained bowed. Undeterred, he lifted Jenkins' chin, looking long and hard into his cold and defiant eyes.

"A man of spirit, I see," he said, turning to Terry. "Don't give this one an inch! He'll turn on you in a heartbeat." He flicked his hand from the rebel's chin, ignoring the man's cold gaze cast in his wake.

"Yes, I agree Captain Caldwell," Terry said, plopping down from the saddle. "He's a damn rebel through and through, a lieutenant of the Twenty-fourth Connecticut Regiment."

"I could tell he was of Wyoming by his obstinate stare," Caldwell said. "Those Wyoming rapscallions are so intense."

"Yes, we are," Terry said.

"Oh, yes, yes, my good man," Caldwell said with a laugh. "No offense," he added with a pat on Terry's back.

"None taken, sir," Terry said, nodding toward the packhorses.

Caldwell quickly examined the packs of plunder strapped to the horses, paying close attention to the rifles. "Smashing!" he said, nodding to each of the men, save the rebel. "Good show for you all!" he added, motioning for some other green-coated men to come and take charge of the men's tired and cold mounts. "Here, my good men, they shall take care of your mounts and your prisoner," he explained, grabbing proudly at the lapels of his new green coat. His eyes sparkled down to it. "These are our new uniforms, right sharp indeed, if I do say so myself."

Terry gave the proud peacock of a man a long look from head to toe. The dark green coat pulled tight against Caldwell's stout torso by his proud tug upon its scarlet lapels, exposing a green waistcoat. Buckskin leggings covered his legs from his moccasins to his waist. A tight black leather cap covered his head, bearing a cockade on one side and a brass plate on its front, bearing the letters *GR* and the words *Butler's Rangers* etched upon it.

"Yes sir, right smart indeed," Terry said. Rubbing his own soaked buckskin trousers, he frowned. When would he get his fine uniform? he could not help but ask himself. Or didn't he and his men rate them?

"Come," Caldwell said, reaching his arm out to him. "All of Butler's Rangers shall soon be uniformed the same. We've now enough men recruited for a full company under Captain Walter Butler."

Terry's odd look upon hearing the younger Butler's name demanded an explanation. After all, Walter Butler and Ten Broek had been prisoners of the Americans in the Albany jail for some months now. "I shall act in his stead until he is liberated," Caldwell said. "Which I might add shall be soon." he added with an uncertain smile. He pointed to the large cabin's door. "For now, come warm yourselves and dry your clothes by the warmth of a fire."

Jenkins watched them enter the warm cabin, looking with a

glaring eye to the stock shelter near it. No warm fire awaited him, but perhaps enough straw to fashion some sort of covering against the cold. His green-coated guard did not need to coax him to the shelter, he went willingly.

The ranger looked confused by the prisoner's attitude. Usually rebel prisoners kicked and spat at him. This rebel did neither. This rebel didn't even curse him. It clearly puzzled him.

Jenkins nodded to the puzzled man; exhausted and cold, no fight remained in him even if he wanted it. He only thought of survival and his dear Beth. Rubbing his hand, he backed into a far corner in the shelter; one with an ample supply of straw. He eyed the straw and then the ranger. He started shivering uncontrollably.

The ranger bent down, carefully checking the rope binding Jenkins' hands. He lifted the looped rope from around his head and put it over his wrists, tying the free end of the rope to a post at the entrance of the shelter. Looking down upon the shivering man with a look of pity mixed with disgust, he turned and walked out of the shelter, but soon returned holding a blanket. With a gentle hand, he draped the shivering prisoner with it, helping him scoop some more straw around his person.

A slight smile slid across his face in response to the prisoner's puzzled, but appreciative look, before he rose and took his post at the shelter's entrance. Drawing his own blanket tight against the cold air, he stood to his duty, no matter how unpleasant.

War brought out the worse in some men; but sometimes the best of men overcame such feelings, and let simple humanity guide their actions. Acts of kindness, however slight, showed a hint of divinity some say dwelled in all men. To be mean and cruel somehow came naturally to men. Kindness came from the depths of the human soul from where faith and other hints of grace came, however slight. To draw it from the depths required a desire which eluded most men.

Jenkins, alone and shivering, smiled back at his enemy for his act of kindness, for he feared such acts to be far and few between before this nightmare ended. He mouthed a silent prayer for all men, despite the cruelty he faced. It brought hints of hope, and he needed all the hope he could muster now, be it from friend or foe.

## Chapter Seventeen
*Red Jacket*

Jenkins sat in the corner of the stock shelter, silently cursing the snoring sentry. He pulled his blanket up, tucking it tightly around his chilled body. Of all the sentries throughout the night this one seemed the most indifferent. He hadn't said a word to him or even checked his bonds when he relieved his predecessor. He just plopped down into a comfortable position and tucked his hat over his eyes. The snoring commenced almost immediately. The rangers, with the exception of the one whom had been Christian enough to get him a blanket, made his confinement miserable in many ways.

Just before he began to pull the blanket over his head and suffer through the snores the shadow of a man caught his eye. The man slowly walked around the corner of the shelter and stopped, staring down at the snoring ranger. After a few moments he shook his head and advanced to the rear of the shelter. A few horses shifted about, but none neighed an alarm. Somehow the man calmed them. The finely embroidered scarlet jacket adorning the man shone even in the pale light just before dawn. Silver ornaments glistened from his ears and under his nose. A lone feather danced about his head, dangling from a leather cord attached to his hair. His sharp features somehow gave the man a regal bearing, and here, observing the Indian's features silhouetted in the dim light, Jenkins understood why some called the Iroquois the *Romans of the West*.

Jenkins also watched the blanket covering the Indian's torso for any sudden movement. If the Indian pulled a knife he had better make his first strike count, for bonds or not, he would waylay him. Then he would take care of the snoring sentry and make his way back to Wyoming. Perhaps a fatal act, taking on two heavily armed men, but he intended to go down fighting.

But the man stood still. His dark eyes shinning down on Jenkins chilled him more than the frosty air. He seemed aware of Jenkins' apprehension and made no sudden movements. Kneeling down, he sat cross-legged in front of Jenkins. His hand slid from under the blanket and he raised it high in the air. "This no good," he said. "No good."

Jenkins' wide-eyes answered him. What was he all about?

The man's lower lip rose. His eyes fell low to the ground and he said, "Brother! Long ago when the white eyes first come they were feeble, while we, the Indian, were strong as the great trees of the forest!" He waved his hand in a great sweeping motion. "Now, after many moons, I fear we shall become the feeble ones, our numbers culled by fighting in this terrible struggle between the white brothers. This quarrel is not the Indians'. Ours is not to take sides, but to live, free of cords which bind us to either of the white brothers!" He stopped as if considering the wisdom of his own words. "This, I, Otetiani, say at many council fires!" His hand fell loosely to the cold ground. "But my words fall on dead ears! None listen! The ghost of *Warraghiyagey* lives in their hearts!"

Jenkins sat silently, not knowing how to take the sudden intrusion, or the strange Indian himself. He only wished him to hush his words so as not to disturb the sentry, if he could even hear over his own snores, that is. But he recognized the Indian's reference to Sir William Johnson, or Warraghiyagey (Big Business), the King's long time Superintendent of Indian Affairs-whom had died in July, Seventeen Hundred and Seventy-four, and had to agree. Johnson's shadow loomed large, even in death. He nodded to the strange stern-eyed Indian.

Otetiani sat perfectly still with his eyes still on the cold ground, deep in thought. The deep lines in his leathery skin seemed too deep for a man with eyes as young as his. Jenkins guessed his age to be no more than his own, reasoning the man's deep thoughts and overexposure to the sun must had prematurely aged his skin. He remembered the man before at Queen Esther's Town when he and Sutton had visited it, and had barley escaped with their lives. He had heard of the Seneca chief the English called *Red Jacket*, but had never been introduced to him, before now, that is. Introductions had not been forthcoming at his last visit to the Indians. He decided to stay silent and listen.

"I know of you," Red jacket said. "And of your father. Yankees, both, you stand strong against the winds blowing against you. If they make you fall, you rise again. You stubborn!" He finally lifted his eyes from the cold ground, pulling his pouch around to his front. His swarthy fingers emerged with a small loaf of cornbread, which he handed to Jenkins.

Jenkins grabbed the bread and eagerly devoured it, all the while warily watching the strange Indian.

Red Jacket nodded. Looking to his pouch, he pulled out some jerked meat, seeming to be much pleased by the welcoming look in Jenkins' eyes. So much so, he pulled several more small loaves from his pouch, eagerly handing them to grateful man. He also placed a small gourd of water on the ground before him.

Jenkins ate and drank as fast as he could, mindful of the snores from the ranger sentry. If the snores ceased, so would his feast. He looked past the Indian, though grateful, and watched the sentry.

"*Assaroni*," Red Jacket scoffed. "No worry, they sleep through anything!"

Jenkins managed a quick smile and nod between bites, but kept his eyes locked on the sentry just the same.

"*Aquanashoni!*" Red Jacket said, thumping his chest. "We strong! Others say we fight this war like we fought Champlain." He looked sorrowfully down to the ground. "But those days gone. Those people gone. They no see wisdom Otetiana sees. There come day, as always comes, when this struggle over, we must not be enemies to either side, but friends. Then when war over we free to trade with both and keep our land." He shook his head. "Warraghiyagey, he spoke of day when America be free."

Jenkins stopped eating and turned his eyes to the red-jacketed Indian. The Indian's words took root.

"But he had much interest in way things were," Red jacket continued. "He want to keep things the same way as long as possible. If he keep peace with Bostonians, King George and Indians give him more land. He love land, but he say one day America independent and free."

Jenkins thought Sir William to be a staunch Tory, but this revelation by one whom had actually spoke to him of his thoughts on American independence shocked him to say the least. Sir William was a complicated man, a friend to some, an enemy to others, but apparently a man of vision few others could comprehend. Jenkins remembered it was Sir William whom launched the '*Snowshoe Campaign*' against the Delaware 'Hornet Nests' along the Chemung and Susquehanna Rivers after the *Wyoming Valley Massacre* of Seventeen Sixty-three. The Oneida and Mohawk Indians he sent against the Delaware Indians in January of Seventeen Sixty-four in retaliation for the massacre had worn snowshoes, thus the 'snowshoe campaign'. Led by Andrew Montour, a relative of Queen Esther Montour, they took the Delaware villages completely by surprise, burning many of the villages and taking prisoner a young *Captain Bull*, son of the great chief *Teedyuscung*, and leader of the hostile Indian raiding parties. From Chemung they had delivered Captain Bull and his hostile comrades to Albany to face the stern hand of justice. Johnson treated the Iroquois justly and used his great influence to keep the peace. Now, the Six Nations being free of his great influence, Jenkins shuddered at the thought of their unbridled power, and wrath. Perhaps Johnson had more depth to his character than history gave him credit.

"*Uraghquardirha*, Sir Guy, he no Warraghiyagey," Red Jacket said. Jenkins nodded in agreement to the reference to Sir Guy Johnson, Sir William's nephew and son in law, whom he had appointed his successor upon his death. Even Jenkins heard of his hard drinking. It interfered with the man's thinking, perhaps a good thing, Jenkins thought; for our cause at least. He continued munching madly on cornbread.

Red Jacket turned and looked over his shoulder. The moonlight dimmed and the ghostly light of false dawn coated the shadows around them with a reddish glow. He faced the light penetrating the spaces between the boards of the rough shelter. It shone on his regal face, magnifying its features.

Jenkins stopped eating long enough to look through the great cracks between the boards to the image of the steep mountains and the light coming over them. It reflected in his eyes. Red Jacket noticed. "Do not worry to face a new dawn," he said, somehow seeing a vision in the light reflected in the rebel's eyes, or perhaps just within the essence of his eyes alone. "You, like your nation, shall survive these days," he continued, raising his hands to some unseen force in the sky. "You shall survive and light the day with hope for many new days, not just for yourselves, but for all peoples."

Jenkins' jaw dropped. Apparently some Iroquois saw the vision of the new future. Some saw the light of this *'Revolution.'*

"The morning comes," Red Jacket said, lowering his hands. "Brother, I shall do all I can in this storm of madness to see that as many Aquanaschoni live through it as possible." He looked up, contemplating his words. "Even if it means they must run and hide, in the end they shall live. We must live! I, Otetiani, of the *Nundawaono*, declare this, I shall do all I can to return you to your people."

A few dogs started milling about the snoring sentry. Red Jacket held his hand out to the gourd Jenkins clutched greedily to his chest. Jenkins jerked it back, taking one last great gulp from it. Red Jacket gestured toward the uneasy snores. Jenkins promptly handed him the gourd without any further argument, realizing soon the horror would return. Soon the Tories would awake.

Red Jacket slowly took the gourd and pulled some more jerked meat from his pouch. "Keep it hidden and nibble it slowly," he said. "On this day they take you to Niagara. Must pass many villages to get there. No say any words but keep head bowed. Brother, I shall see you wear red paint." He placed his hand on Jenkins' shoulder. "I shall go along with the party." He then rose and turned about, walking slowly past the noisy sentry. The dogs raised their heads, sniffing the air at his passing. One of them lifted a leg, spraying the stock of the musket sitting next to the ranger before scampering off with the others.

Jenkins waved at Red Jacket, but he did not turn to see it. As soon as his new friend and the dogs disappeared the snores became more labored. With a loud gasp and lip smack the snoring abruptly ceased. The ranger adjusted the black cap on his head and slowly rose. After rubbing his eyes, he glanced back into the corner and sighed upon seeing the huddled rebel. Clearing his throat, he spat a large glob of phlegm onto the ground. Raising his canteen to his lips he took a long drink, paying no further heed to his prisoner, or his wants and needs.

For an instant Jenkins wanted to rise and knock the ranger from behind but a few muffled voices made him reconsider. Rangers soon appeared at the entrance of the stock shelter. One of them peered back at the prisoner. "I bet you had a restless night indeed," he said with a snort. The sentry punched him in the arm for the comment.

"Here you men!" a commanding voice suddenly called to the rangers. "Be about your business! Prepare for the day!"

The rangers perked up upon hearing the command and quickly scattered, leaving their comrade alone at his post. The sentry snapped to attention, raising his musket in salute of his approaching commander. But his hand slid along the slippery stock. He grunted in disgust. Instantly dropping the musket, he sniffed his suddenly slimy hands.

Captain Caldwell shuffled past him without so much as a passing glance. Marching back to Jenkins, he stood before him with his hands cocked on his waist. "'Today you are off to Niagara," he said.

"I've already heard," Jenkins said.

The Tory captain turned a cold eye to the sentry.

"What?" the sentry asked, furiously wiping his hands on some straw. "Sir, I said not one word to the damn rebel!"

"Stand easy!" Caldwell commanded. "I have no doubt he heard nothing from you but snores!" He moved his foot about the straw until it caught the end of the rope binding Jenkins' hands. Lifting it up in his hands he pulled it taunt.

Jenkins' hands rose from the jolt to the rope. He snarled.

"It is only these bonds that held him here, you inept fool!" Caldwell exclaimed. "Thank God they held tight!"

"What?" the ranger said. "I kept an eye on him all the night!"

"Yes," Caldwell scoffed. "Perhaps between snores!"

The ranger shook his head and glared at Jenkins.

"Well, he shall not escape his escorts to Niagara, for they are regulars of the King's Eighth Regiment of Foot!" Caldwell said, turning to walk out of the shelter. "See that he is fed!"

"See that you're fed, aye?" the ranger snarled, spitting a huge glob of phlegm down at Jenkins' feet. "There! You're fed!"

## Chapter Eighteen
*Off to Fort Niagara!*

Jenkins stood sullenly by the ranger holding the tether attached to his neck. He pulled his blanket tight around him against the morning chill. At the same time he slipped his fingers under the blanket to feel the meager stash of jerked meat nestled in his shirt front tucked into his rawhide britches. He feared it to be his only source of food as he watched the rangers munching and drinking around him. None, not even the kind ranger of the day before, offered him anything, not even a crumb.

Chemung Village slowly came to life around them. Indians huddled around the many open fires speckling the village in an effort to ward off the morning chill before starting their necessary tasks of life.

The sharp creak of a cabin door turned heads from the fires near it. A finely dressed officer stood full in the open door, carefully surveying all around him. The eyes turned away from the arrogant officer, with slight hints of disgust escaping many throats.

Raising an eyebrow at the look, the officer raised his nose high and marched toward the rangers. Captain Caldwell immediately gave them the once over before sauntering over to their prisoner. "Has he been fed?" he asked, shifting his haughty eyes to the ranger holding the other end of his tether.

The ranger shrugged his shoulders.

Caldwell cocked an eyebrow and sunk his hand gruffly into the ranger's haversack, giving the stunned man a start. "Here now, sir!" the ranger protested. "Is that necessary?"

"I am afraid so, old chap," Caldwell said, pulling a biscuit from the haversack. Kneeling down, he handed it most graciously to an equally stunned, but appreciative, Jenkins.

"Here now, men," Caldwell said, standing tall and adjusting his uniform. "Sergeant! Form the men for drill! At once!"

"Yes sir," Sergeant Newbery groaned, slowly rising with rest of the men. He gestured for the man holding Jenkins' tether to sit the rebel prisoner by a nearby fire surrounded by other white men; loyalist civilians.

Caldwell spoke for him. "Gentlemen," he said to the indifferent looking white men. "Would you mind keeping an eye on the King's prisoner while we drill?"

The men glanced up at him and nodded.

"Very well," Caldwell said.

The ranger dropped the lead of the tether down to one of the men. The man stopped eating just long enough to slide his boot over it, laughing at the sorry-looking soul tethered to the other end. "You mind your manners and you'll be fine," he said. "Just eat your fine breakfast and stay quite."

Some of the Indians slowly mixed with the white loyalists, while others seemed quite content to avoid them. Several native women and children poked and prodded their prisoner with sticks and quick jabs. The warriors ignored him. The ever-present dogs howled at them all, eagerly devouring morsels flung at them from firesides.

Jenkins sat with his head bowed and nibbled at a biscuit, mindful that he now fell in status below the begging dogs, whom at least had their freedom. He ignored the taunts and jabs from the sour-faced Indian women and giggling children. The white men, mostly displaced settlers with an odd trader among them, did nothing to curb the cruel attention the Indians gave their new charge. Jenkins recognized several of them, but they did not even offer him a second glance.

Crisp commands tore everyone's attention to the odd formation of rangers. Caldwell barked confused orders, struggling to guide his men in the art of close order drill. Several amused Indian children stood at his heels mimicking his increasingly exaggerated movements. He glanced down at them, especially when they tried to mimic his voice, but thought better of scolding them in front of their parents and relatives. So, mostly he ignored them, giving them the evil eye every now and then.

His men faired no better under his eye than the Indian children mocking him. Finally, in a fit of desperation, he pulled Terry from the confused ranks and ran him through the manual of arms in front of the others. Terry fumbled with his firearm a little better than those in the ranks. "I thought you had experience in the American ranks?" Caldwell finally asked in desperation. Terry just shook his head at him.

Laughs and taunts erupted from the other white men by the fires.

Caldwell finally raised his hands to the heavens in a fit of desperation, finally ordering the men dismissed. They had no trouble obeying that command.

"We are a new unit!' Caldwell loudly announced. "But have no doubt, after a few months of drill we shall be a most formable force!"

More laughs answered his declaration.

Caldwell frowned and marched over to a group of regal looking Indians also enjoying the show. Several white men wearing the tattered remnants of British uniforms stood among them. Shreds of scarlet jackets, torn and worn by the rigors of wilderness campaigning, hung about the shoulders of two of the men; their pride forbidding them to simply disregard the symbols of their great army. They needed to know they belonged to something higher than this Godforsaken wilderness. Then they could maintain their bearing. A soldier's bearing.

In comparison, two other white men, apparently British soldiers also, appeared more Indian in dress with their blanket coats and buckskin leggings. Their jackets had apparently disintegrated against the rigors of the wilderness.

The soldiers eyed the Tory captain advancing toward them and properly snapped to attention, appearing all the more foreign among the Indians around them. They presented their arms and exchanged a few smart words before following the Troy captain back to his irregulars. Several of the Indians trailed them, one of them wearing a fine scarlet jacket, much to the envious eye of the regular soldiers.

The rangers, soldiers, and Indian warriors talked among themselves, several of them occasionally glancing over to the civilians and the rebel prisoner huddled by the fire. Their voices scratched through the air, but Jenkins, as well as the civilians, seemed indifferent to their words. In fact, Jenkins lowered his body to the ground, eager to take advantage of a few desperate moments of sleep. He soon drifted off to sleep when a gruff kick struck his feet.

"Why, who have we here?" a loud voice asked mockingly.

Jenkins lifted his eyes at once, hearing a familiar voice. He locked eyes with a familiar face which matched the voice. Moses Mount, late of Wyoming, stood tall over him, sporting a brand new green uniform. "Moses?" he asked through the haze of sleep.

"Yes, Johnny, it is," Moses said, kneeling down to him. "I hate to see you in such a bad way, Johnny, but such is war."

The mention of the word brought a numbing feeling to Jenkins. He melted back down into his blanket, dejected and forlorn.

"How are things about Wyoming, Johnny?" Moses asked. "Is Wilkes-Barre Fort finally raised? What of Pittston Fort? I hear a right smart and solid stockade surrounds your father's house."

Jenkins pulled the blanket tight around his head.

"Come now, Johnny, that's no way to treat a friend! Where's your manners? You used to be the proper sort!"

Jenkins ignored the man.

"No matter, we probably know more of Wyoming than you, anyways."

The words dripped with pride from the ranger. Jenkins found it impossible to hold his tongue. "Then you, fine sir, will not find it hard to just leave me be!" he growled.

"Leave you be, you say, well if others had just left us all be, perhaps matters would not be so desperate!"

"How can one be left alone in the raging fire of war started by a tyrant and his minions?" Jenkins scoffed.

"Oh, my dear Johnny, a fire it is indeed, a right smart one, and it shall not stop until Wyoming burns clear of rebel scum."

"You best hold a high torch, for if you don't, do not be surprised to see it knocked from your hand!"

The other white men perked up, seeming to become enamored with the conversation. Their silence caught Moses' attention. He smiled at them while Jenkins kept his head cloaked with the blanket.

"I often wonder how a man can turn against his God-given government and sovereign," Moses said. "For only heathen do not abide the scriptures. Have you not read the *Book of Romans*? Everyone must submit oneself to the governing authorities, for they are established by God. He whom rebels against authority rebels against God!"

"Then submit yourself to the Continental Congress."

"My word! *Saratoga* has made you rebels all the more impudent!" Moses' face turned three shades of red in an instant. He rose, cruelly kicking Jenkins.

Jenkins immediately rose, standing tall and full in Moses' face.

Both men stared deathly at each other without flinching. The other white men and Indians formed around them, anxious for a show.

"Here!" Caldwell called, hurriedly marching over to the two men. He gruffly pulled them apart. Moses growled in disgust, pulling his knife. Caldwell pushed him back, glaring at him. Moses took a few steps back, panting and puffing in anger. His eyes shined with pure rage.

"Sergeant Mount! Leave this place at once!" Caldwell ordered.

Mount stood his ground, his muscles flinching with anger. He ignored Caldwell, tossing his huge knife from hand to hand.

Jenkins raised his bond hands to the stunned captain. "Are you to cut these and give a man a fair chance or are am I to be slaughtered like a dog?" he asked, his eyes shining with an equal rage.

Caldwell raised an eyebrow at the mere suggestion. These frontier people are too intense, he thought. They wore their emotions close to their skin. Too close. He stared at both men swelling with anger. The Indians started hooting and yelling. A few whites joined them.

"No! No!" Caldwell finally said. "There will be none of that!" He looked over to his stunned rangers. "Sergeant Terry!" he said. "Escort Sergeant Mount from this place at once!"

Terry plodded through the growing crowd before stopping full in front of Mount. "Now Moses," he said, "put the knife down and step aside, orders you know, old man."

Mount snarled, baring his teeth. "You fine Rebel bastard!" he said, shaking his knife at Jenkins. "We'll get you and your lot soon! Before the fall sets again! Wyoming will burn!"

"Sergeant!" Caldwell said, hardly containing his own anger. "Mind your tongue or feel the lash!"

Mount's bulging eyes glared and darted about. He swallowed hard, spitting on the ground at Jenkins' feet. Jenkins didn't flinch. Terry squarely placed himself between the men. He stood firm.

Mount snarled. He shot an angry glance at Terry and Caldwell before storming off to one of the cabins.

"You, sir, would be wise to mind your tongue, "Caldwell said, grabbing the loose rope dangling from Jenkins' neck. "Private Hoghtailer!" he called to one of the British soldiers. "Come at once and take charge of this prisoner!"

The private marched up and with a smart by your leave grabbed the rope from the infuriated officer. He turned, ready to march off, when Caldwell cleared his throat as if he had more to say but his anger choked it down his quivering throat. Hoghtailer stopped and waited.

"Prisoner!" Caldwell said with an icy stare at Jenkins. "You are to be escorted by Private Hoghtailer here of the King's Eighth Regiment of Foot and his party to Niagara. You shall depart at once!"

With that Caldwell waved his hand in the air as if to bid good riddance, turning his back to the prisoner.

Hoghtailer took the hint. He marched quickly away with the prisoner in tow, gesturing to the other three regular soldiers. They all took their place in line, Indian file, as he passed them. He did not stop a second, feeling it paramount to separate these colonials before their emotions truly did get the best of them. An emotional lot indeed, he thought.

A group of a half dozen warriors, led by a chief in a scarlet jacket, took up the trail behind them, watching them like a hawk.

## Chapter Nineteen
*Painted Post*

Hoghtailer led the party swiftly along the trail. Jenkins struggled along behind him, occasionally casting a wary eye to his rear, comforted by the cushion the three other soldiers provided between him and the grim Indian warriors bringing up the rear. An 'Eyes front!' order accompanied each of his glances, but he turned often, despite the command. The soldiers appeared intensely interested in gaining as much ground as possible between them and the lower settlements. Fort Niagara seemed to beckon them. Though a rude post on the fringes of the frontier, it offered a more secure and familiar place than the Indian villages.

Now and then fire-cracked orange rocks marked a place along the trail where others had enjoyed the warmth of a fire. Rotting and charred wood posts in several large clearings showed traces of deserted hamlets, probably burned and abandoned every since *Andrew Montour's* raids on the *Hornet's Nests* in 1764. Squash plants gone wild and scars from digging sticks among many small mounds of earth told the story of garden patches of days now past. All around the ageless forest dominated the mountains as it had from time immortal.

They skirted a few villages still alive and vibrant but failed to stop in them. At every step Jenkins feared the doors of the cabins would burst open and spurt fire at him-the demon rebel. Thus, he needed no coaxing to hurry along. Only a few nips at his heels from the ever-present Indian dogs at every village actually assaulted him. The few eyes glancing at the party seemed indifferent to their passing.

Jenkins welcomed the trail exiting each of the villages. The well-trodden trail felt as hard underfoot as any post road. The forest, with its tremendous trees, inspired a sense of awe no matter how many times people witnessed it, from a lifetime to a few seconds. Nature, with its virgin magnificence, always inspired men. At certain places brown pine needles, springy to the touch, blanketed the ground. If Jenkins had a decent meal in his stomach, in place of the crumbly and stale cornbread and ancient jerked meat, and if the warriors in the rear suddenly faded away, he felt he could almost enjoy this jaunt to Fort Niagara.

More and more people passed them the farther they trod up the trail. By the widening trail Jenkins reasoned they neared some important village or fork intersecting two great trails. He figured they now trod along the old *Andaste Trail*. Though he had never traveled it, he knew from talk among Indians, and sundry traders, that the Andaste Trail forked where the *Conhocton* and *Canisteo* Rivers met to form the Chemung. The even more hurried pace of the British private in the lead, plus the growing chill, chased away any pretended enjoyment of the jaunt. As time passed, the water gourd passing along the hurrying men touched his parched lips far fewer times than the others' lips, and Jenkins ached for the trail to end or for the sun to set. Either offered hope of a respite from the soldiers' mad pace.

Finally, with the sun setting behind the great trees, the mark of man showed in the wilderness in the form of a village carved from its heart. Each man, friend and foe alike, let out a collective sigh. They clambered down the hillside to the ample village at the fork of the rivers.

Rambling past other travelers, they made a beeline toward the far edge of the village. The Indians of their party melded with the other Indians, quickly disappearing into welcoming lodges. White faces greeted the remainder of the party approaching a few hewn-log cabins by the river's edge.

"Welcome! Welcome!" a solid framed buckskin-clad man said, smiling and holding out his great hands. His grizzly beard seemed out of place on his face, he having the manners of a proper man, one whom would otherwise be clean shaven. But this man lived in the wilderness, and the wilderness demanded little beyond a man's natural appearance. At least a white man. "Welcome to *Kanhanghton*, or, as some say, the *Painted Post!*" he continued, gesturing toward an ancient oak tree dominating the center of the village. The few branches surviving the ravages of time sat atop a great hunk of wood. Several spots showed rolled bark on the edges of bare spots, apparently retreating from constant hands tearing it away before it had a chance to grew back. Red figures of all sorts speckled the bare spots; no doubt the many pictographs told of past deeds of great war parties.

Other whites soon emerged from the cabins to greet them. Among them, much to Jenkins' surprise, showed the smiling and innocent faces of children and women.

A smile stretched full across Hoghtailer's face at the sight of the young white ladies. He most graciously removed his hat, courtly bowing to each of them. Curtsies answered his gesture; a curious sight not missed by the ever-present Indian children always watching the strange white devils. They laughed and giggled, vainly trying to imitate the whites before an old wench shooed them away. Her loud scolding momentarily interrupted the whites, but they stood patiently and waited for the sour-eyed old woman to depart with her brood.

Taking advantage of the distraction, several white children and a curious young lady slipped past the soldiers. They huddled around Jenkins, whom had collapsed on his knees to the ground. The young woman waved to an accomplice, another fetching young lady, to further distract the soldier holding his tether with her coy smile. The soldier's eye turned from his charge and onto the beauty before him. He too removed his hat and took a few steps back, now ignoring his charge.

"So you're a Rebel?" one of the boys asked.

Jenkins shrugged his tired shoulders.

"John!" the young woman immediately scolded him. "Mind your manners! Do not be so rude and insolent!"

"What?" the little boy asked, scampering off with his fellows. "That's what he is! He's a Rebel!"

"I am so sorry for my brother's forward ways," the young woman said, rolling her eyes toward their surroundings. "But we are not exactly among the civilized." Clearing her throat with a slight sound, she gazed at Jenkins, but her eyes did not bear the curious look of the others, only a glow of true compassion. "Have you supped?" she asked.

Jenkins slowly raised his head to her welcoming eyes. Her gentle tones rejuvenated his soul. It put him in mind of another woman's voice, Beth's. Shaking his head, he rubbed his hand.

"Never you mind the prisoner, Miss," the soldier said, suddenly regaining his sense of duty. He tugged at the tether, bringing Jenkins to his feet. "He's in the King's charge now! And he shall be treated accordingly."

"Don't be so silly!" the young woman said, pleading with her eyes for her accomplice to distract the gruff soldier again. Her accomplice only lifted her hands and shrugged her shoulders.

She shook her head at her and rolled her eyes to the soldier. Her accomplice immediately took the hint, interceding with her coy smile and charming looks.

"Look, Miss," the soldier said, battling with himself to resist the charming beauty before him. "You must stand away!"

Her frustrated accomplice raised her nose and strutted away, clearly insulted by his indifference to her wiles.

"Rebel or not, he is a man!" the young woman argued. "Is he not? Why must war make such brutes of men?" She stared deathly into the soldier's unmoving eyes.

"Oh, you'd be smart to let this one have her way," another white villager said, approaching with a great disarming smile. "She's a stout one, this lass," he continued, placing his hand on the soldier's shoulder. "She's John Hart's daughter. She'll have her way afore it's all said and done. She will at it fer sure," he added with a slight wink.

The soldier glanced to her and then down to the beleaguered

man for whom she pleaded. "You may feed him, I guess," he said, glancing about the bustling village. "He'd be a fool to try and make a break for it here, and that's for right sure, it is. He would oblige many a brave by such a foolish act, one for sure would have his hair for it!" He dropped the tether to the ground. "You may do as you wish," he said. "As long as you keep within my sight, that is, Miss."

The woman nodded, gingerly lifting the leash. After giving the soldier a slight curtsy, she ushered Jenkins to a bench in front of one of the cabins.

"You mind yourself and the soldiers, Millie!" a voice called from the crowd. The stout man whom had initially greeted the party walked over to her and her new friend. He looked down at both of them sitting on the bench. "You mind the lass and things will be fine for you, sir," he said with a cocked eyebrow before turning back to the others.

"My father," Millie explained, dipping a noggin into a bucket near the bench. She lifted it to Jenkins' lips and let him take a long drink. "He's a good man, my father, here to try his hand at trading. We've done rather well so far. It's a rich land if one deals with the inhabitants as equals rather than savages." She dipped the noggin again and let Jenkins drink freely of it. His gulps startled her. "Have not you drunk yet this day?" she asked.

Jenkins' rolling eyes answered her question.

"Wait here," Millie said. "There's stew in the pot over the fire with plenty of spoon meat. Made it myself. I'll fetch you some."

She returned in no time, handing Jenkins a bowl.

His eager hands immediately grabbed it. He clasped it in his tightly bond hands and raised it to his lips, ignoring the spoon in it.

"Here," Millie said, easing the bowl down from his lips. Sitting the bowl in one of her hands, she fed him with a spoon from the other. "We have to do it this way," she said. "I don't think I dare ask that your hands be untied."

A man in a red scarlet jacket suddenly appeared in front of them. The silver dangling from his ears and his painted face precluded him from being a British soldier. Red Jacket stood full over them and stared down at the two of them. "I see you have made your way," he grunted, folding his arms over his chest.

"Be easy on him Chief," Hoghtailer said from behind. "We have orders to deliver him to Fort Niagara, hair and all! " He raised a mug full of rum high in the air. Fires now blazed all over the village to replace the light of day. Eerie shadows danced against the light behind him. Wails from dancing Indians filled the air. "Here now!" he said, approaching them. He glanced over his shoulder and then to the light in the cabin behind them. "Be a good soul and keep an eye on him for us Chief, so as we can warm ourselves in the cabin."

Red Jacket grunted an affirmation.

"That's fine! Between you and the young lass here I'm sure he'll be no trouble. We'll be out to secure him after we supp." He looked down at the bowl Millie held in her hands. "I'm sure good food awaits us, say Miss?" he asked.

"Oh yes sir," Millie answered him. "There is enough for all."

Hoghtailer laughed and followed his companions into the cabin.

John Hart marched up in his wake with a young man in tow. A pistol sat tucked in the young man's belt. "Millie," he said, "Pratt here will keep an eye on things whilst we entertain." He looked at Red Jacket and then at the Indians dancing around the fires below. "I think it might be best for everyone's sake," he added, looking nervously at Jenkins. Patting young Pratt on the shoulder, he sat him down next to Jenkins on the bench. "Bring yourself in soon, Millie, it's not proper for a lady to be out here at night for long." he said, entering the cabin. "We must always be mindful of whose land we are in, it is not our own."

Millie smiled and nodded her head. She raised the spoon among the haunting calls of the Indians below to feed Jenkins with it. The yells seemed to vibrate from the soul of the earth itself, as if these ancient native people spoke for it. She tried not to stare at the strange Indian standing before them, but his dark and penetrating eyes caused a great chill to run down her spine. She glanced nervously at Pratt, whose eyes remained fixed on the Indians below.

As soon as Jenkins gobbled down the last bite she gracefully excused herself, retreating back into the comfort of the cabin, ever mindful of the tense and complicated web which war wove through men's souls. She feared for all involved, be they Rebel, Tory, or an indifferent sort. She had done all she could to ease the suffering of one poor soul caught up in the ravages of war. She feared it might be the last comfort he would ever know. Oh, this terrible war! These troubled times!

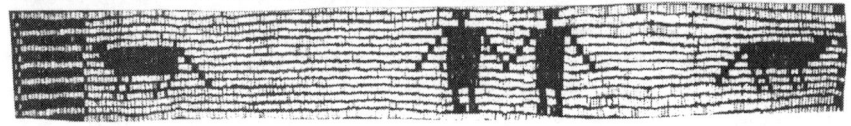

## Chapter Twenty
*Old Man Fitz*

Old Man Fitz, the settlers of Wyoming affectionately called the honest old Dutchman of Standing Stone. But Richard Fitzgerald didn't mind. He thought it a pleasant nickname, in fact. Now, standing in the early morning light on a slight rise of ground just before his cabin, he let a warm sense of pride bathe his thoughts. Any man would do the same, he reasoned, what with such a fine farm stretching out before him.

"Been a nice winter, so far," his neighbor Lemuel Fitch said beside him, shifting his hands on the fence they both leaned upon.

"Yes, that it has," Fitz slowly answered, "in more ways than one."

"Yes, though it's been most unfortunate what has happened to Gordon and poor Jenkins," Lemuel said. "What with being snatched right under our noses and all."

"Jenkins is a fine man, indeed," Fitz said, letting his gaze fall to the fence before them. "Just the kind of man we need here in these troubled times."

"It's always the good on which misfortune befalls."

Both men stood silent for a moment.

"We're already well into December and the river still has no sign of ice," Lemuel said, gazing at the winding Susquehanna River. His eye caught Fitz's large bateau docked on a low part of the bank. "I still wonder how you got that thing all the way down the river."

"Stout hearts and stout minds can do wonders, my friend, you keep that in mind."

"Stout backs? Your William had a part in that, no doubt."

"My nephew's a stout fellow, he is." Fitz stopped for a moment, reflecting on the hard trek down the river. "There were many obstructions in the way until we got to Unadilla, but from then on we proceeded to Standing Stone with little problem," he said.

"William's gone down to Forty Fort, has he not?"

"That he has. He is not so sure about Denison's feeling that we may be fine until spring. He's gone to try and make them down there reconsider and come up to fetch us downriver to the lower settlements."

"Boyd has moved down to Wilkes-Barre because of what happened to Jenkins. They say he reported what happened even before Jenkins' party reached the Fort of the Forty and demanded immediate action against the Tories."

"Yes, he's got a bit more to worry about, seeing the way he left John Bull's army and all. They hang British deserters, they does. He and

Pike have been a blessing for training the Twenty-fourth..." Movement down by the river caused Fitz to stop in mid-sentence. Both men stepped upon the lower rail of the fence and peered down to the river.

Canoes lazily made their way on the current. From the distance the men in them appeared to be white men, which caused more than a slight sense of apprehension in both men. They both watched silently, praying for the current to carry away their worries. The first canoe drifted by the canoe landing, but then suddenly turned about. The second landed just above the first. Eight men poured out of the canoes, paying special attention to Fitz's large bateau. All held their rifles at the ready. They examined the few small barrels and odd things Old Man Fitz had left it and then looked up the riverbank. All of their eyes locked on the two stunned men standing by the fence.

Old Man Fitz immediately turned and backed away from the fence. The sudden movement upset Lemuel's rifle leaning against the fence beside them. Lemuel reached down for it just as he heard the distinct sound of a rifle being cocked behind him. Several similar sounds followed shortly after the first. He looked up at Old Man Fitz staring behind him. His eyes widened. They bore a look of shock and disbelief.

"That'll be a far reach fer you," a voice cracked behind him.

Lemuel recognized the voice at once with a crawling sense of dread. Parshall Terry! The scourge of Wyoming!

A series of loud whoops and triumphant yells filled the air. A pair of hands pulled the men back from the fence, grabbing at Lemuel's fallen weapon. The culprit raised it high above his head and loudly yelled. His face showed radiant through the black paint covering it. If Lemuel had not known better he would've swore the man to be an Indian. Several others rushed forward and grabbed both men roughly by the arms, pulling them back and away from the fence. Another ran a stick through the crook made in each of the men's bent arms at the elbows while another tied their hands.

A man still at the landing yelled while two others discharged their weapons into the air. They ran toward the farmhouse. The others quickly followed, pulling their new prisoners along by tethers tied to their necks.

The blue-eyed Indians raced to the cabin. Shots rang at the chickens milling about the cabin door. A frightened and shaking old woman squeezed past the wild men and fell to the ground, weeping uncontrollably.

"Why? Why?" Mrs. Fitzgerald cried to Parshall Terry.

"Do not ask me, dear lady, I am not in charge," he said, nodding to a large man striding past them and into the cabin door. The man stopped just long enough to glare at her for an awful moment, somehow manipulating the tattoos on his face into a fierce expression. This devil painted his face forever.

"You play to the whims of a savage?" she gasped.

"My dear lady, he holds a captain's commission in the King's army!" Terry said. "Now mind your place! You have all brought this upon yourselves! It is time to pay for your misguided ways!"

Old Man Fitzgerald winced at the sight of his crying wife, while at the same time silently thanking God that his daughters chose to accompany his nephew to Forty Fort. Suddenly jerking himself loose, he knelt down beside his wife. The painted whites guarding him at first trotted after him but then the decided to join their fellows in the cabin. Lemuel did not fare as well. The men guarding him forced him to his knees with their rifle butts.

Terry watch the commotion with an indifferent eye. A smirk slid across his face as more and more of the Fitzgerald's household goods flew out the cabin door. He walked among some of the items, kicking them with his boot. "Oh, such fine things!" he said. "It is indeed a good day's plunder." With a cruel laugh he looked over at Lemuel. "It sets my mind to a wondering what we shall find in your cabin, Lem."

Lemuel clinched his fists and tried to jerk away from his captors. Rifle butts promptly knocked him back to his knees.

Terry strutted over to him. Drawing his sword, he pointed it down to Lemuel's white knuckles. "Temper, temper," he said. Two of the Indians accompanying Tories yelled and sprinted from the cabin, turning Terry's attention, and sword, from the rebel.

The object of the Indians' delight seemed to be a feather mattress they held high above their heads. Yelling like demons, they trotted down to the waterside. Drawing their knives, they savagely cut into the mattress. An explosion of feathers burst forth. They yelled and danced all the louder among the feathers, throwing them into the air and spilling them onto the waters. They stood mesmerized, watching the feathers drift on the current with the awe of a schoolboy.

"Simple pleasures for simple minds," Terry muttered in response to the Indians' odd behavior. He held his tongue, though, when he noticed the Indian captain standing in the doorway watching his fellows below.

The Indian laughed while tossing several tied bed sheets full of plunder onto the ground. Several other blue-eyed Indians in the barn herded more than a dozen sheep from it. Others shooed away several cows, firing their rifles in the air behind them to hasten their retreat to the hills beyond. Another led three fine horses behind him.

"Well, well," Terry said, examining the horses. "Fine indeed!"

The old woman wailed in grief at the Tory's announcement.

The Indian captain emerged from the cabin yelling at the top of his lungs in triumph. Waving his long rifle over his head, he stood full and tall in front of the others. After emitting a few more spine-tingling yelps he lowered his rifle, spreading out his arms to the huge pile of plunder before him. "Take down to boat!" he ordered. "More in cabin! Come! The day, it grow long!"

His fellow Indians whooped along with most of the painted whites.

The old woman stared at him through tear-strewn eyes. "I know you," she declared. "You are Indian Hopkins of *Sheshequin*!"

"Now, now," Fitz said. "Mind your tongue, Mother."

Hopkins' lower lip rose in disgust. He looked down at the two old settlers and drew his tomahawk from this belt.

Terry instantly walked in front of the two huddled settlers. "Now, now, Captain, you are right, we need to get on the move," he added, gesturing toward the sun. "The day does grow long!"

Hopkins did not follow the white man's hand to the sinking sun. Instead, he locked his eyes on him. The whoops and cries ceased. All eyes shot to the two leaders. A sly smile slowly crept across the Indian captain's face. "Load up," he said, waving first to Lemuel, and then to the Old Man Fitz. "Bring them Bostonians!" he ordered.

Fritz promptly rose, knowing the sooner these villains started moving, the better for his dear wife. He nodded his head toward Lemuel. Lemuel took the hint and rose, willingly submitting to his tormentors for the Fitzgerald's sake. An Indian herded the two together with a gruff hand. "Thank you, Lem," Fritz whispered just loud enough for his comrade to hear. "We've got to get them out of here afore they put the place to the torch."

Lemuel sadly nodded.

The Tories and Indians promptly grabbed the fully loaded and tied bed sheets sprawled on the ground in front of the cabin. In their haste several small items spilled from the crudely made bundles. Mrs. Fitzgerald scrambled on the ground, eagerly collecting as much of the spilled articles as possible, putting them under the folds of her dress.

One of the Tories shoved her to the side with a gruff kick.

"No! No!" she protested to no avail. "Oh God! Oh God!"

"You'll not find him here in this wilderness," the Tory scoffed.

He raised his rifle to shoot a stirring chicken that had somehow escaped the earlier carnage. The ball exploded in the earth just in front of the bird's feet. The chicken spurted around the corner of the cabin and into the barn. The Tory drew his long knife, quickly chasing after it.

"Here! Here!" a voice commanded behind him. "Be about your business! Leave the chicken be!"

The Tory stopped just in front of the barn door. Inside several hogs milled about the few chickens that had somehow survived. He turned to report the oversight when an Indian darted from a corner, scooping up two of the birds in one smooth motion. He stopped just long enough in front of the stunned Tory to snap the chickens' necks. Pulling a cord from his pouch, he tied the dead chickens' legs together, and quickly slung them over his shoulder, grinning at the white man. Sauntering out the barn door, he cast a disgusted look down at the sobbing white woman on the ground. He stopped and taunted her in his native tongue before rambling off behind his departing comrades.

"What God is to be found in this wilderness?" the Tory said under his breath. Turning, he shuffled past the crying old woman, dropping one of the bundles of plunder back down onto the ground in front of her. The old woman stared up at him in awe. He only shook his head and ran to catch up with his retreating fellows.

"God bless," Mrs. Fitzgerald found herself calling behind him before biting her tongue. "My God, your ways are truly mysterious," she sobbed to herself. "But ours is not to judge."

## Chapter Twenty One
*The flax break*

A slight mist spread over the Susquehanna River. The moist air held the smoke from the fires along its banks close to the ground. The balmy air eased the apprehension of the Tory party, that, and the fact they remained unopposed. So, they talked loudly and freely, despite the proximity of their camp to the Strope and Van Valkenburg homestead along the Wysox Creek. Both families held rebel sentiments; so much so, the Indians had taken to calling Sebastian Strope-the leader of the families-Boss Strope, short for Bostonian. In Indian eyes, Massachusetts, in particular Boston, harbored the most revolutionary sentiments. Thence, from Boston the spirit of revolution spread through the other colonies like a plague. Therefore all opponents to the King carried the nickname Bostonian in the Iroquois Confederacy. Boss's voice boomed so loudly in praise of the new nation the big man held a monopoly on the name in the upper reaches of the Susquehanna.

Smoke from the rebels' cabin wisped through the trees not far from the Tory camp. Across the river lay the Fox's cabin; but the threat there had been removed with Rudolf Fox's capture months before. Anyway, the rebels' numbers precluded them from any action against the loyalists, for upriver the loyalists sat as a majority. In fact, the Tories felt so confident they made their camp in the Strope's flax field.

Terry stood next to the riverbank just to the side of the field and stared down to the river, watching low swirls of smoke from the chimneys of the cabins of both Rebel homesteads rising in the distance.

"What of them?" a fellow Tory asked from behind him.

Terry looked down, scuffing the dirt with the toe of his boot. "What of them indeed?" he said. He caught sight of a clearing by the mouth of a creek just opposite to them. A raft and two canoes sat back from the water line.

His mate walked up next to him. He looked down to the river and spat. "Yeah," he said, looking at the fully loaded bateau on the bank next to them. "I guess we do have enough plunder for now."

"Yes, Newberry, we have," Terry said. "Besides, I do not think our good captain sees them quite as the enemy as of yet, the way they appease the Indians and all, but that shall not stop us from attaining their rafts and canoes. We shall load the plunder into them carried by the others whom are now driving the livestock."

"Yes, more canoes shall help." Newberry said, looking back over his shoulder. "I hope the good captain shall not object." They both laughed. "Esther herself visits them quite often," Newberry added, shaking his head. "The fools think by not causing any trouble and staying on the good side of the Indians their lives shall be preserved. They have no idea what this war is becoming. There'll be no safe place for any damn rebel afore long. Their scalps will probably end up on some buck's lodge pole afore it's all said and done."

Terry looked up to the darkening sky. "That is their problem. They have made their bed, now let them lay in it."

Newberry nodded. He glanced at the camp and to the two rebel prisoners. "Damn Rebels!" he said. "I don't understand that lot!" He marched toward the two bond men, parting the sheep milling about between them. He eyed them for a long moment without saying a word. The two men stared back at him. Hatred beamed from their eyes. Lemuel held himself well, but old Fitz shivered, despite the mild temperature.

Captain Hopkins noticed the Tory sergeant and walked up to him, raising his hand from the folds of his blanket. "He make it to Niagara," he said, pointing to Lemuel. "The old one no make it."

"If he were to huzza for the King perhaps we could see to release him back to his family," Newberry said.

Hopkins shrugged his shoulders. "Younger one go to Niagara, old one no go if he huzza," he said, walking back to the fire.

"You hear that old man?" Newberry asked.

Fitz just sat shivering, ignoring the brash Tory.

Newberry strutted forward, gruffly pulling the old man away from his partner. He slid the cord from around his neck. Lemuel stood and started to follow before his tether stretched tight. Several other Tories rose from the fires.

Newberry rudely dragged the old man a few yards into a nearby flax field and to a flax break left in it. He threw the old man upon it. "Now huzza for the King!" he demanded.

Fitz glared at him through hate-filled eyes.

Newberry motioned to two of his fellow Tories. Following his lead, each grabbed one of the old man's arms. The old man's back arched against the flax break. He groaned in pain, but still stared indignantly at the Tories.

Newberry stood tall, mindful of the eyes of his growing audience. He bent down full in the face of the old man. "Huzza for the King! Old Fool!" he yelled in his face.

Old Man Fitz promptly spit in the Tory's red and glaring face.

Newberry instantly jerked back, wiping his face with his sleeve. "You will be sorry about that!" he screamed, promptly fumbling about some rocks lying along the edge of the field. Locating a fair-sized one, he raised it high and his hands. Stumbling back to the flax break, he held the rock over the old man's head. "Now huzza!" he said through gritted teeth.

The old man's lip rose in disgust. "I am an old man and will not live but a few years more at the longest, so I would rather die now, a friend to my country, then live a few years a damn Tory!" he declared loudly.

Newberry grunted, totally enraged by the old man's defiance.

Lemuel watched the spectacle in awe, apprehensively noticing Newberry's eyes swell even larger in anger. The huge Tory's large muscles flexed as he raised the rock ever higher, ready to slam it down onto the old man's head in a fit of anger.

Lemuel looked all about for any sign of an intervening hand. The Tories, as well as the Indians, now surrounded the flax break. Their eyes watched the rock, anxious for the blow. Panic flooded Lem's whole body. He stepped forwards until the tether around his neck stretched taunt. Fitz, whom had never harmed a soul, now lay at the mercy of people he called friends just a few short months ago. The insanity of war engulfed them all, blinding their eyes to the past. War lived in the madness of the moment, a moment that may cost the life of this innocent man. Lemuel wanted to speak out in hope of curbing the madness for but a fleeting moment, but the pain in his chest still burned from the blows of hard rifle butts to it. More blows awaited him if he spoke out, for sure.

Newberry lifted the rock even higher. "Huzza or die!" he yelled.

"No!" Lemuel screamed in protest. Several Tories promptly marched over to him with raised rifles.

"You mind your tongue or you are next!" Newberry screamed back at him.

"Don't do it!" Lemuel said. "Words escape even the most guarded tongues! Word of this shall spread!" Rifle butts slammed into his chest, knocking him to his knees. "Terry!" he yelled through the pain. "This is Old Man Fitz! You helped to raise his cabin and barn as well as mine! Are you to let this madness go on!?!" Several more cruel blows knocked him to the ground.

Terry stood by the riverbank, watching the water flow past. He fumbled with a few stones in his fingers. His tongue remained silent.

"There's your answer, you rebel bastard!" Newberry said. "Your scalp is mine!"

Terry suddenly threw the stones into the water and turned about. Marching up the bank, he forcefully parted the gathering of men around the flax brake. "That is enough Newberry," he said. His hand fell to the pistol stuck in his belt. He stared deathly into Newberry's eyes.

Newberry snarled and took a few more steps toward the riverbank. With Herculean strength, he flung the great rock into the river. A loud resounding splash echoed through the deathly quiet camp.

"Thank God," Lemuel muttered, rolling about the ground in great pain. He fought the pain to stop just long enough to see the Tories release Fritz from the flax brake.

Fitz stumbled to his feet, defiantly standing tall before his tormentors.

"Be on your way," Terry said. "The King does not make war on old men, women, or children."

The other Tories parted from around the flax brake, leaving a space for the old man to exit. Fitz looked over his shoulder to his comrade writhing in pain on the ground. He wanted to go to his aid but the cold and hateful stares in the Tories' eyes forbade it.

"Be gone! Now!" Terry commanded.

Fitz needed no more coaxing. He quickly rambled straight down the trail leading south along the river. A deep sigh escaped from his chest. "I shall see to Rebecca, Lemuel. This I promise, old friend." he called over his shoulder before disappearing into the trees.

Lemuel groaned in response to the reference of his wife. For a moment the pains ceased upon reflection of the comforting pledge from his friend, but then came back in full force when a yank to the tether lifted him to his feet by his neck.

"Time to be on our way, is it not Captain?" Terry asked the Indian captain kneeling by the fire. The Indian sat as he had all through the commotion, picking meat from a chicken on a spit over the fire. The ways of the whites puzzled him, but he felt it best to leave them to their own ways amongst themselves. Their quarrel seemed to be an unnatural one, appearing to be a quarrel between brothers, and, so, as such, the Indians chose to stay out of it as it was not their way to meddle in family squabbles. He, as well as most of the other Indians, still could not fathom why the English fought amongst themselves in the first place. Be they Bostonians, Tories, or Whigs, they still belong to the same tribe. In this, tribe fought tribe, seemingly oblivious to the fact that war within the tribe brought death to all. The Indian would profit in the confusion of the struggle while it rode its course, but as for understanding the struggle, the Indian would leave that to the whites. He looked up, giving the white man a nod of his head before rising and taking a place in one of the canoes. He could not wait to be back at Sheshequin, and amongst his own people. At least they made sense to him.

## Chapter Twenty Two
### *The Foxes of the Susquehanna*

Mother Fox stood outside the cabin door and took a deep breath of the chilled air. A slight rain began to fall but she did not mind. She needed the air. She needed time to think, and time from the children crowded about the cabin. She eased down to sit on a bench by the door.

"Do you think this will do Mother?" a voice broke through her thoughts.

She looked over to Catherine, her oldest at thirteen, and sighed. The load of wood she carried nearly covered her whole face.

"Oh my child, it will do fine," Mother Fox said. Rising, she guided her daughter toward the door.

Catherine quickly shifted the load away from her mother as she tried to grab a few of the pieces of wood from the top of the load. "No Mother, I am fine. Do not trouble yourself," she said.

"Such good children I have, so dutiful, so brave," she said, gently patting Catherine on the shoulder. "Go and attend to your brothers and sisters. I shall be along directly."

Catherine plopped the wood down by the side of the door. Turning about, she smiled at her mother before slowly closing the door.

"Brave indeed," Mother Fox said to herself, sitting back down on the bench. "Much like their father."

The thought of her dear Rudolf sent a chill racing down her spine. Oh, Papa, she thought, what has become of you? What shall become of us all? She thought of the time soon after his abduction when she asked the Indians, whom were frequent and troublesome visitors, of the fate of her husband. "He killed. He not good King's man!" They had curtly replied. She immediately came back with her own reply, though a bold-faced lie, but she would say anything to learn of his fate. Searching their eyes she said, "As he should be if he were not a good King's man." Their laughs convinced her that her husband still lived. Thus, she found the faith and determination to stay, despite the advice from others to move downriver to Wilkes-Barre.

Raising her eyes from her memories, she looked all around, thinking of the Indians. They haunted them in more ways than one, coming at any time of day, searching and taking whatever they might fancy. They had become so watchful for plunder she found it necessary to secret provisions in the cellar and eat them at night. She shivered at the thought of a gathering the other day across the river. Loud and boisterous voices echoed across the river to her cabin. She had grabbed Rudolf's rifle and pistols, and gathered the children into the cellar for the whole day. Some of the voices could have been those of white men, for the river teamed with Tories. She had breathed much easier when she had gone to find the Strope's flax field empty of any miscreants; be they white or red. But the theft of their canoes and rafts reaffirmed her fears of the visitors being hostile.

    She tightened her shawl around her shoulders against the growing chill. The rain started turning into sleet, pinging off the cedar shingles on the cabin's roof. Muffled voices and bustling noises crept through the cabin's door. Slowly rising, she placed her hand on the cabin's door latch. A strong gust of wind paused her for just a moment to readjust her shawl before she looked back over her shoulder at the darkening forest. A chill rushed through her body thinking of what could possibly lie in the forest's dark folds. She felt many eyes staring at her. Putting her hand to the latch to free her from the eyes of the forest, she stopped just before she lifting it. Another feeling stopped her dead in her tracks. The wind whistled amongst the trees. It whistled deeper and louder with each new gust. Tree branches whined against its force, but some other noise sounded faintly between the whines. She listened intently. A faint voice struggled against the wind. A human voice. She ran toward the edge of the cabin and cupped her ear toward the river.

    "Hallo!" sounded through the wind. "Hallo in the cabin! Mine goot! Hallo!" She recognized the voice in an instant. Jumping up in spite of herself, she ran back to the door. She flung it open to a group of wide-eyed children. "Catherine grab the rifle and come with me at once!" she ordered. "It's Papa! Mary, stay here and mind the others! Go to the Stropes if we do not return." With that she grabbed the rifle and pouch from Catherine and burst through the door. Catherine followed closely, carefully latching the door behind her.

    The promise of their Papa's return weighed too heavily on each of the remaining children. They immediately all burst through the door behind their mother and sister and stood by the corner of the cabin, watching their plump mother trot down the trail toward the river with the grace and speed of a deer. They listened to the voice calling from the river. "It is Papa!" Mary cried to her younger siblings. "It is!"

    Running to the riverbank, Mother Fox stared across the wide river. She let the rifle in her hands fall to the ground, placing both her hands over her eyes to block the sun. "Rudolf!" she cried at the figure waving from the opposite shore. "It is true!" Turning, she hugged Catherine by her side. "It's Papa!" she screamed. "He's come back! By the grace of God, he's come back!"

    "Elizabeth!" Rudolf cried across the gulf separating them. "Are you all well?"

"Yes my dear!" Mother Fox called back. "Oh yes we are, especially now that you have come back!"

Rudolf raised his hands in the air, waving them frantically over his head. Mother Fox and Catherine waved back. He paced up and down the riverbank, his eyes searching the opposite shore. "The canoes and raft!" he called out. "Have they been taken?"

"Yes, I'm afraid so!" Mother Fox called back.

Both stood and watched each other for the longest moment in the pale light of dusk and in the pelting freezing rain.

"There is no light!" Rudolf finally yelled across the river. He looked down to the swift flowing river at his feet. "I'se has dir flint and steel! I make fire in dir pines," he said, waving back to the thick grove of pines behind him. The sleeting rain turned into a wet snow. "We figured dis out tomorrow!" He stared back across the river. "Now you get back to das cabin! Think of dir children, Mother! I'se love der all!"

Mother Fox gazed down at the child she held tight to her waist. She nodded. "Yes Rudolf!" she cried. Turning the excited child about, she shooed her toward the trail. "We must go back," she said. "Papa will be fine. We shall come back at first light and somehow get him across the river."

"Yes Mother," Catherine said, turning to catch one last glimpse of her father.

Mother Fox lifted the rifle from the ground and backed toward the trail. Tears flooded her eyes, flowing freely down her red cheeks.

Rudolf watched them disappear into the growing darkness and snow. He patted his arms to his body and turned toward the pine trees, gathering what dry wood that remained under the shielding the branches of the pines. He thought of the Stropes, but then reconsidered. The long trek from Québec back to his cabin had taught him to be wary. People seem to change their loyalties on a whim. He knew Queen Esther frequently visited the Strope's cabin. It would be too great a risk of capture again to seek out the Stropes. It would be best if he just stayed to himself.

In no time he built a blazing fire under the shelter of the pine boughs of the thick trees. Piling several boughs into a great pile, he crawled into them, hoping his fire could be seen from the cabin to reassure his long-suffering wife and children. He would be with them on the morrow come hell or high water, he promised himself.

The winds slowly died and the night turned blistering cold. A still settled among the frigid pines. Nothing stirred save the howl of some lone wolf calling in the frozen twilight. Rudolf hunkered down in his haven in the pine boughs, daring not to move, lest he break his fragile blanket of pine boughs against the deadly chill. He listened to the cracks of the huge fire die down during the night; but still, he dared not move, even to revive them.

As daylight filtered through the branches of the pines he awoke to a few dying embers glowing under the charred logs of the fire. Lifting himself from under the pine boughs, he walked to the riverbank. A withering chill immediately assaulted him. His nose hairs instantly froze. His skin tightened against the chill. Still, he stumbled through the snow down the riverbank. There, spread out before him, lie a solid blanket of snow over the entire width of the river. He ran down the bank to the edge of the frozen river, putting his foot gingerly on the ice. It felt solid, but a loud whine and cracking sound made him beat a hasty retreat.

Shrugging his shoulders against the cold, he turned to look back to the pines. The thought of returning to them, even for a little while, made him cringe. Glancing across the river, he noticed a slow trail of smoke rising through the trees beyond the river. The warmth of his own cabin beckoned him. Mother would soon brave the cold with the children in order to rescue him. The cold cut him to the bone. The thought of exposing his good wife and children to its frigid hand brought new chills to his already frozen body.

He glanced across the frozen barrier separating him from his family and the warmth of their cabin. His toes grew numb. His fingers tingled. His nose stung against the raw cold. Drawing a deep breath, he pulled his ragged coat tight around him and sprinted onto the ice, ignoring the whines of protests under his feet. In no time he rambled up the opposite bank and collapsed. Rolling over, he took a long breath. Strangely, he thought of ice fishing.

Shrugging off the strange thought, he rose and hurriedly trampled through the snow toward his cabin. Nothing would take him away from his farm again, he swore with an oath to himself upon this frozen breaths. No, nothing, no Tories, Indians, Pennamites, or Yankees, would ever take him, or his family, from this ground again! Never!

Bowing his head against the cold, he charged forward, fueled with a new determination. Suddenly, a series of loud gasps sounded from the trail ahead. Raising his eyes, he saw his good wife and children braving the cold on the trail to his front. Raising his arms wide, they all melded together in a massive warm clump on the frigid trail, embracing each other tightly. They rose and with frozen tears racing down their cheeks marched to their home; their bastion in the wilderness.

## Chapter Twenty Three
*Collecting Tories*

"Move along," Lieutenant Colonel Dorrance urged his men from the side of the trail, lowering his thick wool scarf from his face to speak. "Make haste so we may catch as many devils as we can this day!" he added, reining his horse back from the grumbling men in the cold ranks. The icy wind howled with a vengeance. Winter definitely returned to Wyoming, leaving the unseasonably warm temperatures they had previously enjoyed but a wistful memory. Nonetheless, the men marched steadily in the late December snows, hoping by their swift pace to take the Tories like the blistering weather they endured, by storm.

"Less than an hour's march at this pace and we shall be about Sheshequin!" a mounted man reported to Dorrance on chilled breaths.

"Very well, Boyd," Dorrance said. "It will be best when this whole damn affair is over and all of us return to our own warm hearths."

"Huzza to that, Colonel," Boyd said. A few approving grunts from the ranks also approved of his sentiments. Two other chilled men slowly plod up to the them along the trailside.

"Captains," Dorrance greeted them with a nod.

The captains nodded in return.

"We shall be at Sheshequin soon," Dorrance said, gesturing up the trail. "Franklin, you take your men to the left, Harding, you take your's to the right. Boyd will take his men to the north, while I and Captain Buck shall approach from the south. We should take them by surprise and encircle them, just like a mountain hunt. Collect all the white men, but let all the Indians be. We are not to bother the Indians! We need not fuel the Crown's argument that they join them. We need the Six Nations to remain neutral! Do all of you understand?"

"Not even that Tory-loving copperhead Hopkins?" Stephen Harding immediately responded.

"None of the Indians!" Dorrance said. "We are to pacify the Tioga Indians and assure them that we are not their enemies. We have enough burdening us with those damn Tories."

"Jenkins was, or rather is, my friend," Harding said.

"Aye," Buck said with a nod. "Mine too! Many a man in these ranks call him friend!"

"Yes, it is most unfortunate what has befallen him, but we must mind our orders, for they are quite explicit," Dorrance said.

"A misfire or a stray bullet could find its mark," John Franklin said. The tall man raised himself high in the saddle, pressing on the pommel of it to add to his height.

"That will be enough of that talk!" Dorrance said. "Mind your men and make sure there are no accidental discharges."

All of the men sourly nodded their heads. Dorrance raised the scarf over his mouth and waved the men off before riding to the front of the column.

"To hell with that, Hopkins had a hand in the mischief with Fitch and Old Man Fitz as well," Harding said. "He's worse than a damn Tory."

"They're all a bad lot up here!" Boyd said. "Deserters, vagabonds, and such, not just Tories and Indians. What of Secord sutlering for them all at Tioga Point?"

"Yes, there are a lot to be dealt with on this trip," Franklin said "I hope our one hundred and eleven men shall suffice to do the job."

"Our numbers are more than adequate!" Harding said. Reining up his horse, he galloped up the trail past the single file of men. Boyd and Franklin quickly followed, urging the men to check their flints and cartridges.

Advance scouts soon appeared at the head of the column, causing a momentary halt. The men busied themselves checking their firelocks while whispers passed up and down their shivering ranks.

"They all sit cozy in their cabins," the scout reported loudly to Lieutenant Colonel Dorrance. Slight cheers rose from the ranks.

"Mind your tongues!" Dorrance quickly scolded them. "It would not do to ruin the element of surprise when we are so close."

The ranks quickly fell silent.

"You have your orders," Dorrance said to the officers crowding to the front upon hearing the news from the scout. "Now let's get to it!"

The ranks parted, melding into the icy forest around the trail. Each man as silent as the next, they fell upon Sheshequin, taking the village completely by surprise.

Men burst through cabin doors, searching them quickly then exiting, some with a white man in tow, while others led a few startled and confused Indians. In no time they covered the entire village, assembling their captives in its center under the eyes of their approving commander.

Lieutenant Colonel Dorrance pushed his cloak aside, exposing his finely tailored uniform and fine red sash, the sign of an officer. He slid down from the saddle, eyeing each of the captives.

"Jacob Anguish," he said, recognizing one of the men. He shook his head.

"Here now!" Anguish said. "What's this all about, rousting a man from his bed whilst in the dead of winter?"

"Hold your tongue, you Tory dog!" Franklin said from Dorrance's side.

Dorrance raised an eyebrow to Franklin, but said nothing. He continued his walk of inspection, talking to his gathering officers.

"We've took some two dozen of the Tory dogs, sir!" Harding reported, rushing to the group of officers. "We got the Hicks, Philip Buck, Berry, Kentner, Bruner, and John Phelps, just to name a few."

"Yes, yes, that's fine," Dorrance said with a wave of his hand. "I know many of the faces, but just the same, see many which are missing. What of Bowman, Hoover, the Pauling brothers, and Parshall Terry?"

"We can't expect to nab them all, can we?" Captain Buck commented from behind. The cold eyes of his fellow officers glared back at him. He only shrugged his shoulders. Did Congress expect to secure the entire frontier with the Twenty-fourth Connecticut Regiment?

"Search the village again!" Dorrance barked at them before anyone else spoke. "But be mindful of our Indian friends!" he called to them as they tromped away, casting a disarming smile to the brown faces staring blankly at him. None of them smiled back at him.

The loud neigh of a horse turned everyone's attention to the stables. A horse suddenly bolted from the stables bearing a frenzied half-dressed man on its bareback. Several soldiers raised their rifles toward the mad horse before one simply slung his clubbed firelock full into the passing man's chest, knocking him instantly from the saddle. He struck the frozen ground with a violent thud. Rolling over, he gasped for air, flailing his arms in the air at the men collecting him up from the ground. The horse continued its mad dash, disappearing into the north end of the village, alone.

Dorrance and his officers immediately rushed to meet the soldiers dragging the gasping man toward them.

"Well! It's Henry Hoover!" Dorrance said. "Where are you off to in such a rush, my fine Tory friend?"

Hoover huffed between gasps, managing a snarl at the gloating rebel officer.

Dorrance drew his sword, leveling its point on the man's chin. "What's that you say, Tory?" he said on a frosted breath. "Come now, it's cold and my men grow weary of this. Now be a good fellow and answer. What are you all about? Mischief, no doubt!"

Hoover coughed, but otherwise stood silent.

"Come now, my fine man," Dorrance said, nodding his head toward his gruff soldiers standing eagerly about them. "Or do I have to leave you to these rather anxious fellows to get a reply?" Captains Franklin and Harding took the hint. They advanced, parting their rough soldiers. They each drew long knives from their belts. Both ran their fingers along the blades. "Come now," Dorrance said. "Lieutenant Jenkins is their friend, as well as mine." He pushed his sword toward Hoover's throat, slightly piercing his skin. A slight bead of blood trickled down from the wound, but he held the sharp blade firm, applying a slight bit more pressure to it. The blood flow grew.

Hoover reconsidered his plight. He glared at the rebel officer. "Hopkins," he said under his breath.

"What was that, man?" Dorrance said. "Speak up man!"

"Captain Hopkins!" Hoover said, mindful of his shivering body causing the blade to cut even further into his neck. "He's across the river at the cabin just below *New Sheshequin*. Terry, Bowman, and Hopkins were all there as of yesterday."

"You don't say," Dorrance said, slowly withdrawing his sword point from the shivering man's neck. "Captain Buck, dispatch a party at once to secure Mr. Hopkins and make prisoners of his guests!"

His words did not need repeating. Franklin and Harding, both large men, bound through the men, jumping into the saddles of their awaiting mounts. They galloped hard for the river with Captain Buck and a dozen eager men running madly behind them.

The horses and men dashed across the frozen Susquehanna, ignoring the crackling sounds of the ice under their feet. Franklin and Harding quickly outdistanced the men afoot. The click of the metal horseshoes faded up the far bank of the river well ahead of the men afoot.

Bearing down fast on the cabin Franklin hastily stopped his mount, and reined it back on its haunches, yelling, "Buck! Surround the cabin!" He then turned and galloped hard for the cabin, reaching it just as Harding jumped down from his mount. Twirling about, Harding drew his pistols from his belt and kicked down the door. Franklin quickly followed him.

The startled inhabitants of the cabin rolled off rude bunks lining the cabin's walls and plopped down onto the floor, all of them fumbling for their rifles near a fireplace before Harding's and Franklin's pistols clicked in their ears. They immediately stopped, raising their hands to surrender.

A third man slowly rose from a bearskin pallet on the floor. Showing his hands empty, he stared curiously at the two pistol-bearing men. "What this?" the tawny-faced man asked.

"There're Rebels, Captain!" one of the surrendering men yelled.

The Indian's sleepy eyes immediately widened, locking on a pair of pistols hanging on a peg a few feet to his side.

"I wouldn't!" Harding said, leveling one of his pistols at the Indian. "You bloody Tory-loving rat!"

Several other rebels burst through the door, spreading all about it. They all raised their weapons at the stunned inhabitants. The clicks of their locks cocking sounded in the tense air.

Captain Buck burst through the door behind them and pushed his way through his men. "Bayonets!" he gasped, trying to catch his breath. "Fix bayonets and take these Tory bastards in your charge!" In an instant a new click sounded and a half-dozen glistening bayonets glittered in the firelight.

"You, fine sirs," Bucks announced to the Tories, "are my prisoners in the name of the Continental Congress!"

None of them said a word.

"Shoot any of them that so much as winks!" Franklin added to Buck's orders. Tucking the pistols in his belt, he shuffled past the Indian, gruffly searching all of the berths and the rest of cabin. "There's places for five here!" he said, glaring at the Indian. "But I count only four rats!"

"You're right!" Harding said, looking toward the door. "But I kept my eye on the door all the way! No one left!"

"Have your men surrounded the place?" Franklin asked.

"No sir," one of the men answered. "The others are well behind."

Buck nodded in conformation.

Harding groaned in frustration, silently cursing both he and Franklin for their haste. "The privy!" he said, raising one of his pistols from under a Tory's chin. "Where is it?"

"Out back!" the Tory said. "Where else?"

"Buck, take these Tory bastards outside!" Franklin said. "We need to search the woods for the Tory Terry afore he gets too far!"

"Fine!" Buck said, waving his men to the door. "Baldwin! You stay here and keep an eye on this Injun!" he called behind him before scampering out the door behind his men.

Baldwin let a great grin slide across his face, exposing a row of tobacco-stained black and yellow teeth. Spitting a great glob of tobacco juice onto the floor, he raised his rifle to the Indian. "You just stay still, copperhead, and all will be fine," he said, watching the last of his fellows exit the cabin door. "But if you so much as twitch the wrong way it'll be your last move in this life, and don't you fer doubt it none!"

A sour look engulfed Hopkins' face. He very carefully sat down on one of the bunks, all the while watching the grinning rebel.

The men spread all about the cabin and the nearby woods. Harding violently pushed open the privy door, leveling his pistols at its empty seat. "Damn!" he said, looking down in disgust. "What a smell!"

Standing by his side Franklin followed his eyes down to the snow-covered ground. "Here!" he exclaimed, stepping back to wave his pistols at the ground. "It's the Tory rat's tracks, it is!" He ran along, following the tracks to the edge of a gully. "Quickly!" he said to the men gathering around him. "He's heading toward the creek so as we'll lose his trail in the water!" He ran down into the gully, directing the men to spread out wide to search its banks. To his disgust, the creek below him somehow ran clear of ice, despite the cold.

"Get up the creek!" he ordered the men. "He can't be far!"

Just then a sharp crack rang in the air from the cabin. Franklin and his men immediately sprinted toward the noise.

Rufus Baldwin stood full in the door, greeting them with a wide grin while carefully reloading his rifle. He spat out a large glob of tobacco before speaking to his wide-eyed captain. "Damn fool tried to run so I blistered him, Capt'n," he said.

Buck pushed him to the side and entered the cabin, finding Hopkins writhing about on the floor in intense pain. A widening pool of blood lay under him. Buck cocked his hand on his hip and said, "Serves you right, you made your bed, now lay in it!"

One of his more sympathetic men bent down to the writhing man. Rolling him over, he quickly examined him. "Looks like the ball went clear through," he said, placing a rag over the wound. The Indian stared up at him in anger at first, but then helped him apply pressure to his bleeding wound.

Franklin swaggered over the Indian, waving the soldier aside. "Leave the rat be," he said. "It may be Jenkins' blood on this one's hands! Let him bleed! It'll teach him a lesson or kill him, either's fine with me!"

The soldier looked up to Buck whom did nothing but wipe his runny noise on his sleeve. The soldier wanted to speak, but the hatred in all the officers' eyes forbade it. He stood and backed away.

Captain Harding burst through the door, joining his fellow officer in gloating over the writhing Indian. Thundering hooves swiftly approaching the cabin turned their heads to the door.

Dorrance soon appeared in the door, staring oddly at Baldwin. Baldwin promptly gave way for him, nodding his head toward his trophy laying on the floor.

Dorrance cast a cold gaze around the cabin. "What has happen here?" he asked the silent officers.

"Had to put a ball in that damn fool Injun, Colonel!" Baldwin said. "He tried to make a run for it, but I stopped him!"

Dorrance's cold eyes looked to him, silencing his bragging tongue. The officers parted to give way for the colonel. "Who is this man?" he asked.

"It's Hopkins himself, it is," Franklin said. "Saves us the time to put a ball in him now rather than later!" Stepping forward, he bent down to the Indian under the colonel's glaring eye, pulling at a small golden plate attached to a cord around Hopkins' neck. He held the crescent-shaped piece of metal up to Dorrance. "It's a gorget! The lobsters must've made him a proper officer! Ain't that right, copperhead?"

Hopkins let out a miserable groan in response.

"Yes, it appears so," Dorrance said. "His wounding goes against orders, but such are the fortunes of war." Looking down his nose to the Indian, he sauntered to the door. "Prepare the men to move out," he said over his shoulder, watching the other men herding the captured Tories to the cabin. "All in all, we've done a good days work," he added, stepping aside for a muttering group of Indian women pushing their way past him and through the door.

Almost immediately their mournful wails filled the cabin. They pushed the other rebels aside and started caring for their wounded companion, lifting him gently to one of the bunks.

Dorrance put his hands to his ears and quickly exited the cabin. Franklin and the others followed, each bearing a self-satisfied grin.

"See to your men for the march ahead!" Dorrance said, turning smartly toward them. "And wipe those smirks off your faces!"

"That copperhead got what he deserves," Harding said. "It's payment long overdue for poor Jenkins' troubles!" Gathering his horse, he quickly mounted it under the colonel's harsh stare. "Good work Baldwin!" he said before riding over to his assembling men.

Baldwin raised his hand, quickly spitting another great gob of tobacco juice onto the ground.

"See to your work, man!" Dorrance ordered him. "Join your company!"

"There's one that was in the privy, sir," Franklin said. "We tracked him up the gully but ain't found him yet. Could be Terry!"

"Yes," Dorrance said, looking to the deep gully beyond the cabin. "He's long gone by now, what with all this excitement. We dare not push our luck. We have done enough for now. We have over thirty of their number. I think we should leave well enough alone, for once."

Franklin nodded his head. "Yes, there has been enough bloodshed this day," he said, looking at a grieving Indian woman in the cabin door. Her gaunt face bore a look of true horror. Even Indian tears seemed human to him now, somehow. He almost felt ashamed, but then quelled the feeling with the hard heart required of every soldier in the field. War is absolute hell, no doubt of it. A cold, absolute, hell.

His eyes fell to a man rushing toward them from the north. He appeared quite anxious at the least. More trouble. He ran from the direction of Esther's Town. Perhaps they had pushed it too far this day? He mounted and spurred his horse toward the panting man. Dorrance reined his horse up behind him and followed.

"Yes Crooks?" Franklins asked, reining his mount up next to the exasperated man. "What is it now, man?"

"It's Esther, sir!" Crooks reported, leaning against the horse's flanks to catch his breath. "She's pissed, or her people are, either way her village is all in a hubbub! Word's already flown on the wind, for they've all heard of Hopkins somehow, and like I said, they are royally pissed!"

Dorrance reined his horse to face Franklin. "Can't you control your men, damn it?" he asked.

"Begging the Colonel's pardon, " Franklin answered. "But Hopkins was shot trying to escape, and the copperhead is also a British patsy! Baldwin's actions were just, no matter how it rubs ill against a certain gentlemen's fancy."

"Mind your tongue, Captain," Dorrance said. "And be about your damn men! See to it no more trigger-happy fools start a war with the Six Nations! Pray we have not!"

"Yes sir," Franklin flatly said, turning to gallop toward his men already crossing the river again. Crooks followed, along with the disgruntled colonel.

None of them felt the cold eyes staring at them from the lone and shivering soul watching them depart with great cheer, or perhaps they would never have left, no matter how Esther felt about it. For this man drew the greatest ire from them, perhaps even greater than the famous Brant or Indian Butler, for he had once been one of them. His blood had once flowed with them. He also once marched off to war with them, swearing the same oath, and sharing the same love of the Wyoming Valley. His treason cut a certain holy cord with them. His betrayal cut the deepest in their hearts. Each one of them would love to end his life, and therefore his betrayal.

Parshall Terry plopped down from his perch in the crook of a great pine tree on the mountain just behind the cabin. The rough bark tore at his bare feet and the snow ran red under them. He once again cursed the departing rebels. Pulling his thin blanket tight around him he glared down at them from the mountain, suddenly realizing if he saw them, they could see him. He immediately scrambled around the far side of the tree, well out of sight of any prying eyes from below.

He once again cursed the rebels, struggling to put his bloody feet into the folds of his ragged blanket. They would pay for this! And they would pay with blood! He would see to it! The damn fool rebel rats!

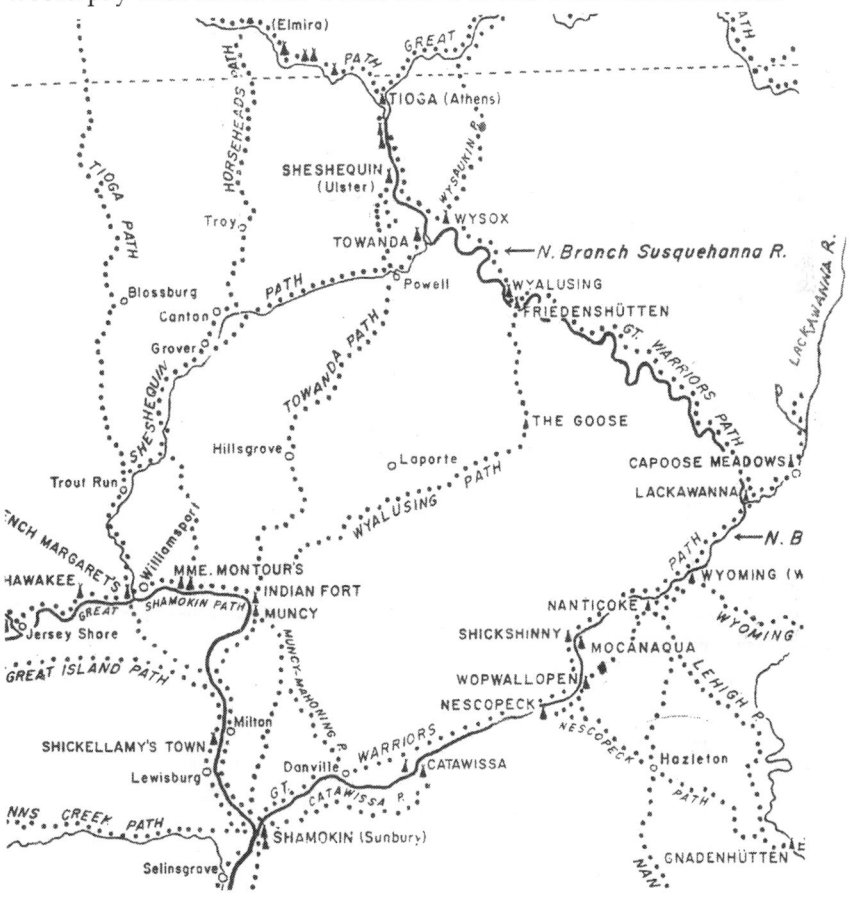

## Chapter Twenty Four
### *A Neighbor's Betrayal*

"I don't like it Amos!" Lucretia York said, pulling her shawl tight around her against the falling snow. "Look! He's watching us!"

Amos stole a glance over his horse's back but continued to busy himself saddling it. "Yes, it is strange, but I'll ride over and find out what's going on now that the snow is letting up."

Lucretia edged her way toward the barn door, casting a wary eye to the curious black man pacing to and fro in front of their barn. His dark eyes watched her intently from under the wide brim of his slouch hat.

"Every since the snow started falling two days ago Billy Lee's been milling about our place on some trifling excuse," Lucretia said back to her husband. "Gives me the chills worse than this dreadful weather."

"Now Lucretia," Amos said. "We're not ones to turn anyone away, especially in this weather."

"Every night he returns to the old Indian village only to pop up again about our place the next morning!" Lucretia said. "I know he's the Pauling brothers' man, but I think they've headed up Tioga way with the rest of their lot. What mischief could he be about?"

"That's what I'm about to find out by riding over to the village," Amos said. "We've been peaceful, obliging, and generous to all whom pass our door. None will hold our political sentiments against us." He looked away as he spoke. Lucretia could always read his eyes.

"Oh, if only Colonel Dorrance had not been in such a hurry! He moved by like the devil was at his heels!" Lucretia said, positioning herself to look into her husband's eyes. She saw the doubt in them. "We would have been down in Kingston Fort now, safe from all this trouble."

Amos looked up, staring her straight in the eye. "Look about Mother," he said. "This is all ours, and all we have, made with our own sweat and blood! It is why we stay! It is why we should stay!"

Lucretia's eyes fell to the ground. "Yes, but the children."

"If things are no better come spring we shall depart to the lower settlements fer sure, at least until this foul wind of war blows by."

"Why Colonel Denison hasn't sent an escort to fetch us downriver is beyond me," Lucretia said, thinking of tall Captain Franklin waving his hat as he passed their house extolling the success of their march, announcing loudly that they had cleared the entire river all the way up to Tioga Point of Tories. A handsome man with pleasing features, the man sat on the borderline of a being a fool or a very brave man, indeed. The division between the two was quite thin, she had to admit to herself, but something about the man's confidence rang hollow with her. She remembered thinking that as he passed, sitting tall in the saddle. His sharp eyes radiated a supreme and absolute confidence, no matter how false. When he removed his hat his fine locks flowed gently in the breeze. His deep blue eyes beamed all the more. The thick fur on the collar of his fine heavy coat somehow fit the man, though it might appear a bit over-the-top on a lesser man. He was all the soldier, exuding an absolute belief in their cause, and himself. Such men were needed now, she mused, wondering if he bore a fool's confidence or if he actually believed his own delusions. After all, he was not the one to be left up the river, they were.

Besides, all they counted as the triumphant, but rushed column of harried men passed their house, were a mere thirty Tories. Secord's face, nor any of the most severe Tory's faces, showed amongst the ragged captives. What of Provost's plantation further upriver and the nest of Tories about Chemung Village? Dorrance's expedition had only slightly pricked the boil on the body of the whole, allowing it to fester and threaten the entire body. And they lay on the extremities of that body.

"Spring's only a month off, Mother," Amos said, breaking her thoughts. Turning, he mounted his horse. "See to the children. I shall return directly."

Lucretia lifted a hand to her lips and waved with the other. A strange, hollow fear swept over her, taking her breath away. She wanted to scream for Amos to stop, but the great lump in her throat forbade it, especially when Billy Lee scampered off behind him. Calm down, she scolded herself. Amos was right! They were all neighbors up here, and friends. How could mere politics cause friend to turn against friend after all they had been through together?

She let her hand fall to the head of her curious young son braving the nasty weather to be with his parents. "Miner," she said. "What are you doing about, son?"

"Pa said the stock needed tending to, Ma," he said, watching his father fade into the thick white snow. He scowled at Billy Lee following him.

"Well perhaps the animals can wait," Lucretia said.

"No Ma!" Miner protested. "Temperance is a comin' to help!" He pointed toward his sister wrapped tight in shawl also braving the snow.

Maybe they should busy themselves, Lucretia thought. It might keep their minds off their plight. Idle hands bred the devil's work. "Well, you children are spry," she said as Temperance approached them. "How, I do not know in this dreadful weather."

"What was Billy Lee all about?" Temperance asked, craning her head to gaze into the barn door. "And where is father?"

"He's gone on a errand to Pauling's is all," Lucretia said, struggling to keep her concern from showing on her face. "Be about your chores now, if you must, both of you. The storm is letting up anyway." Turning her careworn eyes toward the sky she trudged through the snow to the cabin. The deep snow crept up her dress, despite her many petticoats, feeling cold on her legs. "Brrr," she muttered. "It ain't a fit day fer man nor beast!" Stopping to brush the snow from her dress she looked back over her shoulder.

The children still stood by the barn door, staring at her with soulful eyes dripping with worry.

"We'll be fine," she called to them. "Like I said, it ain't a fit day fer man nor beast, so none will be about bothering us, so don't fret on it!"

Temperance let a half-smile creep across her face. She shooed her younger brother ahead of her and into the barn, pausing to cast a last concerned look to her mother.

Lucretia lifted her hand in a slight wave before turning to the cabin door. Five more concerned sets of eyes greeted her inside the cabin.

"Where has Father gone?" Sarah, her fourteen year old daughter, asked. Her other daughters looked to her in anticipation.

"Oh, just to the Pauling's on some errand," she said almost on a whisper. She always found it hard to tarnish the truth.

"Billy Lee too?"

"Yes, so don't concern yourselves. Billy Lee is just a crazy old man." She walked over to the fireplace, mindful of the eyes still watching her. "The storm's letting up. There'll be a lot that needs tending to after it ends. It's best to get to what we can now. Keziah, you tend to the floor. Sarah, you make up the bedding, and the rest of you find a way to make yourself useful or stay out from underfoot!" She poked at the fire with a long poker, hoping for her worries to rise with the smoke rolling up the chimney. Sparks flitted among the flames, giving an omen which made her skin crawl. Fire lie in the smoke, and fear in the snow. Wiping her brow she turned to see her children still staring at her.

"Oh, come here, my darlings," she said, no longer able to contain her emotions. Spreading her arms she welcomed them all into them. They all embraced in a grand hug. Tears flowed down every cheek.

"Come now," Lucretia finally said, regaining her composure. "Be about your chores, fer you are all fine, dutiful, children. God shall be with us this day, I pray, but it's best we remain strong fer your father's sake. Come, let us busy ourselves to relieve our idle thoughts." She released her hold, allowing the children to slowly leave her side, each wiping the tears from their eyes. They all halfheartedly went about their chores, each haunted by their foreboding thoughts.

Lucretia sat down at the table and fingered a hole in a pair of britches she had been mending before Amos left. That man wears his britches thin every week, she thought. But he is a good man, always industrious and hard at work. It was his hands, and his dreams, which led them here to carve their own niche out of this unforgiving wilderness. She wondered of it, slowly pulling the needle through the cloth. Most of the time such work relieved her thoughts, but not this time. It only increased her foreboding sense of dread.

"That old village is a haven for all sorts of vagabonds since the Moravians left to go to the Ohio country!" Wealthy Ann said in the eerie silence. As the oldest still at home she felt it her duty to voice her siblings' concerns.

"Now, now, my child," Lucretia said. "This weather is not fit fer man nor beast. No one will bother us this day."

Wealthy Ann looked soulfully to the floor. "Yes, Mother, you are right, of course, I am sorry."

"Oh, do not fret, my child." Lucretia said, looking to each of the children in the pale light from the fireplace. "Don't any of you fret. We will all be fine. Soon the storm shall break and we can all get some sun."

A thud sounded at the door. Every eye looked to it. Miner burst through, giving them all a start. The little child's chilled cheeks showed crimson below his eyes growing wide with excitement. "Injuns!" he gasped, looking to his gaunt-faced mother. "And they got Pa with 'em!"

Temperance dashed to the door. The others stood perfectly still, looking toward their mother. She stood frozen in fear. She looked to the rifle hanging over the mantle and then to the children.

"They are coming!" Temperance said from the door. Stepping back she gave way to a line of snow-covered men. Snow dropped from the wide brims of their slouch hats to the floor. Not a mumble escaped any of them. Long, deep, hoods covered those faces not covered with slouch hats. Dark eyes peered out from under them. Silver trinkets dangled from some of the noses under the hoods. Numerous tattoos covered some of the faces in the shadows of the hoods. The spears some of them held marked them before they pulled back their hoods and huddled around the fire. The hoods revealed Indian faces.

All of the children's eyes searched for but one face among them and fell hollow by the deep look of despair upon their father's face. His slackened jaw offered no explanation to them.

Another white man swaggered from the fire, rudely pushing the others huddled around it out of his way. Yanking back a chair from the table he plopped down into it, throwing his wet slouch hat onto the table. Shaking his head he slammed his feet on the floor to knock off the snow before brushing back his shoulder-length locks.

Lucretia's eyes widened in recognition. "How do you do, Mr. Terry?" she found herself asking the gruff man.

Terry gave her a sour look and pulled a pipe from his pocket. Fumbling with some makings he quickly stuffed its bowl. Waving a hand toward one of the men around the fire he said, "Pass me a lighted spill, will ya?"

One of the men reached into the small woodened box near the mantle and pulled a small curled piece of wood from it. Bending down to the fire he lit one end of the cone-shaped swirl of thin wood and passed it to Terry.

Terry grabbed it and put it to the pipe. After a few long draws on the pipe he waved the spill out in the air before throwing it to the floor. Smashing it under his foot he leaned back and took another long draw on his pipe, exhaling a long trail of smoke in Lucretia's direction.

Lucretia bowed her head and collapsed on her knees to the floor.

"Father!" Sarah blurted out. "What is the matter?"

Amos stumbled past his wife and sat trembling on the edge of a bed. Through tear-strewn eyes he stared at his family, finding no words to pass the great lump in his throat. Betrayal did such to men. His face fell into his hands. Clenching his fists he slammed them against his eyes before Sarah went to him and stopped his hands. Tears immediately started streaming down her cheeks also.

"Mrs. York," Terry said, rolling his eyes away from Amos. "I am sorry to see you."

"Why?" Lucretia asked, creeping over the floor to her despondent husband. She placed her hands gently on his knees. Gasping in total despair and frustration he slammed his hands all the harder into his face before Sarah stopped him once again.

"What is this?" Lucretia asked again. "Have you taken my Amos prisoner, God forbid?"

"Ask Tom Green," Terry said, clenching his teeth down onto his pipe.

"Tom!" Lucretia cried to the other indifferent white man warming himself by the fire. He ignored her and kept rubbing his hands.

"Tom! Oh my God! Answer me!" Lucretia said. "Is it true?"

Tom Green glanced out of the corner of his eye to the woman

and then gazed back down into the flames. "Yes," he flatly said.

Lucretia, along with all the children, gasped.

"But he shall not be harmed!" Green said. "He need only swear an oath to the King and all shall be fine, in fact, right as rain, or snow."

"You know he will never do such a thing!" Lucretia exclaimed.

"Then he shall have to accompany us to Fort Niagara!" Green immediately answered.

Muffled noises drifted through the cabin door. Chickens clucked and roosters cock-a-doodled in protest. Sheep baaed. Snorts and moos crept from disturbed oxen and cows. Horses neighed. No doubt the others started gathering their stock for plunder. Lucretia's eyes shot apprehensively to the men still standing by the fire. None of them moved yet to gather plunder from their home, but she feared only their chilled bones stopped them. What would they do?

"We are peaceful!" she finally blurted out to Terry.

Terry took a long drag on his pipe and stared coldly at her.

She rose, looking down to her distraught husband. "Terry, you know there is no more a generous, obliging, man on the whole Susquehanna than my Amos! You yourself have benefited from his kind nature! He has helped your family many a time, as well as Tom's!"

The two men said nothing.

"Look to these children!" Lucretia said. "What will become of us? Are you to leave us destitute in the heart of this wilderness?"

"My dear Mrs. York," Terry finally said. "Did you really expect to remain unmolested with the din of war all about you?"

Lucretia tumbled backwards as if the words struck her like a ton of bricks. She collapsed, resting her sobbing head on Amos' lap. His shaking hand fell to her.

"It is growing late," Terry said, unmoved by the rebel woman's words. War changes everything. Friendships are the first to suffer. He smacked the bowl of his pipe on the side of the table to empty it. "We must be going," he said. Rising he advanced toward the door, slowing his steps from the sounds of his men starting to ravage the cabin for plunder. Stopping by the latch he stood still for the longest moment, trying hard to quell the roar of his conscience in his mind. "It is war, that is all," he muttered under his breath before lifting the latch string and stepping through the door. A cold wind blew in his wake.

Several other white men and Indians crowded through the door, anxious to claim their right to plunder. Soon the cabin became a shadow of its former self. Chests of drawers flew open from rude hands. Everything within them soon littered the floor. Sheets torn from beds lay spread about the floor, the repository of the best of the cabin's furnishings.

Lucretia and Amos sat stunned, their life flitting through the great tears falling down their cheeks. The great lumps in their throats forbade any cries of protest. The children tried to huddle close to their parents, pushed aside now and then to make way for the searching and plundering miscreants. None of the gruff men seemed to pay them any mind. War hardens the heart, giving the thief license for his cruel acts.

After bundling a dozen or so sheets and blankets full of plunder together an Indian pointed his sharp spear down to Amos.

The point pricked his knee, making him rise before it sank further into his leg. The Indian immediately prodded him to the bundles. Lifting one with his free hand, he placed it over Amos' shoulder. After loading him to the hilt he pushed him through the door.

With a loud war whoop of triumph at the frightened mother and her children the last Indian stumbled through the door, weighed down by copious bundles of spoils.

A few of the children followed them to the door, much to the protests of their prostrate mother. Oh, rude war, did you ever visit the peaceful vale of *Wyalusing*? Yes, with a vengeance born of the heart of the demon of war himself! The suffering innocents bore witness to your cruel hand, forever etching them, and the land, forever. The poor York children stood watching through bleak eyes out the cabin door, listening to their mother's grieving cries of anguish behind them, watching all they had ever known being carried away on the backs of friends turned enemies. In this, the Tories and Indians etched themselves in the hearts of Wyoming as enemies for all time. As well they should be.

Terry, sitting high in the saddle atop their dear father's mount, reined the horse to the door and stared down indignantly at the huddled and shivering children. His cruel heart, hardened forever by war, seemed not to thaw in the least upon sight of them. His eyes bore an indifference which allowed soldiers from time immortal to rape and pillage the innocent on the whim of their cause. Such injustice needed such failed causes. More of the human heart is lost in one moment of war than in centuries of peace.

The children watched men drive their cattle, horses, and sheep behind the cruel-hearted man whom had once been a staunch friend of their father. Now this man took everything they had in the dead of winter, only offering a cruel gaze upon them in return. Would this cad be as bold to strike down innocent children and a distraught woman? Lo, even Terry's heart shuddered from the threat of revenge if they struck down the innocents from his late family and friends. If he had any part in such an act the barbarity it would surely reach beyond this war. The men of Wyoming would have him, at any cost, for such an act. He knew them. He had once been one of them. Considering this, he reined his mount away from the door and rode over to Amos standing knee deep in snow, weighed down by great bundles on his back.

Before he could utter a word Amos stood tall in defiance of his mere presence. His cold eyes glared indignantly at the traitor in front of him. "Just one thing," he said through gritted teeth. "A word with my wife?"

Terry raised his lip in disgust but then surprisingly nodded. "A moment is all," he said, waving toward the crying woman now standing in the door behind her children.

Hearing the words Lucretia instantly parted her children. She stumbled through the deep snow to her husband, past the disgusted grunt of the gloating Tory traitor on horseback.

Amos took her by the hands, staring soulfully into her teary eyes. No words being needed, they both stared at each other for the longest moment before a ruff kick at Amos broke their trance-like stares. The endless love of a man to his beloved wife flowed in that moment, interrupted by the cruel hand of war.

"Swear an oath to the King and you can join us as a comrade and not a prisoner!" Terry screamed, suddenly overcome with an inkling of compassion. "That is the way of it! Who could blame you in the present circumstances? What is this madness of you rebels? You give your life for politics?"

"It goes much further than the practical heart of a conservative Tory can understand!" Amos said, suddenly finding his voice. He looked to the children. "It is for more than the here and now for which we fight! It is for those living as well as those who shall come! We shall govern ourselves! We have been under the boot of every tyrant in the world, we middling people have, but here, on this new land, in this America, all men have a chance. If there be cruelty or injustice played upon us, it shall be on own account, and therefore more easily addressed! The idea that some men are better by breeding or social position has weighed down man for too long! We are to be free of it, here and now! Every man is his own judge here, and is to be judged as he is, not as his father! This is the heart of it all! You people whom think lowly of man are always in dire need of oppressing his free ideals and heart for fear of it! You are so bleak! If the government of the people be foul it is because the people are foul! Man needs to be free to know this, and correct it on his own accord, not from some gloating and false master! This is the Wyoming man's heart! This is the American heart! Tories be damned! You damn bullies!"

Terry eased back in the saddle, completely overcome by the outburst. This man, as all men in Wyoming, save himself and present company, felt as he did. The pangs of memory flashed in his cold heart for but a moment before he quelled it with a practical sense of the day.

"Move on, fool!" he said, pointing the disgruntled man up the trail. Soon they disappeared up the bleak trail to the north, oblivious of what they left in their wake.

## Chapter Twenty Five
*Secord's Word*

The day did dawn again, despite the restless anticipation of the cold night. Lucretia gazed at the welcoming glow on the greased paper covering the small lone window of their cabin, but somehow her feet felt as tired as her beleaguered soul. But she must rise, she told herself, gazing at her children crowded on the bed together for warmth. Their tired eyes betrayed they hadn't slept a wink, either. The threat of the Indians and Tories returning in the night plagued them all.

Lucretia stared blankly at their inquisitive eyes. Her mind, as well as her heart, pulsed empty. She rubbed her hand along the cold steel of the lone pistol resting on her lap that had somehow escaped the plundering Indians and Tories.

A loud crack from a log on the fire snapped her out of her lethargic trance. The younger children cried, rushing to her side.

"Come now my darlings," she whispered to them. "We must be strong."

"Oh Mother, what of Father?" Sarah asked, slowly rising from the bed. She fell to her mother's side also, sobbing. Her mother's hand fell softly to her head. She gently stroked her long and flowing locks.

"We must pray and keep our hearts strong against the arrows of hate," Lucretia said. "Your father shall return. We must not lose faith."

Wealthy Ann slowly rose and grabbed her mother's hand, lifting it from the pistol. "Oh Mother," she gasped. "What shall become of us?"

Lucretia's throat went dry. She wanted to speak but the words sank in her throat. Cupping her hand to the child's cheek, she tried to dry her tears. She looked into those wide-eyes, still alive with the fear of the previous day. The day they had watched her father led away in the deep snow, burdened with a great bundle of their own belongings on his back. The glow through the window reflected softly on her smooth skin.

"Oh Mother!" all of the children sobbed at once.

Lucretia's heavy heart still forbade her to speak. She shook her head against the heavy feeling, trying to think of something to relieve their angst. The village, she thought, reflecting on how after the raid yesterday she and Wealthy Ann had gone to it in hope of finding some succor. But they found only two other women, the wives of Page and Berry, hired hands of the Pauling's, and their children. Though they held sentiments definitely contrary to their own, safety lay with numbers.

"Get up and get your things together!" Lucretia said, suddenly finding her voice. "We are going to the village!"

The children slowly stood, all watching their mother for

inspiration.

"Come, gather anything of use you can carry," she said, kneeling down to the hearth. Bending toward the dying fire, she blew on some embers until they glowed anew. Placing a tin before them, she carefully scooped some of them into it. "I have fire," she announced, waving her children to the door.

"I've found what quilts and blankets I could," Wealthy Ann said, holding up a few of the poor examples, wriggling the fingers of one hand through one of the holes in a worn quilt. "They took all the best."

"The hogs, Ma!" Miner suddenly interjected, eager to participate.

"Hogs, child?" Lucretia asked. "What of them?"

"The Injuns missed 'em Ma!" Miner quickly answered. Running to the door, he push the others aside, eagerly grabbing the latch string.

"The corncrib has not been disturbed either, Mother," Temperance added, putting a hand on Miner's shoulder. Miner scowled at her and put his shoulder to the door.

"Now just hold on Miner!" Lucretia said. "You mind your sister!"

"Yes, Ma," Miner said, still scowling at his sister.

"You two go and let the bottom out of the corncrib so as to make the corn so them hogs can get at it," Lucretia ordered them. "We may need 'em later, and they won't stray far from the corn. It'll keep 'em big and fat."

Miner lifted the latch and burst through the door into the snow with Temperance at his heels.

Lucretia threw a couple more logs on the fire, gesturing the other children to the door. "Come now," she said, lifting the tin up. "We must go afore the embers cool in the tin. Whatever else we may need when we get to the village we can always come back and get." Tucking the pistol into the waist of her apron, she lifted one of the bundles from the table.

She led her brood through the deep snow toward the many cabins of the abandoned Moravian missionary village of *Freidenshutten*. Struggling to a rise of ground overlooking the village, she halted her column of refugees. Smoke curled in the air from two of the chimneys on the far end of cabins lining the long street through the village. She put a hand to her eyes, looking for any sign of movement around the cabins.

"Lookin' for Injuns?" little Miner asked.

Lucretia looked down at his concerned little face, managing to crack a half smile. "We must all be on the guard for them now," she said. "If any of you see any sign of 'em you must raise the alarm immediately!"

"Even Job?" Little Miner asked.

"All, and any of them," she answered, looking to the snow leading to the stables at the far end of town. Besides the trampled snow of the day before, no sign of man or beast showed about the stables. "Let us go," she said. She pointed to the cabins on the end of the street opposite the occupied cabins. "We shall stay in one of those cabins."

The cabin door let out an eerie creak. Lucrietia took a quick look around its dark interior. A table sat in the middle of the floor along with a few chairs around the otherwise sparse room. The far end of the abandoned village seemed to have escaped the ravages of vagabonds and stray travelers more than the more centrally located cabins. "This will do," she said after a long moment.

The children immediately burst into the room, eager to gain any relief from the biting cold. Several sat on the bunks along the far wall, huddling tightly under their ragged blankets. Miner, though next to the youngest, took his place next to his mother by the hearth. He bent down, helping his mother blow on the embers from the tin. Scraping together a few twigs they carefully placed them over the embers, carefully blowing on them. In no time a blazing fire illuminated the darkness.

"We shall need to collect some more wood," Lucretia said to the other children huddled together against the cold. "These few logs won't last the night."

Temperance slowly rose, pulling one of the ragged blankets from her shivering siblings. Wrapping it around her, she lifted the latch on the door with Miner zealously at her heels.

"Sarah," Lucretia said over her shoulder from hearth. "Take the bucket and fetch some water."

Sarah rose with her own blanket tightly wrapped around her. Scooping up a bucket she walked out the door, passing Miner and Temperance coming in from the cold. Temperance stared blankly over her shoulder. Sarah, curious of what captured her sister's eye, stopped, gazing in the direction of her stare. There, standing a few cabins away, stood several children staring curiously at her.

"Sarah, what is it?" Lucretia asked, walking to the door. She peered over her shoulder. "It's only the Page children. You know them. They mean no harm." Gently nudging Sarah from behind she reached down, grabbing another bucket before following her out the door. "Here, I shall accompany you, but we need to close the door against the cold. Wealthy Ann, watch over your brothers and sisters." She nodded her head toward the pistol lying on the table. Wealthy Ann nodded back.

Lucretia and Sarah trudged past the children without a word

and reached the well near the end of the village. The Page children followed them slowly, one of them disappearing into one of the cabins along the way. The cabin door suddenly creaked open. A woman stepped outside the door, pulling a shawl tight around her shoulders. She stood watching Lucretia and Sarah without saying a word.

Lucretia turned and waved at her but the woman just stared coldly back at her. Sarah turned and stared back, noticeably shaken by the woman's cold stare.

"Don't fret of her," her mother said, grabbing the bucket from her hands. "We have as much right as her to the water." She looked at Sarah and then turned her eyes toward the other side of the river. "We would go over to Eaton's if'n we had a way to cross the river. As soon as the weather breaks we'll head down to Vander Lippe's. I believe the Fitzgerald's have already headed that way."

Sarah's concerned look melted into a half smile, more for her mother's sake than for anything else. The depth of the Page woman's stare still sent chills down her spine. The woman's blazing eyes of hatred mirrored no pity, so it seemed. Sarah turned with her mother and walked with the buckets past the woman. They ignored her glaring eyes of defiance.

Lucretia stopped just short of their cabin door and turned to look back at the woman. The woman shook her head, defiantly tromping into her cabin. The door slammed behind her. "These are troubled times, Sarah, say nothing of this to your brothers and sisters," Lucretia whispered.

Sarah slowly nodded her head, following her mother into the now well-lit cabin. Blazing pine knots stuck into the chinking in the cabin's walls brightened the small cabin. A large pot hung over the fire, attended to by a smiling Temperance. The other children flew from under their blankets and gathered around their mother, hugging her tightly.

"Why, come now children, we only went to fetch some water," Lucretia said with a new smile.

"I am starting a stew," Wealthy Ann said, turning toward the table. She cut up a few pieces of jerked meat and sat some corn on the table. She stopped long enough to pull a chair from under the table for her mother.

"Oh, such fine children I have," Lucretia said. "Your father will be proud of you, as I am now." She barely sat down before a sharp rap came at the door. Everyone froze solid. The rap sounded again. Lucretia reached for the pistol, quickly hiding it in the folds of her dress on her lap. She nodded for Sarah to lift the latch.

The door slowly slid open. A man stood full in the frame of it. The wide brim of his hat covered his face. He held no rifle, much to their relief. Lucretia took a deep breath of relief and said, "Come in."

The man took a few cautious steps, slowly closing the door behind him. He lifted his hat from his face and stood with it hanging before him.

"Mr. Secord?" Lucretia asked. "Is that you?" She cocked the pistol under the folds of her dress.

"Oh my dear Mrs. York, there'll be no need for that," Secord said in response to the clicking sound. Lifting one of his hands high in the air, he pointed down into the folds of his blanket coat with the other. "May I?" he asked. "It is only a letter. A letter from your dear husband, written at Tioga Point. He's well and swore me to deliver it. I do this out of pity for his poor soul, and for you, Mrs. York." The children perked up upon mention of their father. Lucretia lifted the pistol from the folds of her dress. "You may sit, if what you say is true," she said.

"Oh, it is, by the grace of God, it is." He slowly put his hand into the folds of his blanket coat, carefully pulling out the letter.

Wealthy Ann stepped warily toward him, taking it from his hands with a quick jerk. Lifting it to the light of one of the pine knots, she read a few lines. "It is in Papa's hand, yes it is," she said, eagerly passing the letter to her mother.

"I know not what blackguards and vagabonds you have dealt with afore," Secord said, slowly stepping forward. "But I assure you I am not of their like."

Lucretia squinted in the light from the fire and read part of the letter, handing her pistol to Wealthy Ann. After a long moment she sighed and sat back down into the chair. Amos was well, from what she read, that is all she wished to know at the moment. Her drained soul felt a slight relief. She held the letter up and gestured for Wealthy Ann to lower the pistol. "We thank you for the good word you bring Mr. Secord," she said.

Secord stepped up to the table and sat in the chair opposite Lucretia. He smiled and looked to all of the children. "Went by your place," he said. "I figured you would have come to the village."

Lucretia grabbed a large mug from the table and waved it to Sarah. "Get Mr. Secord a bit of cider," she said. "We have not much, because of our dear Mr. Secord's associates, but we shall share what we have. It is the good Christian's way."

She looked over at the pot hanging over the fire. "We shall sup soon. Mr. Secord, you are welcome to join us. Tioga Point is a fair piece off."

Secord gratefully accepted the mug and took a long drink. "I thank you, Mrs. York," he said. "Tioga is a fair bit off indeed."

Wealthy Ann lifted a large spoon from the table and tended to the pot. The fire crackled under it. Picking up a log, she placed it on the dying embers. "Go fetch some more wood, Miner," she said.

Miner looked over to his mother. She looked to Secord.

"I am alone, I assure you of that, Mrs. York, your children have nothing to fear," he said with a smug smile. "Even blackguards do not wage war on women and children."

"Go," she said, "but be quick about it."

Miner sprang through the door in a rush, appearing back through it in what seemed the same breath. He stood wide-eyed with his back leaning against the door. He could not speak past his heaving chest.

"What is a child?" Lucretia asked.

"Three men is a comin' Ma!" he gasped. "They got guns!"

Secord jumped up from his seat with a start. "Mrs. York! For God's sake hide me!" he gasped.

Lucretia stood up in front of the short and stocky man. His hollow eyes bore a look of absolute fear. His disheveled locks added to the stark terror in his eyes. He must truly be alone, she thought, and the men must be ours, from the Twenty-fourth. She thought of just letting them take him and string a rope tight around his neck to stretch him from the nearest tree, but looked down at the paper clenched in her hands. Amos! She must think of him! If Secord did not return to Tioga Point Amos would be sure to suffer. "Blankets!" she cried to the startled children, gesturing for Secord to lie on the floor in a disheveled corner of the cabin. She hastily covered him with the ragged blankets. She and the children threw some stray straw and sticks of firewood on top of the blankets for effect. "Now you children mind yer tongues, for yer dear father's sake," she warned. Straightening her dress, she tidied her hair before walking to the door. She opened it just a crack as the three men approached it.

A bit startled, the men raised their rifles.

"No, no, there is no need for that!" Lucretia pleaded. "Why Aholiab, it is good to see you! You as well, Miner, how is your family? And welcome to you Joel Phelps!"

Aholiab Buck lowered his rifle and bowed his head. Removing his hat, he placed it over the pommel of the saddle. "We came as soon as we heard," he said. "How are the rest?"

Curious eyes peered from the cabin door behind their mother.

"Fine," Lucretia answered. "They are all fine. And how is my darling Lucretia?"

"Your daughter is also fine," Aholiab said. The tall and handsome man's piercing blue eyes suddenly bore a curious look. The captain of one of the companies of the 24$^{th}$ *Connecticut Militia Regiment*, he had been trained to keep a sharp eye for anything out of place. His mother-in-law's eyes had never seemed so empty and hollow, bearing a fear in them he had never witnessed before. He glanced out of the corner of his eye to see if his fellows also noticed her strange behavior. They seemed not to notice it.

"We've come to take you downriver," Captain Buck said, looking over his shoulder. "But seeing how late in the day it is, it is best we start on the morrow." They all started to dismount.

"No!" Lucretia yelled. She stared wildly behind her, her eyes alive with fear. "We have young girls here! It would not be proper for you and your men to stay here." She locked eyes with all the men, one after another. "My fine gentlemen, I think it would be best if you all crossed the river and spent the night at Eaton's. Seeing how he's the last man about."

The men eased back down into their saddles, each staring in confusion to one another.

"At first light I and the children shall be ready to go with you," Lucretia answered their odd looks.

"But Aunt Lucretia," Miner said, "shouldn't you want us about this place?"

"No, my dear nephew, this may be the wilderness, but certain rules of civility still survive. With Wealthy Ann, Sarah, and Keziah, it's best to do as I ask." She spread her arms full in the doorway. She cocked her head and pointed to curling trails of smoke rising from the chimneys across the street. "As I said, there's only woman folk and children about this place. Eaton is the only man and he's well across the river. It will be proper is all. The others are only Page's and Berry's wives and their broods."

"It is best we do as she asks," Captain Buck finally said, placing his hat back onto his head. Nodding, he turned his horse up the street. The others slowly turned their mounts and followed their captain.

Lucretia slowly closed the door behind her, suddenly not certain of what she had done. She backed away from it, lowering her hands for all to be silent. She listened for the sound of the hooves to fade in the distance. Opening the door a crack, she stared out into the empty street.

"They've gone," she finally said.

Secord suddenly burst from under the sheets. His hat twirled off his head, causing his wiry gray hair to spread pell-mell about his head. But his beaming eyes suddenly lit up the room. "Thank you my dear Mrs. York," he said, grinning and sitting down at the table once again. "I am starved! All of this tension has increased my hunger threefold! Is your invitation to sup still standing?"

"Why yes, Mr. Secord, it is," Lucretia said, all the while wondering if her husband received such kindness in the hands of his comrades. She sat at the table and fumbled with some bowls. Wealthy Ann pulled the pot from the fire, sitting it in the middle of the table. The children stood all about the table, each eyeing the pot in anticipation.

"Let us all bow our heads," Lucretia said. The children all bowed their heads. Secord absentmindedly ran his fingers through his hair in a vain effort to try and mat it down. He suddenly felt the need to be civilized. Finally noticing the stares at him, he too bowed his head.

"Thank you dear Lord for all we are about to receive," Lucretia said, raising her eyes to the heavens. "Please keep our dear Amos safe and hasten his return to us. Let his captors see your light in his eyes and I am sure he shall be seen safely through these troubled times. Amen."

Wealthy Ann placed a long spoon in the pot and plopped stew into each of the bowls.

All eagerly ate their portions without a word. Lucretia watched Secord with an eagle eye. But his eyes remained fixed on his food and showed empty of any other thought. He ate with seemingly no other concern than to satisfying his hunger. After his third helping, he belched and leaned back in the chair, placing his hands upon his satisfied belly. He patted it, belching again.

After picking at his yellow teeth, he belched again, but this time said, "Begging your pardon, Mrs. York." Reaching for the mug of cider before him, he gulped down the cider, slamming the mug on the table. "A fine stew indeed," he said, looking about the cabin. "In the present circumstances and all, that is," he added. He stood and walked over to the blankets, lifting his hat up from the floor. "Well, Mrs. York, you have saved my life and now I shall save yours."

Lucretia shook her head at the man.

He smiled and slowly placed the hat over his wild hair. He pulled it down tight over his head and pulled his blanket coat snug around him. "My son James is out there at the head of a body of Indians close by. He has sent me as a spy to see if there are any armed men about." Turning, he lifted the latch from the door. "I shall inform him of the full company of rebels here abouts. He shall not bother when he learns of the numbers he's facing. The Indians do not fight until all is in their favor. It is for certain he shall not be able to convince them otherwise, I assure you." With that, he turned and walked out the door without even a second glance over his shoulder. The sound of his crunching feet on the snow soon faded in the distance.

"My God," Lucretia finally said. "This war is terrible. But in striking a truce with the devil, we have saved our lives. The Lord does work in mysterious ways, indeed."

The children all gathered around her, eagerly seeking her succor in this strange and horrible place that had once seemed so comforting. This place they had once called home. But now it had been touched and ravaged by the cruel hand of war, forever changing it.

"Do not fret," Lucretia said, drawing them all close in a great hug. "God is looking after us, as well as your dear father, I am certain of it."

Gaunt eyes stared up to her, but she had no more words of comfort. This night would indeed be a long one.

Lucretia clenched the letter from her husband tightly in her hands, wishing for his strength and love to ease her angst. She hugged and touched all the children, promising herself to finish reading the letter after sleep eased her children away from this dreadful place for a few hours. She knew her husband's words would do the same for her.

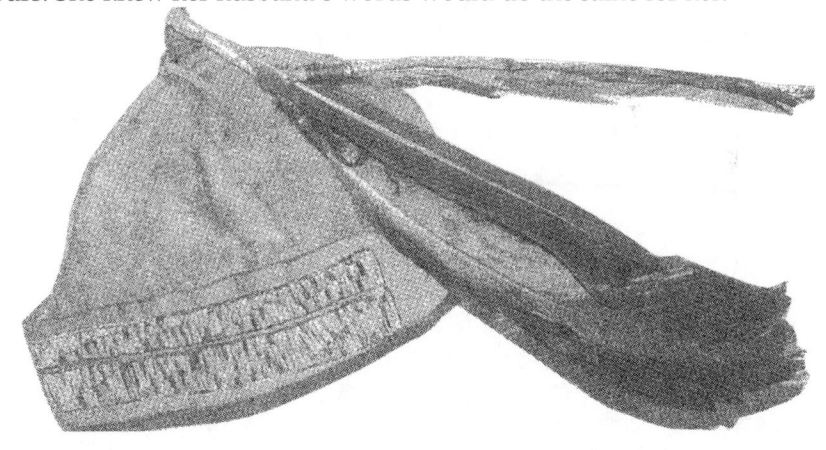

## Chapter Twenty Six
### *Upriver Rescue*

A chilly wind blew in the late March morning. Lieutenant Colonel Dorrance of the Twenty-fourth Connecticut Regiment pulled his collar tight against it. A man priding himself on his immaculate dress, he eased down his collar, imaging it too high for a proper gentleman. He carefully adjusted it to his liking, glancing down at the roughly dressed men darting about him. They bustled all about the abandoned Indian village of *Wyalusing*, popping in and out of cabins.

Dorrance reined his horse up to one of the open doors swinging in the brisk breeze and stared into its dark interior, marveling on just how well-built the structure appeared. The Moravian missionaries built them to last, attesting to their determination to bring the lasting word of God into the wilderness. But, alas, in the end worldly exigencies beyond their control spoiled their divine plans.

Nonetheless, the buildings rivaled anything in Wyoming in sturdiness and longevity. Longevity, Dorrance pondered of the abandoned buildings. Now they seemed only a monument to man's peaceful desires torn asunder and trampled under the gruff boots of war.

Thoughts of his previous expedition in December flooded his mind. He had rounded up men whom just a year before they had called neighbors and friends. But these upriver people, made up of many diverging peoples from the other colonies, carried a diversity in thought foreign to their Connecticut brethren of Puritan stock. Up here men from the Hudson Valley of New York, of Dutch descent, mingled with Pennsylvanians, Scotch-Irish, and Palatine Germans such as Rudolf Fox. Their diverging minds created new dynamics upriver, which showed themselves when the call to form the Twenty-fourth Regiment echoed from Wilkes-Barre. They were to make up their own company, the ninth, or upriver company, of the regiment. They had elected officers, nonetheless than John Secord as their captain. All had went well until their talk of wishing for a peaceful settlement to all of this hubbub rang hollow in the fiercely patriotic ears of the people of the lower settlements. Discussing it, they demanded the ninth company drill at Wilkes-Barre, under their watchful eye and with the rest of the companies. The upriver settlers came once, feeling most uncomfortable with the more stern Connecticut settlers. To the Connecticut settlers one either huzzaed for the Congress wholeheartedly or huzzaed for the King, with no middle ground. Middle ground which most of the upriver settlers trod. Under this, the upriver people complained of the drill, because of diverging thoughts and distances away from Wilkes-Barre. They proposed to drill upriver under their own officers, but would come to assemble at Wilkes-Barre if called to action with the rest of the regiment. This did not set well with the almost overbearing and fanatical beliefs in the cause of the settlers in the lower settlements. They started to question the upriver men, even to the point of harassment, refusing to let their suspicious brethren drill without being under their watchful eyes. So, on the second muster of the regiment, and under the increasingly suspicious eyes of the other companies, they stormed off the green at Wilkes-Barre, telling them to just leave them be. If called they would come, but in the meantime, they preferred to drill amongst themselves. This did not bode well at all about Wilkes-Barre, nor did their suspicions bode well to the upriver people. They complained to nearest people around them, notably the Indians, whom in turn carried the word to loyalists' ears at Fort Niagara. The Indians, always feeling protected by the good treatment of many years from the great *Indian Superintendent for the King, Sir William Johnson*, always sought succor from the pangs of the encroaching land-hungry white settlers from the King. The King's representatives hailed from Fort Niagara now that Sir William had passed, so upon hearing and hearing the many complaints of the upriver settlers, the Indians forced some of them to go to Fort Niagara, whether they wished to or not. Most likely enticed by the King's agents about Niagara, anyway, the Indians did what they felt best in their eyes, oblivious of any agents with ulterior motives. There, about Niagara, men such as John Butler, a person hailing from Connecticut also, but a lieutenant of the late Sir William, with large land holdings which could be threatened by all this colonial hubbub, found a new way to fill the ranks of his Ranger Regiment to protect the King's interests on the New York and Pennsylvania frontiers. He drew from the upriver settlers' unrest and enhanced it, until he, along with others, such as the famous *Mohawk Chief Joseph Brant*, filled their ranks from the new found reserve of manpower-the disgruntled upriver settlers of Wyoming. But some, such as Samuel Cole, James Wells, Robert Carr, Lemuel Fitch, Amos York, the Stropes and Van Valkenburg families, along with Rudolf Fox, stayed true to the cause of American freedom, despite any overbearing persons professing the same belief. This is how it stood, Dorrance concluded in his thoughts, for a moment wondering of the thirty men he had collected in December and sent to Hartford to be tried for treason. Had the thirty merely been reacting to an impossible situation, and being caught in the middle, chose the other side out of sheer necessity? He shuddered at the thought, cursing himself for pondering such things. Their hearts, in the end, showed their true colors. Their sentiments, whether forced upon them or not, be damned!

The men of the lower settlements had been right of their suspicions in the end, and if he caught any more of the rats up here he would surely place them immediately in irons, such as a Tory deserved!

"Colonel! Colonel!" a man suddenly cried from behind him. He welcomed the intrusion into his thoughts. Sometimes he did dwell too long on such matters. They were what they were. The upriver people had made their bed, now let them lay in it, no matter what vermin infested their sheets. He sat up stiff in the saddle and reined his prancing mount about.

The man backed away a few feet before regaining his composure. He nodded at Dorrance and toward a group of huddled women and children being ushered out of a nearby cabin. "Sir," he said, "all that's about this place is these here women and children." He raised a sour eye to his commander. "They are Page and Berry's lot, whom are in the employ of the Pauling's." He let out a loud snort. "The Pauling brothers are known Tories, they are that, sir!"

Dorrance rolled his eyes and nodded to the man. Reining his horse toward the women and children, he gazed down upon them with his own sour expression. "Despite your husband's politics, we cannot leave you up here in good conscience and all," he said to the women. "It would not be Christian, what with all the turmoil here abouts. You shall accompany us back to Forty Fort." He turned his mount about, oblivious to their protests. "See they are ready for the march!" he ordered the men around them.

"Yes sir!" a man with a red strip of cloth attached to the shoulder of his blanket coat said. He smartly turned about, waving the people back into their cabins. "You heard the Colonel, so shut your traps and be right smart about collecting your things!" he ordered them.

Dorrance watched them from afar before another hurried horseman trotted up to him. "Captain Franklin?" he said to the man reining his horse to a gruff stop at his side.

"Colonel!" Franklin said, touching the brim of his wide slouch hat. Several other horsemen reined their mounts to a stop just behind him. "Strope and Fox are well, but won't hear of leaving their farms," Franklin reported, shaking his head. "Strope said he would keep an eye on things and fetch us if things get tight up here. Both of them still think by treating the savages fine they will be spared from any distress. A fool's folly, I dare say!"

"Well that is their decision," Dorrance said. "I can't say I share their reasoning, but it is their decision. We cannot force them." He reflected on his words to the Tory woman, but shook off the hypocrisy of it. They were a different lot. "Our orders are to secure the effects and families of York and Kingsley which have escaped the savages, and collect the family of Benjamin Eaton. We'll take along as many of the others as are willing to go."

Franklin cast his eyes down to the ground and said, "They took all the true men besides Strope and Fox prisoner. I don't feel good about leaving them so close to Esther's band, but they do think Esther shall protect them. I hope they are right, and not just foolish!"

"Esther does hold sway over all that happens up here," Dorrance said. "If we were to force them downriver it just might agitate her into some sort of action, from suspicion alone. We need her peaceful, so we'll let them be, if it be folly, or not."

"I guess you're right," Franklin said, watching his horse's feet slip and sink into the muddy ground. "Despite the chill in the air, the ground's still mighty soft," he added, lifting his eyes toward a nearby pine tree swaying in the wind. "Wind's a changing to the south, going to get warmer yet, it is. The trail will be nothing but mud!"

Dorrance glanced down at the mud and then to the rows of well-built cabins lining the street. Twitching the flanks of his horse with his heels, he trotted toward the nearest one. He stopped near a cabin already partially demolished for some unknown purpose. Leaning forward, he touched one of the fine hewn logs. "Good wood," he said to Franklin, who followed him. "It's well seasoned. The river is high. I think these logs shall make a fine raft. A flotilla is the answer." Turning, he galloped toward another of his officers standing about with his men. "Have we any axes and such, Captain Geer?" he asked the officer.

"Why, yes sir," Geer answered with a puzzled look.

"Then put them to good use, my man, dismantle these cabins and assemble some rafts from the wood, for we are to use them to float downriver to Forty Fort," Dorrance ordered.

Geer nodded, immediately barking the appropriate commands. His grizzly bearded and rough men instantaneously buzzed about the village, selecting the best cabins to demolish for their wood. They seemed to relish the command. In no time walls and roofs fell under their crashing axes. Awaiting horses promptly pulled the hewn logs down to the riverbank to another party of men whom bond the logs together.

A loud series of huzzas accompanied the first successful launching of a raft into the swirling brown waters of the Susquehanna. It floated fine, creating a platform well above the splashes against it from the swift currents. Many soaked feet awaited dry footing, curiously on the river, and not on the soggy ground on which they now stood. Not a dry foot showed among any of them, even the mounted men.

"Right smart operation," Dorrance said to Franklin. "The Twenty-fourth is a fine lot indeed!"

"Yes it is, sir," Franklin agreed. "There's not a hardier lot of men on the whole damn frontier. But, sir, my scouts report a lot of savages about Tioga Point and Esther's Town, along with those rascal Tories egging them on. Chemung shall be buzzing with them too, no doubt."

"Yes, my good man, the sooner we depart the better," Dorrance said. "I fear the upper reaches of the river are becoming the nests from which the Tories and Indians shall strike south, despite our best efforts."

Both of the officers' eyes turned toward a disheartened woman trudging toward the raft landing with her children in tow. Wet, muddy, and dreary, they presented an awful sight. The hollow look in their eyes haunted both of the officers, churning up great pity in their souls.

"The good man John Slocum has willingly taken responsibility for them, God bless their souls," Franklin said. "Nathan and he were fast friends before he was taken. They'll be fine, as well as Mrs. York and her brood, now that she'll be cooking for the garrison at Forty Fort."

"Are any of us going to be fine? For a storm is brewing up at Tioga Point, and when it strikes we shall all shudder from its force," Dorrance muttered under his breath.

Another officer approached the sad-eyed officers, Captain Hewlett-the newly appointed leader of the Continental Line Company Congress had ordered to be formed in light of the constant pleas from the people of Wyoming. Just the kind of help they needed, authority to form a company from their own people. But the one hundred and seventy five firelocks along with 200 weight of powder, 800 weight of lead, and 500 flints sent to them, did compensate for the lack of men, somewhat. Hewlett's beaming face shone in great contrast to the crestfallen senior officers. "I dare put any of my men up against thrice their number!" he proudly proclaimed.

"I fear it may come to that, my dear man," Dorrance muttered back. "I fear it, indeed, and do so hope you are right in your boasts!"

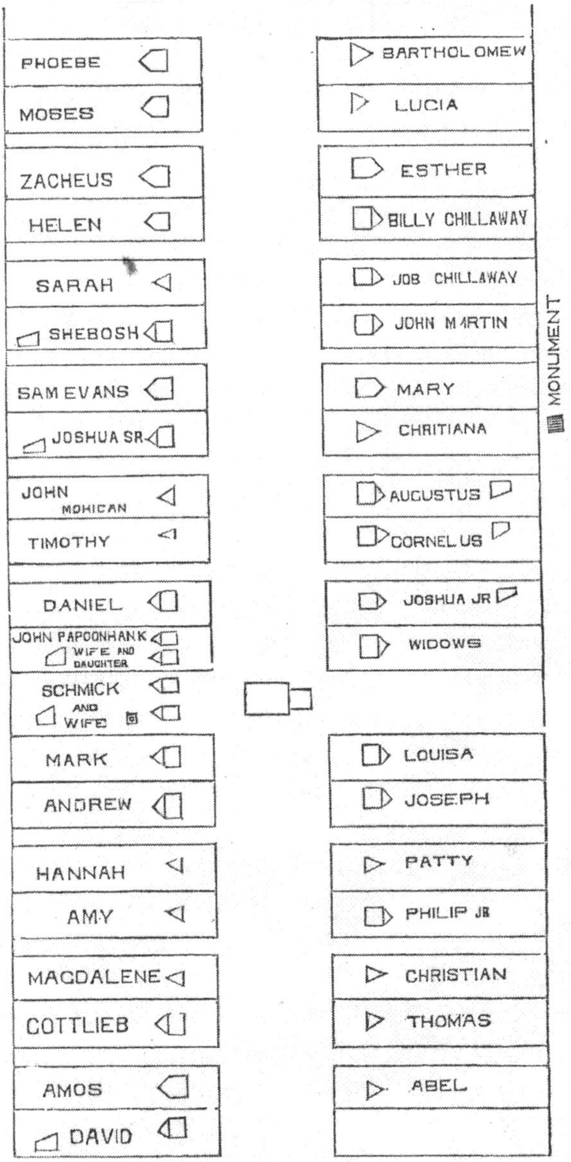

## Plan of Friedenshütten in 1771, Looking West

**West row (left column, top to bottom):**
- PHOEBE
- MOSES
- ZACHEUS
- HELEN
- SARAH
- SHEBOSH
- SAM EVANS
- JOSHUA SR
- JOHN MOHICAN
- TIMOTHY
- DANIEL
- JOHN PAPOONHANK, WIFE AND DAUGHTER
- SCHMICK AND WIFE
- MARK
- ANDREW
- HANNAH
- AMY
- MAGDALENE
- GOTTLIEB
- AMOS
- DAVID

**East row (right column, top to bottom):**
- BARTHOLOMEW
- LUCIA
- ESTHER
- BILLY CHILLAWAY
- JOB CHILLAWAY
- JOHN MARTIN
- MARY
- CHRITIANA
- AUGUSTUS
- CORNELUS
- JOSHUA JR
- WIDOWS
- LOUISA
- JOSEPH
- PATTY
- PHILIP JR
- CHRISTIAN
- THOMAS
- ABEL

MONUMENT

PLAN OF FRIEDENSHÜTTEN IN 1771, LOOKING WEST.

Legend:
- House of round logs.
- " " squared logs.
- Hut.
- Stable.

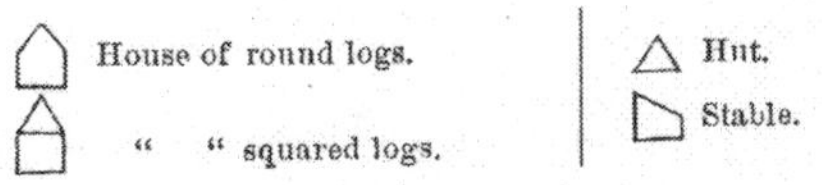

## Chapter Twenty Seven
### *Prisoners of Fort Niagara*

They each took turns sitting against the cold and rough stone wall to catch the sliver of light shining through a crack in a huge door overhead. Jenkins took the first turn, he being in the hole the longest, followed in turn by Lemuel Fitch, Amos York, and David Pickering; all men late of Wyoming, taken to this hell by the gruff hand of their friends turned enemies. Though each one cherished the light, the one thing they looked forward to in their dismal prison, they also made sure each received their turn every day. It kept them sane, the light. It reminded them the world still existed outside this cold, damp hole in the floor of Fort Niagara. A world they hoped to return to after enduring this living hell.

Now and then footsteps shuffled over the door, sending dust down through the beam of light. All of them remained silent then, waiting to hear the tone of the voice from above. If it had the nasal twang of the white man, they breathed easy. If it had the guttural sound of an Indian tongue, they shivered in fear and retreated far into the cold and dark corners of the filthy hole.

The Indians' losses at *Oriskany* the previous August greatly exasperated them still to this day, months after the battle. They seemed to vent their frustrations on the hole filled with rebels, their now hated enemies. The door would creak open and a crude ladder would plop down from above. Soon Indians followed, their dark eyes bearing a certain cruelty the white man seemed to lack. They would raise their spears and poke at the terrified men as if sizing them up for a meal. Their visits grew more frequent the longer the Winter stretched, seeming never to end.

The Tories and British soldiers did little to stop them, in fact, they seemed to have changed their policy of no Indians allowed in the fort just to accommodate their harassment of the hated Wyoming men. Thus, they seemed indifferent to the Indians' visits, giving them free reign over the prisoners. The only white face they saw in months came when the door crept open and a few maggoty biscuits dropped from it. Then, without a word, the door would slam closed, shutting them in the darkness again. So here they sat in the hole at Niagara, their only human contact that of cruel Indians and shunning and silent white men, feasting on stale and maggoty biscuits, while drinking water from a filthy bucket rarely filled by their tormentors. This was Niagara, garrison fort on the New York frontier. Hell had nothing in comparison.

"Rebecca faired well after they took me, eh, Amos?" Lemuel's voice scratched through the darkness.

Amos had heard the same question a thousand times since they had been thrown down into this horrible prison. He found it increasing hard to speak, let alone repeat his tired response for the hundredth time. So he sat silent and still in his corner of their little piece of hell, glumly staring at the sliver of light. Lemuel now took his turn standing in it. It seemed foreign to his blotched and sickly pale skin. Now and then Lemuel smiled in the light, exposing his yellow teeth. His matted and wiry hair spread in a dozen different directions on his head. His rags barely covered his emaciated frame. Fort Niagara, the bane of Wyoming.

Lemuel's eyes widened, looking to the dark corner he knew Amos occupied. Each of them laid claim to their own corner and the rest respected the claim, keeping their distance, for the meager space remained all any of them had left to call their own, besides their memories, which fed the indispensable need of them all, hope.

Lemuel did not mind his friend's silence. But he had to keep asking him to confirm the only thing of promise left in his soul, the hope of seeing his beloved wife again. Turning, he looked at the remarkably still plump Pickering, the last to be imprisoned in this hell. How he maintained his weight baffled him. Shaking off the thought, he turned his face to the dank stone wall again. "I due hope your dear Lucretia has faired as well as Rebecca," he said. "And Beth as well, John."

Jenkins let a tried groan creep from his lips upon mention of his dear Beth. He rubbed the back of his hand, now chafed red and bare. It didn't matter, the memory the action triggered in his heart far outweighed any pain of the moment. It numbed the true pain; the pain in his heart.

Amos remained silent.

"Dear Amos, do not lose faith, for it is all we have," Lemuel said, glancing back into Amos' dark corner. A movement in the sliver of light tore his eyes from it in a flash. He stared up to the door. His eyes caught a familiar shadow standing just to the side it. "The ghoul is back," he whispered.

From all the glimpses they had caught of this eaves-dropper, sometimes merely a shadow, they knew him to be neither an Indian or from the rank and file of the British troops. His fine outline and finely embroidered red scarlet coat identified him as an officer; an officer seeming to gain a certain delight from witnessing their tortured existence.

"You! Listen!" Fitch yelled through his clenched teeth in a fit of anger. "You are a right fine bastard!"

The outburst drew no response from the shadowy figure, only

Jenkins responded, rising to pull him from the sliver of light. "No!" he whispered to his fellow inmate. "Do not give the fiend the satisfaction!"

Both men turned their hate-filled eyes up to the crack in the door. After a few moments boots shuffled away from it.

"He's gone," Jenkins said, releasing his hold on his friend and slowly backing into his corner. "Amos! It's your turn in the light," he said before plopping down onto the cold and filthy floor.

Amos blinked. After a long moment, he slowly rose to his feet. He shuffled toward the light, staring gauntly at Lemuel standing just to the edge of it. A sudden pain in his mouth brought his hand up to it. Fingering a tooth in his bleeding gums, he pulled it easily from his mouth. He held the black tooth up in front of Lemuel whose blank eyes still showed no emotion. He held it in the sliver of light for all to see. "I'm falling apart," he finally gasped.

"No Amos," Jenkins said. "It's only a tooth, we've all lost them. We dare not dwell on it. Think of Lucretia and your young ones. It will keep you strong. You must draw her memory from your heart and soul, and you must believe in her now, as I know she does in you, my friend."

Lemuel put his hand to his head, then let it fall to his heart. He seemed stunned at Jenkins' words. He laughed, something most foreign in the dank hole. All of his fellows stared oddly at him as if he spoke a foreign language. Grabbing Amos' hand, he held the tooth higher in the light. "Flesh doesn't matter, Amos," he gasped. "In the end it's what's in the heart that matters!" He laughed again before slowly retreating from the light. His jovial face seemed most odd to Amos.

"We'll get through this," Jenkins added to his words, raising his swollen right hand up to the sliver of light. "We must!"

Amos' jaw dropped. He stared blankly into the darkness of Jenkins' corner.

A tired shuffle sounded from the darkness and Jenkins soon emerged into the light. He held a rusted tin cup up to Amos' lips. "Drink, my friend," he whispered. "Drink for life, for ours has not ended yet."

Amos took a long drink of the brackish water, slowly smiling.

As long as Wyoming men stood together, they stood strong, he thought, knowing his fellows thought the same.

## Chapter Twenty Eight
*Poor Pickering*

Jenkins watched the plump little man standing in the sliver of light, perplexed of how he managed to retain his weight, while he and the others wasted away. He didn't mind that Pickering turned to see his questioning stare every now and then.

He watched Pickering huff and play at the matted hair hanging from the back of his neck. Pickering had worked the hair into a matted rectangular mass; a sort of ever-ready pillow, simply needing to be flipped up to provide a barrier between his head and the cold floor of the dungeon when he laid down. Rather ingenious, Jenkins thought, though he himself lacked the energy needed to weave his own matted locks into a pillow. He lifted a hand to his coarse beard, wondering what a sight he and his fellows must present to the infrequent rats they heard scurrying about the filthy stone floor in the darkness.

Pickering started to giggle, which continued growing, instead of fading in light of their shared misery. His eyes lit up in the sliver of light. He lifted his hands high in a fruitless attempt to feel the light. He soon jumped and jumped madly toward the sliver of life, the sliver of light.

Jenkins wondered of his sanity, but he wondered of all their sanity. Only an oath to the King and a signed statement renouncing the Rebel cause separated them from their release from this miserable hole. But he thought of Moses Mount and Parshall Terry, knowing upon release, they must join their ranks. Their treason burned in his soul. He knew he could never join them, the hardhearted rats. The conservative devils be damned! Their King be damned! Their ways be damned!

He let his head fall to the wall against the thought. Pulling a clump of filthy straw from under him, he slipped it between his head and the cold wall. The frost on the wall seemed thicker this day. He snuggled as best he could in his rags against the cold breeze slipping through the cracks in the door.

He sat deathly still, intently listening in the deathly silence, thinking of how the normally unending clamor of barking and howling dogs, Indian children at play, chattering squaws, and bragging braves had died down in the past few days. Lately only the lone call of the Corporal of the Guard sounded in the cold air every few hours. Their ration of maggoty biscuits also began to come more irregularly. Winter, in all its fury, descended on Fort Niagara. Its frigid hand threatened famine about the isolated post.

More abrupt, and carrying a foreboding far worse than the breeze, the door suddenly creaked open. Pickering staggered back from the sudden influx of light, raising his hands to shield his eyes from the blast of daylight. A crude ladder abruptly fell in his place.

Well bundled feet crept down the rungs of the ladder. Many blankets coated the Indians, giving them the false appearance of plumpness. But their eyes, hollow, deep and dark, betrayed the empty stomachs beneath the blankets.

The Indians ignored the starving skeletons in the corners of the hole and circled Pickering, the plump one. Pickering gazed at the stark eyes staring at him and did as he always did, he giggled. The Indians did not share his jovial mood. One of them rudely lifted Pickering's arm, exposing his plump belly. Another Indian poked it with his spear point ever so gently. All of the Indians watched the plum man with an odd fascination, though through stark eyes of hunger. After a long moment, they looked to one another and grunted.

"Make good broth!" one of them finally said in English.

Pickering giggled all the louder.

"No laugh!" another Indian said. "No joke this! Many children's bellies empty! Many women's bellies empty!" He cocked an eye to his companions. "Many braves' bellies empty! Children cry from hunger! They must be quieted!"

Several of them harshly grabbed Pickering by the shoulders, gruffly prodding him toward the ladder. He stopped giggling. Stumbling toward the ladder, he collapsed. His eyes looked up to his captors in total despair. Crying, he begged to be let loose. Seeing no hint of the virtue of pity in the Indians' cold eyes, he let his body fall limp.

His dead weight proved too much for the starving Indians to lift, but they struggled on anyway, driven by mad hunger.

Pickering flailed his arms and kicked his legs, all the while muttering prayers and pleading for divine intervention, or human. No spark of humanity showed in the feverously struggling Indians, only stark hunger shone from their hollow eyes. All of life flashed before his eyes. Thoughts of green grass on a summer's day danced through his mind. Fragrances of flowers, a good meal cooking over a fire, and of his dear wife, flooded his senses. The crackle of a warm fire on a cold winter's day flashed along with the other thoughts. The expressions of loved ones and the simple joys of life flooded his beleaguered mind. All of the human emotions sparked to life in an instant. Oh, Mother! All of his thoughts suddenly ended on her, and he cried for her across the lonely miles of the frontier, to her in far away Connecticut.

Finally, a frustrated Indian yanked a tomahawk from his belt. Swinging it down on the blubbering man he just missed him, catching the tail end of his greatly matted locks. The Indian fiercely yanked against them, ripping them from back of his head.

Pickering's cries grew to a fantastic pitch.

The Indian grabbed the matted locks from the end of his tomahawk, holding them triumphantly in the air. Blood dripped from them down his arm, but he held the prize high, screaming almost as loudly as Pickering. Chatter rose from a group of women hovering over the door, gazing down at the spectacle with a certain awe.

His starving comrades, somehow energized by Pickering's desperate struggle, jumped to his aid. A war club immediately checked Amos York, sending his reeling back into his corner. Another doubled Fitch over in excruciating pain. Another slammed down on Jenkins' shoulder, barely missing his skull. The cruel blows promptly neutralized the Yankee threat. All of the injured men rolled about the stone floor, cussing and cursing the Indians with every gasp of their breaths.

Several more warriors spilled down the ladder into the mayhem. Roughly grabbing Pickering, they forced him up the ladder by brute force, ignoring his pleas for mercy.

One last warrior stood behind his fellows, watching them struggle desperately with their equally desperate quarry. He stopped with one foot on the bottom rung of the ladder, seeming overwhelmed with disgust. He bowed his head, catching the other prisoners rolling on the floor out of the corner of his eye. Their groans replaced his disgust with anger. Spitting on the floor, he turned toward them, his face turning dark and sour. "You white eyes' hunger for land cause all this!" he exclaimed through gritted teeth. He put a hand to his stomach. "Your hunger makes our hunger all the deeper, for in your lust for land you forsake all before you! Your lust sweeps the land, changing it forever! Now others starve because of your quarrels! Which in the end are about land!" He shook his head at the ragged white men crawling to their corners to shield themselves in darkness from his wrath. His hand fell to a tomahawk in his belt, but he quickly jerked his hand from it as if it burned. "No, too many have died already," he muttered. "Cannot the white eyes see?" He turned and slowly climbed up the ladder, feeling the eyes of the white men on his back. "Now we see about hunger!" he added before slamming the door.

"What hell is this place?" Jenkins gasped. Amos York grunted, struggling to wrap a filthy rag around his bleeding skull. Fitch still lay on the floor, rolling about in pain. Jenkins fumbled for him in the darkness, trying to comfort him. "Be still," he said, vainly trying to stop the man from rolling in pain. "Let the pain pass."

"If those bastards return they'll take us all or no one!" Amos yelled at the door.

"Yes," Jenkins agreed. Fitch groaned in approval through his gasps of agony.

A loud scream suddenly echoed through the thick door; a spine tingling wail which seemed to vibrate through the soul of the cold fort. Each scream grew in pitch after the other. They all recognized the voice, knowing it would never bear a laugh or nervous giggle again. Each agonizing scream drew visions of horror beyond mere imagination.

How could any white man bear witness to this horror without protest? Jenkins wondered. Where were the Tories? Where were the British to stop this madness? Perhaps the Indian was right, the greater lusts of the white men overpowered all of their other senses. "How any civilized man could bear witness to that horror without protest I dare not wonder," Jenkins finally said aloud.

"Whilst he suffers, we suffer," Amos said. "But tortured or not, he shall find relief in heaven in the end." A particularly long scream scratched through the cold air, silencing Fitch's groans.

"They are cold hearted bastards indeed, born of the heart of the wilderness," Amos said. "And the King fondles them for his own purposes! We must gain our liberty from him! And all tyrants!"

"That we must," Jenkins agreed, staring into the sliver of light. "Dear God deliver us from this horror, and please have pity on poor Pickering's soul. Amen."

"We must deliver ourselves!" York yelled over the lingering screams.

Fitch gasped, pushing Jenkins away. Crawling back to his corner he openly wept.

Jenkins stumbled to his feet and stood in the sliver of light. Looking up through the crack in the door, he started praying for deliverance from this hell. Pickering's wails slowed and suddenly died. Jenkins had no doubt why. The man passed into the next world, tortured and betrayed by this one. He muttered another prayer for the poor man.

"Come now, John," Amos said. "Sit back down in your corner. What do you expect? A deliverer from this hell? There are no angels here but the ones whom dwell in our hearts."

"But is that not where all angels reside?" Jenkins asked, pointing his finger up to the door. He rolled his eyes in disgust.

"What?" Amos asked. "Is that ghoulish bastard about the door?"

Jenkins slowly nodded his head.

Amos York threw the bloody rag from his head and stumbled

toward the sliver of light. Wiping the blood from his eyes, he peered up into the light, catching a shadow pacing back and forth through it. "Hell be about your conscience, fine sir!" he yelled at the ghoul behind the door. "Poor Pickering! He never harmed a soul in his whole life! Is this the King's justice!?!"

A quick huff answered his call, dripping with disgust. Boots shuffled away from the door.

"Cruel Tory bastard!" Amos said, collapsing against Jenkins in total exhaustion. Jenkins eased him back to his corner. Ripping the sleeve from his ragged shirt, he fashioned a bandage over his bleeding head. He then turned, stumbling back to his own corner of the dark and cold hole. Fitch's piteous moans only magnified the great agony sweeping over his soul. What despair. What a sacrifice he and his fellows lay at the alter of freedom. Though he doubted if Pickering would have sworn allegiance to the King he would have been spared, he did not hear the man utter one word of it in his total desperation. He gave his life here, in this British hellhole, for others. For America. He would not be forgotten.

A rage burned in his heart through the pains of his mortal body. The British had done nothing to save the poor innocent man from the savages. In this, their greatest indifference, they proved themselves the most cruelest fiends.

As the sliver of light faded and the sounds of feasting died above the door, he nestled himself in the filthy and soiled straw below him. He rubbed his hand, calling upon the only memory which could save his sanity from this hell, the promise of his dear Beth.

"Beth, oh, my dear Beth, shall I ever see you again, my love?" he muttered under his breath before drifting off into a restless sleep. He silently feared he would only see her in his memories again.

## Chapter Twenty Nine
*The Hole at Niagara*

Jenkins sat huddled in his corner, his face to the cold stone walls, vainly trying to lick the drops of condensation on them to relieve his terrible thirst. Every since poor Pickering's ordeal, they saw nothing of anyone. For days they lay in their filthy hole without so much as a new pail of brackish water to relieve their thirst. He turned his eyes toward his fellows. Lemuel lay moaning in the darkness of his corner. Amos sat staring blankly at the sliver of light. No shadows, good or bad, broke it.

He turned his face back to the wall, rolling his swollen tongue against the bricks again. It scratched against the rough stones with little moisture to quell his raging thirst. Bowing his head, he listened past Lemuel's constant low moan. Let the door open again, he thought, carry me out as you did poor Pickering, you savage fiends! End it now! You can have my body, but you will never possess my soul! This, only God holds! This you shall not have! If I die now, it shall be with the satisfaction that I pass bearing true faith in God and everything I and my family hold sacred. My soul, my soul, Beth, my soul is one with yours. This is, and shall always be, no matter what distance or horrors separate us. It is everlasting. It is the eternal gift of love. He found himself chanting her name on his parched lips, rubbing the back of his right hand profusely. The pain meant nothing. Only Beth meant something now.

Somewhere in the back of his mind he heard the door creak. But he felt numb and beyond it now. He kept his face against the stones, chanting the name of the only one to bring him any sort of relief, beside God himself, whom he felt certain to soon meet in heaven, anyway. He ignored the sound of one of his fellows scrambling across the cold floor and the thud of the door closing again. Strangely, he almost heard a faint thank you in the cold air, but it made no difference now, anyway.

His mind drifted further away. He felt his soul sink down through his cold bones and into the dank floor. A memory, seemingly from nowhere, pulled it back into his body. Visions of Wyoming, his beloved home, flashed through his mind. Its crowning mountains sat coated with a fresh blanket of new fallen snow in his mind. The trees speckling the mountains glistened with a beauty all their own. The snow made all clean and still. Nothing stirred but a slight motion out of the corner of his eye. He turned slowly, about to witness another vision of beauty; a woman with gentle features graced by the hand of Providence. Her radiant beauty shone under the hood of the cloak covering her. Pure and gentle as the snow. A cabin sat nestled on the mountain behind her, smoke curling from its chimney into the crisp air above it. He stared at the woman, hoping by sheer will to coax her to push back the hood and reveal the full beauty he sensed beneath it. As if sensing his will through a silent language only they shared, she responded. Her smile shone as the light of the first day, perpetual and pure. The smile sent rays of warmth tingling through his frozen bones, invigorating his senses to life again, flooding the empty reservoir of his heart with the elixir of love, faith, and hope. But the demon of fear, always close at hand near love, hope, and faith, showed its ugly face from the shadows to her rear. His elation melted into solid fear. A shadowy form, cloaked with a blanket thrown aside to reveal a painted body, lunged forward, the feathers about its head bobbing wildly from gruff motions. The painted demon's cold eyes locked onto her, defenseless and still. Her questioning eyes looked to him, too fearful to turn about and face the horror. Save me! Oh, my love, save me! A raised tomahawk appeared behind her head. A gruff hand twisted her about. The tomahawk cocked further back in the demon's hand, certain to bring a death blow. He wanted to scream. He wanted to burst forth, but his feet suddenly felt heavy like lead. He forced his feet painfully forward. He forced a scream of warning past the great lump in his throat. He had too! He had to save Beth from the savage!

Suddenly, a cold and clammy hand fell against his shoulder. He awoke, finding himself screaming at the top of his lungs. He flailed against the cold hand. The touch of a human hand, no matter how slight, felt foreign to him. He shuddered. "John! John!" sounded loud in his ears. Somehow it felt familiar, as if from another time, and far away, far into the past. He stopped flailing his hands and opened his tired eyes.

Amos stared back at him, his eyes suddenly alive with a faint glimmer. A glimmer he hadn't seen in a long while. A foreign glimmer. A glimmer of hope. "Come John!" Amos' voice echoed through his madness. "Snap out of it man! Snap out of it!"

He ignored the voice and only muttered "Beth" in response.

The hand grew firmer, turning his face from the wall. He opened his eyes again to a filthy and wiry-bearded face bearing bulging eyes. "Snap out of it!" the face said again, gobbling down a biscuit between pleas. The man beamed with each new bite, holding up his estimable prize between ravenous bites.

"Yes, John!" Amos said between bites, finally noticing a faint glimmer of recognition in his friend's eyes. He shoved one of the biscuits under his nose, watching the eyes liven even more. "It's real John! It's food, by blessed God, yes it is!"

Jenkins instinctively grabbed the biscuit and immediately

devoured it. He choked and coughed for an instant, but still ravenously forced the biscuit into his mouth.

"Wait, John," Amos pleaded, leaning back across the floor to grab a bucket. A new bucket, filled with fresh, pure water. He dragged the bucket across the stone floor. Dipping a noggin into it, he raised it to his choking friend's lips. "Yes, this is good water!" he said, taking a quick drink from the noggin before putting it to his friend's lips. His friend ceased choking on the dry biscuit. "And these are good biscuits too!"

Jenkins' weak hands reached for another biscuit, marveling at the ample haversack full of them Amos stuffed into his hands.

"Yes, man, eat your fill!" Amos declared, scrambling over to another corner. "We've plenty!" he added while tending to Lemuel, whose eyes also glared with an equally stark stare of disbelief.

Jenkins watched them, suddenly realizing more light shone into their dark hole. He looked over to the ragged, filthy, and bearded men, wondering how he himself appeared. He continued eating ravenously, looking up to the open door in awe. "What is this?" he asked through gulps of biscuits and water.

"It's life, dear John!" Amos answered from across the floor. "It's life, by God, John, it looks as if our prayers have been answered! We are to live after all!" He looked down to Lemuel cradled in his arms, grinning from ear to ear, suddenly full of the promise of life. Lemuel grunted between bites of biscuit and tried to yell a huzza, which fell short in his parched throat. Amos quickly raised a noggin of the fresh water to his lips.

Jenkins laughed in spite of it all. Amos and Lemuel quickly joined him. Soon all three lie huddled in the middle of the dank stone dungeon, staring up at the light and eagerly praising God for their feast. Each soon became lost in the promise of the outside world, silently contemplating their lives. Their eyes looked beyond the door and their imaginations flashed with visions of Wyoming and their homes. Oh dear, sweet, home! Oh, sweet Wyoming! Its promise never seemed so great.

## Chapter Thirty
### *The Ghoul*

Jenkins found his strength increasing with the regular and plentiful rations provided to them over the past few days. He took to basking in the increased light, standing under it for hours, closing his eyes and raising his face to its soothing rays. He often looked to the open door a half dozen feet above them and imagined scampering through it in the dead of the night. But after examining the smooth stone walls, he knew it to be impossible. But one could dream. Dreams kept the spirit alive, he thought, glancing out of the corner of his eye to Lemuel lying on the floor next to him.

"Forget it," Lemuel said, as if reading his thoughts. Rolling over on some fresh straw, he mumbled another warning before wrapping himself in a few of the ragged blankets thrown down to them along with the fresh straw and better food. He slowly crept into his corner.

Of all of them Lemuel appeared the weakest, Jenkins thought. Groans of agony still crept from his throat every now and then. But Amos seemed to be coming along fine. He turned toward Amos' corner and smiled. "Must be late March or perhaps early April," he said.

Nothing but a lip smack and a grunt answered him from Amos's corner. Straw and blankets covered him completely, and except for a foot sticking out from under the pile, he saw nothing of the man. He stepped over to him but stopped upon hearing a bustle above them. "Sounds all a fuss up there," he said, looking up to the open door. "If a man could just get up to the edge of the door he could lift himself right out of here."

"Oh, yes," Lemuel scoffed. "No one would notice a living skeleton bathed in months of filth, with matted hair, a wiry beard, and clothed in rags. He could just saunter right out the front gate, fer sure. Forget it!'"

"Sounds not unlike many a frontiersman I've seen," Amos said, popping up from under his covering of straw and blankets. He chuckled. Neither of his comrades laughed with him, but he rose anyway, joining Jenkins in the light. He looked the man up and down and said, "Perhaps Lem has a point, John, we do look quite a sight."

"But at night, Amos," Jenkins said. "At night."

"I'm sure the sentries would love that," Amos said, shaking his head. "They're cold British regulars, they are, with no thought at all of mercy or liberty, or any other damn thing, but just their orders. You know it as well as I. They'll point and fire their muskets in any direction they're ordered to, with no regard at all. They don't give a damn whether America remains part of their empire or not. No sir, you'll find no sympathy with that lot!" Stumbling back to his corner, he plopped down on the straw and blankets. "Give it a rest, dear John," he added, lifting up some of the fresh straw in his hands. "Things are getting better, they is. I say we wait it out. Perhaps an exchange awaits us! God shall grant us liberty again, we must keep our faith in him."

"Tell that to Pickering's wife," Jenkins said. "And I am sure Pike and Boyd wouldn't appreciate your thoughts of their kind."

"They're different John," Amos said. "They are men of good sense who came over to the light they saw from the darkness of their ranks. And we all mourn poor Pickering, God bless his soul."

Jenkins rolled his eyes, squatted, then leaped toward the open door, falling well short of it. Rolling on the floor to regain his footing for another leap he gasped, "Did you see? I almost made it!"

"You fell well short, man!" Amos immediately said. "Look about you, dear John! I may make it with you, but what of poor Lem? He's still in such pain he can barely straighten up! The rascals did something to his innards. What say you? Are we to leave him to suffer whilst we escape? I am sure the savages would love that, and make a broth of him too!"

Lemuel groaned in answer.

Jenkins looked down to him and then to the back of his raw hand. "I must get back to Beth and out of this hellish pit!" he gasped.

"I know, dear John," Amos said, recognizing the zeal in his eyes every time he heard the word Beth. "I do miss my Lucretia and young ones, too, as Lem does his dear Rebecca. We must keep our faith! Thy will be done! When it comes down to it, faith is all we have left!"

The strong thud of marching feet hushed all. They listened in the silence of their dark hole, daring not even to breathe, lest it muffle the sounds. The footsteps stopped just to the edge of the overhead door. A few footsteps shuffled forward from the rest.

"Jenkins!" a voice of authority boomed down into the silent hole. A ladder immediately plopped down through the door. "Lieutenant Jenkins!" the voice boomed again. "Present yourself! Come forth!"

Jenkins retreated back into his corner. Amos and Lemuel both nodded to him. Amos brought a finger to his lips.

A head popped over the edge of the doorway. Gasping from the stench, it popped back from the edge. "They aren't moving a muscle, Sergeant!" a voice reported above the door.

"Come now, you filthy rebel!" a voice roared. "If you make us come down into that horrid hole to fetch you, you will be regretting it for the rest of your days!"

Amos slowly crept forward, peering up through the doorway.

"Them's regulars, they is," he whispered, sinking back into his dark corner. "Bloody lobsters fer sure!"

"Yes!" a voice boomed in response. "Of the King's Eighth Regiment of Foot! Come now, you filthy lot! Don't dally! I warn you for the last time, for if we have to descend into your mucky hole you'll regret it, that I grant you!"

Jenkins looked over to Amos and Lemuel. Both stared at the door with faces filled with resolve, but looking at their still-gaunt faces and hollow eyes, he reconsidered his stubbornness. He stumbled toward the ladder. "Hold fast, you lobster bastards!" he called up the ladder, placing his foot on its first rung. "I'm coming, if you promise to leave my mates alone!"

"You're in no condition to make demands, Rebel!" the voice snarled back.

Jenkins looked to his mates before slowly climbing the ladder. A gruff hand welcomed him at the top of it, yanking him up the last rungs of the ladder. "Here now!" a voice behind the hand demanded. "Look smart for the sergeant here, you rebel rat!"

Red-coated soldiers immediately stood all around him, threateningly leveling their bayoneted muskets at his person. One of them parted their number and strutted full in front of him. Raising his upper lip in disgust, he waved a regal hand toward some steps not far from the door. Musket butts immediately pushed him toward the steps.

"Now if you don't mind, rat, get a move on!" the regal man said with a boot to his rear.

The glaring sunshine made him hesitate for another moment to raise his hand to shield them from its foreign rays. Another kick forced him up the steps, followed by the unmistakable prick of a bayonet. He struggled forwards, braving a glance out of a nearby window as his eyes finally adjusted to the light. The bright clothes of the Indians drew his eye. They bustled all about the parade ground of the fort. Feathers danced about their heads. The tired rhythmic thud of corn mauls into wooden mortars echoed about the fort's walls. Endless chatter, in a dozen different languages, added to the clamor. Whites, some dressed in the most primitive frontier garb, walked among finely dressed gentlemen. The whole place reminded him of a large fair of some sort. They also all appeared well fed and almost jovial, and the thought of poor Pickering drew nothing but hatred from the depths of his soul, as well as for the indifferent soldiers, whom now seemed ample in number. There could be no excuse for their indifference, which in turn, had allowed poor Pickering's demise.

A glaring set of eyes from the top of the steps he climbed fueled his hatred all the more. A man stood there all dressed in green, staring indignantly at him. Locking eyes with him, the brazen man stood full in the threshold at the top of the staircase, showing no signs of giving way.

"Well, Jenkins, my friend. You're looking rather pale, man, you should get some more sun," the green-coated man said, crossing his arms. "My, what a few months can do to a man!" he added.

"Go to hell you traitorous bastard!" Jenkins replied, coming to a stop in front of the man obstructing their progress.

The British sergeant eyed both of the men. "Come now, Ranger, be a good chap and clear the way," he said, motioning him aside with his hand. "Carry on your colonial bickering some other time. We here are about the King's business, so make way!"

Terry stood firm, his hatred overpowering him. His hand fell to a pistol tucked in his belt.

"I wouldn't, you colonial devil!" the sergeant said, positioning himself between the two men. He plowed forward, pushing the disgruntled ranger aside. "I am not about to play silly games, you rascal! Now get!" he said, waving the rest of his detachment forward.

They all marched past the ranger, grumbling in disgust before rambling down the steps. His muffled curses followed his every step down the steps, but soon dissipated with distance. Ignoring him, they marched down the corridor, coming to a stop near the end of it.

The sergeant stiffened up and cocked back his head, his eyes suddenly full of purpose. He pulled on the bottom of his fine red jacket to pull it taunt against his frame before stepping through a door. After a few seconds, he emerged, pointing toward the door.

Jenkins stood still between the guards, waiting for their prod.

"If you would be so kind, sir," the sergeant said, nodding his head toward the door. "Major Butler wishes an audience with you."

Jenkins stepped back for a moment, overcome by the gruff sergeant's change of demeanor. Quickly regaining his composure, he stepped through the door, suddenly self-conscience of the filthy rags clinging to his body.

A white haired man sitting at a desk looked up from under his spectacles. He slowly sat the pen and paper he held in his hands down. The glaring light from the window behind him caused Jenkins to squint and raise a hand to shield his eyes.

The white haired man cocked an eye behind him, gazing upon the seemingly endless face of Lake Ontario through the window. He pushed the spectacles up on his forehead. "Yes," he said. "Vast and great, worthy to be part of the empire, don't you think?" he asked.

Jenkins shook his head and lowered his hand. "To hell with that," he said.

The white haired man slowly turned, raising one of his bushy black eyebrows. He too shook his head. "Stubborn to the last," he muttered. "But one does not expect reason from such an unreasonable lot as you rebels. Truculent devils." He shuffled a few of the papers around and looked to the cocked pistol near the edge of the table, making sure the obstinate rebel's eyes followed his. "A moment, a moment," he said, raising his pen to the paper. He lowered the spectacles to his eyes and started scribbling on the papers. "Always paper,'" he said. "The King wants his documents proper, you know. Dot all the I's."

Jenkins glanced about the room. A cabinet sat in one corner, a lone chair in another, with the only other furnishing, a coat rack, gracing the other corner. A green coat, one he had come to despise, hung from it. A finely plumed cocked hat sat on the other end of the desk. Another door, apparently connecting it to the row of rooms along this side of the building's wall, sat to the right of the door. Muffled voices sounded through it.

Jenkins suddenly wondered just why Butler had summoned him. To watch him do paperwork? On second thought, he didn't mind. Anyplace from the hole seemed great, even in foul company. He would stand here all day to be free of the hole. He glanced to the window behind Butler. Blue, speckled with glints of pure sunlight, stretched out as far as the eye could see. Cherry blossoms covered a flat stand of ground between the fort's wall and the edge of the blue water. He drank in its splendor, overwhelmed by God's work, even in this horrid place.

"Yes, now," Butler said, removing his spectacles and standing. "Well, my rebel, Lieutenant Jenkins." He pushed back the chair and walked to the window, pulling a snuffbox from his waistcoat's pocket. He glanced out the window at the sight that so entranced his guest, his sour expression betraying his thoughts. He quickly lifted a pinch of snuff to each of his nostrils and stepped back behind the desk, closer to the cocked pistol.

Jenkins finally tore his eyes from the beautiful lake and glanced down at the rags cloaking his filthy body. No doubt the major found the need to draw snuff to quell his smell. Raising his hands, he stared at his long and dirt-caked fingernails. Only the red spot on the back of his right hand showed clear of filth. Shreds of his buckskin trousers clung to his legs. His hunting shirt hung in ragged strips rag about his bony frame. The hint of his long and scraggly beard spread below his eyes. His moccasins had long ago rotted from his feet, which appeared black with filth. He felt the thick yellow film on his neglected teeth. He only wished he could smell, imagining his odor to be quite strong, but his nose had become too long accustomed to it for him to bear it any notice. A smug smile grew across his face imagining the assault his smell caused his enemy's senses. Any victory, no matter how insignificant, brought comfort to him.

"Yes," the major said, noticing the odd smile. What in heavens did this man have to smile about, anyway? "I realize your confinement must be most unpleasant, but you people must be taught a lesson." He shook his head. "You perplex me, and many others, to say the least."

Lifting his handkerchief to his mouth, he let out a muffled cough. "I am Major Butler, commanding the King's Rangers, Butler's Rangers, in fact." Smug pride overcame him, lifting his nose in the air.

Jenkins' smile dripped into a frown. John Butler and his son Walter; the word treason drew no better description in his mind.

"I shall never understand your treason against your God-given sovereign," Butler said as if reading his mind.

"The Lord giveth, and the Lord taketh away," Jenkins answered.

"Yes," Butler said with a huff. "We do all have our opinions, we do at that." He shuffled some papers on the desk. "Anyhow, now to the matter for which I have summoned you." He picked up one paper in particular, raising it high in his hand. "This is an order I have drafted to exchange your two comrades at New York, seeing how they were not taken in arms." He looked up at Jenkins. "Your matter is quite different, I daresay, what with you being an officer in the service of the so-called Continental Congress. Your exchange may have repercussions among our faithful Indian allies." He glanced over to the open door and nodded his head. Two Indians promptly strode through it, one wearing a bright red jacket.

"However," Butler said. "I have made arrangements with our faithful allies to exchange you with one of their chiefs captured at Oriskany, that is, as long as they are the ones overseeing the exchange."

Jenkins straightened his back and stood tall. The Indians walked up to him, not in the least bit seeming to be bothered by his smell, and appraised him. Folding their arms, they glared at him and then looked to each other. After a long and silent moment, they looked to Butler.

Butler raised his eyebrows, bearing the look of a cocksure nobleman. "Before you are to depart I have arranged better accommodations for you and your fellows," he said to Jenkins.

Another figure shuffled by the open door, seeming to gauge the mood of the room before entering. He soon marched into the room.

"Colonel Bolton," Butler said with a smart nod of his head. "Colonel Butler," Bolton said, choosing to refer to Butler by his militia title. He nodded back at him. "Have you explained it all?" he asked with a slight glance to Jenkins.

"Yes sir, I have," Butler answered.

Jenkins stiffened and did not move, somehow recognizing the officer. The ghoul, he realized, the ghoul! He tightened his fists. The Indians notice his actions, laughing deeply.

The British officers cast and annoying look to them and then turned back to the papers on the desk. After mumbling something to Butler, Colonel Bolton turned toward the door. "Very well," he said, raising his nose to the stiff colonial officer before him. Lifting a pristine white handkerchief, he gently wiped his nose. "I am sorry for any inconvenience you may have endured, Lieutenant, but such is war, you know." He gracefully exited the room without so much as another glance behind him.

"Sergeant!" Butler called, sitting back down behind the desk.

Sir!" the sergeant immediately answered, entering the room smartly.

"Escort the lieutenant back to his cell," he ordered, pausing only long enough for a quick glance up from the papers covering his desk. "See that he and his fellows are bathed and given decent clothing."

"Bathed sir?" the sergeant asked.

"Yes!" Butler answered, pointing his quill pen over his shoulder. "We have plenty of water. Have we not?"

"Why yes sir, the whole of Lake Ontario," the sergeant answered.

"Well I don't think the stench of three rebels, no matter how intense, is enough to foul those great waters," Butler said on the hint of a laugh.

"No sir," the sergeant said, taking Jenkins by the arm. He glanced indifferently at the Indians and pushed his prisoner out of the room. "I don't pity you on your sojourn," he said under his breath to Jenkins. "They'd just as soon scalp you Wyoming people as to look at you! I've seen it! What you have done to deserve such ire is beyond me, but you have a special place in their hearts, indeed you do!"

Jenkins shrugged at the words. He flooded his thoughts with his sweet Beth, and Wyoming. He must keep faith, it, and only it, may deliver him from this living nightmare, this living hell called Fort Niagara.

## Chapter Thirty One
### *A Friend, an Enemy*

Jenkins sat with his back against a tree, curiously watching three Indians around a nearby fire. They seemed more jovial to say the least, chattering and joking among themselves. He had barely witnessed one smile between them on their long journey from Niagara. Now smiles seemed to be the normal. No doubt their proximity to Albany had a lot to do with their changing mood, sensing an end of their long trek and an successful exchange. *Ghalto*, he heard the word many times on their trek, and now heard it more and more between their words. Apparently, they thought well of the man, and he must be the chief for whom he was to be exchanged. He wished he knew more of their language to learn more of this Ghalto. He also wished the man well, for he feared his own fate if some bad will befell him, for his fate now entwined with his own.

He wriggled against the tight leather thongs binding his hands and holding his neck rigid against the rough tree bark. He moved ever so slightly, not wishing to draw any of the Indian's eyes. Finally gaining some slight relief, he eased back, always locking eyes with his escorts. He watched them intently, noting all their actions, customs, and manners, for one of the rules of war stood out in his mind: Know thy enemy.

He flashed his mental notes through his memory, wishing to keep them fresh with repetition. The visions of the great number of Tories and Indians assembling about Niagara before they left the fort flashed greatly in his mind. The fort showed all the makings of a great campaign this season. He prayed for it not to be against Wyoming, but the hushed whispers he overhead all pointed to it. Another reason he wished for this exchange to be concluded; he had to get word back to Wyoming!

All the Indians suddenly stood, looking anxiously up the trail. They danced and whooped in anticipation of news from a returning party. But their eyes, and their hearts, fell sullenly to the ground noticing Ghalto did not show among the party. A haunting low whoop sounded in the still air, its report finally squashing any hope of the waiting Indians. All of them immediately let out their own low whoops in answer. Soon loud whoops of despair echoed through the lonely pines, only to cease all at once a few moments later.

The silence did not bode well for Jenkins, and he knew it. Perking his head up against the tree, he watched the crestfallen Indians file into camp. They all slowly sat down around the fire, silent and still. He craned his head to see Ghalto and sighed. Something had happen to the chief, and, because of it, something would definitely happen to him.

With a sinking feeling, he noticed another missing, Red Jacket. Now he had no one, and no hope.

He kept perfectly still, watching the crestfallen Indians sitting so still around the fire. None uttered a word or even looked to one another. It sent a cold chill down his spine. He tugged against the leather thongs to no avail. Tales of the tortures he had heard many a time around Wyoming suddenly cut through his soul. They seemed stark and ever so real to him now. Oh, dear Beth! Oh, dear God!

A large brave suddenly stood tall. Muttering something, he wiped the backs of both of his hands as if some imaginary foul substance stained them. Jutting his head back, he emitted a loud mournful wail. Lowering his head, he locked eyes on the white devil tied to the tree. The hatred he felt for all white eyes surged through his soul and glared in his eyes. He took one angry step after another toward the white devil, never taking his dark eyes from the terrified white man.

Jenkins flexed his muscles against the thongs, fueled by a desperate thirst for life. If he could just wriggle loose he would sprint away from the dark devils of the forest, denying them of their cruel sport, and thus, saving his life. His new burst of strength flexed his muscles against the thongs making them whine. His bulging eyes watched the awful brave draw closer. His heart thudded in his ears. He tugged with all his might, closing his eyes against the pain and the vision of death approaching him. Each of the brave's slow steps sent new shards of terror surging through his soul. He watched the brave's hand fall to the sheath on his belt, yanking his knife from it. The blade glistened in the sun. My God man! Yank yourself free and bolt past the demon and into the folds of the dark forest! If you could only gain them, no one, devil or not, will catch you! Closing his eyes, he struggled against the thongs with all his might. My God! My dear God help! The stern footsteps sounded closer. No! No!

Another rush of footsteps sounded behind the braves', suddenly stopping them both. He opened his wide eyes. The brave stood but a few feet from him, glaring at him with the gleaming blade clenched tightly in his fist. He felt his heaving and angry breath on his face. A hand to the warrior's shoulder had checked his advance and now he turned his glaring eyes to the red jacketed chief standing to his side.

Red Jacket stared back just as intently into the brave's stark eyes. His angry tongue rebuked the warrior as his free hand flailed in the air, giving emphasis to each of his loud words.

The other braves quickly gathered around, anxious to see the victor of this clash of wills. They, too, quickly drew the scorn of their leader and the sharp words of his severe tongue lashing.

The large brave finally spouted a long protest, which seemed to hit a brick wall against Red Jacket, a master of oratory. Some fought with the tomahawk, others fought with words, but none with words as sharp as Red Jacket's. They rivaled the sharpest blade, and somehow cut deeper, at least to this brave.

Finally, the disgusted brave flung his arms high in the air and stomped off toward the fire, drawing several of the other warriors along with him. A few of the others stood staring at Red Jacket and to the white devil he so avidly defended. The suspicion in their eyes spoke for their silent tongues.

Red Jacket huffed. Shaking his head, he stared deathly at the white devil struggling madly against the tree. Raising his hand in a great sweeping motion, he stepped toward the man, bringing his hand down hard against his face. The hard slap resounded throughout the camp, silencing all their tongues. All eyes shot to the chief standing tall in front of the white devil.

To everyone's surprise, Red Jacket slipped a hand under his coat and drew a tomahawk, sinking it into the tree just above the white devil's head. His tongue came alive with curses and taunts in the face of the devil. The devil's eyes showed wide, apparently getting the gist of the tongue lashing, despite the language. Somehow Red Jacket's actions spoke louder than his words in the tense moment.

Several of the warriors danced, drawing their own knifes and tomahawks in anticipation of sport. One of them approached the devil with his tomahawk held high and ready to strike until Red Jacket's cutting words checked his advance. After rebuking the brave, he slapped the white devil again, yelling at him with such anger his spittle sprayed full in his face. "Ghalto dead!" he screamed in English. "Killed by the pox! The curse you white devils brought with you across the great sea!" He chattered some more in Seneca and then slapped Jenkins on the face again all the harder, seeming to ignoring the tears sliding down the white devil's face. Cocking an eye to the warriors watching him, he checked his last slap, raising his hands to the heavens instead. He danced about, yelling with such fury his booming voice cracked several times.

His hand suddenly fell to his belt. Yanking his knife from it, he swooped down with one smooth motion onto the devil, checking the knife's blade against the man's Adam's apple. He locked eyes with the bulging eyes staring at him. "No!" he exclaimed, making sure he spoke in English. "This death would be too easy! *Kanadasaga* and the gauntlet await you, white devil! Then we see how you cry at the post!" Pulling the knife away, he spat onto the ground. "Yes! Then we see!" He spat again, gesturing for the others to follow him back to the fire. They reluctantly followed the urging of their chief, talking and waving their hands in angry motions. Pure contempt burned in their eyes.

One of the braves suddenly bolted back toward the prisoner. Stopping just short of him, he stared deathly into his eyes.

Jenkins stared back indignantly.

The brave looked to the rebel's crimson cheeks, running his knife blade gently over them. He wetted the knife's blade with his Jenkins' tears without actually cutting him. Finally, he jerked the blade toward the white devil's mouth. Running it across his own tongue his eyes glared, relishing the taste of the white devil's tears, the taste of his fear.

Jenkins still did not flinch.

The brave's lower lip rose, exposing his teeth. Snapping his jaw, he contorted his face in the most gruesome manner, snarling and grunting.

Jenkins' stoic eyes stared back at him. "Do your worse you cruel red bastard," he muttered. "You'll gain no satisfaction from me!"

A smirk stretched across the brave's face. "I will kill you at Kanadasaga," the brave answered. "We will see how brave the Bostonian is with his skin peeled away by my knife and yanked down to his feet. We will see when I hold his bleeding fingers in my hands. We shall see when his pumping heart is held in my hands before his eyes."

Red Jacket's scolding voice sounded behind him, turning his scornful eyes away. Running his fingers over the knife's edge, he screamed before standing and heeding his chief's warning. Spitting on the ground, he rose and slowly joined the others circling the fire.

Red Jacket immediately rebuked the warrior, but the warrior only waved his hands in disgust at him as he would a pesky fly. The other warriors welcomed him into their folds. They soon became engrossed in a deep conversation of their plight with one another, so engrossed they little noticed Red Jacket meandering away from the fire.

Red Jacket at first paced nervously about, giving the appearance of one deep in thought, and wishing to be left alone with his thoughts. He meandered from tree to tree, slowly growing closer to the prisoner tree. When certain no curious eyes followed him, he carefully sat down in front of the gaunt-eyed white man tied ruthlessly tight to the tree.

"It bad," he said, almost on a whisper, casting a nervous eye back to the loud warriors arguing around the fire. "It bad," he said again, staring Jenkins straight in the eye. "But I make promise to you and in that I shall not fail." His eyes shot to the knife in his hand. With a slow and careful movement he slowly cut one of the leather thongs and lowered the knife to the ground, covering it with a few leaves.

Jenkins gasped and flexed his muscles free, stopping as Red Jacket raised a warning hand to him.

The Indian looked back over his shoulder to the fire and then back to the perplexed white man. "Wait until night," he warned.

Jenkins slowly nodded, promptly ceasing his telltale movements. He stared in amazement at the Indian.

"Your death means nothing but waste," Red Jacket explained on a whisper. "War, it make all men crazy. Take blade, but wait until night falls, and warriors sleep." The hint of a smile broke through his serious stare. "Brother, go, you live with your family, and allow us to live with ours. I hope this message lives in your heart."

Shouts from the fireside gave both of them a start. Both men's eyes darted nervously about in fear. Hearing no more shouts, Red Jacket nodded to Jenkins before quickly changing his demeanor and standing. He yelled his familiar curses, giving Jenkins a kick. "Kanadasaga!" he yelled. "We see how you cry at Kanadasaga! White devil!"

Spitting on the ground in front of Jenkins one last time, he turned and marched back to the others, using his gift of oration to quell any doubts or suspicions of him, and also to divert the warriors' rage. With his tongue he weaved a tapestry which soon totally engrossed the angry warriors' conversation, keeping them occupied and away from their helpless enemy in their midst.

Jenkins watched and listened with a new respect and appreciation. Though he barely heard or understood Red Jacket's words appeasing the warriors, their cadence and tone did have an almost hypnotic effect. Some men of true heart rise above circumstances, even amidst madness, he reasoned. Some men, but not all, he whispered to himself, watching the warriors now painting their heavily tattooed bodies in the flickering light of the firelight in the dusk.

Turning his attention to his own plight, he carefully wriggled one of his hands free against the severed thongs and clutched the knife in his hands, careful to give the appearance of still being helplessly bond to the tree. He flinched and wriggled to conceal the knife behind him upon the sudden approach of one of the warriors. He looked to Red Jacket, whom did not even cast a curious eye at the warrior. He clenched the knife tightly in his hands, ready to slice the warrior's throat, but only laughed when the warrior smeared his face with black paint.

The warrior cocked a curious eye to the crazed white man and shrugged his shoulders, returning to the fireside to finish painting himself.

Jenkins thought it odd that they paint themselves before sleeping, but reasoned they intended to depart well before the sun rose and did not wish anything on the morrow to slow their trek to Kanadasaga. It did not bode well for him, thinking of the black paint smeared upon his face. Red paint meant life, and adoption into the tribe, but black meant death by torture. All of the warriors even painted themselves black to covey their intent to their prisoner. No, it did not look good.

He moved his hand ever so slightly to rub the back of his other hand. Thoughts of Beth calmed his anxious mind, giving him the patience to wait for the darkness of the night before he moved. He waited until well into the night and for the crackling fire to die before carefully rising from the tree, moving as a mere apparition for fear of the painted demons' ever watchful eyes. He moved as one with the shadows of the night before he slipped into the dark folds of the deep forest, never noticing the one pair of eyes watching his every move.

Red Jacket watched his friend disappear into the night, running a few thoughts through his mind of how to mislead the others on the hunt for their escaped prey on the morrow, and then rolled over and slept.

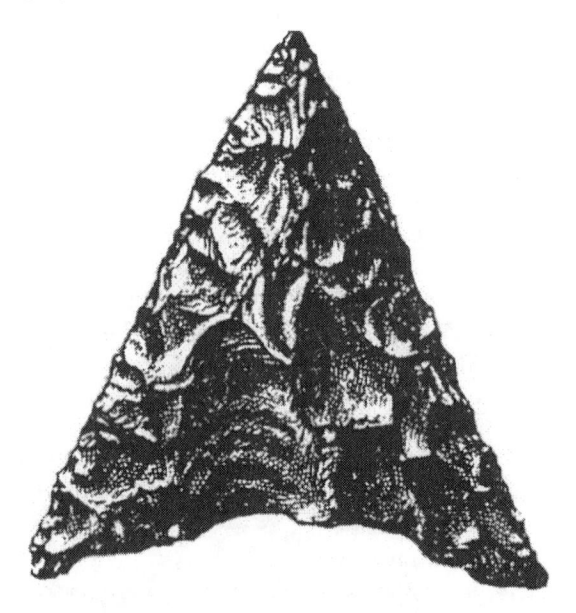

## Chapter Thirty Two
*The Stropes are taken!*

Rudolf Fox stopped dead in his tracks just up the riverbank. He stood perfectly still, listening for any telltale sounds of the danger he sensed around him. It didn't bother him what he could hear, but rather of what he couldn't hear. A deathly silence blanketed the forest around him. No birds sang. No squirrels chattered in the trees. Nothing stirred.

He glanced to his canoe about a half dozen feet away. His rifle sat nestled in it. He silently cursed himself for not having it in his hands, but he had only landed to check a field just a rod away from the riverbank. It wasn't too late to plant corn, even though it would be a late harvest. Standing deathly still, he let his hand fall to the knife is belt. The dark eyes of the forest weighed heavily upon the nape of his neck. He felt them. Would they strike or pass if he feigned indifference?

He moved ever so slowly toward the canoe, ready to spurt toward it, and hopefully beat the devils to it. He took a few more slow steps, praying not to trigger the miscreants forward with his act. Just a few more steps, he told himself, and you will be out of here.

A whoop made him jump, despite his forewarning knowledge.

A warrior instantly burst from the scrub brush, stopping just in front of him. The warrior's wide eyes, full of the excitement of the hunt, glared at him. Several more warriors moved up behind the first warrior and quickly formed a half circle around the stunned white man.

The glaring warrior stood defiantly. His eyes grew wider and he bared his teeth in a threatening manner. His free hand slipped a tomahawk from his belt with one smooth motion. He held it high, as if to throw it, just as a grunt from behind stopped his motion. He shook his head. Another disapproving grunt sounded from behind him.

Rudolf slipped his knife from his belt in the momentary confusion, waving it toward the greasy-haired painted warrior. Every muscle in his body flexed against a perceived blow from behind, but he stood firm, determined to at least strike down the foe to his front before succumbing to blows from his rear. "Mien goot! I take you with me!" he yelled into the tense and silent air.

The warrior grinned, raising his tomahawk all the higher.

"Fox, drop your knife!" a voice sounded from behind. "We take you only so you may not raise the alarm to Boss Strope and his brood. We come for him, not you!"

The voice seemed vaguely familiar to Rudolf, perhaps some chief he met while trading with Secord at Tioga Point. He looked past the grinning warrior and to his canoe. His family! Apparently this war party did not travel by canoe, but by foot. They must've come down the east side of the river, thus saving his family living on the west side.

He instantly plunged forwards in a mad rage, pushing the astounded warrior aside and into the water. He kicked his canoe just enough to send it swirling down the Susquehanna before many hands grabbed him from behind. Painted hands quickly wrestled the knife from his hands. He surrendered immediately, confident he had done all he could to secure his family's safety. The miscreants would have no way across the river to his farm. He watched the canoe spiral off despite the efforts of several warriors to swim after it.

The warrior splashing violently in the river rose from the rocky river bottom full of rage. He grunted and turned back to the water, bending down to look for his tomahawk in the waters. Finally finding it, he burst from the river, lunging at Rudolf. A strong hand checked him just before he reached the Dutchman, pushing him backward again. He yelled in defiance, plunging into the water again. Two Indian women laughed at him from the riverbank.

"No!" a chief firmly scolded him. The warrior slammed his tomahawk down onto the rocky shore, madly arguing before the stern eye of the chief silenced him. Stomping off in frustration, he clambered up the riverbank, roughly pushing the two Indian women aside, but failing to hush their laughter.

The chief immediately motioned for others to bind Rudolf. In no time rawhide thongs held his hands fast behind his back. Other thongs held his arms to a strong branch set through the crook in them. The chief circled him, tugging at his bonds. Nodding his head, he ran his fingers across his lips. A warrior quickly wrapped another thong around Rudolf's head and through the corners of his mouth. The warrior tied it so tight trickles of blood dripped from the corners of his mouth. The chief raised his lower lip and nodded again. A gruff push from behind forced Rudolf up the riverbank and to the trail leading to the Stropes' homestead.

They moved silent and still along the path through the forest. Just before reaching the Stropes' cabin along the *Wysox Creek,* they split up, stealthily fanning out all around the homestead.

Smoke curled in the air from the chimney of the cabin. The dull thud of an ax sounded near a nearby barn. The chief waved to two of his skulking warriors. They nodded back an affirmation. The chief then made a long sweeping motion with his arms. The warriors all advanced as one, slowly closing their circle around the cabin.

Rudolf stood watching it all just to the side of the path. His aged warrior guard, noticing his stare, held a spear point to his throat. The two Indian women stood to his rear with their knives drawn. He drew a deep and regretful breath. The fate of the Strope family made him shudder. He groaned through the tight rawhide thong in his mouth. The old warrior pushed the spear closer to his neck in response. His groans promptly ceased.

The thudding ax fell silent. Two warriors stood by a huge white man, one with a rifle, the other with a spear. The goliath of a man raising the ax high above his head looked all about. Warriors fanned out all around the cabin, surrounding it. The huge white man's anxious eyes stared at both of the warriors, then darted back to the converging warriors, betraying his confusion.

The warrior holding the rifle cocked the weapon and pointed it squarely at his head, quickly quelling his confusion. The warrior with the spear smirked, jabbing it in the air toward him. Big John Strope shook his head in disgust. Realizing the futility of a struggle, he slowly dropped his ax to the ground. In no time rawhide thongs held him fast.

The chief whooped in triumph, dashing through the cabin door with a half dozen screaming warriors in his wake. Smashing sounds and horrified wails crept through the door.

Big John straightened against the thongs and turned toward the cabin, his eyes alive with fear and purpose. He took a few great steps toward the cabin, easily pulling the two warriors along with him. They tugged and pulled him back, all the while screaming with rage. One raised a tomahawk and struck with the blunt end of the weapon, having little effect on the entranced big man. Big John shook it off and took a few more steps, intent on helping his family in the cabin. The warriors yelped and struggled, embarrassed and enraged. Baring their teeth, they tried with all their might to hold the huge white man to no avail.

Big John, driven by a blind sense of duty, ignored them and trudged forwards, wishing for all the world he had not dropped his ax.

A shocked white woman, followed closely by two girls and a tearful boy, stumbled out the cabin door, pushed from behind by two rough warriors. The women and children cried, raising their hands toward the heavens in despair. Another woman immediately followed in their wake, clutching a huge book tightly to her chest. An old man staggered through of the door behind her, wearing a stunned look of outrage and disbelief. The chief appeared in the door behind him and whooped loudly in his wake, hastening the old man's steps.

The two Indian women promptly abandoned the old warrior and his charge. They ran toward the cabin, chattering all the way in anticipation. Pushing the chief aside in the doorway, they disappeared into the cabin. The chief turned and followed them.

The chattering women soon emerged with their arms full of iron pots and garments of all manner. After plopping down their plunder on the ground near the terror-stricken captives, they reentered the cabin, their faces full of glee.

The triumphant warriors sauntered about the cabin dooryard, their chests swelled with pride. In their hands they held several rifles, knifes, and tomahawks, comparing each of their prizes to the others. Two other warriors stumbled from the cabin with a feather mattress in tow, whooping and hollering in their native tongues. One of them stabbed violently into the feather mattress, spreading feathers in every direction. Other Warriors joined their festivities and soon great amounts of feathers danced in the air. Immense joy spread across each of their faces. The captives stood mute watching the feather-fest with anxious eyes, not sure how to take the strange behavior.

One of the Indian women burst from the cabin with a large and brightly colored tablecloth stretched between her hands held high. The other Indian woman struggled behind her, jealously grabbing at one end of it. The first woman yanked and scolded her, wishing for all the world to be rid of her, the jealous vixen. She sauntered near Rudolf and his old warrior guard holding the tablecloth high in front of her, examining it with her beaming eyes. The other woman cursed her from near the cabin and rummaged through the plunder already accumulating on the ground about the cabin door. They hastily gathered the plunder into bed sheets and tied them secure.

The chief whooped for attention and motioned toward the barn. A pair of warriors immediately ran into it. Livestock soon wailed and cried behind the barn doors. The chief stepped back into the cabin and promptly emerged with two fine pine knots burning bright in his hands. Passing one to a nearby warrior, he cocked his head toward the barn. The warrior instantly grabbed the flaming pine knot and set the barn to the torch, seeming oblivious of his fellows still in the structure. Smoke started billowing from the barn immediately, giving birth to a pair of coughing warriors stumbling through it, leading a cow behind them along with a team of great oxen. All of the animals bellowed in protest, seeming to sense their fate. The warriors sneered at their fellow with the torch, who only whooped in response, seeming indifferent to their scowls and complaints.

The chief stepped back from the cabin door, nonchalantly tossing his pine knot into it behind him. Flames soon crept up the walls and flared through the windows.

"Why?" the white woman with the large book cried, falling to her knees. Tears of anguish flooded her cheeks.

The chief looked down upon her with disdain. "Where Boss Strope? He rebel!" he asked on a snarl of contempt.

"Downriver!" the woman bawled. "He's far from here, you devil!"

The chief growled, full of disgust.

"Esther!" the white woman said. "She will hear of this! She is our friend! Her word is powerful!"

"Esther words loud but Great Manitou speaks louder," the chief said, thumping his huge chest with his hands. "He speaks here! To the heart! You white eyes, your time over around here! Many braves at Tioga! Soon all Yankees hit in head with tomahawk!" Bending down, he snatched the book from the woman's hands, flinging it into the flames, despite the women's pleas to the contrary. "Your word false! Your words empty from this book!" he said. "Let them be lost in the ashes!"

The old white man instantly darted past both of them and ran to the flames, grabbing up the book. Frantically, he wiped its smoldering pages with his hands, age losing all of its discrepancies. Triumphantly, he raised the book high, proclaiming it saved. He clamped it tightly to his chest before any warriors reached him.

"If your words mean so much to you white eyes then why do you not follow them?" the chief asked the man.

The old white man only shook his head. The rest of his body shook on its own.

The chief growled in disgust, waving some warriors toward the old man. "Jogo!" the chief said to the shaking old white man. "Take your book with your false words, perhaps now you learn from them! But me think not. White man's hearts too empty. Them words never be true to false hearts."

The old man stumbled past the fierce chief, still shaking, but zealously shielding the book from his grasp.

The other warriors lifted the tied sheets full of plunder from the ground and burdened Big John Strope's back with them. John wilted and stumbled under the grievous load, but quickly regained his feet. The warriors ignored his groans, placing a rope around his neck. With a sharp tug at the rope about his neck, the big man stumbled to keep up with them. Big John finally gasped and collapsed under the immense weight of his burden. The warriors taunted and kicked him, but carefully stayed just out of the huge man's reach.

The chief watch the spectacle and scowled. Growing tired of delays, he gestured to the old warrior guarding Rudolf Fox. "Fox!" he said. "You come!"

The old warrior pushed Rudolf toward the chief. He stopped Rudolf beside Big John, whom sat frustrated with his hands holding his crestfallen head.

"You help with bundles," the chief command Fox. He pulled out his knife and quickly cut the rawhide strip in Rudolf's mouth. He then cut the thongs around the stick holding his arms. "You behave, and remember, we know where you family are, you just do as you told."

Rudolf nodded.

The chief turned toward the others and spoke in the Indian tongue, ordering and waving them into some sort of order for the trek to Tioga Point. The warriors quickly assembled the captives into line.

Rudolf picked up a bundle from Big John's back and filed into line. They moved silently along the path until the Indians started chattering among themselves. Soon hushed whispers began to pass among the captives, also.

"Rudolf," Lydia Strope whispered from behind him. "What is to become of us?"

"Wir are fine for now," Rudolf answered. "But I'se fear not fer long. Perhaps Esther will help you, but I 'se fear for mien family."

"Sebastian has gone to Forty Fort to fetch help," Lydia said. "He left us just afore they fell upon us. A squaw came by last night with a warning. We did not think they would move with such haste."

"I'se heard of the horrors of war before but never see what dey was till now!" Rudolf gasped.

"I fear for us all," Lydia answered, watching a warrior turn to them.

"No speak!" the warrior ordered, his face full of rage. With a gruff push, he reminded Rudolf he meant what he said. He raised his hand threateningly at Lydia but then lowered it, reconsidering his action. White or not, she still was a woman.

Fear for his family raced through Rudolf's mind. He feared for the Stropes also, but knew in his heart nothing could be done for them now. He must get back to his family and get them downriver or they would be sure to suffer the same fate. His feet suddenly stumbled hard against the narrowing trail, sending a rock rolling down the steep mountainside to the river below. Regaining his footing, he looked up. No warriors seem to pay him any mind. Only a few gasps from the other captives to his rear betrayed any concern for him. His mind raced with thoughts of how he had lost a cow over the steep mountainside just a few weeks before. The cow had lost its footing just along the trail and plummeted down to the river below. He had thought it lost when he heard a great splash in the river, but to his amazement, he found it stumbling along the lower bank as he descended the trail down the mountainside. Breakneck Hill, the Moravians had christened this part of the trail. Amply named, Rudolf thought. He then remembered noticing a thick covering of leaves blanketing the mountainside. In fact, if one fell, just as the cow, one would simply slide down the slick leaves to the river below. A risky venture, but he feared it to be his only chance of escape without being pursued.

He stole glances all along the side of the trail. It grew steeper and steeper. Slowing his steps, he awaited the right moment. Everyone now slowed their steps in respect to the narrowing path. The oxen and cattle stumbled. Rudolf thanked God for their place in line behind the cattle. He watched the cattle, especially their footing; for when one slipped, he would slip also, and in that moment slide down to the river, and thus to freedom.

"What are you thinking?" Lydia whispered to him again. Apparently his actions did not go unnoticed. "Don't, you'll fall to your death fer sure." An ox stumbled in the same moment. It fell hard against the trail but quickly regained its footing, causing a slight moment of confusion. The warriors all turned toward it, eager not to lose any of their plunder, especially the potential feast of such a huge beast.

Rudolf instantly flung the bundle from his back and into the nearest warrior to his front. With the same motion, he spilled over the side of the trail, tumbling head over heels for the longest moment, folding his arms and legs tightly against his body. He stopped and grabbed for a small sampling, but it gave way, and in another instant he lost all control, sliding on the leaves just as he had foreseen. He rolled head over heels. Dirt flew from all around him. Leaves flooded his vision. Closing his eyes, he trusted his fate completely to God, mouthing a quick prayer. A rifle cracked to his rear. Balls thudded into the trees, whizzing around him. Mien Goot! Just hang on! he told himself, sliding pell-mell by trees and rocks. Everything a blur, he suddenly felt a hard surface checking his tumble, followed immediately by the strange sensation of flying through the air. Water flooded up his nose and into his mouth. The blue-green waters clouded his eyes, flooding his senses. He flailed his arms wildly about, somehow righting himself against the current. Pushing his head up, he took a deep breath of sweet air. The sweetest air he had ever breathed. He swam madly for the shore, quickly pulling himself up onto a large flat stone. Gasping, he cursed his painting breaths and listened.

Muffled shouts crept down the mountainside, but soon disappeared in the distance. Sighing in relief, he let his lungs fill with the sweet breath of freedom. Rolling over on his back, he peered to the heavens, whispering a hushed prayer thanking Providence for his deliverance from evil.

Suddenly a loud splash jolted him upright again. Staring in the direction of the disturbance he witnessed a great tale disappearing into a swirl on the river's face. Allowing himself to breathe again, he looked across the river. "Mother," he muttered to himself. "Children." After a brief moment of despair his darting eyes caught a glimpse of a log jammed between large rocks to his front. Easing himself into the water he swam to it. Wrestling it clear of the rocks, he grabbed it and floated upon it downriver. His, as well as his dear family's only hope, lie downriver. War came to their doorstep in all its horror. Only by retreating would they find any solace from its repulsive face.

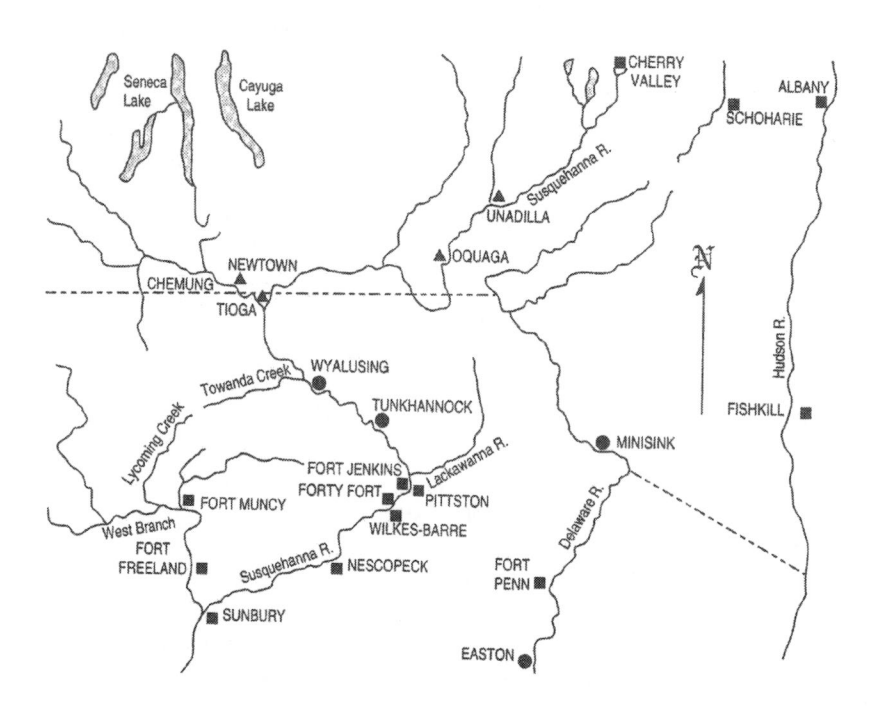

## Chapter Thirty Three
*The Babe Rudolf*

Rudolf ran up the trail from the river to his cabin, his thudding heart pounding in anticipation in his ears. Bursting into the dooryard in front of the cabin he collapsed in exhaustion.

"Father!" a chorus of surprised small voices suddenly said all at once. All the children immediately gathered around their panting father. Rising to his knees he eagerly embraced all of them one by one.

"Rudolf!" A voice gasped from the cabin door. Dropping the bundle in her hands Mother Fox ran to the huddled group, quickly embracing her husband.

"Oh, Mother, Children," Rudolf gasped. "So goot to see ihr all!"

"What has happened?" Elizabeth asked through her tears, suddenly noticing columns of dark smoke rising in the air over the trees just across the river. Her heart sank.

Rudolf recognized the fear in her eyes and slowly shook his head. He wished with all his heart to spare her, but she must be told. "The Stropes," he said. "Sie all taken by der wildens."

Elizabeth tenderly examined the scratches and cuts on his face, staring at him through hollow eyes. "Oh my dear Rudolf," she said.

"Sie got me, but ich got away," Rudolf explained. The children all let out a simultaneous gasp. "It was not easy, but God," he said, pointing up to the heavens, "he helped. He helps us all but wir must move, and now!"

Elizabeth promptly rose to her feet. She straightened her apron and fixed the few strands of her wild hair dancing about her face. Their daughter, little Elizabeth, ran up to them holding a pair of pistols in her hands. She handed them to her father.

Rudolf looked soulfully down at the pistols and then to his dear daughter. He slowly took the pistols from her, keeping one for himself while passing the other to his dear wife. "Best we both keep one" he explained. "Lost dir rifle in das river." A rustle along the path opposite the trail from the river hushed his words. He and Elizabeth immediately pointed their pistols at the path. The children parted and gathered behind them, staring anxiously around them.

A buckskin clad figure promptly emerged from the path. "That's not very hospitable," the tall white man said, lowering his rifle. "Not the proper way at all to greet a neighbor! Not at all," he muttered in the face of the shocked eyes glaring at him.

"John Neely," Elizabeth gasped. "You nearly scared the life out of us!"

"Herr Neely!" Rudolf said, "Das wildens! Sie's burned out dir Stropes and taken them!"

Neely, a strong man bearing the heart of a true patriot, glanced toward the telltale smoke trails rising in the air behind the huddled family. Scratching his head he pulled the reins of the pack horse to his rear. The fully laden horse trotted into the open dooryard. "Figured something was amiss, the way the Indians have been acting all spooked as of late," he said shaking his head. "When I saw that smoke trail I figured it was time to pull up stakes if one wants to keep his scalp. Had to make sure you were all well, though, before I made tracks me self."

"And dien cabin up dir creek?" Rudolf asked.

"It was fine, last I saw of it," Neely said with a sigh. "And will be if the Indians and Tories don't bother us on this side of the river, but I daresay I fear they shall."

"John," Rudolf said, lowering his pistol. Shaking his head he gazed all around. "Wir must all leave." Marching up to Neely he smiled. "Will you help mich with mien family?"

"Of course," Neely answered.

Rudolf nodded and gestured back to his family. "Come now children! Mind your mother and gather all you can to put in dere bateau. Make haste!"

The children obediently obeyed and swarmed into the cabin. Soon they emerged with all the necessities of life they could carry in their little hands.

"John, wir gather dir cattle and drive them down dir bank while Mother takes dir children down in das bateau," Rudolf said, motioning to the barn.

In no time they all assembled in front of the little cabin in the midst of the lush forest. The trees which once seemed so familiar now sired nothing but a sense of dread in them all, for in their dark folds the harbingers of death awaited, ready to strike at any moment. Each of them moved slowly and quietly. Even the cattle picked up on the sense of dread and behaved accordingly. They gathered easily and silently. All seemed so unnatural.

Rudolf gestured for them to all move down the trail without a word. They all moved simultaneously and in good order, knowing their lives truly depended upon it. The cattle took the lead, followed by Neely's horse, and then Neely himself, his rifle held at the ready. The children dutifully followed their mother cradling the babe Rudolf and her arms. The elder Rudolf brought up the rear, his keen eyes fixed on the forest with both of the pistols held tight in his clenched fists.

Upon reaching the bateau they all placed their bundles hastily into it. The children filed into it without a word, but then suddenly all turned at once to look with soulful eyes at their parents.

Rudolf helped Elizabeth into the shallow draft vessel. Looking to his younger sons holding the long poles over the side of the boat he said "you all pole well, work with dir current, not against it," Casting a quick gaze at all the children he added "you all listen to your mother. Wir need all good and dutiful children just now. You keep I and Neely in sight. After wir get over the slide out," he said, pointing to the huge swath the river had cut into the mountain to their front. It produced a great cut in the side of the mountain overlooking the tireless river. "You watch along the tip-top of das mountain. Wir all meet on the other side. Wir be fine."

With one last long and soulful look to his family, he and Neely pushed the boat into the water and marched up the bank. Quickly driving the cattle along the riverbank they guided them up and over the edge of the steep slide-out cut into *Tip Top Mountain*. Prodding the beats onward they urged the beasts along the mountain, pausing every now and then to look down through the trees to the boat on the river below them. It moved slowly down the serene waters draped with the lush greenness of the thick forest bordering its banks. The long smoke trail from the Stropes' burned-out cabin and barn rose high into the air just beyond the river, hastening both men's steps through the forest. They both breathed easier down the other side of the slide-out when a flash of red in the trees before them stopped them dead in their tracks.

Freezing just behind a huge oak, they anxiously peered around the edge of it to the low ground below. Neither said a word for fear of spooking the placid cattle behind them. A red-jacketed devil stalked through the trees, followed by more dark-painted demons with swirls of white paint about their grim faces. Both men carefully eased back down behind the tree, praying their movements did not betray their position. They stared wide-eyed at the curious cattle standing obediently about the trees, barely a sound escaping from any of them, for they sensed their master's fear. The men waited a few more anxious moments before peeking back around the tree. Nothing stirred to their front, thank God.

"They were moving to the right," Neely whispered, still wide-eyed. "Away from the river and back down over the mountain." Turning, he gazed toward the river. Suddenly Rudolf ran before him to the edge of the cliff. Standing by a slight break in the trees he waved his arms at the slow moving bateau below them. Neely carefully approached, anxiously looking about the valley below for any telltale movement of the painted demons. Arms waved from the boat to acknowledge them. Both sighed in relief. "They see!" Neely said, patting Rudolf on the shoulder. "They see! They're pulling up onto the shore below." Rudolf stared back at him in horror.

Shaking his head Neely looked back to the cattle. "We've got to leave the cattle, by God, we'll be lucky to get out of here without going to hell or Tioga ourselves!" he said.

Rudolf nodded without saying a word. Turning with Neely he ran down the mountainside. In no time they burst through the trees and onto the riverbank rambling toward the bateau.

"What is it?" Elizabeth asked the men. Without muttering a word they splashed into the river, hurriedly wading out to the boat. Spilling into it they stared anxiously toward the all-encompassing and great forest along the bank.

"Wildens!" Rudolf explained on a whisper, gesturing to the riverbank. "Many Indians all around. Wir must make haste."

A scream from the opposite shore turned his darting eyes toward it. Whoops and shrieks immediately answered the scream, echoing across the river. All watched the trees on the bank for any telltale movement, their hearts thudding in their ears. The dreadful noises drew ever so closer. The men stood absolutely still, knowing it to be too late to hustle all the children from the boat, for their movements would certainly draw the attention of the unseen yelling demons on the far bank. So they did what they could. They sat perfectly still and pray.

Rudolf slowly brought a finger to his lips in answer to the questioning eyes darting between him and the screams. Carefully pushing one of the poles into the water he quickly nudged the boat into the current, hoping it to carry them silently away from the terror.

A sudden movement burst through the dense foliage blanketing the opposite riverbank. An exasperated white man plopped down onto the shore, his eyes full of absolute fear, darting to and fro. Whoops turned his eyes back behind him before he witnessed the crowded bateau of terrified faces slowly drifting down the opposite shoreline. He bolted up the bank, disappearing into the dense underbrush again.

The next second another white man plopped down onto the shore just after him. Gasping and falling to his knees he bowed his head, exposing a festering and bleeding red spot about the crown of it. Closing shrieks, the call of the hunters pursuing hot on his heels, forced his head up. His terrified eyes danced all about in his head, despite the blood pouring down his face. With trembling hands, he wiped the blood from his eyes and darted up the bank.

Painted demons spilled down the bank immediately after him.

Their eyes, intent on the hunt, searched up and down the bank for a second before a whoop from one of them guided them back up the bank after their terrified prey. The hunt resumed.

Their whoops suddenly intensified. Spine-tingling screams answered them for a spit second before being forever silenced.

The forest turned deathly quiet.

Rudolf looked wildly about, his heart sinking in his chest.

Neely crouched down behind the gunwales and leveled his rifle at the far riverbank, his darting eyes searching for the oncoming assault. A tug to his rear turned his eyes about.

Rudolf's hollow eyes widened and he gestured ahead of the boat to an island downriver. Neely nodded back and rose, helping him silently pole the bateau toward a densely overgrown bank on the island. Fearful of any telltale splash they poled the boat under the shielding branches of some overgrown trees bending down toward the water, finding a ready-made haven to shield them from the prying and searching eyes of the painted demons, and certain death. After carefully and silently adjusting a few of the branches to totally shield the boat, they all nestled down into it and eased back into an uneasy silence.

Nothing stirred for the longest moment. No birds chirped. No crows cawed. Not even a fish jumped in the still waters. A wave of death swept over the Susquehanna, hushing it and draining it of all the sounds of life in its wake. All sat motionless and listened in the eerie silence.

A sudden cry widened eyes and produced hushed gasps. Every eye darted to Mother Fox and the babe she cradled in her arms. Mother Fox, her eyes alive with terror, held the babe Rudolf closer to her chest and anxiously tried to hush him. To her absolute terror all of her efforts only produced new cries. She immediately tried to suckle the babe, but he refused, emitting even louder cries of protest. She rocked and shushed him to no avail. The cries grew louder, a call for life acting as a beacon for death.

All of their throats went dry. All stared at Mother Fox. She stared back with hollow eyes wondering what to do. The Indians will surely hear! John Neely shook his head and checked his rifle. Rudolf stared blankly at his wife, whom stared back at him in a growing panic. No one uttered a word. They couldn't! What horror!

The babe's wail grew higher and higher in pitch. Mother Fox stared in horror at the bundle in her arms. Catherine, her eldest daughter, grabbed at a branch just overhead, stripping it of its leaves. She looked to her mother with the leaves in her hands and offered them to her. Mother Fox's eyes grew wide. She shook her head to her daughter. The struggling babe flailed against her arms, singing with rage. In desperation she grabbed the leaves and crammed them into the babe's mouth. The babe shook his head, spitting out the leaves and crying all the louder. Tears began to roll down the other children's eyes.

Mother Fox's eyes swelled with tears and horror. In desperation she looked over the side of the boat to the still waters. Her eyes flowed hauntingly up to her husband. His jaw slackened and he slowly shook his head. With tears clouding her eyes she slowly lowered the crying babe down to the water, but quickly lifted him back up from it. Her tear-filled eyes looked to Rudolf and then to the crying babe. Her desperation tore her apart, heart and soul. One had to die so the others may live. Her mouth dropped open. She lifted her eyes to the heavens in desperation, hoping for an answer from the most high to relieve her of her angst.

The babe only cried louder. Rudolf raised his hands and shook his head again; his eyes now full of despair and disbelief. Neely gasped and pointed his long rifle toward the island, noticeably disturbed.

Mother Fox closed her eyes and lowered the crying babe down to the water again, but picked him up the second she felt the water on the back of her hands. She tried again, but failed, for the instant the water touched her hand she instinctively raised the babe back up again. The babe's wails grew even louder. She closed her eyes tightly again and took a deep breath, painfully aware of all of her other children's eyes upon her. She lowered their brother one more time, trying with all her might to quiet her conscience so others might live by this horrible act of self-preservation. The water again touched the back of her hand. She tried to relax her fingers to no avail. Groaning, she lifted the babe from the water, closing her eyes tightly against the horror. No! She just could not do it! No, they must all live, or they must all die!

A hand reached out to her, a tender hand, a familiar hand. One filled with strength, but somehow gentle. She felt the hands reached down to the babe. She opened her eyes to stare at Rudolf, now kneeling beside her. His great smile eased her concern. He gently pushed the babe to her chest. Clasping the babe ever so tightly, she felt she never held anything so delicate; anything so innocent. She smiled and gazed through hopeless eyes to her husband. "I cannot," she gasped.

"I know Mother, I know," Rudolf said. An instant later the babe's cries ceased, seeming to sense his parent's unconditional love; a love tested beyond endurance, but holding true in the end. He relaxed in his mother's arms and drifted into a peaceful sleep, safe and sound.

"Thank God," Neely gasped in relief. "I could not live with the babe's blood on our hands. Let the devils come, it'll be all or none!" he added, raising his rifle to the shoulder.

"Yes!," Rudolf said, suddenly oddly tilting his head. "Listen!"

Chirping birds once again sang their songs of life. A dragonfly buzzed over the face of the smooth waters. A fish splashed nearby.

"Listen to what?" his daughter Lily asked.

"Ja, all is right!," Rudolf explained. "Das forest es at peace again, for dir devils have passed."

Neely nodded his head. A grand smile stretched across his face. "You are right! By jingo! You are right! They have passed!" he gasped.

"Ja, but more will be about fer sure," Rudolf said. "Wir stay here until dir night." He paused and looked about the faces in the boat. His eyes grew hollow and empty. "Wir go to Fort Augusta." Bowing his head he stared at the bottom of the boat. Tears dropped from his eyes. "I fears soon dir wildens paints our pictures on dir trees along das trail, too, I'se fear." He looked up and said, "Wyoming, es ist verlorn!"

Neely stared at the man with a puzzled look. He knew and encountered many of the trees along the trails the Indians had stripped of bark on their return from raids to the south. They had painted pictures onto them, bragging of their exploits, but on the other hand he wished for the Dutchman to speak in one language and stop mixing his words. He wanted to ask what he had meant about Wyoming, but shook his head in frustration instead.

"Papa," Catherine said for her crestfallen father. She put her hand to his and sighed. "He says that Wyoming is forsaken! All is lost!"

## Chapter Thirty Four
### *Tioga Point*

John Jenkins wriggled and carefully crawled through the thick scrub brush along the west bank of the Chemung River. Stopping just to the edge of the brush he carefully parted it. Gazing across the waters to the opposite bank he gasped at the sight unfolding before him.

Canoes blanketed the whole riverbank. Indians moved all about the canoes and on top of the bank, engaged in all types of activities. Men worked on canoes dragged just to the top of the bank. A pair of woman struggled with a great iron pot down to the water's edge. A cradle sat strapped to one of their backs. Bells jingled on their moccasins and from the fringes of their bright dresses. With a simultaneous gasp they splashed the pot into the water and pulled it out, laughing and chattering to one another. Further up the riverbank more cradles hung from branches; their occupants nestled comfortably within them. Ever present dogs scampered down to the river once in a while to lap up a drink.

Jenkins sat perfectly still and watched it all, ready to scramble back into the thick scrub brush in a heartbeat. He felt the caked mud he had smeared over his face slowly dry. Carefully he let the leaves fall back into place. Fingering some fresh mud, he covered his face again and slowly parted the leaves, ever mindful that his discovery meant certain death. But death had hung about him every since his capture and escape into this wilderness. He grew almost accustomed to it, but then another sense; his sense of duty, sounded loudly and his heart. He could not pass Tioga Point without gaining some intelligence of the enemy's intensions and operations. He let these thoughts guide him peeking through the leaves, but then suddenly his heart sank at the sight before him.

White men, many white men, marched in the clearing above the riverbank. He recognized the portly figure striding among them with all the pomp and circumstance signifying his important position, Butler! Indian Butler himself! A green coated man to Butler's side loudly ordered all the white men into ranks. After the ranks formed Butler marched between them looking all the part of a regal general inspecting his troops. He waved and gestured a few times but his words faded with distance and mixed with the chatter and movements of the Indians bustling about them. A few Indians walked right through his ranks, parting them right in the face of the pompous man. He stopped and patiently waited for them to pass, probably muttering a few bolts of fire under his breath before the intruders passed. Regaining his composure he jutted his chest, motioning his men back into ranks. He promptly resumed his inspection.

Jenkins now watched with a new purpose. All of the rumors rang true! Not only the Indians, but the British, gathered to march upon Wyoming! He shuddered at the thought of it all. His eyes darted all about the camp, mentally noting everything, from the number of men to the number of canoes. His busy eyes suddenly locked on one figure among the many; a man swaggering from the Indians and toward Butler. The Indian's bright red jacket showed familiar to him.

Jenkins watched with mixed feelings as Red Jacket; a man to whom he owed his life, talked with his most hated enemy. Touching the back of his right hand ever so softly he rubbed it. A great shard of fear crept through his soul and his mind flashed with the image of his dear Beth. Beth, and all he knew and held dear, now lay under the threat of his friend's knife. A hollow pain twisted his empty stomach into a knot.

Red Jacket spoke a few words to the whites then suddenly drew a tomahawk from his belt. With a bloodcurdling shriek he raised the weapon high over his head in a great circling motion. Waving it ever higher, he danced about, screeching and whooping at the top of his lungs. A chorus of yelps immediately joined his cries. The whole Indian camp, including the whites not in Butler's ranks, danced about for a few heart-wrenching moments. Devils at play singing a demon's song.

Jenkins slowly let the leaves fall back into place and bowed his head in grief. If it came down to it he knew he might have to fell his friend; his odd friend. A friend threatening to lay waste to all he knew and held dear. He thought of the rich land he had passed on his trek for freedom and how he had skirted many a farm, not sure whether patriots or loyalists inhabited them. The country lay torn apart from within. Now it lay under the threat of total destruction. He must get to Wyoming and warn them! He must! He must save them from the devils' tomahawks!

He parted the leaves for one last look. A man, a dreadfully familiar man, strode down the bank to the canoes. Rage surged through his body upon sight of the rascal. His knuckles turned white around the knife handle clenched in his fist. Silently he wished the man closer to the water's edge, somehow fueled by a new strength. He felt ready to burst from the bushes, swim a few mad strokes across the river, and knife the scoundrel if he moved but a few more steps to the shoreline.

Parshall Terry stopped dead in his tracks, haunted by some foreboding sense of danger he couldn't explain. It fed a tingling on the nape of his neck that held his feet still. He looked to his rear and to both sides of the riverbank. Nothing out of the ordinary stirred about, but nonetheless the tingle remained. His hand grabbed the pistol in his belt and he scanned the whole area again. Something out there planned his demise. Somehow he felt it. A pure hatred seemed to taint the air. He peered into a thick tangle of scrub brush engulfing the opposite bank. Nothing stirred but a few leaves in a faint breeze. Still, the feeling clung to him. Something haunted the scrub brush with a rage burning so intense he felt its heat from the opposite shore. His eyes brought him no insight, but his heart blared a stern warning with each thundering beat.

Suddenly a pair of Indian boys scampered down the bank behind him, splashing wildly into the river. They seemed indifferent and ignored the strange white man nearly jumping out of his skin. They paid no mind to the pistol he leveled at them.

Terry cursed the indifferent boys and looked back to the brush. Nothing stirred. What a time for your conscience to flare, he scolded himself. What? I've done nothing wrong, he reassured himself. They are the rebels. They brought about this war, no matter what your estranged and smug family might say to the contrary. They were smug, he thought, thinking of his brother's last words to him before he left them. "You not only betray us, but yourself, Parshall," he had told him. There is a rebel for you, talking of betrayal. A right smart fool! Some family! Indeed!

With a devious grin he thought about finding his brother at Wyoming in the upcoming campaign and battle. Then they would talk of betrayal again. He had not felt the back of the Indian Butler's sword yet, as he had Captain Ransom's when he foolishly had joined him in the rebel ranks, nor did he know of any of his fellow rangers whom had felt it. He had been welcomed wholeheartedly into the British ranks and had been promoted to sergeant. He doubted if he would have ever gained the rank of corporal in the ranks of the misguided rebels, the poltroons!

Advancing a few steps to the canoes he pulled a bundle from one of them, no longer paying heed to the strange feeling. Nonetheless, his hand rested on the butt of his pistol, ready to yank it from his belt and fire at any cowardly devil trying to dispatch him. Turning slowly he walked backwards up the bank, facing the opposite shore. Reaching the top of the bank he looked back one more time, admonishing himself for such fears. "Damn rebels," he muttered to himself. They haunt me. But we shall see soon whom shall haunt whom after this campaign and battle. With that thought of burning revenge he turned and walked into the comfort of the ranger camp.

Jenkins watched Terry retreat with a hard heart. He too cursed the Indian boys under his breath. If they had not come he might have dispatched one of the most vile traitors to ever betray Wyoming, and America. Rising to his weak knees he painstakingly crawled out of the scrub brush. Esther's Village and Sheshequin lay down the footpath before him, but he would give them a wide berth before cutting back toward the river. Then he would carry word back to Wyoming. Then he would see Beth again, sweet Beth.

Nothing mattered but carrying word of warning to Wyoming and seeing sweet Beth once again. Cursing the painful burning feeling in the pit of his stomach he struggled onward, his mind flashing with the sights he had witnessed at Tioga Point. The distant echo of a water drum hastened his steps all the more. Each thud echoed a warning deep into his soul. He took it to heart.

Wyoming must be warned! He must live to warn it if nothing else! The distant thud of dozens of water drums pounded their warnings in his aching soul, drowning out his own thudding heart echoing in his ears. He must not fail! He mustn't! Wyoming must be warned!

## Chapter Thirty Five
*Jenkins Returns!*

The pale tips of the pointed logs of the stockade wall shone in the pale moonlight. Suddenly John Jenkins felt incredibly tired and sore. Every muscle in his body screamed for attention, and rest. He scolded his aching body to march but a few more steps, for true comfort awaited him in the fort ahead of him. Struggling a few painful steps to the fort's gate, he collapsed against it. A loud call sounded from within the fort and the doors promptly parted, exposing a sea of astonished faces staring at him. Squire Jenkins burst forth and stood before his emaciated son. Mrs. Jenkins and a surge of others quickly followed.

Jenkins stumbled toward his father, collapsing in his arms. Hushed whispers and gasps echoed throughout the crowd. He lifted his tired eyes toward them. His ears rang with their familiar tones. Home! He had made it home! He saw them! He heard them! They welcomed him! He strained to hear Beth's voice but her gentle tones did not sound among the sea of voices.

The aches of all of his months of struggles suddenly cascaded over his entire body. He felt drenched in them. His back pulsed with pain. His empty stomach burned. His feet tingled. Sores and scratches covering his whole body suddenly screamed for attention. His eyelids felt heavy, but he forced them open a crack with his staunch resolve; the resolve which had delivered him from his hellish odyssey. The resolve to see but one face again. One face he now probed the sea of sympathetic eyes to see but once more, before he succumbed to his exhausted body's pleas for rest. A flood of emotion overcame him upon sight of its beauty.

Bethiah's face wore an expression of great relief mixed with horror, but she forced a smile through it all, cupping the loving face in her hands which bore the soulful eyes staring back at her. "Oh, my brave soldier," she gasped. "What horrors have you endured?"

Jenkins smiled and raised his hand to her cheek with all of his remaining strength. She gently clasped his hand and brought it to her lips, gently kissing it.

"That is all well and fine," Squire Jenkins suddenly announced. "But we must get him inside at once! He needs food and rest, bless him!"

Bethiah stood, but stayed close, always holding the hand which refused to release its hold on her hand. She tried with all her might to quell her tears but his moans opened a floodgate of tears from her eyes. Weeping profusely, she walked along side of the men carrying Jenkins into the house in the center of the fort.

At his mother's direction they placed him upon the finest

featherbed in the house. Moaning, he let his body melt into the comfort of the soft bed.

The others all stood back for a moment, the shock in their eyes amplified by the ample light of the lanterns in the room illuminating the disheveled and filthy skeleton of the once strong and vibrant man lying before them. War definitely broke his body. Had it broken his soul?

His beaming eyes, betraying an everlasting spark ignited from his soul, shone above his hollow cheeks. Eyes locked onto Beth's eyes. Love lit the room brighter than any lantern. Its light soothed all angst from the others. They all stood silently watching the two lovers speak the silent language of love through their eyes.

Both seemed oblivious of the others, for in this moment their love outshone all. Their hearts finally beat as one again. Beth held his hand all the tighter, her eyes swimming in love, and great pity.

"That's fine," Squire Jenkins finally said, looking over his shoulder to his wife and other women scampering up the steps with their arms full of food and drink. "Let us make way, for now that he has fed his soul, let his body feed as well," he added, stepping aside to make way for the women. Mugs of rum and plates of food immediately passed through eager hands down to the returning hero.

The men all slowly turned about, each casting a last glance at the poor soul before stepping through the door, wondering of their own resolve if placed in similar circumstances. Squire Jenkins stopped just outside the door. Leaning against the wall he let out a long sigh.

"I durst say that I would not like to experience the hell those eyes have witnessed," Captain Harding said stopping halfway down the steps turning back to Squire.

Squire Jenkins raised his wet eyes toward him and waved his hand. He slowly descended the steps with his friend, promptly finding a chair at the table. Harding took a seat in the chair opposite him.

"Word has been sent to Forty Fort," Harding said.

Squire Jenkins slowly nodded his head. "My poor boy," he gasped. "I feared I would never see him again, oh, but now the good Lord has answered our prayers and has delivered him back to us."

"That he has," Harding said. "That he has." He paused for moment. "I hope he continues to answer our prayers and saves us from the torments which threaten us."

Squire Jenkins raised an eyebrow. "Amen to that, but I fear nothing can save us from it, for the Tories possess a certain hell-born hatred for us, beyond all doubt and reason. But alas, all we can do is continue to prepare and pray for deliverance from their wrath."

"Do you think your son may bear word of what the devils are up to up at Tioga Point?" Harding asked, lighting his pipe.

Jenkins raised his lower lip. "Oh, I am certain of it! He's much too fine of a scout to not do such, not with all our necks hanging in the noose."

"Yes," Harding said, exhaling a long trail of smoke from his lips. "He is a stout fellow and a fine scout. He was well missed."

"Captain Hewitt's scouts are just as fine," Squire said, his eyes staring far off in contemplation.

"Franklin and his band bring word that both Joseph Brant and Indian Butler are hanging about Tioga," Harding said. Leaning forward he offered Squire makings for his own pipe lying on the table. "A good smoke shall ease your anxious thoughts."

"I fear it will take more than the finest tobacco to ease my angst," Squire said. "There is a horrible storm coming, the likes of which we have never seen afore, I'm afraid."

"We have no choice but to face it," Harding said, removing his hat and plopping it down on the table. "All I have is here, one cannot simply uproot his fields. The grain within them is precious. Congress and the army have already expressed interest in our crops to feed the army." He took a long drag on his pipe. "I fear for my fields upriver. Soon they will need tending or the whole crop may be lost." He lifted his eyes through the pipe smoke and stared deathly at his friend. "We need the grain ourselves. Do you remember the starving time back in Seventy-four when the crops failed? I wouldn't want to suffer through another winter like that, no sir! If those plucky fellows hadn't braved the wilderness to the settlements along the Delaware to fetch back bags of flour, toting them on their very backs like packhorses, I dare not wonder what would have become of us all!"

"Yes, I remember Stephen, we all do," Jenkins said. "What we have endured and suffered is threefold what we would have suffered if we had all stayed back in Connecticut. But it is hope which feeds our spirits, hope and faith of the new day to dawn, perhaps not for us, but for our posterity, for in the end that is all we truly have, I dare say." He stopped and leaned forward on the table, clasping his hands before him in deep thought. "Soon John will recover enough to speak. What with Sebastian Strope's, Franklin's, and Hewitt's reports, all fine scouts, we shall be able to paint a better picture of what is to come." He drew a long breath. "The warnings of the Dutchman Fox whom came by late last night still haunt me. With all this placed before Colonels Denison and Butler, they must act soon! And I most certainly think they shall!"

"Do you think they will order a march against Tioga Point?" Harding asked.

"No, my friend, I think it is much too late for that, if anything, it shall be the opposite. Tioga, with her bevy of crazed Tories and Indians, shall march upon us, but I think we are equal to their threat by far."

"With men such as your son, I do believe we are," Harding agreed. "One of his like are worth thrice the number of Indians and Tories!" he added with a stern nod.

Squire Jenkins smiled but it soon melted in the face of the uncertainty threatening them. This time he truly shuddered for them all.

## Chapter Thirty Six
*Tunkhannock*

James Secord watched the rebels milling about his father's abandoned house with a growing sense of anger. Scraping his hand against the rough bark of the tree shielding him from their eyes he tore some of it away in a fit of anger. Visions of happier times flashed through his mind, temporarily soothing his anger, and thus quelling his impulse to raise his rifle and dispatch the intrusive and bold Yankee men.

He drank in the visions and peaceful thoughts now corrupted by war. His father, John, loved this land, he thought, gazing about. He felt a deep frown weigh down his jowls and empty his mind of the now painful visions. Those fanatical Wild Yankees! It had always been those damned Yankees with their stern ways even before the winds of war swept through Wyoming. To them you held their fanatical sentiments or none worth considering. No middle ground lay between their ways and the world. You were either with them or against them, black or white, no shades of gray. What big-headed arrogant and self-important fools!

A rustle to his rear instantly turned him about. He instinctively leveled his rifle on the disturbance. He lowered it from the wide-eyes staring back at him. Parshall Terry raised his hand and slowly approached. A few warriors and a pair of rangers scampered behind him. They all stopped and knelt down next to young Secord.

"Is it only the pair of them?" Terry asked.

"Yes," Secord answered through gritted teeth. "The rats!"

"What are they about?" Terry asked, craning his neck to gaze around the tree.

"They seem to be sizing up my father's land with an eye for seizing it for themselves, the opportunistic rats!" Secord said.

"Well then," Terry said, suddenly becoming more animated. "It appears we may have some sport!" Easing up to the tree he rested his rifle in a crook in its trunk. Gazing down the sights he leveled them on one of the unsuspecting rebels. "Bold bastards, aren't they," he said, easing back the hammer of his rifle. "Up here about Tunkhannock, just the two of them. Look at that one, standing content as he can be in the doorway, surveying your land with an eye intent on making it his own!" He heard the click of a hammer in his ear. He looked to see Secord and the others rangers taking their stances and leveling their weapons toward the house.

"A ball is the only thing they understand, and I intend to bring an understanding to them," Secord muttered.

"Wait now just one second!" one of the other rangers said. "The other is around the back of the house! If we all blister this one you'll give the other rebel rat the alarm!"

"To hell with him," Secord snarled, barely lifting his eyes from the sights down his rifle's barrel. He looked over his shoulder to the Indians. "He's yours! You can have him! Advance and take him the instant we fire!"

The Indians grunted and nodded, seeming very pleased with the offer. Scalps of rebels brought thirteen pounds each back at Fort Niagara. They moved into position in the scrub brush beside the tree, ready to pounce.

"But this one," Secord muttered under his breath. "The bold one, he's mine."

Terry looked out of the corner of his eye to him and then to his fellow's cold eye. Suddenly he felt good about his defection from the Rebel ranks to the King's ranks. They shared his view on things, and his manners.

"Let's give this gentleman his due," Secord said. An instant later four rifles cracked all at once, sending four balls into the stunned rebel's chest. He fell backwards in a mist of red.

The Indians instantaneously emitted an ear-splitting wail. Rushing forwards, they dove toward the lifeless body lying in the doorway, one of them quickly slicing away the hair on the crown of his head. Rising, the painted warrior lifted it high in the air, emitting an eerie cry of triumph. His fellows joined him with their own loud cries.

"The other rebel! The other rebel!" a ranger yelled from behind the tree. "Get after him or he'll get away! Damn it! Get after the rat!"

Shrieking Indians darted all around the house. Their rifles cracked at a madly retreating man sprinting away from them into the woods beyond. Their curses announced their disappointing aim to the rangers rushing up behind them. Their rifles also cracked at the shadow disappearing into the dark folds of the forest. "Damn it!" Secord yelled. "Missed the bloody rat!"

The lead warrior gruffly stuffed the bloody scalp into his pouch and ran after the rebel with his fellows following closely at his heels. Their yelps and cries soon dissipated with distance into the dense forest.

"Do you want us to follow?" an anxious ranger asked Secord.

"No," he said, collapsing to the ground. "I'm sure they'll make short work of him." He sighed and looked back to the house. "The bastards, anyways. Why couldn't they just leave us be?"

"No worries," Terry said, sensing his concern. "When the war is finally settled we shall have our pick of land in all of Wyoming. We shall be the lords over these disobedient rats, and I grant you I shall keep them on a short leash, for sure I will." He waved his hand all about. "All of this shall be Secord land, all about Tunkhannock, this I assure you, for we cannot fail, for we are in the right and recognize our rightful sovereign. He shall reward us, the king shall, his right faithful subjects!"

"Tell that to that poor bastard back in the doorway," Secord snarled back. "I, for one, wish this bloody mess would have never had happened!" He slowly rose and looked with disgust down to his rifle. Stumbling back to the doorway he gruffly kicked the dead rebel from it. "Rotten bastards," he said. Solid disdain blanketed his face.

"Now your very doorway is covered with a traitor's blood," Terry said.

Secord just scowled back at him and walked into his war-torn home, fearing and knowing nothing would ever be the same again, even if the war stopped this very day. This revolution changed all, and forever.

"Live by the sword, die by the sword," he mumbled to the lifeless body in the doorway before him. "Words we all need to heed. If we only had the ears to listen. War is such a cruel business in the end."

## Chapter Thirty Seven
*Fate's Warning*

Asa Budd ran with all his strength, fueled by a thirst for life. Branches pushed aside by his failing hands snapped and broke in his wake. He stumbled, rolling head over foot before jutting back up on the momentum of his fall. Shrieks and blood-thirsty wails echoed through the trees to his rear. He barely stopped long enough to gasp and catch his breath before the yells urged him on again, madly leaping over fallen logs and boulders. Gripping branches grabbed at his clothes and his rifle pouch, but he ignored them, letting the branches rip them from his body. Not until one tugged at the rifle held in his tight fisted hand did he slow, pulling it free of a clinging and tangled mass of vegetation.

The whoops and shrieks sounded all the nearer. Glimpsing a rushing shadow to his rear he instantly fired his rifle at it before giving up the spent weapon up to the clinging branches. Running all the faster he finally caught a glimpse of the river through the trees ahead. He sprinted to it with a great burst of strength, sliding down its muddy banks into the water with a splash. Raising his head, he searched along the shoreline for any sign of their canoe. The shrieks echoed through his ears and above his thudding heart in his ears. Wiping the sweat from his eyes he fought for each step along the muddy river bottom. There, finally, sat the canoe just around the bend. He dove and swam madly toward it.

Reaching the canoe he yanked it into the water and dove into it. Feeling wildly around the bottom of it his hands finally clutched a paddle. In another heartbeat he slammed it into the water.

Angry spurts erupted in the water around him, followed by angry cracks in the air. Scrunching down he paddled with all his might for the next shielding bend on the river, praying to God, his mother, and all that ever was or ever would be for strength. "Just get me out of here! I shall never return! I get it! I get it! Mere land is not worth one's lifeblood!" he muttered to himself through his gasping breaths.

The shrieks grew, fueled by anger. More shots cracked in the air, this time cracking into the fragile birch bark canoe. A splintering crack sounded along the top of the gunwale of the canoe, sending a sharp burning pain through his side. Fearing the worse, he glanced down between mad strokes, relieved to see a long splinter of wood protruding from his side and not a round hole. With a cruel yank he pulled the wood from his side and scrunched back down into the canoe, muttering more oaths and prayers until he rounded the bend just ahead of him.

Rounding the bend he stopped only to catch his panting breaths before paddling all the harder. Each stroke gained distance from the heavy breath of death panting down his neck. He paddled and paddled until sheer exhaustion overcame him. Finally, he collapsed down into the canoe, trusting the strong current to carry him out of harm's way.

Running his anxious fingers over his bleeding side he quickly examined it. Not deep, he realized with relief, only a flesh wound. The current is strong. It will carry you away. Away from this horrid land. Oh, poor William Crooks! Why in heaven's name did he allow the man to talk him into accompanying him up the river? Free land, he had told him. Do not worry of the Tories, they will never show their faces around these parts again, if they know what is good for them, anyways, the cowards. Some cowards! And some free land! Alas poor Crooks, nothing is free, and now you paid with your life from those not quite the cowards you thought them to be. The blue-eyed Indians in these parts seemed more savage than the true Indians! It is a particularly cruel war in this part of the country, for it is waged between family and friends. More quarter is given to a stranger on the field of battle than it is to a former friend, neighbor, and brother. He found his love of life to be greater than anything else after living through this experience. He promised himself to follow the river far away from this dark and blood-tainted land, for he saw no end to it, and no peace even after the war ended. For a passion born of this land itself fueled the rage of war in these parts. How could any conflict born of such passions fade but with the passing of generations? Only the deep shadows of time could veil the rage born of the love of land in these parts.

After his heaving chest finally began settling, he raised himself up in the canoe, staring all about before his thudding heart also settled in his chest. He felt transferred into an alien world, for birds chirped in the trees blanketing the lush banks. Great trees bent their ancient branches down over the riverbanks as if to drink from the beautiful Susquehanna. An eagle gently glided along the face of the serene waters. Another dove into the river just to his side, rising into the air with a huge fish clutched in its talons. The ancient trees bathed the surrounding mountains in a deep green. Wyoming appeared so beautiful, but death lurked under the dark folds of its great trees. A threat which outweighed all of its other attributes. Death's darkness tainted its beauty.

He paddled steadily down the river. Scattered fields soon broke the endless forest on the banks of the river, not round, as Indian fashion, but square, in the white man's fashion. Further on cabins dotted the shoreline, then, much to his relief, Fort Jenkins and Pittston Fort showed on opposite banks of the great river. He sighed, suddenly thinking the forts a feeble attempt for defense from the terrible tide sweeping down from the north. He ignored the waves from people along the shore and paddled all the harder, anxious to gain Forty Fort.

Reaching the landing by Forty Fort he pulled his canoe onto it and stumbled up the bank. After a few steps he stopped and looked back to the canoe, quickly examining its damage. All the bullet holes seemed to ride high above its waterline. Good, it will get him down river. That is all he wanted.

"Asa Budd?" a man asked behind him. "My God what has happened? Where is Crooks?"

"Dead," Asa answered, turning slowly to look at him.

The man's eyes widened but Budd said nothing in response. He walked past the man without a second glance and marched steadily toward the fort.

The man followed him without saying a word. Budd's hollow eyes precluded him from asking any more questions. The man soon carefully passed him and spurted ahead of him to the fort. "Fetch Colonels Denison and Butler," the man said between pants to the sentry by the gate. "And be Goddamned quick about it!"

The man stood aside, giving Budd a wide berth through the gate.

Budd marched right to one of the cabins along the fort's walls and crammed his traps and belongings into anything that would carry them. He then turned and marched back to the gate, noticing the many eyes now following him, paying no one heed to them except for the two small boys helping with his things. Two men stood by the gate, one wearing a regimental uniform of the Continental Line and the other clad in a fine hunting shirt. Both wore cocked hats sporting cockades. They both carefully stepped into his path to block him from exiting the gate.

"Asa Budd, my dear man, what has happened?" the man in the hunting shirt asked.

"Colonel Denison," Budd said, stopping just to their front. "I do not wish to cause a panic." Turning, he looked all about. Many eyes watched him, some old, some young, but all concerned. "Hell, maybe I do at that, if it will awaken you to what's to come!" Shaking his head he dropped his bundles down to the ground. "Crooks is dead, felled by a half dozen balls up at the Tory Secord's place! The Indians and Tories are coming! A hell of a lot of them too! That I grant you, fer sure!"

"What? Indians and Tories?" the man in the regimental asked. Both he and Denison curiously noticed the bloody spot about his waist.

"Colonel Butler it don't matter none," he said. "Both hate us all just the same. And both are coming! Hell, they almost got me!" he added, noticing their stares at his wound. Picking up his bundles he slowly looked all around. "All you good people get out while you can!" he shouted, kicking at the ground beneath his feet. "It's just dirt! And there's plenty more! Life is not so plentiful! Get out of here whilst you still got ye hair and come back if ye want after this is all over!"

"That is enough!" Denison said. "Our blood is in this soil! We fought Pennamites, diseases, famine, and savages for it and I'll be Goddamned if anyone's going to take it from us now!"

"Suit yourself, fine sir, I'm off down the river as far as it can carry me!" Budd said. He took a few steps toward the men. Hesitating for a moment he sternly stomped between them, shaking his head in disbelief. Stopping just to the other side of the gate he turned about to the two men, now engaged in a hushed conversation between them. "May God bless and protect you all," he said, running his eyes all along the tall hewn logs doubled backed upon one another making up the walls of the fine fort. A fine structure, it would take many cannon to compromise its walls. "When they do come, bent of hell's fury, stay within these walls until they pass, for God's sake!" he warned.

The two men said nothing in response. Both rolled their eyes at the man and turned away, slowly walking back into the fort.

"Stay in the fort!" Budd called back one more time before tromping back to his bullet-riddled canoe. "Heed my warning!"

Vision of hordes of Indians swiftly canoeing down the river flashed through his haunted soul. "God, I tried to warn them," he muttered to himself, looking up into the blue sky. Shaking his head in frustration he added, "Their fate is now in your hands, dear Lord, it is fer sure! Bless these headstrong people enough to know when they're beat!"

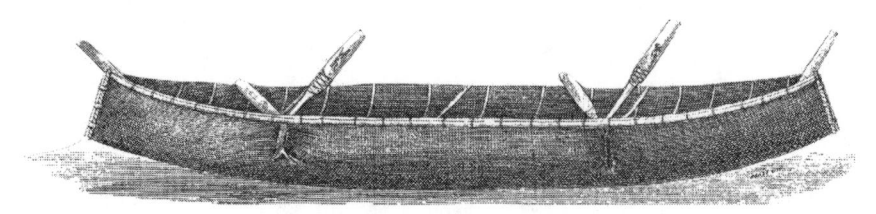

## Chapter Thirty Eight
### *Queen Esther's War*

Here, along the upper reaches of the Susquehanna the question of war lie, waiting on a decision from the Queen holding reign over the region. The Iroquois would strike without her blessing, but it was not their way. Esther Montour, granddaughter of the great French Margret Montour, herself the daughter of a French nobleman and Indian princess, held sway over this part of the Iroquois Confederacy. Her word proved essential for proper cohesion within the mighty Confederacy. It was their way. A way which had brought them all their power. They would not compromise it now for the sake of their blustering British allies.

But the most warlike of the Confederacy, the *Seneca*, always grew anxious when the chance for a fight hovered in the air, and their chief, the mighty *Gucingerachton*, paced to and fro in the Queen's Indian castle, casting an indignant stare down at the Queen lying on a bearskin pallet before a fireplace. The yellow flames from the fire danced in her eyes. Eyes staring into the flames and beyond, deep into the past, but conscious of the future, and of any repercussions a brash act may induce in the future. The Queen did not take the future of her people lightly, no matter how it annoyed a huge barrel-chested chief of the Seneca Nation.

She cast a mournful stare down at the tomahawk placed in front of her. If she lifted it, it meant war. If she ignored it, peace. The monumental decision sent a shard of fear through her soul. A deep shard. The fire crackled, lifting her eyes back to it. Soon she stared into the flames again, seeming to heed a call from beyond within them.

Two other Iroquois chiefs shook their heads and stared at their anxiously pacing third. His eyes widened and reflected the flames straight past them and into the depths of his soul. Pure anger shone within them, fueled by an unquenchable rage. A rage against all white eyes, British, American, French, or Dutch. He made it clear time and time again he trusted none of them, and only agreed to fight along side the British as a means to an end of forever driving the hated white eyes into the seas again. If he needed to bargain with one devil to smite another, so be it. This is what shone in his dark eyes. This is what shone from his heart. He need not his tired words to covey his intentions. His actions spoke louder than any words. Action is what he wanted, and now! He saw no sense in placating this woman along the Susquehanna.

Another stood and paced along with the chief. Gu-cinge stopped and stared indignantly at him, too. The son of the woman held no sway on him either way. "Blood must flow! The Susquehanna must run red with the white eyes' blood before it can ever run clear and pure again, for they pollute all they come in contact with, they, the destroyers of land, of lives, and tradition! They must be dealt with! Now!" the great chief suddenly announced in the Seneca tongue. His words drew many eyes.

The son grunted an affirmation of all he said and reached out his hand toward the chief who only shook his head in frustration and stomped to the far corner of the cabin, grunting and mumbling to himself. His hand fell to the knife in his belt and he gripped it tight, mouthing a prayer for common sense to prevail among his people before it truly became too late.

Esther looked up to the disturbance and smiled, not because of the words, but from the sight of her proud son, *Gencho*. She saw the reflection of her late husband in him, the great *Eghobound*. She smiled all the more when his eyes glared at her.

"He is right! It must be done! It is time to drive the white eyes out forever!" he scolded his mother in frustration. The cold stare his words produced from the other chiefs made his words clump in his throat. He too stormed off to the far corner opposite Gucingerachton.

Esther's eyes glazed over with a dull glare. She looked up to the chiefs now standing over her. Their cold eyes sent chills down her spine. The eldest of the war chiefs, *Sayenqueraghta*, well over seventy years in age, slowly raised his right hand in the air. The time had come. The decision must be made now.

Esther bowed her head and closed her eyes, letting her hand fall to the tomahawk. She felt along the cold steel of its head and the cold metal studs dotting its wooden handle. Locking her fingers around it she lifted it high in the air, staring at it with beaming eyes.

Gencho immediately whooped in pure joy. He bolted out the cabin door, yelping and screaming all the way. A chorus of yells promptly joined him in celebration. "The tomahawk has been raised! The white eyes shall hear *the cry of the tomahawk!*" he announced at the top of his lungs all through the village. Yells soon erupted throughout the village from one end to the other. The yells and cheers grew to a deafening crescendo. The mountains rang with the call to war.

Esther slowly examined the tomahawk in her hands, running her fingers along its sharp edge. Suddenly dropping it as if it burned her hands, she raised both her hands high into the tense air.

*Gayentwahga*, the third war chief, or *Cornplanter* as the whites called him, picked up the tomahawk and motioned her toward the door. Raising it high above his head he followed the other chiefs out the door.

Esther rose and obediently followed them.

Hundreds of shrilling voices greeted the chiefs and the Queen.

They slowly stepped forwards into the excited crowd, nodding their heads in appeasement to the nature of the beast overcoming the hearts of their people. A beast born of rage. A beast called war.

At length a group of warriors, painted head to foot in hideous war paint, and armed to the teeth with rifles, tomahawks, spears, and war clubs, parted the crowd and approached the chiefs. They stopped just in front of the chiefs, demanding recognition and their blessing. The crowd suddenly grew silent.

Esther raised her war tomahawk, emitting an ear-splitting wail.

The crowd promptly erupted with a hundred wails in answer. Men, women, and children danced about, joined by a bevy of dogs howling in the frenzy. Cries filled the air, echoing off the mountains and reverberating back through the village, as if answering the Indians' calls in affirmation. The tired beat of the water drum joined the yells. Feasting and festivities erupted throughout the village. The mountains, dark as midnight beyond the village, drank the lurid flames cast by the many fires growing in the village. The flames lit up the stern visages flitting along the cabins and bark huts before them. Hovering above the dark mountains the waning moon trembled like a crescent of blood on the verge of the western horizon, a sign of the approaching carnage of war.

Esther stood at the apex of it all, her eyes glaring. Conscious of the many eyes watching her, she deferred attention to the Iroquois war chiefs, much to their delight. Backing slowly away, she let the tomahawk fall from her limp hand. Her stark eyes stared at it for a moment, suddenly realizing she may have condoned the impetus for change forever. This white man's war, this *revolution*, touched all of the rest of the world, especially those nations close to its heart.

She picked up the war tomahawk. Tucking it unceremoniously in her belt she watched the chiefs lead the crowd toward a great fire in the middle of the village. There they took their exalted places by the glowing fire. They sat, acknowledging all the congratulatory nods and food passed to them. All of them nodded profusely and praised their warriors, certain of their upcoming victory.

Esther slowly turned and walked to her castle, casting a weary smile to the few faces greeting her. Soon no one seemed to notice her glum face in the crowd of good cheer. She stopped, suddenly noticing the many glowing fires reflecting off the face of the Susquehanna. After a moment of consideration, she walked stealthily toward it. Her mind flashed with the memory of her and her late husband walking hand and hand along it in better times, more hopeful times, dreaming of the future and the hope of their children. They sat for hours along its banks, watching it flow gently and tirelessly past them on its great trek to the sea, pretending to cast their worries upon the face of the waters, there to be carried far way to become lost forever. Such memories warmed her heart and she dearly missed the great love of her life, Eghobund. Family remained her husband's legacy, and her son Gencho carried his seed, a seed she wished to protect. The treat of war endangered all, especially her family. Gencho always seemed to think because of his great father he had to do more than the others to live up to his father's legacy. She feared war for just such a reason, but knew not what to do, for the tide of war swept all before it. She suddenly felt powerless in its face.

Noticing a pine bough hut to her front she stopped and gazed down upon the huddled faces gathered around the small fire in front of it. The faces, though covered with dirt, nonetheless showed the features of the white eyes. An eerie glow reflected from their glum faces, desperate and full of despair. They seemed most out of place. One thing all races held in common seemed to be a love for family and gazing at the hollow eyes of the white woman clothed in rags and her crestfallen children compounded a great sense of pity in her heart. She took a few steps toward the hut and stared sullenly at the fearful and questioning eyes staring back at her. She knew this family of white eyes-the Stropes- and silently thanked the great spirit that their father had evaded capture, for she knew Boss Strope to be a good man whom loved his family. Being free, he would not rest until he reunited his family torn asunder by the cruel hand of war. In this she found hope for them and felt a strange kindred with this family threatened by war as much as hers.

"Do not fear," she said. "Be still and you be fine. I no let warriors bother you. This I command!"

The huddled mass of faces remained blank and hollow.

"Storm of war thunders," she said. "We must bend as the branches of a great tree against its cruel wind!"

"You are bold to say so," the white woman said, turning her grim eyes toward the Queen. "For you are the dark cloud which brings it along!"

Esther shook her head, knowing nothing she said would do anything to ease the hard woman's angst. What was she to do? If she released them how would this skeleton of a woman lead her desperate children many miles down the river, full of beasts, Tories, and *wild* Indians of whom she held no sway? No, they must wait until the winds of war passed, then strong Boss Strope would find them and reunite them. It was all she could do to keep them safe in this very village, let alone in the wilderness. She tried to smile, but feared it to be too inappropriate. She turned toward the solace of the Susquehanna. Her eyes followed a log floating lazily down its waters. She wished to cast her woes upon it and be done with this whole messy business.

Lydia Strope rose, no longer able to contain her anger. She could not let this betrayer, this person whom apparently only feigned friendship with them all these years, escape without a piece of her mind, damn the consequences! She wanted to strike the woman whom had betrayed her entire family's and all of Wyoming's trust, but feared the blow to be fatal, not to the Queen, that is, but rather to her. She still had the children to think of, so she held her angry hand in check.

Solemnly, she fixed her ragged dress the best she could and strode face to face to the devil, hoping the hatred cut into the scoundrel's conscience, if she possessed one, that is. She thought of her warriors visiting their bark hut after their raids, throwing reeking and bloody scalps at her feet proclaiming one of them to be Boss's hair. She tearfully examined each one until satisfied none of them belonged to her husband. The warriors always laughed their cruel hearts out. They never seemed to tire of their cruel game. These cruel rats had the sanction of their Queen. Nothing happen in this whole valley without her approval. Nothing!

"My child," Esther said to the woman glaring at her through eyes raging and overflowing with hatred. "You know not of what you think!" She shook her head and looked to the log. "You eyes blinded by hate as many others! I have no power over such thing!"

"You are their Queen," Lydia managed to say through her gritted teeth.

"Queen, yes," Esther said, feeling down to the cross hanging on her necklace, "but not their God, no!"

Lydia did not move or even blink an eye.

"Did I no save you men from gauntlet?" Esther asked. "I make sure they take to Niagara, it best I could do! They die if stay here!"

"Niagara!?!" Lydia gasped. "I've heard of that hole! I saw the fetters digging into their skin afore they marched a foot toward Niagara! I am sure they shall bear those scars the rest of their lives!"

"They may, but they still have life!" Esther turned her pleading eyes toward the dancing and hooting braves assembling around a post near the center of the village. "See post! No one there! If Strope men here they be at it! Can you no see? Cannot white eyes see?"

"We see enough!" Lydia quickly answered, gripping tightly at the rags clothing her thighs to prevent her hands from striking the devil. Exasperated, she turned and ran into the bark hut, no longer able to stomach the fiend of the Susquehanna.

The Queen raised her hands in despair, watching Lydia's children trail behind her and disappear into the small hut. Their cries filtered through the boughs. Lydia's anguished cries rose above them all.

Esther stood stunned, staring at the hut and praying with all her might to her ancestors, her dear late husband, the *Great Manitou,*

*Hawenneegar*, and *Jehovah*, to relieve the Susquehanna of the plaque of war. Her mind swirled with dread. Why? Why must this be? Blaming the whites' hunger for land seemed too trivial in the face of it all. Something more operated here; something greater and beyond all their control, even the greatest of them. Red or white. The thunder of war sounded. No one could control it no more than they could the natural thunder. Once unleashed it had to play out until it spent its rage.

Her eyes suddenly fell on a shadowy figure scampering along the riverbank, apparently not noticing the Queen, for his eyes remained fixed on the hut full of crying whites. Grasping his tomahawk tight he bent down to the entrance of the hut, his dark eyes alive with anger.

"No!" a commanding voice suddenly startled him. He jumped in spite of himself, nearly dropping the tomahawk. "You jogo! Now!' the voice scolded him again. He turned to see his Queen standing tall before him, pointing her long bony finger back to the village.

Another warrior, somehow noticing the disturbance in all the hubbub, ran toward the hut.

The Queen locked eyes with the Iroquois warrior. She had never seen him before, she realized. Was he an omen of what was to come? How could any one sovereign control a people fueled by such pure rage?

The warrior's eyes shot back at her, full of defiance.

The approaching warrior raised his own war club in defense of his Queen. Grabbing the Iroquois by the shoulder, he gruffly pushed him away from the hut. The painted Iroquois warrior growled in defiance.

Two other warriors suddenly appeared, looking with questioning eyes at the three before them. What was this? Indian against Indian?

The Iroquois warrior, suddenly bearing the look of a child caught in some mischief, shook his head. He looked beyond the Queen and her warriors to the growing festivities behind them.

Esther let her eyes speak further, staring down the warrior.

The warrior slowly placed his tomahawk in his sash and walked toward the village without so much as a passing glance behind him.

"You stay," Esther said to the first warrior before turning toward the river. "Make sure white woman and her children stay safe!"

No, nothing would ever be the same. Tonight it changed forever.

## Chapter Thirty Nine
*White Dog Sacrifice*

The evening shadows crept up the mountains on either side of the winding Susquehanna and Chemung rivers. The last rays of sunlight faded over the crest of the western mountains, leaving Tioga Point smothered in a man-made glow of many fires. One fire in particular, nestled in the middle of a five acre plot the Tory John Secord had laboriously etched out of the forest around his cabin, shone brighter than the others. Around it many Indians danced, howling and twisting their bodies in unnatural ways, all in the festive mood the brink of war brings about in men's souls. The festivities in Esther's Town the previous night paled in comparison.

The fierce fires illuminated the quiet faces of the peaceful rivers and the bending trees along their banks in a strange glow. A mighty chorus of chants and war songs rolled down the river, haunting the valley until slowly dying in the lush greenness of the vast forest.

One cry suddenly rose above the tumult. Oddly no tongue of a young man bore responsibility for the unearthly wail, but rather an old man's tongue claimed it. The old man stood by a newly erected post, crying his long high pitched and eerie wail which somehow rose above all the other noises, demanding a certain attention. His head shook with such force the feathers atop it danced to and fro, adding a new dimension to his antics.

Drawing adequate attention he ceased his wail, changing his tone to a low sounding song, timed to the beating of a water drum tucked under his arm, as the ancients formerly timed their music by beating the tabor. On this warriors began to advance, moving forward in concert like well disciplined troops called by the fife and drum, each wielding a tomahawk, spear, or war club. They all moved regularly toward the south; the way they intended to go to war. At length they all pointed their tomahawks toward the confluence of the Chemung and Susquehanna rivers and after emitting their own simultaneous and unearthly wails quickly wheeled about, dancing in the same manner back to the old chief standing vigil by his post. His great beaming eyes, alive with the promise of war, glared back at them. He slowly stepped back, giving way to a particularly fierce looking warrior.

The fierce warrior danced in a slow moving posture around the post, his glaring eyes staring at the tomahawk he raised up and down and waved all about. His war song started, slowly at first, but then gave rise to a chanting *he-uh, he uh,* from the rest of the warriors. The pitch and tenor of the song grew with the warriors' increasingly agitated moves, finally culminating with a sudden stop and turn toward the post, ending with a strong and forceful whack on the post. The warrior, screeching so loud it forced his head back, bared his teeth and shouted his exploits in previous campaigns, calling for the crowd to dance into a frenzy, proclaiming all they intended to do to the white eyes in the upcoming campaign.

Loud shouts of affirmation answered his declarations, echoing off the far mountains only to reverberate back through the entire assembly of warriors, which in turn influenced other warriors not intending to go to war to announce their change of heart with their own war songs and dances. This continued until every warrior present swore to join his fellows in the upcoming campaign. The entire *Six Nations*, even a scattering of Oneida and Tuscarora warriors, soon stood united, much to Tory Major Butler's delight.

He swaggered among them in pure joy. Entranced by the vigor and spirit of the Indians, he started his own dance, much as he had witnessed his mentor, the great Sir William Johnson, do many times before him. Now he understood the power Johnson had harnessed for the British Empire. His admiration for his late superior grew tenfold in his heart. Oh, if only Sir William had lived to see this day! Though he knew no one could replace such a rare and indispensable man, least of all his son, or any of his lieutenants he left behind, he, in this moment, came closer to understanding the great man than he ever did when the renowned man lived. Fearing no one could fill the great man's shoes, he felt confident he alone among all of his lieutenants could walk in his wake; for he knew his spirit. He saw glimpses of it now, though he had long passed. Somehow it lived again, influencing from beyond the grave.

Noticing a gathering around a dancing medicine man leading a pure white dog behind him on a leash, he ceased dancing and followed him. The dog turned its head to and fro, seeming to be equally entranced by all the commotion. The dancing medicine man seemed to revere the dog, gently leading it with no tugs at its loose leash. He heightened his dance, coming close to a fire with an iron tripod sitting beside it.

The dog, sensing the change in the man's demeanor, suddenly pulled back against the leash, seeming to sense something. A cruel tug yanked him toward the medicine man, his eyes now alive with purpose. The dog whined, staring up in confusion at all the attentive eyes watching it.

The medicine man started a chant, slowly kneeling to the frightened dog. Whispering something to it, he gently started caressing its pure white coat in admiration. Then, changing his stance in an instant, he slipped a looped leather thong over the its hind legs and yanked it into the air. It whined and snapped at the cruel hands lifting it to no avail. It howled and twisted all the more at its indifferent master until totally exhausted. It finally emitted a long mournful whine and dangled limp on the tether around its feet, much to everyone's delight.

The medicine man slowly and patiently tied the end of the leather thong to the tripod, chanting a soothing chant to the exhausted dog. The dog jumped against the heat from the rising flames, trying with one last burst of strength to free itself. It nipped close to the decorated fringes of the medicine man's buckskin shirt, tearing away one of the many silver trinkets dangling from it. It spat the trinket down to the ground, furiously trying bite the cruel man.

Lifting a hand to the dog the medicine man chanted a soothing song, turning his head to the heavens. The dog jerked all the more. Its pitiful howls sounded against the tired drone of the medicine man's chant, having no more effect on it than to increase its rhythm.

The medicine man looked about the gathering circle and nodded his head to them and to the heavens. Raising his knife from its sheath he pointed it high to the heavens, swirling it in the air. Dancing closer to the jerking dog he lowered the tone of his chant, seeming to have a calming effect on the beast. He slowly lowered his hand to the dog's muzzle, clamping it between his long and boney fingers in triumph.

A single roar sounded from hundreds of Indians' throats all at once. Butler backed away, suddenly feeling totally out of place. Another roar stopped his steps. He looked with all the other eyes to the medicine man chanting all the louder and raising his ceremonial knife high in the air.

Hearing the crowd grow silent, the medicine man ceased chanting. Rolling his eyes wildly in his head he yelled loudly into the air, immediately answered by a louder yell from beyond the crowd.

The silent crowd parted, giving way to the great Iroquois War Chief *Sayenqueraghta, he who goes in smoke,* or simply *Old Smoke,* tall and strong, with sharp features and a glaring eye full of life despite his seventy years. He strode toward the medicine man with a dozen lesser chiefs in his wake. They all spread around the fire to give audience to the great war chief.

Sayenqueraghta stepped up to the medicine man and took the knife from him, provoking another cheer through the crowd. The dog, sensing its doom, suddenly jerked back to life, almost freeing itself from the medicine man's hands.

Sayenqueraghta's strong hand immediately clamped onto the

dog's muzzle, holding tight against its spasmodic body. The medicine man promptly backed away in deference to the great chief..

In one fluid motion the old Indian chief sliced the dog's throat and quickly released its flailing body. Its blood sizzled against the flames with its last gasp and burst of strength. With a last whine it hung motionless, its white coat singed with flames. The old chief glared down at its lifeless body with questioning eyes.

Two braves and the medicine man immediately darted forward. Moving the tripod over the center of the flames the braves bowed and moved back toward the crowd, giving deference to the great chief. The medicine man bent down and quickly examined the dog still spiraling over the flames from the momentum of its last fight for life. Jumping up he emitted an ear-splitting wail, declaring in the Cayuga tongue the sacrifice a great success.

All took his meaning and cheered again. Soon all the warriors would partake in a bit of its blessed flesh for protection against the Yankees at Wyoming when they swept them forever from their land. Then the *Great Spirit* would come and make a tobacco pouch from its skin in the night before the dawn. The ceremony would be repeated upon return from the successful campaign.

The old chief turned his aged eyes to the heavens and muttered a prayer, raising his hand with the bloody knife high to the heavens.

Gucingerachton, overcome by sheer emotion, swaggered up to his fellow chief and grabbed his upraised hand declaring no white eyes could stand against such magic! Thumping his huge barrel chest he yelled at the top of his lungs, joined by all the remaining chiefs.

Butler, taken aback by the whole spectacle, finally pushed his way through the crowd to the rear, feeling something heave within the pit of his stomach. No doubt he knew his own ancestors must have behaved in the same manner and wondered of all of mankind, and of Sir William. He must have taken part in many such rituals, but for the life of him he could swear he had never heard mention of any of it by him. The sheer spirit of the act forever etched it in his mind for it betrayed the true spirit of these Indian people. A strong spirit. An indomitable spirit. An ancient spirit. A fierce spirit to be revered, and feared.

He shuddered for a moment thinking of the fate of the misguided Yankees about Wyoming. But they had brought all of this onto themselves, he reminded himself. If they did not learn a lesson from this, he feared they never would. He once again thought of Sir William and thanked him for securing these *Romans of the West* as their fateful allies. He feared for it to be any other way.

## Chapter Forty
### Brant and Butler

Major Butler, fully recovered from the late spectacle of the *white dog sacrifice*, strode back through the crowd of celebrating Indians, stripped down to his shirtsleeves and with his face painted as gruesome as any other warrior; much as he had seen Sir William Johnson do many a time at great councils. He glanced back to his own second chief, Captain Caldwell, dressed in his fine green uniform marching proudly behind him. He bowed and nodded his head profusely to all the warriors hooting and gallivanting all around them.

"We will do it!" Butler said in his limited Seneca tongue to the braves. "We will drive the Yankees from Wyoming with such a thrashing they shall never return!" he added, switching to English for the sake of Caldwell in his wake.

A hearty huzza answered him from his captain.

He suddenly emerged from the crowd only to run into the gloating chief Gucingerachton. Hastily stopping, he instinctively offered his hand to the suspicious warrior. The warrior's cold eye made him withdraw his hand, realizing how he may have offended the warrior. Sir William would have never had made such a mistake. "Do your work along the West Branch well and we shall be rid of the hated Yankees forever!" he attempted to say in broken Seneca. He nervously stepped back to Caldwell who bore a befuddled look.

Gucingerachton glared at both of the white men for the longest moment before a slight smile betrayed his true feelings. He drew a certain glee from spooking the white devils, and reminded himself one had to use to tools at hand to take the first step in ridding the land of the white eyes forever, even if he had to play one white tribe against another. He nodded at the white men, showing he caught the gist of his butchered Seneca. He acknowledged the white man in the true Seneca tongue, as he, unlike his brethren, had never learnt the white man's tongue, English or French. He promised himself it would never taint his lips.

In another instant he screamed and spurted to a nearby war post. Waving his stud-handled tomahawk at a pretend prisoner he struck the post with a sharp thud, boasting of his previous feats in war.

Butler, caught up in the fever of the moment, followed the great chief with a confused and anxious Captain Caldwell in tow. Both white men stopped upon the approach of another warrior; a Mohawk they instantly recognized. Gucingerachton also stared at the haughty figure strolling up to him.

Gucingerachton loudly announced his disdain for the Mohawk

for having refused to allow he and the others sport by not placing his recently captured Yankee prisoners from a raid on *Cobleskill* on the post. It proved an insult to the entire assembly of warriors. A scalp brought as much as a prisoner at Niagara. It made no sense unless this Mohawk, educated at Reverend Wheelock's white school, had ulterior motives of some sort.

The Mohawk said nothing in the face of the accusations, despite all of the unfavorable attention it drew to him. He stared deathly at the Seneca war chief and to the nervous whites standing uneasily behind him. He grunted a greeting to the white men.

Butler said nothing in response. In this matter he shared the feelings of the overly suspicious war chief, though for different reasons. He stared silently at the Mohawk, mostly out of pure jealously of the upstart Mohawk's prestige in the Indian Department. Prestige, he, being a mere interpreter for the late Sir William did not deserve in his eyes, especially with the fact he owed most of his undeserved prestige to Sir William for calling his sister his Indian wife. He did not appreciate this rival and would be certain this glory hound did not partake in this glorious campaign and claim more underserved prestige from it. Not on his watch, anyway!

Thayendanegea stared back indifferently at the white man and Gucingerachton. He slowly turned to Old Smoke standing nearby and smiled.

Old Smoke returned the smile and raised a welcoming hand to the Mohawk *Joseph Brant,* or *Thayendanegea.* The two embraced and walked away arm in arm, leaving the jealous white man and suspicious war chief to stew in their own contempt. After all, he, Sayenqueraghta, held the high post of war chief for the entire Six Nations and in the end it only mattered what he thought. Thayendanegea had the best interests of the Six Nations in his heart. If he outshone the others with the light which shone from his pure heart, what of it? The Iroquois Confederacy needed men of such staunch character and charisma now. Thayendanegea schooled with the whites. He had been to England and seen the Great Father with his own eyes. The old chief looked on him as a bridge between the perplexing whites and his people; the *Aquanuskion* or *ye Covenant people.* He welcomed and sought out his council, even though others may look upon him with a suspicious eye.

They did not go ten feet before Butler approached them from the rear, suddenly finding his words. "Joseph!" he said, preferring to call the Mohawk by his Christian name. "Here are your orders," he added, full of pomp and circumstance. "After Gucingerachton departs on his expedition to the West Branch after which he shall rendezvous with our main party about the mouth of the Tunkhannock Creek, you are to depart to harass the Yankees about the Delaware or Mohawk Rivers, keeping them on edge in that area, which I do not care, it is your choice. You must also collect as many supplies and sundries for our forces."

The Mohawk merely nodded in response, eyeing the British officer from head to foot. A sly smile betrayed his amusement of the man's dress.

Butler eyed the man back, suddenly embarrassed by his appearance. From the look in Brant's eyes he felt he mocked, rather than enhanced, Sir William's memory. He felt truly naked and exposed without his traditional badge of authority, his uniform.

"Joseph!" Caldwell said, sidestepping his awkward superior with a graceful bow. He eagerly shook the Mohawk's hand. "It is good to see you, old man! I've not had time to greet you properly yet, what with all the preparations and such to attend to, right jolly good to see you, old friend!" Suddenly becoming aware of Butler's cold stare at him, he gracefully backed away with a cordial wave of his hand.

"Old Smoke," Butler said, reluctantly addressing the great chief in English so as not to betray his broken Seneca to Brant. An officer must keep proper bearing at all times, he reminded himself, and must always possess tact, especially with dealing with such fickle allies. "I hope you have no objections."

The old chief frowned and shook his head. "I have none, unless Thayendanegea has one," he said, rolling his eyes at Butler.

Brant shook his head. He preferred to be on his own anyway. Yes, he and his warriors and white volunteers did best on their own, anyways, away from the jealousies and spite of their brothers-in-arms.

Gucingerachton suddenly appeared from the crowd, followed closely by a dozen warriors. He held a piece of the roasted dog in his fingers and raised it above his lips before eagerly devouring it. "*Hawenneegar* has blessed this war!" one of his accompanying warriors announced, devouring his own piece of dog in a like manner. All of the warriors simultaneously whooped and fired their rifles straight into the air. "Soon the white eyes shall feel our pent-up wrath!" the warrior added, staring directly at Butler and Caldwell.

"Yes, soon they will," Brant said. "But war shall not always darken the land. We must be conscious of the day of peace to come and act accordingly as not to ignite an undying flame of hatred in our misguided enemy's hearts, for we must always think of our children!"

"In that day no white eyes shall dare threaten our land in

memory of what happens in these days!" Gucingerachton's outspoken spokesman proclaimed in Brant's face. Gucingerachton promptly pushed him aside and took his place staring defiantly in the Mohawk chief's face. Brant seemed much too white in manner for him to ever trust the man. The whites corrupted everything they touched in their lust for prestige gained through property. It blinded them to everything. In that light nothing mattered but their own personal gain. It made him wince just to consider it. It was not the Indian's way to turn a blind eye to his brother's suffering and think only of self-gratification. Such a selfish people would be easy to conquer, if it were not for their guns, diseases, and steel. Their pox alone killed more Indians than all of their rifles combined. If not for it, the *original* peoples would have driven them back into the seas long ago. Thus, he believed the only hope for his people remained in ridding the land of the whites forever with might, trickery, or any deception which gained the desired end. Appeasement with them only brought more despair in the end. This, he tried to convey to the upstart through his eyes. Noticing nothing but defiance, a trait of the whites, in the eyes staring back at him he huffed and turned back toward the fire, there to find people of a like heart. There to find people of sense.

"He is headstrong," Brant said, " but he will do fine. His hatred for the whites burns deep within his soul, even against the whites we call friend." He turned and looked directly at Butler.

Butler raised one of his black and bushy eyebrows and brought a handkerchief to his face. Nodding to the chiefs, he wiped the sweat-streaked paint from his face. "I must return to my tent," he said, turning away. "I've much more to plan."

Caldwell smiled to both chiefs. He then turned and followed his own chief through the festive crowd.

"I pray this battle to be the last," Old Smoke muttered under his breath.

"No," Brant said, "it has a long course to run before its embers of hate burn out." He stepped over to the nearest fire and kicked at some dying embers. Fire flecks swirled and danced into the dark heavens above. "May God have mercy on our souls."

Old Smoke nodded.

An energetic warrior swaggered up to them and presented them with long strips of the stringy meat of the dog. Tilting their heads back they both slowly fed the meat into their mouths, gazing at the stars above with a prayer of victory in their hearts. They then turned to the welcoming arms of their brethren and joined in the festivities, hoping it to clear the foreboding cloud covering their hearts.

## Chapter Forty One
### *The Scouts*

Stephen Jenkins watched the riverbank with a keen eye. The thought of Crook's fate, along with Asa Budd's and his brother John's warnings, haunted him, but someone had to scout the river. Glancing to his front at his two companions in the canoe, Joel Phelps and Miner Robbins, he noticed they scanned with riverbank with an equally intense eye.

"Tunkhannock Creek lies just around the next bend," he announced. "We should make Wyalusing before nightfall."

The two men looked back at him with a start.

"Come now," he said, "you really don't expect to come into any trouble 'til we reach Tioga, do you?"

"Ask Crooks that question," Phelps said, raising his paddle and waving it toward the riverbank. The dark shadows under the great trees never seemed so deep.

"Part of our task is to stop and bury him proper," Stephen said. He motioned to Phelps to put his paddle back to work and steady the drifting canoe.

"If you are weary Joel, I'll take the paddle," Miner said from behind him.

"No, I'm fine," Phelps said, gazing back over his shoulder. He wiped his sweaty brow with his sleeve and stared at the dark folds of the forest surrounding them. "You just keep your eye peeled sharp on them banks and keep that rifle at the ready!" A few pulls of the paddle against the increasingly strong current made him reconsider the offer. "Perhaps you can take over for a spell after we round this next bend, if'n you'd like," he added.

Both Miner and Jenkins chuckled.

"What?" he asked. "My arms still ache from paddling through Cowyard's Riff. Current's mighty strong there, it is at that fer sure."

"Maybe I will spell Stephen first," Miner said. "After all, Denison did put him in command."

Phelps smirked. "That's the way of it, is it?" he said, looking back at the rifle lying across Miner's front. "Seems you'd want the better shot to be about that rifle if we should have the misfortune of coming into any mischief here abouts!"

"Oh, I do, I do," Miner said, looking back over his shoulder at Jenkins. Phelps looked back too. Jenkins smiled at first, but quickly blanched at the sight unfolding around the bend to their front. Miner and Phelps instantly turned about.

An enormous camp spread out on the flats to their left. Smoke spiraled and danced on the summer breezes from numerous campfires dotting the camp. Dozens of tents and pine bough huts blanketed the flats. Hundreds of canoes, rafts, and bateaux lined the shore. Warriors, white men in green uniforms, and dozens of women and children scampered about the tents and huts, engaged in all sorts of tasks.

All of their jaws immediately slackened. They all instinctively froze for fear of any splashing noises and let the current carry them back down the river and around the bend. They all watched the many people bustling about the busy camp with their mouth's agape, praying none of their eyes caught sight of them.

The life-saving current finally carried the canoe downstream, giving rise to a simultaneous sigh of relief from all three white men. Jenkins lightly tapped his paddle on the edge of the canoe to draw the attention of his wide-eyed fellows, breaking them from the shock of the moment. They promptly paddled silently toward the shoreline.

"Do you think they saw us," Miner asked on a hushed whisper.

"No, by God, no," Phelps answered. "If they would have they would have swarmed to their canoes and been upon us in a heartbeat!" He felt his own heart loudly thumping in his chest at the reference. Dropping his paddle he clenched his rifle.

"They didn't see us," Jenkins said, gesturing up the riverbank. "We'll beach the canoe and climb up onto this plateau, we should be able to see their camp quite well from there."

"What!?!" both men gasped back at him.

"We've come to scout," Jenkins said. "So let's scout!"

"I think we've seen enough, Stephen!" Phelps said. "There's hundreds in that camp! They have scouts too, need I remind you!"

"No they don't," Jenkins said, "or we would have been discovered long ago!"

"I ,for one, am not up to pushing our luck!" Miner said.

"They're confident none dare venture this far upriver," Jenkins said, pointing his rifle up the steep bank. "We need a proper scout! We need to know their true number and intent!"

"Intent?" Phelps scoffed. "I can tell you their intent! It's to lift as many scalps as they can! Let's not make it so easy for them!"

Jenkins pushed his paddle in the water, forcing the bow of the canoe into the shore. Gently stepping into the water he motioned for his despondent men to do the same. "Don't beach it too far up the bank," he said. "Just in case we have to make a hasty withdrawal."

The words drew cold stares from his fellows struggling with one hand to beach the craft, unwilling to release their other hand from gripping their rifles.

"Not too far up the bank," Jenkins warned them again, taking a long and careful look around the river. "If we have to make a hasty withdrawal we'll make for that island below. It'll cover our retreat."

"Three against an army," Phelps said. "If they catch sight of us you needn't worry about a withdrawal, only about the afterlife!"

"We've a soldier's duty!" Jenkins flatly stated.

Phelps answered with a nod and looked to Miner. He too shook his head, his face turning a shade crimson from embarrassment. They both checked their rifles and looked up the bank, ready to follow, if Jenkins still had a mind to lead.

"They won't be expecting us," Jenkins said. "In that we have an element on our side!"

He received no argument this time.

Nodding at the two men he carefully stared up the steep bank, grabbing on some of the rough Indian grass and scrub brush to pull himself up it. His two fellows silently followed. Upon reaching the bank's summit they scrunched down behind the bushes and grass to conceal themselves and readjusted their powder horns and possible bags twisted about their torsos by the hard climb.

"No, they won't expect us to crawl up that damn bank," Phelps said under his breath. "Not even a savage thinks a Yankee to be such a fool!"

"Now," Jenkins said, turning a cold eye to Phelps, "we'll see just what mischief they are up too, by jingo!"

He looked up and started to rise when a rush of birds burst from the wood line down the plateau. A large party of green-coated white men ran steadily toward them, seeming oblivious to the threat of their weapons.

"Damn it!" Phelps said, raising his rifle. A yell from the man in the lead of the Tories sent a chill down his spine, for he knew the voice, and knew it well. He glared down the sights of his rifle at the familiar eyes running toward him. Blessed God no other than his own brother's eyes shone back at him. He moved his rifle to the side at another of the green-coated traitors and squeezed the trigger. Two more shots rang out from his comrades at his side, but none of the shots seemed to bother the rushing men besides making a few of them duck slightly.

Suddenly turning he locked eyes with both of his unnerved fellows madly trying to reload their long rifles in the tangled scrub brush. Frightening yells approaching them hastened their efforts. Three cracks sounded again, this time winging one of the painted and yelling red devils joining the Tories. At a loud order the Tories stopped, leveled their weapons at the stunned rebels, and fired.

The whizzing balls hastened all three rebels about. Stumbling and tumbling they rolled madly down the bank with yells, sharp cracks, whizzing, and thudding sounds chasing them all the way. None said a word but scrambled frantically into the canoe before all hell descended from the tall bank behind them. Pushing it out into the waters they all dove into it, hurriedly replacing their rifles with paddles.

Paddling with all their might none turned to witness the pandemonium to their rear. The little gouts of water erupting on the face of the waters around them proved all the witness they needed of the fury of their enemy. The spurts and gouts drew closer and closer along with the many yells and curses breathing down their necks. With a sickening thud Miner fell forward, gasping and spitting out blood all over the canoe. In another instant Phelps twisted and yelped from a stinging ball in his shoulder, cursing all the louder at the demons on the shore.

Jenkins, paddling for his life, jumped from something reaching out and cracking his paddle in two in his very hands. Looking in amazement at the splintered ends of paddle in his hands he turned toward the cursing man in his rear. Grasping the paddle Phelps handed him with his good arm, he took it and furiously put it to work, locking his eyes on the shielding island to their front.

Phelps, beseeching God and praying for a groaning Miner, struggled to lift his rifle up to his burning shoulder. Turning about he squeezed off a shot at the masses on the riverbank, changing his prayers once again to curses upon sight of the devils, both red and white.

Jenkins' mad strokes finally brought them to the edge of the island, shielding them from the fury behind them. Mindful of the balls cracking into the leaves, trees, and underbrush of the island he did not let up his furious strokes. Bowing his head he put every ounce of strength from his burning arms into each stroke, oblivious of Miner's moans, Phelps's curses, the thudding and whizzing balls, and his own pain. Only distance would free them from certain death. Only distance. His mind flashed with horrible visions of hundreds of canoes swarming about them, pushing his arms all the more. No! He told himself, mindful of the groans of agony and curses behind him. I got these poor fellows into this and I will get them out! And damn any fuddled-headed fool about Wyoming whom doubts whether the Indians and Tories meant them harm! They most certainly did, you fools! They most certainly did! If it took blood to awaken a fool to danger, he had the wounded men to do it!

## Chapter Forty Two
*Escape!*

The thrill of terror subsiding in his soul, Stephen Jenkins lifted his eyes to the sights around him in the waning sunlight. Paddling the canoe into the swift current he lifted the paddle and rested it across the rails of the craft, listening intently while the current carried them silently downriver. Scolding his heaving breaths he waited patiently for them to slow.

A welcoming silence surrounded them. Turning he looked over his shoulder to his suffering fellows. Miner sat motionless and face forward, cocked in an odd, but apparently comfortable position in the bottom of the canoe. Phelps sat silently rocking back and forth in rear of him, tightly holding his shoulder and wincing in pain. Blood covered both of the men's torsos and lay in pools in the bottom of the canoe.

He didn't say a word, noticing both men's groans had ceased, and silently thanked God no hoots or calls chased them down the river. The demons had not pursued them, yet. Suddenly his own arms burned, but knew his exhaustion paled in comparison to his friends' pain.

Marking the landmarks around them he knew Forty Fort lay far downriver. Too far to risk canoeing the river in the dark night, for any submerged tree or rock easily seen in the light of day may prove deadly in the night. If he swamped the canoe Phelps and Miner would surely drown. He bent his exhausted head low, trying to think.

"It hurts so," Phelps gasped from behind him.

He followed Phelps' eyes to Miner. The man still lay motionless. He suddenly feared the worse. "We have to stop," he said. "I need to see to Miner the best I can afore he bleeds out, and you as well, my dear friend."

Picking out a secluded and sandy landing along the shore he paddled for it. Rolling out of the canoe into the shallow water he eased its prow onto the sandy beach. He then stepped out into the water to the middle of the canoe. Ever so gently he lifted Miner up from the bottom of the it. Miner groaned and looked at him through glassy eyes. He carefully lifted him from the canoe and laid him on the beach, immediately tearing off strips of his shirt and fashioning a hasty bandage over the man's wound.

A splash turned his bed back to the canoe. Phelps stumbled in the water, nearly upsetting the canoe. "No, damn it!" he scolded himself, struggling with his uninjured arm to set the canoe right in the water.

Jenkins immediately helped the struggling man from the water.

"Set that canoe back on the beach afore it drifts away with our rifles!" he gasped through his pain before Jenkins sat him with his back against a great Elm. "Get them rifles!" he yelled through his delirium, "and load 'em all! The devil's is a chasin' us!"

"Yes, I shall load them all, just relax," Jenkins said, grabbing the prow of the canoe and dragging it well up onto the beach. Pulling the rifles and a bundle from them he sat them down onto the beach. Hastily unwrapping the blanket around the bundle he placed it's contents on the beach. Carefully rolling Miner onto the blanket he redressed his wound while Phelps sat watching, rocking back and forth in pain.

"Doesn't look good, does he?" Phelps asked. "Poor soul."

Jenkins said nothing but just scampered toward him across the beach on his knees with a bandage for his wound. "You need to stop rocking," he said, examining his shoulder. "You'll rip it open again!"

"Hell, I can't, it eases it somehow," Phelps said. "Ain't never been shot afore."

"Yes," Jenkins said, finally managing to examine the wound on the rocking man. "Looks like it went clear through," he said with a nod, "should be fine, but I ain't no Doctor Hooker Smith."

"None of us are," Phelps said, picturing the odd man in his mind. "God only made one of him, and that may be a good thing, but don't you go spouting and telling him I said so, for that old bird will be the one seeing to my healing. Wouldn't do to upset him."

Jenkins let the hint of a smile show on his face despite their predicament. "You'll be fine," he said. "Like I said, it went clear through and missed the bones and vitals."

Phelps lowered his eyes to Miner. "And what of Miner?"

"His went clear through too, but in his back to front, unfortunately, but I think he'll make it just fine," Jenkins said.

Phelps' wide eye locked on Jenkins'. He shook his head. "You Jenkins' ain't much on lying, the truth always shows through your eyes."

"He'll make it, don't you pay it no more mind," Jenkins said. "I'll see he makes it!" Turning his attention back to the ailing man he quietly attended to him.

"He's my brother-in-law," Phelps said in the quiet of dusk. "What will his family say? Least of all my sister, damn it."

"You're not to blame," Jenkins said, turning a soulful eye to him.

"Nor you, my friend, nor you, so don't fret on it none too much, it'll corrupt the soul, it will at that," Phelps said. He rolled his head from side to side and suddenly stopped rocking. "Did you see?" he said more to himself than to anyone else.

"It's growing dark as all hell this night," Jenkins said, attempting to change the subject. "I do not think it prudent to move either of you downriver at night. Too easy to upset the canoe on some unseen rock or submerged tree or such. We'll move on at first light."

"Did you see?" Phelps asked again.

Jenkins ignored the question, pulling some jerked venison and biscuits from a haversack. "Too risky to light a fire," he said, passing a piece of the meat and a biscuit to Phelps. "We'll have to eat cold."

"Damn," Phelps said, gesturing to a small barrel in the bundle. "I'm hankering for a spot of that rum something fierce, my friend."

Nodding, Jenkins pulled the barrel from the bundle. Filling a noggin he passed it to Phelps's eager hands. Cradling Miner's head in his arms he poured some of the rum through his bloody lips. "Hold fast Miner," he whispered to the glassy-eyed man. "We shall make Forty Fort on the morrow."

"Did you see?" Phelps asked again, holding the noggin limply in his free hand. Taking a long drink he let the empty noggin fall from his trembling hand.

Jenkins eased Miner's head back down and crawled over to Phelps. Refilling the noggin he raised it to the weakened man's lips.

Phelps took another long drink. "Did you see?" he asked one more time, this time locking eyes with Jenkins before he could turn away.

The man's horrified gaze kept him at bay.

"It was Elijah!" Phelps yelled, shaking his head. "It was he in the lead of the rascals come to do his own brother in! Come to do us all in! Kith and kin! What a horrid war this is to turn brother against brother!" Bowing his head he looked to his bloody shoulder. "It could be his ball in me shoulder or in poor Miner there! Oh what horror! Damn this war!"

Jenkins sat back, struck by the full weight of Phelps's words. He thought of his own brothers and the horrors John had already endured in the hands of former friends and neighbors, taken away to a suffering hole in cold Fort Niagara and returning a mere skeleton of man to them, his eyes hollow and full of grief, scarred for the rest of his life. His heart sank. A war of brothers indeed, he thought. His mind flashed with their recent encounter, recognizing many of the faces, though contorted with hate, advancing against them in that horde of demons.

He drew all three rifles closely to him and loaded them, watching the folding night encase their meager camp along the winding Susquehanna. He welcomed it, hoping it to shield them from the red demons lurking upriver and the wayward turncoats from Wyoming.

## Chapter Forty Three
*Jenkins' Wedding*

John held her hand. He stared so deeply into her eyes it swept away all his aches and pains, carrying him away to that safe place in his soul only she occupied. Once a dream, now a reality. He broke his gaze only once, ever so quickly, to look down at his right hand. The back of it still showed red, but also showed the signs of healing, much as his heart. But none of the past's pain mattered now in the face of true love with its immortal healing magic. Life, he realized, gazing deep in her eyes. Life is what she meant to him, pure and simple.

Bethiah gazed back into his eyes with wonder. What did those eyes see? Her imagination swirled with images of the hell he must have witnessed in the wilderness and in that horrible hole at Fort Niagara. But now his hard eyes began to soften and gaze at her with a wonder born of all men from the first gaze of Adam onto Eve. Such a purity shines through the eyes of love, totally forgiving, totally innocent. Watching the eyes widen as if reading her thoughts she let them sweep away the dark imagines and replace them with the wonder and hope of the future. A future together. Somehow she saw children aching to be born in his eyes. Born of this love shared by he and she, born and blessed within pure love. What a gift to give to a child. What a gift to give to one another. Her heart rose in her gently heaving chest at the thoughts and visions shining back at her through those eyes of love. Strangely, she felt an odd impulse to just gobble him up, heart and soul. Her love throbbed with an ache so deep it echoed beyond her own wants and needs. Through her reflection shining in her beau's pure blue eyes she realized his soul already meandered and entwined with her own soul through the threads of true love stretching across time immortal. Their hearts lie with each other and somehow beyond this moment, somehow beyond eternity.

"Come now!" a familiar voice interrupted them. "Reverend Whittlesey's just arrived!"

They stood locked in their trance immortal on the platform along the walls of the fort, blissfully oblivious of their friend's calls and of the other activity of the bustling crowd filling the fort proper below them.

"My word," John Murphy called down to his wife standing with her head cocked and hands on her hips at the bottom of the ladder he stood upon. "I do believe they are in a trance of some sort!"

"Yes," Elizabeth called back up to him, rubbing her huge belly with a smile. "I recall the same look in your eyes and look to the result now!" she added, patting her belly.

"Now is that any way to talk Mrs. Murphy?" he asked her with an equally great smile.

She smile again, lifting her hand to shield her eyes against the glaring sun. Taking a few steps she gazed up at their love-sick friends. "Come now, my dear Bethiah!" she called. "The table board's all set and the good reverend is finally about! It's time to sanction your love!"

The familiar tones of her friend finally broke Beth's stare, much to John's dismay. Sensing his sadness she gently stroked his shoulder-length locks and let the back of her hand gracefully brush against his cheek. Cupping her hands she gently held his clean-shaven face. "Strangest thing I ever beheld," she said with a slight chuckle, "was that beard about your face when you first returned from the ravages of the wilderness. You, my love, do indeed look much more civilized."

"Civilized and in love," he whispered. Drawing a long breath he turned to the people assembling below them. His mother and father now joined Elizabeth, anxiously staring up at the lovers. He finally noticed his friend John Murphy standing on the ladder to his side. "Just how long have you been there?" he asked him.

"Long enough, my friend, I assure you," John answered. "Long enough." Smiling he waved his arm in a great arcing motion behind him, almost upsetting the ladder. "See!" he said, leaning forwards on the ladder to steady it once again. "All is ready but the bride and groom!"

Noticing them finally heading for the ladder he scampered down it to make way for the honored couple. Turning his eye to the open gate he cast a long look into the dark folds of the forest beyond. He glanced at the sentry turning about to witness the hubbub in the fort. "Your eyes should be about the river and forest beyond," he said.

The young man abruptly turned about, upsetting his rifle. His fumbling hands caught it just before it fell to the earth. Quickly regaining his composure he locked his eyes to his front. Casting a slight glance out of the corner of his eye he noticed Murphy approaching him.

"Never you mind," Murphy said, putting a hand to his shoulder. "No need to fret. I'll make sure they save some of the victuals for you."

Young James Hadsall nodded, turning toward him with a smile.

"Uh, uh, " Murphy scolded him, pointing with a stern hand toward the tree line. "Eyes front! Remember, lad! Eyes front!"

A murmur of greetings turned his attention back to the bride and groom. He followed the growing group assembling around the couple walking hand in hand to a place on the green before the reverend.

The reverend, decked out in his finest black coat and sporting a fine powdered wig, cleared his throat to quiet the crowd. He stared at the skeleton of a once robust and vibrant man in front of him. The man's clothes, which fit fine last fall, hung loosely about his slight frame. The dark bags under his otherwise bright eyes betrayed the true state of his weary body. He wondered of love's resolve, recognizing its gleam in spite of the man's hollow eyes, and wondered of its power and from what part of the soul it arose. The eternal part, he reasoned.

The reverend caught himself in the stare and quickly adverted his eyes. He slowly lifted a small black bible in his hands and kissed it before opening it. "Our most dearly beloved," he said in a booming voice. "We are gathered here, in the face of an all loving and protecting God." He paused, lifting his eyes to the heavens and then slowly to the obedient flock surrounding him. The rifles lying close at hand, including his, made him consider his words all the more deeply.

Clearing his throat he continued, "Here, at this meager outpost of civilization amidst an increasingly hostile wilderness we find grace and eternal love." Slightly bowing, he smiled at both bride and groom. "A love reunited by a most gracious God after delivering young John here back to the folds of his loving family, kith and kin, in due time to start his own family. Thus, even under the threat of violence, God's love endures. I must say I have personally prayed most earnestly for young John's deliverance from the hands of the traitorous Tories and unmerciful savages, a devilish hand which threatens us at this very moment." He took a long slow gaze around the sea of assembled faces, locking eyes with every man for a moment. "I would say that if any has reason to contest this union let him speak now or forever hold his peace, but it is clear there is no dissenting voice in those gathered here to witness this faithful union of two souls most evidently in love. In this let us all find comfort." He looked deeply into John's eyes. "Do you, John Jenkins, promise to live in the covenant of love, and take Bethiah Harris as your most beloved bride, to have and to hold, for better or worse, and promise to love, honor, and cherish her as long as ye both shall live?"

Turning his head John looked deeply into the eyes of the radiant beauty beside him. "I do," he said.

The reverend turned to Bethiah. "And do you, Bethiah Harris, promise to live in the covenant of love, with John Jenkins to be your husband, and promise to love honor, and obey him, in sickness and sorrow, for better or worse, as long as ye both shall live?" he asked.

"Oh, I do," she quickly answered with beaming eyes.

"John, you may place the ring on her finger," the reverend said, noticing the eager young man pulling it from his waistcoat pocket.

John gracefully slipped the silver ring he had personally hand forged onto her finger.

"And now by the power invested in me by our mutual faith in God almighty I do pronounce you man and wife, you may kiss the bride," the reverend said. "May you enjoy many years of happiness. Let no man, be he white or savage, tear asunder what God has blessed. Be it this here marriage or Wyoming!" he added to a cheering crowd and passionately kissing couple to his front.

Such ceremonies took their minds off the Tory and Indian threat. Joy, no mater how fleeting, overcame the foreboding sense of dread, if for but a moment. They drank in and relished it, letting it blanket their fear with a sense of optimism born of this union of two souls.

John Murphy and his wife broke through the joyful crowd carrying a long handled implement with a flattened end high in the air. Stopping full in front of their recently united friends they presented the implement to them with a smile stretching from ear to ear across both of their faces. "Here you be, Mrs. Jenkins, as custom demands, here is your very own bread peel," they both said at once.

More congratulating cheers sounded from the crowd.

Beth grabbed the symbol of her new household with a slight blush upon hearing her new name for the first time.

"Yes, Mrs. Jenkins," Murphy said, noticing her blushing cheeks growing more crimson. "It has finally come about! Believe it! I made that peel months ago in anticipation of this union!" Stepping forward he placed his arm over John Jenkins' shoulders. "I'm proud of you both, me is at that!" he declared, ushering them both toward a long table board. "Here! Eat hardy! You need to put some meat on them bones of yours anyways, as to deal with the rigors which await you!" he added, casting a sly smile to Beth and a wink.

Beth blushed again. "What a fine feast!" she said, gazing at the feast spreading out on the long table board before her in awe. A fine linen table cloth ran the entire length of it. A silver salt cellar sat at its center. The many clumsy wooden trenchers placed about it did little to deface it. Round pewter platters heaping with stewed meat and vegetables ran from one end of it to the other. Many wooden and pewter spoons dotted the tablecloth along with a few precious silver spoons for the guests of honor; the bride and groom. Great wooden noggins and mugs along with leather jacks of all sizes finished the setting, all filled, of course, with the ever-present rum, the drink of choice.

"Oh ladies, it is such a fine setting," Beth said to the woman around the table board, running her hand along the fine table cloth. "Mother Jenkins, this is your best cloth," she said.

"The best for the best," Squire Jenkins announced for his shy and unassuming wife. She followed the best of the Puritan tradition, seeking no praise for expected work. One must be humble. Her husband did not seem to share her passion for tradition, especially when it bordered on impracticability, such as the fine for not showing up at church every Sunday. Squire noticed the slight hint of ire in the reverend's eye but waved it off with the thought of the money provided to him by paying the fine every week. The good reverend should be happy with that, at least, and stop pestering him about his opening his sawmill on Sunday also. Sometimes business had its own demands. To Squire a good soul ran hand in hand with good business sense. It, in the end, provided the money for the whole community to thrive and allow the church in the first place. But he knew his logic to be lost on the other suspicious and scorning eyes he noticed about the assembled crowd today. What of it? In his mind a full belly came first, and tradition a far second.

Noticing one of the stern stares he reached for one of the leather jacks. Raising it high in the air toward tall John Franklin he waved it to him, urging the man to lift his own from the table. Franklin's sour eye melted upon the invitation. Grabbing up a leather jack from the table he raised it with spirit. With a quick nod both men took great simultaneous gulps from the huge leather jacks, bringing them down with equally great smiles of cheer.

The whole of the crowd quickly descended upon the table, each feasting and partaking in the bountiful feast.

"Let us all drink and be merry!" John Murphy shouted to officially announce the beginning of the feast. Raising a mug he lifted it to the cheering crowd, running it all along the beaming faces until stopping at the sight of a pair of stark men standing behind the crowd. Their haunting eyes shot a confused look back to him. It stopped his mug just before it touched his lips. He slowly lowered it, staring at the hollow-eyed men. The blood-soaked bandage covering one of the men's shoulders suddenly made him feel cold.

Stephen Jenkins shook his head and looked to his side at Joel Phelps. He wanted to speak and bless his brother's marriage but the lump in his throat prevented it. Every eye followed Murphy's hollow eyes to the pair of men, just lately returned from a scout with their lives. But one of their number did not come back at all, and his memory showed on the two men's faces, chasing away all the joy of the moment.

"Let us all drink to the memory of Miner Robbins whom just lately has fallen in defense of Wyoming!" Murphy announced to the now hushed crowd. "May God bless his immortal soul."

Amen filled the air from many solemn voices.

## Chapter Forty Four
### *Gucingerachton*

Whoops and shrieks erupted throughout the Indian and Tory camp at the mouth of Bowman Creek on the flats just west of the Susquehanna River. Crowds rushed to welcome a huge party coming down a path along the side of the creek. Warrior greeted warrior with shrieks and whoops which multiplied into a deafening crescendo.

Gucingerachton strode confidently at the head of the column of warriors pouring from the path. He swaggered to the awaiting chiefs standing with arms folded just to the west edge of the camp. Yelping warriors surrounded him, holding plunder of all sorts in their hands. The warriors closest to the swaggering chief held the true trophies of their campaign high in their clenched fists-scalps.

Gucingerachton stopped just to the front of the chiefs. Raising his head high, he stared down at them without uttering a word. Baring his teeth, he gestured toward the scalps and plunder held high by his warriors. He then slowly stepped aside, revealing a motley group of some thirty odd white prisoners stumbling down the trail behind him. Sensing the chiefs' approval he whooped in triumph.

"You have done well!" Sayenqueraghta said to the proud chief in the Seneca tongue.

Gucingerachton's eyes lit up. He jutted his huge chest.

"All is now ready," the chief Gayentwahga, known as Cornplanter by the whites, added, turning his head to gaze upon the vast camp spreading across the flats behind him. "No more shall we be cursed by the white eyes of Wyoming, for with this might, we shall wipe them forever from the land!"

"Your words are true!" Major Butler interrupted from the other side of the group. Profusely nodding his head, he marched to the front of the chiefs, ignoring Gucingerachton's snarl at him. "After we construct but a few more rafts we shall float downriver and deal with the rebels of Wyoming. We shall depart on the morrow."

"The rats shall have no quarter!" Gucingerachton said in Seneca.

Butler nodded, knowing enough of the language to catch the gist of the brash chief's words. He glared at the chief for a long moment before turning back to the other chiefs. "Old Smoke, Cornplanter," he said in English, purposely addressing the chiefs by their white names. "If the rebels surrender, we must respect them. It is the King's way."

Gucingerachton raised his lip and glared at Butler. Grabbing a rifle from the hands of a nearby warrior, he fully cocked the weapon. After giving the white man another anxious look, he fired the rifle into the air with one hand. Dozens of shots immediately answered his shot, igniting a new series of whoops and shrieks.

Butler looked down to the ground, straightened his uniform, and looked the chief dead in the eyes. "You have done well, Gucingerachton!" he tried to state clearly in Seneca. "The King appreciates such a brave and noble ally!"

Gucingerachton rolled his eyes and spat onto the ground. Thumping his chest, he hastily turned away from the white man. He suddenly bolted back to the startled white devil. Locking eyes with him, they both stared defiantly at one another. After a few more tense moments, Gucingerachton screamed and sprinted toward the camp, carrying a slew of warriors in his wake.

"Gucingerachton holds great influence among the warriors," Butler said.

Both Old Smoke and Cornplanter nodded their heads.

"He fights, but fighting it is not always the only way, or the most wise way, to solve differences," Cornplanter said.

The tired and fearful eyes of the haggard prisoners just off to their side caught their attention. Butler noticed their questioning eyes glaring at him. Most disturbed, he stared back at them for the longest moment before turning and marching back to the camp, suddenly seeming oblivious to their pleading eyes.

Old Smoke and Cornplanter waved their hands toward the prisoners. "See they are fed," Cornplanter ordered the warriors guarding them. "Take them to the river so they may drink," Old Smoke added.

The warriors herded the huddled and forlorn group forwards, prodding the old men and women bringing up the rear by spear point. Cornplanter strode forward, lifting his hand to stop the cruel behavior. The stunned warriors glared at him with unbelieving eyes before noticing Old Smoke nodding behind him. They reluctantly lifted their spears and pushed them along with their hands instead, one or two of them pulling at the tethers around their necks to hasten them along.

Butler, noticing the commotion, suddenly stopped and turned about. The warriors led the prisoners past him, but he pretended indifference, rubbing his eyes to shield them from their pleading stares until they passed.

"We will take them to Niagara," Old Smoke said, approaching Butler from behind with Cornplanter.

Butler jumped, apparently not sensing the chiefs walking toward him. "That is well and fine," he said. "The King shall be pleased, as I." Bowing his head ever so slightly, he gave leave to the chief. Clasping his hands behind his back he walked toward his tent, deep in thought.

The two chiefs watched the white chief walk away, wondering of the demons which haunted his soul. This war between whites truly seemed a war between brothers. They only hoped they had joined forces with the winning side, for they silently feared the worse if they had not. But they shook off the thought, after all, the decision had been made, the winds of war now blew, nothing could hold them back. They shrugged and marched into their own camp to the welcoming fanfare due them.

Great bonfires soon dotted the flats with the setting of the sun. Shrills and wails sounded from the camp and dissipated in the veil of nature surrounding them. The Susquehanna River glistened from the bright flames of many fires. White and Indian now intermixed in joyous festivities, each certain of their impending victory.

Butler slowly paced back and forth by his tent, his mind alive with the many details of the campaign. But, through his thoughts specks of the pleading eyes of the prisoners shone, haunting his soul. Bucking up against them, he cast them out with his strong sense of duty and loyalty to his King, and his true government. They had made their beds, now let them lay in them, he told himself, finally turning toward the festivities, hoping to find relief from his anxious thoughts within them.

His duty remained to the King. The Rebels suffered from the King's hand, not his. May God have mercy on their misguided souls.

## Chapter Forty Five
### *A Tory's Promise*

The sun set slowly through the trees along the creek bank. Its fading rays danced across the water to the front of the young man and boy busily washing their faces and hands. Both stared anxiously between splashes to their faces to the woods surrounding them. The shadows grew long.

"Sun's going down," the boy said.

"Just get to finishing yer washing, Pete, so's we can get back to Uncle Ben," the older boy said. Wiping his face with his sleeve, he watched the younger boy pull his waistcoat up to his face to wipe it.

"That sure was a lot of hoeing, Stephen," young Pete said, looking down to his blistered hands. "Never seen so many weeds afore!"

"That's why it's so rightly important we tend to them just now," Stephen said. "Pa and Uncle Ben was right. If we would have heeded John Jenkins' warning to hold off, we would have lost the crop!"

Young Peter Roger's eyes looked into the darkening forest surrounding them. "We ain't back at Fort Jenkins yet, just the same."

"No, but we will be soon enough," Stephen said, rising to his feet. "Now come on, we've got to fetch the horses!"

The two trotted toward the fields along the river bottom. In no time they met a fork in the trail. One path led down to the river and the other up the river to the fields. Stephen stopped and looked around, nervously rubbing the back of his head before leading them on the trail upriver, pulling the younger boy along by his hand.

"The horses are back down the other way," Peter said, shaking his hand free and stopping.

"I know," Stephen said, looking around. "But I got a bad feeling. Let's check on Uncle Ben and the others first."

"But he sent us to the creek to wash up 'cause the bank ain't so soft there and the water's clearer," Pete said, reluctantly following his elder. "He'll be fit to be tied if'n we come back without the horses he told us to fetch!"

"I know, young 'un," Stephen said, turning to look down to the boy, "But I told you, I got a bad feeling and can't shake it!" He suddenly stopped dead in his tracks, staring straight down the trail ahead. Pete almost ran square into him.

"What ya stopping so short fer?" he asked. "You see a rattler?"

Stephen's hand fell to his lips too late. A pair of men standing in trail looked up to them.

"Here now!" one of them called, lowering his rifle. He peered into the fading light to the crest of the trail. "Is that you Stephen Harding, the lad?" he asked.

Stephen stood absolutely still for the longest moment before lowering his hand from Pete's lips.

Both of the strange men turned toward them and took a few steps up the trail, rifles held at the ready.

"Sure is!" Stephen finally said, deciding it best to play their game just now. "Is that you Michael Showers and Jacob Anguish?"

"Blessed be it is," Showers answered, stopping just in front of the lads. "What brings you young 'uns so far upriver?"

"Just tending to the fields up in these parts," Stephen said. "Had too or the weeds would have choked the life out of the crops. They was higher than the corn and such in some places, they was. You all remember what happen back in seventy-three when we all run out of grain for the winter?"

"Why, yes we do," Showers answered, resting his arm and rifle against a tree. He looked with a sly eye to Anguish.

"What brings you two to these parts," Stephen asked, noticing hints of black paint speckling their necks and the backs of their ears, despite the fading light. "We ain't seen hide nor hair of either of ya these past few months, where you been?"

"Oh, we've just been a huntin' is all," Showers said.

Pete suddenly pushed past Stephen and stared at the two men. "Where's yer game then?" he asked. Stephen's cold stare made him retreat back behind him.

"Hain't saw none yet," Anguish said. "But I've a feeling our luck's sure to change shortly."

"Who's them others in the fields below?" Showers asked.

"My Uncle Ben," Stephen said, glancing toward the river and down at Pete to mind his tongue. "He's got a fine lot with him. A clever body of men, all armed to the teeth, what with the Injun trouble and all."

The two men looked at one another with concern. After a few moments Showers straightened himself up against the tree he leaned against. "We ain't seen hide nor hair of any Injuns," he said, smacking his lips. "You can tell yer uncle, and his clever body of men, to call in their watch, if'n they got one, for they're ain't no call for it."

"But what of the Tories?" Pete asked from behind Stephen. Children never played the art of deception well. Stephen rolled his eyes to him, pushing his hand against him to quiet him.

"No need to push the lad," Showers said. "What boy? Do you mean that fool Butler's lot? An ungoddamlikelylooking lot of sogers I pray you'll ever see than that fool lot! Don't you 'fer doubt it none either!

I'se seen 'em! We both have!" He gestured with his rifle barrel over to his partner. He shot a foul look back to him. "Yes, tell yer uncle you've nothing to fear from those crown fools. We'll be right about hunting. Tell 'em we's all the guard they needs."

"Well that's right smart and fine of you," Stephen said, raising his hand to the fading sunlight dripping through the dense trees. "But daylight's fading and we've yet to fetch the horses."

Showers nodded. "Well then, ya best be about your business and we'll be about ours, if'n you like," he said. Anguish lifted his rifle up with a quick motion before his friend waved him to lower it. "What? You see a squirrel or something?" he asked his flustered partner. Nodding to the two boys again, he tipped his hat to them to give them leave.

The confused lads looked at them for a moment and then hurriedly disappeared over the crest of the trail.

"What are you doing, fool?" Anguish asked, anxiously watching the lads disappear. "They'll be sure to spread the alarm!"

"And so shall we, by jingo!" Showers said, turning back toward the trail leading upriver. "They won't get far, so don't you fret about it!"

## Chapter Forty Six
### *The Harding Massacre*

The boys hastily trotted a few rods back along the trail and stopped. Both Stephen and Pete knelt down by a huge fallen pine, staring wide-eyed back at the trail behind them.

"They following us?" Pete asked

"No," Stephens said. "But they're trouble sure as day! I saw Injun paint on both their necks!"

"Injuns!" Pete gasped.

"Yeh, but these are the blue-eyed ones!" Stephen said. Bowing his head, he listened. "We've got to warn the others," he added. He slowly stood, taking one step forward before a rifle shot cut through the air, stopping him dead in his tracks. Both boys listened intently, standing perfectly still. One, two, then three more shots rang through the forest in rapid succession, followed by the terrible shrill of an Indian war whoop.

"You get down behind that tree!" Stephen said. "Ya hear!"

Pete sank down behind the tree, shivering in fear.

Stephen carefully looked around and inched his way up the trail. The shots and terrifying yells grew in pitch the further he crept up it. Crouching down, he crawled along on a bed of fallen pine needles, slowly advancing toward the growing commotion. Stopping on the edge of a ravine leading down to the fields, he stared down in horror.

Ben and Stukeley Harding fired one shot after another from behind a group of rocks. As one fired, the other reloaded and fired, thus holding the miscreants bent on their destruction at bay. Two yelping Indians twirled about from their sure aims, quickly dragged back into the trees by their swarming comrades. A third man, John Gardner, sat crouched behind the rocks just to the riflemen's rear. Without a rifle, he fidgeted about the rocks, searching vainly for any avenue of escape.

A veil of smoke from the Indians' and the besieged white men's rifles quickly blanketed the darkening ravine. In the shielding veil of smoke, the Indians finally swooped down upon the rocks, overcoming the whites by their sheer numbers. But, to their dismay, the stubborn white men clubbed their rifles and met the onslaught, swinging to and fro at anything moving in the smoke. Cracking bones, sharp twangs and thuds echoed up the ravine, along with wild shrieks and mad yells.

Gardner rolled out of the rocks in confusion, tumbling down into the ravine. A half dozen spear points immediately pointed at his neck. Raising his empty hands high, he looked up in horror of the hovering warriors above him.

Triumphant Indians swarmed all about the rocks, seeming

unable to comprehend only two rifles held them at bay and caused so much damage to their numbers. Some looked beyond the rocks, searching for more white men, others, holding broken limbs or clutching at bullet wounds to their person, moaned and sat about the rocks. Their agonizing wails oddly mixed with the triumphant yells of their more fortunate fellows.

A particularly fiercely painted warrior raised a bloody scalp high, parading it around the wounded. Rolling his eyes to the blood dripping down his arm, he yelled in triumph, wishing to raise their spirits with his gruesome trophy of their victory. Despite his efforts, the victory seemed hollow in the face of their pain. They ignored him and rocked back in forth, seized with pain. They also ignored another shrieking warrior rising from the rocks with another scalp. Both triumphant warriors ignored their indifferent fellows, jubilantly dancing about the bloody rocks.

Another warrior rose from his pain. Dancing and pacing about for far different reasons, he clutched his bloody arm and with an excruciating wail let the useless limb fall to his side. Despite his great pain, he grimaced, lifting a tomahawk from his sash. Stumbling past the triumphantly dancing warriors, he fell upon the dead bodies below them, striking the bodies with a furious rage. Blood splattered and bones snapped with each of his furious blows.

The others watched in awe of him at first, but soon joined him. One picked up a severed arm, circling it wildly over his head before sending it sailing off into the trees. In no time the bodies bore no semblance to human or animal, but merely appeared clumps of red flesh splattered among the rocks.

Stephen, choked with fear, finally found the strength to slowly push himself back on the pine needles, knowing full well if they caught sight of him it meant certain death. A horrible death. His eyes bulged with fear. Gripped by fear, he stopped his movement. Scolding himself, he closed his bulging eyes and let his senses melt away, allowing his instincts to move his muscles away from the macabre sight below him. Hearing the wails of the gruesome devils fade, he opened his eyes and slowly rose. Seeing no sign of them, he turned, madly running up the trail, pushed onward by every throb of his aching heart. Upon reaching the fallen pine Pete hid behind, he stopped just long enough to grab Pete's hand and pull the startled boy along behind him. The boy struggled to keep up with Stephen's mad pace. The solid fear mirrored in his eyes kept his tongue quiet.

Stephen's head darted to and fro, searching all the surrounding area. A glimpse of black, speckled with white, suddenly caught his eye, causing him to immediately stop. Pete, caught in the momentum, twirled around to his front. A gruff pull on his hand pulled the wide-eyed boy back behind his elder.

Pete looked up at Stephen's bulging eyes and followed them to the trail ahead. Squinting, he caught sight of a few shadows gliding about the trees in the fading light. Upon closer look, he made out their painted bodies, mostly by the specks and swirls of white and vermillion showing in contrast to the base of black paint covering their sleek bodies.

Fortunately, no eyes turned toward them. They seemed intent on hunting some unseen prey, or persons, to their front.

Suddenly distant rifle shots echoed through the forest, stopping the painted Indians dead in their tracks. Their eyes turned toward the sounds, and in the area of the two frightened boys.

Stephen yanked at Pete's hand and in one fluid motion they slipped into the descending darkness of the trees surrounding the trail, away from the trail teeming and swarming with painted demons of death. Another movement to his front immediately engaged Stephen's feet again, but this time in the completely opposite direction. His scampering feet plowed through scrub brush and over mossy rocks and rotting logs in a mad effort to evade their foes, either real or imagined. Thorns and snapping twigs tore at Pete's clothes, slapping his face in his wake, causing him to blurt out "Stop Stephen! For God's sake stop!"

The words echoed through Stephen's frenzied mind. Something familiar rang in them, breaking through his prickling fear, and making him stop. Releasing his vice-like grip on the poor boy's hand, he collapsed in a gasping heap to the ground.

"What's the matter?" Pete asked. "You hit or something? Or rattlesnake bit?" He looked all about his feet for any sign of the slithering snakes and turned back to Stephen with questioning eyes. Nothing stared back at him but eyes alive with terror. He too collapsed. Cradling his head in his arms he sobbed, overcome with fear. Crawling to a nearby bush, he pulled his knees to his chest and continued sobbing.

The quiet sobs finally broke completely through Stephen's fear. Shaking his head, he glanced around, his eyes now free of their blinding fear. He looked to the small boy cowering under a small bush and suddenly felt ashamed. He had to buck up, he told himself, if not for your own sake, for Pete's.

"Pete, oh Pete, it was terrible," he said, trying to explain his solid fear. "Poor Uncle Ben and Stukeley! The Injuns killed 'em!" He suddenly checked his words, knowing they did little to ease the lad's overpowering sense of fear.

But to his surprise, Pete's head perked up from his arms, apparently just glad to hear his clear voice instead of his mad mumbles. Nodding, he wiped his eyes, starting to pull the many thorns from his burning flesh.

Stephen just stood and stared blankly at him, seeming completely overwhelmed by their ordeal again.

Pete slowly pulled the last of the most burning thorns from his body and rose. Taking his stunned elder's hand, he eased him down to the ground. "We need to keep low, Stephen," he said. Stephen tired to mouth a response, but in the end just sat staring blankly at him. Distant yells did little to ease his mind.

Pete slowly looked all around in the darkness, trying to gauge just how far the yelling miscreants lay from them in the dark forest. He crawled back through the path they had plowed through the thick brush, peering down the mountainside through it. Pale flickers of light showed just below them. He stared at them for a moment, trying to count the number of Indians by their shadows against the flames. Counting more than a dozen, he slowly crawled back to Stephen.

"There are fires just below us," he said, noticing the depths of fear returning to his elder's eyes. He felt tears of desperation starting to cloud his own eyes. "Stephen, you've got to snap out of this. You're all I got! You've got to get us safely back afore it's too late," he sobbed.

Stephen suddenly blinked his eyes and shook his head violently, trying to regain his composure. Wiping his eyes, he stared at the sobbing boy before him, this time truly ashamed of his behavior.

"I'm fine now, I got my senses back," Stephen assured the sobbing lad. "I'm back, and I'm a gonna stay."

"It's alright," Pete said, wiping his eyes. "I don't know what you saw, but by the look of things you saved us by getting us out of there!"

Stephen nodded his head and pulled at the many thorns cursing his own body. He drew a long and deep breath of relief.

"Did ya hear?" Pete said, perking up. "There's fires a blazing down by the river!"

Stephen cocked his head toward the distant wails and pulled a few more of the painful thorns from his body before stumbling toward the noises. He peeked through the thick brush at the flecks of light. A sense of pure dread descended over his soul. He peered down to the river in the moonlight. Noticing which way it flowed, he turned toward Pete and said, "We're upriver, not down, must've got twisted up a running all about trying rid ourselves of the savages." Actually, he thought, maybe fate had intervened to save them, for more Indians and Tories definitely lay downriver than upriver. They would be scouting and looking all about, probably for he and Pete. For a painful moment, he thought of the others in the fields below the ravine. The unknown fate of his friends, the Hadsalls, and Quocko Martin, particularly bothered him. What had become of them? He blocked out the terrible visions of his Uncle Ben's and his cousin's demise, it bothered him too much, and would probably haunt him the rest of his days. Buck up, he told himself under his breath. You've got to get Pete here to safety, no matter what haunts your mind! Looking down to the flickering fires again, he sighed. "Well, one thing's fer sure," he said, "we can't go that way." He looked up to the full moon through the treetops and thought for a moment. "We've got to get back and warn the valley." He grimaced, thinking of the rest of his family. "We've got to!"

"We'll skirt around 'em," he said. "They won't be expecting us, so we'll turn west and then strike south, and hope we get there afore these rats strike." He stared glumly at Pete. "Are you up to it little man?"

"Are you joshing me?" Pete asked. "Any place is better than here!" he added, tugging at his hair. "I like my scalp where it is!"

With that, the two young souls stumbled into the night, carefully skirting the flickering fires of their enemies, their hearts full of a resolve to free themselves of their threat, and warn their kith and kin of the terror descending upon their homes.

THE WYOMING VALLEY, FROM PROSPECT ROCK.
From an old print.

## Chapter Forty Seven
*Bailey's Farm*

Daniel Carr tried to advert his eyes from the gloating Indians to his front, but a hemp rope held his neck fast to a tree. The more he struggled against it, the more it seemed to tighten. Some form of torture, he thought, knowing the Indians to be masters of it. Giving up, he simply closed his eyes.

The old and bedraggled woman watching over him promptly slapped his face hard with a hickory stick, laughing. Her soul purpose seemed to be to make sure his eyes bore witness to the sight unfolding in the clearing to their front.

He finally gave up, still feeling the welts from the hickory stick upon his face. He watched the busy warriors to his front hack with their tomahawks at four stout logs. After furiously hacking away for a few minutes, they let out a simultaneous whoop upon finishing tying the four logs together in the form of two giant X's.

With a call to the far edge of the clearing, other warriors forced sullen-faced James Hadsall Sr. and Quocko Martin to the posts. Clubbing the men down, they forced them onto the logs. Fueled by a certain fear for their lives, both men struggled furiously against their antagonists to no avail. Through sheer numbers and cruel force they bond them both to the logs; their arms and legs stretched apart on the form of an X.

Piling a huge pile of brush and logs before the posts, they broke out flint and steel and ignited it. Laughing in anticipation of sport, they raised the logs and set them in hastily dug holes. Terror reflected from the hot flames in the captives' eyes, but neither man screamed, much to the Indian's dismay.

One of the warriors lifted a firebrand from the growing fire to the helpless prisoners' faces, seeming to draw a certain glee from the men's terrified eyes. He brushed the firebrand close to their faces and down to their crouches, pulling it away just before it actually touched their person. A sudden whoop from the trail broke his attention to a party of warriors pouring into the abandoned farmyard, hooting and yelling at the top of their lungs. They held another white prisoner in tow.

Yanking their own white prisoner up to the fire, they yelled and danced about, grimacing and sneering at the two men stretched across the logs. Their chief swaggered up to the doomed men and raised his tomahawk high, emitting a blood-curling wail. Baring his teeth and contorting his face in the most unimaginable ways, he danced and thumped the logs bearing the captives with the blunt end of his tomahawk. The thud echoed through the men's terrified souls.

Another chief sauntered up to him and drew him aside, much to his dismay. They chattered to one another for the longest moment, gesturing to and fro, and at the prisoners. Finally, one of them grabbed the tether tied to the new white captive's neck, yanking him toward them. They both glared at the crestfallen man for a moment and then turned their attention to the men spread across the X-posts. They harshly dismissed the tethered white man, passing his tether to a brave.

Both chiefs raised their hands to the sky and slowly lowered them to their sashes, pulling knives from them. Clutching the knives tightly in their hands, they advanced toward the men tied to the posts. Standing before the men each ripped the shirt from the man they confronted. Slowly, they lifted the knives and carefully cut across the men's chests. The sight of the trickling blood drew immediate cheers from the assembled warriors watching the spectacle with glee. The chiefs both turned toward the cheering braves and raised their bloody knives high in the air. Glaring back at the bleeding men, they unexpectedly turned and walked away, leaving the tortured souls time to consider their fate. They had mastered the art of emotional torture, as well.

With the unwelcome pause in the entertainment the brave holding the tethered white man yanked him over to a nearby tree. Kicking the man, he rudely forced him down to the trunk of the tree. He hastily tied the man to it and barked some orders to an old woman hovering about the captive with a hickory switch.

She screeched back at him and waved him off, drawing his ire.

Waving his hands in an angry fashion, he barked his orders again, only to draw a sneer from the old hag. Finally disgusted, he turned and walked back to the posts, anxious not to miss the upcoming spectacle when the chiefs returned.

The old woman shook her head at the brave and ignored his scolds, turning her full attention to the suffering and downcast soul tethered helplessly to the tree below her. She paced back and forth, laughing and waving her hickory stick in his face. Eliciting no reaction from the morose man, she smacked him with the stick, laughing all the louder at the shock in his suddenly wide eyes.

"John?" Daniel Carr suddenly yelled. "John Gardner is that you?" He craned his head against the rope holding his head fast to get a better look at the man tethered to the tree opposite him.

Gardner looked back at him with tired eyes, drained of all life and hope. A tired roll of his eyes is all he could manage in answer.

The old woman scampered over to Carr, silencing him with a strong smack of her hickory stick across his mouth. Snarling back at old hag, he spat a bloody glob of phlegm at the disgusting woman.

Angrily wiping the phlegm from her buckskin dress, she cursed the man in her native tongue. Realizing her words had little effect on the man, she pointed with her stick to the post and said, "You see? That you soon!" in English. The horror in Carr's eyes drew a even more heartier laugh from the hag. Lifting her switch high, she brought it down across his face again. Wails from other women hastily turned her head around to a less enthusiastic group of warriors stumbling into the farmyard.

Women flocked to the wounded warriors, wailing and gnashing their teeth. Their gentle hands relieved the warriors carrying the wounded along. They gingerly escorted the wounded warriors to deerskin pallets lying along the tree line by a series of small cooking fires. There they dressed the wounds and set the broken limbs of their brave warriors, cursing and beseeching the Great Spirit, through the ears of their chiefs, to exact vengeance from the Yankee prisoners.

The old woman stood stunned watching it all. Raising her hands to her face, she cupped her jowls with both of her hands, dropping her switch. She wailed and bent over to snatch up her switch before scrambling over to the wounded warriors. She stood gawking at them for the longest moment before turning with tear-strewn eyes back to the prisoners tied to the trees. Waving her switch angrily at them, she raised her eyes to the heavens, beseeching the Great Spirit for revenge along with the rest of the chanting women. After praying, she turned a cold eye to the fires the chiefs sat around talking. She whipped her switch in the air toward them, scolding them and warning them of Hawenneegar's anger if they did not act for revenge. She turned her anger in an instant to the white prisoners by the trees, cursing them all over again. Wobbling up to them, she mercilessly whipped them with her switch. To her increasing anger, neither man uttered a word, but just watched the warriors and chiefs rise from their fires and circle their poor comrades on the X-posts.

The warriors slowly paced around the posts. Some shrieked fearful oaths at the Yankees. Others paced silently, letting the hate in their eyes speak for them.

A few woman, anxious of the chiefs' slow movements, rose from the pallets. Clutching firebrands in their hands, they burst through the circling warriors, prodding the hated Yankee demons with them. The sound of their sizzling skin hissed in the air. Provoking no response from the men, they returned to the fires, grabbing larger branches. Running back to the demons, they pushed the red hot ends of the branches mercilessly into their flesh. A brand to the face finally drew a mournful cry from poor Hadsall. To his side Quocko remained indifferent to their cruel ways, for it was all his people had ever known; in this land, anyway. He endured silently, holding in his crying spirit as his father before him had done to endure the many blows from the slave masters.

Hadsall's wails drew the attention of more women. They rose from their firesides and pallets with children in tow. A particularly old and brightly dressed woman crept up to the torture posts and pushed the women bearing the firebrands aside, the bells on her dress jingling an odd chorus to Hadsall's pitiful moans. Wildly waving her hands, she spoke in a fast tongue, directing some of the women to one place and other women to another. "Proper rituals adhere to proper procedures," the old woman scolded a few of the uncooperative women in her native tongue, "or the Great Spirit will not except their sacrifice!" The women, with their curious children at their heels, obediently spread about the camp, only to return a few minutes latter with bundles of small wooden splinters and sharp knives.

The warriors, seeming to lose interest, backed away and sat leisurely about the camp. At the direction of the chiefs a few of them stood near the posts should something go astray with the ritual. The chiefs themselves directed some women to lay some pallets on the ground near the posts, also. There they sat, awaiting the spectacle.

With a high shrieking voice, designed to reach high into the sky to reach Hawenneegar, the old woman directed some women bearing the bundles to the posts. They stopped in front of Quocko, but suddenly turned to Hadsall, preferring his pale skin to the darker man's. They mercilessly tore off the remaining rags clothing the shivering man. Carefully selecting long pine splinters, they poked them into every inch of his skin, even the bottoms of his feet. He twisted and cried, beseeching God for mercy from the methodic women to no avail. Their God wouldn't listen to such a demon, anyway. Completing their gruesome task to the old woman's satisfaction, they stepped back, seeming to admire their handy work.

The old woman bearing the switch shrieked in triumph and stumbled over to the women holding the splinter bundles. Yanking some of the long pine splinters of wood from one of the women, she ran back to her own prisoners, giggling all the way to the scolds of the other women. With wide eyes, she approached both men holding one of the pine splinters high in the air. She jumped to Carr, but then suddenly turned toward Gardner. She slowly lowered the splinter and looked at it before waving it threateningly under Gardner's nose.

He turned his head away, repelled by the pungent smell of

turpentine. "White man's bad water make them burn all hot," she said, noticing him scrunch his nose. His action drew a long laugh from her, exposing her black and yellow teeth and her horrible breath in his face. He preferred the turpentine, but did not show it, not wishing to give the hag the satisfaction.

A sharp yell abruptly turned their attention back to the posts. A dancing warrior pounced onto the back of one of the posts brandishing a gleaming knife in the firelight. He circled the knife over the head of Quocko, whom craned his tired head to see him. His rolling eyes squinted in pain, feeling the knife blade cutting into his skull, but still, he did not cry out, knowing it to give the bully too much power. His people had learned this from many years at the hands of cruel bullies. He himself had learned it. But he saw hope in this revolution, for something bearing such great change must hold something for his people, and all people in the end, he hoped. For hope he would endure. For hope he would fight against all enemies of change. It was simply all he, or his people, had at the moment. Hope only dwelled within change, not with conserving the failed establishments of men for a false sense of order. Keep searching, mankind, keep searching, in the end it is all we have. Those content with the corruption of the day doomed the world and all mankind in the end. But not he. He fought for hope. He fought for this new turn, this revolution.

The infuriated warrior lowered the blade to silent lips and cut them, watching the blood flow from the gurgling man's mouth with glee. "He has no need for lips for he does not cry!" the warrior announced to agreeing nods around him. With one fantastic and agile leap he sat atop the opposite cross, staring down with his wide and darting eyes to the white devil below him. Careful of the splinters covering the devil's body, he carefully carved the hair from the crown of his head. Invigorated by his cries, he stood atop the cross holding the two bloody scalps high for all to see. Rejoicing and dancing, the people reveled in the taking of the trophies, which in itself, proved their superiority to the white devils and their like. The warrior jumped down and raced toward his fellows around the perimeter of the great fire.

The women and children cheered his passing and rushed to Hadsall's cross with flaming firebrands. Several of them carefully and methodically lit every splinter, casting a strange light over his quivering body.

All of the warriors suddenly screamed in triumph. They advanced in one solid group, parting the women and children assembled around the X-shaped crosses of wood. They stopped squarely in front of

Quocko, gloating and taunting him to cry out in sheer agony.

Quocko stared defiantly at them, coughing up blood from the pungent odor of Hadsall's burning flesh and from his cut lips.

The warriors all simultaneously raised their knives and cut over all of his body. Some emerged from the frenzy holding a bloody ear or stub of a nose in their bloody red hands, jumping and dancing with pure joy in honor of the brave man whom did not squeal like a coward. This dark-shinned man held more quiet dignity than all the bragging whites that fell under their knives had so far in this struggle. With this respect, the chief's blade slid across the brave man's neck, relieving his tortured soul of this world forever.

Carr and Gardner both watched in horror. Hadsall's painful wails crept through their very bones. Gardner gasped and let his head collapse to his chest, totally despondent and dripping with despair. Carr watched the growing spectacle of death with an overwhelming sense of dread. His stomach heaved, much to the entertainment of the gloating hag. He watched the light from the huge fire glisten off Quocko's red flesh as the women carefully peeled his ravaged skin. He imagined the thousands of blows endured by people of his race over the years, and thus felt a thousand fold pity for the man. Though he never knew William Martin to treat him with cruelty, he knew not of his life before he came to Wyoming. Perhaps the treatment of the men of his race bred a certain resolve in him, and with that resolve, a bravery few free men knew. Now, here, in this wilderness, Quocko Martin, called slave in life, proved himself the freest man in death. Here a courageous man departed his tortured life. Here, he had come on his own, for the good of all, not ordered by William Martin. And here he suffered for something he had never known, but willingly gave his life, that others may enjoy the sweet taste of freedom his lips had never known. Carr lifted his head and stared at the brave man's tortured remains. Pride swelled his chest, despite the horror. Such men should never be forgotten, he thought.

He stared with a grim eye to painted men yelling and strutting into the farmyard. Noticing green-coated white men among their number, he realized some painted men to be white-the hated blue-eyed Indians! He watched them stroll to the posts, jeering and taunting the poor lifeless souls spread across them. A knife rose in one of their hands. Several Indians joined them, curious of their actions against their fellow whites.

"Sergeant Terry!" a voice suddenly boomed above the jeers and taunts. "See to your men! We will have none of that!"

A man instantly burst toward the painted whites, pushing them back from the posts. He stared sternly back at the indignant eyes glaring at him. Lifting his rifle to his chest, he nodded his head for them to step away. They stood firm, shaking their heads in defiance. The man with the knife stepped forwards, only to be leveled by the butt of Terry's rifle.

"Here now," he protested from the ground. "We're only about a little sport, lighten up man!"

"Move on!" Terry commanded through gritted teeth. "Now!"

The man slowly rose, carefully slipping his knife back into its sheath. Shaking his head in disbelief, he turned away and stomped off, followed by the other painted whites. The Indians yelled in defiance, but to little effect. Growing tired of the crazy white men, they also turned away from the posts.

Terry sighed in relief and glanced at the tortured bodies behind him out of the corner of his eye. Their smells made him wince and he hurriedly walked away, leaving the dead to the dead.

Finally breathing clear air, he stopped and bent over, taking long breaths to clear his tainted lungs. Approaching boots made him stand straight again. "I don't know what got into them Colonel Butler," he said to the man stopping to his front and glaring at him.

"See to it!" Butler scolded him, slapping his gloves on his thigh. "I will have none of it, I tell you! My men shall not behave as savages!"

Terry nodded and looked about, glad none of their allies stood within earshot. He straightened up and stood at attention.

Butler shook his head and gestured to the abandoned farm cabin at the edge of the clearing. "Ready that cabin for I and Captain Caldwell this night," he ordered. "And keep your men from these posts!"

"Yes sir," Terry said. Quickly gathering his men, he led them away from the posts and to the cabin, painfully conscious of Butler's cold eyes upon them. His commander's scorn burned the nape of his neck.

"Sometimes I think they're more bloodthirsty than our tawny allies," Caldwell said, approaching Butler from behind.

Butler turned his hard eyes toward him and sighed. "As long as they save it for the battlefield, it will be fine," he scoffed.

Caldwell put a hand to his chin and gazed to the tree line, noticing the still-breathing white men tied tightly to the trees. "What have we there, sir?" he asked.

"Let us find out," Butler said, marching boldly over to the trees. He cast a sour eye to the old hag chattering at him. Sauntering past her, he looked to the two souls tied tight to the trees. One of them stared blankly through hollow eyes at him. The other glared at him through eyes of defiance. He ignored the sullen man, turning his attention to the defiant man. Rage, a pure emotion, opened the soul, which in turn could be manipulated by twisting it into relaying information.

"I am Major Butler of the King's Rangers," he said. "If you value your life and wish not to suffer the fate of your most unfortunate brethren, I pray ye answer my questions quickly and accurately."

Carr spat at his feet. "How could white men allow such to go on in their presence?" he said through gritted teeth. "Bloody Tory or not!"

The old hag laughed. "He see!" she said. "He see!"

Butler cast an indignant stare at the woman. "What our allies do is their concern. If you wish to live, speak. It is that simple."

Carr glared at him. His tongue remained silent.

"How many troops are about Wyoming?" Butler asked. "Have they any cannon?"

"Oh God!" a voice suddenly gasped from the other tree. "There's one cannon, but there's no shot for it. As for men, I pray they have had the good sense to have departed by now, for their family's sake!"

Carr groaned, turning his glaring eyes to Gardner.

"What, Daniel?" Gardner said, letting his head fall to his chest. "Look about you man! Look to those posts! Hell hath come downriver from Tioga! My dear family! My dear friends! I hope all below had the good sense to leave! It's only dirt! Do you think it worth our very lives?"

"Yes, John, I do!" Car said. "Our blood and toil's in that soil!" he said, turning a hatful eye to the Tory gloating over them. "All good men shall muster against your number, seven or eight hundred strong! They won't retreat a foot from you and your cruel bastards and savages!"

"Why thank you, gentlemen," Butler said, raising a handkerchief to his mouth against the lingering stench of burned flesh. "Seven or eight hundred muskets and no cannon. You have been most informative."

"You smug traitorous bastard!" Carr called behind him, struggling against his bonds with pure rage. The old woman scolded and whipped him, but it did little to quell his rage. A few warriors glanced over to the enraged man, laughing at his fruitless efforts. He cursed them all until his voice cracked with rage.

"That man is insane," Caldwell said, following his commander into the cabin. They both walked over to the hearth and stared down at the fire. Butler removed his hat, dismissing the man tending the fire.

"Somehow I almost wish Wyoming is abandoned," Butler muttered under his breath.

"Sir?" Caldwell said with his mouth agape.

"No, no, James," Butler said, backing to a chair by the table. Sitting his hat on the table, he ran a hand through his white hair. Raising his bushy eyebrows he said, "Think of it James! If Wyoming is clear nothing but Fort Augusta lies between us and the rebel stores at Carlisle! To the east of Carlisle Colonel Rankin has already promised to deliver up his five hundred man militia about Lancaster to us!"

Caldwell raised his own questioning eyebrow.

"Yes, Colonel Rankin, the supposed rebel, he has been in touch with our agents all along! The Rebels are not quite as united as they think! Officers in their own ranks sit on the knife's edge, reconsidering their treason. All they need is the opportunity! There are many a unsuspected Loyalist between Carlisle and Philadelphia, I assure you! They shall surrender up all between Carlisle and Philadelphia just on the threat of our approach! Then we shall unite with General Howe and split the rebellious colonies in twain by the Susquehanna, just as General Burgoyne tried to do with the Hudson! Think of it! Glory awaits us and only Wyoming lies as a bump in the road between us and victory. We shall besiege Fort Augusta and bypass it, starve them out. It is perfect! Washington, and his fools, do not see it, save Generals Lee and Arnold, whom they dismiss, the blind fools. Wyoming is the key, and we shall turn it, opening the door all the way to Philadelphia!"

"Some key," Caldwell said. "I hope you do not underestimate the of Wyoming men's resolve. They seem to bear a great allegiance and heartfelt belief in the rebel cause. They may prove quite a bump in the road, indeed."

"Damn it man, it will work, I tell you!" Butler said. He gestured to a pouch hanging on a peg by the door. "Hand me that pouch," he said. "It contains a quill and paper. I shall write a dispatch and send it to General Howe at once, for he awaits word. Fetch me a courier at once!"

Caldwell grabbed the pouch and placed it on the table, gauging the depth of his commander's convictions by the look in his stern eyes. Yes, he believed in his grandiose dream, he concluded. He had discussed it with him a few times before, but thought both of them realized it to be only a dream, or hope.

"What?" Butler said, noticing the captain staring at him. "Fetch me that courier!" he ordered, hurriedly scribbling on a piece of paper.

"Yes sir," Caldwell said, turning smartly toward the door. A haunting feeling tugged at his soul. Wyoming, the key to it all, but did they have enough muscle to turn the key, and if they did manage, would they have strength to carry on, especially the natives? He shook off his feelings, reminding himself his was to serve the best he could, and follow the orders of the ones placed over him. Defeat or victory lay in their hands, not his. He quickly called for a courier, thinking no more of it.

## Chapter Forty Eight
### *Young John Hadsall Survives*

Young John Hadsall lie motionless in the water. The twelve year old poked his head just high enough above the water for his nostrils to draw breath. He left the leaves and branches clinging to his head alone. It covered him from the eyes of the painted devils searching relentlessly along the riverbank for him.

He hadn't seen one of them since well after sunset, but still did not move. Pa always told him an Indian moves like the wind. You don't know he's at your back until you feel your scalp lifted by his knife. He listened to his father's words now, below this clump of debris along the riverbank. A tear slid down his cheek at the thought of his father.

His thoughts slipped from his father and reverted back to the horrible screams and shots which had started this whole ordeal. They still rang in his frightened mind. Visions of how he, his brother Jim, Uncle Ebenezer Reynolds, and Dan Wallen, heard the shots from the shore, flashed in his mind. The terror in all their eyes still burned hot in his mind, probably forever, he feared. He remembered how they all dropped their hoes and scrambled to the canoes. In no time they paddled to the bank from the islands and beached the canoes. His brother Jim, Uncle Ebenezer, and Wallen, all grabbed their rifles and clambered up the riverbank, calling back to him to attend to the canoes and stay put. He lifted his head to acknowledge their order just in time to see rifle balls cut into them. Jim felt like a rock. Uncle Ebenezer twisted and grabbed at his lower arm. Wallen's rifle barked at the painted devils. Ebenezer and Wallen immediately disappeared over the top of the riverbank, followed by the report of dozens of rifles.

He had then turned instantly to the canoes. Several balls splashed in the water around him in angry spurts. He instinctively dove into the water, swimming under it for as long as he had the breath. He luckily popped up from the water under some life-saving debris. He raised his head just high enough to see warriors searching about the canoes. He drew a long breath and slowly disappeared under the shielding debris, where he now struggled, his eyes staring blankly up through the water at the brave walking out onto a fallen tree crossing over the debris. He froze every muscle in his body and watched the warrior search for him, swearing he would let himself die of drowning before rising to take a breath. Just then he felt a tingle along his side under his shirt. His eyes rolled to see a great bubble rise from his shirt. He watched it slowly ascend to the surface and prepared for the struggle of his life. To his relief the bubble burst under some leaves. He locked eyes on the brave again.

As his last breath burned in his bursting lungs, the brave suddenly turned about. Shaking his head in frustration, the brave jumped off the log and back onto the shore.

He rose slowly in the water just so his lips broke the face of it. He drew a long breath as silently as possible, being careful not to gasp, and let the balance of his head slowly roll out of the water. The braves hurriedly searching the canoes caught his eye. Finding nothing of value, they raised their hands in disgust and rambled up the riverbank. In their wake, his ears still echoed with the angry thuds of their tomahawks into the body of his fallen brother. He shrank from the thought of the abuse of this dear brother's body, letting his head fall into the water to wipe away his tears, and perhaps, wash away all the horrible memories. But just then something plowed into his head just at the moment he found peace from the visions, making him jump in the water. He punched at the intrusion, much relieved to find it a branch. He froze. Had he exposed himself by his rash act? The branch flit back into him, nearly poking out his eye. But this time he gently pushed it to the side. His eyes darted all about, searching for any movement. He perked his ears and listened. Nothing stirred. His rash movements had not betrayed his position to his deadly enemies.

He looked to the canoes through the milky darkness. One of them twisted and danced against the current. It's bow shifted on the muddy bank, slowly giving way to the strong current. He watched it turn away with the current, far down the Susquehanna. He wished he could join it. He looked to the second canoe, watching it twist against the same current which pulled away the first. Fearing it his only avenue of escape, he had to reach it before the current pulled it too down the river.

Drawing a deep breath, he moved his feet carefully over the muddy river bottom. Breaking through the debris, he slipped through the water, expecting to hear shrieks from the upper riverbank. But silence remained, so he locked his eyes on the canoe, moving through the water with grim determination. He crept closer and closer to the craft, careful not to lose his footing and make any unnecessary noises.

At last his reaching fingers touched the canoe. Running his hand up to the its bow, he eagerly grabbed it, clutching it for dear life. He quickly glanced up the riverbank. Only his brother's bloody foot showed over its edge. Grabbing the canoe with both hands, he pulled it into the river current. As soon as his feet lost the river's muddy bottom he swam for the islands, kicking his feet and guiding the canoe before him. The current drew stronger, but he welcomed its angry pull. Easing himself slowly up and into the canoe he collapsed into its bottom. For a moment his eyes caught the starlet sky and he forgot all. All the agony, pain, and suffering slipped from his tortured mind. It lasted for just a few heartbeats before he clutched the paddle in his hands and paddled feverishly toward the west bank of the river. He turned his sight downriver, down to his home, a home he feared would never be the same after the horrid wave of war swept over it, but his home, nonetheless, no matter what pestilence cursed it.

His palms burned against the heavy paddle strokes but he blocked it from his mind with sheer will. The more water you push the closer you get to home, he told himself. Rolls of skin slid from his waterlogged hands from the paddle. Finally, he let the paddle fall to the bottom of the canoe, raising his hands to his face in the pale light. Tears rolled down his cheeks, tears burning his raw palms. Angrily wiping them with his sleeves, he gasped in relief at the sight before him. Campbell's ledge rose over the river, silhouetted against the bright moon just behind it. The Lackawanna gently poured into the Susquehanna beyond it on his left. Bending his head down, he feverishly paddled again, despite his burning palms. "Just a few more strokes and it's home! Just ahead! A warm fire and oh, my dear Mother," he muttered to himself to subdue the pain of his blistered hands and aching body.

Plowing the canoe onto a rocky landing, he darted from it in one fluid motion. He rambled up the path toward the awaiting silhouette of a fort atop the bank. His body suddenly felt numb, but he paid it no heed. He stumbled to the gate, oblivious to the warnings from the sentry.

Falling to his knees a few feet from the gate, he looked up through his tears. "Johnny!" he called. "Johnny Jenkins? You there!?!" He heard the lock of a rifle click in response. "Jim's dead!" he cried. "I don't know what happened! Uncle Eb and Wallen ran off in the woods with the Indians right on their heels! It's just terrible!"

A bell instantly rang inside the fort and "Alarm! Alarm!" rang throughout it. The gate burst open with John Jenkins running through it with two men holding rifles on either side of him. Kneeling down to the boy, he stared into his horror-filled eyes. He tried in vain to stop the torrent of tears pouring down the lad's cheeks.

"My God what is happening?" one of the riflemen gasp.

The lad tried to explain, but his words fell mumbled on his trembling lips.

"You're safe now, so you needn't try to talk, you're home, John," Jenkins said, carefully picking the exhausted boy up in his arms.

"You're home!"

## Chapter Forty Nine
*Gencho's Ambush*

Colonel Denison anxiously watched the scrub brush along the trail. Instinctively, he let his hand fall to the pistol in his belt, lifting it against the belt in order to be able to draw it at a moment's notice. Clenching the reins of his mount tight in his grasp, he looked down at the two men flanking the trail. The stern no-nonsense look about them reassured him. Both held their rifles at the ready. He sighed. No better men than Zebulon Marcy and Stephen Harding existed in Wyoming when it came to Indian warfare, he reassured himself. Both possessed keen eyes and lightning reflexes, indispensable qualities when it came to fighting the savages in their own domain. He suddenly thought of John Jenkins, but knew the man much too weak from his own grueling ordeal to tramp through the woods just now.

A stern look from the other horsemen to his side made him straighten in the saddle. "No," Colonel Butler seemed to say with his eyes. "No, Nathan, a look of concern is fine, but a look of fear, no. Command with confidence, mirror it in all you do." He heard the words so much from the regular army officer of the Continental Line over the last few apprehensive days they rang in his head every time he drew that certain look from him. Easing his hand from the pistol butt, he faced his eyes to the front, as a proper officer should.

The haunting look on young John Hadsall's face still cursed his thoughts. The sight of Stephen Harding Jr. trotting to the gate of Forty Fort in the early morning light with Peter Rogers at his heels played at his mind also. When Dan Wallen helped blood-drained Ebenezer Reynolds through the gate nearly a half of an hour later, he knew the circumstances facing them to be dire, indeed. Hell hath come to Wyoming. A painted, vengeful, and cruel hell. He had ordered a rescue party to depart at once. Two full companies immediately responded. His second act placed Colonel Butler in full command. He felt confident of both decisions. Glancing over to the stern-faced colonel, he nodded to him.

"Harding's tannery's just ahead," Zebulon Marcy said from the trail without turning to look back. He slipped silently into the forest around the trail, disappearing before either colonel could utter a response. Both colonels reared their horses and sat staring all around, suddenly aware of the eerie silence surrounding them. The men to their rear all stopped without uttering a word, also. Their darting eyes scanned the spooky forest. Many raised their muskets and rifles ready to fire.

Harding suddenly darted in front of the colonels, peering into the forest for Marcy. Ignoring their pleading eyes, he turned his head to and fro, eagerly looking at something. Denison kicked his horse's flanks, sending it trotting behind Harding, whom still ignored him. Reining his horse to a stop, he put his hand to the pistol tucked in his belt and squinted to look into the trees.

Marcy popped from the forest a rod up the trail from where he entered it, waving at Harding. Harding waved back and read his friend's strange hand signals before turning to look up to the curious colonel behind him. "It's clear, sir," Harding said on a whisper. "But have the men on their guard just the same." He promptly scampered up to Marcy.

"Very well," Denison answered with an equally hushed voice, waving Butler and the column of men silently forward on the trail. They all carefully advanced into the tannery yard by the river and into the fields surrounding it. The men fanned out in every direction with just the wave of Colonel Butler's hand to guide them. All remained silent. In no time they searched the entire area and reformed by their officers.

Marcy and Harding both approached the mounted colonels with grim looks on their faces, with Marcy looking back over his shoulder at an opening to a trail at the far end of the tannery yard. "It leads down to the river," he said. "That's where they be, from what the lad Stephen said."

Harding bit his lip and marched steadily toward the trail. Marcy looked at him and with a surprised look said "He wants to finish this business!" to the colonels. He quickly followed his partner.

"Follow them," Butler said to the awaiting column watching the scouts sprint across the yard. "But keep a keen eye about and stay sharp! Watch the flanks!"

The colonels watched their men file smartly and in good order behind the scouts. A sense of pride flooded Denison's mind at the sight of his well-ordered troops. He felt them equal to any lot of regulars. He nodded and smiled at Butler whom returned his nod.

"They are a fine lot," Butler said. "We've nothing to fear if they keep their present resolve and sense of good order and discipline."

They spurred their horses forwards behind their column of men. The men poured down into a gully in a wide formation, with flankers spread wide on each side of them, combing the woods to prevent their enemy's favorite mode of attack-ambush. Their advance halted among a great pile of boulders placed there by some ancient forces long ago.

Harding rambled up to the boulders, placing his hand on a red substance dripping from one of them. "Blood," he said, feeling the red substance between two fingers. He took another step before he and Marcy stopped. They both knelt, examining something unseen by the others among the rocks. Harding suddenly rose, throwing his hat angrily down to the ground. Curses rolled across every breath he drew. Marcy stood with his glaring eyes scanning all about, his rifle clutched tightly in his hands.

Denison and Butler reined up their horses, quickly dismounting. Scrambling up the rocks, they stopped and stared at the clumps of flesh below the two furious scouts. Blood splattered all over the boulders, drenching them in a sickly red. They suddenly understood the scout's fury. Another man winced, calling their attention to a nearby tree. He slowly held up a severed arm.

"Those gruesome fiends!" Denison said, struggling to quell his heaving stomach.

"Yes," Butler said. "It's begun now, damn it, and hell's to pay!"

Hastily mounting, his startled eyes shot to a sudden movement among the rocks to the side. "There!" he screamed, reining his mount back on its haunches. Two dark figures immediately burst from the rocks, stopping only long enough to fire two quick shots at the bevy of white men surrounding them. Denison's horse reeled back, grazed on the neck by one of the balls, the other zipping harmlessly through the leaves over his head. He stared starkly at the leaves drifting down on him while trying to settle his wounded horse. "Get the rats!" he screamed.

Dozens of firelocks barked in response, instantly felling the running savages. Huzzaing and reloading, they stealthily approached the downed red men, wary of any sudden movements. Moving feathers atop one of their heads hastened their steps, only to watch one of the Indians jump up and run like a bat out of hell for the river. He dove under the water from angry rebel rifle balls whizzing about his person.

Small gouts of water peppered the river from men ignoring Zebulon Marcy's warning not fire until sure of their target. Watching the feathered head appear after the hail of lead ceased, he carefully raised his own loaded weapon. The feathered head promptly disappeared under the water. "Damn it," Marcy said. "Rifles is deadly, but are the devil to load! And them damn muskets couldn't hit the broad side of a barn! Hold your fire until sure of your shot, damn it." Shaking his head to Harding he added, "There may be more hiding back there, take a good look around!" Watching Harding run back to the rocks, he edged his way through the thick brush along the riverbank. Roswell Franklin, quick to reload his rifle, followed him while the others madly tried to reload.

The two men moved smoothly down the riverbank, watching the

river for any sign of the submerged angel of death. A bubble bursting to the surface promptly rewarded their patience. Both men gently eased down to their knees, one resting his rifle steady on a rock, and the other in the crook of a tree. Both licked their fingers, touching the end of their sights for luck.

A head popped up from the water, gasping for air. Two sharp cracks sounded at once. The head twisted and rolled back, trailing a long line of red in the swirling Susquehanna. The body slowly rolled over and over in current until finally disappearing in the murky depths.

Both men rose in triumph, each eyeing one another to see if the other would be so bold as to the claim the shot his own. Neither spoke a word, but just nodded at one another. "Scratch one redskin," Marcy finally said, leading them back to the others.

They burst from the brush to the see men on the bank watching downriver. "We seen it," one of them said. "You blistered him good!"

"That we did," Marcy said with a wink to Franklin.

Franklin nodded back, looking down to his rifle with pride. "That we did, Zeb," he said. "That we did."

"That red devil won't be bothering us again," Marcy said to the two colonels reining up their horses near him. They all looked to a growing disturbance below them. Harding stood with a few of the other men cursing and kicking at the body of the other dead warrior. Soon all the men gathered around the dead body of one of their hated enemy, whom many a time struck from the bush and then quickly retreated into the forest time after time, elusive and deadly in the most sinister way. But not this time. This one sat dead before their eyes, strange because any they did kill before were always carried away on the backs of their comrades, so they barely saw their elusive foe, until now. A strange awe shone in the eyes of the men, even the colonels. Here they had killed one whom had laid in wait to ambush any rescuers for the Harding party. Here lay one whom had underestimated them, and paid with his life.

"I'll have that son of a bitch's hair!" Harding snarled, kneeling down and abruptly drawing his knife. He gruffly grabbed the tuff of hair about the crown of the warrior's head, quickly slicing it free. Raising it high, he stared at it with a certain glee, his eyes rolling to and fro. In a fit of emotion, he flicked his knife around in his hand, bringing it straight down into the face of the dead brave. A sickly cracking sound echoed through the hushed air. "There, you red son of a bitch!" Harding said. Pulling the knife out with a sucking sound, he gazed at the bloody blade with a crazed look of revenge, stabbing the face time and time again.

His actions flowed like a contagion among the others. Many a knife and tomahawk sunk mercilessly into the body, tearing and ripping it to shreds among an eerie chorus of curses and threats. One skillful blade cut the genitals from the body, its owner placing them in its twisted hand above its head. Other blades removed eyes, ears, and skin in acts of cruel vengeance. The wet sound of peeling skin haunted the air. Some men rose brandishing pounded silver arm bands. Others rose with bloody feathers and little silver trinkets. All rose with something of a trophy, relishing the blood tainting it with a thirst of pure revenge for the Harding party. One man rose clutching a bloody silver necklace in his upraised hands, cheering with all his might.

Oddly, Zebulon Marcy and the colonels just stood watching, seeming to become lost in it all. A detached foot flying near his head quickly snapped Denison out of his hypnotic trance. His horse reeled about, tearing open its wound. It tramped about the bloody rocks, filling its master's eyes with the clumps of flesh and blood covering them. "Madness!" Denison muttered, finally reining his horse under control again. Firing his pistol in the air, he drew all eyes to him, "You men cease at once!" he commanded at the top of his lungs. "At once!"

The frantic look in their eyes suddenly melted against the disgusted glare of their commander. They all looked down at their bloody trophies in awe, almost as if someone else had placed them into their hands. The man holding the necklace immediately dropped it as if it suddenly burned his hands. All looked to one another in amazement, except Harding. He rose from the mutilated body, spitting on it.

Marcy sauntered over to him, placing his hand on his shoulder. "The bastard deserved every bit of it," he said, also spitting on the corpse. "It's a shame the river took mine," he added, touching the scalp in Harding's hands with the end of his rifle.

"This is all hell," Denison said.

"A hell for him," Marcy said, leading his friend away from the body. Both men collapsed by a nearby tree, proudly examining the scalp.

"Lieutenant Colonel Dorrance!" Butler said, regaining his composure. "Have a detail collect the remains! We shall take them back for a proper Christian burial! God rest their souls."

Dorrance immediately barked some crisp orders and guided some men to the bloody rocks. "What are we to put them in?" one of his men asked in disgust. "A sack? For that's all that's left of 'em!"

"Just look smart about your work," Dorrance barked back. "We need none of your tongue just now!"

The other men staggered around in a sort of trance, sullenly looking down to their bloody hands and then to the river.

"War makes beasts of all men," Denison said, reining his horse up to Butler.

"Yes, it does," Butler said. "But such is the way of the world."

"There's no sense in searching anymore," Denison said.

"No, there isn't," Butler said. "There may be far greater numbers about than we suppose, I fear." He looked down to the sullen men staring blankly at the river. "We must make haste to Forty Fort and prepare. We'll give them a fight, if they be bold enough to keep coming on, despite their numbers. Damn them all to hell!"

Upon hearing a series of orders from Lieutenant Colonel Dorrance, all the men filed into ranks without a word passing among any of them. A respectful silence hovered over them. None felt shame, but rather the shock of war when it shows a man what he is capable of when provoked.

The long silent line soon filed down the trail behind the packhorses bearing the remains of their fallen and mutilated comrades. All eyes front, without any hateful gazes back to the body of their slain foe torn to bits by their rage. Let the wolves have the bits left in the dirt.

All of the sudden every man felt dreadfully alone despite their number. Onward they marched through the darkening folds of the forest, feeling an awful weight upon their backs, most probably the eyes of the children of the forest they knew watched them. It haunted each man's thoughts and clouded his mind with visions of the threatening clouds and raging storm of Tories and Indians descending upon their peaceful valley. They must turn it back, or die in the process.

## Chapter Fifty
*Esther Mourns*

The fire crackled, sending embers spiraling high into the starlit sky. The two men sitting around it sat silently watching the embers rise into the heavens. The elder took a long draw on a pipe clenched in his teeth, watching the younger man poke at the fire with a long stick. Suddenly ear-piercing wails gave both men a start, nearly knocking the pipe from the elder's jaw. They both passed an annoying glance to a pine bough hut near the river.

"Is that woman to wail all the damn night?" the elder man asked, readjusting the pipe in his mouth.

The younger man just shook his head, turning back to the fire.

Curious Indian women slowly began gathering around the entrance to the hut, some of them bending down to peek into it. After each rose, they started wailing as well, raising their shaking hands to the heavens. Some merely collapsed to the ground in a frenzy of grief. The spine-tingling wails multiplied with each gathering woman, echoing throughout the whole village.

"Well," the elder man said. "We'll have no rest this night!" Taking the pipe from his mouth, he tapped it on the butt of his rifle lying near him. Leaning back, he folded his arms across his chest. "There was nothing you could do, eh, Terry?" he asked.

"No sir, Colonel Butler," Terry said, glancing to the hut again. "I now certainly wish we could have, but there were simply too many of them. Well over a hundred at least, they were. I told those two braves they were much too close, but as you know, an Indian has his own mind. They both had a certain bloodlust in their eyes, especially the Queen's son. Young bucks full of piss and vinegar!" He poked angrily at the fire, sending a geyser of sparks into the air. "We watched it all from the trees across the river, thought they might send a few, maybe a dozen, that we could have blistered with a sudden volley from the far bank. If the damn fools would have advanced but a rod more upriver I would have poured a volley into them which would have staggered them and sent them limping back to Forty Fort with their tails between their legs!"

Butler rolled his eyes at the young upstart. He was not sure about such men whom turned coat. If they did it to their own kith and kin, why would they not do it against a far away king? "No worries," he said. "We shall all have sport before it's all over." He looked over to the wailing Indians. "Perhaps then we shall have some rest in this land!"

"Amen to that!" Terry said.

"If the Wyoming Yankees would have just kept to themselves,

and kept their noses out of the King's affairs, perhaps none of this would be necessary, but they supply men, as well as food, to the rebel army, and their views are quite contrary to good order on the frontier," he said, suddenly remembering he spoke to one of them; or one whom had once been one of them.

"Well here is one man who couldn't stand their blue-nosed ways and bullshit anymore!" Terry said. Tossing his stick into the fire, he pulled his long knife from its sheath. Twirling its glistening blade in the firelight his eyes showed something of the nature of his soul, his lost soul, in them. "Be they brothers or not, their traitorous blood shall flow from this knife!" he muttered, more to himself than anyone else.

Butler found himself rolling his eyes again. He couldn't seem to help it. The dire hatred these Wyoming people professed for one another still shocked him even after hearing it dozens of times. Sure, those on the other frontiers professed an equal hatred, but none bore the intensity of these Wyoming people, on both sides of the coin. He thought of relatives of his own and for a slight moment of his counterpart, Zebulon Butler, wondering if any blood flowed between them through the ancient threads of time. Shrugging his shoulders, he reassured himself duty demanded he perform his assigned tasks regardless of any distant blood flowing between he and the enemies of the Crown. Still, Terry's intense stare at the glistening blade slowing turning in front of his eyes gave him the willies. Thankfully, silence from the hut turned his attention, and thoughts, to it.

Queen Esther eased through the door, slowly rising to her full height over her bowing and grieving minions below her. She stood deathly still, glaring down on the women, all of them silent and sneaking glances at her. Her dark eyes sat amid large white circles painted around them. Tears etched streaks through the paint. Black paint covered the rest of her tall, half-dressed frame, along with other great white swirls marking her well formed and bare breasts. She slowly stepped forward, the bells on her moccasins breaking the eerie silence. All eyes watched her strut to the fire. Abruptly stopping, her eyes rolled down to the two white men bearing a solid stare of hatred.

Butler unfolded his legs from sitting Indian fashion, slowly rising to face her. Brushing off his backside, he stared right back at the Indian Queen, showing no sympathy.

Terry sat still. Ignoring them both, he kept twirling the knife in front of the flames. He started whistling the odd tune *Gary Owen* in the tense air.

A few others advanced from the white camp, led by a concerned

Captain Caldwell. He slowly formed his men to the rear of Colonel Butler, quickly posting them as a show of force.

A few warriors cast an indifferent eye to the painted Queen from their own fires. Only women gathered to the rear of her.

"I sympathize for your loss," Butler said to the Queen, rolling his eyes to Caldwell and the men behind him. "Your son was a brave man. His loss is a loss for all of the Six Nations and our Great Father, the King." With a slight bow of his head, he gracefully turned, walking back toward the cabin. The stench of Hadsall's burnt flesh still tinged the air despite his body's disappearance from the post. A dark clump of flesh, the remains of poor Quocko, hung limply on the other post. He glanced at it out of the corner of his eye, drawing quick breaths to avoid the stench before he finally reached the cabin door. He put his hand to the latch in anticipation of escaping the harsh smell when a scratchy voice commanded his attention.

"Old Butler!" the Queen said loudly. "Much blood must flow to avenge my Gencho! I promise you! Yankee blood!"

Butler winced against the thought of drawing enough air to respond. Oddly, he thought of how the Indians' command of the English language seemed to greatly improve when they truly wished to express themselves. Getting a word out of them otherwise seemed to be impossible but in their own guttural tongue. He wondered of their transparent games, but such were their cunning and wily ways, he reasoned. Much to his relief, a commotion from the trail saved him from the awkward moment.

Two of his green-coated rangers escorted a stout little civilian to him standing with his hand anxiously on the latchstring. They cast a curious eye to the half-naked painted Indian Queen standing near a fire with the light casting an eerie glow over her. All three stopped at the door with their eyes still turned toward the devil Queen staring at them. Only a quick ahem from Butler turned their eyes back to him.

The stout little man, his eyes beaming upon sight of the British officer, bowed his head and removed his hat, tucking it under his arm.

Terry rose from the fire and jaunted over to the cabin, smiling all the way. "Sir," he said to Butler with a nod to the man. "This here is Helmut Wintermoot! He has a fort just below Fort Jenkins." He smiled at the man. "He is a good King's man," he added, patting the man on the shoulder. "It's good to see a familiar and loyal face from Wyoming!"

"Well, Mr. Wintermoot," Butler said, opening the door. "It is good to see not all of Wyoming is infested with rebel rats!" He waved the man through the door, noticing his nose starting to curl against the smell.

Butler tightly closed the door behind him in the face of Terry and his rangers, ushering Wintermoot to a chair by the table. Pulling up his own chair, he faced the man, smiling.

"It is good to see a King's officer," Wintermoot said, shaking his head. "I, and others, have awaited you for so long, my friend. You are most welcome, that is to my fort, at least. I built my fort to protect us against Pennamites and," he paused, casting a nervous eye around, "savages, I dare say! It was in no way built to harbor insurrectionist and crazed rebels! The insolent fools! My God, how headstrong they are!"

"Nicely said," Butler said with a sly smile. "I am most glad to see reason still prevails in some about Wyoming."

Terry paced nervously to and fro in front of the cabin door, soon joined by Caldwell. They muttered a few words of concern between them, each painfully aware of the Indian Queen's cold stare. The cabin door suddenly creaked open after what seemed an eternity.

"Be ready to advance on the morrow, at first light," Butler announced, standing tall in the door. He glanced over to the Queen. "We shall see to the rebels on the morrow, Esther!" he yelled over to her.

The Indian Queen wailed and shook her whole body, causing the bells about her moccasins and skirt to jingle the oddest tune. Her convulsing body seemed to focus about the swirls painted on her finely formed breasts. Overcome in anticipation of the hunt, she turned back to her horde, lifting her hands high over her head. The Indians immediately started wailing, which subsided into a series of individual yelps. They too danced in anticipation. Many of the rangers, drawn by the Indians' unbridled emotion, joined them, dancing and yelping around the fires with the best of the braves of the Six Nations.

The door closed behind Wintermoot standing aghast at the sight unfolding in front of him. Seating his hat tightly on his head, he sprinted toward the trail leading back to his fort, anxious to be free of the heathen celebration of death behind him. He breathed much easier the further his feet carried him away from it all, shunning the foreboding sense of dread haunting him. What had he done? he asked himself, before quelling it with pure reason. They were rebels, inciting mob rule against their God-given sovereign to whom they now had to answer, for he had come calling. He bucked up, filling himself with a resolve from the knowledge that he did what he did in the end for the sake of all, though the haunting wails crept through his soul long after they faded with distance.

Oh, what horrible sacrifices war demands, he told himself.

## Chapter Fifty One
### Fort Wintermoot

Dan Ingersoll nervously cleaned his rifle under the parapets of Fort Wintermoot. Now and then he looked up to Lieutenant Scovell on a low platform just above the gate. The calm in the man's eyes unnerved him. He did not seem to share the anxious look haunting most of the other faces in the fort. Their commander knew something the others did not, he reasoned, but failed to share with others what so set his mind at ease.

"Wintermoot went out late last night," his wife said by his side, noticing the concern in his eyes. "He went all by his lonesome and didn't come back for quite a spell, they says."

"Yes, my dear," Ingersoll said. "Something's afoot and I don't like it. Wintermoot and his lot are all breathing a might bit easier than most this day than they was yesterday."

"I don't feel comfortable with him and his brood insisting on standing watch in place of all us," his wife said, staring at his rifle. He quickly loaded it.

"Them and the Van Alstynes give me the willies," she declared. "I wish we'd gone to Fort Jenkins instead of this nest of interlopers!"

"Maybe we shall, if things don't stop getting so suspicious," Dan said, raising his rifle to prime its pan. "I'm going up there myself for the next watch. No Tory or Indian shall pass my sights without getting some lead in passing!"

His wife slowly bobbed her head.

"You go about gathering up our things and the children," Dan said, giving her a kiss on her forehead. "But do it so as not to draw any undue attention or concern," he added.

Scovell turned and looked squarely down at the pair, seeming to sense their words. Tugging at the sleeve of a man standing next to him, he gestured down to them.

Ingersoll glared back at him and marched headlong toward the ladder leading up to the platform.

"That won't be necessary," Scovell called down to him. "We have things well in hand up here!"

"That's what I'm a feared of," Ingersoll called back.

Scovell shook his head. The man next to him suddenly shook his arm, pointing wildly to something outside the fort's walls. His wide-eyes caught Ingersoll and his wife's attention.

Scovell turned about. His face suddenly turned sour, then pale. After due consideration, he raised his hand to wave at someone unseen below the fort's walls.

"What are you two about?" Ingersoll asked, putting his foot on the lower rung of the ladder. "I dare not wonder!"

"Stand fast!" Scovell immediately said. "Get away from that ladder Ingersoll, and behave yourself!" He looked over to the two men standing at the gate, gesturing for them to open it. It slowly opened to a flood of green-coated rangers and fiercely painted Indians pouring through it, immediately spreading out en masse about the fort.

Ingersoll raised his rifle, his eyes glaring up to Scovell. "You betraying Tory bastard!" he said.

He blanched in the face of the dozens of firelocks, spears, and arrows suddenly pointing directly at his head.

"Wait!" Scovell called from the platform above, waving his hands frantically at the rangers and Indians. "We'll have none of that!" He looked down to a frozen Ingersoll. "I'd lower that weapon now, Dan Ingersoll, and very slowly at that! If you value your scalp," he said.

Mrs. Ingersoll screamed. Grabbing a two-tined pick fork, she marched forth, standing between her husband and the fierce intruders. Snarling profusely, she poked the pitchfork threateningly at the intruders.

They did not flinch. Stone cold eyes stared back at her, daring her to take one more step toward them.

"That's the spirit!" Ingersoll said, cocking his rifle. "We'll drop a few of the bastards at least!"

"No," his wife said, lowering her pitchfork. "Daniel, there are simply too many of them! Think of the children, my dear." She turned and looked halfway over her shoulder to her husband. "Think of me."

Ingersoll growled, but then lowered his rifle gently and slowly to the ground. His wife simply opened her hands, letting the pitchfork fall straight to the ground.

Scovell slipped down the ladder in a flash, quickly intervening between the rangers and Ingersoll and his wife. "Don't!" he said, halting the rangers. "I have things well in hand!" Bending down, he carefully picked up Ingersoll's long rifle, passing it to the nearest ranger.

"We'll keep an eye on this one!" the ranger said with a cold eye to Ingersoll. Raising the rifle up for closer examination, his eyes rolled from one end of it to another, growing wide with satisfaction. He balanced it in one hand against his musket he held in the other. With a huff, he slung his musket over his shoulder and gripped the rifle tightly in both of his hands, looking to Ingersoll's pouch and shot bag. "I'll be having those, too," he said, "for I don't think a Brown Bess's ball will fit down this barrel!" Stepping toward the man, he gladly accepted his reluctant offering. "That's fine!" the ranger said, turning about to his fellows. "I told you even rebel rats can be tamed! And look to this fine rifle! I'll do fine service with this in what's to come!"

Ingersoll angrily kicked at the ground. "Damn it all to hell!" he said to his wife.

"Keep that man under guard!" a voice commanded from behind the rangers. The rangers and Indians slowly parted to make way for their somewhat portly commander. Major Butler strode through them and stood full in front of the disgruntled rebel. "Relieve him of those, too," Butler ordered a nearby Tory, gesturing down to the long knife and tomahawk stuck in the rebel's wide black belt. "We may find use for this one," he added, looking the man up and down.

Ingersoll spat at his feet.

Butler shook his head, sly smirking. "Impudent devil, as all rebels," he said. He promptly turned his eyes away from the insolent rebel as if the mere sight of him soured his stomach and turned to the sea of welcoming faces behind him.

Helmut Wintermoot pushed through the crowd and stood in front of the officer. "Colonel Butler," he said, "it is grand to see you!"

Butler nodded, but rolled his eyes back to the rebel.

"Sir," Wintermoot said, "we agreed none would be harmed."

"There are always unforeseen exceptions to every rule," Butler said. "I may in this case have to alter our bargain." He gestured to some rangers to take the dangerous rebel in their charge, for the pure hatred shinning through the rebel's eyes forbade any other action.

The rangers gruffly handled the man. Dragging him to one of the posts holding up the platform around the walls of the fort, they hastily tied him tight to it.

Ingersoll struggled against the ropes at first, but then let his body fall limp with despair against the ropes.

One of the Indians, intensely watching the entire spectacle, walked up to the gloating ranger now examining the rebel's tomahawk.

The ranger, knowing what along the handle of the tomahawk so drew the Indian's intense eye, offered it to him, rolling a sly eye to the rebel tied to a nearby post. "Luck be with you, my fine fellow, for they have noticed those notches about the handle of your tomahawk," he said to the rebel. "Every notch means one Indian," he added.

Ingersoll turned pale and slumped down even further against the ropes. The sight of most of his so-called friends openly mingling and greeting the Tories with great smiles across their faces made his heart sink in his chest. Noticing a group of rangers gathering his wife and children together and forcing them into a secluded and particularly unpleasant part of the fort sank his spirits even further. All seemed lost. But upon seeing the rangers relieve everyone in the fort of their possessions shortly thereafter, whether they bore a welcoming smile or not, brought a slight smile of irony to his crestfallen face. Witnessing their surprised looks drew a certain satisfaction to his beleaguered soul. What did they expect with a bargain with the devil?

All eyes, even of the crestfallen prisoner tied to a post, watched some proud white men swagger to a table set in the middle of the fort for all to see. One of them quickly unrolled a paper and set a pen and inkwell on the table. With a few words and nods to one another, they all took their turn with the pen to sign the paper. Then Lieutenant Scovell lifted the paper, announcing all seemed in order, finally.

The Indians immediately starting wailing and dancing about, seeming more at liberty to search any bundle or any Wyoming person, rebel, neutral, or Tory.

Ranger and Indian alike gathered more of the fort's inmates around Mrs. Ingersoll and her children. Once there, they poked and taunted them before some other cry or commotion at the other end of the fort caught their attention. They all rambled toward it with no more thought to the gathered rebels.

Mrs. Ingersoll, looking to the neglected gate which still sat wide open, nonchalantly guided everyone in their huddled group toward it. Nearing it, a scant few Indians strode into their path, demanding a quick look into their bundles and about their persons before ordering them on through the gate by saying '"Jogo! Jogo!"

Ingersoll's wife and children, suffering through the humiliating and gruff search of their persons, all gazed with tear-strewn eyes at him, nodding profusely as the Indians pushed them along after stripping them of anything catching their fancy.

Ingersoll perked up, and managed a tortured smile at them, finding little solace from their departing this nest of betrayers. Where would they go? Were all the forts being surrendered in like fashion, or just their fort? And even if they managed to make the trail would the Indians pursue them and ambush them out of sight of their white allies? These thoughts haunted him to his core. Slumping down against the ropes again, he watched them stride through the gate, feeling altogether a failure. But wait! You must do something! He convinced himself. Bucking up against the ropes, he swelled his lungs and cried out "Leave the valley my dears! Head to Easton! I shall find you there! Easton!"

## Chapter Fifty Two
### *Fort Jenkins capitulates*

The sun set on the small fort now bearing the brunt of the oncoming Tory and Indian invasion. Uneasy eyes peeked over pointed logs. Every leaf fluttering in the breeze or snap of a twig caught the attention of the anxious inmates of the small haven. Rifles, fully loaded and waiting, sat along the inside of the wall, by every loophole, and upon the low platforms along the walls.

Plenty of rifles, John Jenkins thought, stealing a glance at two nervous fellows manning the walls next to him, but not enough men to fire them. John Murphy and William Martin shot well, but they could not be everywhere at once. He looked over to Stephen Harding Sr., recently arriving from Forty Fort to assess their situation, and sighed, noticing he had arrived alone. Was he to take on the whole world by himself?

Harding noticed Jenkins' look and went straight to the heart of the matter. "Abandoning this fort and retreating to Forty Fort is the only reasonable thing to do, John," he said, coming right to the point. He gazed over the walls. "No matter which way they come you do not stand a chance!" He rolled an eye toward Murphy and Martin straining to hear their conversation. "See John," Harding said. "They all know and are just waiting for your word to go to Forty Fort."

Jenkins looked at Harding and scratched his head. He let his eyes fall to the darkening forest beyond the walls, imagining the terrible hordes he feared hid within it. He thought of his mother and father, whom he had insisted retreat to Pittston Fort on the *'safe'* side of the river. He thought of Beth, and her refusal to accompany them, along with her friend Elizabeth Murphy, whom both insisted their place was with their husbands. He had had a garrison of nineteen men just a few days ago. Now he had but three able-bodied men.

"I hear your words, and must admit your reasoning is just," he said, turning back toward Harding. The older man smiled. Sliding his wide-brimmed hat back on his head, he slapped his hand on his buckskin trousers, nodding his head all the while.

"How did it come to this?" Jenkins asked. "This is madness!"

"All war is madness," Harding said. "I fear sane men will lose their scalps, as well as their families, if we stay. Bravery is one thing, but madness is another," he added.

Jenkins' jaw dropped. He looked down the steep bank to the side of the fort. It gave them a great command of the river below. Nothing could flow past without coming under their fire. He hated the thought of surrendering the fort. It just seemed the wrong. "Look at that," he said, gesturing toward the opposite bank and Pittston Fort. "If they come by canoe and bateaux we should catch them in a fine cross-fire, indeed."

"What, with just us four men here, John?" Harding said. "Some cross-fire, and what if they gain the shore?" A commotion below turned both men's eyes down the fort's walls.

John Phelps struggled up the ladder. Blood still stained the sling and bandage about his shoulder. Groaning, he stepped off the ladder and drew a pistol from his thick leather belt with his free hand. Stumbling past the two men, he stared into the forest. Stopping a few feet away, he leveled the pistol in the crook between two of the pointed logs. "I know what you're about, Stephen Harding," he said, glancing at the man out of the corner of his eye. "We all do!" He turned toward Jenkins. "You are in proper command John, what you say will go. We will all stand by you, but I tell you a rage the likes of which I've never seen afore lurks in the forest! I've seen it myself, I have, in my own brother's eyes, nonetheless!"

"John! John!" both Murphy and Martin interrupted, both men madly gesturing to the mouth of the trail in the trees. "Injuns! Tories!"

Phelps cocked his pistol. Jenkins put a hand to his arm and cautioned "Be easy! If it comes to that we must make every shot count!" Both he and Harding eased their rifles up to the wall beside him.

A drum thumped and a fife squealed, breaking the uneasy silence and giving every man along the wall a start. Their rifles clicked to full cock and aimed at the green-coated men strutting proudly out of the folds of the forest and onto the green before the fort's gate. A white flag of truce fluttering on a pole one of the rangers held high. Jenkins' order to stand easy precluded any shots at the brazen Tories.

The music suddenly ceasing, they smartly stopped just a rod in front of the gate. A rather tall and slim man in a fine uniform stepped two paces in front of the others. "I am Captain Caldwell of the King's Rangers," he said, staring straight ahead. "I demand you surrender this fort in the name of the King at once!"

Jenkins glared down at the man, but did nothing but wet the end of his sights. The others' rifles remained leveled at the bold Tories.

"By God, it's come to it," Murphy gasped. "Right to the gates of our very own fort. I'll blister every bastard I can John, I grant you that!" He looked around to the others and added, "We are all with you!"

The Tory officer, apparently hearing his words, promptly slid his sword from its sheath, raising it toward the gate. Dozens more green-coated men showed themselves briefly from the forest in every direction. The haunting shadows of their Indian allies drifted in the shadows of the forest behind them. Several wails announced their presence.

"As you can see," Coldwell announced. "I do not propose your surrender idly! If you surrender now your terms will be most favorable. If not," he added, looking back over his shoulder. "I cannot be held responsible for what may happen."

"You just stay right where you are, my fine fellow!" John Jenkins said, eyeing down his sights to the two white straps crisscrossing the officer's chest. "I will be responsible for felling you, my fine fellow, if one of your men fires! So you best pray they don't 'til we settle this all!"

"Outrageous!" Caldwell said, shaking his sword at the man.

"Yes, aren't we?" Jenkins said. "We get that way when pompous intruders with large arses invade our land looking to lift our bloody scalps!" Slowly lowered his rifle, he walked to the ladder. "If anything should happen be sure to drop him first!" he said to the questioning eyes following him. He suddenly stopped on the ladder and looked to Harding. "Stephen, will you accompany me to parlay with the rascals?"

"You bet!" Harding said, turning toward the ladder.

Beth and the other women anxiously met them at the bottom of the ladder. "John, how many are there?" she asked.

"A heap of a lot of hell lies out there I'm afraid." Harding said.

"Don't worry," Jenkins said, giving Harding a hard look. "Don't none of you worry," he added, gently pulling her to him and lightly kissing her on the forehead. Feeling a wisp of her hair touch his cheek he winced at the thought of her beautiful long and flowing hair on some brave's pole. "We'll be fine," he managed to whisper. "We'll be fine."

The gate slowly crept open in front of Caldwell. Jutting his chest, he slowly slid his sword back into its sheath. After the longest moment he stared at the gate, befuddled by no one appearing through it. He looked nervously behind him and took a few careful steps backwards, painfully aware of the rebel riflemen behind the walls. Two well-armed men suddenly marched through the gate, stopping his anxious retreat. They stopped dead in front of him, coldly glaring at him. My, he thought, how tall these rebels of the frontier are, they must eat well.

He quickly shook off the thought. "You are in command of this fort?" he flatly asked one of the towering men.

The rebel only smacked his lips, slowly cocking his head so the wide brim of his hat covered his face. The other man just stared all the more indignantly at him.

"Your rank, sir?" Caldwell asked.

"Lieutenant Jenkins of the Twenty-fourth Connecticut Regiment," Jenkins said, slowly raising his face from under the wide brim.

Caldwell gasped. "My God! It's you!" he said, recognizing him from Fort Niagara. His eyes glared as if he had seen a ghost. "You live! Well now, isn't that just fine? By jingo!"

"It is fine," Jenkins said. "Leastways I think so." He cocked an eye toward Harding. "This here is Mr. Harding. I asked him to accompany me, seeing how he suffered such grievous losses as of late."

Caldwell's eyes widened. The torture posts flashed through his mind. Yes, one of the men did call himself Hadsall, Harding, or such a name. No doubt a relation to this man glaring at him. That would explain his cold eyes. "Most unfortunate," Caldwell muttered to him.

"Yes it was," Harding said. "Leastways I think so."

"Bloodshed is always most unfortunate," Caldwell said.

Both rebels smacked their lips.

"Let us see if we can curtail any further bloodshed," Caldwell said, rolling an eye to some curious warriors stepping from the shadows of the forest behind him. "Here it is, if you surrender now nothing shall be taken from the fort, or from any person, except for such items which may be used against His Majesty's forces and allies, and even those items shall be compensated for from the King's treasury. All persons within the fort shall have the liberty to return to their farms and such in peace as long as they promise not to take further action in this most unfortunate struggle, this war. Excluding all regular Continental soldiers, of course."

Both rebels stared blankly at the man without muttering a word through their stunned lips. They had not expected such liberal terms. Wondering if their true numbers be known such favorable terms would be offered, Jenkins decided to strike when the iron was hot for the sake of the women and children. He would not have their innocent blood on his hands.

"Well gentlemen?" Caldwell asked the silent men again.

"Most certainly," Jenkins finally said, "most certainly, indeed." Both he and Harding nodded at one another and then to Caldwell.

Caldwell managed a slight smile in return.

A ranger slithered from behind the trees. Swaggering up to Caldwell, he whispered something to him, holding his rifle at the ready.

Though black paint with red swirls covered his entire face, Jenkins instantly recognized the man. A chill, quickly subdued by intense flames of hatred, surged through his body. You cannot mask the face of treason with paint, Parshall Terry! No you can not, he thought.

Terry rolled an suspicious eye to Jenkins and pulled Caldwell further to the side, talking in hushed tones to him. Caldwell watched both rebels out of the corner of his eye. His expression grew more sour the longer he listened to Terry.

Finally finishing their conversation, both Tories stepped forward. "Gentlemen," Caldwell said, looking sternly into their eyes. "It has come to my attention Captain Harding here has been, and may still be, a soldier of the Continental Line." He raised an eyebrow. "I am sorry, but as such, he must be held at Major Butler's discretion."

Anger flooded both rebel's faces. Harding bowed his head and stomped the ground, musing about whether to sprint back into the fort or not.

Dozens of yelping Indians from the forest seemed to recognize his dilemma, daring him to turn and run. Green-coated troops appeared from the forest all around in preparation of taking charge of the fort. No avenue of escape remained.

Terry marched up to the frustrated man stomping his feet in rage. He cocked the rifle held tight in his hands. "Are we to have trouble?" he bluntly asked.

"No, not yet, you Tory son of a bitch, but it's a comin' if you be fool enough to proceed any farther down the valley! I grant you that, for sure I do! For who knows what the morrow may bring? Hopefully your destruction! God willing!" Harding proclaimed through gritted teeth.

"Yes, but the morrow is the morrow, and today is today," Terry said, gesturing with his rifle for the glaring rebel to step toward the forest.

Harding took a few angry steps forward before stopping and turning back to Jenkins, much to Terry's disgust. "I go for their sake this day, John," he said, glancing up to the eyes staring down at him in shock from the fort's walls above them. "To spare the innocent, I shall go."

Jenkins nodded, glaring with eyes of pure hatred at Terry.

Terry ignored the indignant stare and shoved Harding along with jabs from his rifle butt. Two other rangers immediately joined him and they rushed their prisoner down the trail.

"Do not worry," Caldwell said. "They are to present him to Major Butler. I shall personally guarantee no harm will come to him."

Spreading his hand toward the fort, Caldwell nodded. Both men slowly marched to the gate under the sad eyes staring over the pointed logs of the wall down to them.

Things did not bode well for Wyoming this day. Already two forts had fallen without a shot fired in anger, but the enemy had slipped down upon them as a thief in the night. Who was to know what the dawn would bring, and the light of day when the thieves could be seen?

## Chapter Fifty Three
*Parley*

John Jenkins struggled through the bustling crowds in the green of Forty Fort. Some familiar faces brought a sense of comfort to him, while others he hadn't seen for a while awoke a deep sense of concern within him. All of Wyoming seemed to gather about the fort, backwoodsmen, gentlemen, and townsmen alike.

"There they is!" John Murphy announced with a tug at Jenkins' sleeve from behind. Murphy pointed and hurried off to one of the cabins along the fort's wall. "Come on, John," he added, waving toward the cabin.

Jenkins followed a few paces behind him, his mind flooded with all of the events of the prior day. He hoped he hadn't left anything of importance out of his hasty report to Colonel Denison. He thought of their arrival yesterday at Pittston Fort, exiled there on their own parole from the captured Fort Jenkins. It too had bustled with activity. He and his two able-bodied men had stayed just long enough to make sure everyone in their charge found some comfort and security, especially Beth and the pregnant Elizabeth Murphy. After tearful and hasty farewells, he and his men set out for Fort Wilkes-Barre, and from there, across the river aboard Yarington's ferry to Forty Fort.

Upon reaching the cabin Murphy eagerly shook hands and greeted the Gore family all huddled together in front of the cabin. Smiles cut through their serious looks for a moment. Silas Gore grabbed at the hair on the nape of Murphy's neck and said, "Glad to see you still got yer hair! Remember what I told ya afore about the only way to get away with yer hair when they're hot on yer heels after you've fired your load and lost your tomahawk is to go where the rabbit won't go, no critter, be he savage or wolf, will follow you there!"

Murphy laughed and thankfully accepted a fowler piece, pouch, and shot bag from them. "Saw you didn't have a weapon, and ya sure look bare without one!" Silas said to his grateful smile.

"They took all ours," Murphy explained, "despite their word to the contrary, the rats." He shook his head. "Then they allowed us to canoe over to Pittston Fort, there to take no part in the mischief brewing about." Chuckling, he loaded the fowler with a load of buckshot. "But we don't see how we're bond to their word which they already broke, damn 'em!"

"And Elizabeth?" Silas asked.

"Oh, my fine spring lassie's just fine, she is at that," Murphy answered with a nod toward Jenkins. "Beth Jenkins is looking over her and promises to see her through this all, God bless her soul. A finer woman you'll not find is these parts!" Waving Jenkins forward, he put a hand to his shoulder. "Man and wife, there're both fine, indeed!"

Jenkins looked down to the back of his right hand at the mere mention of Beth's name. His heart already ached for her. He quelled his urge to rub his hand and instead held it out to the Gores.

"Don't fret none," Daniel Gore said, shaking his hand. "We'll soon run that lot out of here with a lickin' so great they'll never return! I swear it on oath or my name's not Daniel Gore!"

A series of huzzas erupted from his assembled brothers, uncles, and brothers-in-law around him.

Another cry turned their heads to see Colonel Denison making his way through the crowd shouting John Jenkins' name. The loud and commanding voice from the cabin behind them hushed the crowd. The crowd, recognizing their leader, quickly parted to make way for him. Denison headed for a near ladder leading up to the platform, calling for Jenkins and Lieutenant Colonel Dorrance to join him. Other curious officers also followed, but gave way for Jenkins and Dorrance.

Climbing the ladder, Denison removed his hat, rubbing the sweat from his brow. Gesturing over the walls he said, "The devils are afoot everywhere and approaching this very gate!"

The shrill of a fife and thump of a drum, sounding so familiar to Jenkins it filled him with dread, blared as if on cue from Denison. All of them looked down to the Tories advancing under a flag of truce toward the fort. All looked with wide-eyes to Denison.

"I'll take Jenkins here, along with George, and see what they're all about," Denison said to the other officers, placing his fine beaver-skin hat back on his head and carefully adjusting it. The concern in everyone's eyes made him pause. "I'll accept no capitulation, have no fear of that! The rest of you see that your men are ready, for we may soon have some sport!" The officers all turned and scrambled down the ladder, each peeling off to his own section of the fort where his men assembled.

Denison and his two hand-picked officers followed them down the ladder. Facing the gate, Denison adjusted his hunting shirt, gesturing at the anxious souls manning it. It slowly slid open a crack, just wide enough for Denison and his officers to squeeze through it. They marched out to meet a trio of men advancing from the rigid musicians. Soon both parties stopped face to face.

"Damn it!" Dan Ingersoll immediately said to their surprised eyes. Frowning, he kicked at the ground. A Tory jabbed his elbow into his side to straighten him up and stop his distracting movements. The Indian on the other side of him glared at the rebels through his dark eyes set deep upon his red and black painted face.

Denison shook his head, staring back at the indignant Indian.

"Sir," Ingersoll said with a prod from the Tory. "I am being forced upon the pain of death to deliver this message to you."

Denison slowly bobbed his head.

"This here is Lieutenant Chrysler, my guard," Ingersoll said, gesturing toward the Tory. The Tory ranger smirked under the thick black paint totally covering his face and neck. A small piece of silver dangled from under his noise. His piercing blue eyes cut through the paint with a strange mixture of the new and the old. His eyes and his green-coat hinted of his white features, but other than that, he strongly resembled his Indian ally standing on the other side of Ingersoll.

Ingersoll rolled his eyes to the Indian.

The Indian stood mute. His deep, penetrating, and cold eyes cut into the white men's souls.

Ingersoll noticed their growing uneasiness. "This here is Blue Throat," he said. "He's a right proud Seneca, the bloody fiend!"

Blue Throat did not even blink to acknowledge his introduction. Standing perfectly still, he continued staring down the rebels. A rifle sat cradled in his arms, partially concealed by a deep blue blanket with red trim hanging loosely over one of his shoulders. Buckskin leggings rose from his moccasins, tied by red sashes just below his knees. A long white shirt speckled with black spots covered him from his lower thigh to his shoulders. Silver bands covered his wrists and upper arms. A gorget hung shining about his neck. Many ear rings dangled from great loops of skin cut and stretched from the outer edge of his ears. A silver ring with a triangular piece hung dangling from pierced his nose. Red paint completely covered the top of his shaven head, stopping in a line which circled his entire head just below his eyes. Black dots speckled the rest of his face. A lone tuff of greased black hair glistened in the sunlight, standing erect through a silver band atop his shaven head. A lone erect feather sat atop the greasy tuff of hair. The Indian seemed unmoved by all the attention to his person. He had become most used to it over the years.

"Anyhow," Ingersoll said, breaking their attention away from the elaborately dressed Indian. "Major Butler has taken Forts Wintermoot and Jenkins, as you most assuredly already know." He rolled an eye toward Chrysler. "Wintermoot's is their headquarters, they have already demolished your fort, John, but I've seen their num..." a sharp jolt to his side immediately silenced him. Gasping for air, he glared at the Tory officer staring at him with a grim eye.

"Anymore vague attempts to betray our numbers and it'll be your neck when we get back to camp!" Chrysler warned him.

A slight smile crept across Blue Throat's face.

"Wait a minute!" Chrysler suddenly said, staring gauntly at the lean rebel in front of him. "You're Jenkins!?!"

Now John Jenkins let a smile creep across his face.

"You have broken the terms!" Chrysler exclaimed. "Have you rebels no honor!?! You were released with the understanding that you and your men were to refrain from any further involvement in this!"

A sharp whistle raised his eyes to the wall above the gate. Both Murphy and Martin waved down at the infuriated man.

"More of your brood of liars, no doubt," Chrysler said, scowling at Jenkins. He turned his angry eyes to Ingersoll. "Continue!" he ordered him with a gruff push. "As for you, Mr. Jenkins, your treachery will be duly noted, I do assure you! You can expect no quarter, or mercy!"

"Indian Butler," Ingersoll said, letting a slight smile perk up the corners of his mouth on managing to slip in the insult of the Tory leader. "He demands all the forts, and stores therein, be surrendered to him as a due representative of our good King George the third, he does at that. If you comply, he is willing to let all noncombatants depart in safety with their possessions intact. All militia are to turn over their arms and swear on their honor that they will no longer participate in this rebellion against our good King George. After these terms of capitulation are met, they shall also be allowed to live without further reprisal from the King's forces. With the exception of regular troops of the Continental Line, of course, I am told they are an altogether different lot, though Indian, eh, I mean, uh, blast it, Major Butler, ensures all of his erring subjects will gain the King's mercy, if they surrender, that is" He looked to Chrysler, raising his upper lip in disgust. "I guess that's it, it is at that."

Chrysler cleared his throat, his eyes staring deathly at Jenkins.

"Oh," Ingersoll said, "I'm told there's another matter. One of four men."

Chrysler cleared his throat again, slowly raising a stiff finger to Jenkins.

"Oh," Ingersoll said, taking the hint, "that would be five men, in all. Lieutenant Colonel Butler and Captain Hewitt, seeing as they're sworn officers in the Continental Line, then there's the deserters from His Majesty's forces, known to be about Wyoming and training rebels, Malcolm Boyd and the Irishman Pike, and of course, our own Lieutenant Jenkins here, they are the exceptions to be dealt with by the King's justice. Major Butler says that if these terms are not promptly complied with, there is no alternative but the complete and utter destruction of all within the walls, since after he releases the Indians there will be no way to curb their anger. There will be no way to stop them, and Major Butler strongly recommends that you destroy all stores of intoxicating drink, whether you except these terms or not, for a drunken savage cannot be controlled!" He let out a long, sad, sigh, bowing his head in shame.

"Well?" Chrysler snarled. "What say ye men of Wyoming?"

Denison glared at the man and looked over to Ingersoll, whom immediately adverted his eyes in shame. He felt mixed emotions about the man, not sure just which side of the fence the man preferred. He turned a cold eye back to Chrysler. "I don't know why you tortured this poor soul to do your lip service, but we would have believed you just the same without you cruelly humiliating this man! If this be the King's way, perhaps we are not so errant in our ways. Furthermore, I sincerely doubt you have enough men to take this valley away from its rightful inhabitants, and damn you if you try! I dare say you shall regret it! So I advise you, fine sir, and your Major Butler, to turn about and get whilst you still can! For we will defend our land to the last extremity, damn you all to hell!"

Chrysler stared blankly at him as he would a buffoon.

Denison bit his lip and took a few steps back behind Dorrance and Jenkins. Chrysler and the Indian anxiously watched him. They both looked up to the rifles slowly rising over the fort's walls.

Denison, also noticing the rifles, waved them back down, quickly curbing his anger by swallowing hard against it. He stepped forward again.

"Be it as it may," he said through clenched teeth, "I am only the ranking militia officer. Our Colonel Butler is the ranking officer. I shall have to confer with him upon this matter, for you quite well know how I feel! That is all I have to say, you damn Tory!"

"Colonel Butler requires an answer now," Chrysler flatly stated.

"He has my answer!" Denison said. "For official word, he shall have to wait!"

After locking eyes with the Tory Chrysler one more time, Denison smartly turned about and marched back to the fort. Jenkins and Dorrance immediately followed, leaving Chrysler standing with his mouth agape. After a moment, he gruffly grabbed Ingersoll and turned him about in front of his own person as a human shield, carefully backing away from the fort. Blue Throat leisurely strolled to his side, seemingly oblivious to the threatening calls and jeers from the fort's walls. The Tory musicians turned without playing a note and marched away. Soon they all disappeared into the deep shadows of the forest.

No sooner did the gate close than Denison turn to the two officers following him. He held up his hand to wave back the herd of officers forming around them. "Well?" he asked. "What do you think?"

"They aren't ready to attack," Jenkins bluntly stated.

Both Denison and Dorrance raised an eyebrow at his remark.

"I am sure of it," Jenkins continued in answer to their puzzled looks. "The Indian, a Seneca by the way, just as Ingersoll said, I could tell by his one erect feather. One standing feather means Seneca. Anyhow, he wasn't dressed for war. No Iroquois goes into battle but with a breech cloth, war club, tomahawk, pouch, scalping knife, spear, or firelock. Plus his loops weren't tied back."

"Loops?" Dorrance asked.

"Yes sir," Jenkins said. "You've seen them and are aware of their custom to cut and stretch the skin from around the cartilage of their ears as to have more room to ornate them. They believe the more silvery and shiny things they have about their faces, the more it wards off bad spirits. You can imagine them catching on twigs and branches and such, or being pulled off by an enemy in battle, so they tie them back afore every tussle. That Seneca was not dressed for war, but for a Sunday stroll to the meeting house."

"Loops indeed," Dorrance said, straightening his finely tailored uniform. "But you ,sir, know them, and their customs, much better than any of us. Besides, knowing how fickle and superstitious they are they may have abandoned Indian Butler already. He may only have his rangers, Johnson's Royal Greens, and such sundry Tories with him now, and is only feigning a threat of an assault on the fort. I am certain he has no cannon, also, so his threats may be merely braggadocio."

Denison pursed his lips and nodded, immediately gesturing to the awaiting officers. "Send a runner at once to fetch Colonel Butler at Wilkes-Barre Fort! Also send one to Captain Franklin to bring up his Salem and Huntington Company and to Captain Clingman and his garrison at the lower Fort Jenkins." Putting a hand to his chin, he thought for a moment. "I do hope Captain Spalding is advancing with all due haste, for we may need all the men we can muster to face this upcoming storm! That we shall, I am most afraid. May God protect us all. Amen."

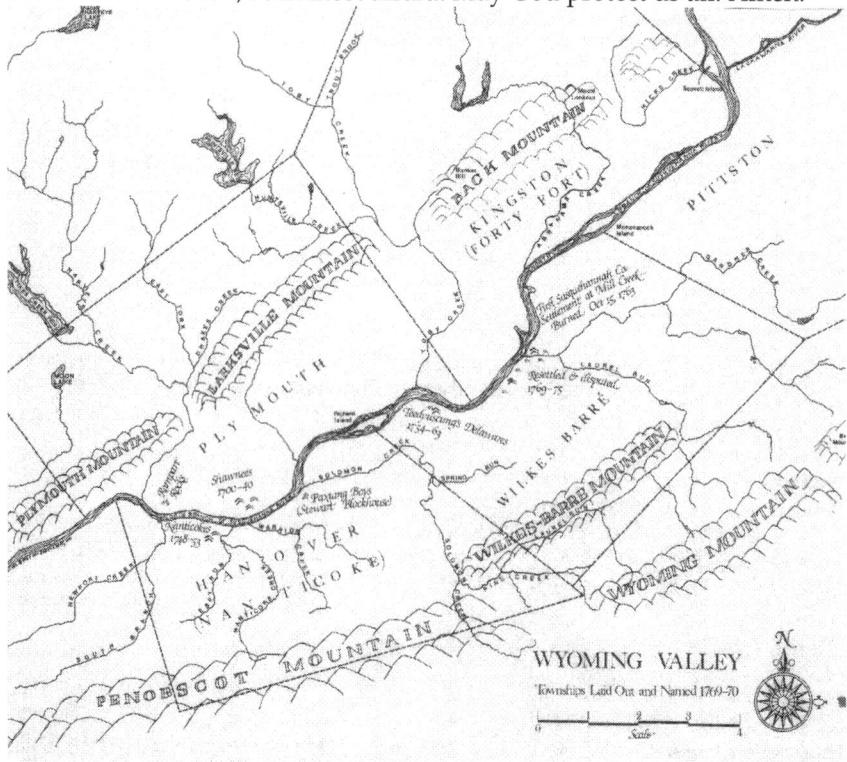

## Chapter Fifty Four
*Muster for battle!*

Nathan Denison's call to muster for battle rolled like thunder through the whole Wyoming Valley. Farmers strode forth with their barn rifles and fowlers. Every soul, both young and old, answered the call. Strong and stout Connecticut women strode to the nearest fort, ushering along their children and carrying what humble belongings they had gathered in their arms. Congress had siphoned off the cream of Wyoming's manhood to fight the greater war, so now the women waved their young, old, and those deemed unfit for regular service, off to war with worried cheers. A few brazen women of the lower settlements armed themselves and stood defiantly on their own thresholds, ready to fight off any intruder.

Lieutenant Colonel Zebulon Butler, on leave from the regular army, and ordered to stay in the valley through the upcoming crisis, led the two Wilkes-Barre companies into the gates of Forty Fort to rousing cheers. He took off his hat in recognition of the peoples' welcoming cheers and stood tall in the saddle, searching for Colonel Denison in the crowd. A smile stretched across his face upon seeing his friend stride through the parting crowd with his hand outstretched to greet him. Jumping down from the saddle, he immediately shook his hand.

"It is good to see you all!" he said to Denison and the group of officers following him.

"Not as good as it is to see you," Denison said. "And your men," he added. Putting a hand to his friend's shoulder, he led him to a center cabin along the fort's high double-posted and hewn-timbered walls. Overcome by his anxious feelings, he stopped at a hogshead by the corner of the cabin and turned toward his friend. "There's the devil to pay, and his name is Major John Butler!" he said.

"Yes, just what is our situation?" Butler asked, removing his gloves and leaning a hand against the barrel.

"Indian Butler sent Dan Ingersoll under guard to parlay with us in his stead this morning on the matter of capitulation," Denison answered. "Ingersoll looked greatly distressed. I have no idea why he sent the man but to humiliate him and show he already masters the upper reaches of the Valley, but who knows what exactly is on a fiend's mind? I told him the valley is not mine to surrender and sent for you."

"Yes, yes, I already know of his mischief upriver," Butler said. "What do you know of his numbers?"

"Well," Denison said, turning to one of the officers surrounding them, "I have sent out many a scout under Captain Hewitt's direction."

Hewitt stepped smartly forward. Raising his bandaged right

hand to lift his hat in salute he reported, "A number of our scouts have come under fire." He glanced down at his wounded hand. "Tory lead," he explained. "I already lost one man dead to it, and another, Sam Finch, has been captured. But, from what I can ascertain, their numbers are no greater than our own, sir."

"I see," Butler said, putting a hand to his chin. "What are our stores and just what are our numbers at present?"

"Our stores are adequate for a few days, but not for any extended period of time," Denison said, looking to the bustling crowds of civilians, soldiers, and militiamen growing every second inside the crowded fort. "I have not a had proper muster as of yet, but, I reckon with the arrival of the Wilkes-Barre companies and the Hanover company we number about three hundred and fifty plus another thirty *Reformadoes*, as the alarm companies like to call themselves. I have sent urgent dispatches to Captains Franklin, Clingman, and Spalding."

Butler rubbed his chin. Looking to one of the men close at hand he said, "Baldwin! Prepare a dispatch for the Board of War at Philadelphia informing them of our present circumstances."

Isaac Baldwin immediately responded, drawing paper and a crude lead pencil from his pouch. Placing the paper atop of a hogshead, he hastily wrote down all the particulars of what he had heard the officers discuss. He then handed the paper to Butler, whom quickly read it. After Butler signed it he carefully folded and sealed it before hurrying off to his mount. In no time Baldwin galloped out the south gate.

"There goes a proper adjutant," Butler said. "I shall be hard pressed to replace him." He then noticed the distinguished looking man standing next to Denison. "Anderson Dana!" he said. "It is good to see all good men gather to the call of Wyoming's defense! Rode all the way from the assembly in Hartford, have you?"

"Yes sir," Dana said. "I must say it was a damn hard ride, but here I am, sir."

"I surely wish more felt as you do, fine sir," Butler said.

"I have made Mr. Dana my adjutant," Denison said.

"Very good choice!" Butler said with an approving nod. "A man of fine caliber to replace Baldwin!" Patting Dana on his shoulder, he scanned the rest of the officers, walking up to two in particular. "Speaking of men of caliber, it is very good to see Captains Durkee and Ransom," he said with a sincere nod to both of the officers. They both gave a courtly nod in return, though interrupted by a rider thundering through the south gate.

They all looked to the anxious man parting the crowd.

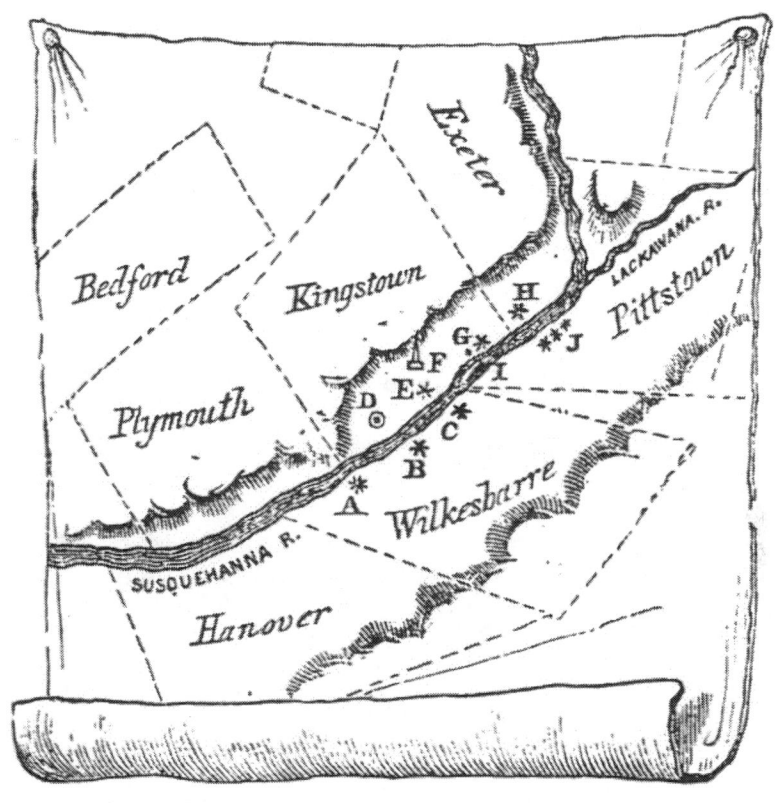

POSITION OF THE WYOMING FORTS.4

*The several divisions, Hanover, Kingston, &c., mark the districts into which the town of Westmoreland was divided; in military language of the day, in different beats. A marks Fort Durkee(demolished well before the battle in the Yankee-Pennamite wars); B marks Wilkes-Barre Fort; C marks Fort Odgen(also demolished in the Pennamite Wars); D, the village of Kingston; E, Forty Fort, also referred to as Kingston Fort. F the battleground proper; G, Wintermoot's Fort; H Fort Jenkins; I, Monocasy Island; J, the three Pittston stockades. The dot below the G marks Queen Esther's Rock.*

Reining up his horse, the rider gazed all about. Finally locking eyes with the officers about the hogshead, he plopped down from his horse, hastily advancing toward the officers, madly trying to straighten his torn and ragged brown regimental. He stopped and stood ramrod straight in front of the officers, removing his hat in salute.

"Lieutenant Pierce?" Butler asked.

"Yes sir," Pierce said through panting breaths. "Sir, Captain Spalding sends his compliments and says he will arrive with his company by Sunday at the latest!"

"Very well, Mr. Pierce," Butler said. "My God man, how you do look famished! Take a breath and settle down. Have a morsel of food, at the least, my good man!"

Dana stepped forward and took the exhausted man by the arm. The Gores met them halfway to the cabins, heartily cheering their brother-in-law. Pierce's longing wife immediately embraced him. A long, passionate kiss ensued. Eyes turned away and ignored the affront to their social code, after all, these were the most trying times. Intense times fostered intense emotions.

"If all coming to our relief are as passionate as he, we have nothing to fear, indeed!" Butler said.

"Nothing to fear but the scalping knife and a torch in some Tory's hands setting our homes aflame!" a voice exclaimed from the mingling troops.

Butler, recognizing the voice, rolled his eyes and leaned back against the huge wooden barrel. Denison reacted the same. They both knew the voice. They all knew it well.

Lazarus Stewart emerged from the crowd, raising his rifle over his head to lure attention to himself. "What say you all!?!" he shouted. "Are we to just sit here on our fat arses whilst the Tories and savages have free reign outside these very walls!?!"

"Come now, Lazarus," Denison said, trying to calm his friend. He did get so emotional at times. "No one has decided anything yet, let alone decided upon a plan of action!"

"We elect officers to lead!" Stewart answered. "To lead us against our enemies and protect our property from the same! By damn if you'll not lead us we'll go back to our homes and defend them the best we can without you!" Swaggering up to the officers, he slammed the butt of his rifle down hard on top of the hogshead, breaking it open.

Denison and Butler stared wide-eyed at the crazed man and stepped back a few steps.

Stewart ignored their looks and grabbed a nearby half-gourd shell from a peg on a nearby post, thrusting it through the hole in the top of the barrel. Raising it high, he victoriously took a long drink from it, seeming to relish it. After satisfying his thirst, he passed the gourd to a sea of awaiting hands around him. "Come!" he called. "Come partake in the rum, so as we may have a proper council!"

Denison suddenly regretted excluding the huge barrel of rum

from his order to spill all intoxicating beverages into the Susquehanna. He figured to use it for medicinal purposes, for who knew how the tide of battle might sway. Now, he reluctantly accepted the rum offered to him in a large mug. Butler joined him, seeming none the more anxious about it. Eager mugs, gourds, and leather jacks full of cheer, passed among the hands surrounding them.

Little groups of men splintered off on their own to discuss their predicament. Denison and Butler watched them all, gauging their words by their animated gestures. The gourd-shells and mugs quickly gave way to buckets.

"I say the only prudent action is to stay in the fort and await reinforcements," Butler said after a particularly long drink.

"I agree," Denison said. "The problem is to convince them."

Butler pursed his lips, slowly shaking his head. How he longed to be back in the disciplined ranks of the Continental Line, where orders needed no approval from the ranks, only compliance, that is, after you explained the reason for it, of course. But these blue-nosed Puritans of New England decided everything through the town meeting. He knew his orders would only be obeyed with popular consent. In such lay his dilemma, to lead through popular consent. Freedom had its price.

"I sent two flags to parlay with them before you arrived and both were promptly fired upon, along with numerous scouts," Denison said, looking up to the blue sky. "Their numbers could be decreasing or increasing as we speak, for the Indians are so fickle and unpredictable. Knowing how the fortunes of war turn so unpredictably I also ordered all the rum barrels emptied into the river." He gazed down into his mug. "All but this barrel, of course," he added, drinking the rest of the rum.

"Yes," Butler said. "You've done well. I would have ordered the rum spilled into the river when I got here anyways, for as you say, the fortunes of war turn so unpredictably. We must think of the innocents, the women and children. A drunken savage is most dangerous, indeed. But now it is time to resolve this matter one way or the other." Standing tall, he drank all of the rum in his mug before speaking any further. "And I have decided that it would be most prudent, as we do not properly know the size of the force opposing us, to wait for Franklin's Company and Spalding's fine Continentals, before we advance one way or the other. We must weigh our situation very carefully, for captivity and slavery, perhaps even torture of our women and children, may be the result of any acts made in haste! We must be of sound mind and reason!"

Men within earshot suddenly bolted toward Stewart, feeding

him all they heard Colonel Butler just say.

Both Denison and Butler watched them with regret, both wishing they had gone into one of the cabins before discussing such things in public. A loud roar growing from the men around Stewart proved it.

"What is this claptrap!?!" Stewart screamed. He paced slowly around, locking eyes with all around him. "Are we to stay cooped up in this fort like so many poltroons whilst those filthy Tory bastards burn our cabins and crops, steal our cattle, and trample our very livelihoods!"

Butler stepped toward him, shaking his head.

"Step back sir!" Stewart said. "I have no stomach for poltroons!"

"Now just a minute!" Denison yelled in defense of his stunned comrade. A poltroon indeed! Marching up to Stewart, he looked him dead in the eye. "Come to your senses man! Look to whom you speak!"

"Nathan," Stewart snarled, "I never thought I would see the day when your tongue spoke in defense of such cowardly ways!"

Barely containing his rage, Denison shook his finger to a nearby officer. "Captain Mckarrachan place this man under arrest immediately!"

"Can't do it," Mckarrachan said, shaking his head. "With all due respect sir, I happen to agree. Whilst we sit here Indian Butler may be sacking Pittston Fort and sneaking down the east shore to take Fort Wilkes-Barre, and from there cross the river and take us from the front and the rear! Right through Hanover! Some of our wives and children are still down there!"

A loud cheer of approval followed his remarks.

"Dana!" Denison said. "Place Private Stewart under arrest!"

Dana marched forth with two reluctant soldiers in tow. They half-heartily took positions on either side of the boisterous Paxtang Ranger, careful to keep their gleaming bayonets turned away from him and harmlessly pointed in the air.

"Take him at once!" Denison screamed, his voice on the verge of cracking with rage.

A groan of disgust answered his order.

Mckarrachan marched between the infuriated colonel and Stewart, throwing his sword at his feet. "There! Damn it!" he exclaimed, glaring down at the sword. "I resign my captaincy this instant!"

The men of the Hanover Company huzzaed and stepped toward their fuming former captain. Flailing his arms wildly about, he marched through them. A grin stretched from ear to ear across Stewart's face. His guards stepped even further away from him, followed most reluctantly by Dana.

Mckarrachan suddenly stopped and turned about to face the

cheering men. "My pursuits in life thus far have been ones of peace," he said, quieting the crowd. "What, with me being a schoolmaster and all. Stewart here has been used to war and accustomed to command. On parade I can maneuver you men just fine, but in the field no unnecessary hazard should be run. A mistake may prove fatal." He locked eyes with Stewart. "Take your lead! I will fight under you with my men, as an aide, or a mere private in the ranks. Your presence at the head of the Hanover Boys will impart confidence. And confidence is what we need in this moment of uncertainty facing us!" With a slight bow of his head, he melded unceremoniously into the ranks of the Hanover Company.

The men took the hint. Roswell Franklin, the lieutenant of the company, stepped to the forefront. "I say we elect Lazarus Stewart as our new captain!" he yelled. "All those in favor say aye!"

A resounding chorus of ayes filled the air.

Butler stepped forward, interposing himself between Denison and the newly elected Captain of the Hanover Company. Raising his arms high in the air he said, "I discharge Captain Stewart from arrest! The matter has now been decided! We shall march out against the enemy, if he is to be found, that is!"

## Chapter Fifty Five
*Drummer strike up!*

Whirling grinding wheels sharpening many a tomahawk to a fine edge rang in the air. Men crowded around them, passing tomahawks and long knives to the men hunching over the twirling wheels one after another. Other men took turns at the handles of the spinning wheels, keeping them constantly spinning and sharpening the deadly edges needed for war. Just a few yards away men hovered over barrels of gun powder, scooping up the black powder to fill many a powder horn. Many a man hovered over hearths in the cabins and small fires dotting the fort's green, melting lead ingots and pouring the hot lead into bullet moulds. Women and children put their agile hands to work rolling countless paper cartridges to hold the bullets and powder. A drum beat a steady rhythm, giving it all a flowing cadence, while the shrill of a fife followed the beat. Wyoming prepared for war. Tories and Indians beware!

Despite all of the activity the dull edge of doubt rubbed across the tightly wound cord of confidence stretching through everyone's mind; especially those of the older women. They watched their old and young men bravely prepare for war with mixed emotions. They tried to quell their hints of doubt from showing on their faces, but some found it much too difficult. One woman flung her apron over her head to hide her telltale tears. Others offered words of encouragement through quivering lips. All felt ashamed of their tears and struggled in vain against them for fear of extinguishing the fires of patriotism burning in their sons', husbands', fathers', and grandfathers', hearts.

Most of the men, young and old, dismissed the tears and tried to reassure the frightened women. Fathers and sons stood side by side in the forming ranks along with grandfathers and grandsons. Gray hair, along with white wigs to hide silver hair and balding heads of other more vain men, peppered the ranks, showing in stark contrast to the heads of other thick-haired youths in the ranks.

Younger women, their husbands and beaus off fighting in General Washington's army, tried in vain to console the older women. Giddy children, overcome with the excitement in the air, tugged at the women's apron strings and dresses, all clapping with glee and gazing about through eyes filled with the wonder of the innocent.

The call to form up outside the north gate of the fort brought a great burst of tears flowing down the cheeks of all the women. Some elderly women scampered away to the cabins, overcome with grief. Others tightened their hugs on the men and boys they loved so, as if trying to burnish their memory into their souls for all time. With some reluctance, the men pulled away with puzzled looks, which soon faded as they fell into the spirited ranks.

A freckle-faced redheaded boy rambled to the top of a hogshead by the gate and danced barefoot atop the huge barrel, grinning from ear to ear at his approaching father. "Go fetch me back a scalp Pa!" he said, welcoming his eager father. His father nodded, smiling at him as he passed. The boy's smile followed him all the way through the gate

Another somewhat elderly man, surrounded by a ring of concerned souls, removed his hat, hugging each one around him. His powdered wig danced about his head from his wife's forceful kisses. He gently pushed her back, slightly embarrassed by her sudden and overwhelming show of emotion. Passing his rifle into the eager hands of his young grandson, he bent down to his knees, carefully removing his silver knee buckles and handing them to his wife. He managed to say a few heartfelt words past the growing lump in his throat before grabbing his rifle and passing through the gate. Refusing the gourd shell of rum offered to each man passing through the gate, he struggled to fight back his growing tears.

Colonel Butler held his wife's hand all the way to the gate from atop his fine mount. Colonel Denison followed, turning his head to watch his wife before following Butler through the gate. Lieutenant Colonel Dorrance followed just behind him, a fine figure of a soldier in his tailored uniform. He bid his wife and family a hardy farewell. Major Garrett, the last of the mounted men, called back one last heartfelt goodbye to his weeping wife. All the senior officers straightened smartly in their saddles and passed through the gate, each casting one last look behind them, cherishing the lingering goodbyes of their loved ones.

Filing past the forming troops, they rode into position to their troops' front. Without being ordered, the men raised their weapons to their shoulders. The men's barn rifles, fowling pieces, long rifles, and wide array of muskets formed an uneven line above the men's heads. Few words rose from men, even from the Hanover Company and their new captain. Each man seemed to feel the weight of the moment upon their shoulders. They all found their place in the ranks of their companies, save a few souls standing just to the right of the line. Four of their number marched up smartly to the mounted officers.

"Sir," Captain Durkee said with a slight touch to his hat.

"Oh, yes," Butler said. "Captains Durkee, Ransom, and Lieutenants Ross and Wells." He looked over to the twenty or so soldiers that had followed the officers back home when word had reached them of the danger threatening Wyoming. "Have your men fall in with

Captain Hewitt's company. It'll be good to have men of the same like together."

Denison reined his horse about to face Butler. He wanted to object to the pooling of all the experienced men together, but minded his tongue after Butler's stern eye admonished him without a word. His horse danced about, forcing his eyes along the men of the ranks. One pair of eyes in particular caught his own, those of his recent friend, Lazarus Stewart. He again minded his tongue, not wishing to cause any dissension in the ranks. Besides, Colonel Butler knew what to do better than he, being a regular officer of the Continental Line and all.

"As for your lot, Captain Durkee," Butler said, almost in compromise to Denison's silent criticism, "I would like you officers to scout ahead to find a suitable place to disperse the troops in proper line of battle. I would think the bridge over Abraham's Creek would be such a suitable place, but you gentlemen are free to allow your own experiences and judgment to guide you. Should you find such a place, mark off the ground on which to form the order of battle."

Durkee and his officers nodded and sped up the trail. A round of cheers suddenly rose from the ranks. The officers glanced back to see a small group of soldiers filing through the gates to join the ranks. The sight of more troops livened their hearts.

"Lieutenant Bowen!" Denison said, riding up to the men. "It is good to see your company, well, at least part of it. What of Captain Franklin and the rest of the Salem and Huntington men?"

"They should be arriving presently, sir," Bowen reported.

"Very well," Denison said, gazing over the lively faces of the men in the ranks. "Form your men with Captain Whittlesey's company."

Bowen and his men melded into the ranks greeting them with great huzzas.

"Drummer strike up!" Colonel Butler ordered. The beat of assembly echoed through the still air.

An old soldier lumbered to the gate, answering the call. Fumbling with his dangling accouterments, he became painfully aware of John Jenkins' critical eyes upon him. Jenkins shook his head, but then cast a disarming smile to him before helping him with the straps twisted over his torso. A woman, dirty and sweaty from cooking over hot pots all day, followed Jenkins. She too helped the man with his straps.

A tired soul, just returning from an all night scout, leaned back against the gate and then stumbled toward them. The woman's cold stare stopped him dead in his tracks.

"Yes Terry, what have you to report?" Jenkins asked.

The man bobbed his tired head. "The devils are up there alright, dancing, hooting, and howling all night, a couple of them even shot at me! There is hell to pay up there!" Jonathan Terry reported.

"We have things well in hand here, Terry, get some sleep whilst you can, for I may have need of you soon," Jenkins said.

The woman turned with a scowl, clasping the old soldier's musket barrel between her palms to pray. "Good Lord," she said, "bless this piece to be the instrument of justice that sends a ball through the skull of Parshall Terry!"

Jenkins stood dumbfounded at the prayer. The drum beat loudly again. The old soldier eased his musket from the woman's palms, turned, then trotted out the gate.

Mrs. York turned and stood firm in Jonathan Terry's path.

Terry rolled his tired eyes down to the belligerent woman. "I, nor any of my family, have anything to do with my brother's failings," he flatly stated.

"Of course not," Jenkins said. "Mrs. York! Please give way!"

Her glaring eyes melted upon hearing Jenkins' voice. "Oh, dear Johnny Jenkins," she cried. "You were there. You know what my poor Amos went through, for you went through it too. For your sake, and none other, I'll tolerate this Terry, but never his brother!" Tilting her head to the side, she spat onto the ground. Turning, she stomped back to her pots, swearing an oath against Parshall Terry.

"She's been through a lot," Jenkins said. "We all have. No one doubts any of your family's patriotism. You all serve well, of course with one exception, but as you say, he is no longer of your family, or of any family of Wyoming. Now go as I ordered and think nothing more of this. We need all good men just now!"

Terry nodded his head and walked to one of the cabins along the walls, stealing one more anxious look back at Jenkins before disappearing in a cabin door.

The shrill of a fife tore Jenkins' gaze away from the cabin door. It struck up the lively air of *St. Patrick's Day in the Morning*. The drummer quickly joined in with a strong beat and the column of men marching four abreast followed them up the trail. The music seemed to uplift the men in the ranks. Their steps grew in spirit with the spirited beat and a growing sense of confidence swelled their chests.

Another man trotted toward Jenkins, blind courage burning in his eyes. Jenkins silently wished obedience to orders burned just as intensely in them. "Our people need all the strength they can get on the field! My being here in the fort will do no good," the man said. Sensing no objection from Jenkins, he touched his hat and hurried off to be with his fellow neighbors in the ranks.

"Godspeed, George Cooper!" Mrs. York called behind him.

Jenkins shook his head, watching the man jog to catch up with the column of men. Standing his rifle on its butt, he leaned against it, oblivious of the hand closing on it from behind. With a quick jerk from behind, the rifle flew from under his arms. Surprised by the sudden movement, he fumbled in the air for it, running a few steps after the fleet-footed culprit stealing it. His mouth fell open in amazement to the youthful face turning to look back at him. "Jabez Elliot!" he gasped. "Get back here!"

His eyes wide with excitement, the fourteen year old turned his eyes to his front again. "Sorry Johnny!" he yelled behind him. "But I got to catch up with Pa and Joseph! Can't miss out on this! No way! No sir!"

Jenkins slowed in frustration, anxiously watching the boy easily outdistance him. Finally stopping, he stared helplessly at the boy carrying away his rifle to the winding column marching up the trail. He watched the boy run along the side of it, madly searching for his father and brother, and sighed when he melded into the lively stepping ranks. Rousing cheers from behind him turned his eyes to the south gate.

He watched ragged old Mrs. York hobble anxiously toward the gathering crowd waving a long wooden spoon over her head. She soon shouted, "God bless your dear brave souls! Glory be! Glory be!"

Jenkins pushed his way through the crowd to a young sentry shouting, "They're a comin' Johnny! They're a comin'!" and pointing wildly toward the gate.

Jenkins stood on a barrel to see over the heads of the crowd. Four horsemen, all sporting brown regimental coats with red collars and cuffs, trotted madly toward the gate on lathered and spent mounts. The horses' heads bobbed up and down, trying madly to draw air to continue onward from the urging of their master's heels in their flanks and the sharp whip of the end of their reins. The lathered horses finally trotted through the gate. Their masters dropped down from their backs, leaving them standing to their own account. Panting and huffing, they welcomed the eager hands of some boys whom hastily led them to the stables.

"We are faint," one of the men gasped, reaching out to the many hands welcoming them. "Give us bread! We have not broken our fast today!"

Commanding female voices in the crowd demanded food immediately. The men panted and fell to their knees, gratefully accepting the food quickly offered to them. They ravenously devoured it. One of them grunted through great mouthfuls of food to the boys leading their mounts away. "They are spent!" he finally managed to yell. "Just like us! We fetched them along the Delaware, treat them well, for they have served us well!" He looked up to see a skeleton of a man standing over him. "Johnny Jenkins?" he gasped. "My God man, is that you?"

Jenkins nodded. "Yes, I've been to Niagara," he said.

"My good God," the man gasped again. "What the hell did they do to you man? They certainly didn't feed ya! But you've always been a stout man, your vigor will return!" The man raised his head and looked all about. "By God where are they? The troops proper? Have they already marched? Have we missed them?" All of his fellows perked up at his words.

"You've just missed them," Jenkins said, craning his head to look out the gate behind them. "As soon as the rest of the company..." the hollow look in the man's eyes answered all his fears.

"We's all there is, John," the man said. "We rode all night to get here! Spalding and the company's about Stoop's Tavern, a day's hard march away, by God." Rising to his feet, he picked up his rifle he had laid down upon the ground to free his hands to eat. The others rose from his example.

Jenkins stared gauntly at them.

"We best catch up!" the man said, leading his men at the long trot past the stunned officer. "The horses are spent, we'll have to advance on foot, make sure your rifles are ready, my brave fellows, for hell's surely awaiting us up the road!" he added.

One of the men trailing behind him stopped just long enough to tug at Jenkins' arm. "Captain Durkee?" he asked. "How is he?"

"He's fine, Gershom," Jenkins said, turning to watch the others trot through the north gate. "He's up there, marching with the rest."

"Thank you, Johnny," Gershom said, shaking his hand. "Thank you most heartedly," he added, his eyes suddenly shining on his dark face. The smile faded at the call of his fellows to hurry along and he locked eyes with Jenkins as if he knew he would soon breath his last air on this earth. "You stay strong, my man, you've always been one of the good sort," he said with a nod before rambling after the others. Women passed more bread and canteens of rum to he and his fellows as they passed, urging them on with heartfelt praises of their bravery.

Jenkins watched the tall black man thank the women for the food and hurriedly stuff it into every one of his pockets, all without slowing his gait. Clearing the gate, he enthusiastically trotted to meet the enemy with his fellows in arms. The man's heart truly beat to the drum of the new country, and with a strong desire to defend his hearth and home.

Odd, Jenkins thought, how men of color like Gershom so willingly took up the fight for liberty, something few people of his race knew in this land. The irony of it all perplexed him, especially his great concern for his ex-master's fate. Fate and liberty entwined here, he reasoned. This war would change things in this land forever, and perhaps, in the entire world. But here, now, it threatened their very lives.

John Jenkins rubbed the back of his right hand.

## Chapter Fifty Six
### *A spirited march*

The spirited march slowed just below a narrow stone bridge spanning Abraham's creek. Captain Durkee and his officers stood on the road leading north, promptly waving the column to a stop. After a few quick words with Colonel Butler, they ushered the troops into position along a slight ridge a hundred feet or so south of the bridge.

Soon Captain Durkee smartly reported the deployment of the troops in line of battle along the ridge a success. "Splendid work," Butler said. Drawing a long breath, he clasp his hands on his saddle horn. Turning with a smile to Denison he asked, "Do you see?", gesturing toward the deep gully through which the creek ran. "It's deep, giving us the edge, they'll have to bottleneck by the bridge to get at us! We'll mow the rats down then, I tell you! It is a great position to defend against an assault and only a fool would attack it!"

"Hell is full of fools," Denison said.

"Well, it'll soon be more crowded if Indian Butler proves to be fool enough to attack us here!" Butler said.

A freak gust of wind cracked the tree branch of a great dead tree near the bridge. All the men around them perked up, immediately leveling their firelocks at the bridge. A rolling click sounded down the line.

"Hold now, men!" Butler warned. "It's only the wind!"

"Perhaps another scout should be sent on ahead," Denison said, easing back in the saddle. Without a word six proud volunteers rolled from the nearby ranks, all of them standing proudly in front of him.

"Fine, men," Denison said, nodding toward the north. "Find out what the rascals are about, but do not bring on a fight. You are to scout, not engage the enemy. If you fall in with them get back here at once."

With a nod the six men proceeded cautiously toward the stone bridge. Quickly crossing it, they trotted up the road, spreading out into the trees on either side of it. They soon disappeared into the dark forest.

Denison and Butler both turned and rode along the ranks, each reassuring the men by telling them to stand fast at the first shock and all would be well. The Indians were not known to tolerate standup fights well. It was their Achilles heal. If you stood strong, they would retreat, no matter how much greater their numbers. Anxious, yet confident eyes, stared up to them.

Nary a noise sounded from the long line of men along the ridge. Each man kept his words to a minimum. Only a few hushed whispers sounded from their throats. Every eye and ear searched the other side of the bridge for any telltale movement. Every chirp of a bird received intense attention, for the Indians mimicked birds well.

The distant crack of several rifles aroused the line. Firelocks instantly rose to many a shoulder. Denison and Butler galloped toward the bridge, meeting a pair of men madly scampering across it.

"They're up there! They're up there!" both of the men hastily reported.

"Calm yourselves!" Butler immediately admonished them.

Both men bent down and leaned against the sides of the bridge, trying in vain to catch their panting breaths. Their wide-eyes glanced over their shoulders and then up to the two stern-faced officers hovering over them.

"They've scattered all about!" one of the men said. "Didn't see any real concentration of them, but they were all over and seemed to be everywhere at once, like hornets from a upset nest, they was! Fired on us they did, the hornets! Killed one, the others are bringing up the wounded. They told us to beat feet to report." Both men looked behind them, seeming to be torn between common sense and the need to go back and help their fellows. Just before they turned to run back up the trail two men scrambled into view, one cradling a bloody arm, and the other with a stream of blood trickling down from a crease across the his forehead. They rambled right past the men and mounted officers on the bridge without a word. The wildfire in their eyes spoke for them. Several men from the ranks rushed forward to help them.

Butler and Denison watched the men with great concern, knowing the report from the scouts and the sight of their wounded brethren threatened the frail discipline and continuity of their ranks. It might also ignite the flames of passion which might lead to rash decisions. Shifting nervously in their saddles, they flinched at the sight of a man suddenly bursting from the forest along the road, running headlong toward them. With clumps of earth and grass flying up in his wake, he ran as if the devil himself chased him, breathing his hot, foul breath on the nape of his neck. Sliding to a stop by the officers, he gasped, "They're burning everything!" Bending down to his knees, he tried to catch his heaving breaths. Turning, he pointed his rifle barrel toward a dark trail of smoke climbing in the sky over the trees to the north. "They're pulling out! Leastways the ones I saw was!" he added.

"Now, now," Butler said, turning to face his already grumbling troops. He knew once they decided to sally forth, no force on earth could stop them but death itself. "Our very future, and lives we have sworn to protect, depend upon the actions we take at this time! We can not afford to go off half-cocked, for we've a cunning foe whom will take advantage of any folly which mistaken emotions may hasten us into! I recommend very strongly we stay here in this great defensive position and see just what develops. No matter what mischief has befallen our brethren up the trail, we can hold here, so mayhem does not spread like a flood through the rest of the valley! We are the dam to stop the raging hordes from flooding our homes!"

Lazarus Stewart stomped from the ranks, his face growing more crimson with each step. Jabbing his finger in the air in a spasmodic gesture he screamed, "You, sir, are a damn coward! I have a mind to report you to headquarters as not fit to hold the rank you got!"

Denison jumped down from his horse. Howls of protest followed his every step toward the agitated militia captain. "Lazarus, listen to reason for God's sake!" he bellowed at the man. "Danger lies in acting hastily, you damn pigheaded fool!"

"To hell with that!" Lazarus yelled back. "The Tories and savages are here! Now! If we stay here fully armed and ready, or worse yet, retreat back into the confines of Forty Fort in the face of the enemy, we, every one of us, shall carry a shame in the face of our dear country which shall never be forgiven or forgotten!" He stopped, suddenly noticing the silence around him. He had everyone's attention and intended to have his way and sway all of them into action. He simply must. Honor demanded it. Wyoming would rise to full honor, or sink in miserable defeat; to him it was one way or the other. It was black and white. "By the morrow more of our homes will be put to the torch whilst we sit here like poltroons or in that damn fort! We have to act now! Who is with me!?!"

Many voices rose in answer to him.

Turning, he looked Denison straight in the eye. "Either we march now against those bastards or I and my men will go home and protect our homes on our own!" he flatly stated.

Denison reared back, suddenly feeling a bitter rage against the man he called dear friend but an hour ago. He had even named his son after the man whom now so completely stood against all rhyme and reason; a man filled with an overwhelming bloodlust which threatened them all. Putting his hands to his face, he rubbed them over his eyes, opening them to see all of the captains of the other companies mustering around Stewart. Was madness a contagion? His rage overcame him. He strode headlong toward the man, screaming obscenities and almost blubbering, for his anger sabotaged his tongue. Finally gaining a moment of composure, he simply screamed, "I will not hear of it!" and clenched the hilt of his sword. "You can go and die! You can venture yourself in it, but I won't let you sacrifice us all, damn you!"

Butler knew when the pot had boiled too long. He reared his horse back on its haunches, sinking his spurs into its flanks to force a loud and angry neigh from it. As it fell back down on all fours its master drew his long sword. Pointing it across the bridge he exclaimed, "Neither I, nor Colonel Denison, agree with your views!" He glanced down at his red-faced comrade with a burning stare. "But he and I shall lead you wherever you dare follow! To the gates of hell, if need be!" he added, rearing his horse on its haunches again.

Heads nodded all around the agitated colonels. After a few self-satisfied murmurs and grumbles, the men all formed into column, four abreast.

Lazarus Stewart grinned from ear to ear. He ignored the cutting stare from his recent friend and shuffled past him to join his men forming in the column of march. He felt lively and sure, so much so, he only smiled at one of his men now snoring on the ground by a stone wall.

"It's Inman," Roswell Franklin explained, walking over to give the man the boot. "He was on guard duty all the night, and he partook quite freely of the rum this day."

"No, Lieutenant," Stewart said. "Let him sleep it off. He can catch up with us when he wakes up. I want all fresh eyes sighting down those savages and Tories."

He did not look so favorably to another old volunteer nervously pacing back and forth the stone wall, cursing and running his hand through his hair. Noticing Stewart's cutting stare, he turned to him. "You best not go ahead, the colonels are right, by God, they is! I told you all afore we left the fort I'd march out to defend the valley, but not on the enemy's terms! It's the truest folly, it is!" the old man said.

"Suit yourself old man," Stewart said. "But if you're going to do one or the other, you best make up your mind, but I do warn you if you join these ranks I don't want to hear another peep out of you, for with us, it's all or nothing, it is!"

"Fine," Thomas Bennett said, turning to walk back to the fort. "An ambush lies up there, I dare warn ye, it does fer sure!" he muttered under his breath, knowing his words fell on deaf ears.

## Chapter Fifty Seven
*Every man to his duty!*

The column marched steadily up the road to face an enemy many believed had already fled. Eyes darted from the column to the trees and scrub brush along the road, anxiously searching for any sign of the enemy. The eyes at the head of column stared dead ahead in anticipation of witnessing the few stragglers which always plague a fleeing army, fleeing upon sight of Wyoming's bold display of force.

For some, pulled along by the confidence exuding from the others, including the two colonels, their apprehension faded with each new step forward. Perhaps their mere showing of force had chased off the miscreants bent on their destruction. Calling a bully's bluff always worked, for all bullies were cowards in the end.

Denison and Butler glanced to one another, noticing a sense of vigor and resolve replacing the angst in their eyes. Their lingering doubts faded.

Both looked to the call of a scout ahead on the road. They looked to a widening plane from which the scout hastened them forward. The trees about them grew smaller and smaller, lessening into small yellow pines and scrub brush about the wide plain.

Butler reeled his horse around to face Captain Durkee. "Take your officers and position the troops!" he ordered, waving his hand along the plain to his front. Reining up his horse, he rode along the column of men dispersing into a long line of one rank. His eyes danced along the eyes staring back at him. He suddenly stopped in front of one of the militia officers. "Ensign Hollenback!" he said, pointing down to the man. "Report to Captain Durkee, he shall be in need of your experience in the line just now!" He then hastily turned and rode back down the line with Hollenback trailing in a rush behind him to find Durkee.

Butler reared his horse up next to Colonel Denison and said, "If they're here, they'll soon be sorry of it, no matter what their number!"

Both officers watched the line of men spreading out before them with a growing sense of pride. "Perhaps Lazarus was right," Denison muttered under his breath. "It is always best to strike when the iron is hot."

Butler turned away, pretending not to notice his words. He had enough to worry about.

Durkee welcomed his old ensign with a beaming smile, immediately putting him to work directing the men into line of battle. On gaining Hollenback, an experienced and able officer, he dispatched

Captain Ransom and Lieutenant Timothy Pierce to the left of the line. He also directed Lieutenants Wells, Ross, and Phineas Pierce to organize the center of the line, while he, Daniel Gore, Captain Hewitt, and Hollenback, took charge of the right of the line, the place of honor in any line of battle. Next to Hewitt's men on the right, spreading to the left, formed the eager men of Captain Bidlack, Captain Geer, Captain Buck, Captain Stewart, and finally Lieutenant Whittlesey, along with the aged men of the Alarm List Companies, or the *Reformadoes*, with other men scurrying to catch up with the ranks from the Salem and Huntington Company. All formed admirably with hearts equal to the task before them. "Stand strong ye men of Wyoming", rang down the ranks.

"Well, I must say they have formed as smartly as any regiment I've commanded in the Continental Line," Butler said, looking over to Denison with a concerned eye. The line stretched far, much too long for one man to oversee. "Sir, we shall divide the line into two wings of overall command," he said. "You take Dorrance and oversee the left wing, whilst I and Garrett see about the right, for I think Indian Butler shall concentrate his forces there, and I am very eager to butt heads with the brazen traitor! Remember, sir, these Indians are not much for a stand up fight, stand fast at the first shook and they shall retreat soon thereafter. Remember, stand firm, deliver your volleys, and they shall break! As for Butler and his Tories, I shall see to them, for I think we are indeed equal to the task!"

"What of a scout?" Denison asked, noticing the scouts had taken their place in the ranks. He pointed to a stonewall and a tree line far across the plain.

"I shall take care of that presently," Butler said, turning to gallop to the center of the line. All three officers followed, waving their hands to suppress the slight cheers rolling along the line. Butler reined his horse to a stop, quickly wheeling it about and asking for volunteers to scout forward.

Abraham Pike-the Irish corporal whom had deserted the British ranks at Boston and took a hand in training the militia along with his fellow British deserter Malcolm Boyd-stepped proudly to the front, sure to prove his patriotism to his new countrymen. An Irish friend joined him.

"Very well!" Butler said, "Pike, you are most welcome, for we need a proper and disciplined soldier just now! Scout Wintermoot's Fort, if the devils are still fool enough to be about, we shall deal with them!"

A rousing cheer erupted from the men. Hats flew in the air. Many patted Pike's and his companion's backs before Denison and the other high officers scolded them back into line. Picking up their hats, many continued cheering, despite the officers.

Pike and his companion scampered away, swearing an oath against all Tories. They soon disappeared into the scrub brush.

Anxious eyes watched them disappear, each contemplating the unknown. Brothers looked to brothers. Fathers looked to sons. Grandfathers looked to grandsons. All consoled each other, trying to reinforce their lagging sense of confidence. Bragging tongues suddenly fell silent in the face of the unknown.

The distant crack of a rifle tore all eyes from their concerns and to their front. A hush descended down the line. Another rifle cracked, then another, slowing growing louder, and thus closer, to the line. Keen eyes looked ahead and then to their colonels craning their necks atop their horses at some movement. All tongues remained silent, quick to hush even a whisper, everyone awaiting a command from their officers.

Pike and his companion suddenly burst from the brush and sprinted madly for the line with every eye watching them and many a firelock rising to dispatch any devil chasing them. But, to their relief, nothing but an unseen fear chased the scouts.

"Report!" Butler yelled at the rapidly advancing scouts. "Report at once!"

Pike stumbled to a stop just in front of the colonels, cocking an eye to his rear before standing tall and at attention. His friend turned sideways to him, raising his rifle to his hip and staring deathly back toward the scrub brush.

"They are all about Wintermoot's, they are at that sir, swarming about like hovering bees they are! Sir!" Pike reported. "Got almost back here when one of the devils fired at us, we returned fire, but I fear with little effect."

Butler's eyes beamed at him and then rose to something behind him.

Pike turned an anxious eye behind him and raised his rifle, but to his relief only noticed a long column of smoke spiraling in the air.

"They're burning Wintermoot's Fort!" a loud voice announced from the ranks.

"What are their numbers?" Denison asked Pike.

Pike fumbled with his pouch and proudly produced a small knotted bit of hemp rope. Running his hands quickly along its length, he counted the knots. "A knot for every ten I counted," Pike explained. "I figure there be two hundred and twenty that I seen and counted, sir."

Butler reined his horse about to face the line. "Men of

Wyoming!" he yelled. "Yonder is the enemy! The fate of the Hardings tells us what to expect if defeated! We came here to fight, not only for our liberty, but for our very lives! We stand here, one and all, to preserve our homes from conflagration and our women and children from the tomahawk! Stand firm at the first shock and the enemy will give way! Now, ye men of Wyoming, stand strong, and every man to his duty!"

The line moved forward with the wave of his sword. Grim faces full of determination speckled the entire line. Officers directed their stern men, echoing Butler's warning to stand firm at the first shock. The scorching hot July sun bore little effect on men filled with such determination. Here they stood, and here they marched, alone in their little haven they had etched out of an unforgiving wilderness which now sent its minions to call upon them. Every heart thudded with the same beat, do or die, and every man felt the same marching across that long plain toward an uncertain fate, alone, but with, and for, one another, bearing a nation's hope on this far frontier and defending it against those whom would trample it. Here Wyoming stood tall. Here America stood tall!

Tri-cornered hats dotted the line of grim men along with slouch hats, workman's caps, leather caps, and simple handkerchiefs tied about some of the men's heads. Hunting frocks and fine gentlemen's waistcoats mixed along the line. Moccasins, boots, and buckled shoes stepped lively and boldly to face the invading foe; to face the tyrant and his minions. Mere acquaintances and dear friends marched side by side. The clerk, frontiersman, blacksmith, lawyer, trader, farmer, judge, doctor, surveyor, schoolteacher, joiner, and soldier formed this thin line of defiance; this human wave rolling forth to thwart oppression on the American frontier. America marched here, it's heart beating in the Wyoming men's chests, whom held its faith and promise so dear and so true, if not for themselves, for their posterity, for in the end that is why they settled this land in the first place. America must grow. America must live and be a haven against the tyrants of the world. A haven from oppression for all men in the end, even these misguided people whom faced them now.

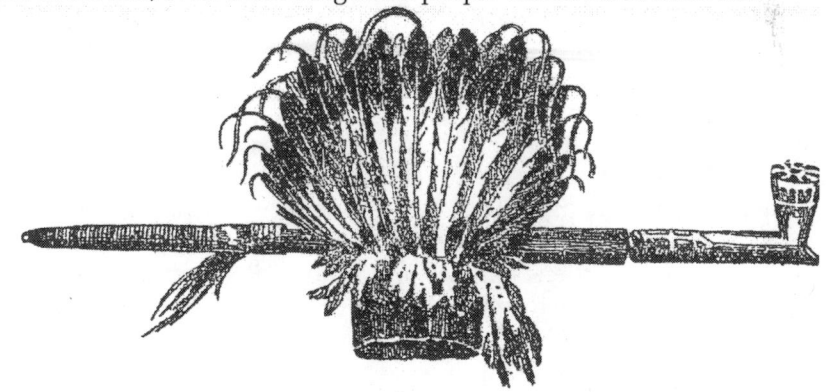

## Chapter Fifty Eight
*Perfect! All so perfect!*

Major Butler lowered his spyglass from his eye and stood aghast. Only an hour before he brainstormed for a plan to bring the rebel rats out of their safe nest in Forty Fort and onto this very plain before him. Nothing satisfactory had come to his mind. It now flabbergasted him how they seemed to be delivering themselves willingly into his hands. Amazing, he thought, carefully sliding the spyglass closed; the rats march right into the trap. The trap closed in his mind as if it had already been tripped. He saw, in his mind's eye, them defeated. The terrain, the time of day, the troops at his disposal, all perfect to spring his deadly trap. Fate blessed him today. He would not turn his back on it or betray it. Destiny had ordained a great victory and place of honor for him, he felt sure of it. Yes!

"Fort Jenkins has been put to the torch," a voice broke through his thoughts. Turning, he looked at Captain Caldwell with a great smile stretching across his face. He couldn't help it. He jerked his hands up in the air, energized by a sudden fit of ecstasy. The spyglass flew from his hands.

"Look at it Captain!" he exclaimed. "Perfect! All so perfect!"

"Yes," Caldwell answered, looking to the advancing line of rebels. "It would appear so, sir."

A groan from behind turned them both around. They looked to see crestfallen Helmut Wintermoot stumbling toward them. Unable to speak, he simply motioned back to the long column of smoke rising in the air from his flaming fort. All he owned went up in its flames.

"Oh, my dear man," Butler said. "Such are the fortunes of war! But look! It worked! It's drawing the rats from the ship and into the drink!"

Wintermoot's sour face stayed silent.

Butler turned from the man, not wishing for the spoilsport to cast dispersions onto this great moment unfolding before him. "Are the Indians positioned to the left in the marsh?" he asked Caldwell.

"Yes sir!" Caldwell said, reaching down to pick up the spyglass. "Old Smoke and the Indians are quite animated, saying they finally get to fight these people on their own terms, in the woods."

"Does he understand they are not to spring upon the rebels until we draw them near the fort?" Butler asked.

"Yes sir," Caldwell said, shaking his head at Wintermoot collapsing near a rock with his head in his hands, openly weeping.

John Butler cast an irritated eye to the blubbering man and lowered his head to think for a moment. He must not miss anything. He must answer fate with his whole heart. "The ferry, canoes, and bateaux between Pittston and Jenkins forts, are they all in our possession? We must keep the Pittston people on the other side of the river, divide and conquer. We shall deal with them latter."

"Yes sir, no help will come from that quarter. And every man jack of them on the west side of the river are now advancing on this position. We outnumber them at least three to one, for certain, sir."

Butler nodded, slowly removing his fine cocked hat. Reaching into his pouch, he produced a large black silken handkerchief. Folding it into a triangular shape, he wrapped it around his head with a great knot tied in the back of it. He then removed his fine jacket, folded it, and placed it next to his hat on a great flat stone. Ignoring Caldwell's curious eyes he donned a black hunting shirt in its stead. He then grabbed his rifle leaning against a nearby tree and checked his tomahawk and pistols.

"Now we shall settle this," he said coldly to Caldwell. He turned toward the rangers and Royal Greens assembling behind him, waving forward a certain handpicked group of rangers. "Remember men," he said to the group surrounding him. "You are just to draw them toward this wall. When you have drawn the rats into position we shall strike them from the right and front. The river shall take care of the left. Victory is at hand, men! Stay true to the plan and we will surely emerge victorious!" He turned toward the red, white, and blue banner fluttering in the wind above the scrub brush, knowing the rebel line marched just below it. "They grow near, the impudent fools! Look yonder, men, to the banner of rebellion and treason, below it many a Whig, each a radical liberal and anarchist, march forth. It is up to us good conservative men to put them in their place, and restore order in these colonies of the British Empire! Their arrogance is their downfall! Now get to it! Draw the rats into the trap and we shall spring it! God save the King!"

"God save the King!" the men answered before scampering into the brush to take up their positions. A few climbed trees.

A man trotting up from his right caught Butler's attention. He turned a critical eye to the man. "Lieutenant Terry, is all well on the right?" he asked the man.

"Yes sir!" Terry answered with glee upon hearing his new title. His field promotion from sergeant to lieutenant suited him just fine.

"Well then, what is it man? Be quick, the rats are advancing!"

"Sir, I would like your permission to implement a special tactic."

"Fine, Terry, fine," Butler said, grabbing his spyglass from Caldwell. He quickly adjusted it and stared at the advancing rebel colors.

Terry stood for an anxious moment, not knowing what to do.

"What, man?" Butler asked, glancing out of the corner of his eye. "Do whatever you think shall hasten our victory, now get back there!"

"Yes sir!" Terry said, nodding profusely. He quickly disappeared into the trees on the right, looking oddly to rangers climbing up trees.

"Strange man," Caldwell said under his breath.

"Yes, a bit," Butler said, "but he knows these men. He is one of them, born and raised. I trust whatever he has in mind shall prove most advantageous to us. Much as these rangers in the trees, if they stay hid."

"Sir, with all due respect, shouldn't you have at least inquired to the particulars of his tactic?"

"No, no, man! I have laid out the plan to all my subordinates. I trust they shall carry out the nature of my orders, if not to the letter!"

"I hope so, sir."

"I know so, sir," Butler said, marching over to a large tree by a stone wall running across the plain a few rods in front of flaming Fort Wintermoot. Leaning down behind the tree's trunk, he peered around it to the bobbing heads of the advancing rebels. Though they had only started marching a few minutes ago, it seemed hours to him and his anxious rangers lying behind the wall. He waved down a few of the heads raised high above the wall. A group of Indians spilling over the wall brought him a great sense angst and he rose, catching himself before he screamed at them to get back behind the wall. Shaking his head in frustration, he looked to Caldwell crouching down beside him.

"They do have a will of their own, sir," Caldwell said.

"A will!" Butler said. "There is room for but one will on the battlefield, and that is of the commander! All others must be subordinate!"

"They fight as they live, sir, much differently than we."

Butler scanned the scrub brush on the plain with his spyglass, ignoring Caldwell's comments. He had much more on his mind and if these warriors fouled his plans he swore revenge. He had waited much too long for this opportunity to prove himself and his rangers a formable part of the King's forces in North America.

The more he watched, the less anxious he became, for the Indians moved as if specters in the brush and scrub oaks. Groups of twos or threes positioned themselves in staggered positions in front of the line of marching rebels, seeming oblivious to them, for none fired at them or altered their march.

Turning to Caldwell he said, "You best see to things on the right." He watched Caldwell get up and scurry away thinking this is beautiful, fate has intervened, thy will be done.

## Chapter Fifty Nine
### *The Battle*

Lazarus Stewart, unable to contain his anger at the sight of the enemy heads bobbing up and down in the far distance, become painfully aware of their deadly intentions from the puffs of smoke, whizzes above his head, and thuds into the ground to his front from errant shots. He furiously yelled at the top of his lungs, *"Come out, ye villainous Tories! Come out if ye dare, and show your heads, if ye durst, to the brave Continental sons of liberty!"* Repeating his oath time and time again, it soon became a chant along the line of patriots.

The objects of Stewart's scorn scurried about in groups of twos and threes to their far front, dodging in and out of bushes before turning to fire a few wild shots at the line. Some of them screamed a curse which faded with distance before bobbing back down. Firing more wild shots they fell back, converging on a long stone and log fence behind them.

Zebulon Butler stood tall in the saddle, seeming oblivious to the random shots. He cast a wary eye down to his chanting men, though, but knew any order to cease would only be met with further discourse from his emotional men. Thus, he held his head high and scanned the bobbing heads to their front, counting each of them before they scurried away, finding their number far lacking to their own. *Fate shines on Wyoming today*, he thought, looking with pride down the long line of chanting men. His eyes focused on a far fence on which their enemy seemed to be converging, no doubt to make a feeble attempt at a last stand before scurrying away with what plunder they had collected to Tioga Point. The few feathered heads scurrying about reassured him most of the Indians had already left Wyoming, just as he had foreseen. *Yes, stand strong ye men of Wyoming, for fate has ordained this be ye day of glory!*

Finally, just two hundred feet short of the fence line, he ordered his men to halt. The chant instantly ceased and the line stopped smartly, much to their colonel's delight.

All of the Tories and Indians rose, running madly for the fence line. The game was up, it was now or never, to die by the first volley and miss out on their certain victory did not bode well to any of them.

"Present!" rolled down the long line of patriots. Firelocks snapped from the shoulder to the firing position. "Fire!" boomed in the silent air. Hundreds of firelocks instantly thundered to life down the line, sending a deadly hail of lead into the fence line. Silence returned after the deadly show of strength.

At the officers' orders powder horns and paper cartridges filled the hands of every patriot. Ramrods clanged down the silent line an instant latter. The solid line advanced a few steps, firing again.

Only a few sporadic shots rang back at them from men rising from the shelter of the fence just long enough to pull the trigger.

Again the smart line advanced and fired in good order.

Confidence swelled the rebel ranks. This is easier than we ever could have imagined, some of them said. Lazarus Stewart's chant started sounding in the air from other voices.

Colonel Butler rode up and down the back of the line yelling encouragement and warnings. "Be careful, do not get cocky! It may get hotter! Be prepared! They could be stronger just ahead! But if ye stand to your tasks the day is ours! Remember your dear wives and children! Save them from the scalping knife!"

A small group of Indians sprang out of the tree line to the left of the line, firing a few wild shots. Denison ordered an immediate volley which peppered them, knocking one of them to the ground. He did not rise again. Another group popped up just to the front and center of the line, this time green-coated rangers. Firing a hasty volley, they immediately turned and scattered, but not before a hail of lead balls peppered them. Several twisted and turned about, groaning in agony. Their fellows rashly grabbed them, dragging them mercilessly back toward the fence line. There they dove, plopped, and stumbled over the fence, some of the more agile leaping it in a single bound.

"See the enemy retreat!" Butler yelled. "Stand fast and the day is ours!"

A hearty cheer rose along the line followed by an equally loud cheer of defiance from those lying behind the fence and wall.

Firelocks boomed all along the line in response. Sporadic fire answered from behind the fence line. Men fell in ones and twos along the line, but the others still stood fast. The smoke of battle blanketed the ground in the humid summer air, no breeze, but from passing musket balls, brought any relief to the sweaty patriots. Ramrods began slipping and sliding in sweaty hands. The Tory fire from behind the fence became more random, but more accurate fire from the trees above started picking off men in the ranks. Officers barked orders to close up and continue firing, nonetheless more than Captain Hewitt on the extreme right. He had waited too long for this chance. His stinging hand from sweat saturating its bandage, only drew more resolve from his soul. He drew his sword, defiantly stabbing it in the ground. Twirling around in the same motion, he faced his wide-eyed men.

"Men!" he yelled. "There are the rats, the Tories who would deny us our freedom and trample our God-given rights as free men!"

Looking down, he placed his hand on the hilt of the sword stuck in the ground. Several balls whizzed past his head but he paid them no heed. "God be with me," he prayed under his breath. "God be with all of Wyoming! This here soil is free because we stand upon it, yonder by the fence, the tyrants' boots trample the ground! Let us march forth and push the tyrants from this land forever! Do not look to me for your strength, look to ye children's eyes and the untold millions yet to be born on this land! Look to your sons! Are they to be free or subjects of an uncaring and distant tyrant? If you are with me give me a huzza and I shall draw my sword from this free soil and carry it forth to make all the soil of this land free by driving the tyrants from it! Are you with me!?!"

A terrific huzza answered him. Gracefully sliding the sword from the free soil of Wyoming, he leveled it at the King's minions behind the wall. His smart line of regulars took a few well paced steps ahead, firing a terrific volley so close the balls' pinging off the stones of the wall echoed in their ears.

"Odds and evens!" Hewitt ordered, leading his well disciplined ranks ever closer to the wall. Closer and closer they advanced, like a well oiled machine, every other man in the ranks firing while the man next to him reloaded, threatening all in their path with their steady rate of fire and strength. They maintained their advanced in good order, with each step in cadence with the man to his side. All of their hearts beat as one. All of their hopes shone as one.

Eyes peered back at them through the smoke just thirty yards away. Eyes filled with their own resolve. A Tory's resolve. They had not marched all the way from Niagara to let up now. As the rebel captain with the sword said, now was the time to answer the call. Now! Grim eyes full of determination faced the steadily firing ranks of rebels, returning fire just as furiously as their foes. The question would be settled today. Would the ancient constitution of the England, governed by the best of kings, stand in triumph today, or the mindless chaos of a rabble? Would good order and loyalty stand in the face of confusion and treason? Would sanity or madness prevail? Would the conservative or the radical liberal win this day and rule this land? Anarchy or good order?

Farther down the line Nathan Denison leaned forward to the neck of his horse, peering through the thickening smoke. His men stood well, but did not advance as far as the men on the far right, for they seemed to be spurred on by an unmatchable force of some sort. Nonetheless, he determined his men would stand steady. "Stand in the face of the first shock," he muttered to himself under his breath, "and all will be well." A spinning man twirled about just to his front, collapsing and holding his bloody arm. The first man to fall within his sight, Denison realized, a miracle from all the lead whizzing about. He glanced up the line to Stewart standing strong and stern to his work, firing his rifle along with his men. All preformed admirably. Another man fell near his horse's feet, sending it reeling back on its haunches. "Stand firm!" he ordered the men around him. "Don't worry of him, worry of what is to your front! Stand firm and the day is ours!" A loud volley and series of screams tore his eyes to the right. Through the smoke painted men darted from the trees along the fence line, firing into the smart ranks advancing on that side of the line. He silently prayed for them not to strike here, on the left, his side of the line.

But suddenly groups of Indians sprung from the trees as if born of the forest itself. Quickly firing, they fled within the same blinking of an eye, leaving momentary confusion in the well ordered rebel ranks; so much so their advance stalled.

Meanwhile, on the right, Lieutenant Daniel Gore felt a shock and a severe burning sensation which spun him around, propelled by a force beyond his own. He watched his rifle fly spiraling into the air from the force of the assaulting ball. Strangely, all time seemed to slow. Hitting the ground, he instinctively clasped his left hand around the his burning right arm, feeling the odd sensation of his own warm blood cascading through his tight fingers, which in turn felt parts of his body they never should; while he lived at least. He saw the pale yellow of his splintered bone. He felt the agony of flesh torn away in an instant. His arm thumped and pulsed with pain. His life-giving blood flowed away with each pulse. He must stop it, and now! Ripping his shirt, he wrapped the torn shreds around his arm. The thumping slowed. The blood slowed. Glancing up, he saw the line falter to a stop. "No! No!" he cried.

Rising in his delirium, he stumbled to the only clear space nearby, the road. Fumbling to tighten his bandage, he noticed feathered heads dancing about in the bushes to his front. Feeling down for his pistol tucked in his belt, his eyes locked on a man waving a sword and marching steadily up the road from the line of men fighting a few yards to the left of it. Wiping the sweat from his eyes, he recognized the man. "Captain Durkee! No!" he yelled. "There are Indians in those bushes!"

Durkee looked to him and clenched his sword all the tighter. With glaring eyes full of valor, he looked to the bushes, raising his sword as if to smite the enemy with the mere fury of his thoughts. "We'll make short work of them with a charge!" he exclaimed. Lifting his sword high, he advanced, seeming oblivious that he had but one injured man bearing a lone pistol. A dozen shots from the bushes brought him down in an instant. He twirled about, his eyes bearing a look of total disbelief before he tumbled to the ground.

Gore cocked his pistol, madly crawling toward him. An ear splitting wail sent a chill clear down through his soul, freezing him instantly. The yell echoed again, one, two ,three, four more times in the distance before culminating into one giant roar. A dozen foreign voices seemed to echo the same command immediately after the roar, the most distinguished to his ears being the sharp words "Attack! Attack!"

Eyes all along the American line looked up in terror, suddenly realizing most held ramrods in their sweaty hands. Some unseen eye had timed the moment of attack at the precise moment most of them had fired. Now, many hands furiously tried to ram their ramrods home and raise their firelocks to no avail, for the furious line of the King's avengers poured down upon them with a fury born of the pits of hell itself.

From the marsh to the left, hundreds of hooting and screaming Indians burst into the rebel ranks. At the same instant hundreds of rangers and Royal Greens popped up from behind the fence and stone wall, firing a point-blank and murderous volley into the stunned American ranks on that side of the line. No patriot could stand in its fury, no matter how blessed and sincere. But the men of Wyoming stood, they would not be denied.

Dan Gore finally reached the writhing body of Captain Durkee. A scream turned his eyes up and his pistol barked, felling a fiercely grimacing Indian bent on lifting his scalp. Quickly pulling Durkee's pistol from his convulsing body, he fired at another warrior advancing behind his wounded friend, sending him reeling backwards. The other Indians cast a quick glance at the bloody man and shivering body he lay upon, and thought better of lifting their hair when more advantageous and easier prey lay just rods way. Yelling furiously, they ran toward the ranks, leaving two old braves to drag their wounded back to the fence.

Gore locked eyes with the old men and hurriedly loaded the pistols despite his torn arm, somehow managing through the pain. He leveled the loaded weapon at them until they disappeared in the brush. Durkee's wriggling body demanded his attention. Tucking a pistol in his belt, he grabbed Durkee by the collar, struggling backwards down the road, desperately seeking any relief from the clouds of war swirling about them. Blood poured down his arm and onto Durkee, but he ignored it. "I'll get us out of this," he muttered under his breath, more to himself than to Durkee. "I sure the hell will! Damn this accursed war!"

Farther down the line, men fell against the unrelenting fire of the

Indians and Tories. Smoke engulfed all, blinding men to what lay just a few yards around them. Cries of anguish echoed through the smoke, along with sickly and sharp cracks of breaking bones from the fierce hand to hand struggles stretching down the line. The thuds of war clubs striking skulls resounded in the air. Yellow flashes shone through the acrid smoke, announcing the presence of deadly fire.

One man lay on the ground amidst the mayhem and carnage, holding his dying brother in his hands on his lap. Phineas Stafford could no longer hold back his tears as he felt his brother's life slowly fade. "I'm done for, Phineas," his brother Darius gasped through gushing blood pouring from his mouth. Locking eyes with his brother, he tried to lift his hand, but it fell limp, his life's blood gushing through his many wounds. "Take care of Lavina!" he finally gurgled one last time. Flashes of his wedding and his dear blushing bride but a few weeks ago soothed his last thoughts, ushering him with a slight smile to the world beyond.

On the far left one man fell screaming from a volley, John Caldwell, and every eye in Whittlesey's ranks fell to him before lifting to a horde of painted men pouring from the swamp to their left and into their line. Many fired to slow the onslaught, only to fall from another more accurate volley from their enemies. Now, many lay in neat little rows as they had stood in life just a heartbeat before; few still drew the breath of life, and those whom did drew it through painful wounds. Some still standing stumbled backwards, clutching their wounded limps.

The few still stood firm, much to the example of their officers waving their swords madly above their heads to show the men they still stood; they still led. War in all its cruelty surrounded them, flashing in the corners of their eyes, but they stood, fired and reloaded; knowing it to be their only hope in holding back the screaming hordes trying to advance upon them. Whistling balls about their ears and the pitiful groans of those lying at their feet made every man aware of the need to stand firm. In it lay their only hope. If they fled, their countless enemies would descend upon them, dispatching them all in ones and twos. Wyoming must stand together, or die alone.

No one knew this more than Nathan Denison. Reining his terrified horse about, he locked eyes with one man standing slightly forward in front of his ranks, calmly directing his men's fire.

Lazarus Stewart glanced up to his old friend for just a second and nodded, knowing all had come to this, all of his life, all of his hopes, and all of his dreams. All this he conveyed in that one last glimpse to his staunch friend, ironically thinking their last words had been in anger. But he hoped their anger not to be carried to the other side, which, by the looks of things, they might soon join. Turning his cold eyes away, he sighted down his weapon, locking his sights on a bevy of painted demons intent on striking his line. Picking the one in the lead, he squeezed the trigger before all went black in his eyes, before his last sensation of falling ceased upon striking the cold, bloody, ground. Then all went black of this world. All faded into darkness.

Denison watched his friend spin about and fall to the ground, blood dribbling from a wound in his forehead. His last look to him seemed most haunting, but also somehow most serine and forgiving. He watched his son, Lazarus Jr., turn to his fallen father. Spurts of blood erupted from all over the lad's body from a deadly hail of lead which struck his father's lifeless corpse as well. A marked man, Lazarus Stewart, Denison thought, suddenly feeling very exposed atop his frantic mount. Reining the animal still, he stared for a moment to Lazarus Stewart and son. Here they fell, the father perhaps a brazen and bold braggart in life, but a hero falling in defense of all he held sacred in the end. Such men should never be forgotten, and to Nathan Denison and the men of Wyoming, they never would be.

A whizzing ball turned Denison about, quickly reminding him of his own mortality. To his absolute horror he watched Whittlesey, Bowen, and Captain Geer fall. Officers! he realized, they are marking and felling the officers! He looked over to Lieutenant Colonel Dorrance promptly dismounting and marching to the line without a word from him. He nodded to the stern-faced officer and spurred his horse up the line in search of any more surviving officers.

He did not have to look far, for Captain Ransom stood tall in the line, shouting orders and maintaining the line immediately around his person. A dead Lieutenant Timothy Pierce lay at his feet, forever silent in a pool of his own blood. A tremendous volley struck the line again, sending Captain Ransom reeling backwards with blood pouring down his thigh. Stout-hearted men to either side of him brushed his blood aside and stood fast. Bullets must fly or all is lost.

Terrible shrills and screams pulled Denison's attention back to his left. Waving to Major Garrett to hold the line, he rode back to the left. More Indians than he had ever seen in his life poured out from the marsh from every bush, rock, and tree, all painted in swirls of black, vermillion, white, green, and blue. Firing their pieces, they threw the spent weapons aside, running forward carrying tomahawks, spears, and deadly war clubs. They mercilessly struck Whittlesey's already distraught and crumbling company. Skulls cracked from the fury of many a war club and many a patriot squirmed from a lance through their mid-section. The

Indians swept through their line, spilling through and behind them, killing any white man they encountered.

Suddenly Denison felt as if his brains oozed out of his ears. In a flash everything seemed apparent. All of the horrible visions vanished. Pure instinct pulsed through his veins, blocking out all his senses but sight. He now saw all, and knew what he had to do. He had to turn the left of the line back at right angles to stop the flow of devils pouring through it to the rear of the line. He must refuse the flank! "Fall back and oblique!" he shouted. "Fall back and oblique to the left!" He spurred his horse toward the failing line, swinging his sword high over his head and shouting his orders at the top of his lungs.

"Fall back and retreat!?!" one of his wide-eyed men screamed. Ignoring Denison's shaking head the confused man screamed "Fall back and retreat!" again. His words flowed like a contagion through the terrified survivors fighting for their very lives. Every part of the line broke, spilling men backwards in a melee toward the bridge, river, or anywhere to escape the furious Indians. Men fought back with anything they could lay their hands on, but to no avail. All of hell burst forth.

Lieutenant Colonel Dorrance would have none of it. He staunchly ordered the men around him to stand firm, despite the reigning terror. A group of Tories running across their front immediately caught his eye. "Fire! Fire!" he yelled, pointing furiously forward with his sword. After one of the Tories fell to the ground, he huzzaed, yelling, "There, that is what we can still give them! Stand to ye work!" He held his breath, noticing several of the Tories turning to see from where the shots felling one of their own came. He ordered his men to quickly reload just before the Tories fired into his ranks, felling several of his men.

One of the men, having enough of the whole mess, lowered his musket and turned about, ready to sprint away before a gruff hand gabbed him by the nape of his neck and spun him back into line. He stared in amazement at Dorrance nodding and pointing his sword at the Tories saying, "Stand up to your work, sir!"

The officer's staunch manner and fine example brought the man's courage back to him. Leveling his rifle at a darting Indian Dorrance pointed his sword at he fired, sending the Indian rolling head over heals into another Indian. Both tumbled to the ground.

"Splendid!" Dorrance exclaimed. "Two with one ball, what!" He turned just in time to see a ball cut across the man's throat, spewing blood all around him, his eyes rolling back in his head. Gurgling for his last breath of life, he fell in a lifeless clump onto the ground.

Dorrance wiped the blood and its foul metallic taste from his mouth, straightening his uniform. Raising his sword again, a sudden pain in his knee sent him to the ground. Clutching his leg, he tried vainly to stand against the pain, but the sight of his own kneecap peeling away from the wound drew his breath away. He rolled about the ground in total agony, trying with all his strength to stem the flow of blood from his destroyed limb. The few surviving men around him finally scattered.

A few rods away another huddled group of men struggled to survive in the unfolding mayhem. Joseph Elliot never loaded and fired his rifle so fast in all his life. He poured, loaded, and rammed no longer than it took to draw a few of his heaving breaths, he had too, he thought, glancing out of the corner of his eye to his younger brother and aged father. He had too! The swarming Indians seemed to pass by the huddled and isolated pockets of resistance, mercilessly pursuing and dispatching the single men running like deer from the line. Running proved no defense, for the Indians dispatched them as quickly as they would any deer. Some with less mercy than they would show a deer.

Noticing more and more pockets of resistance fading around him, Joseph screamed to his father and brother to get while they still could, before they too got singled out and destroyed.

"But what of you?" Jabez screamed back over the yelps, pleas, screams, and shrills surrounding them.

"Damn it Jabez!" Joseph yelled. "I said get!" No sooner had he finished than a dozen Indians stalked forward through wisps of smoke, all of their fierce eyes locking on the three stubborn patriots.

"Get now!" Joseph screamed, his wide-eyes bulging from his head at the advancing hordes of gruesomely painted demons.

The Indians all screamed, madly darting toward them.

Joseph raised his hands from the ramrod stuck in his rifle's barrel and fired, ramrod and all, in the face of the painted demons. One of them twirled about, pulling at the ramrod stuck through his upper torso. Jabez and his father needed no more urging, they turned and scattered, youth drawing all its vigor, and age losing all it discrepancies. Joseph twirled his empty weapon instantly around in his hands, sweeping it in a great and wide arc to cover his family's retreat. It worked; the Indians, seeming to be drawn to desperate men of courage, circled around him.

The Indians darted at him but quickly retreated, like water bugs on the face of a pond, for their tactics demanded they get a scalp without injury to themselves. The scarcity of warriors demanded it of their society. A white man could fight and waste his numbers, for there seemed to be an endless supply of them from across the great sea. But no great reserve of manpower lay open to the Indian, so the loss of one warrior proved devastating to the tribe, thus they never left a wounded man, or dead man, on the field. They proved too precious a commodity to waste.

Two intense faces suddenly popped out of the smoke, earnestly scolding the young braves darting to and fro at the stubborn white devil swinging his long rifle. They looked with angry eyes to the poor unfortunate and stunned braves lying on the ground around the mad rebel.

Infuriated at being showed up, the braves all raised their tomahawks and war clubs, ready for an all-out charge.

A loud grunt from an old chief halted them in their tracks.

Elliot locked eyes on the old chief and choked up his grip on his long rifle.

The old Indian bent down to the ground, never lifting his eyes from the stubborn rebel. He felt with his hands along the ground for a stone. Finally feeling one which fit his hand he rose, bearing a sly smile. With the sharp flick of his hand the rock struck the rebel square in the forehead. Reeling backwards from the blow, the strong rebel's eyes pinched in on his nose, then rolled back in his head. The rifle slipped from his hands and he fell in a clump to the ground, causing the young braves to hoot and holler all the more.

The old chief nodded in affirmation of the young braves' praise, yelling to the brave bending down to the fallen rebel with a scalping knife to cease. "Gather him up!" the old chief ordered in the Seneca tongue. "He is brave and must be saved for the post!"

The disgruntled braves reluctantly accepted his order and quickly tied the tall rebel's hands very tightly. Two of the more hefty braves scooped him up under his arms, gruffly dragging the stunned and muttering man back to their lines, much to the adulation of the two aged chiefs following them. They had gained a fine prize. A rebel prize.

Dozens of other tragedies speckled the line, none the more detrimental than Denison's misunderstood order, though. The word cursed along the line like a fever, rolling it up from left to right. Sensing the disorder and collapse, Zebulon Butler rode madly down the failing line, beseeching his men to stand firm. In total desperation he pleaded, "Don't leave, my children! Don't leave and the day is ours!" But his words fell upon deaf ears and eyes blinded with the instinct to survive.

Colonel Denison fought feverously along the faltering line,

hoping to inspire his men by example. Swinging his sword to and fro, he fired his pistols at any feathered head around him. Blood curling war whoops sounded all around him. Men fell, some begging for mercy before giving up the ghost, others fighting with every last ounce of their strength. The savage whirlwind swept them all, though, no matter what they did, the savage would not be denied this day.

Roswell Franklin, the last surviving officer of the Hanover Company, rallied his men in the mayhem. With stern orders he wheeled them about, firing into the Indians swooping behind them. With his next breath, he turned his men about again, firing into a party of opportunistic rangers advancing on them. Both Indians and rangers scattered before their steady fire, preferring targets of easier opportunity.

Other small groups of steadfast patriots, inspired by the Hanover men's splendid stand, splintered off from their leaderless commands and tried desperately to rally with them. Few made the trek, most of being them cut down like their officers writhing in pain on the field behind them, or simply killed and scalped.

Colonel Butler rode among the confusion, almost in tears. He galloped hard for Major Garrett whom had managed to rustle up a few of the men to make a stand. He sat atop his frantic mount, defiantly waving and jabbing his sword at their enemies swarming around them. After slashing an Indian, he raised his pistol at a group of Tories, ordering a volley. His confused men fired along with him, sending the Tories reeling for cover. "There you fine bastards!" he yelled. "Back to Niagara with you!"

An instant volley answered the enraged officer's words, striking him several times. Gasping, he wheeled about his mount, falling limp in the saddle. He finally slumped down, falling hard to the ground. With its master's feet locked in one stirrup, the frightened horse stood in shock, seeming confused and terrified. A screaming Indian running toward it to claim it and its master's scalp, sent it galloping headlong for the fort, its dead master in tow. It thundered madly through the confused masses of men, trampling both friend and foe. The furious Indian screamed and fired his musket fruitlessly at it. Enraged, he flung his empty weapon to the ground and yanked out his war club, thudding it into the nearest Yankee's skull.

Colonel Butler drew his pistol and leveled it at the Indian, sending a lead ball of justice into his skull. He furiously tried to reload the weapon, painfully aware of the whizzing balls about his person. Pulling on a rein it fell limp in his hands, cut in twain by a passing ball. He instantly spurred his horse toward Garrett's stubborn men. The men scattered upon the approach of his galloping horse, despite his best efforts to stop them. All of the others whom had screamed and begged them to stand now fell dead. They had had enough of it. It now seemed every man for himself. A fool's folly had befallen them.

Butler gazed about in the smoke, firing his pistol at a nearby Indian darting out of the smoke. Feeling totally alone, he looked back to the right, to his regulars, they must still stand! They must! Peering through the smoke, he screamed in triumph at a line of men still standing and still fighting in spite of it all. He galloped toward them, muttering a prayer for himself and all of Wyoming, for they needed Providence now more than ever. They most certainly did for certain.

"The day is lost!" a sergeant screamed at Captain Hewitt. Piles of men lay about their feet, both friend and foe. They had been forced back a rod, but now stood fast at their captain's direction. "Not one more foot back!" he exclaimed to them. "Forward shall this line step, or not at all!"

Another volley, seeming to come from the fence and the trees above, peppered the stubborn ranks, sending more rebels to the ground to speak no more, nor draw a single breath. The sergeant, infuriated by a ball grazing his own arm, pulled his stubborn captain around and pointed at the mayhem to their rear. Feathered heads darted about the scrub brush and saplings, firing and screaming at men running in every direction. "Sir! Do you see!?!" the sergeant asked. "They have gained our rear! Shall we retreat!?!"

"I'll be damned if I do!" Hewitt yelled back at him. "Drummer strike up!"

The drum instantly thundered in the cacophony of war, seeming to ease the frightened drummer boy's nerves. Hewitt looked grimly down to the boy and then to the powder-smeared faces around him. "This is it boys!" he exclaimed, sheathing his sword to grab the brace of pistols hanging about his neck. He raised both of them to a blue-eyed Indian and his painted brethren charging at him, screaming and howling. The crack of his pistols brought them both down at his feet. As the smoke cleared from his pistols, a line of green-coated men formed to his front, leveling their muskets squarely at his line. "Brave bastards ye are," Hewitt said, "I'll give ye that!" His few remaining men fired, but the Tory volley quickly answered, decimating the line.

The sergeant wheeled about and slammed into Hewitt, spurting his life's blood all over him from his torn throat. His hollow eyes locked on his eyes for one awful moment. Hewitt furiously wiped his face, madly trying to reload before all hell swooped down upon him. Spears and tomahawks flew at him all at once, striking his torso in many places.

He gasped, fell forward on one of the great spears sticking in him, and with his last breath cursed all the enemies of Wyoming. A sinking tomahawk forever silenced him.

The stunned drummer boy looked up to the swarming angels of death thudding their tomahawks mercilessly into the dead bodies around him, seeming to ignore him. He locked eyes with one baring his teeth and screaming so loudly it sent his head reeling back from its force. The boy felt his bowels release all at once and a wet sensation run down his leg. In absolute terror, he flung his drumsticks in the air and cast off his drum, running with every ounce of his strength for Forty Fort, oddly thinking of the penalty for the drummer to be without his drum, ten lashes. He would take the lashes in lieu of his hair.

Twenty hardy souls, all that remained of the sixty regulars in the line, stumbled defiantly backwards, only to be met by Colonel Butler. "Form around me!" he ordered, waving his sword in a circle all around his prancing and bleeding mount. "Circle around and form a line of covering fire! It's the only way we shall gain the fort!" The men promptly regained their composure, despite the mayhem around them. They orderly withdrew through the swarming savages and Tories decimating their fellows, forming smartly around Butler, to his immense satisfaction. "Just fine, my lads! Just fine, my children!" he said.

In the center of the line two men stood near a thick bush, praising their luck on being overlooked; for the moment, at least. The aged gentlemen braved their luck with a system of one firing at the feathered heads bounding about while the other reloaded. The process served them well for the moment, but both feared it wouldn't last.

"See, George?" Cherrick Westbrook asked, grabbing George's empty rifle and passing him up a loaded one. "All are retreating! All of the officers is shot dead, they is! We'd best beat feet as well!"

"I'll have one more shot at these devils!" George Cooper answered. He lifted the loaded rifle to his shoulder, but a zipping sound through the air, along snapping twigs, made him scrunch back down against the bush.

"See!?! Damn it man, they've spotted us, fer sure they has!" Cherrick said, flattening his stout frame to the ground. In another instant an Indian burst through the brush, screaming and brandishing a long spear. Cooper's ball immediately answered his screams, slamming into his mouth. He gurgled blood before falling dead to their side.

"Now do you want to get, you damn fool!?!" Cherrick asked.

"One more is all," Cooper said, scrunching down further against his plump friend's body.

"Get off of me!" Cherrick blasted at him. "I ain't yer damn shield!" Rolling his eyes, he crawled a few feet away from the bush. Thudding balls in the ground to his front sent him scurrying back to the thick bush. Hastily swinging his powder horn around, he poured a copious amount of powder down his rifle's barrel. Drawing the long ramrod, he set the ball, ramming it hard down the barrel.

"Watch your load man!" George scolded him. "You'll be doing the Injuns' work for 'em!" Lifting his rifle, he gestured toward a small group of their fellows forming in a circle around a mounted officer. Indians and rangers swarmed all around them, bursting forth firing firearms, and launching spears or tomahawks before melting back behind a bush or tree. Both men watched a huge warrior rise with a great spear. Both fired at once, sending him tumbling to the ground.

"Now that's the way to do it," George said. "By God it is!"

Both men quickly reloaded in the bush and stared wide-eyed all around it.

"Looks like they've forgotten all about us for the moment," George said. "Now's the time to get, it is at that!"

Cherrick offered no argument. He rubbed his hand frantically through his hair, absentmindedly letting his hat fall to the ground. He rubbed so hard he undid the ribbon tying his hair behind his head and his wiry gray-tinged hair spread in all directions about his head.

"Aye," George said, noticing his actions. "It won't do no good making your hair all a fuss, if'n they wants it, they's a gonna get it!"

Cherrick's bugling eyes glared at him full of wonder. "What on earth are you about?" he asked, his eyes wide in his skull.

"Nothing, my friend," George said, realizing absolute fear now cursed through his friend's veins, subduing all rational thought. It had come to this, he thought, looking to the massacre unfolding around him. Perhaps he had waited too long. Another whizzing ball close to his person made him jump up and grab his panicking friend by the nape of his neck. He pulled him along through the mayhem, dodging darting Tories and screaming Indians and stumbling over writhing men rolling in agony on the ground, many with fresh red spots about their skulls. "The river! The river!" George muttered over and over to his frightened friend. "We gotta gain the river, 'tis our only hope!"

Lieutenant Ross lay on the field grimacing against a burning, throbbing, and sharp pain in his hip and left knee. He tried to remain still, and not attract the attention of the Indians swarming about the fallen, slicing one scalp after another from groaning and lifeless men. Watching two of them mercilessly tomahawk a moaning man too weak to stand and follow them, he knew only moments remained in his life. Grabbing his patch knife, he clenched his teeth down on its handle in a vain effort to block out his pain. Rolling over, he crawled painfully toward the stone wall. Just ten feet from it the intense pain overcame him. He groaned and rolled over, dropping the knife from his mouth. Now he had done it. He had attracted attention to himself, no doubt. Craning his head, he looked all about with darting eyes. To his relief, the Indians remained too preoccupied to notice him, at least for now.

Feeling his life's blood drain from his wounds, he grew dizzy. "Oh dear Lord," he prayed. "I'm soon to meet you, but I pray you will give me the strength to help these suffering men but one more time." He pulled his knee up to him, shocked by the splintered bone popping out of the bleeding wound. "Oh Lord," he gasped, tilting his head back against the intense pain. His eyes suddenly locked on a rather portly man standing behind a tree by a stone wall. The man somehow seemed most out of place, like a gentlemen on a bear hunt or such. The man peeked out from behind the tree, obviously taking careful and slow aim at someone. After pulling the trigger, he seemed exhilarated. His glaring eyes shone on his face against the wisps of white hair sticking out from under a black handkerchief tied around his head. His thick black eyebrows pinched together at each shot, widening at its effect. A sickly smile stretched across his stern face.

Through his swirling pain, Ross's mind flashed with recognition. He knew, or at least heard of this man! Yes, the thick eyebrows, the portly frame, and gentlemanly manner. Butler! Indian Butler himself! The fiend himself! "Thank you dear Lord!" he muttered under his breath. Suddenly his pain melted in the face of his exhilaration. Pure hatred replaced it. Yes! A chance for one great blow for freedom!

Rolling over, he felt along the grass for any weapon. Feeling across slippery blood covering the grass, his fingers finally clutched the cold steel of a rifle barrel. Dragging it to him, to his relief, he found its dead owner's pouch and shot bag lying nearby. Crawling over to the body he slid a long ramrod out of the dead man's hands. "Just a few more seconds, dear Lord," he whispered, carefully reloading the fine weapon. The haunting thud of Indian war clubs cracking skulls around him drew closer, but he steadfastly focused on the tree and the fiend behind it. The reverberations in the ground from the sickly thuds echoed through his beleaguered soul. "Just a few more seconds," he prayed.

Finally finished ramming the hard ball home, he slid the rifle along his body and liberally filled its firing pan. Checking the flint, he snapped the hammer closed, leveling the rifle at the tree, and praying for the fiend's head to pop around it but one more time.

To his great frustration only the back of the head bobbed behind the tree. The thuds growing closer, he wanted to squeeze the trigger, but feared wasting his last shot in life. "No! You must wait! The way the fiend's head is bobbing he seems to be in a heated argument with some other Tory bastard. Wait for a clear shot! Wait!" he muttered to himself.

A scream above him vibrated through his aching soul. He sensed a war club above his head sliding through the air in that awful and long moment. The last instant of his life. Putting his finger to the trigger, he pulled it in a moment of intense pain and agony before all went dark for him forever.

The startled Indian jumped back from the barking rifle in the dead rebel's hands, amazed, and feeling certain he had witnessed a ghost firing a shot from beyond. Yanking his bloody war club free of the smashed skull, he gazed at it in amazement. It now had special powers, for it had struck its death blow in a moment between this world and the next. Rubbing his hand all around it to free it of the bloody matter clinging to it, he howled in triumph. He had killed a great warrior! All of his bravery and courage in life now belonged to him! Looking down at the rifle he followed its barrel to a nearby tree and to the shocked face staring from behind it. The startled man immediately started patting at the back of his head. A hearty laugh replaced the brave's spirited whoop at the comical sight.

Butler patted madly at the back of his head, flinging the falling black handkerchief from his face. He glared at the laughing Indian dancing and waving his war club in the air. Sometimes he wondered of these Indians' sanity!

"Damn rats shot the bloody knot out of the back of my handkerchief!" Butler exclaimed to the officer standing before him. "Make sure they are all disarmed before taking them prisoner, for a snake's head is still potent, even if cut from the bloody body!"

The officer nodded and scampered off, barely able to contain his own fit of laughter before he trotted out of earshot of his enraged commander. War did have its moments, he ironically thought to himself. It most certainly did; but all of them seemed cloaked in darkness, even its humor. Regardless, he would be most glad when it drew to a close, wondering if either party within it could truly claim victory from death.

Hearing the death shrieks of the poor wounded he could not help but feel a great pity for them and wondered how any person could strike a blow on the already doomed souls lying about this field. But war, in the end, was its own judge, he realized with a hollow heart.

## Chapter Sixty
### *Targeting*

Parshall Terry accepted Moses Mount's approving nod with mixed feelings. He certainly felt pride, but at the same time wondered from what dark parts of his soul his suggestion came. What makes ghouls of us all? he wondered, letting his sense of pride overcome his sense of dread. War bred battles in a man's soul, as well.

Both men lowered their freshly discharged weapons to ram another ball home. They both approved of the mayhem their well-aimed shots caused in the faltering rebel line. The recent object of their attention twisted and fell from the saddle, pulling it to the side in the process and leaving one unfortunate foot twisted in its stirrup. His horse quivered with fright and reared, pulling its dead master along with it in its mad retreat. Men scattered all around, running pell-mell from the line, despite the pleas of another frustrated rebel officer.

"That there is Rebel Butler himself!" Mount exclaimed, hurrying his efforts to reload. In another instant Mount raised his rifle to the shoulder and fired, ignoring Terry's pleas to wait. Mount cursed himself, and Terry, watching the rebel raise a cut rein in his hands. "If you'd a minded your tongue I would have had the rat! Bloody hell!" Mount said, glaring down at Terry.

"No," Terry said, "I said target all the captains, not the lead rats! We need someone with the authority to surrender in the end! We can't kill them all!"

"Can't we?" Mount asked, rising and targeting another officer whom he once recognized as friend. He hesitated but one second, letting memories of a life past flash through his mind before cracking off another shot. He noticed Terry firing at the same officer now rolling and writhing on the ground, clutching his left thigh and knee. "You aimed at the rat's knees too, didn't you?" Mount asked.

"There is some mercy in war," Terry said, gazing around at the Indians cracking the skulls of the wounded. "For some anyway."

"Wounding them may just leave them open for torture latter," Mount said. "For we are collecting but few prisoners. I am afraid the hatred for these rebels runs deep in both red and white men alike."

"So be it," Terry said, suddenly remembering the pain of his short service in the rebel ranks. "They brought it upon themselves, you know it as well as I. We can only do what we can do, remember, our duty is to serve the King!"

"So be it," Mount said. "Damn the obstinate bastards all to hell! Why couldn't they just leave us alone? Was their fever for the rebellion so deep as to bring it far into the wilderness, where it indeed has little importance? What the hell do they care to whom we swear allegiance? It didn't make a damn bit of difference in our dealings! Freedom they say! They all looked free to me afore all this hubbub!"

"Some men's hearts beat with ideals much different from our own, somehow," Terry said. "But I do not claim to understand a rebel's foul and deluded heart in the least, ours is to but serve the King."

Mounts' hand fell to Terry's shoulder, pulling him back down behind the low stone wall. A heartbeat latter balls pinged off the stones.

"They've still got fight in 'em!" Mount said. "Gettin' a bit hot around here!" he added, rising up from the wall and scampering off in the lead of several other rangers. "Best find a spot less hot!" he called back to Terry. "We've done enough damage here!"

Terry nodded to him, slowly easing his rifle over the wall. He squeezed off another well aimed shot and eased back down behind the wall, urging the other rangers around him to keep up their fire. "Keep them guessing boys!" he said. "For it ain't over 'til it's over!"

The men obeyed, sporadically raising their rifles over the wall to keep up a steady fire at the rebel devils. Terry fired once more before noticing a figure pacing back and forth to his left behind some trees. He recognized the stout figure immediately. Major Butler seemed a bit antsy, perhaps he knew something he did not, he surmised, deciding to report and find out just what plagued his hatless commander.

He crawled behind the stone wall, ever mindful of the thud into the logs atop it and the ping off the rocks below them. Nearing the trees, he promptly rose, running for dear life for them.

"Why Terry!" Butler said, nearly jumping out of his skin. "How is the line along your front?"

"Fine sir," Terry answered his nervous commander, wondering what on earth upset him so. "We're keeping them busy and driving them from the field."

"Yes, things have gone exceedingly well, haven't they?"

A sharp smack to the tree they stood behind made them both flinch. "But it isn't over yet, what? Is it?" Butler commented, feeling for something in his pouch. Producing a torn black silken handkerchief, he waved it before him. "Look at that, will you sir?" he asked, referring to the ragged part of the fine cloth. "The rats shot the knot out of it whilst it sat atop my very head!" Stuffing the cloth back into his pouch, he rubbed the back of his head. "Damnedest thing I ever heard of!"

Terry raised an eyebrow and crouched lower behind the wide tree. "Yes, sir, it is at that," he said, gazing around at the few wounded rangers lying behind the wall. "I'm amazed they haven't struck more of us than they have!"

"They've struck down quite enough!" Butler said, rolling his eyes to a corpse covered with a blanket near them.

"Yes sir, they have, but I made it less myself."

"What are you on about man!?! This is no time for bloody riddles!"

"A snake's no good with its head cut off!"

"Speak clearly, damn you!"

Terry answered him with a self-satisfied grin. Noticing he drew his ire, he quickly responded. "The rebel officers," he explained. "Remember my special tactic?"

Butler stared at him, shaking his head. "Your next breath should be a clear answer, I warn you!" he flatly stated.

"I passed word down the line to the Pawlings, Larraways, Anguish, Mount, Indian Hopkins, the Secords, and all that were quite familiar with them, to single out and cut down their officers! Sir!"

Butler blanched at the thought, knowing the major complaint of the King's forces was that the Rebels routinely targeted officers. However effective on this frontier, he mustn't let word of this get back through proper channels. "Yes," he said, thinking of the knot shot out of his head cloth. "That is well and fine. I do commend you, but things being in the high command as they are, we should keep this under our caps, eh, Lieutenant? Besides, remember the snake's head bears the fangs, which are still quite potent if one treads on them, even in death!"

"Yes sir, but we'll be sure to bury the heads," Terry said, backing away to give room for a hastily advancing Indian toward them.

"Lieutenant Hopkins, what is it?" Butler greeted the man.

The Indian's grim face cracked a sinister smile. Dropping his hands to a string of bloody scalps dripping blood down his painted leg, he snatched at one in particular, holding it high in the air. "Buck's hair!" he shouted, pointing to a healed wound on his bare stomach. "At Sheshequin he think he kill me!" Tilting his head, he stared at the bloody trophy. "At Wyoming I kill him!" Screaming loudly, he ran away.

"See?" Terry asked. "Worked fine, it did, Buck was a captain!"

Butler raised his eyebrows, shaking his head. "You best remember what color your skin is beneath that paint on your face," he said. "Any man you take is to be treated with due regard and treated as a proper prisoner of war!"

Terry's eyes squinted. Due regard, he thought, and this from a man whom turned a blind eye to the hole in Niagara and the Indians' outrageous behavior there abouts. He himself had greater considerations, he reasoned, thinking of his extended family still faithful to the rebel cause. His mind slid to the thought of what he would do if he encountered one of them on the field in arms against him, especially his brother. Yes, his rebel family, whom scorned and ostracized him and his dear innocent wife just because they remained faithful to their lawful government, and their king. These rats, these traitors, had the gall to call him a traitor! Talk of the pot calling the kettle black!

"I cannot vouch for what happens in the heat of battle," he said.

Butler turned his head back to the man, surprised by his comment. "You damn well better vouch for it!" he said.

A reanimated rebel suddenly gasped and sat up on the ground in front of the Tory officers, staring about in stark amazement. Raising his bloody hands up he groaned and cried, realizing the reality of his living nightmare. Feeling down to his twisted and broken legs, then to the burning spot atop his festering skull, he groaned in agony. "No! No, my dear mother!" he cried. "Mother! Mother!"

Both Butler and Terry turned away, only to turn back an instant later upon hearing a sharp cracking sound. The rebel groaned no more.

A warrior raised his bloody war club high in the air, staring defiantly at the two startled white men. The white men should respect their ways and turn away, not stand with their mouths agape as if they witnessed the devil himself. Snarling, he struck the lifeless rebel several more times for effect before strutting away from the ridiculous white men whom seemed to play at war like children. War was war! Perhaps Gu-cinge was right about the white eyes after all. The white men did seem to be greedy, senseless fools, out of touch with true reality.

"Due regard," Terry muttered. "There's your due regard, sir!"

A sickly expression flooded Butler's pale face. Looking down to the rifle in his hands, he drew a long breath. "I can do nothing with them once they are released upon the field," he said, locking eyes with his sour subordinate. "But I can and will do something about you! Now be about your business, for our work is not done, but may merely be beginning! The King's justice stretches the world wide, and don't forget it!"

## Chapter Sixty One
*Go where the rabbit won't go!*

A ball striking violently into the ground before him speckled Dan Gore's face with dirt, waking him instantly. Sitting up, he looked around in amazement. Fearful spine-tingling wails and cries haunted the air. Rifles and muskets cracked all around. Glimpses of painted devils darting about made his skin crawl. He looked to a man crawling on all fours past him, blood pouring from a gaping wound about his stomach. He turned an eye toward him and the man's head exploded, splattering him with bits of flesh. A triumphant wail sounded quickly after the limp body collapsed to the ground.

Gore wiped madly at the bits of flesh, and also collapsed to the ground, not wishing to provide another target for the yelling devils. A warm sensation drew his attention to his arm, still seeping blood, despite the ripped shirts tied tight about it. Carefully loosening the bandage, he stared in horror at the yellow of his own bone showing through spurts of red. Clasping his hand tightly around the blood-soaked bandage, he leaned over it. He groaned, but felt helpless to stop the pain. He needed some relief for the pain, even if only a continuous moan.

Another low moan, more a curse than a groan, lifted his eyes from his bleeding wound to look behind him. Captain Durkee's ashen face shone up to him, his pale blue eyes seeming the only thing showing life upon it. His white lips quivered and he managed to jerk his arm, but otherwise showed no other signs of life.

Crying in total desperation, Gore looked about for any familiar, and live, face. Only glimpses of painted demons showed around him. He looked to the man with the exploded head and grabbed at his fine linen shirt, ripping it from his lifeless corpse with a quick tug. He wrapped his arm again and again with it in a mad effort to stem the blood flow. Watching more blood seep through it, he gasped and held it tight again.

Durkee's arm jerked again, touching Gore's thigh.

Gore looked down to see the dying man trying to purse his white lips to speak. He watched the man in horror, hearing the Indian's yells grow closer every second. His heart pounded in his ears, and with each new thud sent more blood seeping from the makeshift bandage.

"Save yourself," Durkee finally managed to gasp.

Gore grimaced and looked frantically about for anyone to help him drag the brave captain from this horrid field. Finding no one, he bowed his head and clutched his arm again before a sharp thud to his skull filled his vision with stars. He dropped his head down, still clutching madly at his arm. Another thud hit his back. Cursing, he tried in vain to roll away, only to be struck time and time again.

With a quick crack, the thuds stopped. He lifted his eyes to see an Indian tumble face first toward him, the top of his skull spurting hot blood like a gusher all over him. Pushing the dead miscreant away, he stumbled to his feet, gazing down in amazement at the smoking pistol in Durkee's quivering hand. Without another moment's hesitation, he grabbed Durkee's collar and drug him along, away from this horrible field; away from certain death.

Gaining but a few struggling steps, he stopped face to face with another fiercely painted warrior. Streaks of sweat ran through the Indian's face paint, somehow adding to his perfectly terrifying appearance. Baring his grisly teeth, the brave cocked his head back in a horrible yell, his fingers clenching a tomahawk slowly rising in the air.

Gore stood aghast, one arm torn ragged and bloody, and the other clenching his quivering captain's collar. They did not have a chance. He watched the tomahawk rise, bracing himself for the blow.

A rifle suddenly swung from nowhere, cracking hard against the Indian's skull. The Indian's eyes rolled and he fell to the ground, quivering and convulsing against another forceful blow.

A glassy eyed man let the rifle slip from his bloody hands and stared at Gore. "Don't you fret," he managed to mutter through the blood pouring from his freshly scalped head. His entire body appeared bloody, cut, and ravaged. Blood dripped from every wound.

"Thank you," Gore muttered back, noticing the man's knees starting to shake. The man nodded and stepped to the side, stretching his arm toward the rear. "You best get with the captain, there," the man said, bending down to collect a musket from the arms littering the ground. "I'm done for, but I'll hold them off as best I can," the man said, trying to load the weapon with his shaking hands.

My God! Gore thought. How had it come to this? He looked up to the sun still in the sky. They had marched out in the late afternoon, and had advanced onto the field but a half of an hour ago. A half hour ago this man breathed strong and hard of life, with the promise of many more years. They all did. Now, merely a half hour latter, their entire lives seemed shattered beyond repair. What madness!

Nodding, he drug his captain away from the shaking and bloody man bravely standing to cover their retreat. Screams and wails sounding closer and closer made his entire body shake. Turning, he watched a wave of painted men sweep over the bloody man, cracking his skull with many war clubs. Two fierce warriors then turned their bloody tomahawks and attention toward he and Durkee. Releasing his hold on

Durkee's collar, he pulled the pistol from his belt, quickly firing and dropping one of the closing warriors in an instant. The other plunged into him, throwing him to the ground so forcefully it knocked his breath away. Coughing and gasping, he rolled about the ground, all the while watching the Indian turn to bend down to Captain Durkee. Feeling madly about the ground his fingers landed on a nearby corpse. Searching about the corpse's waist, his fingers finally clutched a prize, a small Queen Anne pistol tucked in the man's belt. Rolling over to shield the Indian's glaring eyes from the pistol, he cocked it. Sensing the Indian's approach, he turned and drew the pistol, discharging it into the painted devil's shoulder. The Indian screamed, turned, and ran, much to his relief.

He scrambled along the ground to Durkee, noticing many more Indians scurrying about in the distance. No doubt, their screaming comrade would send them to he and Durkee shortly, after he stopped screaming long enough to tell them, that is.

"Damn it man," Durkee gasped. "I'm done for! You get! Save yourself you damn fool!" His eyes rolled in their sockets and his head fell against the ground from the mere effort of scolding his stubborn fellow.

Horrible screams drawing closer confirmed the pleas of his dying captain. He slowly rose, reluctantly turning away. Dropping the spent pistol to the ground he just started running, clutching his throbbing arm close to his body. His feet gained more momentum from the horrible sights around him. He quickly broke into a steady jog, despite the dizzy feeling clouding his mind.

But somehow his lesser senses never seemed more keen, trotting across the sanguine field. He bowed his head, picturing the strong, double-hewn logged walls of Forty Fort in his mind's eye. He must reach them! He must! His heightened senses suddenly alerted his throbbing heart to closing footsteps vibrating through the ground behind him.

He suddenly felt numb against the pain and ignored his throbbing arm, letting it swing to gain more momentum. He focused on a snake rail fence to his front. On the other side of it lay a thicket. A wide thicket full of briars, thorns, and vines, impassable but for the most desperate prey. "Run where the rabbit won't go!" he started chanting on his aching breaths. "Run where the rabbit won't go!"

He stole a quick glance out of the corner of his eye to his rear, catching sight of a grim warrior closing on him with a long spear held tight in his hands. It brought a sudden spurt of energy to his steps, sending him bounding over the fence in one great leap, tumbling him into the thicket beyond. Feeling thorns prick at his flesh and rip at his ragged clothes, he kept on just the same. "Go where the rabbit won't go! Go where the rabbit won't go!" he chanted over and over. He felt himself being forced down closer to the ground from the pulling and tearing thicket, down to the small trails running below the thick and tangled bushes overhead. Rabbit trails!

Lower and lower he scrunched until his hands scraped along the earth to force himself through the thick brush with a madness born of a pure thirst for life. Onward he pulled himself, oblivious of the pain, the tugging thorns and grabbing twigs. Finally reaching a small pocket of clear space beneath the thick brush, he tumbled to stop, rolling his forlorn body up in small and tight ball.

Gasping for breath, he turned to look back into the thick brush through terrified eyes. A flash of memory instantly soothed his thoughts, the sound of the Indian thudding into the fence behind him, cursing the thick and impassible brush. The sight of his bright porcupine quill adorned skull cap with feathers flying from the Indian's head and to his front somehow brought great joy to him. No, the painted demon would not follow him into this dense brush; this haven of hell from hell.

Despite his new haven, the horrible sounds of war still echoed all around him. Twigs crackled but a few feet away, but he dared not speak and betray his position, for his exhausted body could take no more of this terrific struggle.

He rolled himself into an ever tighter ball under the accursed, but lifesaving, tangle of brush, intent of providing the smallest target possible to his probing foe. All of his strength sapped, and his throat and lips parched and dry, he mouthed a silent prayer of deliverance for he and all his brethren whom still breathed the sweet air of God's earth. Dear God save them from the cruel and vengeful tomahawk!

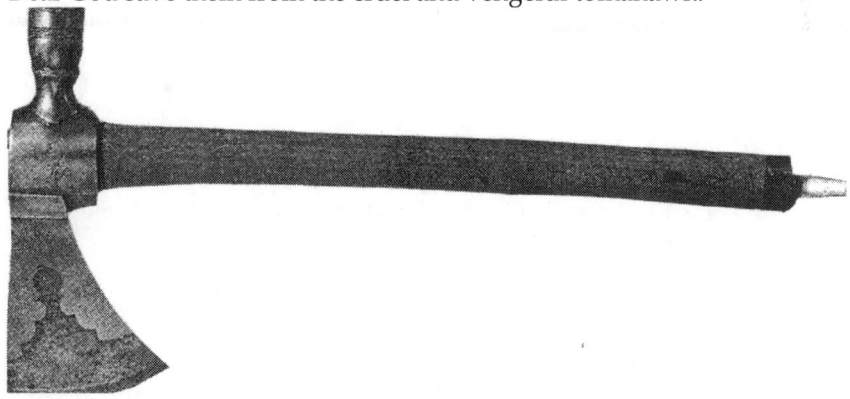

## Chapter Sixty Two
*Forty Fort*

The women of the fort watched a pacing man down by the river's edge with deep concern. Peering over the pointed logs, they whispered among themselves, drawing more of their curious number to the fort's walls. The distant sounds of battle had everyone on edge.

John Jenkins also noticed the chattering women and climbed a ladder to the young sentry standing near the women. His eyes also locked on the odd man pacing back and forth below the fort's walls.

"What's this all about!?!" Jenkins demanded, startling them all.

"Johnny!" the surprised young lad said, smartly turning about and barely catching his upset bayoneted musket. Some of the women turned to him, also.

"Well?" Jenkins asked, stepping from the ladder to the platform.

"Old Tom Bennett's down there a pacing about the riverbank muttering something fierce to himself," the boy answered. The women immediately turned from the officer and stared back down at Bennett. "He marched out with them," the boy continued, "but now he's come back and been a muttering every since." A loud rolling echo, filled with gunshots, screams, yells, groans, and agony, thundered down the valley from the north, seeming to grow every second. The horrible sound seemed to roll down the river. The fervor and thunder of war sent shards of fear tingling down everyone's spines. The boy's eyes grew wide. The women ceased their chatter. Many cupped their mouths in their hands, staring to the young lieutenant for succor.

"It's started," Jenkins said, pushing his way to the edge of the pointed logs. "Indeed it has." He looked down to Bennett throwing his musket and hat to the ground. Bennett fell to his knees, openly weeping and raising his clenched fists up to his eyes. His long, slow, moan rolled through the other sounds, somehow adding to them.

"Bennett!" Jenkins called from the silent fort. "Get the hell up here and into this fort! Now!"

"I told 'em!" Bennett moaned back. "Our boys are being cut to pieces fer sure! Oh, my dear God help them all! It's an ambush, it is!"

"Belay that talk!" Jenkins ordered. "And get up! You'll regret it if I have to come fetch ya, you will fer sure!"

Bennett looked down to his hat and slowly lifted it to cover his disheveled hair. Snatching up his musket, he slowly marched to the fort, so downcast and crestfallen Jenkins wondered of his sanity.

The women along the wall started wailing, just as Jenkins feared. Their eyes dripping with tears, they turned toward the young officer again, too choked with tears to speak.

"Your men will be fine!" Jenkins said. "We must all stand strong, as they do! Keep the faith, dear ladies, keep the faith for your dear men!"

He glanced at the scattered young boys and old men manning the walls and sighed. The dull, mingled roar of battle still rumbled in the distance, seeming to increase instead of decreasing. "You keep a sharp eye out for anything outside these walls," Jenkins said to the lad. "And you ladies find every firelock you can, load them, and bring them up to these walls! Start melting down and pouring shot, and fill horns too!" he added before turning to scramble down the ladder to meet Bennett.

Bennett slowly backed through the gate, facing to the north, and the horrible battlefield.

"What is going on up there?" Jenkins asked behind him, turning the worried man about. "What have you to report, man?"

Bennett's hollow and gaunt stare answered him. He slowly shook his head, overcome with gloom.

Madly thudding hooves approaching the gate alerted his dull senses. He turned, quickly raising his musket to his shoulder.

Jenkins pushed him aside, raising his own rifle, only to lower it and stand back from the gate. "Its back is bare," he explained to the old men gathering around them. "Make way! Let it pass!"

They stood back, all watching in wonder of the terrified and lathered beast running full for the fort. It thundered through the gate past them all, its empty saddle dangling from its side. It ran headlong for the stables and did not stop until it reached sanctuary in a stall.

An old white-haired soul near the stables whispered and carefully approached the quivering beast, waving back Jenkins and the gathering crowd. After a few anxious moments of whispering to the prancing beast, he finally grabbed its bridle, easing it into submission. A boy quickly helped him remove the loose saddle. Throwing it up on a side rail, he raised his slippery hands to his face and gasped, "It's blood! It's all covered with blood!"

Several women gasped and ran from the stable, crying and pleading to the heavens above for their poor men. Others stood in shock and stared blankly at the horse with the distant echoes of war ringing in their ears.

The old man ran his hands all over the horse and slowly showed his palms to the others. "Its whole back is drenched with blood," he gasped. "And it ain't his!" He looked to Jenkins. "This here is Major Garrett's black mare, it is."

The few remaining women's lips trembled. Children hovering

close by began to fidget, sensing their mothers' growing apprehension. One of the innocents looked up to his mother and asked, "Is the Injuns a comin' to get us Ma?" The woman dropped a trembling hand to the child's brow, trying to comfort him. Crying, he hugged her legs. No reassuring words sounded from her choked throat. Distant booming noises and strange howling wails answered for her.

Tears flowed freely down the woman's cheeks. All of the other children now clung close to their terrified mothers, looking up to them with wide-eyes. Their mother's efforts to console them all fell short, for all saw the bloody horse and heard the horrible sounds reverberating from the fort's thick walls. Some gathered their huddled children and retreated into the cabins along the fort's walls, hastily locking and barricading the doors. Other more stout-hearted women grabbed pitchforks and gathered muskets, but solid fear still shone from their faces, no matter how they tried to mask it. The fear seemed to strike some of the old men, older boys, and few wounded men left to garrison the fort. The fear sought out all in the fort, no one escaped it.

Jenkins watched them all, unconsciously rubbing his right hand. He feared for Beth. He feared for all. But he must stand tall, for now they needed strength. "The fort is strong!" he announced. "They cannot breach these walls with musket balls and spears!"

His words fell on ears already relentlessly pounding with fear. Some stopped, only to stare hollowly at him. Others continued crying, while few others busied their hands gathering weapons and such. A shrill voice echoed above all the other sounds, turning a few eyes to it.

Lucretia York walked to the center of the fort, waving her hands to the high heavens and chanting a loud prayer. "All we can do is pray!" she explained to the odd stares. Lowering her hands, she stumbled crestfallen back to her kitchen. Reaching a bench in front of the kitchen, she lowered her shaking hands and eased herself down onto it, painfully mindful of the eyes following her. Slowly bowing her head, she clasp her hands together. "Pray and be silent, my darlings," she said to her gathering children. "Let not your tears muffle your voice to God. Pray for our brave men and boys fighting the ruffian Tories and savages, that they may yet emerge victorious from the awful battle. Trust in God and pray most earnestly for them and all our dear souls!" Her brood all joined in a great hug around their praying mother, all but her eldest daughter. Collapsing to the ground, she held her hands tight against her ears from the horrible sounds of battle upriver. Her tears flowed freely down her crimson cheeks for her dear husband on that horrible field. If the sounds rang true of what truly transpired out there, her heart drained of all hope for him and the others. Her mother rose with all her siblings and tried desperately to console her, but they also became lost in the fear. They all sat on the ground near the kitchen crying uncontrollably for all their struggles in this terrific war for freedom. What a cost must be paid. The devil would have his full due before he allowed any comfort from the Lord above, at least, it seemed to them all.

A red headed boy watched it all, shaking his head. All his friends seemed crestfallen. Every mother and woman cried all about the fort and many a stout hearted man joined them. All of their world crumbled around them. Everyone heard the Indian yells rolling down the valley. Everyone knew Bennett to be right in his assumptions; all, even this freckled-face farm boy of Wyoming climbing to the top of the hogshead from which he had bid his father good hunting when he had marched out to meet the enemy. He too bowed his head, praying most earnestly, and peering out the gate through his tears, waiting for his Pa to return from battle with his trophy.

"All men to the walls!" Jenkins cried. Every man in the fort climbed the ladders, old and young alike. Joel Phelps strode to the ladder, intent on doing his duty despite his wound. He ignored Jenkins shaking his head at him and continued walking past him when he felt a hand to his shoulder.

"I need someone to go to Wilkes-Barre Fort and have Hooker Smith fetch that damn cannon here with all due haste!" Jenkins said before Phelps could protest. "I don't care if Smith has to tote in on his back! Just get it here, mounted or not! And tell Smith to get over here and bring whatever *Reformadoes* he has, for I fear we may need every man jack we can get soon!" The shrill of battle sounded behind his words.

"But what of shot?" Phelps asked. "Cannon's no good without shot!"

"I'll load the damn thing with stones!" Jenkins answered, nervously pacing about. He stopped and listened to the battle, rubbing his hand all the more feverously. "I'll load it with my damn surveyor's chain! That'll drop them!"

Phelps now shook his head at Jenkins.

Jenkins' face turned grim. "I've a feeling we're going to need everything we can get to save our scalps before this is all said and done. They should have brought the damn thing over at the first sign of trouble anyhow! Hell, they should have hauled the damn thing along on wooden runners and fired the damn thing empty at the superstitious fools! They call if the thunder stick! The sound of it alone would have made most of them scatter for Tioga Point! I tell you it'll work!"

Phelps looked down to the pistols tucked in his belt. "I'll do it, damn it! I'll do it!"

"Good," Jenkins exclaimed. "Very good! You're a good man Joel Phelps, just the kind we need just now!"

Screams turned them to the gate. A man stumbled into the awaiting hands of a few women hovering near it. So much blood cover his face neither of the men, or the women, recognized him. The man collapsed into the women's arms. They ushered him to the nearest cabin.

Jenkins followed them but stopped, hearing the man chant "Everyone is dead or dying!" Taking a step back, he let the women continue to usher the man to the nearest cabin. Listening to the sounds outside the gate, he rubbed the back of his right hand. The man's warnings made his spine tingle. He turned and looked at Phelps' gaunt face. Apparently everyone else shared his foreboding sense. Visions of Indians skulking about the fort's walls flashed through his mind.

"You best be on your way presently," he said to Phelps. "Bring back that cannon and men, for I fear soon all of hell shall be at the gate!"

## Chapter Sixty Three
### *The Horrors of War*

Sam Carey looked up at Hibberd, the man in all of Wyoming known for his agility and strength, and paled. Solid fear filled his eyes, his brave eyes. Fear penetrated the bravest heart he knew in all of Wyoming.

But the man still stood stoically, reloading his rifle and carefully picking his targets before firing into the swirling misery engulfing them. All around men fell, some silent, some writhing in pain and emitting horrible howls before succumbing to death. Smoke and dust swirled in the air. Green coated men and painted devils darted about the smoke, dashing forth when opportunity gave them a target. The sharp crack of war clubs cracking skulls sounded all about them. Spears flew from the smoke and confusion, cutting down many a brave soul.

Carey's hand started shaking uncontrollably. He fumbled with his cartridges but somehow managed to load and fire, much to the example of Hibberd. The thud of a spear into a tree just over their heads jolted him, throwing his rifle from his shaking hands.

Hibberd glanced out of the corner of his eye down to his friend and nodded for him to retrieve the weapon, spitting out the end of a torn cartridge from his gunpowder-smeared black lips.

Carey bent down and scooped up his rifle, immediately firing at a black-painted yelling demon in the smoke. The yell promptly ceased.

"I got one!" he yelled, gazing proudly up to Hibberd. "I got one!"

His yells attracted more spears to fly about them, but thankfully over their heads, to their side, and their front. The smoke clouded the demons' eyes as well. One well-aimed spear suddenly struck Hibberd's rifle stock, splintering it in his hands with its force. Hibberd immediately dropped the useless weapon, grabbing his friend up by the nape of the neck. "Time to go boy!" he said. "For the love of God it's everyman for himself! Now be fleet of foot or you'll breathe no more!" In the blink of an eye he broke into a dead run toward the river without looking back.

Carey's feet thundered after him, twisting and turning through great fields of rye and leaping fences with the agility of a deer. Balls whizzed by their ears. Spears flew by them, sticking in the ground. Yells and shrieks followed, growing closer all the time. Both ran all the faster, invigorated by the sight of the riverbank ahead.

Hibberd reached it first, rolling down the muddy bank to the beach. Carey tumbled behind him. Rolling to a stop, he wiped the mud from his eyes, gasping at two fierce Indians standing atop the bank glaring down at them. With a yell, both warriors plunged down the bank with spears and tomahawks held high and ready to strike.

Hibberd met them head on, plowing into them and sending their weapons flying from their hands. All three tumbled through slippery river mud in a mass of arms and legs.

Hibberd popped up from the mud first. Clenching one of the spears in his hands, he struck the nearest Indian full in the face with his huge fist, sending him spiraling into the water. In almost the same motion he plunged the spear into the other Indian's chest.

The Indian grabbed at the spear, holding it with his tight fists against the white devil's strength. Feeling his life's blood flowing from the wound, the Indian forced them both to their knees, vainly glaring in defiance of the white devil.

Infuriated and hearing more screaming Indians approaching the riverbank, Hibberd pushed the spear with all his might. By his brute force it slid up the Indian's ribcage and into his throat, making a sickly, wet gurgling sound. He pushed harder and harder on it with a strength born of pure rage. One must die, and it would not be him.

The Indian gurgled and flailed his arms in a vain attempt to do harm to the white devil, but growing faint, he felt his hands fall limp. His eyes grew wide, finally rolling back in his head. His entire body fell limp as the spear pushed on and through the back of his lower neck.

Hibberd pulled his hands from the spear and let the Indian twist over on the beach, only to turn to face a dozen more Indians spilling down the muddy bank. They instantly gathered up stunned Sam Carey and plowed into the muddy and enraged mountain of man standing defiantly in front of them, sending him tumbling backwards in the mud. Springing to his feet, the mountain of a man threw several Indians aside, madly scrambling for their spears.

A musket cracked from the bank above and several spears flew through the air, all striking the infuriated white devil at once. Gasping, the devil stepped back, his failing fingers trying to grasp the spears stuck in his chest. One of the Indians screamed and plunged forward, sending one of the dangling spears deeper into the staggering white devil's chest. Gasping and gurgling curses sputtered through the blood gushing from the devil's mouth. The white devil's eyes finally rolled back in his head and he fell forward, impaling himself on the other spears. His limp body tumbled over, his fingers twitching in the pangs of death. His bulging eyes betrayed a look of absolute shock and disbelief to his gloating enemies. But for him, all was over.

A simultaneous whoop erupted from the Indians staring at their dead foe. One of them fell to a knee drawing his knife, quickly slicing a piece of scalp from atop the dead devil's head. Another burst toward the corpse and with two quick thrusts of his spear poked its offending eyes out of its head. Grunting in disgust at the matter sticking to the point of the spear, he thrust it into the water, swirling it about before raising it high over his head screaming in triumph. Several of his fellows descended to the corpse, slashing it beyond human recognition.

Carey stared in amazement and disgust. Out of the corner of his eye he noticed the two braves holding his arms starting to eye his hair. His stomach sank and he swallowed hard, playing scenarios in his mind of just how to push them aside and dive into the swirling Susquehanna, willing to take his chances in the strong currents rather than with these brazen savages. A small Indian descending the bank screamed, tearing Carey's eyes to him and his shrill tones.

The little Indian, though much smaller in stature than the braves surrounding him, seemed to be greater than them in social stature, for they all stopped screaming, giving him their utmost attention.

With a malicious smile, the small pot-mark faced Indian strode up to frightened white devil. One of his eyes rolled oddly to the right, pale white, while the other dark orb locked deathly on the white demon. "*Te-te!*" he said, pointing one of his fingers in the terrified white man's face. "Te-te!" he said again to the white man's odd stare.

The other Indians frowned, but then grunted what seemed to be an approval. The two braves immediately grabbed the white man's wrists, tying them tight with leather thongs. Another slipped a loop of rope over the white man's head. With a sharp tug, he drew it tight around the man's bulging Adams apple. At the direction of the waving smaller brave they all scrambled up the muddy riverbank, pulling the white devil along by the rope looped tight around his neck.

Carey gasped at the sharp tug of the rope, managing one last glance at the mutilated corpse of brave Hibberd, wondering whom shared the worst fate.

Reaching the top of the bank, he stared at the swirling mass of people all around the field in a new light, no longer blinded by his mad quest for escape. Men ran everywhere, yelling, fighting, and screaming, both painted and white. Spurts of men occasionally burst from some bushes or trees and ran pell-mell for the river, chased by a merciless foe cutting them down with glee. None of the confused white men dared slow to give aid to a fallen and pleading comrade, or certain death awaited him, too.

Carey watched it all with his mouth agape. Several of the Indians of the party broke off, enticed to join the slaughter around them. A sharp tug at the rope turned Carey's eyes to the front again. A pitted face at the end of the rope grinned at him. A horrible scream tore both their eyes from each other and down to the melee unfolding by the river. The Indian looked down, shaking his head. "Te-te!" he said with a frown.

A pair of white men swaggered past them, pausing only to grin at the small pot-mark faced Indian with the white man on a leash. They walked nonchalantly, as if on a Sunday stroll. One of them noticed something and dropped to his knees. Raising his rifle to his shoulder, he drew a bead on a sprinting rebel running for the river. Following the rebel with the barrel, he cracked a shot off just as the man reached the riverbank, sending his limp body rolling down into the swirling river.

His partner cheered, exclaiming "What a bully of a shot!" and patting him on the back. A smiled stretched from ear to ear across his face and he nodded to the rebel at the end of the rope. With a call from his partner, he turned, following him in search of more mischief.

They did not have to walk far, for coming to the bank both looked down at a rebel standing chest deep in the river, staring at the far bank, but daring not to take another step. "The bloke can't swim, he can't fer sure," one of the Tories commented to the other.

The rebel turned upon hearing them and struggled up the river, desperately searching for a shallower place to ford it. To his dismay he only sank deeper in the water. Spitting river water from his mouth, he turned back to the bank. Taking just enough steps back to clear his mouth, he stopped, staring glumly at the awaiting Tories.

"Why Elijah Shoemaker!" one of the Tories yelled. "It is I, man! Henry! Henry Windecker! Friend!" The Tory slowly eased his weapon to the ground, gesturing for his friend to follow his lead by nodding with a mischievous grin. His companion frowned, but slowly complied.

Shoemaker stood firm, cursing himself under his breath for never learning how to swim.

"Come now!" Windecker said. "You took me in, taught me a trade and all! What sort of a man do you think I am? The battle is lost, we're only to collect prisoners for parole, no doubt! Besides, as I said, we are friends! All politics aside!" The comments brought an odd stare from his comrade. He nudged him to comply with his act. "If we shoot the rat here he'll just float downriver, no, my friend, I want satisfaction from this bloke, I do," he whispered out of the corner of his mouth, all the while smiling at Shoemaker stumbling against the current.

"I durst say I am afraid you shall turn me over to the Indians!" Shoemaker yelled. Losing his footing, his head sank under the water. Stumbling, he raised it from the swirling waters, gasping for air.

"Well, you won't last long in that river fer sure!" Windecker said, waving him toward the shore. "Come now, I can keep my mate here in check, but I cannot vouch for the others who may find you after us!" He looked warily over his shoulder. "I will save you! They shan't hurt you!"

Shoemaker coughed against a splashing wave in his mouth. Spitting out the water, he cursed all the more, looking all around him. Rifles cracked downstream at other men swimming the river. Little gouts of water showed all around a bunch of men madly swimming for an island in the middle of the river. Some screamed and rolled over in the water, quickly silenced by the swirling waters. Bowing his head in defeat, he reluctantly stumbled to the shoreline.

An appeasing smile greeted him from the bank. Windecker scrambled halfway down the bank and extended his outstretched hand, seeming to grasp at some grass or something on the bank behind him. No sooner than his friend's hand touched his before a sour expression flooded his face with pure hatred. Drawing strength from an overwhelming sense of rage, he tightened his fingers around Shoemaker's hand, pulling him up the bank. Screaming, he swung his other hand in a great arc, sinking a tomahawk squarely into the top of Shoemaker's head. For an awful moment, he felt his old friend's fingers twitch in his hand before his eyes pinched together staring at the deadly tomahawk, the agent of his shocking demise.

With a sharp yank Windecker pulled the tomahawk from his friend's skull, watching his bulging eyes roll back in his head before blood gushed down the sides of his head. His hand twitched once more, then went limp. The sudden dead weight almost pulled Windecker down the bank before he released his hold and fell back against the bank, watching those bulging eyes full of shock, horror, and disbelief tumble into the waters.

Turning, he scrambled up the bank to see his friend reel back from him. He stood, wiped the blood from his hands, and turned back to the river to watch the body of his old friend float downriver, rolling over and over in the bloody red waters.

Cries broke both men's gaze to the cruel reality around them. Both men looked at one another for the longest moment before picking up their rifles and walking up the riverbank, only this time they did not raise their weapons to any target of opportunity, but let them pass. Too much blood had flowed from their hands this day. They both feared their brethren did not share their sudden aversion to the horrors of war. In that, the horrible massacre would continue, unabated by any conscience.

## Chapter Sixty Four
*The Hanover Boys*

Colonel Denison struggled to hold his panicking mount in place. He felt every nerve in its body quiver beneath him and sternly pulled the reins tight, intent on keeping his horse in place despite the desperate situation surrounding them. He cursed and yelled at himself, disgusted for seemingly losing control of all around, be they man or beast.

He fumbled with his pistol, trying to reload it amidst the angry storm of Indians and Tories sweeping over his splintering command. Tightening his legs around his horse's flanks, he yelled commands to a dozen or so faltering men trying to stand fast around him. Bones cracked. Blood flew in great spurts in the air from tomahawks and spears assaulting the unfortunate men. Spears flew in every direction along with an occasional arrow, some striking men, while others missed and stuck in the earth, springing back and forth from the momentum of their flight. Groans, cries of anguish, and yells of triumph mixed with the sharp report of firelocks.

Denison twisted around atop his mount, his eyes locking on a man holding an Indian fast to the ground, madly trying to gouge his eyes out with his thumbs. The Indian screamed, shaking his head, vibrating under the weight of the stout soul intent on blinding him. With one great scream from both men an eye rolled from a socket, dangling down the Indian's cheek, etching a streak in the paint covering his face. In another instant a tomahawk cracked the skull of the triumphant rebel and he fell limp on top of the brave. The screaming Indian fumbled underneath the dead rebel, desperately trying to cup his eye in his hand. His Indian rescuer stared oddly at him, cocking his head at the thing dangling free from his bloody eye socket. He watched with a grim curiosity which overwhelmed all his other senses, much to his detriment.

Denison leveled his newly reloaded pistol, cracking off a shot at the tomahawk wielding warrior. The warrior instantly fell dead onto the back of the rebel, burying his struggling comrade under more dead weight. Screaming all the more louder, the Indian convulsed and jiggled free of the dead weight. Standing and cradling his dangling eye, he staggered back toward the swamp, oblivious of the rebel colonel desperately trying to reload his pistol atop of his prancing mount.

Denison watched the Indian disappear into the swamp and the men around him scatter in the winds of fury. Wheeling his horse about, he sank his spurs into its flanks and galloped away, searching for any sign of hope or resistance still standing. His eyes locked on a group of men moving in smart order, turning and firing to their rear, flanks, and front, by the direction of their sword waving officer. The Hanover men, he realized, third company from the left. They still stood and fought! Somehow they maintained their order in the mayhem. Somehow they retreated in strict military fashion while everyone else collapsed in confusion about them. He watched them through fits of smoke and dust, riding to the aid of a pair of men fighting a losing battle with a half dozen circling Indians. He spurred his horse into the fray, breaking it up and sending the Indians spiraling off in a dozen different directions. The men bolted in the opposite direction, leaving Denison sitting alone again on his mount. A ball grazing its neck sent it on a mad rush past the Hanover men. Unable to stop it, he craned his neck to watch a cutting volley drop many of the Hanover men in their dwindling ranks. Indians seemed to run to and fro around them, running from every direction, waylaying a man before scampering away in the ensuing confusion.

Denison tried to spur his horse to them but a rushing Indian blocked his advance, grabbing at his horse's reins and raising his tomahawk to strike. He dispatched him at once with a pistol shot to the brain and fought again to calm his prancing mount. Craning his neck, he looked through the smoke to the now-beleaguered little company of staunch men. "Disperse!" he mouthed to himself, somehow hoping by sheer will to convey his order to the sword wielding lieutenant. "Retreat! Save yourself and your brave men whilst you still can!" he yelled.

Roswell Franklin's sword rose high in the air. As it fell a cutting volley barked from the remaining firelocks huddled around him, creating a great deal of smoke. Franklin's sword swirled above it, gesturing wildly to the rear. Instantly men scattered into the prevailing smoke in every direction, confusing and dividing their pursuing foe.

"Brilliant!" Denison muttered to himself, turning to the men running about him. "We must all get to the fort whilst we can!" he yelled to them. Balls whizzing about his ears answered his order. Ignoring them, he madly reloaded his pistol, intent on being the last to leave the field. He yelled his order to the men about him again to get to Forty Fort.

A pair of screaming Indians, glistening with bear grease and paint in the late day sun, darted toward him, stopping just short to bring their weapons to play at the stubborn Yankee. One fired, sending a ball whizzing by his ear. Another threw his long spear at him with all his might. The deadly missile darted past his cheek, the feathers on its handle brushing it.

Denison tightened his legs about his horse's flanks, not sure if its agitated and rash movements proved a blessing or a curse. Reaching into the shot bag hung about his neck, he finally managed to pull a ball from it, furiously ramming it down his pistol's barrel. Lifting his horn to prime the pan a ball cut its strap, sending it falling from his shaking hands. His eyes followed it down to the ground with terror and disbelief. "What in heaven's name!?!" he gasped, casting a look to the sky. "Dear God! Do you wish me to fall this day!?!"

The pair of warriors screeched, raising their tomahawks to strike. Their heads rolled back from the force of their ear splitting wails.

"My God what hell is wrought on us this day!?!" Denison muttered, firing at the yelling demons. The larger of the two gasped at the blood spurting from his chest. He fell to his knees, struggling and gasping for breath from the frothing and bloody hole in his chest. His comrade stopped momentarily, gazing down in wonder to his friend.

Denison twirled the spent pistol around in his hand, flinging it at the confused brave lock first. It spun through the air, smacking the stunned warrior square between his eyes. Screaming, he fell to his knees by his gasping friend, trying in vain to quell the copious flow of blood flooding his eyes. Denison's horse reared and neighed, galloping away from the melee of death despite its master. Denison jostled on the horse's back before clutching its mane. Lowering himself to its neck, he let it carry him from the whirlpool of death screaming, "Retreat to the fort!" to anyone within earshot. "Retreat to the fort whilst you can! Run! Run!"

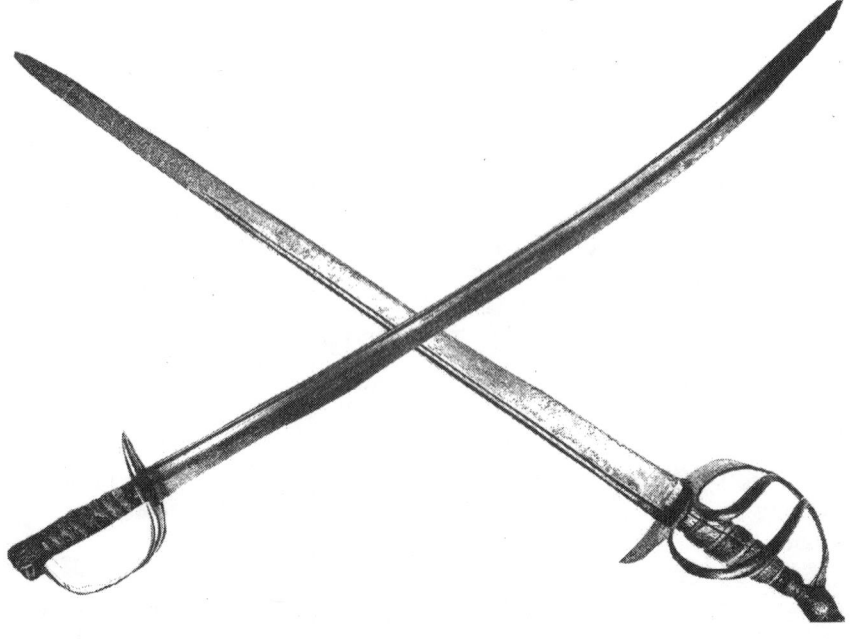

## Chapter Sixty Five
*Save A Guinea!*

Balls whizzed through the smoke but Mathias Hollenback stood firm, firing his pistols and quickly reloading them. The dozen or so stalwart men around him quickly dropped in number to eight from the deadly aim of Tory rangers behind the wall to their front. But the men still stood fast, much to one another's example, firing, reloading, and firing again.

"Fire in pairs!" Hollenback bellowed between shots. A whiz passed close to his ear; so close he almost felt the burn from the ball cutting through the air. Lifting his eyes, he peered through the smoke just long enough to spot a miscreant rapidly loading his rifle atop the wall. The ranger's eyes stared coldly back at him.

Hollenback calmly rammed the ball home in his pistol, raising it just as the ranger lifted his rifle. Locking eyes with the surprised man down the barrel of his pistol, he lightly squeezed the trigger, sending a ball into the stunned man's chest. The miscreant jumped back, let go of his rifle and tore at his clothes, only to fall dead a quick breath later.

Gasping in relief, Hollenback looked along his beleaguered line. Noticing no other officer, save himself, he wondered of the near misses about his head. Two of his men bolted, crazed with fear. A hollow feeling struck him as he turned to scold them when they both fell, cut down from deadly fire on their flanks.

"They've gained the rear!" Hollenback screamed, in spite of himself. Three other men fell from rifle shots from the rear. The other men fired in every direction, turning their wide eyes to their officer. Firing his pistol he shouted, "Break for Kingston Fort at the long trot!"

The three men disappeared in a second, and in every direction, to the shock of their officer. Frantically reloading his pistol, he stared at the fence. Painted devils and green-coated Tories poured over it, all screaming and yelling, bloodlust shining through all their wide eyes. Instinct flooded his body; before he knew it he felt himself instinctively running madly for the river.

With his heart thudding in his ears, his eyes darted all around the field. Muskets, some stuck oddly in the air on their fixed bayonets, spears, tomahawks, bodies, haversacks, cutlasses, swords, hats and many pistols lay strewn about the writhing and moaning wounded men littering the matted grass of the field. Small fires burned here and there, adding to the smoke and confusion. Painted men bearing great feathered headdresses, strange lone strips of hair, and skull caps bearing but a single feather, darted about, raising some of the poor unfortunates to their feet, groaning and protesting all the way. Those failing to rise fell to their war clubs immediately. Hollenback bowed his head and ran headlong for the river, knowing it to be his only hope for survival.

He rambled to and fro, spinning about some startled warriors screaming at his passing, being too engrossed in lifting scalps and gathering prisoners to pay him any mind. Glancing back at them, he tumbled over a lifeless body. Trying madly to gain his feet, he noticed his buckles caught in the dead man's clothing. Rolling and twisting his shoe from his foot, he placed his hand on a groaning man's chest to gain leverage. His darting eyes stopped, recognizing the groaning man. "Captain Durkee!" he gasped, staring at the man's face. "It is you!"

Blood covered the poor soul's entire lower body. Some of it somehow splashed onto his face, drying and cracking on his ashen cheeks. It scaled and cracked from his attempts to mouth a response.

"I'll get you out of here if it's the last thing I do!" Hollenback said. Rising, he grabbed at the red collar of the man's brown regimental, dragging the dreadfully wounded man behind him. Screams from the smoke ahead stopped him dead in his tracks. Relaxing his fingers on the collar, he braced himself for the shock he knew advanced from the smoke. A warrior suddenly popped out of the smoke, locked eyes on them, and ran pell-mell toward them brandishing a spear.

Hollenback immediately dropped and rolled backwards, feeling with his fingers for any weapon lying about the grass. In one smooth motion he rose, clutching a cutlass tightly in his hands. He instinctively slashed the cutlass at the advancing brave, cutting his spear in twain. But the brave plowed into him in spite of it, smearing his whole side with paint before tumbling to the ground.

The brave's hands immediately found a musket lying on the ground near him. Rising, he pulled back its hammer, leveling it squarely on the stubborn Yankee. The weapon clicked, but no fire spew from its muzzle. Casting an disgusted look at it, the brave quickly tossed it aside, reaching for a tomahawk tucked in his sash.

Hollenback plunged forward, swinging his cutlass in a wide and sweeping arc. The warrior dodged too late and arched his back against the cutting blade slashing along it. Dreadfully screaming, he trotted away, all the while reaching back to his bleeding wound. He soon disappeared in the confusion, trailing blood in his wake.

Relieved, but totally exhausted, Hollenback collapsed to his knees, trying in vain to catch his heaving breaths. Twirling the cutlass in his hand, he stared at the blood drenching it in amazement.

"Get!" a shaky voice cracked through the air. Hollenback turned his tired head behind him to see Durkee raising a shaking finger at him.

"For God's sake save yourself man!" Durkee pleaded through pale lips.

A chorus of wails and whoops sounded from the direction in which the cut warrior retreated. "They're coming!" Durkee groaned. "Get whilst you still can!" His eyes widened one last time and stared deathly at Hollenback before rolling back in his head.

"God bless you, brave Captain!" the distraught ensign muttered before rising to his feet. Several rifles cracked near him, announcing the advance of a half dozen infuriated warriors. He turned and ran, his ears burning with the last words of his dying captain. A bone crunching thud echoing behind him silenced the man, and his voice, forever.

Sprinting and leaping over anything in his path, he stripped his clothes while running in anticipation of the river. Nothing would hinder his escape once he reached the waters. Nothing!

His fingers fumbled with a coin he found in his waistcoat's pocket before he finally shed it and his shirt. Twirling, he hopped just long enough to strip off his breeches and fling them, all the while clutching the coin tightly in his fingers. Money always mattered, no matter what. You may have my land, but not my coin, he thought through his smoldering anger. Not my coin! Never!

Reaching the riverbank, he slipped the coin into his mouth and dove off the bank into the swirling Susquehanna, painfully aware of the screaming warriors at his heels. He dove deeply at first before rising for a quick gasp of air. Bullets spurted in little gouts all around him. Diving again, he struggled against the strong current. Bursting to the surface he cursed his thudding heart to quiet it. Keenly listening he swam, one mad stroke after another. To his amazement sounds of laughter crept from the shore behind him. Sporadic rifle shots and sounds echoed off the face of the river from the far riverbank, creating a strange chorus of human agony, pain, hearty laughs, and yells of triumph.

A thud, followed by an intense burning sensation, assaulted his shoulder. Gasping in pain, he dropped the coin from his mouth with a half dozen more little gouts of water erupting around him. His eyes caught sight of a trail of red flowing in the water from his shoulder. Grimacing hard, he blocked out the pain, swimming headlong for the shore. Hearty laughs from the opposite shore hastened his strokes. He must get out of the water before the gloating devils reloaded, he told himself over and over. A whizzing sound in the water infuriated him. The thought of being the object of mere sport for those merciless devils fueled a rage which propelled him to the shore. Finally feeling his fingers touch the muddy river bottom, he bound up the bank, disappearing into the trees beyond, swearing revenge for all he had witnessed.

## Chapter Sixty Six
*Fratricide*

George Cooper fumbled down the riverbank, barely stopping long enough for his winded friend to catch up with him. Bodies lay all about the riverbank. Some, pulled from the shore by the strong currents, started floating downriver. The two men stood dumfound at the sight.

"Who would have thought such horrors could ever have happened, dear Cherrick?" George muttered to his panting friend. "It is terrible, indeed! Most terrible!"

Cherrick rolled his eyes, sullenly leaning on his spent musket. "I have no more shot!" he said.

"Nor do I, dear friend," George answered, looking down to his friend with a sorrowful eye, now wishing for all the world he had heeded his friend's earlier pleas to depart with all due haste.

"Where are the devils?" Cherrick asked, looking all about.

"Off to do their master's bidding," Copper answered, letting his worthless rifle fall from his hands. Stripping off his hunting shirt, he pointed to a few souls madly swimming the river. Little gouts of water erupted all around them from unseen rifles in the brush along the high riverbank. "We must make for the other bank as well, my friend," he said, looking across the swirling waters. "Do you feel up to it?"

Cherrick Westbrook rolled his eyes again before drawing a deep breath. "Have we any other choice, dear friend?" he asked.

Both men instantly started stripping off the rest of their clothing and shoes, each pondering their long swim for life against the strong currents and undertows of the wide river. Struggling to pull his shirt over his head, a crack sounded in George's ears from the bank above them. Flinging his shirt off, he turned and stared at a grinning savage. His eyes fell to his friend lying on the bank below him and to the blood flowing from a slight gash on his upper arm.

The savage threw aside his spent rifle, plowing down the bank yelling and screaming with his scalping knife held high. Plopping onto Cherrick's back he screamed all the louder. Cherrick also screamed, rolling into the water, splashing madly away from the painted demon.

George glared in disbelief and lost all control of his stomach, spewing vomit all over the brave. The brave screamed and backed away, repelled by the insane Yankee's act of defiance. In another instant a spear thudded into the side of the old and sick Yankee, sending him tumbling into the water. The brave stared in utter amazement into the water behind the Yankee, and at his comrade. "It is well the river washes such a Yankee away," he said in his native tongue. It did little to ease his friend's angst, but such is the way of things. Killing a crazy man proved bad medicine, not only to the brave doing the killing, but to all of his family and descendants thereafter as well. You gain one Yankee's hair and lose another, it is just the way of it, the brave consoled himself.

George Cooper rolled over and over in the water, tugging at the spear dangling in his side until it fell free, trailing blood behind it. Feeling the current pull him along he relaxed and let it do its work, all of the sudden praising God for it. He moved as little as possible for fear of showing any signs of life to the devils on the riverbank. Rolling just enough to catch a few quick breaths now and then, his mind flashed with the horrid visions of the day. Poor Cherrick, he thought over and over in his mind, almost welcoming the pain in his side as recompense for their plight. "Forgive me dear Cherrick," he muttered between splashes of water. "Forgive me, for many have made mistakes which have proved deadly this day. Forgive us all, brave, fallen souls of Wyoming!" He looked in the swirling waters for Cherrick but didn't see any sign of him.

Noticing an island ahead, he swam for it with all his might. Stumbling from the water and onto the rocky shore pings immediately sounded all around him. A strange sound, almost sounding like laughter, puzzling him after the reports and sharp pings of balls ricocheting off rocks, but he nonetheless ignored them and plowed headlong into the foliage beyond the island's shore. Bowing his head, he kept plowing through it, urged on by the whizzing balls chasing him.

He finally burst through the brush on the opposite shore, pulling remnants of clinging vines, thorns, and twigs from his body and hair. Bursting onto the rocky beach, he looked up and down it, locking eyes with three startled men further down the shore. They stood still, looking at him with hollow eyes filled with shock, their mouths agape. No words crept from their open mouths, but their eyes spoke volumes to him. He knew of what they spoke, and had no answer for them. Looking down to his bleeding side, he raised a shaky hand and pointed to the east shore of the river, it being the only answer he knew. Sensing no reaction, he stumbled into the water, not waiting for the stunned men to follow. Their fate belonged solely to them, as his own fate did to him. A loud voice to his rear made his heart jump in his chest and he twirled about, ready to claw the eyes out of any Tory or savage who dared step within his reach.

"George!" the voice yelled again. "My God man, I've not the strength to make it across! For you know I can barely tread water as it is! How I made it this far I dare not wonder!"

George's jaw dropped lower than the ghostly men's jaws standing down the shoreline. "John Abbott?" he gasped. For a moment he almost turned and dove into the water, but the haunting vision of poor Cherrick flooded his mind's eye. Recompense, he thought, recompense for the rash and arrogant acts of this day. Shaking his head, he bowed it in shame. Oh dear Cherrick, I hope you survive this day, he prayed.

"My dear wife," Abbott said, stepping out into the water. The rags covering his body trailed in strips behind him. Tears dripped down his face. "All my friends are gone! Everyone has been slaughtered! This is not war! It is murder! Oh, my dear children! What hell hath come!?!"

"Calm yourself, my dear man," Copper said, extending his shaking hand to the man.

Abbott stumbled toward him. "What?" he asked, spreading his hand toward Cooper's bleeding side. "You are wounded?"

"A mere scratch compared to the others suffering on that field," George Cooper said. Reaching out his hand, he grasp Abbott's hand, leading him out waist deep into the water. "What of them?" he asked, nodding to the three stunned men gawking at them.

"I don't know about leaving them," Abbott said.

"Come!" Cooper yelled to them. "You must make it to the other side! The savages are coming!"

Blank stares answered him.

A ball hitting the water to their front hastened him into the water, pulling Abbott behind him by his hand.

"What of them?" Abbott asked again, seeming to hesitate the further they crept into the water.

"They're the guardians of their own fate," Cooper said. "I cannot save all of Wyoming this day. If they do not wish to follow, it is their loss, I cannot force them!" Turning, he pulled the fearful man close. "But I can save you," he added. "Clasp your hands about my neck and shoulders and hold firm until we gain the far shore, but be mindful not to choke me!"

Abbott grunted in response and climbed onto Coopers back, drawing a long deep breath and hoping it not to be his last.

Balls spattered around them again, hastening Cooper's strokes against the current. Pulling Abbott's arms tight around his neck, he swam hard for the shore, letting the current pull them downstream. It didn't matter, for they welcomed any distance gained from the fury of their enemies. At first Abbott fidgeted and groaned on his back, but half way across the river he suddenly relaxed and seemed to flow with him, much to Cooper's relief. Fearing being swept further down and away from the shore, Cooper focused on a great clump of overhanging bushes along the shore and swam headlong for it, ignoring the spouts of water gushing around them and the whizzing balls overhead.

His reaching hands finally clasp one of the branches and he pulled with all his might from the weight about his shoulders. With a great burst of strength, he managed to pull himself up and tumble beneath a shielding bush. Feeling solid ground underneath him, he collapsed, letting Abbott roll off his back to the ground. Gasping for air, he looked over to the man and paled at the wide eyes staring back at him.

All of the sudden the eyes came to life and Abbott stood tall, staring all about. "Thank you, George Cooper," he said. "Thank you fine!" With that, he scampered up the bank and disappeared into the forest beyond, without so much as a second glance behind him.

George tore a piece of his shirt and pushed it hard against the bleeding hole in his side. "Who could have imagined this day?" he muttered under his breath.

A few balls cutting and whizzing through the branches over his head ushered him back to the terror of this day. He mouthed a silent prayer before scrambling through the brush and breaking into a full trot away from it all. The further he gained the sheltering trees the faster he ran, despite his apparent escape. He knew he had only gained a slight reprieve. Soon the devils would swarm this shore, also.

The Susquehanna ran red. The only safety lay to the far Delaware River to the east, or Fort Augusta miles downriver. No other hope remained. He ran, clutching at his bleeding side and promising himself to only stop to warn anyone he encountered and grab a few feeble provisions for his quest for the Delaware. His life depended upon it.

The three men stood and watched Cooper and Abbott's spectacle in awe. A sickening feeling of hopelessness rose in each of their stomachs. Turning to on another with blank stares, they knew none of them possessed the strength to swim the rest of the way from *Monocanock Island* to the east shore of the Susquehanna. A few corpses rolling in strong current in front of them made their hearts sink further in their chests. The enemy would soon reach the island. Everyone had lost their weapons and had only the very shirts on their backs. Not even a knife showed among them.

"I have not the strength," Giles Slocum finally said. Stumbling back a few steps, he collapsed onto the beach. Lifting a handful of sand in his hand he let it dribble between his fingers. "I'll bury myself in this if I have too," he said with glazed eyes.

"Or they may do it for you," Henry Pensil said, listening to the shrill war whoops echoing down the river.

"We must do something!" Thomas Baldwin said. His naked body shook, but neither of his fellows questioned whether he shook from a chill or fear. They felt the same way.

"They shall give no quarter," Slocum said. An eerie screech from the other side of the island gave each man a start. They all looked wide-eyed all about. "They're coming!" Slocum added.

All three men immediately scrambled in different directions. Slocum crawled to a harsh tangle of bushes near a great fallen tree. Surely no one would search there, he reasoned, carefully parting some of the thick bushes to make a place for himself. After scrunching under some of them, he scooped some of the sand and loose leaves over his prone body, leaving a small break in them for his mouth and eyes. Settling down in his living grave, he took long and slow breaths and waited, noticing Pensil scrambling about near a tree. He watched the man's eyes dart toward a noise and grow wide with fear. He slowly turned toward the fallen tree and laid down beside it, hastily scooping leaves and twigs over his body.

Men soon appeared from the direction in which Pensil had been staring. Two of them hovered about the log, silent and still, seeming to be drawn by some strange six-sense to it. One raised his rifle and started scuffing at the leaves around the log.

"What is it John?" his comrade asked.

John ignored him and kept pushing the leaves aside.

"I see nothing," the other man said, looking up and down the beach. "Nor do any of the others. Let us follow them."

John waved his hand at his friend to silence him. He looked up to the fading light of day and back down to the log. "I sense something," he finally said, his eyes alive with the hunt.

His friend raised his rifle, suddenly aware of the potential threat of an unseen enemy. Wiping his hammer dry again from their swim to the island, he looked all around them. Taking a few steps toward the other side of the log, he suddenly noticed some disturbed leaves.

John's eyes followed him and raised his hand to stop him just short of the log. "Stay still," he said, climbing over the log. Stopping atop of the log, he carefully scrutinized the ground around it. Sensing his prey, he cocked his rifle. Its click sounded in the silent air of the hunt. A movement under the leaves instantly drew the aim of both men's rifles.

Peering harshly at a face in the leaves, John asked, "So it's you, is it?"

His friend peered into the leaves, trying in vain to see to whom he spoke.

After a few tense moments the leaves rustled. A ragged man slowly emerged from under them. He raised his arm as if to shield himself from the Tories' cold stares and eased back beside the log.

John's eyes shone in recognition of the man, but he still steadily aimed his rifle at the man's heart. Neither man said a word, but just stared at one another.

John finally took a deep breath and tightened his hold on his rifle in preparation to fire.

"John!" Henry Pensil gasped. "I am your brother! Spare my life and I shall serve you!"

The other Tory gasped, slowly lowering his rifle. This man proved no threat. Oddly, John clenched his rifle all the tighter.

"You!" John finally said through gritted teeth, "are a damned rebel rat!" His body suddenly trembled from the rage surging through his veins. "You are a damned rebel, Henry!" he said, his voice crackling with emotion. "You and I are of different sides as well as sentiments!"

Henry's pleading eyes seemed only to further enrage his brother. "I am your brother!" he said, sinking down against the huge log. He tried to crawl away, but the rifle shook at him to stop. "For our dear mother's sake, spare me! I shall serve you and your cause as long as I live henceforth! Spare my life! You won't kill your own brother will you!?!"

John's face drew pale. "Yes!" he exclaimed. "I will as soon as to look at you! You are a damned rebel!" Putting a foot atop the log, he coldly squeezed the trigger, sending his brother to the ground forever. Henry twitched but once, then gasped his last breath of dear life, killed by his own blood. Killed by this war of brothers.

An eerie silence blanketed the beach.

John stood for a long moment staring down the business end of his rifle to his brother's limp body, ignoring the gasps of shock from his stunned comrade. Carefully lowering his rifle, he advanced toward the body. Drawing his scalping he bent down, slowly slicing the hair from the crown of his brother's head, ignoring the flashes of childhood shared between them in his mind's eye. A soldier's duty forestalled such thoughts. They had too for a soldier to function. This rebel, as all rebels, must be dealt with or their deluded dreams might infest the order of the whole world. Then what? Anarchy? No sir! He would do anything to curtail that, and now he proved it.

John glanced down at the bloody trophy, gruffly stuffing it into his pouch along with the others he gathered this day. "There!" he announced to his silent comrade. "That's the only way a rebel understands! And I plan to bring a lot of understanding to Wyoming!"

"What!?!" his comrade muttered, suddenly finding his voice. "What are you about, slaying your own brother!?!"

"Yes," John Pensil said. "For he was a damned rebel!"

The Tory gritted his teeth, swinging his rifle toward his cruel comrade. "I have a mind to serve you in the same manner!"

Johns Pensil's empty eyes simply glared back at him.

"What?" someone called from the trees. "Did you get one?" Several men stepped out from the trees, each curiously eyeing the two men. They walked around the two men glaring at one another and stared down to the dead rebel. One of them pushed the lifeless body with the toe of his boot. "Scratch one rebel rat," he said, raising his rifle high in the air and whooping.

The others followed his lead and patted both of the men on their backs, defusing the tense situation. "You've both done well," one of them said, poking his fingers into Pensil's pouch. Pulling no less than three scalps from it, he raised them high to show everyone.

"You best put them back," Pensil snarled at him. "I went through a lot of trouble to lift them. More than you will ever know!"

"Yes," the Tory said, frowning. Pushing the bloody scalps back into the pouch, he wiped his bloody hands on his wet trousers. "Such is war," he said. "Bloody in more ways than one, and hell all the way around, but we must not lose sight of our duty to the King. We must be about our duty, it is the lot of a soldier."

Pensil's friend finally lowered his rifle and reluctantly nodded. Turning with the others, he walked back into the trees, leaving their sullen comrade behind to ponder his bloody trophies. Such is war, he thought, horrid and cruel. Let John's brother's blood stain his hands for the rest of his days, for he would have none of it. He quickly subdued his conscience, earnestly replacing it with a high sense of duty to his King and country.

Giles Slocum grimaced in his hiding place. Sand trickled down the corners of his mouth, but he scolded himself to stay still, lest he share poor Henry Pensil's fate. He closed his eyes, but the image of brother slaying brother burned in his memory. He feared the sights of this day to haunt him to his dying day, and perhaps far beyond. Now he convinced himself he must live, if just to tell of the horrors he witnessed this day; this day of horror. This day Wyoming shuddered.

## Chapter Sixty Seven
### *The Horse's Tail*

Zebulon Butler stared in awe of the men falling all around him. Reining his horse around in the swirling smoke, he searched in vain for any pocket of defense. "Oh my children," he gasped to himself, noticing the many bodies lying about. His horse pranced about, trying in vain not to stumble on them. Butler clutched his pistol, spurring his confused horse around the engrossed Indians darting about in the confusion. Finally, through the smoke ahead, he spied a determined little group of men still firing their firelocks at the demons swirling around them. He rode steadily toward the pocket of five men standing firm amidst the terror.

All five noticed the rider galloping pell-mell toward them. Perhaps the officer might deliver some great gem of knowledge and insight to allow them to escape their dire circumstances. Their hopes quickly faded, for they recognized the same wide-eyed and hollow stare they all shared on the face of the savior. And far from delivering them, their savior only brought more attention to them from their merciless foes. A murderous volley cut them down instantly.

Butler reined his horse to a stop in front of the fallen men, knowing in a few seconds, as soon as the demon's reloaded, the same hail of lead which cut them down would pepper the air again. Drawing his sword, he cried in anguish, suddenly feeling a great pity for his men which overrode his fear. After firing his pistol at one of the darting demons, he flung the spent weapon at another before pointing his sword straight ahead to charge the demons. A sudden movement from the five men lying about gave him the start of his life. He stared in disbelief at a young man staggering around in a daze near him. Blood flowing into his eyes, the young man gasped, feeling ahead of him with one hand, while clutching his head with the other. Hearing the horse's neighs, he flailed his arms, stumbling blindly towards it.

"Bennett!" Butler finally gasped. He could save one! He could! He wheeled his horse about to the blind young man. "Bennett!" he screamed above the roar of battle. "Bennett! Grab hold of my horse's tail! Grab the tail lad!" His sense of rage and self-sacrifice melted away. A chance to deliver life, even one, from this bleak and hopeless field surged through his veins. He must succeed! He must!

The young man's hands ran along the horse's flanks, finally clutching its tail. Butler bent down, trying in vain to lift him onto the back of his horse, but bullets whizzing close to his head forced greater prudence. Certain of the young man's iron grip on the tail, he viciously sank his spurs into his horse's flank. The horse bolted, then galloped madly for the fort, pulling the stumbling young man along with it. It galloped through the whirlpool of death, trampling any poor unfortunates beneath its thundering hooves. The young man clung onto the tail for dear life, somehow maintaining his balance by the tug of the tail. Flashes of sweaty men, their faces smeared black with powder and red with blood, showed through the confusion. Fiendish yells and pleas from the living and dying cursed the acrid, smoky air.

Butler ignored it all, waving and pointing his sword toward the fort. He must reach it! He must save at least one poor soul from this field! Spying Abrahams Creek just ahead, he spurred his horse all the harder. Nearly there! Nearly there! he told himself over and over, ever conscious of the tug on his horse's tail whenever they leapt over a fallen tree or large rock. It meant Bennett still clung tight. Hold on man! Hold on! Stealing a glance back to the man his heart sank. A screaming Indian ran headlong after them, brandishing a spear and leading more Indians behind him. His fierce eyes glared at the man's head. Butler felt his stomach lurch. No! Not after all this, he thought. No! You fiendish ghoul!

A motion to his front tore his eyes to it and he yelled a great huzza at the top of his lungs. He spurred his horse all the deeper, galloping headlong toward a confused man lying on the ground bearing a glazed and stunned look. The man groggily fumbled and looked for his rifle, finally clutching it tightly to his chest. His blood shot eyes stared ahead, bewildered by the chaos engulfing him.

Butler waved his sword behind him and shouted, "Inman! Inman!"

Inman leaned up on his elbows, still bewildered after being so rudely awoken from sleep into a living nightmare. His hand instinctively cocked his rifle.

"Is that rifle loaded!?!" Butler screamed at him.

Inman nodded, shaking off the sleep. His bloodshot eyes grew wide.

"Then shoot that Indian!" Butler ordered, pointing his sword at the closing Indian.

Inman's rifle immediately cracked, instantly felling the Indian. The brave tumbled head over heels onto the ground, rolling to a stop just in front of the stunned rebel. The braves following him promptly parted and fell back, dispersing in several different directions.

Butler thundered by Inman, yelling at the top of his lungs for him to follow and get to the fort with all due haste.

Inman wasted no time joining the yelling colonel and bloody young man clinging tenaciously to his horse's tail. Painfully becoming aware of the screaming Indians, rifle shots, and cries of anguish, he wondered how on God's green earth he managed to sleep through it all. Nonetheless, he somehow started loading his rifle while he ran, knowing his life now depended upon it, and upon a prompt response from his feet. He fell to sleep in one world and awoke in another, worse than any hell he ever imagined. All seemed lost of the old, and the burgeoning terror of the new showed stark in his face. A sense of rage slowly replaced his fear. Heeding it, he suddenly stopped his feet and turned about, sighting down one of the painted demons closing on them. He fired, somehow feeling empowered to stop it all, but looking to the wide-eyed and terror stricken men stumbling by him, he thought better of it and turned to run again.

Loading his rifle, he swore an oath under his breath. As long as one rifle or musket remained in the hands of one patriot in Wyoming, defiance to the tyrants remained strong and the burgeoning idea of American liberty lived! It lived as long as one patriot drew breath, and he promised himself to be that patriot.

## Chapter Sixty Eight
### *The Horrible Aftermath*

The thick smoke from the burning fort now and then clouded his eyes, but he preferred it against it the awful sights before him. Both burned with an equal intensity in his eyes. He wriggled his head against the rough tree bark behind him, but found little relief from the tight cord holding his neck fast to the rough bark of the tree.

Cries, horrible cries, forced his eyes open, despite the smoke. He peered through the trees at the poor souls being dragged to the burning fort. The victors dragged them along with little regard for further injury. It only mattered that they reach the fort still breathing, for the moment at least. A broken limb or gushing wound meant nothing. Some struggled and fought back with their cruel captors despite their wounds, only to be quickly subdued by a war club.

Two souls in particular caught his attention, for he knew both, and both held a place dear in his heart. His flowing tears cut through the stinging smoke and much to his relief the wind switched direction, carrying the acrid smoke away. Closing his eyes, he blinked hard to flood the stinging sensation away. Opening his eyes wide, he gazed more clearly to his fellow prisoners tied to the trees around him. One man, Wilcox, sat tied with his arms and legs straddled around a tree trunk in a most uncomfortable fashion; perhaps in prelude of the torture which might await him. Two others, tied in a like fashion, watched the drama playing out in front of them with silent tongues, none eager to draw any undue attention to themselves from the pair of Tory guards about them.

He bowed his head in deference to the women and children clumped together to the their side, some victims of their own foolhardiness for not heeding the word to evacuate to the forts, while others came from the burning Fort Wintermoot itself. Mothers cried and held their frightened children close, most now widows, and none possessing more than the clothes upon their backs. Cry, mothers of Wyoming, he thought, for through your forlorn tears none shall ever forget what happened this day.

More horrible cries turned his head back to the burning fort. A man rolled along the ground behind a steadily advancing brave, groaning piteously and raising his hands from a bleeding wound about his thigh to his hair, vainly trying to gain some relief from the brute dragging him along by it. Another man thrown roughly down to the ground before crackling Fort Wintermoot staggered to his knees, despite them being shattered, and flailed his hands at his tormentors to no avail, for they simply laughed, easily dodging his fists.

"It's Captain Bidlack," a voice whispered from the tree to his right. He turned his head just far enough to see Wilcox.

"Yes, Ingersoll," Wilcox said, noticing his stare. "It's Captains Bidlack and Ransom! May God have mercy!" A sharp grunt from one of the Tory guards quickly silenced him. Whimpers from the huddled children clinging to their distraught mothers crept through the air, but drew no scorn from the Tories, for they somehow filtered and diluted the tortured cries, groans, and shrill war whoops polluting the air.

Contemplating their fate, Ingersoll bowed his head and shuddered, thinking of how Indian Butler had ordered two men to wisp Captain Harding away upriver last evening. He wondered if Harding knew of his lucky break. Anguished cries lifted his head once again.

The Indians dragged, kicked, and shoved both captains closer to the burning fort, stopping just before the dancing flames. One started dancing around them, fingering at the lone tuff of hair on the crown of his painted head, taunting the still-defiant Yankees to lift it from his scalp. The men rolled on the ground, vainly trying to strike the gloating Indian, growling at him through their intense pain. The Indian, confident of his agility, darted near the enraged men, but soon tumbled from a sharp blow to his shin. Bobbling and screaming in shock, he drew the ire of all the other Indians laughing incessantly at him. Quickly regaining his balance, he screamed down at the men, raising his war club threateningly at them. More growls answered his threats.

Another brave appeared holding several pitchforks in his hands he had gathered from a barn. Dropping them to the ground, he raised one of them high in the air. The dancing brave and all of the others stared curiously at him until he advanced, mercilessly stabbing Captain Bidlack in the torso with it.

Bidlack scrunched his body and writhed in pain, managing to curse the Indian through his painful moans. Another brave scooped up one of the pitchforks and prodded at him just the same, seeming to draw great enjoyment from the writhing man trying desperately to jerk away from him. Both braves stabbed and prodded him again and again until blood showed from the many pairs of two pronged points on his skin through his ragged clothes. After many more prods a brute of a brave advanced, knocking the writhing man squarely on the head, dazing him long enough for the brave to pick him up and toss him onto the burning flames of Fort Wintermoot.

Sheer cries of agony erupted from the burning man's throat. Rolling out of the flames, he tumbled onto the ground, moaning in pure agony. Pitchforks immediately prodded and poked him, piercing his crackling skin and forcing him back into the flames, despite his flailing arms. Again he screamed from the deepest part of his tormented soul. With a sudden surge of strength drawn from pure rage, he kicked a flaming log toward his tormentors, much to their amusement.

"My God! My Good God no!" Ransom screamed, trying to crawl away from the macabre scene. The same cruel forks met him, prodding and rolling him toward the flames. "No!" he screamed to no avail. "My God just shoot me! You inhuman bastards! No! Have you no mercy!?!"

Sinister laughs answered him. The forks prodded and pushed all the more. Fueled by Bidlack's unearthly screams, he furiously slapped them aside, gaining himself a slight reprieve.

Seemingly out of nowhere, a tall barrel-chested painted brave marched toward him, clutching a bloody sword in his hands. The huge silver arms bands on his large biceps glistened from the rising flames and in his bulging eyes. Red blood glistened from the string of bloody scalps hanging about his sash. Hesitating for a second, he glared at the screaming man in the flames, his wide eyes betraying his intense disdain for him. All, including Ransom, stared silently at him, seeming mesmerized by his commanding, yet terrifying, presence. The other Indians parted, giving him a wide wake.

Noticing the fearsome brave's cutting and hateful eyes falling to him, Ransom regained his dignity and stared defiantly back at the monster.

A great scowl amplified the brave's sour expression. With one smooth and fluid motion he raised the sword and swung it, slicing the defiant rebel's head from his body, watching it tumble and roll to the side. The other braves immediately yelled with glee and pounced upon the quivering body, stabbing it mercilessly with the pitchforks and plunging spears into it. The large warrior put a foot atop the head, bent down and sliced the scalp from its skull, ignoring its shockingly wide eyes forever bearing a look of defiance. With a gruff kick, he sent it tumbling into the flaming fort. Raising his upper lip in disdain, he yelled and poked a piece of leather through a hole in the scalp. He strung it to his sash along with his other grisly trophies and trotted off with nary a passing glance over his shoulder. More white devils needed his attention.

"You evil Tory bastards!" Wilcox screamed at his Tory guards. He wriggled madly against his bonds with a fury born of pure outrage. Gaining no advantage from the tight bonds, he glared back to the indifferent guards. "You do nothing as Christians suffer such a cruel fate!?!" he screamed at them again.

One of the guards turned from the tree he leaned against. "Be silent, rat," he said. "Be thankful you remain in our charge and not in theirs! Thus go the spoils of war to the victor!"

"You inhuman bastards!"

The Tory marched bluntly toward the indignant rebel, striking him with the butt of his musket. "I like it no better than you!" he exclaimed. "But it is out of our hands!" Turning away from the gasping rebel, he twirled about, flinging his musket to the ground. "If you stupid rebels would have only capitulated none of this would have happened, but no, you stubborn rats would have none of it! Well there is the result of your stubborn nature! Look to it! I hope it sickens you well, you and your boastful Yankee pride!"

"No worries!" Wilcox said. "We shall remember, and so shall our children, for all ages! This will not be forgotten and you Tory bastards shall surely pay for your unholy alliances with these savages!"

"Shut up! Damn you!" the Tory screamed, dropping his rifle and collapsing to his knees. He raised his clenched fists to his eyes in frustration. Stumbling to his feet, he marched back to his friend, but his friend still seemed indifferent to it all, and said nothing. Turning back toward the bond rebels, he blanched from their hateful stares. "You idiots best mind your tongues and perhaps we will be able to get you out of this with your hair! Keep opening your mouths and ye shall see the other way!" he said before sulking down by a tree near his friend.

His friend finally turned and looked down to his exasperated mate. "You are right Horatio," he said, bending down to him. "Do not fret or be sullen, my friend, for it truly is out of our hands." He looked out of the corner of his eye to their indignant charges. A sour expression poured over his face. "They did bring this all about themselves, what with their refusal to let some people upriver be and all!"

A new series of screams turned both of them back to the burning flames of the fort. A burning form tumbled from the flames, swinging its arms wildly at the Indians. Easily avoiding the desperate blows, they simply laughed all the more. Bringing their pitchforks and spears to play, they quickly forced the burned form back into the flames.

All of the women gasped, some falling faint to the ground. Others tried in vain to turn to shield their children's eyes from the horror with trembling hands.

"The little ones, John," Horatio gasped. "Must they endure this?"

"No harm will come to them," John answered, raising his musket up to his chest. "Not as long as I hold this!" He nodded toward the Indians and then down to his friend. "It is their way, not ours," he said. "You, being of *Unadilla*, should know what they are about."

"From Albany," Horatio said, "forced out by Schuyler, the rat!"

"There now, did you see the way that one danced around taunting them with his tuff of hair and all?" John asked.

Horatio looked sullenly down to the ground, shaking his head in disgust. "Every warrior in shaving his head for battle is careful to leave one lock of hair about his crown in defiance of his enemy, as to say to his enemy, take it if you can," he explained. "Taking the scalp is taking a piece of their enemy's soul, for it is taken from the soft spot of the head that is there when one is born, the place they think the spirit enters the body at birth, and thus departs in death. If you take it, you take a piece of their soul and their bravery and such. The stake and torture are his way to test and honor the endurance of his enemy. If they wail, they prove the warrior's superiority, if they remain silent, it is an insult. Every warrior expects torture and humiliation if the tide of battle turns against them, but here alas, it has not, so they deal out the torture. It's their way is all, cruel as it is." His head remained bowed through the whole explanation.

"Yes," John said. "We are about their land now, due to respect their manners and ways, no matter how repulsive. Besides, we're too few in comparison to numbers to do much about anything." He turned an eye back to the rebels. "Major Butler's indifference may appear cold as a December morn, but what is he to do? These rebel rats knew what awaited them in defeat, yet they marched out of their fort brazen and bold, the fools. Now they have it. Do not listen to the Quakers and such whom spout words praising the noble savage and the meek children of the forest! They are no children, I grant you, but warriors of the forest and if ye be fool enough to trod on their ground ye shall live by their ways, not the ones carried in your heart from lands far away. Now, Horatio, we must be good king's men and stand to our duty!"

A low growl, laden with disgust, crept from Wilcox's throat. He shook his head in pure rage. Great tears flooded his eyes. "You are a fine lot of smug bastards, you are!" he screamed. "I share not your summation of the savage, for this is all God's green earth! All of it! A coward's reason slips from your lips, fine sir!"

Several of the Indians noticed his screams and slowly turned their dark eyes toward the rebels tied and huddled under the trees.

"Mind your tongue, rat!" John said over his shoulder. "Or you'll bring more trouble to yourself and your fellows!" He and Horatio both stood tall, the latter finding his composure again. Scrambling backwards, he quickly found his musket. Raising it up, he joined his staunch friend standing between the warriors and the trees.

The warriors glanced at them and marched toward the trees

despite their defiant allies. A blood lust burned in their dark and foreboding eyes, evidence of the rage still burning bright in their souls. They peered past the two white men, ignoring them. Several drew their scalping knives and war clubs.

"Now, that will be far enough, my tawny friend," John said, positioning himself squarely in front of the lead warrior. Raising his musket full to his chest, he stood fast. Its bayonet glistened in the fire cast by the horrid flames of the burning fort.

The warrior stopped and sneered at him. Sweat ran through the swirls of paint covering his face, making him appear all the more gruesome, and menacing. "We go past!" he said, waving his tomahawk at the bond prisoners. "They Yanks! They die!"

John gritted his teeth and shook his head, not giving an inch. Horatio stood tall just to his side. A click sounded from his sharp movements to slide his bayonet into place on the end of his musket.

The warrior rolled his eyes and stomped his foot on the ground. "This our land!" he said, probing the white men's eyes for any sign of weakness. All became silent. The warrior spat at John's feet. "We see!" he said, gesturing with his tomahawk toward the setting sun. "We see when sun go down!"

A grim look overcame John's face. He pulled back the hammer on his musket to full cock, letting its sharp click speak for him. Horatio's sounded behind him.

The warrior screamed in anger, thumping his chest. "Tell Butler I captain too!" he exclaimed, glaring past John to the trees.

"Scream all you want!" John said. "But enough blood has been shed this day!"

All of the warriors laughed. "There plenty more Yankees!" the lead warrior said. Screeching, he turned, then jogged toward the battlefield, leading the other disgusted braves away with him.

"We best make fires near us," John said, easing the hammer of his musket back to half cock. "We'll set them about as to light all under the trees," he added, nodding to the rebels. "It is to be a long night and the devil is at play here, he is. It will be hell to keep him at bay!"

Horatio nodded and also looked to the grief-stricken and miserable prisoners, trying to convince himself they brought all of this onto themselves, but somehow the words did not ring true in his heart. But by the stark looks in the rebels' eyes, he knew they need not express any more warning to them to keep quite. They knew.

"We'll have no more trouble with them," John said, noticing Horatio's stare at the prisoners. "It is the others I fear, as do they."

## Chapter Sixty Nine
*Zebulon Butler Departs*

Forty Fort's gate slid open just wide enough for Colonel Denison and his few followers to slide through it. Mayhem greeted them on the other side. People ran about in confusion and disorder, all wearing the same gaunt look of disbelief. Some tended to the distraught soldiers stumbling through the gate, most of them wounded, bloodied, and battered. Others stood with their mouths agape, stunned and totally shocked by it all.

None caught Denison's eye more than a freckle-faced boy standing on a hogshead just inside the gate. At first he looked to Denison wide-eyed and full of hope, but the colonel's hollow and bloodshot eyes quickly extinguished any sense of lingering hope from his eyes, and heart. His great tears etched streaks through the dirt smearing his face from wiping them with his hands. He bowed his head in total grief and despair. "Pa! Pa's gone!" dribbled through his trembling lips.

Denison reined his horse toward him and stopped. He stared at the grief-stricken boy, suddenly feeling bereft and somehow responsible for his father's demise. The little boy's grief cut deep. He wanted to say something, but the growing lump in his throat forbade it. Tugging at the reins, he slowly turned away, leaving the boy to grieve.

He bowed his head in grief but soon raised it to the demand of many grieving souls about him. The crowded fort moved as one vast sea of misery, with bloodied men exhorting the need for all to buck up and stand fast, for they had witnessed what happened if they didn't, and had barely escaped it with their lives. Looking up to the few wounded men, old men, and young boys manning the walls with great intervals between their posts, Denison shuddered to think of their fate. No cannon, no regiment, few firelocks, and shaking old men and frightened boys manning the walls. It all did little to exhort confidence in his soul.

His sad eyes caught the sight of a crowd gathering around two men. One of the men, lying on a bench with a bandage covering his bloody head, waved his arms at every syllable his fellow said standing near him. His arms waved to and fro, spinning a web of true horror to the wide-eyed women and children standing about them. That would not do. They needed words of confidence just now, or none at all.

"Inman!" Denison called to the man, finally finding his voice. "What are you about man?"

The man stared wide-eyed at the stern colonel, abruptly biting his tongue. The full shock of his ordeal finally caught up with him and he staggered backwards to sit on the bench near his wounded comrade, suddenly mute.

"They barely escaped, Nathan!' a grisly bearded old buckskin-clad man said. "Bennett here took a glancing ball to his head and awoke to see Colonel Butler reining his horse up near him! Grab my horse's tail! he said to him and he right smart did, for the savages was a breathin' down their necks! Old Butler spurred his horse out of the fray and galloped full and hard for the fort, pulling along young Bennett! The savages lit like deer after them and was about to catch 'em when old Inman here rises up and blisters their chief full in the chest! The others beat feet to get away from Inman and they all made it to the fort, just afore you, I might add!"

Denison looked at Inman nodding in confirmation of the old man's words. "You best get you and your rifle up to the walls, Inman, if it draws such fear from the Indians," he said.

Inman rose, clutched his rifle tight, and marched obediently to the nearest ladder rising to the platform below the walls.

A woman's shrill cries turned Denison's eyes to the parting crowd making way for her. "Oh, dear Nathan!" she cried upon sight of him. "Oh! Blessed God! My dear husband lives!" She trotted a few more steps to him, pulling along a boy clinging to the back of her dress and holding a babe tight in her arms.

Denison immediately dismounted and stretched his arms toward his family. The boy let loose of his mother's dress and darted in front of her to his father's awaiting arms. His mother quickly joined him.

"Be still," he whispered to his trembling family. "All is well at the moment, be still. I am here now. Be still, my dears."

Both sobbed, holding him all the tighter.

"Now, dear Lazarus," he said, trying to quell the great lump growing in his throat upon mention of the name. "Stand strong. I tell you your dear Uncle Lazarus did. We must follow his brave example."

Elizabeth suddenly looked at him with eyes of wonder.

"No," he answered, reading the question in her eyes. "He did not make it, but we must be strong in honor of his memory."

A sullen man popped out of the crowd near them and said, "Begging your pardon, Mrs. Denison, but I must report to the Colonel."

"Yes, Lieutenant Jenkins," Denison said, slowly leading his family toward a cabin. He gave a slight nod to a boy collecting his mount and stopped his family just in front of the cabin.

"Colonel Butler is in there, the Bennett's cabin," Jenkins said, nervously rubbing the back of his right hand. Noticing the colonel's odd stare, he ceased rubbing it and shook his head. "All is in upheaval," he added, removing his hat and running his hands through his hair.

"Mothers morn everywhere! Fathers morn! Brothers and sisters morn! All have been touched by the horror of this day!"

"Yes, yes," Denison said. "It is a sad day, but what else, man?"

Jenkins drew a long breath, cursing himself for his emotional outburst. "Yes sir," he said, quickly regaining his composure. "Barely forty have passed through the gate as of yet. We have plenty of ball and powder, but few effective men to man the walls."

Denison motioned for Elizabeth to enter the Bennett's cabin and took Jenkins aside. "Go on man," he said, looking around. "I need not tell you what happened out there, just that we mustn't let it happen in here, my dear man."

"Yes sir, fifteen of the regulars have returned, minus most of their officers, Durkee, Hewitt, Hollenback, Wells, and Ransom, have not been accounted for as of yet, nor Major Garret or Colonel Dorrance!"

"Yes, please go on."

"Phineas Pierce has survived. He and Roswell Franklin are among those manning the walls, they are both fine officers. A dozen or so of those manning the walls are walking wounded, but all still have the spirit of fight in them. A few have entered the north gate only to pass through the south gate, fearful for their farms and whatnot, but most have the wisdom to remain in the fort. I have sent a dispatch to Captain Smith at Fort Wilkes-Barre to repair to this fort with all due haste and bring the four-pound cannon if possible. He has declined my request for the cannon, sighting no proper carriage for it, and says they will stand fast until receiving word from you or Colonel Butler. He reports about a dozen or so have repaired to his fort after swimming the river. Many are gravely wounded, though. He says Blanchard is still unmolested at Pittston Fort, as of yet, and also awaits word. He regrets not being able to repair to this side of the river, but the Tories took all the boats about their landing. Captain Franklin has arrived with five men and says more are rushing to the fort." He looked sadly up to the walls. "He's up there with the others."

"Very well, John," Denison said, looking around the fort. "We are in a bad way, indeed. What of our stores of food?"

"We have enough for a few weeks, I reckon."

Denison looked toward the Bennett's cabin. "What of Colonel Butler?"

"He is grief-stricken, sir, I fear for him, he kept muttering about his children, his children. They had to urge him down from his mount. One of the reins had been cut by a ball, but he was not hit. He saved Rufus Bennett by having him clutch his horse's tail, but he is badly shaken, sir."

"Yes, aren't we all? But you have done well, Lieutenant, keep it up, for we need all good men just now," Denison said, nodding and shaking Jenkins' hand. "I shall now consult with Colonel Butler. You keep seeing to things out here, and my God I hope Clingman and Spalding arrive soon. Keep an eye out for them, my good man."

He stepped smartly to the door of the Bennett's cabin but stopped for a moment to gather his thoughts before pushing it open. Startled eyes turned to him, but then turned away when he did not speak. Two women hovered over a bed in a corner, busily tending to Rufus Bennett's head wound by the light of a pine knot jammed into a hole in the wall. One of them stopped long enough to turn starkly toward him and ask, "Have you seen Solomon?"

"No, Mrs. Bennett, I am afraid I have not," he answered, removing his hat and stepping into the room.

"Afraid," the other woman scoffed. "That is the word for today."

Denison closed the door behind him and stood for a moment, considering their plight.

"Here, Nathan," Elizabeth Denison called to him from a table near a hearth in the crowded room. "We are here, as well as Colonel Butler," she added, nodding to the crestfallen man sitting on the other side of the table gently tapping his fingertips on it. His hat sat near his tapping fingers and he stared blankly at it through strands of his disheveled hair hanging over his eyes. His lips betrayed a mumble from them. Elizabeth rolled her eyes from him and down to the babe in her arms. "We are all lost this day," she whispered.

Little Lazarus ran to him as he walked toward the table. He sat down on a bench next to his wife, sitting the boy on his knee. "It's no one's fault," he said, looking into Butler's blank eyes.

"Is a true shame, it is!" Thomas Bennett exclaimed from another dark corner in the cabin. Stumbling from the corner, he looked deathly into both colonel's eyes in the dim light before retreating back into the corner. "I knew it, and warned them, I did," he mumbled.

"Don't mind Father," Martha Bennett said, barely taking her eyes off of Rufus's head. She tightened the bandage about his head tighter against the flow of blood. Her mother gasped. Rufus squirmed, looking up to her. "Hold still," she said, "afore you bleed out, you've quite a nasty gash!"

"How many more must perish this day?" Thomas asked.

"Father!" Martha said, turning to him. "Rufus will be fine, the bleeding's already stopped." Releasing her hold on the end of the bandage, she stood back, relieved it no longer bled.

Thomas lowered his head, sobbing, "Thank God."

"Father is overcome with grief," Martha said, bending down to pick up 'old trusty'. She shook the old musket and said, "All of our spirits are not broken, though!"

"Yes," Denison said. "I see."

"My children!" Butler suddenly said. "They all lay dead upon the field or suffering at the hands of our merciless enemies as we speak!" His head fell slowly to his chest. His wife raised her hand, cupping his chin. Lifting it, she stared soulfully into his eyes.

"As I said," Denison said. "No one is to blame, least of all the dead and dying. It is for the living that we must be strong now."

A babe cried for attention. Raising his eyes in astonishment, Butler stared at the babe his wife held. "I thank God Hannah and Lord are in Connecticut," he said, looking soulfully at his babe and wife. He locked eyes with Denison. "What do you think they shall do? How much time do you think we have?"

"Not long!" Martha Bennett interrupted. "Indian Butler will have all our hair stretched across scalp hoops if given the chance!"

"Martha!" her father scolded her from his dark corner. "Mind your place, daughter!"

"It is only the truth!" Martha said. "We must face it!"

"I am afraid she is right," Denison said. "Zebulon, you must take your family and depart as soon as possible. I very much doubt Indian Butler can curb the savages' rage against a Continental Officer of the Line. You must depart with all due haste, as well as the rest of the soldiers of the Line. Jenkins should leave also, for they are not showing any mercy."

"The savages' rage!?!" Mrs. Bennett gasped. "What of their blue-eyed brethrens' rage, it is twice as intense!"

"That is enough from both of you!" Thomas Bennett said, this time stepping boldly from the shadows. Marching to the table, he slammed his clenched fist on it. "Do not disturb these officers again!"

Both women shook their heads and sank down to the floor next to a groaning Rufus. "It is our hair, too," Martha scoffed under her breath. Her mother's stern look silenced her before her father could scold her again. He glared at her with an equally stern look.

Butler perked up in his chair, wiping the hair from his eyes. Leaned toward Denison, he rubbed his chin. "What of terms?" he asked. "Are you to accept the terms that I have thus far rejected?"

"I shall try to get the best terms possible in our present

situation," Denison answered. "But no matter what the terms, I would not trust your life, or the lives of the men of the Line, to Indian Butler. After all, what would we do if the shoe were on the other foot? Our men would hang him instantly, along with all his officers."

"Yes," Butler said, slowly nodding his head. "I agree." He looked to a young lad standing by the door listening intently to every word. "You, lad," he said. "Tell Lieutenant Jenkins to have Lieutenant Pierce assemble his men and depart for Fort Augusta at once, but be mindful to draw the least attention to his actions, as not to upset the good people. And fetch my mount at once."

"Yes sir," the lad said, his eyes alive with the importance of his task. He exited the cabin, almost stumbling over his own feet in his haste.

Butler stood and ran a hand through his disheveled hair, placing his hat squarely over it. Nodding to his wife, he gathered her and the babe together. He bent down to a few hasty pouches and things his wife had collected to helped her lift them, throwing the oddest part of her collection, a feather tick, over his shoulder. Bowing his head to Denison, he led his wife and babe to the door.

Denison followed, helping his own wife with a few of the Butlers' pouches.

The lad stood dutifully beside the colonel's mount outside the door. Butler nodded to him and to Jenkins standing by his side. Jenkins acted like he wanted to say something, but Butler's stern look warned him not to protest any of his decisions. The decision had been made.

Butler turned his eyes from the probing young lieutenant and plopped the feather tick over the back of his horse. The lad helped him hastily tie it secure and tie the pouches to it. "This is all that is left of our lives in Wyoming," Butler growled under his breath, more to himself than to anyone else. Turning to his wife, he handed the babe to Jenkins before letting Zebulon lift her onto the horse's back. After waiting for Butler to mount the overloaded animal, Jenkins passed the crying babe up to his anxious mother. Wanting to speak. he held his words once more, noticing huge tears flowing down Mrs. Butler's cheeks.

Butler cleared his throat, swallowing hard against the great lump in his dry throat. "We shall repair to Fort Allen, Nathan," he said. "That is where you can find me. I shall try to assemble some resistance and aid from the good people there and return as soon as possible."

"Yes, my dear friend," Denison said. "I hope to see you again."

"Oh, you shall," Butler said, locking eyes with all around him. "If any brute touches a hair on any of these innocents' heads the retribution shall be threefold! This I promise you all!"

## Chapter Seventy
### *Queen Esther's Rock*

The lingering light of day slowly gave way to the dark veil of night. Deep shadows slid across the battlefield. Small fires flickered to life all over it in man's haste to keep the day from ending; some of the men at least, the victors of the field. To them this day of triumph seemed much too short, but oddly enough, this day would live in the hearts of the vanquished and defeated much longer than in their hearts, forever etched in their descendants', and therefore the new nation's, heart forever.

But at this moment, the heightened sense of victory surging through the victorious braves' hearts seemed infinite and everlasting. They congealed around certain fires which grew with an intensity born of their heightened emotions, which seemed only to be appeased by committing acts born of the same fires in their hearts, which in turn brought them victory in the first place. The Gods called for their pound of flesh and they more than happily obliged them. They dragged many struggling prisoners to the fires, tomahawking some of the more stubborn before they reached the fires to add to the reeking and bloody scalps hanging about their belts and filling their pouches. All of their eyes glowed and their hearts pounded with the thrill of victory. It would not be denied. It would have its fill of Yankee blood this day.

Groans and screams mixed with their yelps and hoots of triumph, filling the air with a strange mingled roar. Naked men tethered to poles at the center of huge fires danced from the flames, prodded mercilessly by spear points. Many other posts father away from the hot flames held others tied tight to them with leather thongs. Smaller flames on the points of many pine splinters poked in every inch of their bodies, slowly burned down to their skin, triggering horrible screams of anguish. The screams brought hearty laughs from their tormentors. The laughs seemed a tonic to the victorious warriors, easing all their angst and proving their superiority to the Yankees, for this day at least.

One dark place along the river lay just far enough below the proper field of battle to provide a certain air of privacy for one particular act of vengeance. A lone Indian Queen stood atop a large boulder dressed only in a loincloth, her bare, well formed, and painted breasts glistening in the light of a large fire blazing and crackling near it. Large white circles encased her dark eyes which bore a solid, deep, stare of pure vengeance. Except for large white swirls painted about her breasts, solid black paint covered the rest of her body, mingling with the darkness so well as to only show the whites of her eyes and swirls from a distance. Beyond, the light danced off the nearby river, speckling its face.

She danced in strange convulsing motions atop the rock, wielding a war club up to the heavens to beseech the Great Spirit's blessing upon it. She screeched and rambled in a strange tongue, drawing curious braves to her antics atop the great rock. They gathered about the rock, lured by the

Queen into bringing their crestfallen captives to her rock. They then stood patiently and watched their dark queen, awaiting her command to bring forth the objects of their scorn. Her war club represented all of their angst against the headstrong and stubborn Yankee interlopers. The justice potentially rendered by it represented all of their desires for justice.

She danced for the longest time, a show in itself, which only attracted more braves to her rock. Seeming to be finally satisfied by the number of offerings the braves collected, she jerked and jumped a few more times before collapsing onto the rock in total exhaustion. Her face fell to the face of the rock and her long fingernails scratched along it. Rolling her convulsing body upwards, she rose like a snake rising from the dark pits of hell atop the rock. A lone guttural command rose from her lungs. The warriors turned toward the huddled and tightly bond prisoners held just beyond the rock, forming them in a long single line of death before the Queen atop the rock.

Sneers greeted the line of crestfallen men, none more intense than those of the strange Queen dancing atop the rock. She collapsed down onto the rock before their eyes, slithering, caressing, and fondling it, laying her entire writhing body on it. Her dark locks twirled and fell over her face, their ends wisping over the face of the rock. With a spine-tingling screech, her head slowly rose from the rock. The dark hair parted, revealing heartless eyes full of rage. Some of the prisoners instinctively stepped back, only to be prodded back into line by spear points. Others bowed their heads in total grief, suddenly aware of the eyes of death staring at them from atop the rock.

A young Yankee screamed in terror, twisting free from the hands holding him. He immediately bolted, running with his arms flailing madly in the air. A dozen warriors quickly chased him down and subdued the desperate lad. Wrestling the crying soul to the ground, they dragged him kicking and screaming back to the rock.

The other prisoners stood aghast at the sight of the boy rolling, crying, and pleading for his life. One of the warriors pleaded with the boy in broken English to be still, because of his hair suddenly turning white he would not be harmed, for it showed his great magic. No harm would befall him because of it. All he would have to do would be to calm down and take his place in front of the line. The Queen would honor him. The Great Spirit would honor him.

The boy stared with stark eyes at the warrior and finally ceased sobbing and wriggling against his guards. He stood, all the while being assured by the warrior he had nothing to fear. The warrior ushered him to the rock, urging him to take a few steps toward the Queen now standing full and erect upon it. The boy's legs still trembled, but he stepped forward anyway, his eyes mesmerized by the sight of the strange queen. With one fluid and smooth motion the Queen swung her war club in a great arc, shattering the boy's skull. His body twitched, trembled, then rolled off the rock. The lad's eyes danced wildly in his head, watching the blood pour down over his face for an awful moment before he fell limp to the ground, much to the delight of the warrior. He whooped danced about, praising the Queen for bringing justice to Wyoming again. Leaning down to the boy, he quickly sliced part of his scalp away with his sharp knife, moving and convulsing even more than the Queen atop the rock. The warrior wailed all the more. Apparently, honor held a different meaning to his like.

The other Indians whooped and wailed with him. The Queen stood to her full height atop the rock, raising her bloody war club to the heavens, her body jerking in ecstasy.

Several of the captives suddenly felt their knees grow weak. They collapsed, only to be jerked angrily back to their feet. Several started to mutter a prayer on their trembling lips, much to the amusement and wonderment of the warriors.

The Queen turned her scornful eyes to them, eyes alive with contempt for the blasphemous words. In her eyes the prayers came from unworthy lips, and therefore must be silenced immediately. She gestured at the captives with her bloody war club. The warriors promptly forced one of the chanting prisoners forward, laying him at the center of the rock with his back facing against it. A painted hand gruffly grabbed his hair, pulling his head back against the hard rock.

He stared up in terror at the painted demon standing over him. Behind her sneering painted face a tapestry of stars shone in the heavens. "Lord," he chanted over and over, much to the Queen's growing disgust. He watched the war club, shaped like a bird's head with a huge ball in its beak, descend from the heavens to his face. All then went instantly dark.

The Queen screeched, twisting her body in ecstasy. "Gencho!" she chanted over and over toward the high heavens. She looked down to see a fresh white face staring back up to her in absolute horror. Raising the war club, she brought in down on the skull with all her might. It exploded, spewing grey matter all over everyone in the immediate vicinity. For a heartbeat all stopped. All eyes shot to the shattered skull.

Two prisoners near the end of the line immediately took advantage of the sudden lull. In fits of superhuman strength, spurned by pure desperation, they threw off their guards. One sprinted one way in the dark night and the other one sprinted the other way.

The warriors, momentarily confused, watched both white devils part and run, not sure which prize proved the most precious to subdue and return to the rock. The Queen's screams broke their confusion. Several warriors immediately sprang after the fleeing men, four one way, three the other.

Lebbeus Hammond's feet thundered under him. He never ran so fast in all his life. He leapt and sprinted past surprised Indians on the trail, leaving them in confusion before rushing away from them. He ran inland, away from the heavily patrolled river, hoping and praying over the loud thuds of his heart to find deliverance in the mountains. Cries of warning to the Indians to his front suddenly rang from behind him. In the pale moonlight, he noticed several warriors turn around far in front of him. He instantly turned and ran pell-mell back the way he came, once again bursting through stunned Indian women and children meandering along the trail laden with all sorts of plunder.

His mind raced. He kept running, not knowing to where exactly, but a moving target proved the hardest to hit and capture. Any destination away from the mad Indian Queen and her rock would do. Rifles suddenly cracked to his front. Balls whizzed past him. Sliding down to the ground, he stared at the yelling demons rushing toward him. He instantly popped up and ran for the marsh, realizing it to be his only sanctuary. Running through a great field of rye separating him from it, he crisscrossed the many trails cutting through it in a vain effort to confuse his tormentors. He did not turn back to look at them, somehow feeling their proximity through his heightened senses. The thud of their closing footsteps vibrated through his bones.

Stumbling up a slight rise and into a sudden growth of thick pines, his feet suddenly flew out from under him from the slick matting of pine needles under the trees. Groaning in frustration, he turned to face his closing foes. In total desperation, he gripped the nearest branch and snapped it from the tree, amazed at his sudden strength to snap the springy pine. Snapping it in two again, he ran his hands to the hard knot at the end of it. Twirling it around his hands, he stood ready to crack skulls with it, or die trying.

Scratching away the pine needles with his feet, he braced himself, standing just within the shadows leading from the trail into the pine grove. His fingers clenched the pine branch, ready to bring it into play. To his astonishment, the braves stopped just before the grove and peered into its dark shadows, seeming reluctant to proceed. Two of them dropped their rifles and fell to their knees, panting desperately for air. The third still stared into the foreboding shadows. After considering them for a long moment, he turned toward a fork in the trail leading downriver. Craning his neck, he peered into the pines again, squinting to try and focus on them. Nervously scratching his head, he panted, trying to catch his own rushed breaths.

The others raised their heads and grabbed up their rifles. They looked to the third man for his assessment of the situation. Looking back to them, he only shook his head, then grunted and rolled his eyes, poking his tomahawk toward the pale moon, then down to the ground. One of the others looked up the trail toward the fork, then slowly back to the spooky pines. He felt something in there, something foreboding, not seeming quite human. Frowning, he pointed his rifle to the trail leading downriver. The others nodded toward the spooky pines, grunting in agreement. They then ran to the downriver trail, away from the pines.

Lebbeus stared in disbelief at the empty trail before him. Gasping for breath, he suddenly realized he held his breath in anticipation of battle. He let his fingers relax on the pine branch. He smelled the aroma of the pines, breathing it in deeply. Lifting the pine knot up to his face, he stared at it in wonder, savoring its sweet aroma like a new babe drawing its first breath. That is how he felt in this moment; reborn.

He listened intently, his ears keenly aware of all sounds instead of those just around him. Cries echoed from the plain below. Voices of all kinds slid through the darkness, some wailing in triumph, others tinged with horror. Confused thoughts flooded his mind. Visions of the well-ordered ranks firing and advancing in unison flashed amid other visions of green-coated and painted men suddenly erupting all around them as if born of the earth itself. The painted men darted through the smoke in his mind again, waylaying everyone around him. Men clutched their bleeding heads and tumbled to the ground, groaning and writhing in pain. Others heads simply exploded from well aimed shots. All of the visions gave way to the painted Indian Queen dancing atop the rock. The same rock bloodied with his friends' blood and splattered with their very brains. For a moment all the flashing visions stupefied him. The chatter of quick, almost clicking, guttural noises tore his eyes to the trail and away from the horrid visions.

Two Indian women strolled nonchalantly down the trail. One held a brightly colored tablecloth in her hands, eagerly showing it to her friend. Her friend laughed and held up her own trophies, a new pot and metal spoons. The silver spoons clinked in her hands and glistened in the pale moonlight. They both laughed loudly and continued walking without so much as a passing glance at the white man standing with his mouth agape in the trail leading into the pine grove.

Lebbeus watched them disappear down the trail in wonderment. Clutching the pine knot to his chest, he backed into the dark and shielding folds of the pines. He instantly turned and ran down the trail, relieved to find it passed by the edge of the marsh; his sanctuary.

He darted off the trail and into the marsh, seeking out its thickest portions in which to hide. Finally locating a particularly thick clump of tangled vegetation, he eased his way into it, carefully positioning the branches and leaves to shield him from prying eyes. He eased down into the muck of the marsh, suddenly filled with a strange sense of exhilaration. He lived! If he stayed quiet and still, he might just live through this living nightmare! His mind swirled with new plots of escape. When the far off yells and whoops died and the flickering fires dimmed in the encroaching night, he figured to skirt the mountains and make his way south. South to freedom! South to civilization!

Joseph Elliot sprang over a high fence before him in one great leap, fueled by a desperate thirst for dear life itself. His feet struck the ground and he instantly burst into a dead run; only this time no rushed breaths sounded behind him. He glanced back out of the corner of his eye to witness his tormentors struggling to climb over the fence. The whiz about his ears and the flash from several of the painted demons' firelocks hastened his feet all the more. He ran pell-mell over the battlefield, leaping over dead bodies and the litter of human conflict. Finally, the rush of the river sounded in front of him in the foreboding darkness, deafening the closing cries to his rear. Tumbling head over heals down the bank, he leaped from the muddy bank and into the swirling and dark waters. Choking down and spitting out great gulps of water, his hands and feet struck and madly kicked through it. He tried to listen past the splashes and the loud thudding of his heart in his ears. Cries of anger sounded from the shore, accented by the sharp report of several firelocks. Balls hissed through the water around him. Putting his head down, he swam with all his might for the far shore, and freedom.

A sudden and sharp pain rolled him over in the water. Quickly steadying himself in the swirling waters with his other arm, he looked to the trail of red pouring from his arm in the moonlit waters. His arm burned intensely, but he still paddled from the other little gouts of water erupting over the water's surface. Yells from the far shore sent a fresh burning sense of anger surging through his veins. "No!" he yelled, gazing to the shore but a rod away. Furiously kicking his legs, he pulled at the water, fueled by a new sense of outrage. The shore seemed so close! Victory from the demons lay just a few strokes and kicks away! He must not surrender to death yet! He must not!

The fingers of his hand finally felt the muddy bottom and he let his legs sink down to the bottom. Rising, he splashed frantically for the shore. Bullets thudded into the muddy bank around him. Cradling his burning and bleeding arm, he scrambled up the bank. The sharp cracks from the opposite shore suddenly increased. Balls cracked through the nearby branches of trees. Stumbling through the trees to a large oak, he scrambled behind it. Flattening himself against its rough bark, he waited for the thudding and cracking balls to cease. Soon only the distant cries of some poor unfortunates still lying on the field echoed in the still night air.

The pain in his shoulder suddenly intensified. He looked down to the warm sensation dripping from the end of his fingers and blanched at the sight of his life's blood pouring from his burning and throbbing shoulder. Ripping off his soaked shirt, he wrapped it tight around his upper shoulder, holding it fast until it slowed the flow of blood.

Collapsing down against the trunk of the tree, he pondered his plight. The stark look in Lebbeus Hammond's eyes flashed through his mind. Some unspoken call for survival flashed through his eyes just before the war club spattered their comrade's brains all over that bloody rock and stunned all around it. In that moment of confusion lay their only avenue of escape, and somehow both men knew it, responding to its call instinctively and at the same moment, further confusing their Indian guards. Just a fraction of a second sooner he felt certain both of them would have shared the fate of poor William Buck, whom had spurted from the rock only a few moments before and had been brought back to meet a cruel death. The boy had just turned seventeen. What a waste.

The throbbing pain quickly demanded his full attention again, tearing him from his thoughts. But then one face flashed through his mind's eye again, a painted face, based in black with white circles surrounding its dark eyes. Eyes he knew. Eyes, which, though masked with hate, still shone familiar to him. Esther's eyes. Esther, quiet and unassuming before these troubled times, now turned into a mad demon by war. Those dark eyes of betrayal still burned in his soul. He feared they would haunt him forever. He feared the war to haunt him forever.

Blocking the horrid visions from his mind, he pushed his feet against the ground, raising himself up against the rough tree trunk. Leaning against the tree, he looked all around with darting eyes. Fort Wilkes-Barre lie just to the south, he reasoned. He must reach it or lay here and bleed to death. Stumbling through the trees, he soon came across the road leading to Wilkes-Barre. He plowed headlong down the road in a daze. The further he crept down the road, the heavier his feet felt. Soon he merely shuffled down the road, forcing one foot forward after the other, chanting on his tired breaths "The fort lie just ahead, just ahead. Must keep moving. Must keep moving."

Through his daze he stumbled onward. For a strange moment he thought of angels. He somehow felt a strange presence urging his heavy feet forward. He raised his eyes, but his swirling vision offered no insight. In his delirium, he beseeched the angels to help this poor soldier of the battle, muttering a solemn prayer on his failing breaths. His mind felt as if it floated in his skull, but he kept up the prayer and his frantic urges kept his feet shuffling along, one slow step after another. He prayed most earnestly, vesting all his faith in each word.

A call abruptly sounded through his daze. He shuffled toward it, but his failing legs sent him to the ground. He tumbled and rolled over, rising again to an angelic voice urging him onwards, hoping to find relief in its beatific tones. Clutching his burning arm, he prayed. His mind drifted, but he scolded himself back to the presence of the angels. Rolling back and forth, he beseeched the angels to come forth and save him. A loud distant creak answered his pleas. Forcing his eyes open, he stared into the starlit sky. A face suddenly appeared above him, staring down at him with heart-felt sympathy.

"It's Joseph Elliot!" the face announced. "Dear God, he's covered with blood from head to foot, he is!"

Arms reached down to him, lifting him from the earth.

"Angels," he muttered under his breath. "Angels."

"That's the first time I've heard you called that, Doctor Smith!" a voice announced.

"He's delirious," another voice answered. "He's lost a great deal of blood. We must get him into the fort with posthaste!"

Joseph relaxed, letting the angels lift him up and carry him into the fort, all the while praising them.

"Be quiet man," Doctor Hooker said to the delirious man. He hastily directed the men carrying the man into Fort Wilkes-Barre. "Let the angels go, Joseph, they have delivered you safely, now let them go to do the same for other poor souls still breathing on that forsaken field."

"Yes," Joseph agreed, suddenly recognizing the voice. He soon felt the welcoming comfort of cool straw on his back. "Must let the angels go," he muttered before drifting off into a deep sleep. "Must let the angels go."

## Chapter Seventy One
*Carey's Adoption*

Sam Carey walked with his head bowed, trying in vain to shield his eyes from the horrible sights around him. An occasional angry tug to his tether raised his eyes, but he quickly lowered them to the ground again. His heart ached and his empty stomach heaved from the glimpses of misery passing on the ground below him. He ignored the festive cheers of his captors and wondered how anyone could draw joy from such a place of total misery. Only the small pot-marked faced Indian holding his tether did not scream or wail. His one good eye darted around nonchalantly, too haunted by some deeper thought to pay heed to the misery.

An overwhelming odor suddenly lifted Carey's eyes from the ground. The acrid smell of death hung in the air, despite his short breaths attempting to expel it. The culprit of the unearthly and rancid smell soon showed ahead of him atop the burned ruins of Fort Wintermoot. A body stood black and burned, but oddly in the manner of a pugilist, still defiant even in death. A few scattered fits of flame illuminated it against the other shadows. Wisps of smoke still rose from the burned hair of the poor man. Carey looked to the face, but could not recognize any of its features. He still stared at it, unable to turn his eyes from the charred man standing with his arms raised in death, inviting his tormentors to a challenge. He had never seen or imagined such a thing. War brought horror to everything it touched. Cruelty bred odd sights.

Suddenly slipping, he looked down to the blood soaked ground and followed its trail to a mangled and headless corpse lying but a few feet away. He winced and moaned piteously before a sharp tug urged him onward.

The pot-marked faced Indian cocked his lone eye back to him, seeming annoyed by his charge's rash movements. His eye darted to the fort and then to the corpse which seemed to annoy the white man so. "Te-te!" he said with another angry tug at the tether tied to his neck. The Indians following to his rear grunted loud disapprovals and walked around them, though without yells and wails of triumph this time.

"It is Captains Bidlack and Ransom!" an anguished voice cried from the trees beyond the fort. "Be sure you remember all you see if perchance you should survive this hell!"

Carey looked to the trees just beyond a great fire in front of them. The flames reached up, singing many a leaf dancing on branches in the faint breeze. The flames reflected off the faces of the poor souls tied tightly to the trees. Two Tory guards sat near the fire with their muskets by their sides. One of them cast an angry gaze back to the soul speaking out, sternly warning him to mind his tongue.

The warriors, especially their leader, paid no heed to the white Tories and their prisoners. One of them gestured with his spear to a noisy celebration up the trail. The others nodded and with a sharp tug to urge on their prisoner, trod onward. In no time they marched into a huge clearing lit by many fires and filled with festive people.

Women cheerfully greeted them with glowing smiles, holding up bright cloth, looking glasses, and other forms of prized plunder. Warriors danced around many a fire behind them, most holding scalps up in the moonlit sky. Others feasted and examined many newly acquisitioned rifles, swords, tomahawks, and others spoils of war taken from their defeated foes. The ground lay littered with pottery, dinnerware, and other implements of daily life. Wails greeted new parties returning from cabins and the battlefield laden with plunder. All, young and old, seemed overcome with their great success. Carey looked to a party passing them on horses, trying to spy their pale-faced brethren, but with most of them also having painting their faces, it seemed impossible to distinguish them from their tawny allies. They, too, seemed to share the Indians' ecstasy over victory.

His captor nodded his head and grunted an approval to each one greeting him holding their plunder high and wailing at the top of their lungs. He cocked his head strangely to a woman demanding he give his prisoner up for torture. Staring at the woman as if she had lost her mind and all her senses, he waved her off and kept marching to a far corner of the field. The woman's bickering fell on deaf ears and she soon turned, rambling off to a fire and cursing the warrior with every breath.

They rambled toward a few pine-bough lean-tos nestled in front of a few blazing fires on the far edge of the field. Strangely clad medicine men danced about the front of each of the lean-tos while grieving women wailed and cried about them. Incense and smoke wafted from under the lean-tos and from little pots smoking in the medicine men's hands. Unnerving chatter sounded from most of the medicine men, others remained strangely silent and still, as if talking to God himself. The pot-marked faced Indian led them to the latter.

A green-coated man sauntered up in their path, stopping full in front of the tethered Yankee. "So you!" he exclaimed, his eyes bulging in his head. He pointed an accusing finger under Carey's nose. "So you are the fellow, are you, that threatened to comb my hair!?!" Throwing off his leather cap, he tugged at his long locks, gesturing toward one of the many scalp dances around the field. His eyes widened even further and a cruel and sinister smile slid across his face, raising his dropping jowls. A tug at the tether pulled Carey away from the odd man, much to his relief, for the Tory's fowl breath nearly gagged him. The Tory laughed behind him and marched away, seeming glad to have vented his grief to at least one Yankee, for live ones seemed to be becoming a more rarer commodity with each passing moment. "Be glad you have Roland Montour to look after you, or I'd have yer hair fer sure, I would!" he called loudly over his shoulder.

Montour scoffed at the man, pulling Carey to one of the lean-tos. Abruptly stopping, he stared down at a lone figure lying on a huge bearskin spread inside the dark lean-to. A worried-looking medicine man rubbed a paste of herbs onto a gaping wound in the man's upper left chest. A few women sat on either side of the man, whimpering and holding their clenched fists to their faces. The Indian Montour looked cautiously at the medicine man.

The medicine man noticed his stare and slowly shook his head.

"*Cocaneuquo,*" Montour said, bending down and stepping into the dark lean-to. Grabbing the wounded man's right hand, he held it tight to his quivering lips. The man smiled and nodded to him. Montour bowed his head in grief, gesturing toward a mystified Carey. "He," he said purposely in English, "is strong and brave! He shall take your place in our lodge!" He bit his lip, barely containing his absolute grief. The women wailed.

*Cocaneuquo* nodded, turning his soulful eyes to Carey.

Montour exploded with grief, collapsing and laying his head on the man's chest. The women wailed all the louder, running their soothing hands over both of the men's heads. The medicine man started chanting, raising a small smoking pot to the heavens. Fanning the smoke into the lean-to, he danced around the front of it.

A similar scene played out in the other lean-tos. A sudden high piercing wail sounded from the one just to their side. A pair of stout braves promptly appeared before it, gently lifting a dead body from underneath it. Gently placing the body on a brightly colored tablecloth, they rolled the body up in it. Lifting the body up, they slowly marched toward the marsh with a bevy of wailing women following them.

Cary stared at the smaller brave bringing up the rear carrying a shovel. Somehow it seemed out of place in his hands. He remembered an even more curious sight of Indians collecting many digging implements earlier. Perhaps his comrades' rifles proved more accurate than they thought. But it made no difference now, dead is dead, and grief is grief, no matter what color the skin..

## Chapter Seventy Two
*Back from the dead*

The sentry perked up, peering over the pointed logs. Something moved up the road, something coming from that horrible field. The last of the survivors rambled through the gate a while ago, followed by an eerie wail sounding from the trees beyond. Forbidden to shoot at anything but a sure target to conserve ammunition, they had had to let the demons scream and taunt them from the trees. It did not settle well with any of them. Raising his rifle to the wall, he leveled it at a figure approaching in the darkness, outlined by the pale moonlight. If one feather showed on his head, they would all fire. They would all strike a blow for their fallen brethren still screaming on that horrible field. Yes, they would!

"Hold steady," Lieutenant Jenkins ordered, suddenly appearing at his side. The lieutenant seemed to be everywhere along the wall.

The sentry pulled back the hammer in spite of the lieutenant. The cry for vengeance rang louder in his ears than the exhausted lieutenant's commands.

"I said hold!" Jenkins ordered again, clutching the sentry's arm. Staring at the wide-eyed man, he shook his head. "We must keep our heads," he added, looking down to the man approaching the gate. "Especially now."

"Don't fire!" suddenly rang out from further down the wall. "It's Hollenback, it is!"

Jenkins released the man's arm, quickly rambling toward the ladder. He slid down it, running to the gate cracking open in the darkness to receive one of their own, one seeming to return from the dead.

"See!' one of the wide-eyed old men at the gate said. "It is him! It's Hollenback in the flesh!"

Hollenback squeezed through the slight opening in the gate gasping, "Yes, it is I, in what is left of my flesh!"

One of the men, rubbing his tired eyes clear, seemed overjoyed at the sight of the man back from the dead. He grabbed Hollenback's hand, profusely shaking it. His smile stretched from ear to ear. "My God it is good to see you, old man, we thought you lost with the rest!" Jenkins said, releasing the man's hand upon seeing his bloody shoulder.

"It is good to see you all too, my friends," Hollenback said to the overjoyed faces greeting him.

"Pittston Fort!" Jenkins suddenly blurted out. "What do you know of it? Have you any word of it?"

"No, John," Hollenback said, eagerly excepting a drink of cider from one of the men. Another looked to his arm, waving for a boy to fetch him a blanket upon witnessing his rags and nakedness. "I know nothing of it," he added after taking a long drink.

Jenkins' face lost what little color it had gained. His eyes sank in deep sorrow.

"Beth, is it?" Hollenback asked. A great pity rose in his chest. "I am sure she is fine. Captain Blanchard's no fool. She's in good hands!"

Jenkins shook his head, suddenly ashamed of his selfish feelings in light of what this poor man leaning against the gate before him must have endured this day. "Yes," he said, "I am sure she is, but what of you, my friend?"

"It was terrible," Hollenback said. "Captain Durkee is lost for sure, along with most of the other officers and men." Shaking his head, he looked down to his naked lower body. "What of Solomon Bennett?" he asked. "After I braved the river, lost a guinea in the river, by the way, I did, well anyways, I had not a stitch of clothing, nor a shilling to my name. I do not know which made me the most uncomfortable. I soon met Solomon in the woods on the way to this place and he gave me the shirt off his very back, he did at that, the fine lad."

"He," Jenkins said, "and all the Bennett men, left this very hour with Colonel Butler and the few surviving Continentals. We all thought it best should we be forced to capitulate."

"Capitulate!?!" Hollenback gasped. "I hope not to that vicious lot out there! I tell you we will find no quarter with them! All of the Continentals of the Line have left, you say? How many survived?"

"Fifteen in all."

"Have you a shot of rum for a parched throat, and soul?"

"Certainly," Jenkins said, ushering the man to one of the cabins. They clambered over people sleeping everywhere to a corner of the cabin. Jenkins moved a few things on a shelf, finally producing a leather jack. "It's my own personal stock," he explained. "Now drink up, man." Hollenback took a great gulp and looked to Jenkins rummaging through a sack near the shelf. He produced a pair of breeches, passing them to Hollenback.

"Why, thank you," Hollenback said, lowering the leather jack and smacking his lips. "That's what I'm taking about." The blanket slipped down from his wounded shoulder and his eyes glanced at it. He suddenly winced with pain.

Jenkins promptly produced a long strip of linen and gestured for the man to sit below the shelf, the only spot in the crowded cabin not covered with snoring people. "It's my spot," he said, tying the bandage fast. He made his way to the hearth, scooping a great helping of the stew from a pot hanging near the fire into a long rectangular bowl. "There you be, man" he said, passing the trencher to Hollenback's eager hands.

"Why, thank you fine," Hollenback said, scooping his mouth full with a wooden spoon. "Butler's departed with all of the men of the Line and then some, eh?" he asked through gulps of food.

"Yes, but if they were to be caught, it would mean the loose no matter what the terms, we all felt certain of it."

"Certain, eh? Well I'm certain not to give up this land soaked with my very blood so easily! We have a strong fort! Double thick walls!"

"Yes, but that was both of the colonels' decision."

"Well, that may be fine as it may be, but I intend to do all I can to save this land and these poor women and children!"

"Keep your voice down, friend, do you wish to cause a panic more than there already is?" A few sleeping people shifted on the floor. Jenkins waited until they settled before he continued speaking, though he fully suspected many feigned sleep and listened to their every word. "Many have been pouring out the south gate and the lower settlements all evening, taking the lower road for Fort Allen, Easton, and the like."

Hollenback's eyes suddenly lowered. "Damn," he said. "All of my life is in this valley, both future and present! My dear wife is at Pittston Fort, too, you know, but I thought it best to join the main force."

"Yes, I know, but what are we to do against such odds?"

"Increase the odds, instead of lessening them, as Butler and Denison have, my friend." Perking his head up, he glared at Jenkins. "Have you a rifle and a horse, my good man?" he asked.

"Yes," Jenkins quickly answered, nodding his head to a line of firelocks leaning against the wall.

Rising, Hollenback stumbled toward the firelocks, almost tripping over the people lying on the floor. One of them rose after him, seeming animated by Hollenback's fine spirit.

"Hageman?" Jenkins asked the man. "What are you about?"

"I'm with him," Hageman said, nodding to Hollenback. He pulled down to straighten his crumpled buckskin shirt and bent down to picked up his wide-brimmed slouch hat. Straightening, he grabbed his rifle and pouch from a peg along the wall. "I'm not about sitting around waiting to have me scalp lifted! I like me hair where it is."

"Have you any provisions?" Hollenback asked, turning to the man while checking the action of one of the firelocks.

"Me pouch is full of jerked venison and biscuits, as well as plenty of shot and powder," Hageman boasted, holding up his pouch and powder horn.

"Fine, my good man," Hollenback said. "That will do!" He winced against the pain of his burning shoulder, but quickly quelled it with his great sense of determination. "Someone must do something to save this settlement," he told himself against his pain. Turning about, he marched out the cabin door with Hageman and Jenkins in tow.

"Shouldn't you report to Colonel Denison first, or at least have your wound looked at by Doctor Gustin?" Jenkins asked.

"Denison be damned!" Hollenback said. "A man must do what he thinks best, despite what others may think! It is the true measure of a man in the end! The truth, Lieutenant, is seen different by all, but I have the utmost confidence in my vision! We must hasten Spalding onward!"

"Very well," Jenkins said, quelling the urge to join him. He happened to be needed here, and did not know of the colonel's plans yet, which he silently feared leaned strongly toward capitulation, even after all they had seen of their ruthless enemy. But he still commanded the fort, and in such, had to wait on his superior's word. But then one thought, that of his dear Beth, made him reconsider. He marched toward the stables beside Hollenback and ran his hands nervously over a horse's flanks.

"Is this not Major Garrett's mount?" Hollenback asked.

"It is," Jenkins said. "But he will have no more need of it."

Both Hollenback and Hageman cast an odd gaze at him.

"Well, he was a fine man," Hollenback said, motioning for a tired boy standing nearby to saddle it. "And such is his mount."

Hageman wasted no time in saddling his own mount and then help the struggling boy saddle Hollenback's jittery horse. Slapping the saddle, he nodded to Hollenback to mount. With Jenkins' aid he climbed into the saddle atop the jittery horse.

"Are you sure of this mount?" Jenkins asked. "It came at full gallop to the gate as if the devil himself were at its tail, still jittery, it is."

"As we all are," Hollenback said, laying his rifle across the saddle to his front. "He's seen the face of battle and has survived. He'll settle down soon and be fine, as well as the men here abouts, if we can only convince them to stay." He looked down to Jenkins. "That is what I hope you shall do, my friend."

Recognizing the objection in Jenkins' eyes he added, "No, you must stay here, we need leveler heads about just now. Tell everyone I ride for Spalding and reinforcements."

Jenkins nodded and watched them gallop out the south gate, suddenly wishing for all the world he rode with them.

## Chapter Seventy Three
*The eerie shadows*

Captain Blanchard cautiously led his small scouting party along the bank of the river, careful to keep out of sight of the opposite shore, lest they invite the screaming hordes of Indians to his side of the river. The groans and cries echoing across the waters made his skin crawl. Raising his hand, he halted his small party near a particularly thick clump of tangled bushes. Waving his men forwards, they crawled under the bushes, cautiously peering through the shielding leaves to the far shore.

Fires flickered all over the opposite side of the river, seeming to stretch for a mile or so along the plain above the bank. Though trees and some bushes blocked their view, in some of the clear spots they clearly made out men silhouetted against the light from the flickering flames. The shadows moved oddly, some seeming to dance, while others jerked and jolted around the fires as if bond to them by some unseen force.

Blanchard put his hand to his pouch, producing a small spyglass. His eager men urgently awaited his word of just what transpired on the other side of the river, though the screams left little to the imagination. Curses and yells in English occasionally mixed with the Indians' hoots and hollers, filling all the men with a certain dread. Apparently white men played a part in the mayhem on the other shore. The thought caused all their hearts to sink in their chests.

Blanchard stared through the spyglass for the longest moment before lowering it from his shocked eye. Passing it to the nearest man, he said, "I can only make out the shadows, but it is not good. They appear to be torturing our men in the most cruel manner, tying them to burning posts, prodding them on with pine knots and such. I am glad they are too far away to make out any of the features of their faces, for I fear many a dear friend is being tortured over there."

"They're cutting the poor souls up and burning them alive!" the man next to receive the spyglass gasped. Rolling over, he lifted his wide eyes to the heavens, wishing to witness no more of the macabre sight. He eagerly passed the spyglass to the next man.

The next man grabbing the spyglass stared through it but a second before raising his rifle to fire. The click of its hammer drew Blanchard's attention. "Hold there, man!" he said. "Are you mad? They are much too far away to do any good! All you would draw from them is their ire! I warn you! Now lower that weapon!"

The man growled in frustration before pounding his fists into the ground. "Damn them!" he yelled. "Damn them all to hell."

"They seem to be making their own hell over there," the next man looking through the spyglass said.

"Are we to sit here and just do nothing!?!" another man asked after a particularly anguished cry crept through the air. "That man is crying with all his heart and soul to be heard at such a distance!"

"I am afraid all that can be done has been done," Blanchard answered. "What are we to do against such odds when four score our number has failed? Do you want to end up as those poor souls?"

"But Captain," a voice countered his remarks. "Hooker Smith is crossing the river with his *Reformadoes* at this very minute!"

"Yes," Blanchard said. "And if any man feels up to it, he may accompany him, but I am to stay here for our families in the fort. It will take far too long to get them all across the river, and the move would certainly invite an ambush, their favorite tactic. No, we best sit and wait until the Tory rats depart or reinforcements arrive. Then we shall see!"

The bark of several rifles drew everyone's attention back to the far shore. A few splashes in the water to their front unnerved the lot of them. All of the locks of their firelocks clicked back.

"Do not fire until you are sure of your mark," Blanchard said.

They all lay still with every itchy finger ready to squeeze their triggers. Soon the splashes ceased and all breathed a deep sigh of relief.

"Just think of it boys," someone said in the darkness. "If they hadn't stolen our canoes we'd be over there too."

"Such are the fortunes of war," Blanchard said. "We must not question the Lord's ways, but only do as he gives us the vision and knowledge to do. He has spared us thus far, for what, I know not, but we must abide by the faith he has given us. We must not lose faith, for it is all we have now."

Another man rolled over and faced about. "I wish not to see it anymore, just the same," he said. "I cannot bear this test of faith!"

"What are we to do if they try to cross the river in force?" another man asked.

"Pray harder than we ever have done, and aim well," Blanchard said. Lowering his rifle, he bowed his tired head over it.

"What shall we do if they besiege Forty Fort on the morrow?" the man nearest Blanchard asked him. "Are we to just sit safe on this side of the river whilst woman and children suffer as those poor souls do?"

"No!" Blanchard said, raising his head. "We shall go to their aid the best we can! We must!"

"Amen to that!" came a sharp reply.

The clouds in the night sky suddenly parted, letting the pale glow of the moon bathe and illuminate the entire plain before the men's sorrowful eyes. Struck by a strange sense of curiosity, tinged with a growing feeling of disgust, they stared at the figures silhouetted against the flames of the far away fires, thankful distance prevented them from recognizing any of the poor souls. Several naked men running around and through the flames attached by long tethers to poles in the middle of the huge fires caught all of their attention. No one reached for the spyglass, they saw just fine. Somehow their vision grew more acute under such circumstances, though many wished it did not. They watched the feathered heads of their tormentors dance about with long spears in their hands, prodding the naked men back into the flames. Around a few of the fires only feathered heads danced about in a strange frenzy, contorting their bodies and leaping in the air. Smaller shadows betrayed the presence of women and children.

"My God," one of the men finally gasped. "Them is women and children about some of them there fires. Raising them right smart, they is, ain't they? No wonder they seem so cruel! They's taught it!"

No one answered him. The horrid orgies continued. One man grabbed the spyglass.

"Are you insane?" the man near him scoffed. "You actually want to see their faces!?!"

"No," the man quickly answered, gesturing down the riverbank to a gathering around a rock under a huge oak. "There," he said, "look at that devil dancing about that rock, through the glass it appears to be a woman! I dare not wonder what mischief she is about?"

"She's creating her own little piece of hell," a voice answered.

Blanchard slowly slid the spyglass back into his pouch, suddenly overcome with a deep sense of shame. The pitiful cries from the opposite shore made him wince all the more. He glanced to the men lying to his side. Hollow eyes lit by the haunting moonlight shone back to him.

"It is enough," he said. A hollow and empty feeling filled his heavy heart, overcoming his whole body. He knew his men felt the same way. Sitting here witnessing the tortured shadows would do no one any good. One of his men coughed harshly, choking down the contents of his heaving stomach.

"Everyone up," Blanchard ordered. "We must return to the fort and take care of our people. There is nothing we can do for those poor souls across the river but pray for them. God have mercy on them."

A long mournful wail sounded in the night after they rose, stretching across the river and etching itself in the men's souls for what they feared to be forever. No one talked, but only hastened their steps to find relief from the lingering cries of misery, for the moment, at least.

## Chapter Seventy Four
*Pittston Fort*

Captain Blanchard watched the enemy scouts slither through the brush toward the blockhouse, not really surprised, but nonetheless somehow hoping against the odds to avoid the humiliation of capitulation. He looked over his shoulder to the men behind him. "Here they come," he said through a choked throat.

"How many, sir," a voice anxiously asked.

"Enough," Blanchard said. Peering through a slot in the wall of the blockhouse, he watched hordes of painted men and green-coated Tories spread out behind their scouts in every direction. A shrill war whoop suddenly echoed throughout the entire blockhouse, making everyone jump. Gasps filled the air. Children cried along with their mothers. Men's eyes nervously darted about, their hands clutching their firelocks. Several crowded around the firing slits and cursed out loud, doing little to settle the women's and children's angst.

"Now be calm!" Blanchard said. "It is all in the Lord's hands now. We must all pray for his mercy and protection now! They can do nothing to us if it is not his will! We must keep the faith, for it is all we have. Stand strong in our faith in the Lord! It is all we have!"

A hush fell over all. Heads bowed. Nervous lips mouthed silent prayers. Women swept the crying children up in their arms and gathered them all together, urging them to join them in prayer. Frustrated men stomped about and shook their heads in despair, with a few joining the women and children in prayer.

"You in the blockhouse!" a loud voice called in the tense air.

Blanchard stiffened his back and passed his rifle to one of the men. The man stared at him with questioning eyes, but knew any argument would prove fruitless. They did not have a chance and with what little food they had in the fort the enemy need only to wait them out. No, they had no choice, the man realized, looking to the huddled and frightened women and children. Blanchard read the man's eyes and nodded to him. Pulling down his hunting frock to straighten it, he swallowed hard against his pride. "I do it for the women and children," he said under his breath to the man.

The man slowly nodded and raised his lip. Watching the proud captain make the hardest walk of his life out of the blockhouse and to the stockade's gate he did not envy him in the least. Nor did anyone else, for he walked alone, bearing the weight of the shame for them all.

The gate slid open a sliver and Blanchard slipped through, only to have it quickly close behind him. The sound of the crossbeam sliding into place to hold the gate fast seemed the loneliest sound he ever heard. Looking back at it, he never felt so utterly alone in all his life. But duty called. He must turn to face it. Looking down to the ground, he swallowed hard against the growing lump in his throat, and turned to face his enemies, alone.

Taking a step into the sunlight, he raised his eyes to a sea of painted faces, all wearing the same look of utter disdain for him. Holding his head high he marched forward nonetheless. Duty demanded it. His faltering sense of pride demanded it. The Indians and their green-coated brethren parted upon his approach, funneling him into the heart of their gathering horde.

They stopped parting around a rather portly looking man standing with his thumbs cocked in his belt and staring at the advancing Yankee captain out of the corner of his eye. His lips rose in what seemed to be a perpetual look of contempt. Other men around him wore smart green uniforms, some sporting fine black leather caps with the letters *GR* engraved on a brass plate on their front. They seemed to pay deference to the portly man wearing a black hunting shirt with a handkerchief tied tight covering his head. A small gorget hanging about his neck glinted in the sunlight. It alone, the only thing besides the deference paid to him by the others, denoted his high rank. "You sir," the portly man finally said, raising his hand to halt the brash Yankee, "have a most pressing decision." He smacked his lips. "I shall not dilly-dally as they say, you know we command the whole valley, are to capitulate or are we to have more bloodshed, fine sir?"

Blanchard stared dead in his eyes, eventually smacking his own lips. "No," he said after the longest moment. "We shall discuss terms, sir. I believe we have spent enough time in the company of death."

"Very good, old man," the portly man said, suddenly smiling. Stepping forward he asked, "Do I have the pleasure of addressing Captain Blanchard?"

"Yes you do, fine sir," Blanchard said with a slight bow. His hand fell to the hilt of his sword.

The portly man noticed the Yankee officer's eyes roll into a hateful gaze to the faces surrounding them. Indians sneered and bared their teeth back at him. Several of the rangers spat on the ground. The portly man stiffened his back and bowed to the Yankee, stepping even closer. "I am Major Butler," he announced with a smart nod and courtly wave. "Now let us be about the business at hand, sir."

Blanchard's jowls dropped and a sour expression blanketed his face.

"Come now," Butler said. "There is nothing you can do. Wyoming has been defeated, further resistance on your part would prove quite futile, and foolish, I might add." Looking about, he spread his arms to the mean faces surrounding them. "Are you to have your women and children depend upon their mercies if you choose to continue this insane struggle?" he asked, gravely shaking his head. "I assure you they have no mercy, and after they do battle no one can do anything with them, for they will not be denied their spoils, and they shall do as they see fit."

Turning about, Blanchard looked back to the blockhouses and to the many eyes peering from firing slots toward them. "What of the women and children?" he asked, turning slowly back to the major.

"If all three blockhouses do immediately deliver up all ammunition, stores, and arms, the lives of the men, women, and children shall be preserved entirely," Butler flatly stated.

Blanchard took a deep breath. "If they are the terms, we shall offer no further resistance," he said almost on a whisper.

"Very well," Butler said, suddenly wincing from the memory of the long night before, especially the peculiar effluvium of burnt human flesh. He had barely slept a wink last night and remembered what he had told his lieutenants whom complained to him. "It is not in my power to help," he told them time and time again, and now he absentmindedly said it again to this rebel officer.

"Excuse me, sir?" Blanchard asked him curiously.

Butler shook his head, embarrassed by his thinking out loud. "Very wise decision," he said, wiping his brow. "For I tell you once they are turned loose no power in the world can stop them, let alone I." He turned toward one of the chiefs standing at his side. "Nor can anyone, even their own leaders, I might add."

He motioned behind him to one of his green-coated rangers. A man immediately marched forward, smartly reaching into his pouch. Producing a paper, he elegantly handed it to his commander. Butler nodded and quickly stepped back, holding up the paper to Blanchard.

"You shall find all we have discussed and agreed upon in this document," he said, eyeing Blanchard for his reaction.

Blanchard glared at the paper. "Had it all figured out, aye?" he asked, reluctantly grabbing the paper from the haughty man's hands.

"It is best to be prepared," Butler answered, lifting his nose high.

"It is proper to write terms only after they have been agreed upon," Blanchard snarled back.

"Do you wish to see the field of yesterday?" Butler snapped

back. "If you keep on so we shall show it to you here and right now! I assure you these terms are most liberal. Why quibble over them?"

"Very well," Blanchard said. "As you say!"

Grinning from ear to ear, Butler waved one of his hands high in the air. Wild whoops immediately filled the air. Once again they gained a fort without firing a shot. They all swarmed toward the stockade's gate, rudely pushing it open. Swaggering past the crestfallen men at the gate, they spread out toward the three blockhouses within the stockade. They knocked heavily on each of the blockhouses' doors, demanding entry. All the doors slowly slid open to the conquering hordes.

They immediately herded the disheveled and shocked inmates of blockhouses out into the stockade. Gruff hands relieved all the men of their prized possessions, their rifles. Some clung stubbornly to them for a fleeting moment, only to have them jerked away with the threat of a war club or tomahawk to the skull. Women pleaded with the men to just give in for God's sake, their sake, and their children's. For all resistance seemed futile and pride just a fleeting emotion which would draw nothing but ire from the crotchety Tories and Indians, and then blood.

Settling down, the men stared at the odd Indians scampering around them holding small clay pots and buckets. Scooping thick black paint from the buckets and pots onto their fingers they smeared it onto every face they encountered. Other Indians followed in their wake, cautioning the irritated Yankees in broken English not to wipe it off, for it marked them captives, therefore saving them from further harm. They also told them to carry a bit of white cloth about their persons as to denote them as prisoners, and therefore save their scalps from the knives of some *wild* Indians. Some of them even took great pains to tie bits of white cloth to some of the mystified children.

Others Indians, too overcome with their great victory, simply stood wailing at the top of their lungs in celebration. Others busied themselves ripping apart feather beds and dancing among the feathers flying in the air, oddly, their favorite amusement. Others flung chests out of the stockade to their awaiting brethren, who promptly busted them open and rifled through their great bounty.

A few braves gathered their newly acquired firelocks and marked out targets on the logs of the stockade, firing one rifle after another until they discovered the one which hit the mark and felt best at their shoulder. Smoke soon rose from one blockhouse, then the other, until all three went up into flames.

Seeking refuge from the flames, many of the huddled refugees scampered about, herded one way and then another while eager hands rifled through their pockets and pouches taking anything that amused them. Indignant eyes and tongues answered their protests, but the Indians and Tories continued searching their persons, stripping them of more than their mere possessions, but also their pride and dignity. No greater humiliation existed to them and their enemies seemed most aware of it.

Blanchard found himself being herded to a small table procured from one of the blockhouses before flames engulfed it. He scratched a pen forced into his hand across a paper laid in front of him. His hand never burned more than gripping that pen, that awful pen, and he eagerly passed it to the gloating British major standing beside him.

After scratching his name on the paper Major Butler rolled it up and stood only long enough to nod at Blanchard before rambling out the gate greedily clutching the paper in his hands.

Blanchard shook his head at Butler, biding him good riddance under his breath, and wishing for all the world to be anywhere but here at this awful moment. He stumbled back and out of the way of the dancing and parading Indians, suddenly gasping at the sight of a few of them passing by him. Though paint covered their faces, he recognized some of them, and paled at the sight of them. Some of them had even supped in his house many a time in friendship. Now they passed by him with his mouth agape, showing no more sign of recognition to him as they did any of his like.

He wanted to call out their names, Anthony Turkey, Tom Turkey, David Singsing, and Anthony Cornelius, but thought better of it, for now they seemed totally different men. Men changed by their sudden prestige. Men showing their true nature and thoughts about him and his kind, no longer inhibited in expressing their thoughts by social taboos. Absolutely no remorse or recognition of their former friends shone in their eyes. They seemed intoxicated with the prizes of their conquests.

Watching them shuffle past time and time again drew hard on Blanchard's soul. Time and time again he tried to catch their eye only to have them ignore him. Why? Why this after all the years of friendship? Was there no pity in their hearts for ones they once called friend? Did all their years of friendship now mean nothing? Finally unable to contain his rage he called, "Anthony! Anthony Turkey!" to the indifferent man passing him.

The Indian turned his eyes to him for the slightest instant, cracking a sly smile. Stopping, he raised a captured rifle over his head, yelling and nodding to the stunned white man, confused by his questioning eyes. Did not he share the joy of his sudden good fortune?

Squinting his eyebrows together, he yelled once more loud enough for both of them, and walked away from the strange white man who played by different rules and seemed to have no hankering to understand anyone else's rules. It was the way of the white eyes. They seemed to think all the world beat to the tune of their own drum and turned a deaf ear to sounds not pleasing to their senses. Well now the whole world collapsed around them, and their ways must turn to a different beat, much as the Indians did in their world. If they did not share the Indian's desire to at least turn their eyes to see the world through other's eyes, then let them live in the blindness of their own arrogance. Closed eyes cannot see. If you think you know all the answers, you have little desire to understand other people. This he tried to covey to the white man through his eyes for a second, but upon seeing the same familiar coldness once again, he turned away. One could not make a man see if the man refused to lift the blanket of arrogance from his face.

Blanchard stared at his changed friend with eyes of disbelief. How could he be so cold? No mercy showed in his dark eyes, but a light of joy. Joy from his misery. How strange they are, how insensitive and cruel. A series of high-pitched wails turned his eyes from his former friends and to the Indian women pouring through the gate smiling at the gallivanting braves, stopping some of them to examine their plunder. They all wore the same smile from ear to ear, seeming oblivious to the misery they caused the crestfallen faces watching them. He would never understand these people. He felt sure of it. Such totally different cultures bred totally different people. A people whom could never find common ground, for the chasm between them remained much too deep.

The white women cringed at the sight of the filthy Indian women, some smeared with blood. A few of the Indian women noticing their stark stares held up portions of their bloody garments and yelled, "Yank-ee blood!" before laughing and turning away. One of them held a bloody scalp high over her head, dancing in little circles all around the sullen whites, seeming to draw great enjoyment from their angst.

Blanchard felt his knees shake in rage. He fought back the urge to burst forth and pummel the red demons with his bare fists, for he knew it would all be for not and only result in his death in a most horrid manner. Collapsing to his knees, he put his clenched fists to his eyes, unable to bear the sight of it anymore. For the longest moment he ignored the hands searching rudely about his person, but finally succumbed to his rage. A loud growl creep from the depths of his soul.

The growl drew the attention of many of the braves. They immediately circled the dejected man, taunting him mercilessly. Their jeers quickly turned to cruel blows and kicks at the growling white man. Prodding him all the more, he seemed to gain great delight from it. The more the growling white man ignored their blows and kept his tightly clenched hands over his eyes, the more they pummeled him.

A sharp rebuke suddenly sounded from the crowd. People parted to give way for an old chattering man scolding the braves kicking at the dejected Yankee captain. The old chief sauntered up to them, gruffly pushing a few of the more stubborn braves aside and shaking his finger at them. After pushing them away, he crossed his arms and stood firm by the white man bearing a great frown on his face. Soon the braves waved him off and scampered away to find new mischief out of sight of the old chief.

Blanchard finally dropped his fists from his eyes and pounded them into the earth. He felt energy surge through his muscles in preparation for his mad attack. Be it foolish or not, simple rage demanded it, regardless of the consequences. A lone word uttered from a guttural throat quelled his rage for but a moment. A moment long enough for him to look up at the old chief standing with his arms crossed above him. He stared at the man with wide eyes.

"Butler," sounded out of the corner of the chief's mouth. The chief noticed the man's stare out of the corner of his eye and scolded the last lingering braves hanging about. After they reluctantly melded with the crowd, he turned to the dejected man and knelt down beside him.

Blanchard locked eyes with the man. Strangely, the eyes neither bore the look of an enemy or friend, but merely showed the wisdom of age.

"I sorry," the chief said on a whisper. "Butler, he say no hurt come to any of you. I make sure for him." Turning, he sighed at the sight of the young hooting braves gallivanting about. "They young," he added. "In that they sometimes foolish. No one must be foolish now. What done is done."

Blanchard stared blankly at him without uttering a word.

"This no white man's day," the chief said, slowly helping the man regain his feet. He looked deeply into his eyes. "This Indian day, so now we live Indian way."

Blanchard did the only thing he could do, he nodded, excepting the old chief's words of wisdom, for they certainly rang true. So true, they quickly quelled his sense of futile rage. He must live to fight another day, and in that day find retribution, for today all seemed lost.

But one must live for tomorrow..

## Chapter Seventy Five
*Godspeed John Jenkins*

Nathan Denison slowly rose from a crowded bed in the cabin. He moved carefully, not wishing to disturb his wife's and child's well-deserved sleep. The longer they slept, the longer they escaped the living nightmare engulfing them in this cruel reality called war.

After carefully maneuvering out of the bed, he rubbed his eyes and glanced down at his filthy sweat-soaked garments. Lifting his shirt up he winced at the splatters of blood staining it. He shuddered to think of just to whom it belonged. Too many fell around him the previous day.

Throwing the bloody shirt aside, he reached for his fine clean hunting shirt his good wife had placed at the foot of their bed before sleeping. Sliding it over his head, he pushed his arms through its sleeves, somehow feeling invigorated by the touch of the fine and clean cloth. Looking about at the sea of dirty and wretched souls lying everywhere on the floor he wondered just how he would navigate around them to reach the door without disturbing them. They also deserved their respite.

He took one careful step after another, ever mindful of the rays of the sun now teasing the greased paper serving as the cabin's only window. Finally meandering his way through them, he opened the cabin door to a blast of sunlight. Quickly squeezing through the door, he gently closed it behind him to see Jenkins sitting crestfallen on a bench beside it. The sad lieutenant raised his bowed head and unconsciously started rubbing the back of his right hand.

"John," Denison said, noticing the great bags under the man's bloodshot eyes. "I pray the night has been free of mischief in this fort."

Jenkins sat silently watching a poor widow parading in front of them. Nervously clapping her hands she muttered, "Oh my dear husband! Oh my dear husband." A child sat cross-legged near her staring up through the streaking tears flowing down his crimson and dirty cheeks. The woman paid no attention to him or the two men. Her eyes bore the same stare haunting all the faces of the men returning from that horrible field. A blank thousand-yard stare so deep it seemed to reach into time immortal. Jenkins looked up to the man standing over him, noticing the hollow stare in his eyes also, though he tried to mask it. He wondered of the horrid shadows haunting their minds.

"Poor woman," Denison muttered.

Jenkins sat up, straightening his back. Suddenly aware of his unconscious gesture of rubbing his hand, he quickly drew it away. Jerking the hand up to his face he stared at it, his eyes full of concern. He somehow saw Beth mirrored in it and gasped at her fate. No one heard about the fate of Pittston Fort yet and he could not help but fear the worse. "No sign of the enemy about the fort, yet, sir," he muttered. He looked to the woman again. "Only the signs of the aftermath of his cruel work of yesterday," he added. "Some say they saw some canoes about the river just before dawn. A few more straggled in the fort last night, some crawling to the gate in the cover of the night. They were all in a bad way, though. Hollenback come in, he did, all bloody and mad as hell."

"Ensign Hollenback you say! What did he report?"

"Only more of the massacre on that field, but he did bring word of Captain Durkee's demise. He is gone for sure. It is a most horrid loss."

"Yes, we have certainly lost too much of Wyoming's fine manhood on that field."

Jenkins' eyes narrowed. He looked to the south gate. "Sir, Hollenback and Hageman have departed to hasten on Captain Spalding, and I fear some mischief has befallen them. I feel I must ride to make sure Spalding is on his way with no mind for his horses! We need them, for whom knows what shall befall us this day? I must ride for dear Beth's, and everyone's sake! We need them or we haven't a chance!"

Denison looked into the man's wide-eyes. Turning toward the south gate he nervously ran his hand through his disheveled hair. "You must do what you think is best, lad," he said. He raised his hand to shield his eyes from the glaring sun rising over the fort's high walls. "As you say, we may need them yet this day."

Jenkins jumped at the affirmation. Nodding profusely, he ran toward the stable. In no time he saddled a horse and hastily mounted it. Turning toward Denison, he raised his rifle high in the air, spurring his horse through the south gate. "I'll fetch 'em!" he called over his shoulder. "You just hold fast!"

Denison raised his hand in a slight wave to the departing officer and muttered, "Godspeed John Jenkins," under his breath. Taking a few steps away from the cabin, he caught sight of a man waving madly toward him from the wall above the north gate. The man scampered down the ladder to meet the colonel at the gate. Both of them raised the crossbeam bracing the door, cracking it open. The man stuck his rifle through the crack, frantically motioning at something in the grass. Denison drew his pistol from his belt and cocked it.

"No sir," the man said. "It ain't no Injun or such! Look down there, just to the side of the road!"

Captain Franklin's tall frame bobbed along the platform along the walls and stopped over the gate. Gazing over the pointed tips of the logs he shouted, "There! There he is! Go fetch the poor soul afore he bleeds to death!" Turning about, he waved at two men to advance to the gate, seeming indifferent to Denison and the man with him.

Denison peered out the gate to a bloody man crawling through the stomped grass just outside the gate. The man moaned upon seeing him, reaching desperately with his bloody hand up to him. Franklin's two men suddenly appeared at the gate and anxiously stood near it. "Go, by all means, go!" Denison said, stepping aside.

The two men instantly darted out the gate with their rifles cocked and ready for action. Sliding to a stop in the grass, they scooped up the man under his bloody arms, dragging him moaning and groaning to the gate. The gate slid open just wide enough to let them pass and slammed closed with Denison himself slamming the crossbeam into the slots bracing the thick doors.

Denison watched them drag the poor man to a cabin and looked up to see Franklin leaning over the top of the pointed logs staring intently at something. He rambled up the ladder and next to the tall man.

"There they be!" Franklin said, noticing the curious colonel out of the corner of his eye. Leaning back down below the wall, he gestured over it. "Look there, Colonel," he said, "just under the tree line."

Denison looked in the direction he pointed and immediately noticed green-coated men standing just behind several trees. They held their rifles up but did not fire, seeming to dare the patriots' rifles to bark at them. One of them lowered his rifle and took a step to the edge of the tree line. Jutting his chest proud, he took another step but then stopped, noticing a dozen rebel firelocks pointing over the wall at him. Carefully putting a hand slowly inside his coat, he pulled a white handkerchief from it. Lifting the cloth high in his hand, he slowly waved it in the air.

"The devils watched it all," Franklin said. "That poor soul's lucky he's still got his hair! I bet they used him for bait, they did."

"Perhaps," Denison said, watching the Tory with the white flag slowly advance toward the fort. After hearing several clicks of hammers being cocked back, he waved to his men to desist. "Don't fire," he said, "but be at the ready, nonetheless. Let's hear what this one has to say."

"But Colonel," one of the men said, "can't you see? It's that bastard Parshall Terry! It is fer sure!" More rifle locks clicked in response. More rifles vied for revenge.

"Hold!" Denison ordered. "Rat, traitor, or whatnot, we are in no position for a prolonged siege! Think of the women and children! And the hair about your own heads! Just wait!" He turned to Franklin. "Have them hold their fire, Captain, we must use our heads about this business, for we see where our hearts led us yesterday!"

Nodding, Franklin eased back his own itchy finger on his rifle's trigger. "Hold fast, men! Listen to your Colonel!" he yelled.

"What is it you say!?!" a woman's voice screeched from below the platform. Shaking a wooden spoon she held up to the wall, she narrowed her eyes.

Denison and Franklin turned slightly to look down at the woman, for both knew the voice. They rolled their eyes from her and back to the bold ranger slowly marching toward the wall.

"I heard you!" the woman screamed. "You uttered the rat's name! The scourge of all of Wyoming! That Tory bastard Terry!" The mere mention of the name, even from her own tongue, infuriated the woman. Throwing down her spoon, she marched toward the ladder, cursing and cussing under her breath all the way.

All of the men ignored her. They had a rat in their sights.

The woman lifted her petticoats and climbed up the ladder.

"Look here!" one of the men finally called to her. "This is no place for a woman! Now go see about your kitchen and leave us to this work!"

"Killing a rat's everyone's concern!" the woman barked back, shaking a finger at the man. "You just mind your place and I'll mind mine!"

The man turned and looked past her to the officers. Both of them shook their heads back to him. The man gasped in a huff and turned his eyes back over the wall. "You just mind your tongue!" he warned the feisty woman. "We are in no need of your lip up here!"

The woman ignored him and marched by him. Turning, she stood tip-toe to look over the pointed tips of the log wall. Gasping, she caught her breath. "It is the rat himself!?!" she said under her gasping breath. "The scourge himself!?!"

Denison leaned an arm over the wall and waved at the ranger. "That be far enough!" he warned. He looked back at the Tories still behind the trees. They stood stoically, but sternly, with their rifles still held at the ready.

Terry stopped, noticeably stiffening his back. "You know why I'm here!" he yelled. "Major Butler wishes to discuss terms!"

Denison glared down at the man, wondering of the brash major sending a traitor to discuss terms. Salt to the wound, he thought, shaking his head. His anger forbade speech for the moment. He remained silent.

"Come now!" Terry said, putting a hand to his eye to shield it from the sun. "Has not there been enough bloodshed!?!"

The sharp click of several more rifles being cocked answered him. "If you surrender peaceable like, not a soul shall be hurt!" he said, gazing up at the rifle barrels now bristling along the top of the wall. Noticing they all pointed at him made him a bit nervous, but he stood fast. He walked right into it, so now he had to face it. Running wouldn't do anything but draw a ball to his back. Perhaps one, two, or three might miss their mark, but not two dozen. And they seemed to be multiplying with each passing second. "But if you refuse," he continued, realizing his only chance lie in intimidation. "Well, then the whole fort shall be put to the hatchet and they ain't nothing Major Butler can do to stop it, so consider that, I pray ye will!"

"Bold bastard, he is!" Franklin said.

"Yes," Denison said out of the corner of his mouth, "but we need more time."

Franklin nodded and spat over the wall. Tightening his rifle to his shoulder, he looked along the wall out of the corner of his eye. "Be a shame if'n one of them firelocks was to fire accidentally," he said.

Denison looked along the wall and felt his hand tighten his grip on his pistol. No, he thought, quelling the urge to fell the traitor. Calmer heads need to prevail now, for everyone's sake. Lifting himself up on the logs, he leaned forward. Terry flinched, much to his amusement.

"Send Major Butler my compliments and tell him he shall have an answer this afternoon!" he shouted.

Distant rifle shots echoed down the river. Terry jumped in spite of himself. The rifle barrels jumped with him. He swallowed hard against the lump in his throat. "Fine!" he said. "Major Butler shall expect you at his headquarters about Fort Wintermoot, or what's left of it, at one of the clock!" he yelled for all to hear, silently hoping the mentioning of the major's name and the authority it represented forestalled any itchy trigger finger. He knew many an eye glaring down the rifle barrels thirsted for his blood. He suddenly wondered why he had accepted this task in the first place. The Lord, like these Yankees, did not suffer a fool. He backed away, careful not to turn his back on the bristling rifles along the wall. He suddenly became aware of every beat of his heart and every breath he drew, fearing it might soon be his last. His mouth grew dry. He scolded himself not to noticeably flinch, though every nerve in his body tingled, especially the closer he gained his fellows in the trees. A hearty laugh from behind him made his heart jump, but he welcomed it, for it announced he had reached the shielding trees. Biting down on his lip, he smartly turned about. Taking a few great steps to the trees he let out a deep sigh of relief.

His comrades all laughed but he ignored them. "Major Butler

shall have his answer this afternoon," he said, trying to catch his breath.

"That he shall," one of his comrades snarled. Looking the nervous man up and down, he chuckled. "A bit nervous after your reunion there, aye?" he asked.

"Not at all," he said, leaning against a tree. He took another deep breath, stuffed the white handkerchief into his pocket, lifted up his rifle, and marched into the awaiting folds of the dark forest. "Now come along!" he yelled back to his men. "And be smart about it! I'll have no more of ye smart lip this day, for I have certainly had my fill!"

Denison watched the last of the green backs disappear under the trees and sighed. Turning away from the wall he suddenly stood face to face with boisterous Mrs. York. Rid of one nightmare to just face the next, he thought, nodding his head to the woman.

She glared at him and did not move.

Franklin stood nervously to the side of the woman, not sure whether to forcibly remove her or not. A slight nod and quick look from the ambushed colonel relieved his tension. He slowly stepped away, not wishing to intrude, or have any part of the hard woman's scorn.

"Colonel!" she said, glancing out of the corner of her eye to the retreating captain, "Terry was the man whom deprived me of a husband and my children of their father! I, for one, cannot bear sight of the devilish traitor! I, fine sir, have not the slightest confidence in anything the blackguard says and if he is allowed to come in I shall go out!"

"Come now, my dear Mrs. York," Denison said. "I sympathize with your loss, but no one should go out of the confines of this fort now for their own protection!" Looking over her head he waved a hand to Franklin. "Captain!" he called to the man. "See that the south gate is secure! No one is to leave this fort henceforth!" Giving Mrs. York a slight bow he shuffled past her to the ladder.

"I will leave if I have a mind to, my dear Colonel!" Mrs. York declared. Stomping by the colonel, she lumbered down the ladder before him, staring at him in defiance. "Children!" she called to her awaiting brood. "Gather what you can! We are leaving!"

Denison scrambled down the ladder behind her, loudly calling for a meeting of his remaining officers. He ignored the woman's hateful and defiant stare, fueling her anger, and outraging her all the more.

Stomping to the kitchen in the far corner of the fort she clanged pots and pans about before appearing again with a hastily completed bundle tucked under her arm. A few spoons and such fell out of the loose bundle, leaving a trail behind her stomping mad feet. Turning, she waved for her swarming children to gather near her. "I have had my fill!" she exclaimed. "I will not even share the same air with such a betraying demon as that fiend Terry, as so he can finish his work of destroying my family! For his like have already destroyed our homes!"

Marching steadfastly toward the south gate she demanded passage from the exhausted sentry.

The sentry, an exhausted old man, rubbed a hand to his face, boisterously commanding her to stop.

Her march did not cease.

Overcome with fatigue, the man raised his bayoneted musket up and called, "Colonel! Colonel!"

Denison craned his head around the assembling officers and promptly marched over to the disturbance. "My God woman!" he said. "You'll be the death of me yet! I swear it!"

Mrs. York ignored the officer and stepped forward to the point of the man's bayonet. Forcing him against the gate he stood firm, shocked by the woman actually pressing the point of the bayonet into her heaving chest.

"Colonel!?!" the sentry pleaded. "Shall I let her pass!?!"

"No!" Denison said. "I shall not have her blood on my hands, or the blood of these dear innocent children! No! I shall not!"

The sentry pushed the bayonet just enough for it to penetrate the first layer of the woman's ragged garments.

She stood fast, glaring down at the trickle of blood showing near the point of the bayonet. "I will go out with my children," she said, turning a burning eye to the stunned colonel, "or I will die here at the gate!"

Denison shook his head in disbelief. "Let her pass, man," he finally said. "Let her pass."

The sentry gladly eased back on the bayonet and quickly barked "Yes sir!" He immediately lifted the crossbar from the gate and cracked the door open.

Denison stood helplessly watching the last of the York children scoot through the crack, suddenly feeling numb. Shaking his head one last time, he turned back to his awaiting officers, trying in vain to come to terms with the scornful look on the last child's face. He feared it to be forever etched in his memory. *You have done what you can in the present circumstances*, he consoled himself in his thoughts, *which is all anyone can do in this madness called war.*

*Your duty lies with the rest of Wyoming. You must see them through the best you can*, he told himself, *you can do nothing with those refusing to listen to reason*, but somehow the words rang hollow.

## Chapter Seventy Six
*The Upper Road*

Bethiah Jenkins sat huddled with the dejected mass of settlers in Pittston Fort. Barely a whisper sounded among them. Shattered and numb, they watched the Indians and Tories rampage through their precious belongings. Trying to do anything to take their minds off the horror, some of them busied themselves by tearing bits of white linen from shirt sleeves and the bottoms of petticoats to tie about everyone's heads. Children sat with dried tears coating their cheeks, their sorrow now turning to fascination of the strange and brightly adorned Indians.

"What is to become of us?" Elizabeth Murphy asked on a whisper, raising her soulful eyes to her friend Beth.

Beth looked to the pregnant woman and knelt down beside her. Grabbing her hand, she gently squeezed it. "Nothing," she whispered, turning an eye in the direction of Captain Blanchard. He sullenly shuffled about the huddled settlers, trying his best to reassure them. "The good captain has agreed to terms, we shall be fine, dear Elizabeth," she added.

Elizabeth shook her head and looked down to her stomach. She bowed her head and gently rubbed her large belly. "Oh my poor child," she muttered. "I know not what ill will has befallen your dear father or what is to become of us!" A torrent of new tears poured down her cheeks, falling onto her and Beth's hands. The tears streaked through the black paint some wrinkled and old Indian woman had daubed onto her cheeks. The hint of her rosy cheeks showed through the streaks.

"Now, now," Beth said, raising her tear strewn hands to gently embrace her friend. "We shall be fine. You mustn't fret so and cry," she added with a choked attempt to laugh. "You'll wash away the paint."

"I do so wish these tears to wash away all of these past days," Elizabeth said. "But I fear not all my tears, or the tears of my unborn children to be enough, or all the tears for two hundred years!"

Beth shook her head, not knowing what to say in answer.

"What of my dear husband?" Elizabeth gasped. "What of both of our dear husbands?"

Beth closed her eyes at the thought of her new husband and their good friend John Murphy. "We must pray that God in his infinite mercy shall deliver us all from the ravages of this war," she said, reaching out to cup her friend's face in her hands. "We must keep faith and be strong," she added, "as I know our dear husbands are!" In the back of her mind she shuddered thinking of the men, and feared the worse, but held her tongue for her friend's sake; and her unborn child's sake as well.

A tall ranger appeared before the huddled masses, promptly raising his arms high in the air to gain their attention. "You are all free to depart the fort and return to your homes, but I must warn you to respect the terms of capitulation!" he announced. Casting a stern look to the blank faces staring at him, he turned to march back among his fellows gathered around a huge fire. With a nod from him many rangers gathered firebrands from the fire, gruffly pushing their way through the startled settlers. They quickly flung the flaming torches into the blockhouses behind them. The settlers needed no more urging, they all simultaneously rose, immediately heading for the gate of the fort.

Outside the gate they all splintered off into little groups, some going one way, others going another way. Many shuddered at the rising columns of smoke from the fort and shuddered even more at the columns of smoke rising from their homes. Captain Blanchard and his officers scurried about the little groups urging them to depart for the Delaware River and civilized settlements to the south with all due haste.

Beth and Elizabeth sat huddled under a tree watching their world crumble before their eyes. They both nodded to a crestfallen man approaching them. The man nodded back, putting a hand to the bloody cloth tied about his head. He looked with a sorrowful eye at Beth and her pregnant friend. He needed no words to convey his deep regret.

"We must do as Captain Blanchard says," the man said, turning an eye back over his shoulder to his own huddled family under another nearby tree. "We must repair to Fort Penn!"

"But the distance is so great!" Elizabeth gasped, her eyes suddenly glowing with fear. "And those awful Shades of Death! How shall we ever manage that horrid, dark, snake-infested hell?"

Both the man and Beth cringed at the thought, also. The dark trail leading under a thick veil of ancient and towering hemlocks and the ground covered with a thick carpet of ferns shielding hordes of deadly rattlesnakes flashed through their minds. After the snake-riddled ferns lay a thick swamp laden with its own peculiar horrors before leading into another dark veil of dense hemlocks; twenty miles of hell in all.

Beth cast an eye down to her bare feet and her friend's. The trek seemed daunting to say the least, but they had no choice, she realized with a heavy heart. She collapsed to the ground, unable to hold back her tears any longer.

A group of screeching Indians filed past the trees making a beeline for the nearest cabin still standing. Beth hushed her tears and lifted her head to a new horror, wondering when, if ever, it would ever end.

The man ran back to his family under the other tree and stood firm in front of them. The Indians snorted at the man and continued on to the cabin. They kicked in the door, screaming, yelling, and rummaging through the cabin in front of the terrified family watching from under the tree. Throwing and kicking chests, pots, featherbeds and such out the door, one of them struck flint to a rag tied about a stick. The flaming torch flared to life in front of his wide glaring eyes. Yelling, he tossed it into the cabin. Kicking at some of the plunder, he grunted, turning toward the huddled family under the tree. His eyes widened upon sight of the bundles clutched in their hands. Yelling to his comrades, they quickly swarmed around the tree, yanking the bundles from the terrified family's hands. Tearing them open, they grabbed a few things from them, and then turned their dark eyes to the people. Swaggering to the man, they yanked his fine waistcoat from his back. He twirled from the force of their act, falling to the ground.

"Poor man," Elizabeth whispered to Beth.

Beth looked down to their meager bundle, stealthily shoving it into the folds of her dress. She had seen enough. Lifting her friend up by the arm she led her away from the tree. "We must make our way the best we can, for we cannot stay here! As for the Shades of Death, we shall not take the lower road, but follow the upper road, as most around these parts shall, I dare say!"

"We have but the dresses upon our backs!" Elizabeth gasped. "Most shall take the lower road as to meet Captain Spalding and the relief column, for that is the way they shall come, certainly they shall!"

Beth stopped and held her by the shoulders. After staring dead in her eyes, she let her eyes fall to her swollen stomach. "Look about you!" she said. "There is soon to be nothing left here! We must find our own relief! What of the child you bear? Do you wish for the child to be delivered amidst this? Come now, Elizabeth, you must buck up!"

Elizabeth jerked away from her, turning away. "We must await our husbands!" she said. "They shall come! They must!"

"We must buck up and mind ourselves for the moment," Beth said, "for our husbands have greater duties just now!"

"Oh, but I am John's greatest duty!" Elizabeth gasped.

"And I my husband's!" Beth said. "We must be good and dutiful wives at the moment and make for the settlements! That is where they shall look for us when they can! They must find us safe!"

Elizabeth rubbed her stomach and turned her eyes toward her pleading friend. "You must calm yourself, dear Beth," she said, noticing the tears streaking through the black paint on her cheeks. "Or you shall wash away your paint too!" Reaching out, she took Beth's hand and let the hint of a smile show about her face, however brief.

Beth let a smile cut through her own sense of gloom in return. The hooting Indians rambled off just beyond the trees to seek greater places of opportunity, much to the women's relief. Clasping their hands together, they both stumbled back toward the burning cabin and the crestfallen family.

The man, still sitting on the ground, nodded his head in shame, but greeted them, nonetheless. He stood tall, but turned a sad eye to his burning cabin and their property scattered around it like so much trash. Staggering to his wife standing stunned by it all, he embraced her. "Oh, my sweat," he said. "It is sad indeed." He looked to the burning cabin and outbuildings and then to the two women. "They drove away all our stock! Not even a piglet remains! All is lost or in ashes!"

"I know," Beth said, slowly leading Elizabeth toward the family. "We've all lost so much!"

"It is all so terrible!" his wife said, lifting the remnants of a bundle up in her hands. Putting a hand to her husband's shoulder, she gently kissed him before turning to the women. "And you," she said, looking the women up and down, "being with child and all! Oh my!" She waved her three children to her side and hugged them all. "We shall make for Fort Penn," she said. "Colonel Stroud shall see to us."

Hoots and familiar wails sounded from the Indians just down the road. A trail of smoke soon curled in the air from the direction of the spine-tingling wails.

"That'd be Ebenezer Marcy's place," the man said. "But they'll find no one there, thank God, for they left from the fort straight away at the insistence of his brother Zebulon, barely stopping for anything."

"It was a right smart thing to do," his wife said, "for if they where to realize just who they had, Zebulon Marcy, Indian slayer and bane of the Tories' existence in these parts, they would have strung him up right smart, they would! In fact they tried it once afore but that man's got a charmed life. You heard of his tobacco tin, ain't ya? It saved his life from a Tory's ball once." She glanced at Elizabeth. "Mrs. Marcy's with child too."

Elizabeth patted her stomach and smiled.

"Won't be long, will it?" the wife asked.

"No, I am afraid it will not be long," Elizabeth answered.

Rifles started to bark in the distance. The man's eyes grew wide and he scampered over to a corner of the burning cabin. Kicking madly at the dirt, he bent down to lift up a small bundle wrapped in an oilcloth. Carefully removing the cloth, he held up a fine pistol, shot bag, and small powder horn for all to see. A self-satisfied grin stretched from ear to ear across his face. "Hid it there, I did, afore I set out for Forty Fort," he explained. He quickly loaded and primed the pan of the weapon. "Yes, I was in that horrid battle and swam the river, I did! Saw many that didn't make it. I shudder to think of their fate. God have mercy on their souls."

"And you'll shudder at ours if'n we don't get a move on!" his wife said, bending down to hastily collect some of the scattered things on the ground to make a new bundle. "We ain't got much food, and just the rags on our backs to keep off the night's chill, but you're both welcome to join us if'n you got a mind to," she said to the two women.

Both women nodded. "We are of Exeter, all we have has been put to the torch," Beth said.

"Yes, and you just being married and all," the wife said. "Your husband is a fine and brave man, Mrs. Jenkins."

Beth blushed upon hearing her new name. "Yes," she said, "and so is yours, I might add."

The wife glanced to her husband, proudly nodding.

"We must go by way of the upper road!" the man said.

Distant yells turned all their eyes downriver. Dozens of columns of dark smoke rose into the sky overtop the trees. Timbers cracked in the flaming cabin near them. Suddenly the roof collapsed with a loud crash, sending thousands of embers flying into the sky. Flames quickly devoured the fallen roof.

The man stopped and staggered to the cabin. All he had struggled to build these past years now rose into the sky in the flames and acrid smoke. A sense of solid dread crept through his soul. He fell to his knees and lifted his hands in despair to the heavens, for what man does not love what he himself has created? Fighting back his tears, he struggled to his feet, turning his back to it all. He simply had too.

His wife, not encumbered by his strict sense of masculinity, let a flood of harsh tears flow down her face. The children stood silently in awe of it all.

Elizabeth and Beth both broke out in tears anew, hugging the grieving wife. All three wailed and sobbed together.

The man waved the children to the road and looked back over his shoulder at the grieving women. "Come now, Mother!" he said. "We must leave, and I mean now!"

The women did not argue, but just released their hold on one another and slowly turned their backs on all they had known these past years. They trod up the road and dared not look back at their hopes rising in the smoke and flames. Their hollow hearts forbade it.

## Chapter Seventy Seven
### Death along the Lackawanna

The large wheels of a two-wheeled cart creaked through the ruts of a rough road. The yoke of oxen laboring to pull it along groaned in defiance of the sharp crack of a whip hastening their steps. The man holding the whip marched along side them, brusquely pushing with his free hand against them to urge them forward.

A deep rut, much too wide to pass, suddenly stopped the cart dead. The cracking whip caused a slight burst of energy from the groaning oxen, but it proved too little, for the cart rolled backwards and sank more deeply into the great rut. The man let out his own exasperated groan, pushing against the struggling beasts to no avail.

"What?" another man called from the cart. "Daniel! Do you need help?"

Daniel St. John looked up to the man tenaciously holding a babe in one hand while steadying himself in the cart with the other. To his side his wife held fast to several bundles in one hand while her other fell to a small child. The child lifted himself up, peering over the side of the cart despite his mother's efforts to hold him down. The small child's questioning eyes stared down at him, making him uneasy.

"No, James," he said, nodding to the lad. "It's just a rut or two, you know this road. We'll be out as soon as the oxen catch their wind." Backing away, he looked down to the wheels. A silent cursed pass his lips before he cracked the whip again, yelling, "Ya oxen! Ya!" The cart rocked forward and out of the rut, much to his relief.

"This accursed road needs work bad," James Leach said. "We'll have to see to it after these troubles pass!"

Daniel rolled his eyes at the comment. He hoped his friend's optimism proved true, but nonetheless did not regret their decision to leave their cabins about the lower Lackawanna River and move to Pittston Fort. Too few settlers and strongly built cabins dotted the river to provide a suitable defense if needed. The only hope for security lay in the forts, after all, that is why they had built them in the first place. Even with this argument, though true, it took a long time to convince James to join him in his trek to the fort. He only hoped their decision did not come too late. A clearing along the side of the road ahead eased his mind, for he feared a certain ambush from the great trees about them now.

Smoke drifted in the air from the chimney of a cabin nestled neatly in the clearing. A man walked to the cabin from a small barn off to its side, nonchalantly carrying a bucket of milk. He stopped and looked to the cart. Waving his free hand to the cart, he turned toward it.

"Mr. Hickman," James called. "You are still welcome to join us."

"Is this all the further you've gotten?" Hickman asked, shaking his head.

"It's this cussed road!" Daniel answered. "It needs work!"

"Yes, it does!" Hickman said with a chuckle. "Peculiar how one doesn't notice things 'til one really needs them, or thinks he does!"

Daniel stopped the oxen and wiped his sweaty brow. "Are you sure?" he asked, gazing at a woman holding a small babe in the cabin doorway. She nodded, but the lines of worry showed clearly on her face.

"Yes! Go on!" Hickman answered. "I've no quarrel with the Indians! In fact, I was fine friends with Anthony Turkey and Cornelius! I don't think them much worse than the next man! Don't bother them, and they won't bother you, I say. Live and let live is my motto, it is!"

"But what of the war?" James asked.

"The war's a long ways off!" Hickman said, turning toward the cabin again. "We should have just left it there! Besides, what on earth would the King want with a little cabin nestled in this far wilderness?"

"The war may be closer than you think!" Daniel said.

"Yes, and what of the Tories?" James asked.

"We're too far from the main settlements to be of any concern to them. They won't bother us if we don't bother them!" Hickman scoffed.

"War makes no sense in itself!" Daniel said. "It's a disease that makes sane men mad and good men bad!"

Hickman stopped and turned toward the man. He stared long and hard at him for the longest moment. "I've staked a lot in this here land!" he said. "It's all I got! Everything's here! If we abandon it, we abandon our lives!"

"In the end, simple life may be all we truly have!" Daniel said.

"I'll be tarred and feathered if you don't put me in mind of Zeb Marcy!" Hickman said. "You're a bit more poetic, but talk just the same!"

"Zebulon's down in the fort," James said.

"Good place for him, God bless him," Hickman said, turning toward the cabin again. "Now I've got to get this here milk to my wife and I've got a pile of chores to get at, so you all get along and don't fret about us here. We'll be fine. I'll see you soon. We'll fix that damn road!"

"If that's your decision, we'll go," Daniel said. "But I myself wish I only heeded Marcy's warning sooner!" Snapping the whip, he slapped a hand to the flank of the lead beast. Both oxen belched a loud groan and trudged forward.

All in the cart watched the cozy cabin disappear through the trees, dreading the crowded fort they knew lay ahead. Daniel's eyes remained fixed on the road, except for one quick glance behind him.

"They'll soon be back and feel all the foolish for their troubles!" Hickman said to his wife. Her stark look did not fade. "It's much too crowded in that stinky fort, plus, it'll spread the fever fer sure! Putrid fever shall have its way with the lot of them, it will, all crowded together like that." The crack of a twig in the trees stopped him dead in his tracks.

Before he turned a lance flew from nowhere, striking him square in the back with a sickening thud. Dropping the bucket, he turned wide-eyed to his horrified wife, then fell to the ground a lifeless clump of flesh. Gasping, his wife turned just long enough to put her hand to the door before two rifles cracked simultaneously, cutting her and the crying babe down in an instant. Painted men darted to and fro from the forest all around, scurrying about the barn and cabin in an unnatural silence. One of them bent down to the road, grunting some remark to his fellows. They all followed him down the road.

Daniel St. John turned toward the sharp report of the rifles and reached into the cart for his rifle. Another rifle instantly barked, sending a ball slamming into the side of his head. Twirling about, he instantly fell dead under one of the cart's wheels.

James Leach's eyes spread wide. He stood for a heartbeat in total shock, holding his child tight in his shaking hands. Out of the corner of his eye he noticed something painted in gruesome swirls burst from the trees firing a rifle. A sharp pain burned his neck. He gurgled, rolled his eyes and fell backwards, feeling all of his life's blood drain from his trembling body. With each beat of his heart great spurts of blood flew from his neck. He crumpled along the side of the cart and onto its floor.

A hand from nowhere reached over the cart, snatching up the babe from its bloody father. With a continuous and smooth motion, the hands passed the crying babe into its shocked mother's arms. "Me no hurt!" the Indian brave to whom the hands belonged declared loudly. The woman gasped, clutching the babe tight to her heaving chest.

Several rifles barked at the terrified oxen. One of them groaned and fell instantaneously to the ground, pulling the other down by the yoke connecting them. Bellowing, the surviving ox spurt forward with a sudden and tremendous burst of strength fueled by sheer panic, pulling its dead partner and cart along a few yards before succumbing to exhaustion.

A sharp rebuke in their own tongue stopped the swarming warriors dead in their tracks. They stepped back from the cart, seeming most confused, some of them quickly reloading their spent weapons. An approaching chief screamed at them some more, waving his hands high in the air. He pointed down the road and the braves quickly departed, some of them chattering among themselves, all of them casting odd stares back at the strange chief. But they obeyed, and kept walking away.

The chief turned and looked over the side of the cart to the bloody man staring unblinkingly up at him. Shaking his head, he slid his tomahawk into the colorful sash around his waist. He struggled with it for an awful moment, for a huge sword also stuck in it weighed it down well below his thigh. After finally securing the tomahawk, he grunted something to the woman and terrified child sinking back into the cart away from him.

Shaking his head again, he held out one hand while reaching into his pouch with the other hand. Lowering his black hand down to the shaking and whimpering woman he smeared her cheeks with the paint in his hand. He reached down further, daubing some black paint onto the child's and babe's cheeks also.

Seeing nothing but solid fear in the white woman's and child's eyes, he eased himself back from the cart and waved his hands madly in the air. "Jogo!" he yelled, pointing down the road. He looked to the bellowing oxen and screamed at it before trotting off behind his braves without a second glance behind him.

Mrs. Leach raised one of her trembling hands to the child cowering beside her and looked down to the crying babe. To her horror she noticed great columns of billowing smoke rising over the trees behind her. The report of many firelocks sounded sporadically all around her. She groaned and cried furiously, just to get it out of her system before swallowing hard against any further cries rising in her chest. Scrambling out the rear of the cart, she carefully laid the crying babe on the ground, motioning for the babe's terrified older brother to watch her. The boy inched his way out of the cart, his wide eyes darting all around him. He laid down next to the babe and nestled it in his arms.

Mrs. Leach stumbled up to the bellowing oxen and fought to free the yoke from the terrified animal. Finally breaking it free, she led it from the front of the cart and struggled onto its back. Motioning down to the boy, she scooped up the babe he handed to her. Holding the babe with one arm, she reached down with the other and pulled the young boy onto the back of the great animal.

She need not whip the beast, for it shared her urgent sense of fear and immediately lumbered down the road, just as anxious as its masters to leave the terror behind it.

But alas, such horrors never fade, not even with time. They haunt the ages forever; as well they should, lest the world should forget.

## Chapter Seventy Eight
*Liberty rises from ashes*

The men stepped through the gate at Forty Fort and stood for a long moment, nervously adjusting their garments while they waited. All of the men's eyes shot to Colonel Denison in his fine hunting shirt and fine beaver hat. The others glanced down at their tattered garments and shook their heads at the colonel, especially Doctor Gustin, straightening his blood splattered waistcoat over his blood soaked shirt.

"It is what my good wife grabbed in the confusion," Denison explained in answer to the odd stares. Shaking his head back at them, he adjusted his fine hat. To his relief the fifth man of the surrendering party finally stepped through the gate. It promptly creaked closed behind him.

Zerah Beech nodded at the men and sighed. Noticing the dark bags under each of the men's eyes he wondered what a sight he presented, gruff, unshaven, and disheveled. He imagined they all looked the part of desperate men, despite the colonel's fine shirt and hat. He shook off their gazes, unfurling a small white flag on the stick he held.

"Well, gentlemen," Denison said, clearing his throat. "Now that we're all here, Obadiah Gore, Mr. Beech, the good Reverend Johnson, and of course, Doctor Gustin, we shall see about this unpleasant business. Wyoming is well represented, I might add."

"Yes, it is," Obadiah Gore, Sr. said, gesturing up the road.

"Yes, we had best start," Denison said. "Remember, gentlemen, no one is to stray away from the group and we must stick to the road, no matter what we see or encounter."

Each man nodded.

With a wave of Denison's hand they all stepped forward, gauging their steps to keep huddled around Beech and his flag, for it proved their only protection. After a few rods everyone slowed to let Beech step to the lead. Glancing back at them he muttered curses under his breath. How on earth did he get this task? he suddenly wondered.

"Hush!" Denison said a few steps behind him. "The flag needs to be in the lead!"

The march slowed to Beech's frustrated pace, but no one complained for fear of the flag being passed to them. Soon their eyes fell to the debris littering the field around them. Pouches lie strewn all about the ground, with canteens, muskets, hats, haversacks, ramrods, swords, torn shirts, and tomahawks. An odd spear or two stuck in the ground showed among the debris, the feathers on their staffs dancing in the faint breeze. They all stepped over the debris, wondering of their reaction when they met the ultimate debris of the battle-the bodies of the slain.

Finally reaching Abraham's creek, they stopped, anxiously looking about for any sign of the enemy. Staring across the bridge all felt a certain fear, wishing their counterparts to show themselves and usher them onward, for the visions of escaping that field just a day ago played heavy on them all, especially Denison. The first bodies lie just beyond the creek, some in the road itself. Oh, to revisit horror and gaze down upon faces vibrant with life just a day ago proved taxing to say the least.

"Where are the blasted buggers?" Beech finally asked, fidgeting nervously about.

Silent and hollow eyes answered him. They all looked to Denison. Nervously rubbing his face, he stared at the bridge. After the longest moment he simply waved his hand forward and stepped onto the bridge. The others silently filed behind him.

All slowed past the first body and stared down at it, each silently thankful the mangled face drew no recognition from any of them. Coming upon more bodies the pace slowed, especially the doctor's. "What am I to do if we come across a wounded man?" he asked under his breath.

No one answered, but just kept marching, some forcing their eyes to the trees above to forestall any such predicament. Their duty lie with the living at the moment. The dead would have to bury the dead, for now, at least.

"It's my duty," Gustin muttered to himself, becoming increasingly agitated the more bodies they passed. He started lagging behind, stopping to get a better look at a few of the corpses. "I do hope Hooker Smith is as expeditious as possible in evacuating the wounded from the fort to downriver somewhere safer!" he said loudly, trying to relieve some of his angst. "We must get them out of here before, well, before anymore of this!"

Denison stopped and turned about. Waving the others past, he shook his head at the Doctor and put a finger to his lips. "Come along, Doctor," he said. "We mustn't dilly-dally, I assure you none of the living occupy this ground but their tormentors! And we don't want to draw any rogue elements of their number to do us harm, do we, Doctor?"

Doctor Gustin rose from one of the bodies, nervously running his frustrated hands through his disheveled hair. He looked quite a sight, all bloody from his previous day's work, standing frustrated and confused. His eyes bore the most helpless look Denison had ever seen. "It is all hell, it is," he gasped before stepping into line again.

"Yes it is," Denison said, putting a hand to his shoulder. "And we must think of their wives and children for the moment, for I am certain they do not want them to share their hellish fate this day."

Gustin nodded and reluctantly marched onward, only to stop with the others a short distance up the road.

"Look there!" Obadiah Gore said, pointing to some movement at the edge of the field. They all watched a furry animal rummaging through the bodies, all fearing it to be a brave cloaked in a wolf's skin. All breathed easier, but with disgust, as the beast noticed them and snarled. It sank its teeth once more into the chest of the poor soul beneath it and violently shook it like a rag doll. Red droplets flew in the air.

"That's it," Gore said, bending down to the ground. Picking up a sizeable stone, he hurled it with all his might at the wolf. With a loud and hollow thud it struck the beast full in the side. The wolf yelped, dropped the body, and ran into the thick folds of the nearby swamp.

Denison watched the whole affair with a sick feeling. Visions of the previous day flashed in his mind, making him wince. He closed his eyes tight against the visions before a sharp yell, familiar in a cruel way, shot through the air. He heard it before, only yesterday, only amplified through a thousand voices screaming it all at once.

He instinctively turned toward the disturbing sound and opened his eyes. There they sat, but a few rods away, atop captured mounts. Long spears rose in the air from some of their hands. Others held rifles in the air, but fortunately none of them leveled on the white men. The feathers tied to their spears, rifles, and about their heads, fluttered in the breeze. Their cruel and indifferent eyes stared down at the white men, unforgiving in their nature.

Beech instantly started waving the white flag tied to the end of the long stick.

One of the Indians replied with a spine-tingling screech. It cut through the white men's souls more than the snarls of the wolf.

Denison suddenly felt a sharp pain run from the nape of his neck and roll through his entire head. "What!?!" he yelled to the indifferent warriors. "Have not you had enough blood to quench your bloodlust!?!" Throwing off his fine hat in a fit of anger, he clutched his head against a sudden migraine headache. What were these people all about? The total slaughter of his people!?! He shot a hand to the flag Beech nervously waved and held it up. "Do you see this!?!" he screamed. "We come to parley, not make war! Damn you!"

One of the warriors reined his mount toward the angry white man and rode up to him. Stopping just in front of the crazed white devil, he bent down to pick up his hat. He noticed the white devil oddly twisting it in his hands instead of placing it back on his head. A movement to his side caught his eyes. Raising his rifle toward a lone wolf, he squeezed the trigger. His horse and the wolf bolted at the sudden and violent noise, but he quickly reined his horse under control again. The yelping wolf ran into the swamp again, holding its tail between its legs.

The warrior slowly lowered his spent weapon and laid it across the front of his saddle. Reining his horse back toward the infuriated white man, he glared down at him.

"Damn you all!" Denison said, locking his cold eyes on the brave. "Damn you and all your accursed Tory brethren!"

The Indian sneered and reined his mount about, leading his party away from the crazed white men. They had a bad air about them.

The white men slowly regained their composure and continued their trek through the horrid remnants of the nightmare of yesterday. Such emotional torture tore at the men's souls, but they kept on marching, for duty demanded it.

The dark and mysterious swamp, from which the hordes of painted men burst forth the previous day to decimate their ranks, lie just a few rods to their left. Looking into the dark folds of the thick swamp their imaginations played at their senses, making them envision many dark eyes staring at them and Indians ready to pounce. It haunted their souls. They all suddenly felt quite alone, despite each other's presence.

Quiet now ruled the battlefield, save the screech of a circling bird of prey surveying it, along with circling buzzards and vultures. The odd sound of a woodpecker pecking away at some unseen tree deep in the dark marsh echoed through the still air. Smells from the bloated corpses mixed with the aroma of decaying vegetation from the mucky swampland. Odd fragrances also tinged the air now and then of wild flowers, rye grass, and the lingering smell of sulfur from gunpowder.

Onward they marched through it all, closing on the smoldering remains of Fort Wintermoot just ahead of them. More and more charred posts stood in the middle of ashes from great smoldering fires littering the field. The peculiar smell of burned flesh tinged the air.

Nonetheless, no one spoke, but only hastened their steps, focusing on the huge gathering of their enemies a few rods from the smoldering ruins of the fort. They glanced briefly at the figure standing burned to a crisp among the smoldering logs. Curiously, most wondered not of the man, but why half a cabin remained along with a few of the pointed stockade posts. It puzzled them why the Indians and Tories had not reignited the blaze to continue their work of destruction; perhaps in grudging deference to one whom shared their sympathies, Wintermoot, or perhaps, the figure of the standing man brought bad medicine to the superstitious Indians. If so, the man gained a victory in death which had eluded him in life.

Ear-spiting yells rose from the enemy camp the further they advanced into it. A scattering of Indian children darted about the white men, some of the wiry little boys punching at them before scurrying away to the protection of their hovering mothers.

Denison felt the small fists, but ignored them. The rage he felt surging through his veins fed his throbbing headache. He bit his lip, imagining the great army which would come from the rest of the country when they learned of this outrage. Wyoming would be avenged. It simply had to be. The thought somewhat eased his pain, quelling his anger long enough for him to raise his eyes to a portly man walking toward them. He had to buck up and swallow hard against his pain, but most of all, quell it long enough to parley with this devil.

He recognized the portly man in the black hunting shirt at once, though he only wore a golden gorget to distinguish him from the others. His cocky manners betrayed him, Indian Butler himself. He watched the odd man cock his head to one side and watch them approach. To his side stood a much taller figure, older, but more muscular and somehow more regal looking, despite his painted skin. He stood bedecked in silver broaches and arm bands with many brightly colored beads gracing great loops of cartilage cut and stretched wide from the ears of his shaven head. A lone tuff of well-greased hair glistened in the sun atop his finely formed skull. A single eagle feather sat perked straight in the air among his glistening black hair. His old, but wise face, brimmed with a confidence born of many years of wisdom. His bright eyes glowed with an ardor marking a true and passionate leader. From the glistening hair atop his head, to the fine and brightly beaded moccasins gracing his feet, he appeared every bit a fine and regal leader. Another chief, with dark eyes betraying a deep passion, perhaps hatred, stood with crossed arms across his great barrel chest. His large muscles bulged tight under his pounded silver arm bands. Though a much younger man, he exuded the same confidence of his elder, but in a much more sinister way. No hope of compromise shone in his eyes. About his colorful sash hung the unmistakable signs of victory, a string of bloody scalps. Behind him stood more chiefs, all dressed in their own significant regalia.

Denison gritted his teeth and stepped out of his party of patriots. Marching up to the regal party, he stopped in front of Indian Butler. Raising his head high, he awaited their word.

"Colonel Denison, I presume?" Butler asked

"Yes," Denison flatly answered.

"I am Major Butler of the King's Rangers and this is Sayenqueraghta, War Chief of the mighty Six Nations," Butler said with a slight bow of his head and courtly wave of his hand toward the Seneca chief.

Denison rolled his eyes to the chief, giving a reluctant nod.

The chief glared back at him, folding his arms across his chest. A slight chatter rose from the chiefs behind him. One of them, somehow seeming out of place, edged his way to the front wearing the scarlet coat of a British officer.

Butler rolled his own eyes away from the Indians and cleared his throat. "Well, fine sir," he said. "Are you to surrender or not?"

"We have come to discuss terms," Denison snapped back, looking over his shoulder to the bewildered faces of his comrades. "These gentlemen are Obadiah Gore Sr., Doctor Gustin, Mister Beech, and Reverend Johnson, whom, I might add, is quite familiar with many native tongues," he added.

Butler cocked an eyebrow at the apparent warning not to speak in any native tongue to disguise his words. Bold even in defeat, he mused, these rebels. For a moment he wondered if such brazen men could ever truly be conquered. Quickly shaking off the odd thought, he stood tall, after all, he did represent the King, and despite what these impudent rebels thought of him, they had been defeated. And he did defeat them. He did not feel up to letting them belittle his fine victory.

"Seeing how you have been so thoroughly defeated on the field, capitulation seems to be your only option," Butler flatly stated.

"Yes, defeated on the field, but not in our hearts," Denison said. "But we shall see if there is but a lingering sense of humanity in our antagonists which shall now allow an honorable peace."

Butler raised an eyebrow, shaking his head and sighing. What arrogant people! Pursing his lips he said, "Balderdash!"

A murmur rose from the surrounding Indians.

Butler looked around. Noticing but few of his rangers about, he wondered where in God's name they could have gotten off to. A shard of fear shot through his veins. He mustn't lose control. His name must not be tainted with a massacre! Forcing his anxious feelings deep within himself, he stood tall, staring at the brash rebel colonel with a cold eye.

"The inhabitants of the settlements are to lay down their arms and the garrisons are to be demolished," he said, looking down his nose at the obstinate rebels.

After looking to his comrades and seeing no objection in their eyes, Denison slowly nodded his head.

Butler drew a pinch of snuff and put it to his nostrils. After two quick sniffs, he slowly placed the snuff box back in his pouch, staring at the silent rebels for the longest moment. "Of course, my dear fellow," he said, "all Continental officers and soldiers shall be delivered up." He rolled an eye to the anxious Indians. "And all persons you have must be delivered up," he added.

Denison looked to the others upon the reference of the two Indian prisoners they held at the fort. They did have some leverage, however slight.

The Indian wearing the red jacket suddenly stood to their front. "If they still breathe, so shall you," he declared. "If not! You shall not!"

Butler raised an eyebrow and rolled his eyes to Sayenqueraghta.

The stately chief shook his head and pointed to the Indian. He bore such an indignant stare the red-jacketed Indian slid into the crowd of chiefs and slowly disappeared in shame among their number. Sayenqueraghta then waved his fingers in the air for the parlay to continue. The red-jacketed chief, a pine tree chief, an orator and advisor at most, had no place among the war chiefs. He belonged back with the women, and would be reminded of that fact after these proceedings.

"Yes, they still breathe," Mr. Beech suddenly blurted out, "but does Finch?" All eyes shot to him. He slowly lowered his white flag and stared coldly at Indian Butler.

"We shall deliver him up, if terms are agreed upon," Butler said through gritted teeth. He did not know who were the most insolent, the Indians or the rebels.

"Very well," Beech said, raising the flag again. He rolled his eyes along the line of Indians, saying no more.

"If the terms are met, the settlers shall be free to remain in possession of their homes and farms, seeing they no longer molest the people upriver they call Tories," Butler said, glancing toward the chief next to him. "All property taken is to be made good," he added.

"None to be harmed, nor any property?" Denison asked.

Butler gave a simple nod of his head.

"So be it," Denison said.

"Well, that was not quite as difficult as one would think, was it?' Butler asked. "I assure you I, as well as Good King George, grow tired of this senseless conflict and hope one day to welcome back into the folds of the empire all its erring subjects."

His enunciation fell upon deaf ears. The rebels stared blankly at him as if he had lost his mind. No hope of reconciliation shone in their eyes, but only the emptiness of defeat.

Butler shrugged his shoulders and cocked an eye to Captain Caldwell. The captain merely raised an eyebrow back to him. Neither of them expected the drawing of terms to be so easy. "Seeing how we have no table for writing up the terms, I suggest we meet at the fort you occupy now at four of the clock this afternoon," he said. "There, we shall formalize the conditions here agreed upon in writing."

Denison glanced at Beech.

"Yes," Beech said, "I shall write the terms up."

"Four, it is then," Denison said. Bowing his head, he slowly turned about, leading his party out of the Tory and Indian camp.

"Keep that flag raised high until you reach your fort, you rebels," a Tory yelled behind them. "That is if you value your hair!"

Butler immediately scolded the man, but offered no apology.

The surrender party ignored the Tory's rants, anyways. They trod slowly along, each contemplating the surrender of their homes, farms, and land. Their lives took a bad turn now and it changed them forever, especially their dreams, for now they no longer dreamed of life, but upon gaining revenge. Though struck down by a blow their enemies thought fatal, they knew better of it. From these ashes Wyoming would rise and grow again, but only after it wiped the land free of the scourge now tainting it. Wyoming would be free again, and damn any King or savage who thought otherwise. For life and liberty always rose from the ashes. And it would rise again here, for their strong spirit demanded it.

## Chapter Seventy Nine
*Curbing the Indians*

The Yankees no more than disappeared from view before a barrel-chested chief stepped forward spewing oaths against them. Many other chiefs nodded in approval of Gucingerachton's words. "All Yankees must be put to the hatchet!" he screamed in the Seneca tongue.

His words sang so vehemently no one dared counter them. He stomped to and fro along the line of chiefs, glaring down anyone offering the least objection. Ranting and raving about all of the white eyes' offenses, he thumped his chest, raising his hands to the heavens. The veins in his neck bulged and his face showed so red it burned through the vermillion paint already covering it. Soon all nodded in affirmation and voices rose to praise Gucingerachton, great War Chief of the Seneca Nation. To them his words rang all to true.

Butler stood back, looking ruefully to Caldwell.

Caldwell took a second look at his stark commander, whom if by magic suddenly drew little resemblance to the confident man he had seen just a few moments ago. His face had turned pale and his eyes stared down to the ground, seeming to contemplate some great error in judgment. He kicked at the ground with his boots, anxiously listening to the Indians talk about slaying all the Yankees. His jaw dropped.

The Seneca War Chief's words seemed to ignite a smoldering flame in the hearts of his brethren and soon the camp bustled with braves all screaming for the Yankees' scalps. Rangers also rose in response to the commotion. Their yells and hoots multiplied the braves' voices into a giant continuous roar.

The bloodcurdling wails echoed throughout the valley, and through Butler's very soul. What had he done? he thought, suddenly gripped with fear. What has he unleashed? This must not happen! Visions of the scalp dances of the night before flashed through his mind. He imagined them in his mind's eye, the white women, the children, all slaughtered, all dead. History would never forgive such an act. He himself could never forgive such an act. He looked with wide eyes to a circle of befuddled rangers not sharing the Indian's bloodlust swarming around him. All looked to him for direction. All shared his fear.

The visions choked his words. The torches and firelight reflecting in wide eyes betrayed an absolute gruesome look of death playing at his emotions again. He saw it all, the frantic and leaping Indians dancing about with their hands full of fresh bloody scalps. He heard their boasts again, saw their darting and glaring eyes full of absolute rage. "No!" he finally yelled, attempting to purge his mind of the horrible visions, "No!"

Some of the chiefs turned to give him a passing glance, but most continued advancing to the posts and dancers forming around them. Gucingerachton turned to him, laughing in contempt. Turning away, he trotted toward the nearest post, much to the gathering braves' delight.

The rangers gathered closer to their befuddled leader. Caldwell took a step to him, shaking his head. "It shall be a massacre!" he said. "My God we must do something or we shall never be able to show our faces in civilized society again! It shall mark us all! Dreadfully!"

Butler looked him dead in the eyes. "No!" he yelled again. Turning to two armed rangers, he gestured for them to follow him. He marched straight toward a war post. Parting a sea of screaming warriors, he pushed the post aside. Glaring down at the post, he turned smartly about and faced the chiefs. They shook their heads and grunted a protest, but he would have none of it. Raising both his hands he stared defiantly at all the braves. The screams and yells slowly subsided.

He looked to the two rangers. "Interpret every word I say in Seneca, Onondaga, Cayuga, Delaware, Chippewa and all of their damn tongues!" he ordered them. Caldwell quickly stood by his side.

"Hear me!" Butler yelled. "I speak for the King! He shall not pay for scalps taken in such a manner!" He waited an anxious moment for his rangers to chatter away in the native's tongues. Silence began to descend over the tense crowd. Many of the braves ceased dancing, glaring at the rude white men. A slow grumble rolled through the crowd.

"If you wish to still have the King's favor, hear me!" Butler yelled over the grumbles. He repeated his words in Seneca and stared at Sayenqueraghta.

Sayenqueraghta nodded and waved his hands in response. The grumbles from the crowd grew silent.

"My brothers!" Butler yelled. "We must not give the rebels reason to degrade our great victory over them! You brave warriors have fought well! We all have! But if you put the Yankees' women and children to the hatchet I shall wash my hands of you all and will certainly advise the King to do the same!"

Loud chatter rose from a group of women off to the side, led by the ever-present Esther. The Indian Queen shook her head and loudly admonished the white man in her native tongue. A cold stare from Sayenqueraghta silenced her tongue and the tongues of her followers.

Sayenqueraghta raised his hands and turned toward Butler. He shouted a few words in his native tongue.

"He says there is wisdom in your words," a chief beside him explained in English to Butler. "We shall listen!"

All over the field the dancers stopped and gathered around the disturbance. A great hush swept over the gathering. Everyone looked on, heeding the great Chief's command, save one. Gucingerachton stormed off in a huff, muttering to himself under his breath. Few followed him. Most stood silent and listened, including Esther.

Sayenqueraghta grimly nodded for Butler to continue his speech.

"Brothers!" Butler yelled. "We shall march into their fort with honor! Both Indian and white! In this we shall prove our hearts are pure! In mercy we shall find honor! They are beaten! Hitting them over the head any further is nonsense! We are better than that! We must have honor for all, for we have won!" He patiently waited for the rangers to repeat his words, trying his hardest to listen and make certain nothing became lost in the translation. The nodding heads rolling through the crowd affirmed the effectiveness of his words, much to his relief.

"Brothers, the King shall honor all of the scalps taken on the field of battle, but no more, for the battle is over," he added for good measure.

A few of the chiefs cheered his words.

"Brothers, I am pleased you all see the wisdom of my words!" he said with a nod to the approving chiefs.

A ranger suddenly burst forth from the crowd and stood next to the post. He ignored Butler's glaring eyes.

"Brothers! We have won!" Parshall Terry exclaimed. "Is not that enough! Brothers! I tell you the King, nor his rangers, will stand for women and children being put to the hatchet! The outrage of such an act will never fade in time! It will always be remembered in shame! A shame that will haunt the *Kanonsionni* forevermore! Brothers! I myself shall not stand for it!" He turned his own glaring eyes toward Butler. "Nor shall any of the rangers!"

"That is quite enough Terry!" Butler said through gritted teeth. "I have control over the situation! There is no need for your words, so shut up this instant!"

"Sir," Terry said with a sneer, "I will right well be damned if I shall let them put any women and children to the hatchet!"

"Now, now, my man," Butler said more to the nearby chiefs than to Terry, "all is settled. We must prepare to enter the fort and take our rightful possessions."

The chiefs looked sullenly to the arguing white men and turned back to their people, speaking in various tongues to them. After quelling a few minor grumbles of protests, they all turned back to their huts and fires, leaving the white men standing among themselves.

"All is well then," Butler said to his remaining men. "Do as they do and prepare to enter the fort in the glory you all so richly deserve." He waited while they all slowly walked away, but cast a stern eye to Terry to stand fast. Caldwell took the man by the arm.

Butler turned to him, staring him dead in the eye. "I know you still have people in these parts, so I will dismiss your foolishness, but in the future I warn you mind to your tongue!" he said.

Terry stood mute and looked down to his arm. Caldwell followed his eyes and slowly released his hold on the man.

"We must be very wary in our dealings with these people of such vastly different cultures and beliefs than our own," Butler said to the captain. "For their understanding is not ours, nor is it founded on the same considerations."

"Quite," Captain Caldwell said., rolling an eye to Terry. "We must strive for a greater understanding in a lot of matters, it appears."

Terry raised his lip, taking a few steps away to distant himself.

"Terry!" Butler called behind him.

He turned about, nodding his head toward his commander.

"Relatives or not," Butler said, "must I remind you to where your sworn allegiance lies?"

"I assure you sir, I am a good King's man!" Terry instantly answered, his back suddenly stiffening with pride.

"Just you remember that," Caldwell warned, "for I assure you that if you should return to your former comrades, the rope awaits you!"

"A good long stretch of rope, I might add," Butler said. "You shall see what happens to turncoats if we should be fortunate enough to find Pike or Boyd among their number, treaty or not!"

"As I said, sir," Terry said. "I am a good King's man!"

"Yes," Butler said. "But a conscience is a strange thing. We must not let it cloud our eyes against the realities of life. It is what it is, no matter what voice haunts us. Duty, we must obey its call! Always!"

Terry nodded his head, removing his hat in salute.

"Now be about your duty and see to your men," Butler said. "And mind your place!"

Terry walked away, swallowing hard against the growing lump in his suddenly dry throat. Visions of the fort's walls bristling with rifles all aimed at his head just this morning flashed through his mind. Butler's warning also echoed in it. He knew he meant every word and he knew he dare not tempt him anymore.

Conscience is a terrible thing, for a soldier, at least. It rang hollow and hard in every soldier's mind, only to be quelled and tamed by the ancient call of duty, as always, from time immortal.

## Chapter Eighty
*Butler claims Forty Fort*

Forty Fort bustled with activity, despite the sinking feeling possessing all within its walls. Though every heart knew no choice remained for them but capitulation, the shame of it weighted heavily on their proud Yankee hearts. Thus, the exodus through the south gate increased, with no admonishing voice calling any of them back, least of all Colonel Denison's. He stood along the platform above the gate watching all below with a heavy heart. He had struck a bargain with the devil. He knew he bore all the weight of such a decision himself. He silently prayed the blackguards abided by it.

Noticing a man standing nearby also watching the exodus, he turned toward him. Perhaps talking to him might ease his mind.

The man watched him approach and nodded his head. "Sir?" he asked under his breath.

"Ah, Lieutenant Franklin," Denison said, nodding back. "I watched you on the field, splendid job, under the circumstances, that is."

"Yes," Roswell Franklin answered. "We must do what we must in such circumstances." He followed his commander's eyes down to the people below. His own eyes caught sight of his nervous sergeant gathering some bundles. "Sir," he said, "my men, they all wish to depart and collect what they can before their farms, well, before the Tories and Indians come. They hold little trust in their respect for property."

"Understandable," Denison said. Removing his hat, he nervously ran his hand through his hair. Drawing a deep breath, he looked to the lieutenant. "You, and your men, have done all they can do, and quite admirably at that. You may do as you wish and no man will say anything less of you, least of all I."

He put his hat back on his head. Gazing at the lieutenant, he noticed a trickle of dry blood running down his neck. On closer examination he also noticed a fine cut along the side of his hat. The man apparently had barely been missed by many balls aimed at his head, unlike many of his other fellow officers cut down on the field. He remembered the whizzing balls about his own head during the battle and wondered of Providence. Why did some survive while others perished, though they fought side by side, and faced the same fury? It perplexed him, but here he stood to ponder it, while others did not. He must carry on in their stead and care for their widows and orphaned children.

"There are still a few firelocks about the blockhouse down below," Franklin said, breaking his train of thought. "I intend to bury them to keep them from the enemy, along with such provisions as I can for when we return."

Denison bowed his head. A good man indeed, he thought, already thinking of reclaiming the land they had yet to surrender. With men of such spirit he knew Wyoming would live again. Raising his hands to the man he patted him of the shoulder. "Godspeed, my good man," he said, offering him his hand.

Roswell Franklin eagerly shook his colonel's hand.

Both men turned and looked to the Hanover men fretfully awaiting their officer. "Well, we must be going, we are not much for surrender," Franklin said. "But it must be done, or they'll lay all to waste." Turning to the ladder, he slid down it to his awaiting men. He gave Denison a wave and hurried with his men out the south gate with barely a glance behind him.

"They fought well, they did," Stephen Fuller said, slowly approaching the brooding colonel.

"Yes, we all did," Denison said. "It was the confusion of battle that did us in. I dare say if we would have held and given them but a few more volleys, the day would have turned out very differently."

Fuller nodded his head in agreement. "We have stacked the arms in the center of the stockade as you ordered, sir," he said. "Preparations to receive the enemy are almost complete, for those who can stomach it, that is." He looked down to the people still pouring through the south gate. The number of people choosing to depart had greatly diminished, he figured only some two hundred remained in the fort to face the humiliation of surrender and take their chances. Most of those departing now moved sullenly through the gate. Some stood by and bid those departing farewell, while a scant few others moved supplies around in a vain attempt to hide them in some safe place in the fort. All seemed to move in a trance, in shock of what had happened to force them into such a predicament.

"What is the doctor about?" Denison asked, watching Doctor Gustin directing people with armloads of provisions into a small cellar under one of the cabins.

"Trying to save what he can," Fuller said. "He and Hooker Smith have some strange notions."

"The terms state none are to be molested," Denison said.

Fuller rolled an eye toward him. "Yes," he said, "the terms. All the same, I am glad to see all depart whom can. I don't trust the Tories or the Indians as far I as I could throw one across the river, no sir, I do not!"

"But all is said and done," Denison said, "or will be soon. The die is cast and the metal is ready to be poured, we couldn't stop it now if we wanted to." He waved his hand toward their now helplessly depleted numbers, especially of armed men.

"They shall be coming soon, then we shall see," Fuller said, easing up the corner of his hunting shirt to reveal the butt of his pistol tucked stealthily in the waist of his trousers. "We shall see."

"Yes, we shall," Denison said, looking down to the bench his wife and son sat silently upon in front of a cabin. A cold chill ran up his spine. He locked eyes with his wife. Despite the distance, he recognized the pure dread dripping from her eyes. He gave her a slight nod and the hint of a smile, but he knew it to be insufficient to mask the concern in his eyes. Besides, he knew his wife knew better, as did all the others restlessly awaiting the victorious enemy and his savage hordes.

"All is said and done," Denison said under his breath, more to himself than to anyone else. "Our terms are with the English. It is on their backs to control their allies."

Fuller looked at him out of the corner of his eye but said nothing.

A call from the sentry by the north gate sent both men scrambling along the platform toward it. Denison slowed his pace the closer he gained the gate, overwhelmed by a great sense of foreboding. He swallowed hard against it. Painfully aware of the eyes about him, he straightened his hunting shirt and strode forward. He looked down to a sea of enemy faces, neatly divided into two parties. On the left stood a long column of men standing four abreast, their ranks dotted with leather caps, hunting shirts, and green uniforms. On the right stood a mass of painted faces, all sneering up at the men glaring down on them from behind the high walls. Denison suddenly had the sense that opening the gate would be like bearing his chest to an Indian's lance. Both he and Fuller gazed down at the pompous and somewhat portly man standing in front of all of them with a great sense of dread.

"What's done is done," Denison muttered again under his breath, staring at the strange Indian woman sitting sideways on a woman's saddle faced the wrong way. How absurd she looked, wearing so many captured petticoats she appeared plump, and wearing a towering sea of bonnets tied one after another atop her head, also facing backwards. He looked down at her for the longest moment and gasped when her face turned upwards to his. "Esther," he gasped. "It's Esther!"

"That witch is short of her senses, she is," Fuller said.

Denison turned his eyes away from the preposterous looking woman and to a man holding a bright banner high behind Indian Butler. The officer holding it, dressed in his finest green coat and leather cap, smartly held it high and tight. The standard fluttered gently in the breeze, showing the red crosses of St. Andrew and St. George about its face. Triangular designs of blue graced the four corners of the bright banner.

"Quite a flag," Fuller said, "but it is not ours anymore. It belongs to another time and age, and people. I do so prefer the new stars and stripes much better. It has more of the true heart of the people about it."

Drums and fifes immediately struck up lively airs behind Butler.

"Prepare to open the gate," Denison shouted over the growing lump in his throat. He slowly turned to the ladder, his heart full of a strange sense of anticipation mixed with dread. Stopping at the foot of the ladder, he slowly gazed about, trying to regain his composure. A few eyes stared back at him, hollow and gaunt. Others turned their ashen faces to the ground. No one spoke a word. Every one of their heavy hearts thudded with the same hollow and empty pain. Everyone stood motionless, as if a heavy string of dread stretched from one heart to the other, keeping them in place by the sheer weight of its shame alone.

The drums and fifes grew closer to the gate. Denison straightened his hat and waved to the men at the gate to swing it open, suddenly hoping for all the world to forgive him.

The odd columns marching through the gate made a curious sight, indeed. On the left, brazen men marched in fine order with their flag flying smartly in the breeze accompanied by fine musicians, though a few painted faces dotted their ranks. On the right a huge mass of mean faces stomped through the gate, sneering and baring their teeth with an absurd woman riding near their front. The fresh paint on their faces amplified their expressions, which oddly seemed to mellow the further they stepped into the fort.

A tall man marched up behind Denison and stood watching the horrid parade of Tories and Indians with a cold eye. Folding his arms tightly over his chest he said, "Though it would be rude, I have a strange urge to slam the gate in their faces."

"Yes, Captain Franklin," Denison said, "I am afraid it is much too late for that, though I do understand your urge. But it wouldn't be fitting to slam it in their faces just now, what with their rude nature and all, but there will come a day soon, I grant you that!"

Indian Butler marched proudly and stopped just to the front of Denison, his face bearing a grin so wide it seemed to threaten to tear his face apart. With a wave of his hand behind him, the music promptly ceased and all fell silent, except for a few chattering Indian women.

Denison and Franklin stood stoically still, neither able to speak past the huge lumps in their throats. Denison let his eyes rise to Esther sitting tall and proud atop her stolen mount in all her glory. The closer she appeared to him, the odder she looked, all twisted in the saddle mounted backwards and all. A slight smile grew across his face.

Esther's eyes widened at the impudent rebel. "Well Den-i-son," she snarled, "you make me promise to bring more Indians!" She slowly turned, spreading her arm in a great arc behind her. "See! I bring all of these!" The devilish grin of her face grew wider than Indian Butler's.

Denison's smile faded in its shadow. A great frown replaced it.

"That woman should be seen and not heard!" Butler instantly bellowed, turning a disdainful eye towards her. His smile also instantly disappeared. Shaking his head, he turned his eyes to Denison.

Denison gave him a polite nod and ushered him aside.

Both the Tories and Indians resumed the march with a wave from Butler's hand. The Tories marched smartly and quickly to the arms stacked neatly in the center of the fort. They halted at Captain Caldwell's order, all becoming deathly silent. For an awful moment the eyes of conquerors glared at the sullen eyes of the conquered.

The settlers moved first, breaking the uneasy silence. They moved nervously about in front of the cabins, backing up against the walls from the eyes of disdain glaring at them. Atop the platforms and the cabins a few men stared uneasily down at the conquerors. The Tories and Indians stayed silent, somehow seeming to relish the moment.

A horse slowly advanced from among them. Its rider reined it toward Colonel Denison. Its master bent down from its backwards saddle and reached her long and boney fingers toward his fine beaver hat. Snatching it off his head, she held it high with a hearty laugh, plucking the feather from it and holding it high for all to see.

The Indians immediately poured from their ranks, storming the startled settlers all at once. At a crisp order from Caldwell, the Tories spread out around the stacked arms, protecting them from the gallivanting Indians. Their swarthy counterparts ignored them and continued swarming around the anxious settlers, earnestly examining the buildings, people, and the stable, but molesting no one.

"Here! Here!" Butler suddenly yelled. He turned toward his rangers and the Yankees' stacked arms. "Here!" he said again, spreading his arms toward the weapons. "The Yankees give you all of these as presents!"

A triumphant yell simultaneously rose from every Indian throat. They immediately rallied around the stacked arms, quickly gathering them up to examine them. Eager hands passed them to one another, all in total ecstasy. Their victory just seemed to get better and better.

Butler stood tall, ignoring Denison's glaring eyes.

All of the settler's eyes shot to the gloating British major, astounded by his insane action. He smiled at them and nodded to each of the Indians passing by him, gesturing them toward their new prizes of war. He even smiled at the disgruntled Yankee Colonel.

Denison did not smile back, but merely waved his hand toward the Bennett's cabin.

"Yes, my good man, is that where we are to formalize the terms?" Butler asked over the hoots and howls of the Indians.

Denison answered him a sour look and walked toward the cabin.

Butler cocked an eyebrow to the man and led his officers forwards, walking past many of the shocked settlers. A pair of probing eyes, blue as the day, shone up to him from the huddled settlers. He smiled down at the bearer of the eyes, a little girl standing in front of her crestfallen mother.

"Mother," the little girl suddenly gasped, "how could such a fine looking man bring the Indians here to kill us all?"

Butler's face turned pale. The smile drained from his face and his feet suddenly felt like two ton of bricks. Stopping dead in his tracks, he stared gauntly down at the little girl turning her face back into the folds of her mother's dress in fear.

Shaking his head, he raised his arms. "I must declare that if the settlers in this valley had remained at peace and not sent food, men, and arms to aid the rebellion against the King, none of this would have happened!" he yelled. "You need only to look to yourselves for blame!"

No one within earshot offered any argument. A few of the settlers even reluctantly nodded their heads in agreement.

Butler clear his throat, tugged down to straighten his hunting shirt, and marched toward Denison standing near the cabin door. Butler stopped at his side and rolled his eyes to him. He opened the door and waited for the haughty officer to pass, scowling at him behind his back. This proved more distasteful with each passing moment, he thought. The sooner it drew to a close, the better! Damn this awful war!

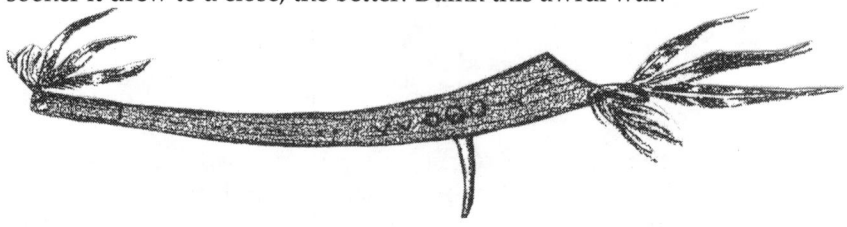

## Chapter Eighty One
*Jenkins' Ride*

John Jenkins rode hard down the narrow trail, barely stopping at Bullock's farm near Bear Swamp and the Shades of Death. Giving a worried old man and woman standing by the trail a quick nod, he continued onwards, seeing no sign of Spalding and his men, or Hollenback. He couldn't find it in his heart to tell them of their three sons' demise in the battle. Others with more time would tell them, besides, by the look in their soulful eyes, they already knew. Though he felt for them, he had no time to waste. He must reach the relief column and hasten their march! Who knew how long Forty Fort could hold out?

After allowing his mount a quick drink from a water trough, he spurred it up the trail, consoling himself that the Bullocks would learn of the massacre soon enough and join the throngs of refugees exiting the valley. By the looks of the scattered debris along the trail, some of them already passed Bullock's, anyway. A sudden gust of wind blew his hat from his head, but he let it go without much thought, much as the refugees had unburdened themselves of any trinkets and such when they faced the dark Shades of Death, twenty miles of a dismal, dark, and snake-infested hell. Trinkets and hats could be replaced, lives couldn't.

Staring into the dark folds of the forest, he checked his rifle, wary of any skulking Indians. Considering the valley their's again, the *Romans of the West* would be everywhere, collecting all whom dared enter their domain without their permission, and inflicting their stern penalties on the transgressors. If Wyoming surrendered, it would truly have a tussle trying to regain the land. A horrible tussle. Wyoming must not surrender, and the only way to secure their land lie with Spalding's men, and whomever else General Washington may have sent to their aid.

He looked to the dimming sunlight over his shoulder, despite the noon hour, for a thick canopy of the towering and great hemlocks started stretching over his head, allowing only enough light for the thick matting of ferns spreading wide under the dark trees. Galloping past more and more settlers, he barely giving them a nod as he passed, hoping to himself their trek to be made in haste. When the reinforcements arrived the valley would be cleared of the Indian and Tory menace, it had to be!

The more settlers he encountered the more he praised himself for not canoeing down the river. He remembered noticing crafts of all types already fretfully crowding the river in the great exodus before he left the fort and how he had smiled upon seeing Abel Yarington still running his ferry across the river between Forty Fort and Wilkes-Barre. He admired the man's pluck and wished more shared it. Oddly, it put him in mind of

Beth. She had pluck in abundance. She could take care of herself and then some, he reassured himself, rubbing the back of his right hand. She would survive.

Another odd memory flashed through his mind with the words 'Monsters! Monsters!' echoing through his memories. They somehow amused him now, despite everything, as much as they did when he had first heard them from a scared man he had escorted back to the valley after tracking him all the way to the Juniata River for stealing a few buckskins. As constable, it was his duty to track down such miscreants, to the ends of the earth if need be, to face justice back at Wyoming. As he led the man through the swamp the man yelled 'Monsters! Monsters!' at each sighting of the huge rattlesnakes plaguing the area. And for good reason, for some of them stretched full over seven or eight feet and were as fat as a man's thigh. "You don't have snakes her abouts but monsters!" the man proclaimed after they finally emerged at Bullock's farm after twenty miles of the thick morass. Jenkins had had to agree. He liked the man, despite his failings, and had to admit relief when the man agreed to work off the fair price of the buckskins with a set period of labor. With a sigh, he realized the man's indentured servitude expired just before the battle. The man had left for the Juniata just in the nick of time. He wondered what he would think of the new 'Monsters' about Wyoming.

A series of rock ledges along the side of the trail caught his attention, turning him from his thoughts. He ignored the tingling sensation about the nape of his neck, though normally he would be wary of the rock ledges. He knew well of the threat of panthers lying in wait. Panthers were known to attack and kill unwary men, dragging them off into the treetops, their stringy skeletons hanging from the treetops the only evidence of their gruesome passing to other men finding their bodies months later. But more important matters pressed his mind. Other lives lay in the balance, he reasoned, galloping hard up the trail.

Suddenly his horse neighed, cocking its head to the rocks. It stopped and reared back on its haunches, almost sending Jenkins tumbling to the ground. He fumbled for his rifle but something struck like lightning from the dark rocks. He felt empty air around him and claws tearing his flesh, along with a harsh snarl in his ears, before feeling the hard ground beneath him. Out of the corner of his eye he saw his convulsing horse neigh and kick wildly in the air, blood showing from long marks torn into its flanks. The gray mass tormenting it suddenly turned and leaped at him, knocking him to the ground in a twisting and rolling mass of gray fur, arms, and legs. Plummeting through the thick ferns, they rolled end over end down the mountainside. Stars filled his eyes, but he nonetheless punched, scratched, and tore at anything not of his own flesh. Feeling something madly trying to clamp onto his neck, he struck at it with all his might. The cat screamed in his ear, its foul and dank breath choking his own breath away. Fiercely kicking along its long slinky body, he finally forced the beast away from him. Snarling and baring its teeth, it sat scrunched a few yards away, its eyes darting from the terrified horse to him. Falling to the ground, he frantically scrambled under the ferns, desperately searching for his rifle.

The beast leaped at his horse again, only to be met by a cruel kick from its rear legs. The beast roared and leapt in the air, this time landing square of the horse's back, sinking its fangs deep into its neck. The frightened horse tumbled to the ground, rolling its terrified eyes to its stunned master.

Jenkins forced his fingers under the thick ferns, madly searching for the cold steel of his rifle's barrel. Finally touching it, he grabbed it and held the splintered weapon before him, gasping and running his eyes all along it. The lock still sat in place. The barrel looked fine, only the splintered stock confused him. His horse neighed all the louder, agonizing in its last moments. Lifting the weapon up, he held it like a long pistol. Cocking it, he fired it point blank at the horrifying beast.

The splintered rifle flew from his hands, sending him rolling backwards into the ferns. He promptly struggled to his feet and felt along his twisted belt for his knife. Drawing it, he stood tall, ready to fight the horrible beast to the last. But only the shocked eyes of his horse met his. It stumbled to its feet, shaking its bloody head. Behind it the panther lay, silent and still. He slowly advanced toward it with his knife clenched tight in his hand. Gazing at the panther's head, he relaxed and let out a great sigh of relief. A great crevasse sat in the middle of its head from the large ball. Its ears fell down into it, creating a curious sight.

The horse neighed at his approach. Its saddle sat askew on its back and blood flowed from neat incisions in its neck. He calmed it, whispering, "You'll be fine dear friend, you did well," in its ear while ripping off one of his shirt sleeves to wrap tight around its neck to stem the flow of blood. He looked to the gashes in its flanks and fixed the saddle. "I know we're both a bit beat up and torn, but we must continue on," he whispered to the horse again. Mounting, he looked to the sea of ferns, wondering whether to search for his broken firelock or not.

A great sense of helplessness overwhelmed him and he gasped. All seemed for not, and hopeless. They had been beaten, he realized with a heavy heart. They most certainly had been. He took the horse by the reins and led it down the trail, suddenly feeling very bereft and empty.

## Chapter Eighty Two
*Life born anew*

Beth stumbled along the narrow trail, looking down at her tattered and ragged dress from the many thorns and briars they already encountered. She shuddered to think of what lay ahead. Her aching feet also protested against the thought of the many miles of stony trial interlaced with swamps, fallen logs, and treacherous defiles full of the ever-present bane of the trail, rattlesnakes. She knew many a face of Wyoming, and wondered how many she would see again after this bloody trek.

The horrid vision of the mounds of earth they had noticed along the trail made her wince at the thought. Already people had perished at the very beginning of the trail. First, two mounds lay next to the trail by the carcass of an oxen peppered with bullet holes and with spears still stuck in it. Three more mounds lay just a few more rods up the trail past a mill in front of a burned out cabin. The small mound next to the larger ones haunted her mind. A small mound for a small soul; an innocent soul. Her heart went out to those whom must have first trudged along the trail to escape and came upon the pitiful scene. But even in their haste they had stopped to do the proper Christian thing and bury the slain. She commended them and hoped all shared their basic humanity in this terrible tragedy. For life went on and needed tending no matter what terrible things cast their foreboding shadows upon it.

She lifted her hand to her sunburned nose and let the burning pain subdue her visions. Which seemed more painful she did not know. Peeling the loose skin away, she lifted her hand to shield her face from the merciless sun. She looked ahead to the man struggling along with a bandage tied about his bloody head. Pieces of it torn from the briars trailed down his back. He clutched his pistol tightly to his chest, ready for whatever demon, be it man or beast, which might burst from the forest. His wife plodded along by his side, ever faithful, even in his wretched exodus. The children, tired and full of despair, trod just behind them. A neat file of human misery. She felt for them all, including her pregnant friend struggling along beside her, and shrugged off the pain of her burned nose and aching feet, suddenly feeling ashamed. Others had it much worse than she.

Elizabeth's groans turned her head to her friend. Elizabeth stumbled over a root and stopped, gasping for breath. Raising a hand to the sweat-soaked white cloth tied about her head, she adjusted it from her eyes. Only streaks of black paint tinged her face now, for her tears and sweat washed the paint away miles ago.

"Don't fret," Beth said, taking her by the arm. "Fretting can only

### The Cry of the Tomahawk — James B. Miller

bring the child all the earlier!"

A loud gasp answered her. Elizabeth collapsed down to her knees, gazing up to her friend with wide eyes. "Too late," she said, putting a hand to her swollen stomach. "Too late!"

"Oh dear God almighty!" Beth gasped.

The man and his family stopped their tired march and looked back to the two women. The children rolled from the trail atop a slight clearing of wild rye grass and collapsed, grateful for a reprieve from the long march, no matter what the reason.

Beth looked down to the ragged dress between her panting friend's legs and noticed it showed wet. "It is time!" she gasped.

"You're telling me?" Elizabeth asked between pants.

The man's wife stumbled toward them. She looked down at the wet dress, shaking her head. Bending down to the two excited woman, she put a hand to both of their shoulders. "For everything is a season, a time to live, a time to die, a time to be born," she said, looking sternly in the women's eyes. "This is a time to be born, and that baby's a comin' and ain't nobody gonna stop it, they ain't fer sure! It will be born here!"

All the women looked about the trail. All of their eyes fell to a thick growth of shielding pines. A bare spot under their branches covered with a thick matting of soft pine needles would suit them fine.

"That'd be best," the wife said, gesturing to the pines. "Nice bed of pine needles and out of the sun."

Beth nodded and helped her gently lift Elizabeth up by her arms. The man watched it all, but kept his distance, as all men knew to do at such a time. A woman's time.

"I'll keep an eye on things out here and mind the children," he said. "Don't fret none on it. Don't fret on nothing."

"Too late," Elizabeth answered.

"Go see if there's water about!" the wife called over her shoulder as she disappeared into the pines.

"We'll see," the man said, slowly turning away. "We'll see."

"He's done tuckered out," the wife said. "And so's the children! Will you be alright while I's fetch some water?"

"Yes," Beth said, easing her friend down onto the pine needles. She soothed her sweaty brow and said, "Be quick!" to the wife.

"I will," the woman said, slowly rising to her tired knees. "Lord almighty help us all."

Beth nodded and started ripping parts of her ragged chemise into long strips, one to tie off the umbilical cord, and the others just for rags. She also started scooping up pine needles for a pillow for Elizabeth.

"Oh dear," Elizabeth gasped. "He's coming soon, by God." Fiercely grimacing, she gripped Beth's hand so tight her knuckles showed white. She looked up to her friend, groaning very loudly.

"It won't be long now!" the wife said, suddenly appearing with a gourd of water. She held it to Elizabeth's parched lips. Elizabeth shook her head away from the gourd and glared at the stunned woman.

"What, my child?" the woman gasped. "It's only water!"

"Water!" Elizabeth gasped. "I'll get putrid fever! Have we no cider, rum, or ale?"

"No, my child, it's all gone," the woman answered.

"Oh my, I am so parched, but I mustn't get the fever!"

"No, my child, we are far from the settlements that breed such. The water's as pure here as if in heaven itself, I durst say!"

Elizabeth peered up to the careworn woman. The pain clouded her mind, but the reference to heaven eased her soul. She welcomed the gourd, taking a long drink. "From heaven," she muttered. "Oh, forgive me dear lady, I do so thank you most heartily." Her eyes suddenly bore a confused look. "My God, I do not even know your name!" she gasped.

"Cary," the woman muttered. "Our name is Cary."

"Well God bless the family Cary for their succor whilst we endure these troubled times! Isn't that so, dear Beth?"

"Oh yes, Mrs. Cary," Beth agreed. But names seemed so unimportant in times such as these. After all, what is in a name? All that truly mattered is whom was there when you needed them. For through great acts of kindness faces would be remembered long after their names faded into the minds of the aged.

A loud scream jolted everyone from their exhausted daze. Elizabeth squirmed in pain. Sitting up, she tired to rise, only to be gently eased back down to the matting of pine needles by the other two women. "Oh John!" she screamed through her pain. "Slain by the cruel savages!"

"Come now," Beth said, "let's be about this business. A new life is to be born out of all this horror. We must let it be!"

Elizabeth nodded and bent her legs at the knees. Both women lifted her ragged petticoats and tended to the screaming woman. Soon a new cry replaced her screams. The cry of a new life started echoing under the dense pines on the lonely trail amidst the wilderness.

"It's a boy!" Beth proudly announced, wiping the new babe clean. Mrs. Cary beamed at the babe and his mother while attending to the other matters of birth. Beth eased the child into his mother's arms.

"Oh, he's a fine soul, he is indeed," Elizabeth said.

Tears rolled down all the threadbare women's faces. Here, in this unforgiving wilderness, they helped usher in a new life whilst many other lives perished. Somehow it brought a great sense of purpose to their struggle. Leaning toward one another, they hugged each other, each somehow conscious of their new found sense of purpose.

Mr. Cary and the Cary children barely raised an eye toward the commotion under the pine trees. Exhaustion dulled their senses. Many other lethargic souls trudged along the trail before them in the same trance. Barely any of their curious eyes turned toward the noise under the pines. Those few which did quickly turned back to the trail and to the countless miles lying ahead of them. The winding trail never seemed to end. The children's minds turned back to more peaceful times by their cabin, their mother working hard, but never seeming to mind, while they played about. All the world seemed a joy then. It seemed a nightmare now. They yearned for their old life, but it seemed so far away, so, so, far.

## Chapter Eighty Three
*The stroke of a quill pen*

Martha Bennett watched a portly, but proud man, swagger into the room, full of himself and looking down his nose at everyone. Strutting to a small table in the middle of the room, he looked down with a critical eye to the paper lying upon it. After a long moment he quickly looked about the room, but adverted everyone else's eyes. Folding his arms across his chest, he impatiently watched the others file through the cabin door, not saying a word. A tall Indian chief, aged, but still magnificent in bearing, positioned himself next to the haughty British officer, edging out two Tory officers. A younger, but fiercer looking Indian, pushed the two officers even further back, taking his place next to the older chief. His glaring eyes showed full of purpose and resolve. He was not a man to be trifled with at all.

Clearing his throat, the portly officer bent down to adjust one of the fine beaded leggings covering his lower legs. His moccasins appeared finer than the two great chiefs' moccasins standing next to him, what with their fine bead work and all. He must have an Indian maiden in the sugarbush, as they say, to tend to his clothing, Martha thought. "That's Indian Butler himself," she whispered into her cupped hands over her friend Polly's ear. Polly gasped in the tense and quiet air, immediately provoking a stern look from Martha's mother. She waved her hand for both of the girls to back away into a corner of the cabin. Martha shook her head, but her mother's glaring eyes quickly subdued her sense of rebellion. She joined her friend in the corner.

Doctor Gustin stood alone in the opposite corner, his hand to his chin. He watched the Tory officers with a certain glare of disdain in his eyes. Mister Beech stood by a small table, pen in hand, awaiting further instructions.

Captain Franklin, his eyes also alive with disdain, stepped into the room. Denison himself closed the door behind him, anxious to be done with the whole sorted affair. The loud creak of the door turned every eye to it.

Denison blanched at the sudden attention. The full weight of the whole situation suddenly fell heavy on his conscience and he bowed his head in shame. He felt like a ton of bricks fell upon him. He swallowed hard against the sudden and overwhelming feelings, trying to collect his thoughts. "Yes," he finally said, clearing his throat. "If you may, Major?" He waved his hand toward the table beside the haughty officer. "We have written up an agreement, if you care to review it."

Butler raised one of his bushy black eyebrows and removed his hat, revealing a fine stock of white hair, meticulously combed and tied with a fine silk ribbon about the nape of his neck. "Your clerk may read the terms aloud for all to hear," he said with a nod.

"Very well," Denison said. "If you will, Mr. Beech?"

Beech nervously sat down onto a chair placed behind the table and shuffled a few papers about. He looked down to the paper and then up to the spectacles perched on his forehead. Lowering them to his eyes, he cleared his throat, and recited the terms in a stately tone:

**Westmoreland, July 4th, 1778**

"Capitulation made,& completed between Major John Butler on behalf of His Majesty King George the 3rd and Colonel Nathan Denison of the United States of America.

"Article 1st That the Inhabitants of the Settlement lay down their Arms and their Garrison's be demolished.

"Article 2nd That the inhabitants are to occupy their farms, peaceably,& the lives of the Inhabitants be preserved entire and unhurt.

"Article 3rd That the Continental Stores be delivered up.

"Article 4th That Major Butler will use his utmost influence that the private property of the Inhabitants shall be preserved entire to them.

Article 5th That the prisoners in Forty Fort, be delivered up, and that Samuel Finch now in Major Butler's possession be delivered up also.

"Article 6th That the properties taken from the People called Tories up the river be made good; and they remain in peaceable possession of their Farms, and unmolested, in a Free trade, in and throughout this State as far as lies in my power.

"Article 7th That the Inhabitants that Colonel Denison now capitulates for, together with himself do not take up Arms during the present contest."

Butler eyed the paper for a moment, silently considering all he had heard. He reached out his hand and Beech handed him the paper. He read it for the longest moment and sighed. "All seems in order," he proclaimed. "Of course, you shall allow my man to make a copy?"

"By all means, but as you see," Denison said, gesturing to more papers on the table, "it has already been done."

"Just the same, if you don't mind," Butler said. Stepping aside, he let one of his officers strut to the table.

The green-coated officer looked down his nose to Beech, loudly clearing his throat.

Beech raised his spectacles to his brow again and slowly rose from the chair.

"As soon as my officer has completed his copies, we shall all sign them, if that is agreeable to you," Butler said.

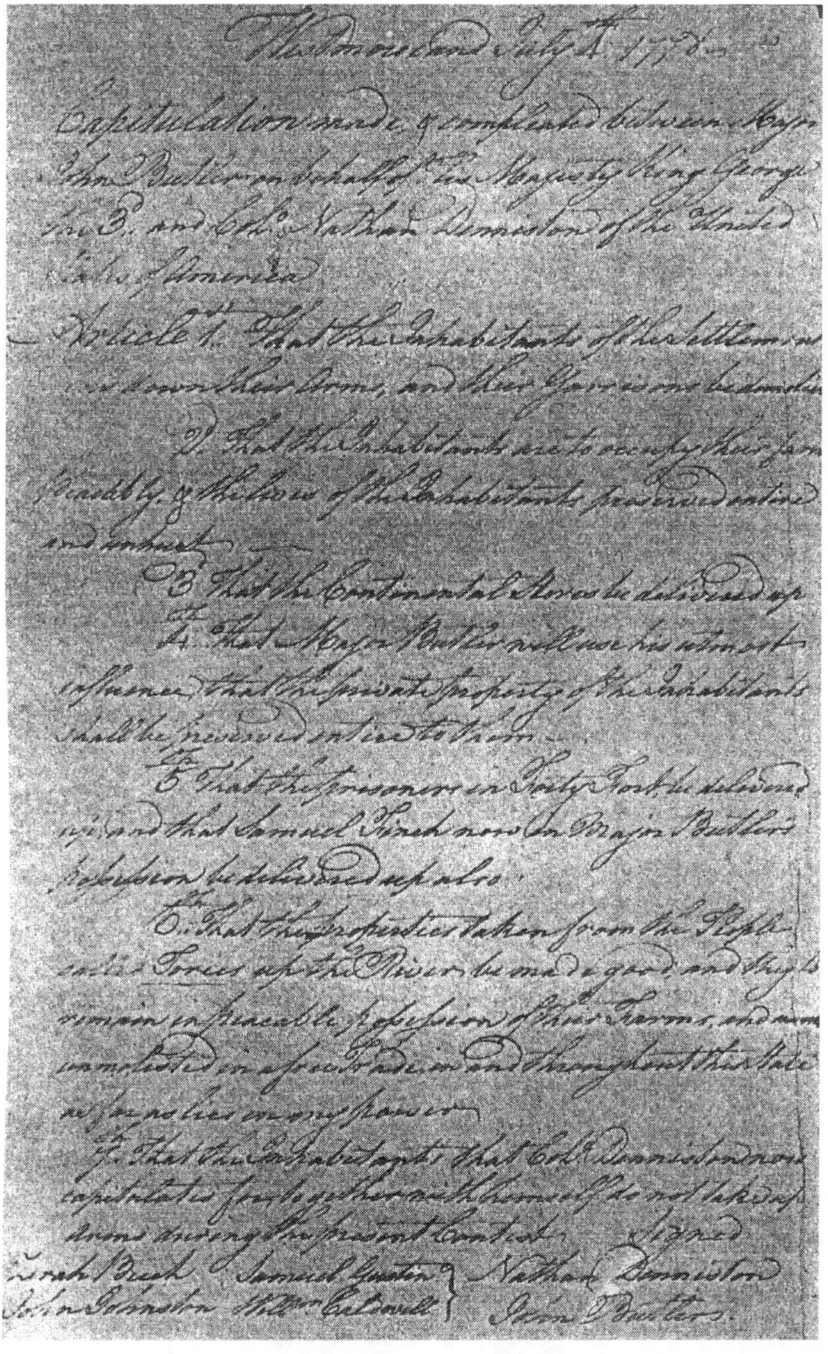

Denison nodded, not sure how to take the victor's accommodating attitude. Biting his lip, he gazed around the room at the assembly of Indians and Tories. None stared back, save one, with eyes dark as the night. A tall Indian chief raised his chin and stared so intensely at him it sent shards of fear tingling down his spine.

Denison's jaw dropped. He had never witnessed such a shocking stare of glaring hatred in all his life. He knew that if this chief had his way all would be put to the hatchet. He felt his eyebrows pinch together and stared at the brazen chief, locking the chief's burning stare in his mind forever, for it told of the Six Nations' true attitude toward the Yankee settlers of Wyoming. He would never forget it. This chief proved himself a true enemy of this new nation. No words or friendly overtures would ever reduce such a pure and absolute hatred. Cocking his head, he listened to the whispers now passing between the Indians for a hint of the brazen chief's name.

"I Gucingerachton! Yank-ee Chief!" the large chief said without taking his eyes off the Yankee colonel. He lifted one arm from his chest while keeping the other folded across it. His finger pointed in the direction of his cold stare. Slowly drawing his arm back, he tucked it under his other arm.

Denison's spine tingled again.

Sayenqueraghta smiled along with the other Indians. Some of them let their hands fall to the tomahawks tucked in their sashes.

"Are you quite finished with that document?" Butler asked, noticing the Indians' actions.

The Tory officer seemed to ignore his commander's question, but his hand suddenly moved all the faster. In no time he finished scratching the pen across the paper and dashed some sand over it. Blowing the sand clear, he quickly handed the paper to his commander's eager hands.

Butler gave it a quick glance. "The sooner this document is signed, the better!" he said, reaching for the pen. He quickly dipped it in an ink well. "Are we in agreement," he asked, rolling his eyes to Denison.

"Quite," Denison answered.

Heads nodded and grunts of affirmation rose from everyone in the crowded room, save one, Gucingerachton.

The Indians gathered around and watched the white men sign their papers with piercing eyes. None of them stepped forward to sign, though, for Sayenqueraghta had told them they had no interest in the paper. For they had won and all the world knew it. If the white eyes wished to show mercy, let them, for now anyways. The *Kanonsionni* needed no paper to proclaim such an absolute and total victory, or the need to show the white man's weakness, mercy. They had taught these rebels a proper lesson. If they forgot, the lesson would be repeated. Nonetheless, the Indians hovered close to the table to ensure the Yankees witnessed their humiliation. They themselves would never forget it.

Denison took the pen with a great sweeping motion and signed his name full and large under the glaring eyes of the Indians. His empty heart thudded in his ears. He felt conscious of every child's, woman's, and man's heart thudding in Wyoming. A cold shard of fear shot through his entire body, as cold as the surrounding Indians' eyes. The pen, though merely a feather, felt heavy in his hand. He tried not to think of the icy feeling surging through his veins as he signed the other copies, but the full weight of many a heavy heart fell onto his hand. Oh, what a legacy, he thought. What a horrid legacy.

Wyoming fell with the stroke of his quill pen.

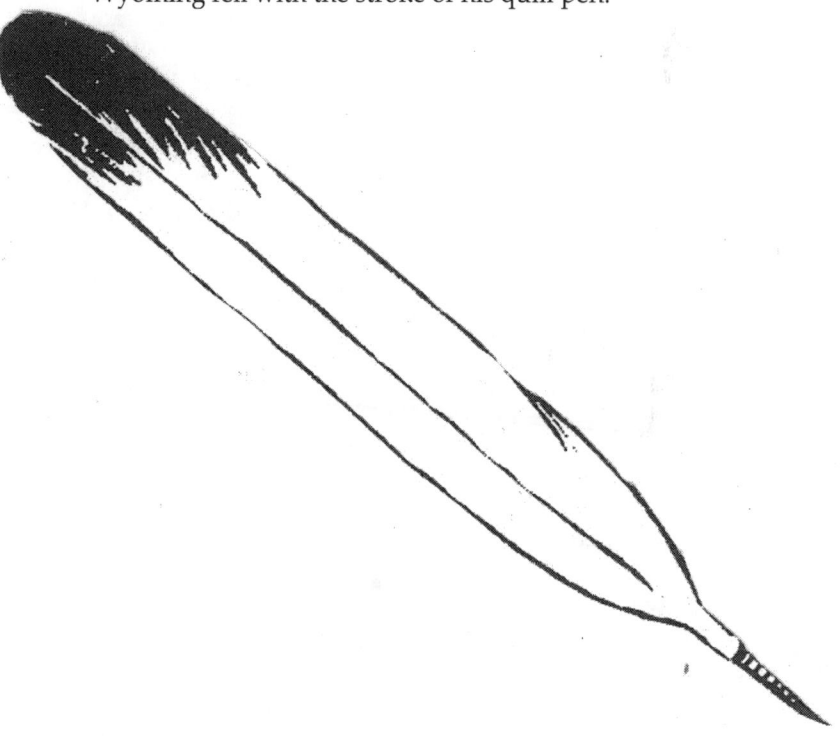

## Chapter Eighty Four
### *We must!*

Mathias Hollenback rode at the front of a meandering line of men and packhorses trudging through a great swamp: the Shades of Death. He stared straight ahead in the direction of Wyoming, barely pausing to look back to the struggling soldiers behind him. His words, and his haste upon first meeting the soldiers last night, urged them on with the same fever possessing him, and he knew it. That is why he had to keep his eyes locked ahead, for now they had to cover some forty odd miles as quickly as possible. Duty demanded it. Decency demanded it.

A crackle in the brush ahead made his heart jump. Had the savages penetrated this far south? Keeping his horse moving forwards at a slow walk, he nonchalantly cocked his rifle lying across the front of his saddle, glancing back to see if anyone else noticed the noise. Sergeant Baldwin, just behind him, perked up, raising his rifle to his chest. He stared into the waning sunlight through the trees and immediately stopped, halting the line of men behind them. The well-trained soldiers readied their arms and made way for their captain. Hollenback pulled back on his mount's reins, also awaiting the captain.

Captain Spalding rode to the front and reined up his horse beside Hollenback. Gesturing forward, he watched Baldwin spread a few of his men in a line and slowly advance toward the disturbance, firelocks held at the ready. Drawing his own pistol, he cocked its hammer. No one spoke, for each knew the drill after performing it on many battlefields. The many hardships and battles these men endured together formed an alliance and second sense of how everyone would react. Hollenback, once a member of the same ranks, shared the feeling.

The noises lessened upon the approach of the stern soldiers. Only the most foolhardy enemy would approach their ranks in such a manner, certainly not Iroquois warriors or Butler's Rangers. Spalding raised his hand in the air and then slowly lowered it. Lowering his pistol, he waited. All the men relaxed at the sight of a man stumbling down the trail leading a bloody horse behind him.

"Why that's Jenkins!" Hollenback blurted out.

Jenkins lumbered toward Baldwin, passing the reins of his mount to him with barely a nod. Darting toward Captain Spalding, he stopped just in front of his mount.

"Jenkins," Spalding gasped. "My God man, what has happened to you?"

Jenkins shook his head and struggled to catch his panting breaths. He glanced down to his torn and bloody clothing and then back up to Spalding. "Never mind me," Jenkins gasped through his panting breaths. "Many need your assistance up yonder! Many!"

"My God Jenkins, what has happened?" Hollenback said, perking up in his saddle.

Jenkins shook his head, finally catching his panting breath. "We must hasten our march to Wyoming! For I do fear for the lives hanging in the balance! Many are starting to leave the valley by the river, this road, and the banks of the river itself!"

"Has Colonel Denison capitulated?" Spalding asked.

"I know not, sir, as I left the fort before dawn, but I dare say I hope not! I do not trust Indian Butler or have any faith in him controlling the hordes of Indians!" Jenkins reported. He looked back to the many wide-eyes of the ranks staring at him. "Our homes, and many a man's dear wife and family, lay in peril ahead, sir!" he yelled. "You are their only hope to relieve their suffering! All other is lost!"

"See?" Hollenback said, turning toward Spalding. "It is as I said, perhaps worse! Look at poor Jenkins here! He is in tatters and many more like him await us at Wyoming! We must not fail them!"

"Now just calm down, Ensign," Spalding said. "We are marching with all due haste, you know that! What more can we do?"

"Clear away the Tory and Indian menace!" Hollenback quipped.

"Ensign," Spalding said, staring at the upset man with wide eyes born of the excitement of the rage burning within his heart. "You yourself faced them with some thirty well trained men of these very ranks, plus Captain Hewitt's fine men, and led by Captains Durkee and Ransom no less, some sixty men in all!" Putting a hand to the rear of his saddle, he leaned to look back at the exhausted column of men behind him. "We barely have equal that number! What magic do you think we possess that you did not?"

"Nonetheless, it is our duty, sir!" Hollenback said, pointing up the trail. "And I intend to do all I can to relieve our people!"

"As all of us do!" Spalding said. "But I've been in many a battle, and I do fear this one is lost! In more ways than one, I might add!"

Hollenback glared at him. "We have not yet arrived, sir, save your judgment until then!" he said through gritted teeth.

"Certainly," Spalding said, "but with our pack train and such, we can only move so fast! We have already come some twenty miles this day alone!" He looked to Jenkins. "And he says they're already leaving!"

"Some," Jenkins said. "But not all, sir, Forty Fort is still full of people. I know not of Pittston Fort, but they too, perhaps, await relief!"

"Yes, we shall resume the march straight away," Spalding said.

"We move as the turtle when we need to be as fleet of foot as the hare!" Hollenback said.

"Sirs," Baldwin interrupted, looking toward the spooky trail ahead. "Let me take Stephens here and scout ahead, Captain!"

"Very well," Spalding said. "Draw horses from the quartermaster and be about it, but do not engage the enemy, ascertain their number and the state of things, then report back with due haste."

"I shall join them, if you have no objection, sir," Hollenback said.

"Of course," Spalding said, "but I must caution you all again, do not let your emotions control you, I feel too much of that has already taken place! Do not engage the enemy or be captured! Be mindful that surprise is our only advantage!" He looked up through the canopy of tree limbs over their heads. "The light of the day fades. I expect you back at first light on the morrow!"

"Yes sir," Baldwin said, leading Stephens back to the packhorses.

"Mind yourself, Ensign, do not let your emotions gain the best of you," Spalding said to a fidgety Hollenback.

"It is much too late for that, my dear Captain," Hollenback said, reining his horse back toward the pack train as well. "We need more emotion now than ever!"

"Of course, Ensign," Spalding said, looking to his bloody shirt. "You should have your wound looked at first, though."

"I haven't the time, fine sir," Hollenback said, galloping back to the packhorse train.

"He is a very brave, but stubborn man," Spalding said to Jenkins.

They both watched a man lead Jenkins' bloody horse to the rear.

"I almost hope to encountered an Indian and not a panther, seeing the damage to you and that poor animal," Spalding said.

"They are both as mean as the other," Jenkins said. "It seems the day has indeed turned against us, I fear. Leveler heads must prevail."

"Fine," Spalding said, "and seeing as I am need of a lieutenant, may I offer the position to you?"

"Yes, sir," Jenkins said. "I shall be honored." Straightening his back, he groaned from some tired muscle cramping in his back.

"I think we have one more good horse to save your aching feet," Spalding said.

"I would appreciate that, sir," Jenkins said, putting a hand to his aching back.

Baldwin and Stephens edged around them on their packhorse mounts and trotted headlong up the trail. Hollenback soon galloped along behind them.

"Godspeed," Spalding called behind them, but none turned to acknowledge his words. "I hope we can do something," he muttered under his breath before waving the column forward again.

"We can," Jenkins said, taking the reins of the somewhat fresh mount handed to him. He quickly mounted and stared up the trail. "We must! For many innocents lay under the threat of the scalping knife!"

## Chapter Eighty Five
*The ludicrous and sad*

Without a word, but with merely a wave of his hand to his officers, Major Butler turned and exited the cabin with his nose in the air. Caldwell gave Colonel Denison a slight nod in his superior's stead and led the other officers out the door behind their haughty commander. Butler met them outside the door, mumbling a few passing orders to them. At his leave, they slowly parted for other parts of the fort.

Butler stiffened his back and marched about the confused settlers, barely acknowledging any of their questioning eyes. No one spoke to him, or he to any of the crestfallen faces staring at him. He soon found himself at the north gate, gazing at an odd freckle-faced boy sitting atop a huge barrel with his knees drawn up to his face. "Pa, oh Pa, he ain't comin' back," the boy gasped between sobs.

Butler raised one of his bushy eyebrows and watched the boy collapse in pure sorrow atop the hogshead, finally drained of tears and spirit. The pitiful boy's anguish reminded him of how his own son had been locked in the infamous Albany Jail by the rebels. Yes, how his dear son Walter had suffered in the rebels' jail, but he still lived, thank God. But he did find some solace in his son's cunning escape from the rebels' prison. Turning, he walked away from the grieving boy, silently fearing the boy's suffering may not have ended, but may have just begun.

A strange skulking man with a painted face caught his eye. The man slid through the gate and scampered along the wall, obviously trying to maintain a low profile. Butler carefully watched the man and suddenly recognized his face, despite the owner's efforts to disguise it. He knew the settlers would easily recognize the face also, and grudgingly admired the man's pluck to waltz into the den of those he had so bitterly betrayed, disguised or not.

Parshall Terry's eyes did not lock on his commander's, though he noticed his gaze. Creeping through the shadows to the corner of the first cabin, he stood watching the glum settlers. Though he searched for other faces, his jaw dropped at the sight of one man in particular.

Butler noticed Terry's surprised look and curiously followed his eyes. The face to which they led filled his body with an instant rage. He promptly drew his sword and marched toward the man.

The man blanched upon his approach, but stubbornly stood fast.

"Boyd!" Butler screamed, barely able to contain his rage. He pointed his sword threateningly toward the man, daring him to move. The settlers around Boyd slowly parted, leaving him standing all alone.

"I would hope that your honor would allow me the rights of a prisoner of war!" Boyd flatly stated.

"Rights!?!" Butler said, almost stammering with rage. Looking all around, he finally locked his wide eyes on a great elm a few rods outside the gate. He pointed his sword toward it, shaking with rage. "You'll have the rights due a traitor!" he screamed, prodding Boyd out the gate and toward the tree. "Now go to that tree without another word!" he loudly ordered.

Boyd marched full and proud at sword point toward the tree. The longest walk of his life. Reaching it, he faced about and stood tall, knowing nothing on earth, short of a miracle, could save him now. Well, everyone is to die, he thought, and if I am to die here it will at least be as a friend to my new country. Looking down at the shaking sword close to his neck, he smacked his lips in disgust. Mind your code of honor now, Major Butler, he thought, daring not to speak. A code of honor which now condemned him, ironically. He raised his head high despite it all. He would die a soldier's death He would beg no more, nor give this haughty British dog the satisfaction. Fetch the bone like a good dog, he thought to himself, glaring with eyes equal to the hatred shinning from the Major's bulging eyes. Be a good mindless idiot! At least he died for a country in which every man had dignity.

Butler stammered, enraged, seeming to read the man's taunts in his eyes. He wanted to plunge his sword into his neck, but thought better of it. The code of honor forbade it, he reminded himself, even here. He looked around, suddenly realizing no rangers accompanied him in his haste. Perhaps he would have to be the executioner after all.

A group of Indians noticing the spectacle and sensing some sport, curiously gathered around the infuriated British officer and his stoic prisoner held by sword point to a tree. These white eyes could be so dramatic and strange in their ways.

Butler, noticing their firelocks and not wishing to waste time in gathering his own men, stared at the dark eyes watching him. "Shoot this man!" he ordered, stepping back.

Boyd swallowed hard against his fear and stood even taller.

The Indians needed no translation. They immediately shouldered their firelocks, firing all at once.

Boyd instantly fell, his body riddled with a half dozen lead balls.

The Indians whooped and gazed curiously at Butler, not sure whether to claim the scalp or leave it to the white man. Seeing no argument in the British officer's eyes, they swooped down onto the corpse. One of them produced a knife and neatly cut a small round spot of hair from the dead man's head. Lifting the scalp high, he wailed in triumph. They then all rambled toward the fort, hooting and yelling all the way.

Butler, his rage spent, gracefully slid his sword back into its scabbard. He turned back toward the gate.

Terry stood there, his mouth agape. He stared blankly at Butler and then over his shoulder to his former countrymen gathering about the gate. He quickly slid along the side of the fort and stealthily disappeared down the riverbank.

Butler looked away from the eyes staring at him from the gate, biting his upper lip. Straightening his hunting shirt, he took a deep breath before marching through the gate, without so much as a passing glance back over his shoulder at Boyd's body. Boyd had played the game. He lost and paid the price. Butler had little doubt that his own neck would be stretched from the nearest tree if the fates reversed themselves. It was just the way of it. The code of war, or so-called honor.

He wasted no time in finding Caldwell and some of his other officers, ushering them into one of the cabins. He suddenly found the need for conversation, but out of earshot of the prying Yankees. Their rebellion had cost the land and people more than they could possibly imagine, and had ripped and torn this whole country asunder. He needed the company of rash and just men right now, no more rebels.

John Franklin and Nathan Denison edged through the crowd just in time to see Butler dodge into one of the cabins with a few of his officers. He seemed all in a huff and the sharp rifle cracks they heard just moments before did not play well to them. They continued onward to the gate, passing a group of oddly grinning Indians. One of them holding a bloody scalp seemed all the more happy than the others. The two Yankee officers passed them with an odd stare. The Indians gave hearty laughs in response.

"Odd lot they are," Denison said, noticing a crestfallen man approaching them from the crowd by the gate. "It's Sergeant Boyd!" the man explained upon finally reaching them, pointing beyond the gate to a body by a tree. "They executed him without so much as a word," the man gasped. "He should have had the good sense to leave with Pike."

Denison shook his head. He too wished the man had had the good sense to leave with Pike, but suddenly remembered how the man had always told him with a stomping foot to the ground, "This is my new country," he had explained, "and this is where I'll stand or fall. I'll run no more!"

Quite an explanation, true words the man had lived by, and unfortunately died by. He now wished he had ordered the man to leave with the others instead of tempting fate. He wondered if a lingering guilt, or the wish to validate his courage for his new country, as he called it, caused the man to stay. Whatever haunted the man's soul after he deserted the British ranks twisted his thoughts and in the end caused his own demise. There was no code of honor in this wilderness. But whatever his thoughts, the man proved himself a brave man and staunch friend to his adopted country in the end, and one whose knowledge had helped the people of his new adopted home. He indeed proved a great loss. Wyoming, perhaps, lost too much this day. "See that he's buried," he said to Franklin. "See to it discreetly. We don't wish to antagonize our guests."

"No sir, that wouldn't do," Franklin said. He turned and looked at the green coats and feathered heads intermingling with their own crestfallen people. Taking off his hat, he scratched his head.

"Wait until dark," Denison said. "Very dark, it won't be long."

Both men climbed a ladder to a platform running below the wall for a place free of grinning Indians. A yell down at the gate turned their eyes to it.

A dozen warriors sauntered through the gate holding wooden buckets. An odd sight, both Denison and Franklin thought, watching them. Coming across the first settlers they met, they dipped bits of cloth into the buckets and daubed the stunned settlers' faces with paint, shaking their fingers at them not to wipe it away.

A grunt and wave from one of the bucket-bearing Indians up to the two men made them climb down the ladder again. The brave daubed their faces the moment they stepped off the ladder. "You no touch!" the brave warned them. "Save you from wild Indians! Show you captured! They no hurt you or knock you on head!"

Both men reluctantly accepted the paint and urged the others to also accept the Indians' strange ways. With faces painted black and burning red beneath in shame, they climbed the ladder again.

"When shall they leave us?" Franklin asked.

"When they tire of their present sport, I am afraid," Denison answered. "I pray they keep to the terms." Looking down to the swarming Indians, he sighed. "I've ordered the release of their brethren. I hope that shall appease them somewhat."

Both men watched the Indians walk among the remaining settlers, profusely nodding their heads and professing friendship in broken English. The stone cold faces staring back at them did little to deter them from their antics. One in peculiar stood out to them. A wiry Indian, possibly simple of mind, shook many a settler's hand, walking from one settler to another like some strange ambassador of good will. His huge overbite pulled his upper lip and pointed his nose out from the rest of his face, which receded into two dark pits of eyes. But a smile stretched from ear to ear across his face and he seemed most sincere, despite his cold reception. He said, "Goot? Goot? Uhum, very goot," to every hand he shook, always looking back over his shoulder at the other Indians, thinking he impressed them with his command of the white eyes' tongue and manners of diplomacy. Ignorance did have its bliss.

At a far corner of the fort a yell rose above the endless chatter of many Indian tongues. A group of Indians danced with joy around two Indians just released from the Yankees' possession.

Black Henry sauntered among the dancing Indians with his newly released partner, both of them holding up their hands to show how the Yankees had tortured them to try and make them talk by pinching the tips of their fingers with bullet molders. But neither had talked, he proclaimed triumphantly, and thus the hated white eyes had been defeated.

Both Franklin and Denison rolled their eyes at their bragging display, neither of them thinking whatever intelligence they would have gained from the spies would have prevented anything, anyways. Black Henry had professed a great friendship to the settlers and a total commitment to peace among the peoples, until he and his fellow had been caught spying on Forty Fort just a week before the battle, that is. After that his tongue remained silent, but the hatred in his eyes spoke volumes. He once even dwelt in Wyoming, much as many of the other familiar Indian faces now taunting the poor settlers, nonetheless greater than the two Indians heartily embracing the recently released Indians, Anthony Turkey and Captain Cornelius. Both had once sworn no harm would come to Wyoming while they still drew a single breath. Well, they still breathed, and many they once called friend now lay dead upon the field of battle. Both Denison and Franklin turned their heads away, shaking them in disgust upon feeling the cutting edge of their betrayal.

At almost the same moment a high pitched yell grabbed their attention. The tone and sharp words in both broken English and the Indian dialects made a curious, almost comical sound down by the gate. There Samuel Finch walked hastily through it, pursued and tugged at by a haggard and very old Indian woman chattering, "Grandson! Grandson," among many others things to the embarrassed white man. Finch turned, berating the woman to no avail. The settlers about the gate stared blankly at him walking through the gate with his new grandmother at his heels. She kept at him until some sympathetic souls led him into a cabin, closing the door in the crying woman's face. She immediately collapsed to the foot of the door, wailing about her recent loss. To Finch's and the settlers' relief, the other Indians offered nothing but a muffled laugh to the woman.

The chatter of another language, neither Indian or English, drew Denison's and Franklin's attention from the door. Denison squinted and pointed to direct Franklin's probing eyes to the speaker of the strange tongue.

Dr. Gustin stood before a group of Indians, fluently chattering away in French while spreading his arms to prevent the Indians from advancing toward a certain cellar door. Some of the Indians answered him in French, waving their arms while others looked puzzlingly at him. One of them, an aged chief covered with tattoos, finally pushed the stubborn doctor aside. He marched toward the cellar door with Gustin madly waving his arms at him and following close at his heels.

Others of the doctor's party stood nervously about the cabin, all wearing dreadful looks on their faces. One of them suddenly strode forward, waving his arms in protest of the chief. "Pox! Pox!" the man yelled, shaking his head and pointing toward the cellar door.

The chief's eyes lit up in recognition of the dreaded word. His wide eyes stared at the door and he quickly turned about on his heels, directing all those near him to follow his lead. They rapidly departed.

Dr. Gustin sighed in relief, biding the Indians adieu. His heart jumped from an old woman carrying a bucket walking steadily toward the door. He raised his hands to protest, but her cutting tongue and waving hands halted him. Bending down to the door, she quickly swabbed it with black paint before scampering off, cursing the stunned doctor behind her. "Bad medicine!" she screamed back at the crazed white man.

Gustin shook his head and smiled at the man standing near him. Offering his hand, he shook the man's hand heartily for saving their meager stash of supplies in the cellar. They needed them for the wounded. It would be a while until they could be moved, no matter what happened. He put a hand to his face to suppress a chuckle.

The Indian woman screamed "Bad medicine!" at him again.

"Indeed, for some," he answered the old hag with a smile.

A touch to Denison's shoulder broke his gaze from the cellar door. Franklin directed the colonel's gaze to a pair of Indians approaching the gate, one of them dressed in the common manner of the Indians while the other sported a finely tailored gentleman's coat and a equally fine beaver-skin cocked hat. Strutting through the gate, the latter paraded in front of a group of admiring Indians, continually chattering about something.

Reverend Johnson edged his way stealthily toward the bragging Indian, listening intently to what he said from the shadows.

The brave noticed him and the other settlers gathering about to hear of his exploits and yelled all the louder, intrigued by the settler's sudden attention.

Reverend Johnson did not share his enthusiasm, but rather blanched from his words. Stepping out of the shadows, he looked gravely up to Denison and Franklin. "They had Colonel Dorrance in their charge," he explained through his choked throat. Swallowing hard, he continued, "They were to bring him here to exchange him for some sort of ransom, but his wounds slowed them down." He shook his head in grief. "They finally dispatched him, fearing by the time they entered the fort, the celebrations would have ceased."

A gasp rose from the surrounding settlers, but none more louder than a woman's listening intently not far from the gate. She recognized the coat and hat immediately, but prayed against all odds for her husband's survival. She collapsed to the ground crying, full of anguish. Other women promptly helped her to a nearby bench.

The finely dressed Indian walked over to the bench, drawn by the sudden commotion. Keeping pace with Reverend Johnson, he reached the bench at the same time as the reverend.

Mrs. Dorrance, overcome with grief, looked soulfully up to the Indian and pushed Johnson aside. She glared with all the hatred she ever felt in her heart to the cold eyes staring down at her in confusion.

The brave finally shook his head and waved Reverend Johnson's equally cold stare off. Backing away, he faced his fellows. "Woman!" he said, pulling at the coat. "She his woman!" He stepped back to her.

Johnson bowed his head and walked to his own family standing not far away, watching the warrior parade mockingly in front of the woman with a growing sense of outrage. He stared blankly at another bucktoothed Indian grabbing his hand and saying, "Brothers! Now goot friends!" over and over as he shook it.

"The ludicrous is mingled with the sad," Denison said.

"As you say," a voice commented from their side. "But war is a rather unpleasant affair."

Both Yankees jumped in spite of themselves, silently scolding themselves for becoming so engrossed in what lay before their eyes, they paid little heed to their surroundings; a mistake which could prove fatal to any frontiersman. They always slept, toiled, and lived with one eye open, always waiting for whatever might leap at them from the forest. But this time their senses had failed them, and in their own fort, no less. Both men stared blankly at the Tories suddenly standing beside them from nowhere, totally ashamed of themselves in more ways than one.

The Tories noticed their uneasiness and laughed. Only one of them wore his green coat. Besides the coat, all three had stripped down to their breeches in Indian fashion, and had painted all of their exposed skin with great swirls and daubs of odd colored paint. One of them grinned at the Yankee officers, exposing his black and yellow teeth, proudly presenting a scalp. "You know," he said, leaning toward the Yankees. "This hair, it's Lazarus Stewart Junior's, it is!"

"That's quite enough Hughes!" the green coated soldier said. "Now be about your business and leave these officers be! Captain Caldwell says we is to assemble to march out, so get to it! You and your whole lot!"

"Caldwell?" Hughes scoffed. "He and Butler can go to the devil!"

"No," the green coated man answered. "I think they've already seen quite enough of you this day!"

Hughes heartily laughed and turned away, running down the platform to a far corner of the platform to meet his fellows. The other blue-eyed Indian ran after him.

"Pay no attention to that lot," the remaining Tory said. "They's part of the horrors of war, they is!"

"Quite," Denison agreed.

"You seem a sensible man, sir," the Tory said, eyeing the Yankee officer, "so's I'll play it straight. If your lot would have held but a bit longer the victory would be yours, not ours, but don't you tell the Major I's said so. It's just between us gentlemen, it is."

"Yes," Denison said. "But such are the fortunes of war."

"Yes," the man answered with a smart nod, "fortunate for us."

"Am I to understand your lot is to move out of the fort this night?" Franklin asked, noticing Denison's sour expression. He felt he had to say something to defuse the situation before the colonel exploded with rage. Perhaps he might gain a bit of information in the process.

The man eyed them suspiciously for a moment and then turned his eyes down to a few of the yelling Indians grabbing firebrands from the hearth in the abandoned kitchen for their fires. Apparently they intended to stay the night in the fort. "Yes," the man said. "We's to leave." Noticing their expression turn sour, he added, "but we is to leave a token force behind to keep an eye on things so's they don't run astray."

With that the man turned toward the ladder. After climbing down it, he motioned for the drummer standing nearby to strike up assembly.

Several of the Indians scoffed and ignored their assembling white allies, while many more gathered flaming pine knots and torches. They ran about the column of assembling rangers, screaming and waving their firebrands wildly in the air. Butler and Caldwell strode through the gallivanting Indians and took their place at the front of the column. With a wave of his hand forward, the whole column followed Butler out the gate to the lively airs of the musicians. Tied sheets full of plunder burdened some backs, but they marched smart nonetheless.

Many Indians filed behind them, led by Esther, heavily laden with even more plunder. Pots and pans clanged and glass crashed in their wake. Their screams added to the strange chorus of noises. The firebrands swirled in the darkening air with embers and sparks flying.

Denison and Franklin both watched the wild column of Indians holding their breaths, expecting them to fling the firebrands into the cabins in the fort and among the terrified settlers. But they held them in their hands well beyond the gate, and the Indians and Tories left behind in the fort only gathered to watch the spectacle of the column marching through the gate.

Both men breathed a great sigh of relief which quickly turned to gasps as the cabins outside the fort went up in flames in the column's wake. They both watched in horror. So much for property being respected and restored to the settlers.

"Well, it's started," Denison said. "Let's hope Indian Butler can keep them under control or the flames shall surely spread!"

"But what of the terms?" Franklin gasped.

"Let us hope they don't go up in flames as I fear everything else shall," Denison said. "Let us hope and pray, but I most earnestly suggest all prepare to get the hell out of here while we still can, for hell hath returned to Wyoming!"

## Chapter Eighty Six
*Bullock's Farm*

Three men lie silently on a great rock jutting from a mountain overlooking the valley. Dots of flames slowly spread before their eyes, each one some poor unfortunate's farm; perhaps even their own, they realized with dread. The flames speckled both sides of the river, growing in number.

"Well, there you have it," Stephens said, rolling to his side and sitting with his back toward the valley. His heart grew too heavy with thoughts of the misery of his people in the Wyoming Valley for him to face it anymore. A cutting sense of failure burned in his stomach, almost bending him over with pain. "We're too late," he gasped.

Baldwin nodded, but still stared down into the valley in the direction of Forty Fort. "None of the flames seem great enough to be Forty Fort, but it is much too far to tell fer sure," he said to Hollenback.

The brooding Ensign remained mute on the rock next to him.

"I hope they are not," Stephens said.

Hollenback crawled off the rock to a tree. Leaning his arm against it, he lowered his head. He remained silent, brooding over the events of the day before. It all seemed too much. His wounded shoulder throbbed with each memory flashing through his tormented mind.

"We must report back with due haste," Baldwin said, crawling off the rock. He walked past Hollenback, wondering of the demons antagonizing his soul. He thought of the horrors of battle he himself had witnessed in the ranks of the Continental Army, but knew none compared to this battle. This battle fought on one's own soil, beside friends, brothers, and fathers, proved most devastating to the souls whom fought it. But duty still called. He intended to answer it.

"Come on, Stephens," he ordered.

Stephens crawled off the rock, stumbling by Hollenback in the early morning light. The man's grief seem to cling to the air around him. He pitied the man and the many men fallen on that horrible field, but as Baldwin said, they must report. Touching the man's arm he said, "Ensign, we must report, sir."

Hollenback's head jolted from the touch to his arm and he stared at Stephens, his eyes glaring with rage in the pale light.

It sent a chill down Stephens' spine. He quickly stepped away and toward his horse. He mounted, painfully aware of Hollenback's eerie stare.

In another instant Hollenback ran to his horse, leaping onto its back. Reining the animal about, he trotted down the mountain.

Baldwin shrugged his shoulders at Stephen's questioning eyes and quickly mounted. "War makes some men spooked, you know that," he said. "You've seen it afore!"

"But never like that, I ain't," Stephens said. "I'm a feared for what's happening down there."

"Ain't we all," Baldwin said, spurring his mount to follow the Ensign. "But we've got a duty, so let's get to it!"

Stephens nodded, obediently following Baldwin through the trees down the mountain. They both peered ahead for glimpses of Hollenback through the trees, sighing in relief at the sight of him waiting for them on the trail at the foot of the mountain.

"Get a move on!" Hollenback said, suddenly animated.

"These accursed packhorses go at their own speed," Baldwin said. "Ain't no sense in forcing 'em any faster, they is going as fast as they can. Besides, riding bareback ain't like riding on a proper saddle."

"To hell with that, Sergeant!" Hollenback said, reining his horse hard about to face the trail. "We're riding hard, come hell or high water!" With that, he whipped his horse hard, galloping it madly down the trail. "Come on!" he yelled back over his shoulder. "Duty calls!"

"Orders is orders," Baldwin said, whipping his mount hard. It burst into a trot, soon galloping hard behind the suddenly vibrant Ensign.

"There is hell to pay," Stephens said, whipping his own mount into a hard gallop. "And it's come to Wyoming!"

They both rode hard behind Hollenback, seeming possessed by the way he bound over fallen logs and small creeks. The distance between them greatly widened, but they kept on, for as Hollenback said, duty called. Coming to a turn in the trail there sat Hollenback, staring through the trees at something ahead on the trail. Both men reined their horses up before they ran into the sudden obstacle of Hollenback's horse.

"Damn it all!" Baldwin couldn't help but exclaim, trotting off the edge of the trail. "What the hell are you about!?!"

Hollenback glanced back at him with a hard eye, sternly pointing beyond the trees. A flickering light showed in the early dawn.

"Ain't that Bullock's place?" Baldwin asked, squinting through the trees.

"Yes," Hollenback said, "and as I remember it was empty when we passed afore."

"It was," Baldwin agreed. Suddenly the Ensign's hasty stop did not seem so rash.

"What do you think?" Stephens asked.

"We haven't the time," Hollenback said, turning a glancing eye to him. "But there's only one way to find out," he said, lifting his rifle up and spurring his horse ahead. A fresh red spot showed about his shoulder from overexerting his wound.

Baldwin and Stephens quickly followed, all with their rifles held ready. Hollenback's horse thundered into the farmyard. Reining it back on its haunches, Hollenback's quick eye scanned the whole area.

Three rifles suddenly poked around the corner of the cabin, leveled on him. Hollenback reared back his horse and quickly lowered his own rifle, ready for action. Baldwin and Stephens dropped from their mounts, training their own weapons on the rifle-bearing men.

"Hold on there!" a voice suddenly demanded. "Ain't that you Hollenback? Mathias Hollenback?" it asked.

Hollenback somehow recognized the voice in the shadows and eased his finger back from the trigger. "Downing?" he asked. "Is that you, my good man?"

"My God it is Hollenback!" Downing said, walking out from the shadows and lowering his rifle. The other men behind him did the same. "And who do you got with you?" Downing asked, squinting at the two men leveling their rifles at him. "Is that Ira Stephens and Waterman Baldwin? My God it is!"

"It is at that," Hollenback said, wincing with pain from his wound and easing his rifle back across the front of his saddle.

"Then Spalding's about!" Downing said. "Where is he?"

"He's still miles back," Baldwin said, gathering the reins of his horse.

A woman's face showed in the shadows behind the men.

"Who do we have here?" Baldwin asked.

The woman walked into the light of dawn, her tears glistening on her cheeks through the streaks they cut through the paint hastily daubed onto them. They recognized her immediately, Mrs. Durkee, their late captain's widow. Her four children slowly appeared behind her, clinging to the folds of her dress. The pleading eyes of Anderson Dana's wife showed behind her, along with her sullen children, along with the rest of the Downing clan.

Baldwin and Stephens nodded with respect to Mrs. Durkee. The bitter taste of defeat, tinged with guilt, caused a lump to grow in both of their throats. They swallowed hard against it. "Ain't our doing," Baldwin muttered under his breath as if reading Mrs. Durkee's mind. "It's the higher up's fault, it is, and cruel fate. So don't fret on it, we's to just do our duty." he added for Stephen's sake.

Stephens nodded, but the words rang hollow to him. Stepping toward the woman he asked, "Are you all fit?"

"As fit as one can be after what we've been through," Downing answered for her. He gestured toward the lone horse tethered to a tree near a fire not far from the cabin. Great bundles burdened its back. "It carries everything in the world we still own," Downing said.

"What of the Bullocks?" Baldwin asked.

"Cabin was empty when we got here," one of Downing's sons answered, finally lowering his rifle. "The Indians are all over the valley now, ravaging and putting everything to the torch. Pa thought it best we get out of there whilst we could, don't know how many are of the same mind, but I recollect most will be on the morrow. I suspect they'll all pour out of the valley by then, if'n they value their hair, that is."

Hollenback sighed and pulled back on the reins of his horse. "We must help those who are coming, I suspect the Tories won't let them have anything but the clothes on their backs!"

"Is you wounded, Mathias?" Downing asked, noticing the blood spot on his shoulder.

"Yes, but it must wait," Hollenback said. "There are others in greater need!"

"Now, you good people gather up your things," Baldwin said. "You are coming with us to the column, they has provisions and such."

Not a word of protest sounded from the grieving faces of the refugees. Gathering up their scant belongings, they assembled to leave the lone cabin on the edge of the wilderness.

Baldwin and Stephens gave up their horses to the women and the infant children. Without another word the party slowly crept down the trail into the awaiting folds of the dismal swamp, ever mindful of what lay behind them. The lone howl of a wolf echoed from the depths of the swampy land, along with the rustle of many unseen beasts in the brush along the dark trail.

Hollenback let Baldwin and Stephens lead, resigning himself to bring up the rear, for his shoulder ached so. In spite of the burning pain, he clenched his trusty rifle tight in his fists, ready to bring it into play at a moment's notice.

There would be no more lives taken while he still breathed, he promised himself. None!

## Chapter Eighty Seven
*Promises made, promises broken*

Each new ray of sunlight cutting into the dark folds of the forest awoke something. As it penetrated the darkness new howls and screeches echoed through the forest. The steady pounding of a distant water drum melded with the noises, creating a strange, unearthly, cadence in the dawn. The rays of the sun shone through many wisps of misty smoke rising from burned out cabins all around the fort. Dark eyes opened to welcome the new dawn, some emitting their own howls in answer to those echoing in the air.

Other eyes, heavy from the little sleep they managed to gain during the uneasy night, stared about the surreal fort. The living nightmare welcomed them again, and many wished to just close their eyes to it, but reality would not let them. Their hearts sank in their heavy chests and their heavy eyes glared contemptuously at the few dozen Indians hooting and yelling in answer to the distant calls of the forest.

Some of the settlers climbed to the walls to stare down at the painted faces converging on the fort from the forest again. The bark of a few of the Indian's rifles firing in the air gave them a start. Oh, it all started again, the settlers thought. They feared it would never end.

The Indians scampering through the gate helped themselves to whatever the dumfound and groggy settlers had left to them from the previous evening's plundering. Greedy and gruff hands even pulled the hats from their heads. Indian women helped themselves to the white women's bonnets and shawls from their backs. Others marched headlong to the cabins, determined to finish their plundering. Pots and pans soon clanged about in the cabins. Brightly colored tablecloths flashed in the early morning light. Feathers danced in the air from many featherbeds ripped open to the Indian's delight, all while the flabbergasted settlers watched in horror and amazement. Their bargain with the devil turned sour before their eyes.

Not all let the Indians befuddle them. Several ran to the Bennett's cabin, eager to awake their leader and put a stop to this sudden breach of the terms.

Colonel Denison met them at the door. Rubbing the sleep out of his eyes and running a hand through his disheveled hair, he asked, "What is it now!?!" Turning abruptly to his wife standing behind him, he took his hat from her hands. "Please Elizabeth," he said, "get back into the cabin for now." A nearby screaming Indian nearly made all of them jump. How they had mastered the art of being a nuisance when they had a mind to it, Denison thought. His wife slipped back into the door with no further argument. Denison watched the latch string disappear and turned back toward the nervous settlers.

"There is the devil to pay!" one of the men said, ducking from a Indian trying to snatch his hat. After the Indian screamed, he took the hat off himself and handed it to him. The Indian laughed and rambled away, joining his fellows in plundering everything.

Denison cast a nervous eye behind him to the cabin door, doubting whether simply drawing in the latch string would prove effective in keeping the Indians out of the cabin.

"Has anyone been hurt?" Denison asked the gathering of men.

"Not yet," one of them said, turning to watch a mounted woman ride up to the cabin. She still sat atop the same mount with the backwards side saddle, but appeared to have added more petticoats to her collection, along with a bright red shawl. Even the tower of bonnets atop her head seemed to have grown. Denison had to take a second look through the many bonnets to truly recognize her, but those same dark eyes glared down at him, full of the hatred.

Esther sneered at the Yankees standing before the cabin. Raising her chin high in the air, she reined her horse about to make sure the Yankee officer noticed all of the finery she had added to her wardrobe since last night. Satisfied she had properly humiliated him, she reined her mount away from him. An Indian woman tying ribbons to her horse's tail stumbled to keep up with her.

"This is not good," Denison said, shaking his head at the gleeful woman trying to tie the ribbons to the horse's tail. She smiled at the Yankees, exposing her rotting black and yellow teeth.

"That woman must have hellish toothaches," one of the men said.

"I would be only too happy to relieve her of her suffering," another said.

"Yes, well that moment has passed, gentlemen," Denison said.

"I would still like to pull her teeth like the *Wyoming tooth*," one of the men said, referring to the method in Wyoming of tying a strong cord to a lead ball and attaching one end of it to the tooth and the other to the ball and firing it. A strange, but effective way, the Wyoming settlers had learned to deal with their dental problems. One which had drawn fame to them in the eyes of the other colonies. "But I would face the rifle about when I did it!" the man added.

"That is enough," Denison said, leading them away from the cabin. A sharp crack behind them turned them all around in shock. In the time it took them to take but a few steps, the Indians snuck in behind them, smashing through the cabin door. Screams sounded from inside of the cabin infuriated Denison so he ran back to it yelling to some of his men, "Get word to Indian Butler I demand to see him at once!"

Two of the men ran toward the gate only to be tripped and kicked at by the swarming Indians. They stumbled to their feet, trying in vain to reach the gate through a sea of blows from hands, fists, and clubs. "We have word for Butler!" one of them finally screamed. The name seemed magic, for the Indians immediately ceased beating them. Exasperated and bruised, they ran out the north gate, dodging all the Indians they encountered, and for once welcoming the sight of a Tory.

Denison burst into the cabin, hastily gathering his wife and babe. He soon found himself cowering in a corner, shielding them and watching a large barrel-chested brave rampage through the cabin. The brave's hands flew along the shelves, momentarily grabbing something and giving it a quick glance before flinging it to the floor. He smelled of sweat, smoke, bear grease, and an odd assortment of herbs they constantly used in cooking. Two other braves and a woman entered the cabin upon hearing the commotion. Scanning about, they looked through everything, ignoring the wide-eyed whites huddled in the corner. The two braves gasped and lifted an esteemed, if not amusing prize, featherbeds. Lifting the fluffy mattresses over their heads, they quickly drew their knives and slashed them, overwhelmed and in ecstasy from the sea of feathers spilling from them. They paraded through the door to their amazed brethren, dancing about in the floating feathers.

The large brave ignored them and made his way to the hearth, flinging its iron implements across the floor behind him. Gripping the handle of a large black iron pot, he rolled it across the floor and gazed at some chests now exposed under a rope bed. Flinging the rope bed aside, he tore into the chests. Rifling through them, he flung whatever caught his fancy into the pot. Mrs. Bennett raised her voice and advanced toward him, but his sneer made her think better of it. She retreated back to her own corner opposite the Denison family.

Denison waved Mrs. Bennett and her frightened daughter to his side, pushing them behind him. He stood tall, glaring at the brave.

The brave scoffed, but kept rampaging through the chests.

A deep and commanding voice from the doorway made everyone stop and look to it, even the brave.

Gucingerachton stood full in the doorway, glaring at the huddled settlers in the corner. He snarled and bared his teeth before stomping toward Denison.

Denison glanced out of the corner of his eye to the frightened women and children behind him and stepped toward the bold chief, showing no fear.

Gucingerachton screamed so loud at him the force of it sent his head reeling backwards. He lowered his piercing eyes to the Yankee.

All, Indian and white, watched.

Denison stood firm.

Gucingerachton glared at the man, seeming mesmerized, not by the Yankee's defiance, but rather by his fine hunting shirt. Lifting his hand, he fingered its fringes under Denison's hatful eye. Grinning from ear to ear, he rubbed the fine linen through his fingers. Noticing the fine hat atop the Yankee's head, he quickly snatched it off his head. Placing it comfortably on his own head, he pointed at the hunting shirt.

The Indian's eyes showed he would not be denied. Denison suddenly felt the bulge of his wallet against his skin from a hidden inside pocket of the shirt. It held all of the money collected in the whole settlement, entrusted to his care. Now this Indian unknowingly threatened it, the key to their future. He did the only thing he could, he let the hint of a disarming smile stretch across his face.

The Indian's momentary confusion offered him a brief window, his only window, to save the money, and thus, their future. He backed until he felt a warm body behind him. Pulling at the shirt he somehow slipped the wallet free of the pocket. Palming it, he feigned struggling with the shirt and backed into somebody behind him. He half turned and faced a wide-eyed girl, Polly, and gestured for her help in tugging the shirt over his head, slipping the wallet to her into the confusion. She quickly stuck it into the folds of her dress and pretended to help him pull the shirt over his head, all the while watching the hard, mean eyes staring at them.

The chief, not one to be trifled with, strode forth. Yanking the shirt from Denison's hands, he stared fiercely at Polly.

Polly back away, staring at him with a question in her eyes.

Denison quickly intervened, raising his hands to the shirt. Rolling some of the fabric through his fingers he said, "See, it's fine, is it not?" to the chief.

The chief raised his lip and snarled, yanking the shirt from the Yankee's hands. Pushing the offensive Yankee back, he sauntered toward the door. Stopping just short of it, he looked up to the hat, suddenly removing it from his head. Placing it on a surprised brave's head standing beside him, he noticeably admired it.

The brave cheered and followed the great chief through the door. A chorus of hoots and yells greeted them as he lifted up the fine shirt to show all his fine prize.

A disturbance near the gate ushered in another chief, a white chief. Butler pushed his way through the throngs of cheering Indians, marching directly toward the cabin to which the two bruised Yankees leading him gestured. Stopping for a moment, he gazed about the commotion, much to the vexation of the two Yankees. Their waving hands finally urged him on to the cabin.

"He's in here, Major," one of the Yankees said, pushing the fallen door aside and stepping over it.

Butler stepped by them and into the cabin to meet Denison's glaring eyes. Looking oddly at the enraged and shirtless Yankee officer, he shook his head. "Aren't you afraid to catch a draft?" he finally said.

"What!?!" Denison asked, biting his lip to contain his rage. "I find no humor in outright thievery, fine sir! This is ludicrous to the extreme, taking the shirt off a man's back while he's still in it!"

"Calm down, my dear man," Butler said, picking up two upset chairs. He slid them to the table and said, "Come sit, we shall parley."

"Parley!" Denison scoffed. "Are you daft? The parley is over, and look to the result!" he added, waving his bare arms in the air. He angrily gestured down at a brave still rifling through the chests, now and then tossing something into a black iron pot beside him. He continued in spite of the angry white people glaring at him. He only looked up when two rangers and two chiefs walked through the doorway. Grunting to the chiefs, he reluctantly rose under their stern eye. Grabbing the pot, he stumbled through the door, casting a sour eye behind him.

Butler waved at the rangers to close the door behind the Indian, despite it dangling on one rawhide hinge. Watching the rangers fumble with the door, he took a long breath and looked to the rebel women glaring at him. "I must profess," he said, sitting down on one of the chairs. "My feelings are also injured by this outrageous behavior." He stared coldly at the two chiefs. "I have pledged my honor that the property of you inhabitants be preserved entire. By this rampant plundering, my promise, and therefore my word, is made mute. It is most distressing to say the least! If I would have known the Indians would have behaved in such a manner I would have marched them all off after the battle and never taken possession of the fort!" He suddenly stopped, fearing he had spoken his mind too long. "Perhaps not," he added.

Both chiefs looked to one another, shrugging their shoulders. One of them noticed Denison's cutting stare at him and perked up as if witnessing it for the first time. Strutting boldly over to the obstinate

Yankee, he pointed his finger under his nose. "Whites! You all same!"

"What are you rambling on about?" Butler asked.

"You white eyes cannot stand the truth, even when it stare you in face!" the chief answered, despite Butler's wave of dismissal in his direction. "You make lies and myths to mask your eyes from truth! You talk of God you yourself hang from tree! You speak his words with your tongue only! Indian speak his words from heart! Yank-ee like all whites! He see only what he want to see!" Drawing his tomahawk, he slammed its blade hard into the tabletop. "You see now? You hear the *cry of the tomahawk*? It scream in your ear! Kanonsionni win! Wyoming ours!"

"Are you quite finished?" Butler asked, rolling his eyes toward the chief.

"White eyes!" he screamed, yanking the tomahawk from the tabletop. He pushed two forked fingers up to his eyes. "You blind and see what you want to see and no more! The world not all white!"

"Yes," Butler countered, "but that does not dismiss the Kanonsionni's actions as of late."

"These are your people!" Denison yelled to the chiefs. "Stop them from plundering at once! You must!"

The chiefs looked to one another again. One of them shook his head, walking out the door. The other chief huffed, leaning back against a wall. Crossing his arms across his chest, he glared at the Yankee.

"Calm down!" Butler said, raising his hand toward Denison. "We shall see about this, I assure you." He looked back to the two rangers by the door and said, "None of my men are in their number, sir."

"That may be so," Denison said, fanning his hands up and down his bare chest. "But what of the losses we have already suffered in property? Cabins are burning all over the valley!"

"Sir, if you draw up a list of all possessions and property damaged, the King shall make good on it," Butler said.

"It shall be a ponderous list, indeed!"

"Be that as it may, it is the best I can manage at present."

A creak from the cabin door turned both men's heads to it. The chief walked to Butler, profusely shaking his head. "I try," he said, glancing at Denison, "but they no listen. Say they hit me on head!"

Butler sighed and tapped his fingers on the table. He raised his head to say something, but shook it instead. Slowly rising from the table, he walked to the door. "We shall see," Butler said, walking out the door. His voice sounded on the other side of the door in the Seneca tongue. A chorus of disapproving hoots and yells followed his words. The door opened again.

Butler took a step into the cabin, profusely shaking his head at Denison. "I tell you," he said, his jaw slackening, " I can do nothing with them!" Waving his hands in the air, he promptly turned about, exiting the door with the ranger and two chiefs in tow.

"My God," Denison gasped. "What has this come to?"

His wife put her hand to her mouth, gasping. The other women shook their heads. The children clung to their mothers, save one rambling across the floor to his father. "Father, whatever shall we do?" little Lazarus Denison asked.

"I tell you, my lad, we must depart with all due haste," Denison answered, bending down and picking his son up into his arms. "All of us! This is getting too far out of hand," he added, listening to the yells outside. "I dare not wonder what the morrow shall bring!"

Mrs. Denison quickly rummaged through the clothing strewn about the floor, handing a shirt to her husband. He let his son down and slipped the shirt over his head, watching his wife continue to search for a waistcoat. "Don't fret over such things, just gather the essentials and leave it at that," he told her, lifting the bulging wallet Polly passed back to him up to her. "This shall take care of us if we get out of here."

The women pooled together what morsels of food still remaining in the cabin into meager bundles, stuffing them with what few personal items remaining in their possession. Denison searched for a hat, but finally settled on a handkerchief hastily tied around his head. "When we get out the door everyone stay together," he said, ushering everyone to the door. "Try not to make eye contact with anyone, just head straight for the south gate." He noticed a concern for the others in their eyes.

"I'll have Franklin spread the word, but anyone with any sense knows to get out," he answered, putting his hand to the door. "Now we must go," he said, easing it open on its one rawhide hinge. Peeking out he said, "Most of the Indians have gone to who knows where, so now is the time, remember what I said!" With that, he stepped through the door, pulling his wife along behind him whom in turn led their son by the hand. The others followed silently through the wailing Indians, who fortunately seemed too engrossed in revelry to notice them. Besides, by now one settler looked like the other to them anyways. If the white faces wished to depart, so be it. Wyoming belonged to the Iroquois now.

## Chapter Eighty Eight
*Hollenback's relief*

Something stirred in the hearts of the exhausted men at the sight approaching them. They all rose from their brief respite in the mud along the trail, rushing forward to meet their returning scouts with their new charges-refugees from Wyoming.

The refugees' tired eyes glanced to the soldiers for a moment, but then fell back down to the trail. They trudged along, some managing to wave a hand at the soldiers, while others just walked along. At the behest of the soldiers, they finally stopped, collapsing to the edge of the awful trail, thankful for a respite with some security from the forest.

Soldiers scanned the haggard refugees for familiar faces, but still few spoke, for the sight of one another choked down all words in their throats, except for the few children complaining of their sore feet. "Be quiet!" a mother's tired voice quickly scolded them, "or the Injuns will get you!" Each of their tongues instantly fell silent and their wide eyes looked in terror at the dark forest surrounding them.

Some of their elders also stared into the dark forest, for the mother's warning rang true to them, too. Death by a tomahawk or war club may spring from the dark folds of the forest at any moment, and they all knew it. Soldiers, recognizing the fear in their eyes, fanned out along the trail, tirelessly searching the great carpet of ferns for the specters which may be haunting them.

A lone horseman rode silently along the line of crestfallen refugees. He too said nothing, but just rubbed his chin and stared at them. Nearing the end of the line, he reined his horse to a stop and slowly dismounted, passing the reins to an awaiting soldier. Nodding to the silent man, he walked back along the trail. All the faces wore the same haunted and empty stare, but one particularly hard gaze stopped him dead in his tracks.

"Mrs. Durkee," he said, removing his hat. "I offer you my most sincere condolences."

"Yes, Captain Spalding," Mrs. Durkee said, rolling her eyes down to her children huddled beside her. "That may be well and fine for some, but may not for others whom suffer from other's slow movements."

"I assure you we left with all possible dispatch the instant we were finally released from our duties," Spalding said. But the words cut the soldier deep, slicing into his sense of pride and honor. He stepped back, still mute from the woman's words. He waved to one of his soldiers. "Break out the stores and feed them all," he ordered. "Now!"

Stephens and Baldwin trudged up to him, raising their hands to their hats. "It is all lost, sir," Baldwin reported, looking down to the torn strips of his ragged clothing. He promptly ripped one of the strips away, stuffing it into his pouch and shaking his head. "The sugarbush plays hell on clothes in these parts. It's leather stocking land fer sure. Anyways, we saw flames spreading all through the valley, and on both sides of the river, yet. I suspect there will be a great runaway from the valley. The whole valley's right smart with Injuns and those damn bastard Tories!"

Spalding looked down to a nearby rotting log and cleared a spot along it with his boot. Turning, he sat down on it. Removing his hat, he wiped at the sweat dripping down his brow, slapping at a huge mosquito flittering about his neck. "Ain't that a fright," is all he managed to mutter past the growing lump in his throat. "We lost the whole valley!" A horde of mosquitoes soon descended over all along the trail.

Another man reined his horse up near him and slid down from the saddle. "Have they told you, sir?" he asked, nodding toward Baldwin and Stephens. "Why do you sit? We must advance in relief!"

"Come now," Stephens said, swatting at the horde of mosquitoes. "What are our numbers against theirs, Mr. Hollenback?"

Hollenback glared at the upstart private. "Mind your place!" he warned. "These here words is between officers!"

"Begging your pardon sir," Baldwin said, in spite of the glaring eyes, "but Stephens here is right, sir, leastways that's the way I's sees it."

Hollenback shook his head, waving a dismissing hand toward the two haggard soldiers. He started to speak but Spalding's hand shot up to stop him. Rising, he slowly placed his hat back on his head after running his fingers through his sweat-soaked locks. He cupped his chin and rubbed his hand against the stubble plaguing it, deep in thought. His bloodshot eyes ran along the sea of miserable and forlorn faces sitting along the trail and to his own soldiers, all furiously swatting at swarming mosquitoes. Frustrated faces etched deep with the horrors of war shone back to him, but also some dim light, some deep serenity born of the knowledge of grace. A grace he himself had witnessed on many a battlefield embodied the faces. These souls now entrusted to his earthy care must not be spent foolishly on some whim born of an irrational desire for revenge. Emotions must give way to simple common sense.

Jenkins, noticing Spalding's quandary, trudged over to him.

"Jenkins!" Hollenback yelled. "Tell them we must march to the relief of the valley immediately!"

"No!" Spalding said, cutting his lieutenant off before he uttered a word. He slapped at one of the huge mosquitoes biting his neck, showing his bloody open palm from the pest's feasting on his blood. "Too much blood has already been spent foolishly! It would be the greatest folly to march forth with my sixty odd men against such odds! No! I'll have none of it!"

Hollenback looked down to Downing and his sons lying exhausted by the muddy trailside. "But we have Downing and his party, and many more of his like are on the trail! We only need gather them!"

Downing stared up at the man and rolled his eyes, but offered no response to the headstrong man's comment. He just shook his head.

Spalding noticed and shook his own head at Hollenback.

Hollenback knew he had lost the argument in an instant. Turning in frustration, he spread his hands out to the settlers munching on army biscuits along the trailside. "Look at them! There are plenty more braving the wilderness with barely a morsel to eat! Women and children alike! We must go to their aid at once!"

"Yes," Spalding agreed, wiping his bloody palm on his buckskin trousers. "But we shall change our line of march to Fort Penn, most of them shall be heading that way, anyways. We'll render what assistance we can to all we encounter and await orders from headquarters when we gain Fort Penn. That is it. It is my decision and I have made it!"

Hollenback snatched his hat from his head in frustration and wrenched it in his hands, gasping in despair.

"My God man get a hold of yourself!" Jenkins said to him.

Hollenback shook his head and turned toward Spalding. "Sir, at least allow me provisions from your stores so I can ride in relief of these poor souls!" he begged.

"Of course, my dear man," Spalding said. "Draw whatever you can manage from the Quartermaster."

Hollenback gathered his horse's reins and trod back to the packhorses. Stopping for a second, he turned back to Jenkins, but only shook his head in frustration before turning away again.

"The captain here is right," Jenkins called behind him. "My God man, look what rash thinking has brought us! Havoc!" From the glazed look in Hollenback's eyes he knew his words fell on deaf ears, but he himself realized the wisdom of Spalding's words. Waving his friend on, he rubbed the back of his hand, thinking of Beth. A deep frown, accented by worried eyes, overcame his face.

"I'm sure she is fine," Mrs. Durkee said from the trailside, reading the concern in the newlywed's eyes. "She's a strong woman, and has an equally strong man to return to, that thought alone shall keep her going if nothing else does." She looked soulfully down at the lad lying by her feet with head resting on his hands upon her lap. "He's a fine lad, is he not?" she asked Jenkins. "There's much of his father in him."

"Yes, there is," Jenkins said, wondering if he would ever share the joy of children with the only woman he truly loved, Beth. Pangs of longing burned through his heart. Raising his hand, he rubbed it all the more, thinking, hang on, my dear Beth, hang on!

Spalding walked up to the man, watching him rub his hand. An odd habit, but thinking of the man's new bride, Bethiah, considered the most beautiful woman of Wyoming, he suddenly understood. "It is the last place she touched you, is it not?" he asked, nodding toward the hand.

Jenkins lowered his hand, looking thoughtfully at it. He must watch this odd habit he had developed as a prisoner in that awful hole at Niagara. He felt embarrassed and ashamed of his selfish thoughts.

"We all feel the same of our own wives and loved ones," Spalding said, looking up the dark and menacing trail. "My own wife is down there in that hell, I can only pray that fate is kind to her," Spalding said. A rage suddenly overcame him. "Damn it, I wish I could just ride to her more than Hollenback, but my duty forbids it! It's the soldier's curse, it is! Damn it all to hell, I worry about her something fierce, I do at that."

"I understand," Jenkins said.

"I know you do," Spalding said, now sharing Jenkins' sense of shame at his own outburst fueled by emotion. But what was man but an emotional animal? he thought. But a wise man must control his emotions, for emotional thinking most likely leads to disaster. Faith fills the gap between rational thoughts and emotions, so he mouthed a silent prayer to ease his anxious thoughts.

"Our duty," Jenkins said, gazing at the refugees. "We must follow it, as painful as it may seem." He closed his eyes tight, trying to come to terms with his worried mind.

"We shall both see our dear wives again," Spalding said. "For I have prayed on it, and as you know, I am a man who rarely prays, therefore, the Lord shall take stock in my request. I know it to be true."

He turned his grim eyes away from the dark trail. "All is not lost of Wyoming," he said, "not as long as hearts such as ours beat! We will rebuild from the ashes! Our honor demands it!"

## Chapter Eighty Nine
*Odd old friends*

He stumbled along in a painful daze to the front of his cabin, there to find his trusty old rocking chair. Easing himself down into it, he reflected on how it had been carried all the way from Connecticut in what seemed a lifetime ago. Clenching his fingers tight around its arms, he fought back his tears. It would not be proper for a man to show tears, especially in front of his wife, daughters, and slew of grandchildren gathered around the forlorn cabin.

His wife, a good strong woman of fine Connecticut stock, gazed at him from the doorway of the cabin. Her whole family huddled around her, sharing her bitter tears, tears running through the entire family; her family torn apart by war. Her sons, Philip, Jonathan, and Bartholomew Weeks, had all marched confidently out the gate of Forty Fort while they all cheered them. Their daughter's husband, Silas Benedict, along with her brother, the sons' uncle, Jabez Beers, and her cousin Josiah Carmen, along with their borderer, Robert Bates, all marched with them. Seven brave souls in all. None to ever return. The news shocked her husband most of all, making him fall into a grief-stricken trance which still gripped him. He had paced back and forth along the road in front of the cabin for the longest time. It eased her heart to see him finally sitting in his favorite chair, rocking back and forth and staring up the road as if awaiting the ghosts of the slain men, his brethren.

The gloating and indifferent attitude of the Indians to the terms agreed upon prompted Philip Weeks to lead his family out of Forty Fort even before the ink dried on the instrument of surrender. They settled uneasily in their cabin just south of Wilkes-Barre and waited. According to the terms they just had to occupy their homes peacefully and all would be well and fine. But they held little faith in *'terms'* and their suspicions grew at the sight of the glowing fires to the north all night. Now the lingering smoke trails rising in the air above the trees up the road confirmed their fears, along with the droves of people now filling the road leading south.

The refugees trod along in silence, their heads bowed, with few of them even raising their eyes to the crestfallen family gawking at them from their cabin. The creak of the old man's rocking chair haunted the quiet march. His glassy eyes stared at them, barely nodding to acknowledge the few raising a hand to wave at him. He knew what would soon come on their heels; an indifferent enemy to whom mercy seemed a foreign word in their vocabulary, as well as in their thoughts.

Mrs. Weeks eased back inside the door, waving the others back into the cabin. The long faces trudging down the road played hard on her already heavy heart. Besides, her husband needed time alone; time to come to terms with their great loss. If the head of the family didn't heal, none would heal. Time, he needed time.

Philip watched his family file through the door and wanted to speak, but his dry throat forbade it. Releasing his grip on the arms of the rocking chair, he fumbled in his waistcoat's pockets for his pipe. He raised it empty to his lips with his shaking hand. The strength eluded him to call for a spill from the fireplace to light it, anyways. Biting bitterly down on the stem of the pipe, he let his mind drift back into time to familiar and safe memories. He let his eyes fall to his knees, remembering how he had rocked each of his boys in the waning hours of a summer's day and told them how one day they would rock their own sons in this very chair. He remembered stretching his hand over their farm and telling them of how it would grow some day to provide a good living for them all. A legacy, he told them on a whisper in their ears. He would pass down more than a farm, but a legacy, etched out of this hard and unforgiving wilderness. But that dream now lay shattered.

He fought against the hollow feeling and again remembered how he had told each of his sons special secrets only they shared. Secrets of the best fishing holes in the river. Secrets of where to catch the best shad in the run up the Susquehanna each March. Each boy shared his own special secret and it bore a special meaning to him. Each had their own special hopes and dreams for the future born of their own unique talents. Now those dreams lay hollow on that horrible field. Now his sons no longer breathed the sweet air of Wyoming. And why? The question haunted his mind. Surely for something more than hearth and home. Something greater, beyond this horrible day. Beyond this all.

He remembered reading in the *Courant*-the Connecticut newspaper delivered by a postal route they themselves established-of this virgin nation struggling to mark out its own place in this world, much as they had done in this unforgiving wilderness. He also remembered the taunts in the paper from some of their own people in Connecticut, calling the people of the Susquehanna Company mere '*land jobbers.*" Not all understood, but it did not stop them from settling this land, a part of the Connecticut Charter of 1662. It null and voided the Pennamite's Charter of 1681 by some nineteen years. They had the rightful claim, and now they bore the burden of the Indians' wrath alone.

He felt his breath slow and suddenly felt conscious of his heart thumping in his chest. He wondered of their critics in Connecticut, if for nothing else, to take his mind from the painful thoughts of the day. They seemed so engrained in the present and so intent on satisfying their material lusts to ever slow down and consider the true intent of their lives; and its meaning. All had a heart, but few heeded it, for it forced them to do impracticable things which would not put a penny in their pockets. Perhaps, in the end, coin proved to be the God in their empty hearts.

He bowed his , soulfully thinking of his sons again. Their hearts beat no longer. He wondered of their last thoughts lying on that field with their life's blood draining from them. They must had been aware of each precious breath and beat of their heart until both ceased. Such a tragedy. Oh! Such a waste!

"Oh God," he finally muttered to himself. "God help us!" His chin fell down to his chest, pushing the pipe from his mouth. Gasping, he picked it up from his lap. Slipping it back into his teeth, his heart soon echoed in his thoughts again.

His sons, his dear sons. They died for hearth and home and at the same time for something much greater. All of them talked of the hope their new nation represented to the world when they lived. All nations bowed before a king or some other monarch. Here, in this land, his sons had said with beaming eyes, men could rule themselves. Here, this land bred a new man, who started calling themselves Americans, and not simply backwards colonists of a distant realm. A new heart beat in their chests. And in that heart beat a new hope.

He remembered reading in the *Courant* how British soldiers landing in New York asked, marveling at the rich land they marched through, why on earth a people so blessed with plenty revolted in the first place? The question rang true in a practical sense, but when the citizens explained to the soldiers something more beat in their hearts, a yearning to be free, their remarks only drew odd stares from the soldiers.

Here, he became aware that his heart, the hearts of his sons, and the hearts of all true patriots, beat not only for their lives, but for all, the whole world wide. In some strange way he felt the connection of all to one another. What happened here would touch people across the ages in ways he could not even fathom. He thought of the Charter stating all land between the forty first and forty second parallels from the Atlantic to the South Seas belonged to Connecticut. Here, they had taken the first steps toward one sea from the other. Here, brave souls took the first steps to answer their deep yearning to be free. The yearning beat in all men's hearts, he felt sure, but some ways of lives and situations simply drummed it out until it sounded no more in those men's souls. But here, upon this virgin land, it awakened, and roared from time immortal.

This new loud heart, this American heart, beat for untold billions to come long after these days passed. It beat for all men, women, and children, of every culture and race, both present, past, and future. Its thunder rang loud and inspired new thoughts in men. It beat hope, one of the eternal gifts from God alone. Listen to your heart, he said to himself deep in his thoughts. There you shall hear your sons again. For they touch the ages with their selfless devotion to the new ideals rising from this new land. Something of the whole heart of humanity beat at this place called Wyoming now, born of its great sacrifices. It should never be forgotten for its part in forming this living consciousness, this new breed of men, these Americans. Wyoming, his sons, and all sons of liberty, lived as long as that nation-that heart-still lived.

A bustle in the people on the road abruptly broke his thoughts. He watched them hurry their pace, melding into the woods surrounding the road as if avoiding the plague.

Wiping his eyes, he watched a plague of painted men descend down the road behind them. Wailing and screaming, they rummaged through the discarded bundles the refugees left in their haste to get away and looked all about with puzzled eyes that suddenly locked on him. He stopped rocking, watching them swarm around him with eyes full of disgust. The eyes staring back at him sent a chill through his aching heart. He knew the eyes of one of them staring at him from painted faces. The man behind the eyes had once supped with this very family huddled in this cabin and shared many a story around their hearth, but his eyebrows did not rise in recognition, only descended into a cold and heartless stare.

Anthony Turkey ignored the old man's probing eyes and put a hand to the rocking chair. He waved his braves toward the door, watching and listening to the muffled screams inside the cabin. He shouted something in his native tongue and the screaming promptly ceased.

The old man sitting in the chair tried to rise, but the point of a warrior's spear urged him to sit still. To his relief, his family soon strode out of the cabin and soon sat huddled in the yard. All of them remained silent and watched the warriors' every move. Several soon appeared in the doorway, feasting on some captured food from a pot. Burping loudly and passing gas, they seemed to take great joy in how it so annoyed the whites.

Philip Weeks sat patiently in his chair, resigning his fate to the dear Lord. You savages cannot stop this heart from beating without the Lord's permission. For he beats in it, he thought, biting down on the pipe. And my dear brave sons' hearts beat in it.

The curious Indians watched the sullen family with a strange fascination. None of the women or the children cried or wailed. An eerie numbness cloaked the entire family. They all sat patiently, offering no resistance, or any aid for that matter. Nothing the warriors did seemed to stir any emotions in them, even when they knocked down fences and herded all of the livestock over their fields to trample their crops.

The braves had no time to destroy and burn crops, no matter what Indian Butler ordered. Let the cows trample it, they reasoned, but these sullen people sure took a lot of the fun out of it, acting so numb to it all. Satisfied with their accomplishments, they all starting departing, seeking a more sporting family and farm to destroy.

Turning away, their leader, Anthony Turkey, stopped suddenly in his tracks and marched toward the old white man in the rocker biting down on the stem of an empty clay pipe. "You leave!" he ordered.

Philip Weeks gingerly took the pipe from his mouth and stared at the brazen Indian. "How can I?" he asked, waving his hands in the empty air. "My whole family is slain, besides the women and children."

Something within the words, or perhaps the white man's eyes, choked down the words of scorn Anthony Turkey had delivered to every other Yankee he encountered. He stepped back, momentarily confused. Shaking his head, he suddenly became aware of all the other braves' eyes upon him. "You get up!" he yelled, baring his teeth. Scooping up the man's hat from his head, he rudely pushed at the back of the chair.

Philip slowly rose from the chair, watching the triumphant brave scamper away with the chair and his hat. "You can have it all, but not my heart, for it belongs to one greater than you or I," he muttered.

Anthony Turkey screamed at his words and hastily stopped in the middle of the road. Seeming totally frustrated, he curiously sat the chair down and started rocking back in forth in it. He threw the hat away and stared at it. Memories from a far different world in the past flashed through his mind. He rocked all the more feverously in the chair, ignoring the inquisitive stares of the other braves.

The glare of a flaming pine knot shone in the corner of his eye. He jumped from the chair and sprinted toward it. Reaching out, he knocked the pine knot from a stunned brave's hands, but then realized his actions to be too late. The cabin blazed before his wide eyes. Looking toward the smoking barn, he ran toward the warriors leading away the horses and oxen from it and grabbed a yoke of the oxen. Chattering away in the Indian tongue to the astonished braves, he pulled the oxen away and grabbed a pouch full of food from another brave. He waved for them to join the other braves leaving with plunder and led the oxen over to the huddled family. "You get! Jogo!" he yelled at the old white man. "Bad Indians come soon! Make broth of you if you no go! You go!" Noticing a small wooden pineapple lying on the ground, he kicked it into the flames of the cabin, plopping the pouch of food down to the old white man's feet. "White man's magic no good!" he screamed, waving madly toward the flaming cabin. "Bring luck you say! Look what luck it bring! Bad luck! Bad medicine!" Turning, he marched away in a huff.

Philip Weeks slowly placed the clay pipe back into his mouth. He watched the Indians slowly depart up the road to the backdrop of a huge billowing column of smoke over the trees. No doubt Fort Wilkes-Barre, he reasoned, pulling the pipe from his slackened jaw. He glanced out of the corner of his eye to his crestfallen wife. "We have to leave now, Mother," he said.

"With what, besides this pouch and yoke of oxen?" she asked.

"With our hearts," he said, slowly walking to collect the yoke of oxen. Watching the last of the feathered heads disappear up the road, he gasped, "We leave with our hearts."

## Chapter Ninety
### The Great Runaway

Boats, canoes, hog-troughs, hastily made rafts, anything capable of floating, sat crowded with women, children, and precious belongings floating down the Susquehanna. Women leapt into the water whenever a shoal or ripple hung up their crafts. Hastily putting their shoulders to them, they pushed and pulled their crafts back into the deep water. Men, holding rifles, muskets, scythes, or pitchforks, walked in single file down the riverbank, ever mindful of the forest surrounding them. The roads thronged with masses of people fleeing for their very lives. Others, watching the spectacle unfold from the walls of Fort Augusta, already called it the *Great Runaway*. Amply named for the evacuation of the entire Susquehanna River Basin from Sunbury and above. Ample indeed.

Colonel Hunter blanched at the sight unfolding before him, closing his eyes to the overwhelming splendor of settlers from the entire frontier running for their lives. What a tremendous blow to this new nation. Canada's borders now stretched from Fort Detroit all the way down to Fort Pitt, eastward to Sunbury, to the Delaware River about Fort Penn, and from there to the Hudson River. A great section of America lost, all from the *Battle of Wyoming*. He now full well understood the importance of Wyoming and how it affected the future of the nation; at least in territory. It remained a keystone on the hinge of the frontier, if you lost it, you lost Iroquoian territory-all of Western New York and Northern Pennsylvania. Now the burden fell onto him, alone on this frontier with but one hundred soldiers. But he would not run, he promised himself, looking about the fort's strong walls. No, he could not, for now Fort Augusta is all that remained between the victorious British and the Continental stores at Carlisle. From Carlisle, Lancaster sat wide open, and from there Philadelphia. The nation would be cut in twain, not by the Hudson, as gentleman *Johnny Burgoyne* had tried to do, but by the Susquehanna. Feeling the terrible weight of it all, he raised a stiff upper lip. No, Augusta would not fall, not while he still breathed air.

Here, America would stand. Here at the conflux of the great Western Branch of the Susquehanna and its Northern Branch. Here the panic-stricken people of the West Branch and Wyoming met, creating a hodgepodge of frightened people, each sharing the same terrified look.

Never in his life had Hunter witnessed such a scene of distress. Words describing the atrocities, carried on the stammering lips of terrified men and women, echoed through his ears all the previous night. So close did the enemy appear that some settlers daring to return for a horse were shot down mere yards from the shore of the Susquehanna.

The blood-strewn face of a terrified woman, her eyes still wide with fear, shifting a bandage on her head to ease a burning sensation from her scalp being lifted, still flashed in his mind. The young red-headed woman, fleeing from an Indian close to the shore, leaped down to the swirling waters, trying to escape. The Indian reached down the bank, grabbed her long hair by the roots, hacking it off before men racing to her rescue arrived. She lived, though no doubt bald, and traumatized, for the rest of her days.

Wyoming lay in total devastation from what he heard from the rushing settlers passing through the gates seeking word of a missing relative or friend before grabbing a quick morsel of food and hurrying out the gate to continue their trek; some of them with nothing but the shirts on their backs. Bare feet tracked blood through the gate, their owners too numb with fear to notice. Their darting eyes searched for a place of security, and they moved on despite Colonel Hunter's pleas to stand with him here to curb this awful tide. "All of the forts of Wyoming couldn't hold them with thrice your number!" rang back to him at every plea. "What makes you think you can stand when they could not!?!"

Duty, he thought, but did not say. For these people had faced the enemy, and duty had proved fatal to most.

In desperation, Colonel Hunter loaded his own family into a boat and sent them downriver to Paxtang, along with dispatches pleading for any help at all. He appreciated the steadfast twenty or more Yankee soldiers from Wyoming answering his pleas, swearing to stand fast along his forty or so men. With the equally staunch *Fair-Play* settlers, it brought his numbers up to nearly one hundred. Not enough to stop the awful tide, but enough to slow it. He knew no one remained to the west, north, or east to the Delaware River. He and his hundred stood alone.

Captain Clingman of Fort Jenkins did not even stop with his ninety or so men. Hearing foreboding words from hordes of terrified settlers pouring past his fort, he wasted no time in heading for York. He must do as he sees fit, Hunter had mused, after hearing of his refusal to help in the fort. Turning, he looked down to the confused settlers swarming about the fort. "My God what has befallen us?" he gasped.

Lieutenant Pierce of the Wyoming men eased a spyglass from his eye, turning toward him. "It is worse than one could ever imagine," he said. "If only Congress could see what we see, perhaps then they would fully realize our plight, dire as it is!" He looked down to the confused settlers. "We've barely one hundred to make a stand at last count."

"I've pleaded until I have no more voice!" Hunter managed to scratch through his raw throat.

"Yes sir, but who can blame them? Butler and his wild horde is coming, emboldened by their victories. They shall show no mercy!"

"That is why we must stand! We have heard men thumping their chests and spouting on about how they would stand for liberty to their dying breath before all of this! Where are they now, when their nation does so surely need them? We need men such as you and your lot!"

"Yes, sir, I know you appreciate my men, but we are too few in number. We will stand, as I have already seen many a soul stand at Wyoming. Their deaths shall not be for naught! We shall stand here, if but just to buy a few more days time for the forces below to come to our aid."

Hunter noticed a certain glint in the man's eye. He liked it and wished the Pennamite-Yankee troubles to stop separating them, for he noticed the same glint in his own men's eyes. It bond them together by something greater than their petty differences. "Assemble the men," he ordered, clearing his harsh throat. "I need to address the brave souls. They need to know they are appreciated."

Pierce waved to his sergeant and the other officers. They quickly motioned most of the men down from the walls and cleared away a patch in the swarming settlers. The officers yelled themselves hoarse to quell the nervous chatter of hundreds of terrified voices. The roar subsided into a dull chatter. Hunter straightened his back and stood tall.

"Men!" he yelled, despite his burning throat, "this fort is now the only Northern outpost against the victorious hordes of Indian Butler! I personally thank you for the great fortitude and courage you display by standing here with me against the awful Tory tide! For it is sure to crash into these very walls!" Drawing his sword, he pointed toward each corner of the fort. "We have cannon! We have good men! We shall give them the devil if nothing else!" He lifted the point of his sword to the sky. "Here we stand, whether the sun on the morrow shines on us free men, captives, or in the great eternity beyond!"

Great huzzas answered him, though the soulful eyes of the refugees watched them in total disbelief. They turned and looked at each other for a long moment before resuming their exodus out the gate.

The men watched the settlers march on and slowly manned the walls again, each silent with his own thoughts, for death, the most personal thought of all, haunted their souls. But each swore to stand for his brothers, his family, his friends, and hearth and home, all which congealed into one word for which they fought-*America*. Their new country seemed to demand the greatest sacrifice in its birth. These United States of America would stand. Come Hell or high water..

## Chapter Ninety One
### *The best laid plans*

John Butler looked out from under the canvas tarpaulin supported by some crude makeshift poles to the burning valley. Sighing,, he put a pinch of snuff to his nostril, inhaling it. Looking down to his waning supply of snuff, he raised an eyebrow. Another whiff of the tremendous smell from the smoldering fort would be his undoing, he mused. He adverted his eyes from the burning form haunting the burned timbers. Such is war, he thought. These rebels brought all of this down upon themselves with their obnoxious ways and fanatical support of this so-called *Revolution*. One does reap what he sows, at least here at Wyoming!

He watched his fellow officers busily talking among themselves, showing items of plunder to one another. Farther away his men bundled together other effects of their efforts at plundering the valley. He wanted to scold them to be about making sure the Indians burned the crops and the buildings, but thought better of it. After all, they had performed admirably. An officer's lot is a lonely one, but necessary, he reminded himself. One must know when to push and when to give a little leeway.

Sighing again, he reached for a map sitting on a table dragged from one of the nearby cabins to his headquarters. He wriggled in the fine chair brought with it, finding it a welcome relief to the hard ground or log around a fire. Comfort had somewhat caught up with him, he reasoned, lifting the map to his face. He ran a finger over it down the winding Susquehanna and stopped for a second at the point marking Fort Augusta, and sighed again. Forts in such remote places could simply be bypassed with a few troops left to besiege them, he thought, letting his finger continue running down to Carlisle. "There," he muttered to himself, running his finger along the map eastward to Philadelphia. We lie on the verge of completing a grand task, he mused, very satisfied with himself. He wondered if he should now order the rest of the supplies and his army down from Bowman's Flats when a movement behind him tore his eye from the map.

"Oh, Captain Caldwell," he said, turning toward the man. Lifting his finger from the map on the table, he lay a pistol on it to keep it from flying away in the wind. "Come, my good man, sit," he said, gesturing to an empty chair.

Nodding, Caldwell palmed the paper he held in his hands. Walking by the table, he glanced down to the map, noticing a circle drawn around Fort Augusta with a question mark beside it. He sighed and sat down in the chair. Removing his hat, he wondered how on earth he could present the information in the dispatch he palmed without breaking his commander's heart.

"Just think of it, my friend," Butler said, rolling his eyes down to the map. "It all lays before us! We have the forces at hand to sweep the entire Susquehanna free of the rebel scourge! Only Augusta and Carlisle can offer us any resistance, but between you and I, I have reliable information that Colonel Rankin will surrender up the whole *Lancaster* militia, many of their number shall aid us in our efforts! Then it's on to General Howe in Philadelphia! Oh, this is something Sir William could only dream of! A knighthood surely awaits the man whom accomplishes such things! Tearing the colonies apart by the Susquehanna, vice the Hudson! Brilliant, my good man, brilliant!"

Caldwell fidgeted about, hastily drawing a deep breath.

"What on earth could be the matter, man?" Butler asked, leaning forward to turning his open palm toward the map. "It is all right there! They have guarded the front door but kept the backdoor wide open! We shall simply push it open and gain a great victory!"

Caldwell's anxious eyes puzzled him. A fierce yell from somewhere down the road echoed through the headquarters. Of course! It must be the Indians which so upset him!

"Yes," he said, shrugging his shoulders at the yell. "I know the Indians grow anxious, but they are superb fighters when put to it. The plunder of all the river settlements await them! We shall have no more trouble with them. Victory shall subdue them and make them submissive to our designs. Their nations shall once again stretch all the way to Maryland. Their chiefs know this, and shall act accordingly."

Caldwell raised an eyebrow, but curiously remained silent.

"The rebels at Augusta shall be swept aside," Butler said. "From there we shall gain Carlisle with all its stores and shall have a surprise for them at Lancaster. We have people there, waiting, officers high in their own ranks! It shall be a breeze! Then this horrid war shall be over!"

Caldwell put an elbow on the table, leaning his head in his palm. With his other hand he held the folded dispatch up to Butler.

Butler looked at it, shaking his head. What on earth?

"It is from the courier you sent to Philadelphia," Caldwell said. "He just returned bearing this dispatch."

Butler took the paper, quickly unfolding it, noticing with a sour eye its broken wax seal. He read it and gasped. The color drained from his face. He swallowed hard a took a step back, putting a hand to the table to steady himself. "Howe is no longer in Philadelphia," he said, plopping down into his chair. "He's been relieved and his successor, Clinton, has left Philadelphia, his troops divided, some to the Caribbean, others join him on a march to New York City. His rear guard fought with the Rebels just this past week in New Jersey." He let his hand fall limp to the table with the paper. He clenched it tightly in his fist, crinkling it. His burning eyes faded into a deep expression of disappointment. Dreams die hard.

"Well," he said, looking to Caldwell, "this does change everything. Does is not?" He rolled his eyes toward the heavens. "Why?" he gasped. "Why must this horrid war last so long?" A loud screech, followed by many more, echoed through the air in the distance. "Yes, we must deal with the present situation. The winds of war do change on a whim. A sour whim at that!"

"Sir," Caldwell said, "the Indians swarm about as if they are mad. I know not how much longer we can contain them, such as we can. Most of the settlers have had the good sense to depart, but some one hundred and eighty are still about Forty Fort. Denison himself has departed. There is word some sort of outrage has occurred on the Lackawanna River, but we know not for sure."

"Yes, rumors of war," Butler said. "I shall address our allies and announce an immediate departure. You are to dispatch a detachment of rangers up the Lackawanna to capture any rebel fools still about for their own good. As for the crops, put them to the torch or trample them, as I notice this is the favorite method of the Indians. Put every building to the torch. They must have nothing for which to return, the rebel rats."

"Sir, there are still some settlers about, the wounded and such."

"Leave a cabin about Forty Fort, but raze everything else. Such are the fortunes of war."

Caldwell slowly rose, crestfallenly looking down to his dejected commander. "Sir, we have gained a great victory and have rid the frontier of rebels for hundreds of miles. Let us not lose sight of that."

Butler turned his sullen eyes up to him. "The cards have been played, my friend. Let them fall where they may."

Caldwell scratched his head. "What of the inmates of Fort Wintermoot?" he asked.

"Set them free," Butler said. "But keep those taken in arms on the field of battle in our possession. My pity goes only so far."

Caldwell did not move.

"Those in the Indians' possession are theirs," Butler said. "Do not push matters. Anyone taken under arms is not to be released."

"And Captain Harding?"

"Oh, yes, the good captain, I had him led off, away from the rest, in fear of the Indians' retribution. Let him go also, whether he keeps his hair after that is his concern, not ours."

"Very well sir," Caldwell said with a courtly bow. He smartly turned about, marching quietly away.

"I shall address the chiefs straight away, see that they are assembled," Butler called behind him. He did not wait for a reply. Caldwell would see to things. He always did.

Butler sighed, thinking of how glory greater than his late mentor Sir William Johnson's march and taking of Fort Niagara in the previous war had eluded him. His thoughts drifted to his men, remembering how Colonel Bolton had stated how week-kneed they would become the further they advanced from Fort Niagara. How some prejudices shall never die, he thought with another sigh. Well, this campaign proved the good colonel wrong. The irony of people from Wyoming filling his ranks rang clear to him. This war proved to be a civil war. Brother against brother. Father against son. He had no doubt of his men's moxie, and even less doubt they would have marched all the way to Philadelphia, taking Carlisle, York, and Lancaster along the way. They would do their duty. But now, that remained nothing but a dream. A dream he feared would haunt him well into old age. He grieved for a moment, not for himself, but for his men. Would they receive the honor and praise they so richly deserved? Somehow he doubted it. Prejudice prevented it.

The chatter of approaching Indians turned his eyes toward them. Taking another pinch of snuff, he quickly inhaled it. Rising from the chair, he placed his fine beaver hat atop his head and cocked it to one side. An officer must look the part. He picked up the offending dispatch, stuffed it into his pouch, and stepped out to meet the chiefs with a cordial nod. Many of his men also gathered around him.

He stopped, raising his arms to gain their full attention.

Sayenqueraghta raised his arms in response. The chattering immediately ceased.

Butler nodded in appreciation, clearing his throat. "Brothers!" he said. "I have received a dispatch from General Clinton, whom now acts as Commander of all His Majesty's Forces in America." Questioning eyes peered back at him, both blue and brown. He pulled the paper from his pouch and feigned a quick read of it. "We are to depart for Tioga Point and then to Fort Niagara with all due haste." Murmurs rose from the crowd. Butler cleared his throat, repeating his words in Seneca. A great shout of outrage erupted from the chiefs. Gucingerachton strode to the front, angrily spitting at his feet.

"Orders are orders!" Butler said, looking coldly into the chief's eyes. "Make preparations to depart at once! That is all!"

## Chapter Ninety Two
### *A woman's suffering*

She rushed through the bands of Indians, trying to gain Forty Fort while confusion still reigned in their ranks. Every since a howling band had come down from Fort Wintermoot, the Indians' demeanor had abruptly changed. At first they raised their arms and stomped about complaining furiously, then turned their attention back to plundering, but in a more furious manner. Indian women rummaged through the scattered plunder lying about the ground, seeming to double-check it for any worthwhile thing they may have missed. Braves slung bundles of plunder over captured horses' backs. Attention seemed to wane from tormenting the settlers.

In this, the woman had made one last effort to search her ransacked cabin before watching the Indians put it to the torch with little attention or regard for her. What few possessions she had managed to salvage went in a white tablecloth slung over her back. All dresses she found, she immediately slipped on, hoping to fool the eager and searching hands of the Indian women swarming about. About her head she wore a ragged white cloth with two ends hanging down by which to tie it, put there by the hands of Indian women to mark her. She hoped the white cloth would keep her and her meager bundle safe from the hands of other marauding Indian women, for only hints of the paint they had daubed on her cheeks remained due to her incessant tears.

She crept along, turning every now and then from some Indians searching the littered ground. Her back slouched under the load of the bundle. She reached one hand behind her to the bottom of it to hold it, while her other held her crying child's hand. She pulled her young son along, scolding him every now and then to try and hush his tears.

A few yards from the gate she stopped, stumbling2 backwards from the force of the gate falling from the fort. Tories appeared behind the falling gate, glancing at the wide-eyed woman and her crying child for the blinking of an eye before turning their axes to the fallen doors. They promptly hacked them to bits.

More eyes turned toward the crashing gate than hers, though. A cry sounded from behind her. She froze, feigning she didn't hear it, though her son turned toward the advancing Indian women. She took one step away when a gruff hand to her shoulder turned her about. She stared blankly at the Indian woman. The Indian's dark eyes narrowed and stared sternly back at her. Surprisingly, the Indian woman smiled and shook her head, twirling her brightly beaded and braided pony tails back behind her. She pointed to the bundle and then down to the ground.

The white woman shook her head, shrugging her shoulders. Her son put a hand to his eyes, crying all the louder.

The Indian woman twirled her around, tearing the bundle on her back open and spilling its contents all over the ground.

Putting a hand to the collar of her bodice, she backed away, pulling her crying son along with her. They both stood watching the Indian woman's eager hands search through all they had left in the world, tossing priceless treasures to the wayside without so much as a passing thought. The Indian woman stripped them of the last thing they truly possessed, their dignity. How one person can so belittle another.

The son curiously ceased crying and wiped his eyes. He watched with a blanched face as one after another of his family's prized possessions fell under the gruff Indian woman's eye, only to be tossed aside or into her own bundle. He raised his eyes to his now crying and grieving mother. She gasped and he followed her eyes to his father's pipe gripped in the Indian woman's dirty hands. Grinning, she put the fine pipe in her mouth before stuffing it greedily into her bundle. Pa's pipe, he had loved it. Pa, who never returned from the battlefield. His red eyes instantly filled with tears again. His mother's shaking hand fell to his shoulder, trying in vain to comfort him. Her tears fell in greater torrents.

More Indians poured around them, some mounted on captured horses, while others still searched the disregarded plunder littering the ground. Feathers danced in the slight breeze from atop many a spear. Shouting warriors waved tomahawks and war clubs triumphantly in the still air.

A loud crack turned all eyes to the fort. A portion of its great double walls cracked again before slowly tumbling to the ground. A slight cheer rose from the Tories. A yoke of captured oxen pushed through the lingering Indians, guided by a pair of shirtless Tories cracking whips. They turned, backing the huge bellowing beasts of burden toward the walls. A great length of thick rope fell down to them from atop the wall. They hooked the rope to a harness and cracked their whips, forcing the great oxen forward. The logs of the fort's walls tied to the rope creaked and groaned in defiance, but finally succumbed to the might of the oxen. Log after log methodically followed.

The gruff Indian woman ignored the Tories, loudly cursing the closing oxen. She only moved when a party of braves pushed her aside, carrying of all things, Yankee chairs.

"My God! Are they to take everything?" the Yankee woman said aloud, more to herself than to her son or anyone else.

"Could be, Missy," one of the Tories by the oxen said, overhearing her. Raising his whip high, he cracked it by the groaning oxen. The ropes went taunt. An awful creaking sound filled the air, silenced by a great thud. Another part of the fort fell.

"Leave her be!" the Tory's partner said, wiping the sweat from his brow with his forearm. He gave the Yankee woman a smile before looking back up to the falling wall.

She did not smile back at him.

"Let a man have a bit of fun, now, old chap!" the other Tory said.

"You've a strange sense of humor indeed," he said, nodding his head toward the fort. "Why not just put the place to the torch like we have the other Yankee forts?"

His partner turned a mean eye to the Yankee woman and her sobbing child. "For her like," he said. "Major Butler says to leave them some sort of shelter. Sometimes I wonder of that man."

"Well, at least something of a heart still beats with compassion within the man, despite this damn cruel war!"

A bloodcurdling scream sounded from the Indians. A mounted warrior trotted among them, waving something brown about his head at the end of a short rawhide thong. The brown strands danced wildly in the air, no doubt a recently acquired scalp.

The Yankee woman pulled her son close, staring in defiance of the howling Indian. He strode past her, grunting at her before stopping at the remains of the gate. More mounted warriors followed and gathered around him. The howl grew contagious among them, even the gruff Indian woman raised her eyes from sorting her plunder, joining the eerie chorus. Arms rose through the crowd. All the Indians seemed to start howling. Spears rose in hands. Firelocks fired in the air. Feathered heads bobbed. The braves with the chairs halted, turning about to join their brethren howling and chattering for joy.

"I thought Major Butler released every one of those Yankee buggers not in arms against us?" one of the Tories commented.

"He did the ones in our hands," the other answered, "but he holds no sway over them in their hands. Apparently another has fallen."

The Yankee woman shuffled toward the neglected bundle behind the Indian woman. She gingerly grabbed at the edge of it, pulling it away. The Indian woman momentarily turned toward something glittering in the trampled grass not far away and did not notice.

The Yankee woman scooped the bundle up in her arms and sprinted toward the fallen gate, pulling her child along after her. She ignored the loose items spilling from it, reasoning anything they gained would be a plus. Reaching the gate, she stopped for just a second to tidy up the bundle and try to explain they needed to buck up now to her child. Profusely nodding his head, he looked back toward the remains of the gate behind them, fearing the mean old Indian woman.

"Now come on, Johnny," she urged the boy. "We've got to get while the getting is good, dear Lord we do!" She grabbed the child's hand and they both sprinted through the throngs of howling Indians, not stopping until they gained the south gate. There, she hastily tied the corners of the bundle tight, slinging it over her hunched and aching back again. She felt her son grab her hand and noticed his half-smile. She smiled back and looked to the other settlers spilling through the gate. She shuddered at the thought of the arduous and long trail ahead, staring down to her bare feet. They had what they had, she finally reasoned, looking to the others who appeared even worse off than they.

What lay ahead, even with all its horrors, paled in comparison to what lay behind them.

Her eyes shot to a group of Indians emerging around the corner of the fort. She hastened her steps, much to the consternation of her son. She pulled at him, stumbling over a rock. Tumbling to the ground, she looked up in terror at the gathering Indians. To her relief, they ignored her. Rising from the ground, her eyes fell in sorrow to a pair of distraught white men being led by tethers around their necks by some braves. She recognized them both. Daniel Carr's and John Gardner's soulful eyes stared back at her as if begging her to do something. She held her child tight and watched the Indians lead them to another group of settlers around a huge elm. Mrs. Gardner stood by the tree with her children and a lone Tory soldier.

The Indians stopped the prisoners just short of the tree. A painted ranger among the Indians doffed his hat to Mrs. Gardner and waved Daniel Carr forward with his other hand.

The woman forgot about the heavy bundle and watched the heart to heart spectacle unfolding in front of her in amazement. Her whimpering son slowly collapsed to the grass and rolled over, falling instantly asleep. She put her hand gently on his back and sat down next to him, content to let him sleep, for a long trek lay ahead of them.

She watched the tears pour down the faces of all of the Gardner family. Mrs. Gardner embraced her crestfallen husband for the longest moment before a cruel hand tore her away. An Indian baring his teeth at both of them angrily tugged at Gardner's tether until he gasped. Mrs. Gardner collapsed in grief. The ranger said nothing to the Indian's cruelty, but only turned and walked back into the falling fort.

The cruel brave yanked Gardner toward a great bundle brought forth by another Indian nearby and threw the pack onto the white man's back. Gardner stumbled under the weight, gasping profusely. Instead of mercy or some form of relief by lightening the bundle, a cruel yank pulled him away from his distraught wife and family. The cruel Indian barked something to the other Indians in his native tongue and soon an equally large bundle soon burdened Carr's back.

The Yankee woman watched both men struggle past her, panting and puffing under the great burdens on their backs, while their less burdened captors yanked them along by the tethers around their necks. The only solace offered from the Indians came from a quick command to them-"Jogo! Jogo, or you die!"

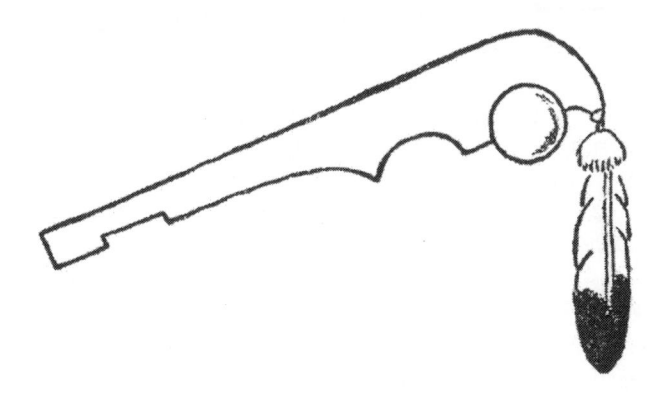

## Chapter Ninety Three
### *Indian Butler departs*

Rangers filed into line with an officer unfurling their flag in front of their column. A self-satisfied look covered most of their faces with just a hint of lost glory. No more so than on the face of their sullen commander, standing rigid and motionless by the ensign.

Major Butler turned from the flag, taking a step or two clear of the column. He looked beyond his forming ranks to the curling smoke rising in the air over the trees from dozens of fires. Only a few wisps of lingering smoke rose from the remains of Fort Wintermoot, though scant remnants of one charred wall still stood. Let it stand, he thought, for nothing else than a reminder of how impetuous men fell when they rebelled against their God-given sovereign. The morbid and charred skeleton of one of the brazen rebel still standing among the ashes bore brutal testimony of that fact. All in all, not a bad campaign, he thought, at least for their Indian allies. They had gained much more than they dared dream. Their giddy laughter still haunted the air.

His eyes fell to the swirling Susquehanna River winding through the valley. Its waters flowed south, carrying away his hopes of grandeur, but such were the fortunes of war. He feared no knighthood awaited him, but only scorn. Such would not be the case if he had gained Philadelphia. All of the little atrocities which follow the footsteps of every great army would have been overshadowed by such a great accomplishment. But he did his duty in spite of it all, and aside from the burning and plundering, no one else died whom had not fought on the field of battle. Considering the ire of the Indians toward the Yankees, he should receive great favor for that alone, but somehow he doubted it.

He marched back to the forming ranks and to the beaming face of Lieutenant Turney holding their grand flag. His smile paled beside the lackluster look on his commander's face.

Butler suddenly felt aware of his sour expression and scolded himself. Do not let your doubts overshadow your men's deeds! he told himself. Straightening his back, he let all the glory of this successful campaign shine across his face. His eyes brightened. One must watch one's continence for the sake of those one commands, he reasoned. He looked beyond Turney to the beaming faces of his men. Nodding, he smiled back at them. Though quite out of character for a British officer, he did it anyways; for no eyes watched in this wilderness.

A huzza rising from the ranks for him only encouraged him more. Removing his hat, he waved it to each of the huzzas, much to the curious looks of the gathering Indians. Had the ranger chief gone mad?

They watched his strange actions and chattered among themselves all the more when he started cheering with his men.

Butler ignored the Indians' odd stares and let the contagious joy of victory surge through his veins, if for but a fleeting moment. They had tramped through hundreds of miles in this unforgiving wilderness to attack a pest and eyesore at the southern gate of the Iroquois Confederacy. In securing this vital border, they had done a great service for king and country. If any future shame tarnished this victory, so be it, but at this moment, all shinned bright.

Strutting up to Captain Caldwell, he gave him a hearty handshake.

"Sir, you wear the cloak of victory well," Caldwell said, astonished by his commander's change of demeanor.

"As should we all!" Butler yelled, waving his hat in the air.

A loud series of huzzas answered his words.

"Captain, are we quite assembled and ready for the march?" Butler asked.

"We are sir!" Caldwell answered, waving his own hat.

"Then it's off to Tioga!" Butler said, drawing his sword to point it north. "In victory we march! Let no man belittle what we have accomplished! Let all of us bask in its glory! For it is well deserved!"

The drummer struck up a lively beat, quickly joined by the shrill of fifes. The column stepped lively to the beat, marching up the winding trail along the river. The brisk march of the rangers melted into the loose trot of the Indians bringing up the rear. In their ranks the few white faces struggled along under heavy burdens placed on their hunched backs. Angry tugs at the ropes tied to their necks yanked them along, the many yanks burning their necks raw. To them the sixty or so miles to Tioga Point seemed a thousand. After that, the trek to Fort Niagara loomed. But onward they trudged, with a resilience born of their strong faith in God. Now their fate lay in his hands and not the brutal savages. Their undying faith fueled one tired step after another. Hope and faith; they remained their only possessions. The only thing not raped by this defeat.

Behind them many Indian women tramped, some wearing more than a half dozen different dresses one atop the other. They stepped and chattered among themselves, seeming oblivious to the sweat pouring down their bodies. Four or five bonnets sat atop most of their heads, mostly backwards. Pots and pans dangled from their captured horses, clanging and pinging with each step. Bedspreads and tablecloths covered the heavy bundles on their backs. Some carried looking glasses in front of them, dazzled by their own images. A few sported dangling small hoops tied to sashes about their waists. On the hoops strung many a Yankees' hair, a symbol of their victory and dominance over them.

Esther, sitting high and bold atop her backwards facing saddle, rode amid the twisting column. Her dark eyes stared straight ahead, still hollow and full of grief. Her acts of vengeance did not seem to lessen the pain in her heart. She feared this war to haunt her for the rest of her days, for it changed whatever it touched with its foul hand. Nothing would ever be the same after this battle. How could it be? A thousand pangs born of the blows inflicted here would forever separate the white heart from the Indian heart. She ached for the generations to come and felt a deep pity for them which belittled her fleeting and hollow sense of victory. She rode in her self-inflicted trance, oblivious to all around her.

Cheers rose from the others around the melancholy Indian Queen. Wyoming belonged to them again, as well as *Otzinachson* and all along the West Branch of the great Susquehanna River. They had secured their southern door forever against the encroaching whites, especially the brazen Yankees of Wyoming. They doubted whether a people so completely broken would ever return, but if they did they would have nothing to return to, for they had burned everything. All would be better now in their eyes and they turned a blind eye to those few remaining bitter-faced Yankees watching them leave.

Yankee eyes anxiously watched the last of the enemy column disappear up the trail. They turned a sour eye to the few Indians still skulking about seeming not as anxious to leave their new bounty. Mostly miscellaneous Indians from Tioga Point and other parts of the frontier, they descended upon Wyoming as soon as the runners spread the word about the great victory at Wyoming through the Indian villages. Now, freed from the restraining eyes of the great chiefs and Butler, they ran wild. Truly wild.

The few cabins and outbuildings surviving the initial onslaught burned from their torches. New fires marked their procession down the valley. Joy beyond belief rose from their lungs in great hoots and shouts. They burned, ravaged, and plundered to their hearts' content, an Indian's paradise. None cared or worried on what the morrow might bring, for now it was loot, ravage, and plunder. Leave nothing for the Yankees to return to but burnt ground. Here in Wyoming the pestilence known as the white man had been eradicated. Let it never return!

Wyoming sat ravaged, shattering the dreams of the conquered, and perhaps the dreams of the conquerors, in the end. For war fueled by the burning fires of vengeance twisted one way and then the other, in the end ravaging all.

## Chapter Ninety Four
### *Fort Penn's Refuge*

They stumbled onward, most staring doggedly ahead at the seemingly endless trail. Groans crept from a few tired throats, but mostly silence prevailed. Exhaustion swept along the ragged column of refugees. Bundles fell from backs to the ground, there to be merely dragged along or abandoned. Pine branches waved over children's tired heads in the hands of their mothers to scatter myriads of mosquitoes. Other mothers, fearful of wolves and other wild beasts, carried infant children whom had breathed their last tight to their chests, refusing to give their deceased babes up to the wilderness. Dazed old men and women struggled along beside them, some to drift off the trail never to be seen again. Among all of this a few women gave birth, rising to their feet soon after to keep pace with the column of misery.

The few soldiers, overcome by the vast number of refugees swelling their ranks, did their best, but exhaustion plagued them, also. They flanked the trail to offer some protection, ever mindful that the threat of death hovered about and could strike from the thick forest at any time. Others aided the refugees, but hunger, sickness, despair, and death overwhelmed them. Their tired eyes gazed to the endless trail ahead also, hoping Fort Penn to show over every passing ridge ahead.

"We'll make it, by God Almighty, don't you fret, none of ya!" an aged voice suddenly broke the silence. Tired heads rose toward the voice. Some shushed it, while others just stared mutely ahead and continued tramping ahead.

Both John Jenkins and Captain Spalding stopped near the sound of the voice, leading their exhausted horses to the side of the trail. They looked up to the poor souls atop their horses' backs and sighed. Neither said a word, but just watched an old woman approach them shaking her finger.

"We'll make it Capt'n, don't you fret none on it!" Mrs. Tubbs told the two officers. Her sagging jowls moved up and down munching on something, or merely her gums. Her grim eyes turned, looking up the trail. Glancing back at the officers out of the corner of her eye, she gave them a wink, tightening her hold on her grandson's hand beside her. Her dirt-caked and swollen feet trailed blood behind her.

Jenkins put a hand to his face, rubbing his chin before shaking his head. "How did this happen?" he gasped to himself.

"Just hold on, dear John," Spalding said. "Fort Penn's only a few miles ahead at the most. I'm surprised we haven't come across any of Colonel Stroud's scouts yet."

"How many have we lost in this column alone?"

"Enough, God rest their souls."

A shout suddenly rang down the column from the front. Both men perked up and watched a scout running madly toward them.

"It's just over the next ridge!" the scout shouted, panting to a stop in front of the officers. "It's Fort Penn, it is! I met one of Colonel Stroud's scouts myself! He's rushed back to Fort Penn to spread the word. They'll be coming with help, yes sir, they will fer sure!"

"Thank you, my dear man," Spalding said, grabbing the man by the shoulders. "Thank you very much."

Nodding profusely, the scout put his own hand to the captain's shoulder.

"Now you run along and spread the word as soon as you catch your wind," Spalding said. "Make sure all of those in the rear catch up."

"Yes sir," the scout said, running back along the column.

The word of hope spread along the column, hastening their steps. All stepped a little livelier the nearer they reached the ridge in front of the column of misery. At the sight of Fort Penn cheers rose from their throats. Others chanted praise after praise to God. Some just walked trance-like to the fort, right past the throngs of people rushing out to meet them. They did not stop until they reached the gate. There, they collapsed to their knees, endlessly praising God.

Cries of joy marked many reunions, mixed with anguished cries of despair. Friends and family crowded around, searching the long line of suffering refugees for any familiar faces. But all soon fell into one another's arms, for all seemed a brother and sister, sharing their grief. Open arms and hearts received the refugees with deep sympathy.

Colonel Stroud pushed his way through the vast tide of human misery to greet the two sullen officers leading their exhausted horses. Stopping before them, he stared in shock at the whole panoramic spectacle unfolding around him. "My God what has happened?" he gasped. "What have you poor souls suffered through?"

Neither man answered, but just stared blankly at the Colonel.

"We must garrison the fort and prepare, lest the Indians and Tories strike here next!" Stroud said to an officer behind him. "See to all these poor souls and their horses as well."

The officer personally took the reins of the Yankee officers' horses and led them toward the fort, leaving the three officers along the edge of the trail to muse over their situation.

Stroud reached into his waistcoat pocket. Pulling out a flask, he presented it to Captain Spalding with a nod. Spalding eagerly partook of it and passed it to Jenkins. He drank copiously of it before finally passing it back to Stroud, whom took a great swig of it himself.

Spalding extended his hand to Stroud. "Yes, Colonel, we must make ready, we are not out of it yet," he said, shaking Stroud's hand.

"People have been pouring in since yesterday, but nothing like this bedraggled column you have here, I durst say," Stroud said.

"What have you heard, sir?" Spalding asked. "Has Fort Augusta been taken?"

"I know not," Stroud answered, shaking his head. "I only know that we have not been bothered as of yet. But who is to tell what you may have brought at your heels. Black caitiffs by the hundreds, perhaps!"

"Our heels are clean sir!" Spalding said.

"Of course, of course, Captain, don't get into a tizzy," Stroud said. "We do hear that Brant is about Onoquaga ready to sweep down the Delaware as Indian Butler has swept the Susquehanna! Danger lurks all about gentlemen. Word has come that your Colonel Butler has reached Fort Allen and is on his way here as we speak."

"He is?"

"Yes, and Colonel Denison has already arrived, quite crestfallen, I might add. I am afraid we now stand on the edge of the frontier, for it has been pushed back some hundreds of miles. I myself always knew the importance of your settlement to hold back the British and Indian tide from Niagara, perhaps now others shall realize its importance, but much too late, I am afraid."

"Your fears are well founded," Spalding said. "Wyoming is ravaged! My scouts report all buildings are in flames and thousands of Indians tromp the crops!"

Stroud turned his attention to Spalding's crestfallen lieutenant. "It seems you have all lost something dear," he said.

Jenkins shook his head at the undue attention. His heart suddenly felt raped of the hope which had carried his spirit through the past year. Rubbing the back of his right hand, he turned away from the other officers to the sea of haggard faces trudging past them. He saw Beth's face in every passing young woman and his heart shuddered to think of her fate. Beth, he thought, I have let you down. I have let down all whom I love. What of my brothers? What of my dear mother and father? Closing his eyes tightly against the pain, he marched to the sound of the footsteps to his front. He wondered of just what his fellow officers thought of him and forced open his eyes, trying in vain to quell the emotions flooding his tired soul. Stumbling, he grabbed a nearby tree branch, following it down to its trunk. Collapsing against it, he raised his clenched fists to cover his eyes. All seemed lost. All seemed hopeless, even in this supposed place of safety. He lowered his fists, watching Spalding and Stroud approach him through his tears.

Stroud and Spalding both stopped by the tree, staring down at him through eyes of great pity. His vacant and tear-strewn stare, full of pure grief, touched both of the hard men.

He tried to speak, only to bow his head in grief. "A moment, gentlemen," he gasped. "I need but a moment."

Stroud raised an eyebrow and put his hand to the hilt of his sword. He felt perfectly content to wait for his fellow officer, for he could only imagine these poor people's grief.

Spalding knelt down to him, only to jump from a scream sounding just up the trail. A woman sprinted past the refugees, running headlong for the officers. Spalding's eyes widened and Stroud stepped back to give the screaming woman way.

Jenkins instantly rose and opened his arms, letting his dear Beth pour into them. They embraced and kissed openly, forsaking all social taboos. They had found one another again in this vast wilderness of misery. Something good and pure lived again. Love, and its sister hope, flooded away all their grief in an instant. They both gazed into the eyes of love again, healing and empowering them against the despair of war.

"Oh John, how I prayed for you," Beth finally gasped between passionate kisses.

"As I have for you, my love," he answered her longing eyes.

Slight smiles crept across Spalding's and Stroud's faces in spite of the misery and anguish surrounding them. The unadulterated outpouring of love embarrassed them, but somehow also invigorated and emboldened them.

Spalding raised his hand, pointing toward the fort. "There you be," he said, "both of you make for the fort, you've a lot to discuss. I'll find you latter, Lieutenant." Stroud turned along with him and they walked away, both immediately starting to discuss their defenses.

"Wyoming," Beth gasped, "all is lost!"

"No, my dear," Jenkins answered, "not as long as you and I, and others of our like still breathe air, it is not. Lowering his hand, he clasp her hand to his heart. "Wyoming beats here, my love, as it does in your heart also." His face brightened and beamed with a sudden firmness and resolve. "Wyoming has heard *the cry of the tomahawk,* now it shall hear the avenging crack of the long rifle in response!" Squeezing her soft hand in his, he clutched her head close to his heart. Both stood, overjoyed at their reunion, feeling certain their faith and love would conquer all in the end. It had to. It simply had to.

Beth listened to the strong thump of his heart and knew his words rang true. Something more beat in all their hearts, she realized. Somehow Wyoming lived, as it always had, in the hearts of men. A new spirit lived in the hearts of all in this new land, an *American spirit*. Soon men possessed of that spirit would seek vengeance on those fool enough to try and trample it out of existence. Nothing could overpower or subdue men possessed of such a spirit for long, for this spirit rose from the land, as well as from the hearts of men. It thudded in the hearts of this new breed of men born of this virgin land. These Wyoming men. These American men. God bless them all and the new country they sired. They would rise from the ashes of despair, they simply had to in the end.

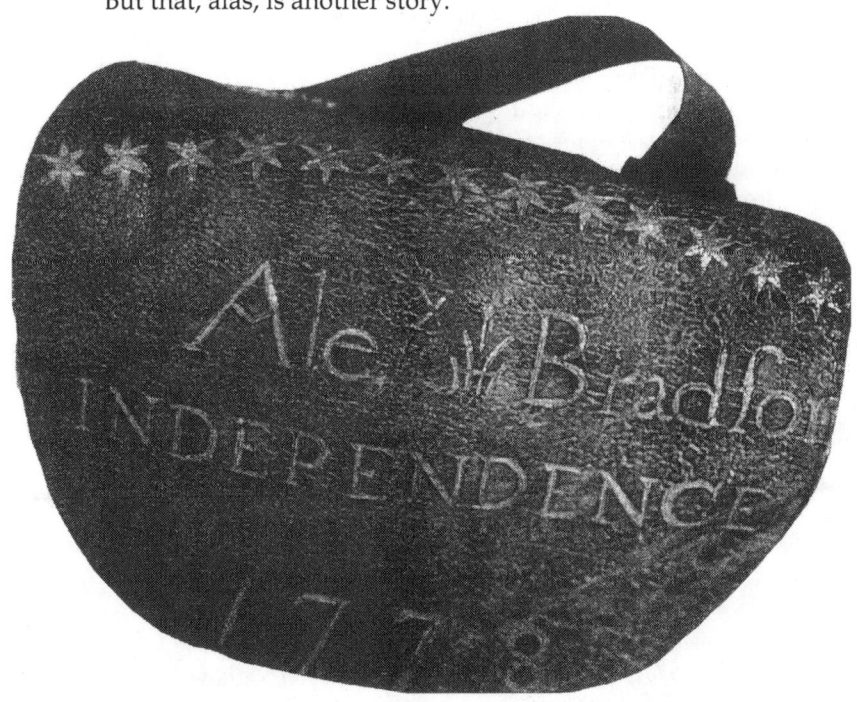

But that, alas, is another story.

*An first hand account of the* **Battle of Wyoming**, *July 3rd, 1778*

At 5 o'clock the Rebels left their strongholds and proceeded to give us battle. We set fort Wintermoot on fire to decoy the enemy, thinking by this that we fled. But they soon found it a mistake to their sorrow, for we immediately treed ourselves and secured every spot that was any way advantageous to our designs. When the enemy came within sight of us, calling aloud, **"Come out, ye villainous Tories! Come out, if ye dare, and show your heads, if ye durst, to the brave Continental Sons of Liberty!"** But we came out to their confusion indeed -- for the Indians on the right under the command of Col. Butler and their King Quirxhta entirely surrounded the enemy, and the white men under the command of Quiskkal ... On the left drove and defeated the enemy on every quarter. They fled to the river and many of them even there were pursued by the savages and shared the same fate as those on the land.

The prisoners that we took told us there were 450 men in the battle and after we went to the Forty Fort to destroy it, not more than 45 returned. The loss on our side was one Indian killed and two white men wounded. One of the white men, Wilson by name, died of his wound. The other recovered. Thus did loyalty and good order triumph over confusion and treason, the goodness of our cause, aided and assisted by the blessing of Divine Providence, in some measure helped restore the ancient constitution of the mother country, governed by the best of kings. This I must say: Every man behaved with uncommon bravery. They vied each other for glory to see who should do most in supporting the injured cause of our excellent constitution.

With the defeat of the Rebels followed a total confiscation of all their property, such as oxen, hogs, sheep and every other thing of that kind. Thus did the Rebellion get a severe shock. The Rebels begged of us to restore them something back, but "No." we replied. "Remember how you served the peaceable subjects of his Majesty at Tankennick. Remember how you took their property and converted it to Rebel purposes, and their persons fell into your hands, you immediately sent them off to prison in Connecticut and left their numerous families in utmost distress. And be contented, Rebels, that your lives are still spared and that you have not shared the same fate with your seditious brethren." This was the argument we made use of to the surviving Rebels of Wyoming. But on the whole, my heart was affected for the women and children, who came after us, crying and beseeching us that we would leave them a few cows, and we told them it was against the orders of Colonel Butler. However, privately we let them have 4 or 5 cows...

Written by Richard McGinnis, a carpenter, who fought under the British Colonel John Butler.

## Nathan Denison to Jonathan Trumbull, Gov. of Connecticut

Lower Smithfield township in the State of Pennsylvania the 28th of July 1778

Honoured Sr as Circomstances have been Such that it Renderd allmost impractible for me to give your Excelency an account of the unhapy affair that hapned at Westmoreland on the 3d of this instant Shall now indever to Represent the affair : on the Last of June We got intelegenc of a Party of the Enemy being up the River about 30 miles Distant from us the party Supposd not to be grate the Next Day after another Scout Returned and gave an account that they had Discovered about fifty Cannoe Loads of the Enemy With Considerable Parties of them on Each Side the River Coming Down Which intelegenc alarmed the inhabitence so that Some Ware for Securing their famalies in our forts others for moveing out of the Settlement in this situation We Collected to the numbr of four Hundred of our men and marched up the River in order to meet the Enemy but not meeting With them Saving a Small Scout Which Ware Killed by our People the Day before this hapned the Enemy fell on a Small Party of our men that Ware at Work Killed four of them the other made their Escape the Next Day after the body of the Enemy Came to a Small fort & Demanded it Which Was instantly given up Whear they mad there Head Quarters During the time they Was in the Settelment there Parties Ware Distroying our Cattle Horses &c the Day that We had the battle With them We had betwen three & four Hundred men Collected at Kingstown fort about three milds Distant from the Enemy in this Situation it Was Concluded best to march out and attact the Enemy upon Which there Was a little over three Hundred that marched out & attact them the Enemy got no advantage of us in the first fire but we ware over Powerd by numbr, our People Ware abliged to Retreet the Numbr Killed on our Sid Can not be Certing Knoon but I beleve not far from two Hundred the numbr of the Enemy Killed not far from Eighty the Next morning John Butler the Commander of the Enemy Sent a flag to Demand the fort I Let him no that I Wold See him at one o Clock after noon after Which I Went to the Loar Part of the Settlement to find the Situation of the People & found numbr of Wimen & Children then in the Roads Som Pushing out of the Settlement Some one Way & Some the other in the utmost Distress & Ankeiety indevering to make thire Escape from the Saveges at my Return to the fort foun that it Was the minds of the gratest Part of the Peopl then Present to Capitulate With the Enemy I Went to theire Camp & Was Put to the Disagreable necesity of Sineing the in Closed Paper after Which no Person Was hurt by the Enemy untill after I Left that Plac the Next Day after I come from there : there Was five Person murderd by the Enemy on the Rode as they Was Coming from there and as the artickle of Cappitulation are brook on the Part of the Enemy I Do not Look upon my Self holden on my Part by them and Expect Soon to Return to Return to Westmoreland to See if Some trifels Can be Saved that the Saveges have Left the numbr of Enemy That Came against us Did not Exeed Sev[en] or Eight Hundred at most by the best information I can git I am Sr With Due Regard your Exlences most obedient humble

Nathan Denison

N B I find that there is Numbers of People in this State Desine to take the advantage of our Distresed Situation to get Posesion of our Settlement Which I think Cannot b alowed of but the gratest Part of them have been very Kind to our Scattered inhabitenc

Colonel John Franklin's account of subsequent events after the battle: "Some persons, in giving an account of the battle, stated that the Tories and Indians brought fresh scalps into the fort and slapped them in the faces of the women. This was not done. I saw but one scalp brought into the fort by a Tory, and he said it was the scalp of Lieut. Lazarus Stewart {Jr.} Some of the Tories and Indians told me they had taken 190 scalps; but I think the number was not so great. They informed us that if Colonels Butler and Denison, with their forces, had stood their ground one minute longer they would have gained the victory; that the Tories and Indians on the left wing were giving way, and that they would not have stood their ground after another fire.

"After the business of capitulation was finished in the fort the enemy withdrew in a body, marching out in the same form in which they had entered. About thirty or forty Indians and Tories remained in the fort, but the main body marched to Wintermoot's Fort. The first house they came to after leaving the Kingston fort [Forty Fort] was set on fire, as was every other house on their way. Major Butler marching at the head of the savages, all was laid in ruins before him-his pledged honor to the contrary notwithstanding."

"It is not known what number of the enemy were killed.* Daniel Ingersoll, who was a prisoner at Wintermoot's Fort, informed me that after the battle the enemy collected all the tools they could find in the neighborhood, and the parties were out all night in the woods where the battle was fought, and went off to the adjoining swamp, where, as he supposes, they buried their dead. In the evening after the battle a council was held in Kingston fort, when it was proposed to send and get a cannon(a four-pound gun) from Wilkes-Barre, and have all the inhabitants from the towns below repair to Kingston fort, and to make a stand against the enemy. I sent one of my men to Huntington for a cask of powder, and notice was sent to the inhabitants below to repair to Kingston; but it was too late-all were flying or preparing for their flight."

*About eighty of the invading enemy were killed, according to the best contemporary evidence.

# The Cry of the Tomahawk

*James B. Miller*

One of the mighty warriors of the "Six Nations."

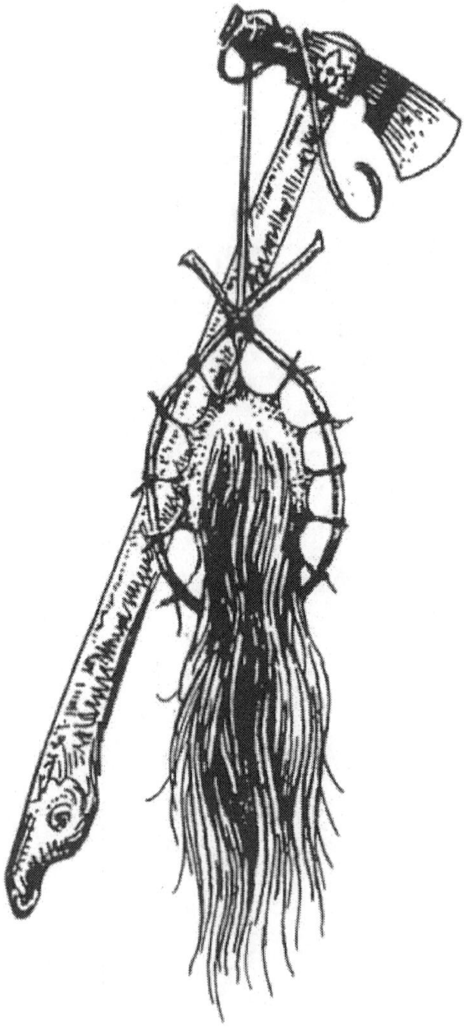

Made in the USA
Charleston, SC
14 June 2012